1978

ARISTOTLE
AND THE PROBLEM OF VALUE

ARISTOTLE
AND THE
PROBLEM OF
VALUE

WHITNEY J. OATES

PRINCETON NEW JERSEY

PRINCETON UNIVERSITY PRESS

MCMLXIII

Publication of this book has been aided
by the Ford Foundation program to support
publication, through university presses, of work
in the humanities and social sciences

WHITNEY J. OATES, Avalon Professor of Humanities
at Princeton University,
has had a long and distinguished career as teacher,
scholar, and administrator.
A member of the Princeton University faculty since 1927,
he has served at various times as Professor of Classics on the Andrew Fleming
West Foundation, Chairman of the Classics Department,
Chairman of the Special Program in Humanities,
Chairman of the Humanities Council,
and Trustee of Princeton University Press.
He is a Phi Beta Kappa Senator
as well as Vice President of the United Chapters,
and Treasurer of the American Council of Learned Societies.
One of Professor Oates's pioneering achievements was the establishment
of the Woodrow Wilson Fellowship Program,
of which he was the co-director in 1951–1952.
He is a regular contributor to scholarly journals,
and the author of a number of books.

Printed in the United States of America

TO THE MEMORY OF
PAUL ELMER MORE
AND
DUANE REED STUART

CONTENTS

PREFACE

THE idea, which this book will attempt to develop, emerged while I was preparing to offer a graduate course in Aristotle at Princeton University in 1936. The first step in my investigation was to examine the entire corpus of Aristotle's writings in the effort to identify all the important passages in which he became involved, either explicitly or implicitly, in the question of value or, as I have called it from time to time, the "phenomena of evaluation." In Chapters V through VIII these texts have been analyzed and interpreted in order to try to validate the major thesis of the book, namely, that Aristotle when he faced the question of value was frequently inconsistent or even incoherent. This situation, according to our argument, resulted from Aristotle's rejection of Plato's Theory of Ideas, a rejection which entailed a philosophical separation of Value from Being. All quotations from Aristotle in the text appear in English translation and are taken from the Oxford version unless otherwise indicated, while the original Greek text appears in each instance in a footnote.

My initial interest in Plato and Aristotle and their relation occurred when as a graduate student in 1930–1931 at Princeton it was my good fortune to be a member of a seminar given by the late Paul Elmer More. My treatment of the Platonic Theory of Ideas in Chapter II owes not a little to Mr. More's writings on Plato, and in Chapters III and IV, which deal with Aristotle's "metaphysics of the individual particular," I have made use of some of Mr. More's lecture notes which were turned over to me after his death. On the present occasion I would like to acknowledge my gratitude for having had the privilege of knowing intimately Mr. More, the quality of his mind, the breadth of his learning, and his profound humility.

It is freely admitted that my argument may not prove to be convincing to those who are stout admirers of Aristotle. Here I would like to call attention to one point. Over the years, as I have discussed the thesis of this book with "pro-Aristotelians," I have become more and more aware of the fact that many of these scholars tended to argue on the basis of interpretations of

Aristotle such as those to be found in Dante or St. Thomas. I can only answer that I have grounded my case on the *ipsissima verba* of Aristotle, and not on what a Dante or a St. Thomas made of them.

Samuel D. Atkins and Gregory Vlastos, Princeton colleagues, were kind enough to read and criticize the entire manuscript. To them more than to any others, I owe my deepest thanks. It should be unnecessary to say that they can in no way be held responsible for its shortcomings. Francis Fergusson of Rutgers University also read the complete text and I wish herewith to express my gratitude to him for his many cogent suggestions. The manuscript was also read by the late Arthur E. Murphy of the University of Texas with whom on several occasions I had a chance to discuss my argument. A most helpful letter from him reached me shortly before his untimely death. It is with deep thankfulness that I acknowledge his invaluable assistance.

President Robert F. Goheen of Princeton read parts of the manuscript, and I am grateful to him for several constructive criticisms. Also I should like to express my appreciation to Professor Edgar Wind of Oxford University who read an early version of the first four chapters. In fact it was he who suggested using the central figures of Plato and Aristotle in Raphael's "School of Athens" as the frontispiece. The contrasting poses of the two philosophers in a way express pictorially the essence of the book's argument.

Finally, thanks are due to Miss Mary Bertagni and Miss Rebecca Fuller who typed the manuscript, to Mrs. Edward Frieman who prepared the Index, and especially to my wife who helped signally in the proof-reading and never failed in offering her encouragement while the book was being written. My heartfelt appreciation also goes to Herbert S. Bailey, Jr., the Director of the Princeton University Press, to P. J. Conkwright, the Press typographer, to Miss R. Miriam Brokaw, the Managing Editor, and to Mrs. Polly Hanford, Editor, whose courtesy and assistance were never wanting.

Whitney J. Oates

Princeton University
Princeton, New Jersey
April 1963

ARISTOTLE

AND THE PROBLEM OF VALUE

CHAPTER I

PRELIMINARY STATEMENT OF
THE PROBLEM

THE incorrigible Lucian, whose eye for the weaknesses in others as well as in himself was unsurpassed, spared none of the great in the Greek philosophical tradition. In one of his well-known dialogues, he singled out Aristotle for attack, and caught in the focus of his satire that aspect of the great philosopher's ethical position which has been characterized often as "practical," prudential, and this-worldly. In the dialogue, which is set in Hades, Diogenes is chiding Alexander, but lately dead, for lamenting his recent loss of his power, his imperial trappings, and all other tokens of his earthly splendour. Diogenes asks, "What, crying? Silly Fellow! Did not your wise Aristotle include in his instructions any hint of the insecurity of fortune's favours?" Alexander retorts, "Wise? Call him the craftiest of all flatterers. Allow me to know a little more than other people about Aristotle; his requests and his letters came to *my* address; *I* know how he profited by my passion for culture; how he would toady and compliment me, to be sure! Now it was my beauty—that too is included under the Good; now it was my deeds and my money; for money too he called a good—he meant that he was not going to be ashamed of taking it. Ah, Diogenes, an impostor; and a past master at it too. For me the result of his wisdom is that I am distressed for the things you catalogued just now, as if I had lost in them the chief goods."[1]

The so-called "realistic" or practical attitude of Aristotle's thought, so skillfully delineated by Lucian, has attracted many of a more pragmatic temper of mind, while to others the Aristotelian position has seemed unelevated and in certain respects distasteful or inadequate. What actually Lucian's critique suggests is the widely divergent reactions to the Aristotelian point of view which

[1] Lucian, *Dialogues of the Dead*, XIII. *The Works of Lucian of Samosata*, translated by H. W. and F. G. Fowler, vol. I (Oxford, Clarendon Press, 1905).

3

have emerged in the course of the history of Western thought. It is true that the more Platonic one's view, the more inadequate the Aristotelian approach appears to be. This in turn suggests the profundity of Coleridge's familiar dictum that all men are born either Platonists or Aristotelians. That this rather ambitious dichotomy of the human race is in a real sense valid is vividly prefigured in the genuine opposition, primarily on metaphysical grounds, which existed historically between the master, Plato, and the brilliant pupil, Aristotle. Though the ground of the conflict lay in metaphysics ultimately, to the individual whose technical knowledge of the more abstruse philosophical problems is somewhat slight, the difference appears most clearly in the area of value. While on the one hand the casual reader of Plato can readily observe in the Theory of Ideas, and in the supreme Idea of the Good, a coherent theory of value that is essentially other-worldly in character, on the other a like reader of Aristotle can see a common-sense mind, aware of things, "as they are" and reacting in value judgments, particularly in ethics and literary criticism, as any "sensible" man would. On closer reading, however, the value theory of Aristotle, appealing though it may be in its "realism," appears in the main to lack the coherence found so clearly in Plato.

The thesis, briefly stated, which the present volume will attempt to elaborate is simply this: When Aristotle rejected the basic metaphysical theory of his master Plato, *viz.*, the Theory of Ideas, he developed an empiricist metaphysics which permitted him to build upon the logical aspect of Plato's Ideas, and at the same time to make startling advances in ontology and epistemology, but which prevented him from coming to grips adequately with the problem of value and its relation to being. In other words, I am inviting a comparative study of Plato and Aristotle with respect to the relation of Being and Value.

There will be two serious difficulties to overcome in the presentation of this thesis. The first lies in the fact that the identification of and speculation about the problem of value as such is a relatively recent phenomenon in the history of philosophy. Consequently a modern interpreter who approaches the thought of Plato and Aristotle with particular reference to its implications for the problem of value lies in grave danger of projecting back modern modes of thought and speculative contexts of value thinking. He may thus be applying them to philosophies produced in a speculative climate which had not recognized value as such as one of the persistent and analytically isolable problems of philosophy. However, the difficulty can with proper precaution be overcome. Though indeed neither Plato nor Aristotle, we can suppose, ever explicitly asked himself the question, "What is value?", yet throughout their writings, as everyone knows, they are both implicitly and explicitly concerned with all the varied phenomena of evaluation. Consequently what the modern philosopher would call "value theory" is to be found imbedded in the texture of the writings of these two monumental ancient thinkers, save in those areas, which are either logical or descriptive or "scientific." Obvious cases in point would be the puzzling second half of Plato's *Parmenides* or the mathematical or physiological sections of the *Timaeus*. In Aristotle, the strictly logical *Organon* or the biologically descriptive *Historia Animalium* should suffice as illustrations.

For evidence wherewith to reconstruct the "value theory" of either Plato or Aristotle, the interpreter will be obliged to scrutinize almost completely the body of their extant writings. He can legitimately use any passages which involve value judgments expressly, as well as those which by implication readily suggest presupposed value criteria. He must only be on his guard not to lose sight of the contexts from which the passages are drawn, for often their meanings will not be confined to that which has a bearing upon value alone. The ancient thinker, even when dealing with the nature of "goodness," was not accustomed to limit his meaning philosophically to "pure value," but rather to have within his speculative range other closely related philosophical areas.

The other difficulty will arise as the negative character of the thesis concerning Aristotle's value theory begins to appear. In fact, as we have already indicated, our argument will attempt to show a serious lack of coherence, and even confusion, in questions of evaluation, which tend to vitiate the effectiveness of Aristotelianism. There may even be adequate ground to contend that the major reason why Aristotle is so frequently obscure and difficult to understand lies in the absence of any comprehensive meta-physical ground for his value judgments. Or, to put it in another way, Aristotle never seems to have consistently felt the obligation to relate explicitly his evaluational speculation with those other aspects of his thought in which he achieved such outstanding success. It will therefore be incumbent upon us to demonstrate as best we can by a careful analysis of numerous specific passages that in fact there is confusion and incoherence in Aristotle's thought when he comes to deal with questions of value.

It would be generally admitted that Plato in his Theory of Ideas has set up a metaphysical hypothesis which, for all its difficulties, has kept Being and Value together in a way that is uniformly coherent. Furthermore, as we shall attempt to show later in greater detail, the Theory of Ideas permits Plato to develop his thinking in the spheres of logic and epistemology in complete conformity with his speculation on Being and Value.[2] Conse-quently, it seems fair to assert that Plato has perforce not seen the question of value in isolation, and hence his whole "value theory" is deeply imbedded in his total metaphysic. Aristotle, by contrast, and, we should contend, as a result of his reaction against Plato, concentrated upon the question of being, in effect in isolation from his consideration of value. From our point of view this Aristotelian ontological "isolationism" reveals its consequences in the lack of coherence that is identifiable in his thought in the area of value. Perhaps we can summarize the point by recalling the phrase which G. R. G. Mure has chosen as the epigraph for his excellent discussion of Aristotle,[3] τὸ πάλαι τε καὶ νῦν καὶ ἀεὶ ζητούμενον καὶ ἀεὶ ἀπορούμενον, τί τὸ ὄν, "The eternal question: What is Being?"[4] The case of Aristotle, and indeed, some of the more recent developments in the field of value theory indicate that the eternal question rather should be "What is Being and Value?"

The history of Western philosophy has produced myriads of views of Reality, of human life and the world, of value, of God and of the supernatural. Though these views are almost infinitely

[2] See below, Chapter II, pp. 43–51.
[3] G. R. G. Mure, *Aristotle* (New York, Oxford University Press, 1932).
[4] *Metaphysics*, 1028 b 2–4.

various in their several details, they can in general be classified into three main groups which may be called somewhat arbitrarily Naturalism, Humanism, and Theism. It is most instructive to observe in each of these classes the characteristic attitude of the view in question concerning Nature, the nature of man, reality, and that which is valuable. Naturalism according to this classification, comprises all those philosophies which are basically materialistic or mechanistic, and above all in the biological sphere adhere to the principle of continuity. The Naturalist is impressed by the haziness of the line which marks off the animate from the inanimate, and in the animate category sees an unbroken continuum, ranging from the most minute unicellular organism which possesses "life" on up to man, traditionally regarded as the most complex of living beings. No difference in kind, *i.e.*, no qualitative difference, is recognized normally in the series, but only a difference in degree, which is at bottom quantitative. Man and the amoeba, in other words, are in the same qualitative category, and are separated from each other by degrees of complexity which can be quantitatively measured. If Reality (that is, Reality with a capital "r," or as Sir Arthur Eddington is alleged to have designated it, "Reality, loud cheers") be defined as comprising *everything* that has existence, the Naturalist makes it coextensive with the universe of space and time and hence would deny the existence of God or of any transcendental element in things. Man's consciousness tends to be regarded as a bundle of conditioned reflexes, or an epiphenomenon. As an inevitable concomitant of the materialistic hypothesis, the validity of the concept of free will is usually denied, and man is conceived as a being determined completely by his hereditary physiological make-up and by his physical and social environment.[5] In the sphere of value, both

[5] This, and the subsequent descriptions of Humanism and Theism, are drawn, it is fully acknowledged, in the most general terms, and are expressed in this way in order to designate the basic tendencies of the three different views. Not every philosophical system fits precisely into one of the three categories. For example, the position of John Dewey, in all its facets, may be regarded as Naturalistic in so far as it places supreme confidence in science and the so-called scientific method, while it is Humanistic in so far as it is a doctrine proclaiming, in the liberal tradition, the rights of individual men, human freedom, and the values inherent in political democracy. An unfriendly critic, however, might protest by pointing out that Dewey ultimately is a Naturalist, and that there is no sound basis in Naturalism wherewith to sanction his humanistic liberalism.

aesthetic and ethical, the Naturalist usually propounds a subjective and relativistic position. Ultimately values are determined by a hedonistic calculus and sanctioned by pleasure and pain reactions. What is pleasurable is good; what is painful, evil.

Perhaps the best illustration of Naturalism, because it is relatively simple, is to be found in ancient Epicureanism. In it, as we may gather from its leading exponents, Epicurus and Lucretius, we have most of the features described above. Certainly, reality is equivalent to the space-time universe, even though the orthodox Epicurean held that the universe is infinitely extended. All things are compounded of atoms and void, and all natural as well as psychological phenomena are explained in terms of this hypothesis. Pleasure is the highest good, and all value judgments are ultimately referred to this absolute norm. To be sure, the Epicurean hedonism is enlightened. The creed is far different from that of the crude voluptuary, and characteristically the pleasures which accrue from elevated intellectual pursuits or from friendship and similar human activities are given the highest place, but they are finally determined by the subjective reaction of the individual. In only one respect does Epicureanism depart from the standard features of Naturalism, since it does maintain the freedom of the human will. Through the well-known attribution of the capacity to "swerve" to the individual atom, the Epicurean could account for the power of human beings to initiate action. It is thus that Epicureanism avoids the trap of a complete determinism, but still the criterion which controls moral action remains the carefully calculated long-term pleasure reaction of the moral agent.

The second great class among *Weltanschauungen* may be called Humanism, even at the risk of some confusion because of the wide variety of meanings which have from time to time been given to the term. Humanism here intends to designate that view of man and Reality which, like Naturalism, sees man as part of biological nature, but at the same time believes that there is a dimension in man, not possessed by the other beings in the biological order yet sufficient to differentiate him qualitatively from the rest. In short, Humanism denies at bottom the principle of continuity. The major ground for thus assigning a special position for man lies in his capacity to have both ethical and aesthetic responses, as well as in his possession of the faculty of reason. Humanism would not limit Reality necessarily to the physical and temporal extension of the universe (specific examples of Humanisms differ on this point) but, at any rate, the view would hold that intrinsic in Reality are certain absolute norms or standards of value. These absolute principles are deep in the heart of things and are external to and unconditioned by any human subject. Yet Humanism would insist that it is possible for man to grasp and know these principles, and govern his life accordingly. Though he does adhere to his belief in the existence of these absolute standards, the Humanist shares with the Naturalist the conviction that no Divine Being lies behind the universe. Man in his view, because he possesses reason and is capable of ethical insight, is in complete control of his own destiny, and will at some future time be able, by virtue of his own powers, to solve the problems presented to him in the human predicament.

In ancient philosophy, despite the fact that both Renaissance and modern Humanisms stem from it, it is difficult to find a system which in every point coincides with Humanism as it has been delineated. Both Platonism and Aristotelianism fall in part within the category. Plato and Aristotle both would deny the principle of continuity in nature, and would assign a special position to man because he possesses the faculty of reason. Plato's Ideas certainly are absolute norms, but Plato would not assert that man could apprehend them completely or could totally exhaust their meaning. Yet Plato would contend that man possesses the power to orient himself properly towards these Ideas, as the ultimate principles in Reality. But, as distinct from the normal Humanism, Plato does postulate the existence of God, who has functioned as the great Artificer of the universe and who does control in some measure the things and events therein. Aristotle, on the other hand, would insist that man through reason is capable, in an absolute sense, of solving his problems, though Aristotle by no means can postulate the separate existence of absolute norms or values. Also, in Aristotle, God occupies a supreme position in his metaphysical scheme, a fact which further would differentiate his system from "normal Humanism."

Historically, it may be observed that Humanism has emerged by a kind of amalgamation of Plato and Aristotle into a view which tends to elevate man and his reason into the supreme position in Reality.

Theism, or the religious view of Reality, shares certain beliefs with both Naturalism and Humanism and to this extent absorbs them within itself. With Naturalism it recognizes the biological aspect of man's nature, and with Humanism it denies the principle of continuity in nature. With Humanism it postulates the existence of absolute norms or standards of value, but unlike Humanism, it postulates the existence of God, who as Creator is the supreme source of these values. Though Theism recognizes the superior status of man among spatiotemporal things, it insists that Reality has within itself a supernatural dimension over and above the natural order, from which man derives his especial worth and without which he is incapable of working out his own destiny. To a greater or a lesser degree most of the great religions of the world maintain this view of man and Reality, and, of course, Christianity gives it its most explicit formulation.

Even in these brief analyses it should be clear that there is an inevitable functional relation between theories of value and of being. If this be so, then any philosophy which addresses itself specifically and exclusively to the one or to the other would appear to run the risk of having its system vitiated by the failure properly to attend to the excluded problem and the relation of it to the sphere selected for analysis. Thus, if a system attempts to be exclusively a philosophy of being, the problem of value will receive short shrift. On the other hand, a philosophy which singles out value for its sole sphere of investigation will suffer for want of an adequate ontology. In fact, this phenomenon, to be found so often among philosophers, *viz.*, to abstract one area from the total philosophical context, and to analyze it to the exclusion of all else, has constituted, as we have been insisting, perhaps the gravest of all philosophy's liabilities. Of course, it cannot be denied that these investigations have produced significant results, but in all but the rarest of cases, these positive results have failed of complete fruition, because they have not been produced by a method which analyzes always in full context.

If it be accepted that analysis in full context is an ultimate desideratum for a philosopher who concerns himself with the question of Being and Value, perhaps the case of Saint Augustine may be instructive. He, almost more than any other great thinker of the West, kept all aspects of his thought simultaneously before him,[6] and as one result, he keeps Being and Value strictly together. His attitude towards the problem is to be found most explicitly in his famous treatise, *On Free Will*. As is always the case, Saint Augustine begins with God, as his well-known "proof" for His existence makes perfectly clear. To review the argument briefly, Saint Augustine points to the fact that man, in his mind and through his reason, is aware of the existence of certain mathematical relations. Inevitably he is able to say that certain mathematical propositions are true, something which he would be unable to do, had he not within his mind a conception of truth. This immediately suggests absolute Truth, which in turn can be no different from God. On this ground, Saint Augustine would contend that there is a Divine Illumination within man which enables him to build an epistemology which can be called an inner empiricism. God, whom man knows through Divine Illumination, is the Creator not only of man but of the whole physical universe. God is infinitely good, all-wise, and omnipotent, and thus it is necessary that that which He creates will possess something of His goodness.

On the basis of this view, Saint Augustine puts forward his doctrine of "natures." Everything which God creates in the universe of space and time is a "nature," no matter whether it is to be found in the mere physical order, or in the order of plant and animal life, or in the human order. God has seen fit to arrange these "natures" in a hierarchy, so that the whole may represent a harmoniousness. These "natures" are not all of equal value or importance, for, Saint Augustine would contend, there would be no way by which a more important "nature" could be identified, unless there were present a less important "nature" with which it could be compared. But the important point is that a "nature," of whatever order, is, by virtue of its being a creature of God, good in some degree or other. As a creature it must

[6] See the remarks on this point in the Introduction to my edition of *Basic Writings of Saint Augustine* (New York, Random House, 1948) pp. ix–xiii.

reflect in some measure the goodness of its Creator. Hence it is not possible to talk about the "being" or existence of a "nature" without taking into consideration its "value" or goodness. God's creation of a "nature" has bound together inextricably in it Being and Value. The epistemological method of inner empiricism leads man to this doctrine of God as the creator of "natures," and hence man, in his ordinary empirical experience of objects external to himself in the universe of space and time, can see them as "natures," can be aware of them as units of Being-and-Value, and can see them properly in their relation to other "natures" as well as in their relation to their Creator.

This is not the place to go into Saint Augustine's theory of "cosmic" evil, which is heavily based upon Neo-Platonism, whereby he would attempt to explain the palpable flaws and defects in these created "natures." Nor in turn is it possible to argue here about the validity of Saint Augustine's so-called demonstration of God's existence, or the relation of these, his more philosophical, views to the data which derived from his religious faith. It is enough to cite his doctrine of "natures" as the view of a thinker who was aware of the main problem which is before us, and who solved it in such a way as to recognize the deep association of Being and Value. Obviously the Augustinian solution will satisfy neither the Naturalist nor the Humanist, but whether the approach be that of a Naturalist, Humanist, or Theist, there emerges the strong suggestion that the investigator should see Being and Value together, because that is the way they seem to be related in actual human experience, which is after all by way of being a final court of appeal, no matter what type of philosophical system may subsequently be developed. A. E. Taylor in his Gifford lectures of 1926–1928 has devoted a long section to a discussion of the problem, and concludes that Being, or as he calls it, "actuality," and Value must be seen together.[7] With respect to the point that Being and Value are always co-present in human experience, Taylor writes that he refuses to admit the ultimate severance of value from existence, and goes on to say, "The point on which I would lay the chief stress is that such severance falsifies the facts of real life, where existence and

[7] *The Faith of a Moralist* (London, Macmillan, 1931–1932) vol. I, 24–66.

value appear always as distinguishable, but always as conjoined."[8]

Now it would be safe to assume that, if this point is sound, those philosophies which see an ultimate severance of Being and Value must do so upon the basis of some metaphysical prior assumption. If such an assumption leads to a genuine falsification of the "facts of real life," then the assumption, it goes without saying, is profoundly suspect. The whole point here is not to state in absolute terms what the solution of the problem of Being and Value should be. It can be, and indeed has been in the past, resolved variously by the Naturalist, Humanist, and Theist. Self-consistent solutions are possible within any of these three general modes of thought, but we should not forget that in a distressingly large number of instances, thinkers have neglected the basic datum which has been so clearly formulated by Taylor. What rather should be suggested is that a philosopher must in his thinking take this basic datum fully into account, and that the degree to which he has done so in his fully articulated system will constitute one of the tests whereby the system may be validly assessed.

As the major task before us consists in analyzing and appraising the systems of Plato and Aristotle with reference to the problem of Being and Value, it is incumbent upon us, at least in brief, to make clear the metaphysical framework within which the analysis and appraisal is to take place. One point should be stressed at the outset. The enterprise is at once philosophical and historical. The proposition that Aristotle's rejection of the Platonic Theory of Ideas had certain identifiable consequences for his system when we seek to discover the relation of Being and Value in it—this proposition is basically historical, and is susceptible of more or less conclusive historical documentation. But the task cannot stop at this point, for the general philosophical problem is raised: Which of the two attitudes towards the problem of Being and Value is superior? Does Aristotle represent an advance over Plato in this area, as he does, let us say, in the descriptive area of biological science, or does Aristotle retrogress from a more enlightened Platonic position?

Now the answer to these latter questions cannot be fundamentally historical, but rather it must be philosophical. It is freely

[8] *ibid.*, vol. I, p. 55.

admitted that a certain view of both philosophy and history is implicit in the very fact that we are supposing that these are valid questions to ask. So far as history is concerned, it is presupposed that the events of history have meaning and significance, and that every historian, no matter how strongly he may deny it theoretically, does in fact discriminate among his various sources according to some consciously or unconsciously realized criteria of significance. As for philosophy, it is presupposed that it is possible upon reasonable and philosophical grounds for men to say that system A is superior to system B. This may be difficult, and enormous errors may be perpetrated in the attempt, but still the possibility exists. Of course, there have been many philosophers, particularly those who propound some variant of relativism, who would insist that one can only say that A is different from B, but never better than B. But even this assertion, in and of itself, in reality argues for our presupposition. Does not the relativistic assertion which says that difference is determinable, but not superiority or inferiority, amount actually to an assertion that in an absolute sense the relativist hypothesis is better and more satisfactory than the hypothesis which maintains the possibility of validly discriminating between better and worse? In fact, has there ever been a case where a writer undertook to compose a philosophical work of any sort without at least the tacit assumption that somehow he would produce something better in some respect than had hitherto been in existence?

On these grounds, we must examine the historical fact of the difference between Plato and Aristotle in the full light of its historico-philosophical significance. And here we might observe in passing that the point of view from which we will attempt to argue for the superiority of Plato over Aristotle in the area of the relation of Being and Value will probably not be acceptable to the Naturalist, though it might be hoped that he would feel the force of the argument for the copresence of Being and Value as basically in accord with the "facts of real life" in Taylor's phrase. Both Humanist and Theist should not find too much difficulty in agreeing with our general position, though, of course, there will be several individual points of divergence. In any event, a sketch of the various assumptions in the light of which we shall compare and contrast Plato and Aristotle may be useful as a background for the analysis which follows. Naturally the full philosophical arguments for our point of view cannot be given here. That is a book in itself—a book, we might say, which has been written by many a Humanist and Theist author. However, the want of a full philosophical argument at this juncture may be in a sense compensated by the fact that the detailed study of Plato and, in particular, of Aristotle should present as it moves along at least some measure of the grounds which support the position which we have taken.

Let us, then, list the several assumptions which we are prepared to make:

1. "Knowing" involves a relation between a consciousness and objects of all sorts and orders which are external to it.[9] In general the epistemologies of Plato and Aristotle agree on this point.

2. The view of A. E. Taylor that Being and Value are conjoined is basically valid.[10]

3. Being and Value, thus conjoined in "objects," are external to the "knowing subject" or consciousness and must be apprehended as such.

4. Consequently, it is incumbent upon a thinker to develop his axiology and his ontology simultaneously.

5. Axiology and ontology must be regarded as completely unconditioned by the "knowing subject." His views are the variables, while the Reality which he attempts to understand is unaltered by them.

6. Any "conjoined" theory of axiology and ontology must face the question of the ground or source of both Being and Value.

7. Any such "conjoined" theory must possess an inner coherence or consistency so as to reflect the generally ordered nature of the Reality, comprising both Being and Value, which is external to the "knowing subject."

[9] The phraseology here is meant to include not only the objects of normal sense experience, but also other "non-empirical" objects such as mathematical relations. In other words, the empirical realm is assumed to have much wider limits than the empiricism of sense.

[10] See above, pp. 12-13.

8. The ground or source of both Being and Value, in the light of the foregoing assumptions cannot be "subjective" but rather must be fundamentally "objective."

If these assumptions may be regarded either as tenable, or at least intelligibly formulated, and granted that they are all essentially Platonic in character, we should be in a position to examine more precisely Plato's theory of Being and Value and then turn to Aristotle to observe the consequences of his rejection of Plato. But at this point one crucial fact should not be overlooked, and this is that the value theorist is faced at every turn with the humanly insurmountable problem of evil. *Unde Malum?* Why is it that with every positive value there is paired an opposite disvalue? The number of such difficult questions is legion. It has been remarked that, of all the perennial problems, philosophy has made the least "progress" in the face of the problem of evil. Consequently, the best that can be done in our present discussion is to be aware of the theories of evil held respectively by Plato and Aristotle, and to attempt *pari passu* to develop as firm a working hypothesis as possible which will take into account the notion that a human view of Being and Value does involve also a conception of disvalue.

To set the stage for the coming examination of Plato and Aristotle against the background of our several assumptions, a remark of Werner Jaeger may be appropriately quoted, "When the [Platonic] theory of Forms was abandoned being and value fell apart, and dialectic thereby lost its direct significance for human life, which to Plato was an essential feature of it. The distinction between metaphysics and ethics became much sharper than before."[11] He here appends a footnote which runs, "This is true of all specifically human values, but not of absolute value or good. Aristotle believed as much as Plato that being and value in the absolute sense coincide in the conception of God. In that respect he remained a Platonist to the day of his death. The highest being is also the highest good. At the point that is farthest removed from human affairs metaphysics penetrates into ethics and ethics into metaphysics." Jaeger is quite right in

[11] W. Jaeger, Aristotle, *Fundamentals of the History of His Development*, translated by R. Robinson (Oxford, Clarendon Press, 1934) pp. 83–84.

asserting that Being and Value fall apart for Aristotle with the rejection of the Theory of Ideas. Metaphysics and ethics lose their vital contact. But it may be questioned whether Plato saw Being and Value coincide in God. Did Aristotle in this respect remain "a Platonist until the day of his death"? What are the arguments by which Aristotle attempts to show that the highest being is the highest good? These, and many questions like them, must be faced in investigating the consequences of Aristotle's refusal of the Platonic theory. The remarks of Jaeger indicate in some measure Aristotle's situation. So close was he to Plato that hardly a page of his does not bear some vestige of Platonic influence. This much of a Platonist he must always be. But he repudiates categorically the heart and soul of Platonism, the Theory of Ideas. This is the Aristotelian dilemma: how to be a Platonic non-Platonist. Nowhere do the consequences of this dilemma reveal themselves more clearly than in Aristotle's doctrines in the field of value.

CHAPTER II

PLATO: BEING AND VALUE: THE THEORY
OF IDEAS

MUCH has been written about the so-called development of Plato's thought. No doubt there were many shifts in interest, as he concentrated now upon ethics, now upon ethics and politics, now upon logic and cosmology. But the best criticism and interpretation has tended to show that there is a basic unity to Plato's thought which in no fundamental way varied from his earliest to his latest writings.[1] Despite the views of many scholars, it seems difficult to see any real difference between the doctrine of the *Euthyphro, Gorgias, Republic, Theaetetus, Timaeus*, and *Laws*. Informing all of these dialogues which are spread over the entire period of Plato's creative activity is an identical view of man, the human predicament, man's destiny, and the realm of eternity. Our problem, then is to get before us, within the briefest possible compass, the essence of this view and its implications for the problem of Being and Value. It will then be possible to consider those elements in the view to which Aristotle objected, and to study the consequences of his objections.

One convenient means of presenting the essence of the Platonic position lies in reviewing the analysis of Platonism developed by Paul Elmer More.[2] More maintains that Plato worked out in parallel two notions: one the Theory of Ideas which receives its

---

[1] The most eloquent and effective proponent of this view is Paul Shorey, notably in his *Unity of Plato's Thought* (Chicago, University of Chicago Decennial Publications, 1903).

[2] *The Sceptical Approach to Religion* (Princeton University Press, 1934) Chapters 2–4. A fuller statement of the position can be found in the earlier volumes of More's series on *The Greek Tradition*. For general works on Plato, the reader is referred to A. E. Taylor, *Plato, The Man and His Work* (New York, The Dial Press, 1927); P. Shorey, *What Plato Said* (Chicago, University of Chicago Press, 1933); G. M. A. Grube, *Plato's Thought* (London, Methuen, 1935); L. Robin, *Platon*, (Paris, Alcan, 1935); C. Ritter, *Platon, sein Leben, seine Schriften, seine Lehre* (München, Beck, 1910–1923); C. Ritter, *The Essence of Plato's Philosophy* (transl. by Alles. New York, Dial Press, 1933.) = *Die Kerngedanken der Platonischen Philosophie* (München, Reinhardt, 1931).

fullest and most compact expression in the Image of the Divided Line at the end of the sixth book of the *Republic;* and the other, the conception of God, which is elaborated to the greatest extent in the cosmology of the *Timaeus* and in the great theodicy of the tenth book of the *Laws*. In More's opinion, the *Euthyphro* is by all odds the most significant of all the earliest dialogues. Here, it will be recalled, as Socrates cross-examines Euthyphro on the latter's motives in prosecuting his own father for murder, *i.e.*, a specific act of impiety, the argument turns to the question of the nature of piety or holiness, ἡ ὁσιότης. Socrates asks whether the gods love that which is holy because it is holy, or whether that which is holy is holy because the gods love it. Though the dialogue is aporetic or exploratory, and leaves open the question of what holiness really is, this particular phase of the argument declares that the gods love that which is holy because it is holy.

It is in this embryonic fashion that these two great aspects of Plato's thought receive their preliminary expression in the *Euthyphro*. On the one hand the Theory of Ideas is postulated, when Socrates at an early stage asks Euthyphro not to give him one or two instances of holiness, but "that Form or Idea itself by virtue of which all things that are holy are holy."[3] It has been frequently pointed out that the language here is the regular technical language which Plato always employs when he is discussing the Theory of Ideas.[4] Furthermore it is likewise thoroughly characteristic that when Socrates introduces the Theory of Ideas in this technical language the interlocutor regularly and without argument accepts it.[5] On the other hand, in the *Euthyphro* is the

---

[3] *Euthyphro* 6 d 10: ἀλλ' ἐκεῖνο αὐτὸ τὸ εἶδος ᾧ πάντα τὰ ὅσια ὅσιά ἐστιν. Socrates then refers back to an earlier admission of Euthyphro (5 d 1–5) to the effect that in every act holiness is identical with itself, that the unholy is the opposite of everything that is holy, with whatever is to be unholy being the same with itself and having some one Form or Idea with respect of its unholiness.

[4] Some scholars would deny that the Theory of Ideas is invoked in the dialogue —or would admit at most a vague anticipation of it.

[5] As is well known, Plato never attempts to give a demonstrative proof for the Theory of Ideas. He merely builds up a large mass of reasonable evidence which will make for its acceptance. This fact would lead one to conclude that Plato held demonstrative proof of ultimate principles to be impossible. An analogous situation can be seen in the various attempts to define moral and aesthetic Ideas. No Idea is ever defined in Plato in any final sense. Working definitions are employed, as, for example, in the *Republic,* δικαιοσύνη, "justness," is tentatively defined as τὸ τὰ αὑτοῦ πράττειν, "the proper performance by each particular

Platonic conception of the Divine, and the whole argument of the dialogue suggests that the gods, or the element of the Divine and the Ideas are extrinsic to each other, though in the argument about holiness it is at least implicit that God or the gods know that which is holy and love it accordingly.

Now, if these two notions, of the Ideas and of God, are taken to be present at the outset of Plato's thought, according to More, Plato first became preoccupied with working out the full implications of the Theory of Ideas. Nor did he neglect the question of human happiness which from time to time obtruded itself in his speculation. A significant step in connection with the Theory of Ideas occurs in the *Gorgias*. Here Socrates by invoking the theory is able to overcome the might-makes-right, Nietzschean, amoralistic position of Callicles.[6] But the *Gorgias* leaves open the question of the nature of justness. The first book of the *Republic* obviously continues the *Gorgias*. Thrasymachus, who repeats the arguments of Callicles, fares no better at the hands of Socrates than his predecessor. But the argument takes a more serious turn when Glaucon and Adeimantus, the brothers of Plato and members of the *dramatis personae* of the *Republic*, take up the discussion. Styling themselves as basically friendly "advocates of the devil," they put the case against Socrates in its most extreme form. They ask, in effect, "Can a man be happy if he really possesses δικαιοσύνη, justness, alone, even when he is deprived of everything else? Who is the happier: the most completely unjust man who *seems* to be the most completely just, and on account of his excellent reputation enjoys all the goods and honours of this

---

thing of its own proper function." *The Greater Hippias* is another case in point. One after another, definitions of beauty are submitted to scrutiny, only to be rejected. The outcome of the argument is that beauty is revealed to be an Idea, and, as such, being an ultimate principle, is therefore incapable of definition. Plato's method, then is not to "prove" absolutely, nor to "define" absolutely, but rather to convince by the weight of reasonable and relevant evidence. The whole Platonic attitude is reflected in one casual speech in the *Republic*, 532 d 2-4, where the interlocutor says to Socrates, "These things are difficult to believe, but they are also difficult not to believe."

[6] Plato's method can be clearly seen in Socrates' argument with Callicles. A vast amount of evidence against Callicles is assembled and is supported by the telling use of moral eloquence on the part of Socrates. All this is designed to persuade the reader, but in the dialogue Callicles does not depart an iota from his original position. Nor is Thrasymachus convinced in the parallel passage in *Republic* I.

world; or the most completely just man who *seems* to be the most completely unjust, and hence suffers all the pains and dishonours of this world because of his unfortunate reputation?" Glaucon and Adeimantus definitely rule out of the argument any question of rewards and punishments in a possible life after death, as well as the presence or influence of God in the matter. Socrates avers that the just man will be the happier. He accepts fully the challenge of his younger interlocutors, and in a sense the remainder of the *Republic* consists in an attempt to validate his answer.[7]

As the *Republic* advances through its succeeding stages, by impressive steps it moves towards the climactic delineation of the Theory of Ideas. As a consequence of the famous paradox which proclaims that kings must be philosophers or philosophers kings if the states of the world are to find any surcease of evil, at the end of Book V, Socrates draws in broadest outline his basic metaphysical schema. On the one hand, there is the realm of Being in which no flux can find its way, a realm of permanence where all that abides unchanged eternally is. Opposing it is the realm of Non-being, and in between the two is this world of ours, this realm of "sights and sounds," of flux and change, in which Being and Non-being are tumbled about together. It is the philosopher whose gaze is oriented towards the realm of Being, where the permanence of its objects makes it possible for him in some sense to have knowledge of them. The philosopher, who is thus oriented towards Being, is able to look at the things in

---

[7] More (*Sceptical Approach to Religion*, p. 81) has drawn an interesting comparison here. Glaucon, in his famous description of the fate of the just man who seems to be unjust, says, "He will be beaten, he will be broken on the rack, he will be bound, he will have his eyes burned out, and finally after suffering every ill, he will be crucified" (*Republic* 361 e 3). Socrates maintains that even in this state the just man will be happy. More cites the passage in the *Nicomachean Ethics* (1153 b 17-21) where Aristotle says, "Therefore the happy man needs the goods of the body, external goods, and the goods of fortune, so that these (or the lack of these) may not stand in the way of his being happy. When men maintain that the man who is being broken on the wheel, or the man who is beset with great misfortunes, is happy if he is a good man, whether they mean to or not, they are talking nonsense." Whether or not Aristotle here is giving a direct answer to Plato in the passage of the *Republic*, the differing tempers of the two thinkers are strikingly revealed by the comparison. Aristotle maintains on the face of it that it is nonsense to suppose that a suffering good man is happy, while Plato strains every nerve to show that the truly just man under whatever circumstance is happy. The contrast between Plato and Aristotle on this point prefigures their metaphysical conflict and their attendant reactions in the realm of value.

the changing world of "sights and sounds," but not to stop there, but rather to see through the things of flux to those permanences which lie behind them. Because things continually change in the world of "sights and sounds" it is not possible to have any genuine "knowledge" of them, but only opinion, δόξα. Hence the thinker who believes that there is nothing more ultimate in Reality than the world of phenomena, cannot be called a philosopher, *i.e.*, a lover of wisdom, but a "doxophilist," a lover of opinion.

In the sixth book, Plato explores the implications of this preliminary statement of his position, and at the close of the book he introduces his more elaborate image of the Divided Line, which, as the most explicit statement of Plato's Theory of Ideas, will be examined later in detail. At the beginning of the seventh book the same metaphysical view of Reality as is in the image of the Divided Line, is repeated in the famous Allegory of the Cave.[8] These two great passages, coupled with the one which describes man's ascent to an apprehension of the Idea of the Good, not unlike the medieval Christian mystic's ascent to and apprehension of God, really amount to a momentary elimination from Plato's thinking of any element of God or the Divine. In other words, the view of Reality contained in these two great images approaches closely a non-theological abstract idealism.

[8] It should be needless to point out that those who try to establish a tight one-to-one correspondence between the image of the Divided Line and the Allegory of the Cave are undertaking a fruitless enterprise. Such a correspondence would imply an absolute identity of meaning for the two images, in which case Plato surely would have been content to employ one only. The plain fact of the matter is that Plato is talking about first principles and among them, the Idea of the Good, which, he consistently maintains, can never be adequately delineated in any words or images. Socrates says explicitly in *Republic* 506 d 6 ff. that he will not speak of the Good, but can only talk of something that is the offspring of the Good and like it, *viz.*, the sun. No wonder, then, that Plato, as he proceeds through this difficult area, seeks to convey his basic meaning by the use of any image or metaphor at his command. Hence derives his use of alternative images. The mathematical imagistic material of the Divided Line can communicate his meaning admirably, but there is a limit to the effectiveness of the communication which is fixed by the mathematical nature of the imagistic material. The material of the image in the Allegory of the Cave is drawn from ordinary human experience, is non-mathematical, and as such has both its strength and weakness as a medium of communication. Each image has the same basic meaning, but each does something which the other cannot. Hence the two images complement each other. Only in terms of some such analysis as this can the presence and the relation of the two images be satisfactorily explained.

Now in More's opinion, Plato was not able to establish his contention that a man could be happy by the possession of justness alone solely upon the basis of the Theory of Ideas, a stark abstract idealism. Nor in the Theory of Ideas by itself was there any possibility of working out even a moderately adequate answer to the question, *unde malum*, "Whence evil?" For these reasons ultimately Plato undertook to develop in the *Timaeus*, a dialogue explicitly in continuation of the *Republic*, a cosmology which would combine the Theory of Ideas and appropriate theological conceptions. And it should be remembered that the religious aspect had never been totally absent from Plato's thought, from the early *Euthyphro* on down through the *Republic* and later. In the *Timaeus* Plato does not use the method of dialectic, characteristic of his earlier works, but instead employs the medium of myth. The cosmology and myth of creation of this highly complex work can be expressed in its essence in the following scheme:[9]

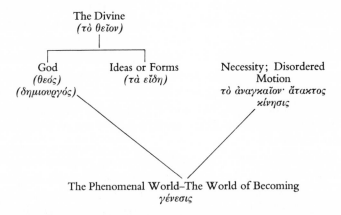

Plato's theory postulates three eternally coexistent elements: God, the Ideas, and Necessity. In the terms of the myth, God, the Demiurge or Master Craftsman (whose nature, Plato says, is difficult to know and impossible to tell to men), is good, and in virtue of his goodness undertakes the act of creation. He desires to forge a cosmos which will likewise be good, in fact, be as like himself as possible. So the Master Craftsman, keeping his eye

[9] The scheme was worked out by More.

23

upon the Ideas, which are extrinsic to him, as models or patterns, proceeds to mould or fashion the cosmos out of the vast mass of preexisting stuff, which is also extrinsic to him and which Plato calls variously, Necessity, Disordered Motion or the Matrix. It is in this way that γένεσις, the World of Becoming, comes into existence.[10]

There are several aspects of this myth which are worth noting. In the first place, God and the Ideas are distinct from each other. Always in Platonic studies there has been the consistent tendency to attempt to identify the Idea of the Good with God.[11] No amount of scholarly argument can avail against the decisive evidence of the *Timaeus* account. God is not *the Good;* He is good, and therefore wishes to make a good world. Thus in the realm of the eternal and unchanging, there are the two elements or aspects, the subjective and active element, God, and the objective formal aspect, the Ideas. These two are distinct from each other, and are related, we may suppose only by the fact that God has a perfect and complete "awareness" of the Ideas.

Secondly, the myth is explicit in its theory of time. In eternity, the realm of the Demiurge and the Ideas, there is no such thing as temporal sequence.[12] In fact, Plato insists that the only "tense" one can use of an Idea is the present. The Ideas *are*, and it is quite inaccurate to say that Ideas *have been* or *will be*. Sometimes we do use these expressions, but actually this is the result of a conventional manner of speaking which is hard to avoid because human beings after all are living in a universe of space and time. According to the myth, time came into being with the creation, and hence it is proper to use past, present, and future to designate things in the phenomenal world which are ordered in temporal sequence. But by the same token, it is not precise to use the expression, "*before* the creation," for actually, time did not exist *before* the creation, and thus any word like "before," which

[10] It is easy to see the relation of the elements of the cosmology of the *Timaeus* if it is restated in the terms of the Aristotelian doctrine of the four causes. Necessity is the material cause, the Ideas the formal cause, the Demiurge the efficient cause, and the purpose in the "mind" of the Demiurge the final cause.

[11] Cf. the conclusive discussion of this problem by H. F. Cherniss, *Aristotle's Criticism of Plato and the Academy*, vol. I (Baltimore, The Johns Hopkins Press, 1944) Appendix XI, pp. 603–610.

[12] Cf. *Timaeus*, 37 e–38 a.

24

depends upon temporal sequence for its meaning, cannot appropriately be employed in that context.

And finally, the myth does supply Plato with a theory of evil, at least a theory whereby to explain cosmic evil, which the Theory of Ideas as it is expressed in the *Republic* was unable to provide. In the *Timaeus*, Plato indicates that cosmic evil somehow or other derives from a kind of recalcitrance or stubborn resistance inherent in Necessity or Disordered Motion to the benevolent forces of creation. In the stuff or material out of which the Demiurge moulds the universe, *viz.*, Necessity, there is that which ultimately prevents him from fashioning an absolutely perfect world. It is a good world, and the Demiurge wants it to be as good "as possible." Consequently, the residual imperfections in the universe cannot be attributed to God. His is not the responsibility. The myth then presents us with a doctrine of a Deity limited in power, but of supreme goodness, who has created a universe marred to a certain degree by defects traceable to the primordial stuff of the creation. In this way the myth recognizes and explains that aspect of the universe which our own contemporary physicists, as a result of their recent experiments, have been led to call, somewhat ruefully, the "inherent depravity" in things. But, at the same time, the myth conveys the view that the values represented by the Ideas have been translated into the universe, for they have served as models for the Demiurge during his work of creation. The universe, then, in its very being, reflects the values after which it has been modelled.[13]

More's account of the Platonic position concludes by calling attention to the *Laws*, especially the tenth book, where the two parallel conceptions, God and the Ideas, are copresent and in the proper equilibrium in Platonic terms. In this book, for example, Plato picks up the three views concerning the nature of the gods mentioned by Adeimantus in the second book of the *Republic*.[14] This triple "heresy," as More calls it, consists in either denying the existence of the gods, or in asserting their existence but denying that they have any care for men, or in

[13] It is in this respect that the cosmological myth of the *Timaeus* expresses the same view of the relation of Being and Value as is found in the Theory of Ideas, which we will examine in detail below.

[14] 365 d 7 ff.

asserting that they exist, do care for men, but can be bought off by suitable sacrifices. In the tenth book of the *Laws*, Plato by means of an explicit refutation of this triple heresy establishes the position and function of Deity in Reality.[15] And furthermore, the Ideas are still present, functioning as ultimate principles but extrinsic to God.[16]

Whatever criticisms may be levelled in one way or another against More's analysis of Plato's basic thought, nonetheless, even in the foregoing brief recapitulation, it cannot be denied that it expresses in bold outline the position which is given in the text of the dialogues. But at the moment it is necessary to examine further the Theory of Ideas, which from first to last is always present in Plato's mind. Fortunately for the reader of Plato, the image of the Divided Line provides an amazingly concise statement of the Theory, and hence he can with confidence seek to understand it by scrutinizing closely the final pages of the sixth

[15] For the purposes of our general argument, we need not be worried by the fact that Plato sometimes talks about God (in the singular) and sometimes about the Gods, where he perhaps falls into the conventional mode, employed in his time, of speaking about the element of the Divine in Reality. It is enough to note that his tendency is profoundly towards monotheism, as can be seen in various key passages. The Demiurge of the *Timaeus* is one. Or, to take another crucial example, when in the myth of Er in *Republic* X, the souls who are about to be reborn are being instructed on how to choose the patterns of their next life, Plato says, αἰτία ἑλομένου· θεὸς ἀναίτιος, "The responsibility is on the chooser; God is blameless."

[16] Cherniss, *Aristotle's Criticism of Plato and the Academy*, vol. I, p. 608, maintains that God must be subordinate to the Ideas, because God has νοῦς. Cherniss cites the *Phaedrus*, 247 d, where Plato in the myth refers to "the nourishment of God's mind by the contemplation of the Ideas." *Phaedrus* 249 c 6 also is adduced, where Plato, according to Cherniss, states that "God's divinity is a result of His relation to the Ideas." Cherniss also cites the passages from the *Euthyphro* (which already have been discussed above (where Plato argues that the holy is beloved by God because it is holy, and it is not holy because it is beloved by God (10 a, 11 a.) Now none of these passages appears to justify the "subordination of God to the Ideas." Rather God and the Ideas seem to be coequal; each by itself is inadequate, but each in relation to the other posits an eternal realm adequate, in Plato's view, to express the subjective and objective elements which are necessary to it. An interpretation of this sort certainly accounts for Plato's phrase that God's mind is nourished by the Ideas. God's mind thus nourished, can act, while the Ideas of themselves cannot. Of course, the *Euthyphro* passages make clear that God did not create the Ideas, but neither did the Ideas create God. As for *Phaedrus* 249 c 6, πρὸς οἷσπερ θεὸς ὢν θεῖός ἐστιν, it must mean, referring to the first part of the sentence, something of this sort: "The mind of the philosopher is ever oriented towards the Ideas in memory so far as possible, towards which God, being divine, is oriented." Thus this passage cannot justify the thesis that "God's divinity is a result of His relation to the Ideas."

book of the *Republic*. Interpreters usually accompany their discussions with a diagram of some such sort as the following:[17]

		Realm of Becoming The Sun ὁ ἥλιος		Realm of Being The Idea of the Good ἡ τοῦ ἀγαθοῦ ἰδέα	
		The Visible grasped by Opinion ὁρατόν δοξαστόν		The Noetic grasped by "Knowledge" νοητόν γνωστόν	
	A D	C	E	B	
Objective	εἴκονες Images	ζῷα, σκευή Natural Objects, Artefacta	μαθηματικά Objects of Mathematics	εἴδη Ideas	
Subjective	εἰκασία "Imagina- tion" Conjecture	πίστις, δόξα Belief, Opinion	διάνοια Understanding	νόησις The "Higher" Reason	

The Line initially expresses the radical dualism of the Theory of Ideas. There are two modes of existence, one the realm of phenomena, the space-time universe, the world of sights and sounds. This mode, represented by the segment AC, is presided over by the sun, and it is apprehended by men through their senses. Since it is constantly changing, men can only have opinions about it. The other mode of existence is the real realm of Being represented by the segment CB. It is eternal, outside of space and time, and unchanging. It is presided over by the supreme Idea of the Good, and because it is conceived to be eternal and unchanging, men in some sense can be said to have "knowledge" of it. Plato then means the whole line AB to comprise within it everything which can lay claim to objective existence of every sort or order, and he means to indicate by its first division at C those two great areas or

---

[17] The diagram is based upon the text of *Republic* 507 b 2–511 e 5. The image of the Divided Line is actually introduced at 509 d 6. Sometimes interpreters of the text have placed the line in a vertical position in order to emphasize the relation between the "lower" and the "higher" segments. If it is represented in the horizontal position as here, I believe that all the relations meant to be expressed can be more easily grasped. It only need be remembered that the "lower" segments are at the left, and that as we move from left to right, we "ascend" to the "higher" segments.

modes of existence into which it can be analyzed.[18] But Plato has said that the Line should be divided into unequal parts, which can only mean that the greater of the two parts is the more important, and is therefore the appropriate one to symbolize the more important mode of existence, *i.e.*, the realm of real Being.

Plato's next instruction in the text, however, is that the two initial segments, AC and CB, be subdivided ἀνὰ τὸν αὐτὸν λόγον, "according to the same proportion." Thus the whole line is divided in the familiar geometrical mode of extreme and mean proportion. From the geometrical point of view, this division sets up a large number of equations, not all of which by any means does Plato either exploit or intend to exploit in his subsequent exposition.[19] Suffice it to say that, at least at the outset, Plato is most interested in conveying the relation he sees between the realm of Becoming and the realm of Being. This he is able to do by examining the subdivisions which appear in the realm of Becoming. In the first segment, AD, are subsumed the images, shadows, or reflections of all the objects, ζῷα and σκευή, that is, all natural objects as well as the artefacts which are to be found in the world of sights and sounds. Hence, in respect of reality and importance, the objects themselves are superior to the shadows or reflections they cast. Now if we assume that it is one of Plato's prime purposes to throw light on the relation between the realm of Becoming and the realm of Being, he does so by prefiguring it in materials drawn from the most ordinary human experience. It is as if he asked, "Do you wish to know how AC is related to

[18] It is my purpose for the moment not to raise the various difficulties which are present in the image of the Line, but rather to give a positive exposition of it as an expression of the Theory of Ideas. At a later stage of the argument, it will be more appropriate to consider the difficulties.

[19] Warner Fite, *The Platonic Legend* (New York, Scribners, 1934) pp. 250–253, makes great capital of the mathematical fact that in a line divided in extreme and mean proportion, as in our diagram, segment DC equals segment CE. Fite argues that the contents symbolized by the two segments must therefore be of equal importance—a consequence which Plato obviously did not intend. But, to Fite, this unhappy result of one aspect of the image reduces the whole to a state of uselessness, and thus becomes nothing but another item of evidence making against the mind of Plato who was dogged by the hopeless tendency to mathematicize everything. It should be unnecessary to point out that Plato meant his image to be grasped imaginatively and not to be pressed too far. The presence of the immediately following Allegory of the Cave should be sufficient evidence for this conclusion. Cf. above, note 8.

CB?" and then replied, "Just as shadows are related to the objects that cast them, *i.e.*, as AD is related to DC."

The situation is not so clear on turning to the subdivision of the other major segment of the Line. Plato first makes the distinction between CE and EB upon methodological grounds. He insists that in dealing with the material of mathematics, the method employed is one which starts with hypotheses, and proceeds from these, not towards a genuine first principle, ἀρχή, but to a conclusion coherent with the hypotheses. In so doing, Plato points out, the mathematician uses as images those things which in the next lowest segment of the line were objects able to cast shadows or be reflected. Whereas, in the highest segment, the method does not involve the use of images but rather treats hypotheses as such, tests their validity, and moves towards a first principle by employing the Ideas themselves.

At this point in the text, Plato quite humorously causes Socrates' interlocutor to remark that he does not understand the explanation very well. So Socrates undertakes to elaborate his point. He cites the odd and even, the three kinds of angles, and other related notions, as characteristic of the hypotheses which geometricians employ. They never give any account of these hypotheses either to themselves or to anyone else, but merely accept them as self-evident, ὡς παντὶ φανερῶν. The geometrician's whole task is then to construct a self-consistent system, the conclusion of which will be coherent with the starting point. Now, Socrates continues, these geometricians use diagrams, and they argue in terms of the diagrams. These diagrams can be seen, and indeed are objects in the world of sights and sounds.[20] The figure of a triangle or square drawn on a blackboard is a sufficient illustration. But, Socrates adds, it is not the diagram about which the geometrician is thinking, but rather those things of which the diagram is an imitation or likeness, namely, the square itself, or the diagonal itself. And here the point is that the real mathematical square and the real mathematical diagonal are as much superior to and more important than their representations in

[20] As such, of course, they can be reflected in a mirror. Plato includes this point, but it is not particularly germane to the whole argument. It functions rather as a means of showing the interconnection of the segment CE with AD and DC.

diagrams, as are objects more important than their imitations or reflections.

The final segment is the realm of Ideas proper, and the appropriate method here is that of dialectric. In this segment hypotheses are treated as genuine hypotheses, starting points whose validity must be tested. The goal is to reach a non-hypothetical first principle and to move from it through its implications, to an appropriate conclusion. In the process, no object of sense is employed, but only Ideas. The dialectician uses them, moves through them, and reaches his conclusions in them.[21]

Much more needs to be said about the "contents" of the realm of Being, and the relation of its two subdivisions to each other, but first we should notice the series of subjective correlates attached severally to the four segments of the Line. These subjective correlates in effect break down the operation of apprehending all that exists on the part of a human being into the workings of four separate "faculties" or "instruments of apprehension." These are distinguished according to the differences of the objects of which they are the correlates. Though the realm of Becoming as a whole is described as visible or "opinable," in the subdivision of the realm, opinion *(δόξα)* or belief *(πίστις)* is reserved as the faculty for apprehending natural objects or artefacts. Plato, in order to complete his scheme symmetrically, postulates a special power, which he calls "imagination"[22] or conjecture, εἰκασία, wherewith the apprehender grasps shadows, reflections, and the like. Efforts have been made to see in εἰκασία a special aesthetic faculty whereby man grasps works of art but there seems to be no ground in the text for subsuming art under the εἰκόνες of segment AD.[23] Furthermore, it is difficult to understand how the relation between "understanding" and the "higher reason" of the upper segments of the line is very much illuminated by the introduction of "conjecture" as distinct from "belief" or

---

[21] *Republic* 511 c 1: αἰσθητῷ παντάπασιν οὐδενὶ προσχρώμενος, ἀλλ᾿ εἴδεσιν αὐτοῖς δι᾿ αὐτῶν εἰς αὐτά, καὶ τελευτᾷ εἰς εἴδη.

[22] To obtain the proper effect of this word as a translation of εἰκασία, it should be pronounced with the accent on the first syllable.

[23] Such a theory presupposes that Plato's views on art stop at the analysis in *Republic* X of art as "an imitation of an imitation" and thus at the third remove from the truth. Plato's genuine philosophy of art is rather to be found in the *Phaedrus* and the *Symposium*.

"opinion." Or, to put it another way, the objective correlates—images and natural objects and artefacts—function powerfully as a means of communicating the relation between the realm of Becoming and the realm of Being, and this because objects and the shadows they cast are an immediate part of human experience. But, unfortunately, there is no comparable experiential sanction for the distinction between "conjecture" and "opinion." Hence, it must be admitted that the postulate of a special faculty correlated with the images constitutes one of the least satisfactory aspects of the Image of the Divided Line.

No doubt many critics would see a comparable weakness in the distinction between the special mathematical faculty which Plato labels διάνοια, understanding, and the dialectical faculty, νόησις, the so-called "higher reason." Quite apart from the difference in method, the question which is really raised is whether the type of intelligence employed by a mathematician is actually different from that put into play by the metaphysician, since they both obviously deal with abstractions, a fact clearly recognized by Plato, for the objects with which they both deal are in the realm of Being. According to Plato, the mathematical intelligence, the "understanding," considers entities which in some way or other may be diagrammed, may be given some kind of representation which can be apprehended by the senses, whereas the dialectician in manipulating the Ideas cannot avail himself of any such sensory support. One can draw a picture of a triangle, but it would be impossible to represent pictorially any one of the Ideas subsumed under the highest segment of the Divided Line.[24]

What are these Ideas in the higher range of Being? Critics usually maintain that there are Ideas or Forms of all entities which can be considered as classes of particular entities in the universe of space and time. There are, it is usually affirmed, two great categories of Ideas: one, Ideas of things; the other, Ideas of qualities, primarily aesthetic or ethical. Thus there would be Ideas of stone, tree, chair, or man, which, strictly speaking, should be called stone-ness, tree-ness chair-ness, or man-ness. Such Ideas would account for that essential element common severally to

---

[24] Clearly this distinction works very well for geometry, but its application in other branches of mathematics is not so apparent.

all stones, trees, etc., which in turn would explain the fact that they can be considered together as groups. In the other category of Ideas would appear the Ideas of aesthetic and ethical values, such as beauty, or courage, or temperance, or justness. These Ideas too can be said to account for that element in objects which causes them to be called beautiful, or that common element in human actions which would cause them to be called courageous, and so on. And presiding over all these Ideas is the supreme Idea of the Good, from which, according to Plato, derives the very being of these Ideas as well as the fact that they can be known by men.[25]

Admittedly there are many puzzles in this account which need illumination. One of the standard difficulties lies in the position which Plato assigns to the objects of mathematics. A common-sense explanation can be found in simply recognizing that the material of mathematics provides Plato with a very easy instance of the kind of thing he means by an Idea, an entity that is by its very nature unconditioned by space and time, literally "outside of" space and time, and an entity which cannot be seen by the eye of the body, but only by the "eye of the mind." A triangle is just such an entity. No true triangle can ever be produced in space and time—for one reason: there is no such thing in space and time as a line, which by definition has only one dimension, length. Yet these objects, the objects of the geometrician, have for Plato a real existence, an unchanging existence which somehow transcends anything that can be found in the world of space and time. The objects of mathematics endure, and mathematical relations abide, no matter how wrong-headed some men may be in understanding them. It is surely this reason which causes Plato to put arithmetic as the very first discipline to be taught those who have qualified for the higher education of the potential "philosopher-kings." He there calls mathematics a study which "in every way draws men towards Being."[26] And in a way, the discussion of the Divided Line makes clear this intermediate position of the objects of mathematics between the world of sense and the realm of the Ideas proper. Mathematics, or at

[25] *Republic*, 509 b 6–10.
[26] *Republic*, 523 a 2, ἑλκτικῷ ὄντι παντάπασι πρὸς οὐσίαν.

least geometry, can be visibly illustrated in the world of sense, *i.e.*, one can draw a triangle on a blackboard, but no one can draw a diagram of honesty, or self-control, or justness—or for that matter, of tree-ness or chair-ness. One can draw, to be sure, a picture of a tree, but that is a far different thing for Plato from tree-ness. Hence, Plato maintains, mathematics gives men practice in manipulating non-spatial and non-temporal entities, with the help from time to time of visual diagrammatic aids. With this practice, we can move more easily into the realm of the Ideas proper where no visual or diagrammatic assistance is available.

There is a well-known passage in the first book of Aristotle's *Metaphysics* on the intermediate position of the objects of mathematics in Plato's Theory of Ideas. In the course of his criticism of the Theory, Aristotle writes, "But further, besides the *sensibilia* (*i.e.*, the objects of sense perception) and the Ideas, [Plato] says there are the objects of mathematics in an intermediate position, since they differ from the *sensibilia* in that they are eternal and unchangeable, and since they differ from the Ideas in that there are many objects of mathematics alike, whereas the Idea itself in each case is unique."[27] According to this interpretation there is an Idea, in segment CE of the Line, let us say, of an equilateral triangle with the dimensions of one inch on a side. This Idea of an equilateral triangle has many others like it, and it is eternal and unchanging. However, there would be an Idea of triangularity, which would fall under the highest segment of the Line, but it would be not only eternal and unchanging, but also unique. Now such an understanding of the passage from Aristotle does not have any explicit support in Plato's discussion of the Divided Line, but on the other hand, there is nothing in that discussion which would make against this interpretation. Hence, it would be quite reasonable to suppose that Aristotle had Plato's Image of the Divided Line in mind when he wrote this passage.

Ross in his note on these lines[28] points to the fact that Plato's

---

[27] *Metaphysics*, 987 b 14–18: ἔτι δὲ παρὰ τὰ αἰσθητὰ καὶ τὰ εἴδη τὰ μαθηματικὰ τῶν πραγμάτων εἶναί φησι μεταξύ, διαφέροντα τῶν μὲν αἰσθητῶν τῷ ἀΐδια καὶ ἀκίνητα εἶναι, τῶν δ' εἰδῶν τῷ τὰ μὲν πόλλ' ἄττα ὅμοια εἶναι τὸ δὲ εἶδος αὐτὸ ἕν ἕκαστον μόνον. In all quotations from the *Metaphysics*, I follow the text of Ross. The English rendering here is my own.

[28] W. D. Ross, *Aristotle's Metaphysics* (Oxford, Clarendon Press, 1924) vol. I, pp. 166–168.

33

conception of the objects of mathematics works much better in the case of geometry than it does with arithmetic as such. This should not be surprising if we recall how Greek mathematicians tended always to think of number in geometrical terms. And further, Plato obviously in the Divided Line is not addressing himself to the specific problem of a philosophy of mathematics but rather, among other things, is relating to one another several orders of existence. Not only does he want to insist upon the absolute existence of the objects of mathematics as separate from all sensible objects, but also he wants to use the objects of mathematics as the easiest illustration to show to the uninitiated exactly what kind of entity an Idea is. This pedagogic purpose, which can rely upon general familiarity with geometry, is thoroughly justified, for if one understands what Plato means by the eternity and unchangeableness of the material of geometry, it is not too difficult to move on to the Ideas of the highest category in which Plato had by far the most interest. Not only do the objects of mathematics as intermediates function in this way as a readily grasped stepping stone to the Ideas proper, but also the distinction between the mathematicals and Ideas proper permits Plato to elaborate the distinction between the method of mathematics and the method of dialectic. And indeed, Plato in the Image of the Line dwells most upon this methodological distinction. The mathematician asks no questions about the fundamental character of the entities with which he deals, but only seeks to construct a coherent system. The dialectician, who deals with Ideas proper, asks every question about the entities and relations which he investigates, and seeks to test and improve such first principles as he may reach. If such is a fair account of Plato's purpose in the Image of the Divided Line, then it is surely not justifiable for criticism to seek in the Line a thoroughgoing interpretation of a philosophy of mathematics.

There are some additional points which have to be borne in mind in order to understand more completely the Theory of Ideas as it is expounded in the Divided Line. It is by way of being a statement of the nature of the external Reality, in all its dimensions, with which man is confronted. For Plato's views on the human nature which confronts this Reality and must exert effort to understand it, we must look at other portions of the dialogues than those which treat directly of the Theory of Ideas. Obviously the meaning of the Theory of Ideas in Plato cannot be understood apart from his notions in regard to the nature of man. As for human nature, Plato insists that within man is an immortal soul, which abides for a time in the body,[29] and on death will leave the body. The soul possesses moral responsibility and after death it will be rigorously judged, and rewarded or punished for its deeds on earth. Under the influence of Pythagoreanism primarily, Plato holds that the soul has to endure a cycle of rebirths until it shall have become sufficiently purified to merit the bliss of eternity, or alternatively, if it persists in evil, to be consigned to the everlasting punishment of Tartarus. The one guarantee which the soul has, according to Plato's great poetical myths, is to attain an abiding vision of the Ideas while in death and awaiting reincarnation. If this vision is profound, it will stay with the soul, even in its new birth, and will permit man to see through the jumble and flux of human affairs to the Ideas which lie behind all. But this is not easy, for Plato characteristically portrays the soul in man as having three parts: first, the lower desires and passions; second, the nobler and higher emotions; and third, the highest element of all, the reason.[30] This analysis, to which Plato compares the three classes of the state in his famous analogy in the *Republic* that the state is the individual writ large, is reexpressed on two occasions. One, towards the close of the *Republic*,[31] likens the soul to a vast monster consisting of a man, a lion, and a chimaera. The other is the famous image of the soul as a combination of a charioteer (the reason) and an ill-matched team of horses, one white and noble (the higher emotions) and the other black, mean, and ugly (the desires and appetites). The life of the soul in this image consists in the difficult struggle on the part of the charioteer to drive the pair.[32]

[29] I shall make no effort here to do more than summarize very briefly the familiar Platonic doctrine of the soul of man, which is to be found in the main in the great myths of the *Phaedo*, *Gorgias*, *Phaedrus*, and in the Vision of Er at the conclusion of *Republic* X.

[30] *Republic*, 435 c 4 ff.

[31] *Republic*, 588 b 6 ff.

[32] *Phaedrus*, 246 a 6 ff.

35

Plato's technique of exposition, particularly in these mythical flights of his creative imagination, requires that interpreters be on their guard lest they take him too literally. So here, in these portrayals of the soul, we should not construct a rigid tripartite psychology for Plato, but rather see in these passages poetic insights into the essential nature of the human soul. Thus it would be a mistake to say that the λογιστικόν, i.e., the rational part of the soul, the reason, should be broken down into the four subjective faculties of the Image of the Divided Line. It is much better to say that Plato believed the totality of man's inner being, i.e., his soul, to be a complex unity.[33] From the moral point of view it possesses drives and appetites which somehow or other must be overcome and controlled. From the epistemological point of view, that is, from the point of view of the soul as a "knowing subject," it has certain powers and attributes by virtue of which it can apprehend with some degree of validity all that which is external to it.

Similarly, Plato's famous doctrine of knowledge as recollection, ἀνάμνησις, perhaps should not be taken too literally.[34] In the medium of the myth, Plato in effect says that the soul, before it comes into a new incarnation, has a vision of the Ideas. This vision becomes latent when the soul enters a new body, but the substance of it can be recalled under proper stimulation. The well-known experiment in the *Meno* exhibits Plato's meaning. The ignorant slave-boy, in response to adroit questioning by Socrates, reveals that he "knows" relatively complex mathematical relations. Plato explains this phenomenon by suggesting imaginatively that the slave-boy "saw" these truths prior to his birth, and now is merely "recollecting" that former knowledge. In all probability, it is a mistake to equate this doctrine of knowledge as recollection with any fully developed doctrine of "innate ideas." Rather, it is better to assume that Plato is attributing to the human mind a kind of capacity or ability to contemplate its manifold of experience, and see through it in some measure to the true nature of Reality as it really is, and that which is permanent in it.

---

[33] Such clearly is the force of συμφύτῳ in *Phaedrus*, 246 a 6. Cf. A. E. Taylor, *Plato, The Man and His Work*, p. 307.

[34] Cf. the exposition of this doctrine in the *Meno*, 80 e ff.

So much then for the general Platonic attitude towards the subjective aspects suggested in the Image of the Divided Line. So far as the correlated objective aspects are concerned, there is still the very difficult problem involved in the relation between the realm of Becoming and the realm of Being. How are the particulars of sense-experience, the objects in the world of sights and sounds, related to the Ideas? This problem is indeed one of the most difficult aspects of the metaphysics of the Theory of Ideas, and one which Plato fully recognized and continually struggled to resolve.[35] Plato uses four terms (which come to be almost technical) to designate the relation, μέθεξις, "participation," κοινωνία, "communion," παρουσία "presence," and μίμησις, "imitation." The first three are employed virtually as synonyms. Particulars are said to "participate in" the Ideas, or "have a share in" the Ideas which correspond properly to them. Thus a chair, in the world of Becoming, participates in the Idea of chair-ness, and achieves such reality in this world of Becoming as its degree of approximation to the Idea warrants. Similarly, an act of courage or of self-control would be said to participate in the great ethical Ideas of ἀνδρεία or σωφροσύνη. And in turn the degree of courage or self-control exhibited can be identified, according to the Platonic view, by the closeness of its approximation to the Idea. On the same ground, Plato would explain why beautiful objects in the world of phenomena are so regarded, viz., because they to some extent participate in the Idea of beauty. All objects and events in the world of Becoming, i.e., chairs, acts of moral virtue, and beautiful objects, are transient. They come into being and they pass out of being, but the Ideas, in which they have had a share, exist eternally.

Plato used the terms "participation" and "communion" to indicate the relation of particulars and Ideas much more frequently in the earlier dialogues whenever the Theory of Ideas was under discussion. But as time went on, and as he probed deeper into the implications of the Theory, he tended to abandon these terms in favour of the conception of μίμησις,

---

[35] Aristotle's attack on Plato in connection with this problem will be discussed later.

"imitation."[36] Particulars are what they are by virtue of the fact that they "imitate" the Ideas. So in his later treatment of the Theory of Ideas, Plato consistently holds that particulars are related to the Ideas as a copy is related to its model. And, of course, this is the relation expressed in the myth of the creation in the *Timaeus*, where the Demiurge fashions the universe, while keeping his eye upon the Ideas as models or patterns.

However adequate an explanation this may be of the relation between particulars and Ideas (and many, most notably, Aristotle, have thought it to be hopelessly inadequate) at least it is Plato's best thought on the problem. One of the consequences of the whole Theory, though this is not very thoroughly discussed by Plato, is that a single particular may, indeed must, "imitate" more than a single Idea. A chair, for example, is modelled after the Idea of chair-ness, but also, if it is brown, must "imitate" the Idea of brown-ness, and so on. And furthermore, in the realm of Being, Plato comes to see that there are relations between the Ideas themselves. The fact that the Ideas are in some sense hierarchically ordered is at least suggested by the Image of the Divided Line where the Idea of the Good is assigned the supreme position. In the later dialogues, in particular, the *Sophist* and *Parmenides*, Plato attacks the problem explicitly and concludes that there is such a thing as the so-called κοινωνία γενῶν, i.e., the communion of the Ideas with one another. Of the various Ideas which have "a communion" among themselves, Plato, in the *Sophist*, singles out for special discussion those which he conceives to be exceptionally important and which exhibit interdependence in the highest degree. These are the Ideas of being, motion, rest, identity, and difference. With this analysis can be coupled the first two hypotheses of the difficult second part of the *Parmenides*. It will be recalled that there Plato examines first the hypothesis, εἰ ἕν ἐστιν, "if it is one,"[37] and concludes that an attempt to analyze unity absolutely by itself ends really in what some have called a *reductio ad absurdum*. The second hypothesis,

---

[36] This point was established by D. O. Robbins in an unpublished Princeton University doctoral dissertation, "The Paradigmatic Interpretation of Plato's Ideal Theory" (1939).

[37] *Parmendies*, 137 c 4 ff.

ἓν εἰ ἔστιν, "if there is one,"[38] upon investigation reveals that it is impossible to conceive of unity apart from being. No matter what other meanings may be found in the study of this hypothesis, at least it is quite justifiable to connect it with those sections of the *Sophist* which deal with the communion of the Ideas. Here in the *Parmenides* is an instance of the Ideas of being and unity where they are shown to be in "communion" with each other.

These two illustrations from the *Sophist* and the *Parmenides* represent the kind of investigation Plato undertook in the later part of his life when he was interested in ramifying the Theory of Ideas. But it is a mistake to see in these efforts at ramification any basic departure from the essential character of the Theory as it is expressed in the Image of the Divided Line. Indeed, the *Timaeus*, a dialogue roughly contemporary with the *Parmenides* and the *Sophist*, bespeaks the same essential Theory of Ideas as that found in the *Republic*. But there were certain other difficulties inherent in the Theory, to which Plato turned his attention in the first part of the *Parmenides*, one of the most remarkable pieces of self-criticism ever to be found in the writings of a philosopher.

The dramatic setting of the opening section of the *Parmenides* is most arresting. The dominating character is Parmenides, pictured as an older man, the great philosopher of Being, really at the height of his professional career. Discussing with him is Socrates, who is depicted as a young man, a young philosopher of great promise who has hit upon a metaphysical theory, the Theory of Ideas, which he wishes to submit to the criticism of the older man. One by one, Plato, in the main through the character Parmenides, raises the metaphysical difficulties inherent in the Theory of Ideas, and as they are raised, Parmenides subjects them to the most penetrating scrutiny. For example, at the outset, the Theory of Ideas is sketched in its barest possible form. To paraphrase the passage,[39] Parmenides asks if on the one hand there are Ideas and on the other particulars which participate in the Ideas. Such Ideas include likeness, unity, plurality, or justness, beauty, and goodness. Socrates asserts that this is his belief. Then Parmenides asks if there is an Idea of man in which all men

---

[38] *Parmenides*, 142 b 3 ff.
[39] *Parmenides*, 130 b 1 ff.

participate, or an Idea of fire or of water. Socrates then replies that it often has been difficult for him to decide whether he should agree here, *i.e.*, assert that there are Ideas of such things. At this, Parmenides asks if there are Ideas of hair, or mud, or filth. Socrates' reply is most interesting. He admits that he fears to postulate Ideas of such things, for he thus might become involved in nonsense, and yet, on the other hand, sometimes he has suspected that what is true in one instance may be true in all. More or less to avoid the difficulty, Socrates admits that he returns to the Ideas which were first mentioned and spends his time busying himself about them. Parmenides allows that Socrates behaves in this way because he is still young, and philosophy has not yet the firm grip upon him which some day it will have. At present, Parmenides believes that the younger man is much too sensitive to public opinion.

Thus Socrates at the end of this first bout is somewhat shaken about the extent to which Ideas must be postulated for the things of sense. Next, the discussion turns to the precise meaning of "participation," or "partaking of." Does a particular "participate in" the whole of an Idea or only a part of it? Can the Ideas be divided into parts? How do many particulars "partake of" a single Idea? And so on, Parmenides keeps pressing the case against the Theory of Ideas. But in the end, just when Socrates is about to give up and admit that perhaps the Theory of Ideas should be abandoned, Parmenides pulls him up short. After all, the older thinker points out,[40] if out of regard for all these difficulties one refuses to postulate the Theory of Ideas in some form, he will have no direction whither he can turn his thought. If there is not some unchanging Idea underlying the various particulars of sense, the whole power of dialectic *(τὴν τοῦ διαλέγεσθαι δύναμιν)* will be destroyed. In other words, upon the acceptance of the Theory of Ideas depends the whole possibility of mind communicating with mind.

In the light of this section of the *Parmenides*, and of the passages already mentioned in the *Sophist*, it should be clear that Plato was prepared to hold to the Theory of Ideas substantially as he had expressed it in the Image of the Divided Line, but at the

[40] *Parmenides*, 135 b 5–c 2.

40

same time was thoroughly aware of the difficulties in it. It is true that he felt the puzzle inherent in his notion that particulars are related to Ideas by virtue of "participation" or "imitation." Likewise he was troubled by the necessity of admitting that there are Ideas of all sorts of things, when his overwhelming interest lay in the moral power for the living of human life which derived from the view that Ideas of justness, self-control, and the like abide eternally in the realm of Being. Furthermore, he evidently was not entirely happy about the fact that the Theory of Ideas does not function too smoothly in the face of the problem of negative values, or disvalues. Are there Ideas of disvalues? Is there an Idea of evil?[41] If there is such an Idea, how is it related to the supreme Idea of the Good, which presides over the hierarchy of the Ideas, and which gives the fundamental orientation of the teleology in Reality, and to the degree to which this teleology is reflected in the universe of space and time?

No sensitive reader of Plato can be unaware of these problems, and, it should be noted, Plato takes great pains to make his reader know that he himself fully recognized them. For the most part, it must be admitted that they remain unresolved in Plato's thought. In connection with the question of the relation of particulars to Ideas, he may be regarded as having made some progress by giving up the notion of "participation" in favour of the conception of "imitation." Also, as we have already pointed out, the myth of creation in the *Timaeus* goes at least part way in offering a theory to explain the phenomenon of evil. But still, even in the face of these metaphysical liabilities, Plato insists that the Theory of Ideas, or something very like it, provides the most satisfactory mode of analyzing Reality. He insists that there is a reasonably high degree of correspondence between his Theory and the Reality which it is attempting to interpret. And in this connection, there seems to be a bit of extraordinarily accurate autobiography on Plato's part, when he makes the young Socrates say to Parmenides that he much prefers to speculate about the Ideas of likeness, unity, plurality, justness, beauty, and goodness than to worry about Ideas of hair, mud, or filth. Plato's overwhelming

---

[41] Cf. Cherniss, *Aristotle's Criticism of Plato and the Academy*, vol. I, pp. 266–269, and especially notes 175 and 176.

moralistic and religious predilections directed his attention to problems of that order, problems which had a bearing upon the good life for man either in time or in eternity, and away from problems, let us say, of a strictly logical or ontological character.[42]

If we are correct in asserting that the Theory of Ideas, as it is presented in substance in the Image of the Divided Line, summarizes the core of Plato's thought, from which he never essentially deviated even in the face of its attendant difficulties, we should be safe in using it as a means of readily identifying Plato's attitude towards the perennial and pervasive systematic problems of philosophy. But before discussing this point, it is well to remember Plato's general attitude towards the enterprise of philosophy. One datum of human experience is always recognized by Plato, and that is the fact of the finitude of the human mind. In this sense Plato occupies an intermediate position between that of the relativistic sceptic and that of the rational absolutist. The sceptic denies the existence of absolute principles, and tends to reduce "knowledge" to the sense contents of the human consciousness. The absolutist not only asserts that there *are* absolute principles but also that the human mind, via the reason, is capable of knowing them absolutely. Plato, in contrast, maintains that there are these absolute principles, but that the human mind, so long as it is in the phenomenal world can only approximate to a knowledge of them. It is in this spirit that he makes Socrates refuse to talk about the Idea of the Good (a point which has already been noted) but willing to talk about that which is like the Good. It is this spirit which explains the much disputed passage in the famous *Seventh Epistle* where Plato says he will never put on paper his final thoughts on philosophy.[43] The same attitude informs his method of dialectic, which really amounts to a continual examination of presuppositions in the effort constantly to improve their character. No other approach to philosophy than that of process, of unending quest, could be in the

---

[42] As Cherniss has pointed out (see note 41 above), this does not mean that the Theory of Ideas did not admit the existence of Ideas of κακίαι. However, it can hardly be asserted that the Theory of Ideas in and of itself actually throws much light on this aspect of the problem of evil.

[43] *Seventh Epistle*, 341. This letter, in my opinion, should be accepted as genuine. Cf. G. R. Morrow, *Studies in the Platonic Epistles* (*University of Illinois Studies in Classical Philology*, XXXII, 1935), pp. 47–60.

Plato who produced the dramatic character of Socrates, who chose the dialogue form for this philosophical exposition, and who used so often the medium of the poetic myth for the communication of his insights.

Philosophically, the Theory of Ideas is outstanding among the various metaphysical hypotheses which have been evolved in the history of thought because it is designed, as a single theory, to function simultaneously in four great areas of speculation. These spheres are logic, ontology, epistemology, and value, or axiology. Cherniss in an article entitled "The Philosophical Economy of Plato's Theory of Ideas" has suggested briefly the fact of the multiple function of the theory, though he merely sketches in its terms the relation which exists between ethical, epistemological, and ontological problems.[44] He cites in particular the *Meno*, where Plato indicates that investigation of an ethical question inevitably, and indeed very soon, leads to the problem of knowledge. And from here Cherniss points out how ontology is likewise involved. Actually, the Theory of Ideas has a wider purview, including, as it does, a logical aspect as well as an aspect which covers all values, and not merely those of ethics. The fact that the single Theory does have these four functions bespeaks Plato's firm conviction that the various subdivisions of philosophy have no real independent existence of their own, but actually are completely interdependent. And, obviously, as such, the Theory of Ideas commends itself because it does recognize the basic principle that Being and Value cannot be considered apart from each other.

The logical function of the Theory of Ideas should be readily apparent. From the early *Euthyphro*[45] right on through the Platonic corpus an Idea is that which designates a class of objects, and offers an hypothesis on the basis of which a term for a "class" can be validly predicated of a particular. When we say, "This is a chair," chair is actually a logical universal, as any student of logic knows, which indicates the class of objects to which the particular "this" belongs. To be sure, Plato would insist that the Idea of chair, or chair-ness, has an existence apart, but by virtue

[44] H. F. Cherniss, *American Journal of Philology*, LVII (1936), pp. 445–456.
[45] Cf. above, note 3.

43

of the "participation" in or "imitation" of the Idea of chair, all particular chairs have within them that common element which warrants their being grouped together as a class. In one sense, this logical function is explicit on every occasion when Plato introduces the Theory of Ideas for discussion. Typical of such passages is the introduction to the exposition of the Image of the Divided Line. Socrates remarks, after warning his interlocutors to be on their guard lest he in some way deceive them, "I am reminding you of what we have agreed upon, points which have been mentioned previously, and which have often already been discussed elsewhere." Glaucon asks what these are, and Socrates continues, "We have maintained that there are many things which are beautiful, and many things which are good, i.e., particular instances, and we have distinguished them in our discourse." Glaucon agrees. Socrates then says, "And that predicate by which we call each thing 'what it is,' we designate as Beauty itself, or Good itself and thus concerning all those things which we supposed then to be many particular instances, we in turn assume to be grouped under a single Idea of each thing, as though the Idea were a single entity."[46] Nor is the logical function absent from the famous section in the *Phaedo*[47] where the Theory of Ideas is postulated and Plato attempts to describe the relation between Ideas and particulars as causal. And finally we should not forget that it is really the logical function of the Theory of Ideas which provides Parmenides with the decisive argument with the young Socrates. After all, he insists that without the Ideas, and primarily Ideas as logical universals, there will be an end to all thought and all communication will be impossible.[48]

The ontological function of the Theory of Ideas can be most readily observed in the Image of the Divided Line. Ontology asks, "What exists? What is real?" Plato, via his image, gives his philosophical answer. In considering this answer it is useful

[46] *Republic*, 507 a 7-b 7. Διομολογησάμενός γ᾽, ἔφην ἐγώ, καὶ ἀναμνήσας ὑμᾶς τά τ᾽ ἐν τοῖς ἔμπροσθεν ῥηθέντα καὶ ἄλλοτε ἤδη πολλάκις εἰρημένα. Τὰ ποῖα; ἦ δ᾽ ὅς. Πολλὰ καλά, ἦν δ᾽ ἐγώ, καὶ πολλὰ ἀγαθὰ καὶ ἕκαστα οὕτως εἶναί φαμέν τε καὶ διορίζομεν τῷ λόγῳ. Φαμὲν γάρ. Καὶ αὐτὸ δὴ καλόν καὶ αὐτὸ ἀγαθόν, καὶ οὕτω περὶ πάντων ἃ τότε ὡς πολλὰ ἐτίθεμεν, πάλιν αὖ κατ᾽ ἰδέαν μίαν ἑκάστου ὡς μιᾶς οὔσης τιθέντες, "ὃ ἔστιν" ἕκαστον προσαγορεύομεν.

[47] *Phaedo*, 100 b 1 ff.

[48] *Parmenides*, 135 b 5-c 2.

to introduce a distinction between the terms existence and reality, a distinction which is certainly implicit in the Divided Line.[49] The whole Line represents or is meant to include everything which can be said to exist in any sense at all, whereas the four constituent segments of the Line distinguish among different degrees of reality. Thus, as it is used here, existence means to connote the fact of being, at any level, and no more. Existence, in other words, is a completely colourless word. However, reality is the term which admits of being differentiated into various degrees. Reality, then, should be regarded as a colourful word. Plato's Line comprises all that exists, but from the ontological point of view, the Line is important because it breaks down existence into those elements which possess greater or lesser reality. As men in their common experience distinguish between "shadow and substance," so Plato's theory of existence and reality insists that the things of space and time, since they are impermanent and changing, exist, to be sure, but are far less real than the Ideas, which are fully real. Plato's ontology maintains that only that which is permanent and unchanging can be said to be real.

Plato's answer to the problem of epistemology runs absolutely parallel to his ontology. In other words, the answer to the questions "What do we know?" and "How do we know it?" cannot be given without a simultaneous consideration of the question, "What is real?" The Theory of Ideas, via the Divided Line, gives an unequivocal reply to the inquiry into the nature of knowledge. It simply holds to the position that the human mind can only be said in any full sense to know, when the object of its knowledge is fully real. One cannot really "know" any object, if that object is continually changing. A changing object cannot be "known," for by the time, so to speak, that a knowing subject apprehends it, it has already changed, *i.e.*, has become different. Hence the true object of any genuine knowledge must be permanent, and it is here, of course, that Plato can introduce for purposes of his exposition the objects of mathematics; these can be "known," for they never change. In Euclidean space, the square on the hypotenuse of a right triangle will always be equal to the sum of the squares of the other two sides. Ideas, in

[49] *Republic,* 509 d 9 and 511 e 2–4.

Plato's epistemology, since they are fully real and unchanging, are the only legitimate objects of knowledge. We can have "opinion" about objects which change, and these opinions can be more or less accurate, *i.e.*, can be either "right" or "wrong," but opinion can never be equated with knowledge any more than the objects and events in space and time can be equated with the real objects in the realm of true Being, *i.e.*, the Ideas.

Perhaps it would be fair to say that for Plato opinion, δόξα, is an inferior kind of "knowledge." Just as the objects in space and time exist but are less real than the Ideas, just so the apprehension by the mind of the objects in space and time, which Plato calls "opinion," is "knowledge" of a sort, has a legitimate status, but should never be confused with knowledge in the full sense of the term. Plato makes his position perfectly clear on this point. Those who attempt to live by right opinion, and right opinion alone, he compares to blind men going down the right road, without any intelligent understanding of the reasons why it is the right road.[50] But Plato here is attacking "right opinions without knowledge," τὰς ἄνευ ἐπιστήμης δόξας, and thus implicitly approves of right opinion accompanied by genuine understanding of the grounds for its correctness. This, in the terminology of the Theory of Ideas, would depend upon a man's ability to grasp the true nature of the objects in the world of sights and sounds, that they are continually changing, and that whatever degree of reality they possess derives from the degree to which they have a share in the Ideas.

Plato is completely consistent on this epistemological problem. He always holds that what man knows most fully is what is most real, the position ultimately to which the elaborate scheme of the Image of the Divided Line may be reduced in so far as its epistemological bearing is concerned. The whole system of objective and subjective correlates propounded in the Line boils down to this. That Plato never varies in the epistemology of the Theory of Ideas is apparent in the later dialogue, the *Theaetetus*. Critics have often contended that this dialogue, since it never mentions specifically the Theory of Ideas, therefore represents a new and "later" development in Plato's thought. Such an

[50] *Republic*, 506 c 6–9.

46

interpretation obviously misses the point of the work, as Cornford in his masterly translation and commentary has clearly demonstrated.[51] The whole dialogue sets out to examine the implications of the theory that knowledge equals experience. Plato has taken great care not to mention the Theory of Ideas, but wishes rather to analyze the empiricist position on knowledge completely upon its own merits. The several empiricist propositions are examined in turn and each is in turn refuted. The whole dialogue ends inconclusively, and thus has frequently been compared to the earlier dialogues of search. But the unmistakable significance of the inconclusive nature of the work is that it is impossible upon empiricist principles to arrive at an adequate theory of knowledge. In other words, Plato, by omitting to mention the Theory of Ideas and thus being unable to reach a tenable position, is saying in effect that the problem of knowledge demands for its proper solution the Theory of Ideas or some other similar metaphysical hypothesis. That Plato had this intention in mind is made clear by the presence of the famous interlude in the *Theaetetus*.[52] Here Plato in his characteristic fervour of spiritual eloquence, which recalls many passages of the same sort in the *Gorgias*, *Phaedo*, and the *Republic*, compares the free life of the true philosopher with the narrow enslavement of the so-called man of practical affairs. The interlude presupposes the Theory of Ideas by its very tone and language, and indeed has no meaning except if the true philosopher be seen in the context of Reality which has within it the dimension of the Ideas. A. E. Taylor finds difficulty in seeing the connection between the interlude and the argument of the dialogue.[53] Cornford rather is correct when he argues that Plato inserted the interlude, which presupposes the Theory of Ideas in its standard form, in order to make perfectly clear to the reader why the Ideas are not mentioned in the main argument which is concerned exclusively with the empiricist claims to a theory of knowledge. Plato's theory of knowledge, or alternatively the epistemological function of the Theory of Ideas, can be summed up in repeating a remark of Cherniss to the effect

---

[51] F. M. Cornford, *Plato's Theory of Knowledge* (London, Kegan Paul, 1935).
[52] *Thaetetus*, 172 c–176 c.
[53] *Plato, the Man and His Work*, p. 336.

that to dispense with the Ideas results in equating right opinion and knowledge, and really amounts to asserting that phenomena are stable.[54]

One further point is connection with Plato's theory of knowledge should be repeated here, since it is frequently overlooked, and thus often leads to a rather serious misunderstanding of Plato's entire position. Plato distinguishes between "opinion" and "knowledge" (δόξα and ἐπιστήμη) according to the lack of stability or the stability of the objects of each. Because Ideas are in the full sense stable, it is only proper to designate as "knowledge" the apprehension which a man may have of them. The mistake which can be made here is to equate the "knowledge," i.e., the awareness, which a man may have of the Ideas with an *absolute* knowledge, such as, we may suppose, would exist in the mind of God or the Demiurge when He undertook the work of creation. Plato again and again makes clear that the only "knowledge" available to man is the finite knowledge which is all that man as a finite space-time entity can hope to attain. Thus when Plato says that man can only "know" the Ideas, he really means that he can "know" them finitely but not absolutely. Critics unfriendly to Plato, in particular those who wish to make him the remote ancestor of totalitarianism,[55] really assume man's knowledge of the Ideas to be absolute knowledge. Plato repearedly makes clear his belief that man can never completely exhaust the meaning of an Idea.[56]

The fourth and final function of the Theory of Ideas is that which provides Plato with his theory of value. In broad general terms, this theory of value follows the principle that as there are ascending degrees of reality in all that which exists, so these degrees of reality mark ascending degrees of value. As can be seen in the image of the Divided Line, as one moves from the left segment on through the Line towards the right, the objects subsumed under each segment become progressively more real

[54] Cf. Cherniss, "The Philosophical Economy of Plato's Theory of Ideas," p. 456, and the sources in Plato there cited.

[55] One may well wonder how long this essentially superficial interpretation of Plato will endure. It is tantamount to saying that a doctor is a fascist when he orders his patient to take a certain medicine.

[56] Cf. above, pp. 42–43.

and more valuable. The Theory of Ideas presents then an analysis of Reality wherein Being and Value are kept together; indeed they coincide. As in the phenomenal world, shadows and reflections are less real and less valuable than the objects which cast them, so the whole phenomenal world is less real and less valuable than the true realm of Being which is the locus of true reality and true value in the full sense. As the sun is that which is most real and most valuable in the realm of Becoming, so the Idea of the Good is the most real and most valuable entity in the realm of Being. Certainly such must be Plato's view when he describes the Idea of the Good in the extravagant language of the sixth book of the *Republic*. The Idea of the Good gives "truth to the objects of knowledge" and "the ability to know to the knower." It is "the cause of truth and knowledge." And however "beautiful truth and knowledge may be," the Idea of the Good is "more beautiful still." Knowledge and truth are "like the Good," but they are not "the Good." "The possession of the Good must be still more greatly honoured." "The capacity to be known is present in the things known, by virtue of the Good," and "the being and essence" of things "comes to them by the Good," though the Good itself is "above and beyond essence in its dignity and power."[57] Plato could hardly be more explicit in expressing the full reality of the value Good.

Ontology and axiology are thus closely interfused in the Theory of Ideas. The very distinction of the varying degrees of reality among objects in itself brings Being and Value tightly together. But by no means does this imply that the Theory of Ideas has completely resolved all the difficulties involved in the problem of Being and Value. For example, an object like a chair gets its degree of reality by virtue of its association with the Idea

[57] *Republic* 508 e–509 b 10. The key phrases in the Greek which I have translated are as follows: τὸ τὴν ἀλήθειαν παρέχον τοῖς γιγνωσκομένοις καὶ τῷ γιγνώσκοντι τὴν δύναμιν ἀποδιδόν. . . . αἰτίαν δ᾽ ἐπιστήμης οὖσαν καὶ ἀληθείας, . . . οὕτω δὲ καλῶν ἀμφοτέρων ὄντων, γνώσεώς τε καὶ ἀληθείας, ἄλλο καὶ κάλλιον ἔτι τούτων. . . . ἐνταῦθα ἀγαθοειδῆ μὲν νομίζειν ταῦτ᾽ ἀμφότερα ὀρθόν, ἀγαθὸν δὲ ἡγεῖσθαι ὁπότερον αὐτῶν οὐκ ὀρθόν, ἀλλ᾽ ἔτι μειζόνως τιμητέον τὴν τοῦ ἀγαθοῦ ἕξιν. . . . καὶ τοῖς γιγνωσκομένοις τοίνυν μὴ μόνον τὸ γιγνώσκεσθαι φάναι ὑπὸ τοῦ ἀγαθοῦ παρεῖναι, ἀλλὰ καὶ τὸ εἶναί τε καὶ τὴν οὐσίαν ὑπ᾽ ἐκείνου αὐτοῖς προσεῖναι, οὐκ οὐσίας ὄντος τοῦ ἀγαθοῦ, ἀλλ᾽ ἔτι ἐπέκεινα τῆς οὐσίας πρεσβείᾳ καὶ δυνάμει ὑπερέχοντος. . . . It is needless to mention the vast number of times this passage has been quoted.

of chair. The Idea of chair is both fully real, and, we might say, ultimately valuable (or important) because of its over-arching relation to all particular chairs in the phenomenal world and because of the "perfection" which the Idea of chair-ness connotes. This seems to be Plato's answer to the question, "What is the value of a particular chair?" Perhaps the Theory of Ideas does not totally solve the difficulty. The answer it gives (and note that Being and Value are kept together) lies in the fact that things as such, e.g., chairs, in the perspective of the Theory of Ideas are to be valued far less than the great normative realities, the Ideas of Good, beauty, self-control, courage, and the like. Their complete being and their complete value, placed at the very heart of Reality, finally provide the ultimate pattern in terms of which man can understand the relation of Being and Value in all the objects and events in the world in which he lives.

The teleology postulated by the Theory of Ideas should not be overlooked. In the *Republic*, for example, when the emphasis is almost entirely on the Theory of Ideas in and of itself, the Idea of the Good, as it has just been described, sets the direction of the teleology. When Plato says that the Good is the "cause" of the "being and essence" of things *(τὸ εἶναι τε καὶ τὴν οὐσίαν)*, he means that their purpose and their value constitute actually that which makes them be what they are.[58] But, of course, the full Platonic teleology does not appear until the Ideas are put into relation to God or the Demiurge in the myth of creation in the *Timaeus*. Cosmic teleology, to be completely significant, must have an appropriate metaphysics of time to go with it. Indeed, it does not seem possible that one can conceive of the universe as going in any direction, *i.e.*, as dominated by any purpose, unless it is conceived as having a starting point, *i.e.*, unless it is created. Plato surely was exhibiting profound insight when he asserted in his myth that time came into being with the universe, for the very concept of purpose demands that there be a time dimension in things. Whatever may be the limitations of Plato's cosmic teleology (and this point will come up for fuller

[58] P. Shorey, *Plato, The Republic*, vol. II (Loeb Classical Library, Cambridge, Harvard University Press, 1935) in his notes on 508 e 1 and ff. (pp. 102–107) tends to support this point, although I personally should not see as much of an element of sheer "rhetoric" in the passage as apparently Shorey does.

discussion in connection with the teleological doctrine of Aristotle), it does give the final setting to Plato's view of the universe of space and time and its relation to the whole of Reality.

Such, then, is the Theory of Ideas and its fourfold function. Whenever Plato invokes the Theory, he may involve one function only. At times and according to the context two or three of the four functions may be put into play simultaneously. And, as we have seen, the Image of the Divided Line presents the Theory of Ideas with full relevance for logic, ontology, epistemology, and axiology.

And it is this basic metaphysical Theory of Ideas which Aristotle categorically refused to accept. Now it is not necessarily to the point here to go into great detail with respect to all the reasons why Aristotle rejected the Theory of Ideas. Nor is there any need to argue at length about the nature of Aristotle's criticisms of Plato—whether, for example, Aristotle misunderstood Plato, whether he consciously or unconsciously misrepresented Plato, whether Aristotle was relying upon Plato's oral teaching for some of the remarks which the modern reader finds difficult to expain in the light of Plato's written dialogues, or whether Aristotle may have been directing his attack not so much against Plato himself as against Plato's immediate successors in the Academy, and their well-known mathematicizing tendencies which Aristotle found so objectionable.[59] The fact remains that there is a profound and radical difference between the philosophies of the two men. Platonism and Aristotelianism are simply two different ways of looking at Reality. To be sure, there is a current tendency which maintains that after all Plato and Aristotle are far closer together than we might suspect. A case can be made for such a view, because there are many points of similarity. But such similarities pale into insignificance when we come face to face with the overwhelming fact that Aristotle explicitly and repeatedly asserts that an Idea, separate and apart,

[59] All these tasks have been ably undertaken by Cherniss in his book, *Aristotle's Criticism of Plato and the Academy*. Perhaps the only valid stricture which may be laid upon the book, at least the first volume (up to the present the second volume has not appeared) is that it exhibits on the whole a somewhat pro-Platonic bias. Cherniss is a shrewd, thorough, and penetrating critic, but he sometimes permits himself a little too easily to make Aristotle the villain of the piece.

so to say, outside of space and time, cannot exist.[60] Anyone who does not accept Plato's Theory of Ideas, as eternal, non-temporal and non-spatial entities, cannot avoid formulating a philosophy which will be radically non-Platonic.

Aristotle's objections to the Theory of Ideas can, to all intents and purposes, be reduced to his reaction to two principal difficulties which he believes were unavoidably inherent in the Theory. And these two difficulties are the main grounds for Aristotle's rejection of the Ideas. The first is the question of "participation." Even the most sympathetic follower of Plato will admit that Plato's explanation of the relation of the particular to the Idea via some kind of mysterious "participation" (from the metaphysical point of view it really does not make much difference whether the term "participation" or "imitation" or any of the other alternatives is used) leaves much to be desired. Aristotle is categorical in his attitude. He dismisses "participation" and the other terms as "empty verbiage," mere metaphors which do not explain or account for anything.[61] The other difficulty lies in the question of "efficiency."[62] Aristotle is quite prepared to recognize that the Platonic Idea was a more or less successful anticipation of his own doctrine of the formal cause, but he felt at the same time that the conception of a formal cause did not depend upon this cause being hypostatized, *i.e.*, having an existence separate or apart—χωριστόν. The substance of Aristotle's attitude amounts to this: he in effect asks why we should talk about Ideas, or postulate their separate existence, when they cannot be shown to *do* anything. They simply serve to complicate the picture. The poor philosopher already has enough to do to try to analyze all the data that are ready to hand. Why add to his burdens by gratuitously creating this whole realm of Ideas which parallels the world of phenomena? The upshot of the Aristotelian argument, based on these two difficulties, is simply that the Ideas do not exist, they are not separate οὐσίαι, substances.

No doubt Aristotle has fixed upon the two most serious

[60] *Metaphysics* A, chapter 6 and 9, should suffice as evidence for this point, quite apart from the numerous other passages from the Aristotelian corpus which might be cited.

[61] Cf. especially *Metaphysics* Z, chapters 14 and 15.

[62] Cf. especially *Metaphysics* A, chapter 9.

liabilities in the metaphysics of the Theory of Ideas, but at the same time it is puzzling that Aristotle never alludes to the fact that Plato himself was thoroughly aware of precisely these difficulties. For example, Aristotle does not refer to the extended self-criticism contained in the first part of the *Parmenides*. Furthermore, it is noteworthy that Aristotle, particularly in those passages where he is pressing his attack most vigorously in the *Metaphysics*, uses as examples Plato's Ideas of things and of the objects of mathematics. In this context, he never gives any evidence that he is aware of the aesthetic or ethical Ideas of Plato, those Ideas which are always at the focus of Plato's attention owing to his own intense moralistic drive.[63] Aristotle's preoccupation with the objects of mathematics is likewise puzzling, and from this preoccupation and the frequent attribution to Plato of views on *mathematica* for which there is no support in the Platonic corpus, arises the vexed scholarly dispute over the question whether Plato actually in his later life identified Ideas and numbers.[64]

In any event, it is true that Aristotle concentrates much of his argument upon Plato's Ideas of things. One of his favourite instruments of attack, therefore, comes to be the so-called "argument from the third man." It runs something like this: if one postulates an Idea of man, let us say, beside and apart from a particular man, it will be necessary to postulate a more ultimate Idea to represent that which is in common between the particular man and the Idea of man, and under which these two may be subsumed. This new situation, in its turn, will demand a still further and more ultimate Idea to comprise within it the first Idea of man, and its next subsequent and more ultimate Idea. And so, Aristotle would contend, the series may be produced *ad infinitum*. Aristotle will never accept anything which involves such an infinite regress, and consequently, he regards the

---

[63] A notable exception to this point occurs in the *Nicomachean Ethics*, I, chapter 6, where Aristotle attacks Plato's Idea of the Good. We shall have occasion to consider this passage in detail later.

[64] Typical of the scholarship on this problem is the well-known work of L. Robin, *La Théorie platonicienne des idées et des nombres d'après Aristote* (Paris, 1908). Aristotle may also keep returning to the problem of the ontological status of *mathematica*, because actually there is no adequate solution to this problem in terms of Aristotle's own ontology. Any continuous reading of Aristotle's text reveals how much he was troubled by the problem.

"argument from the third man" a powerful and even decisive refutation of the Theory of Ideas. Plato's retort to the argument would appear to be simple. He would merely point out that the Idea of man and a particular man, according to the metaphysic of the Theory of Ideas, derive from such a radically different mode of existence that it is not possible to postulate some third term or Idea under which the two could be subsumed. A particular man is in the realm of Becoming, and hence is an entity so different from the Idea of man, which exists in the realm of Being, outside of space and time, that no ground exists, not even a logical ground, upon which they can validly be grouped together.

Why, then, does Aristotle consider the third-man argument a genuine refutation? It is extremely difficult to answer this question. Certainly, by selecting an Idea of a "thing," and not an aesthetic or ethical Idea, as his example, Aristotle gives the argument a superficial persuasiveness which it might not otherwise have. Aristotle also seems to conceive the Idea of man as though it were spatial and temporal. If the Idea is spatial and temporal, then the third-man argument in some sense might apply. The real question then becomes this: Why did Aristotle treat Ideas as spatiotemporal entities? Did he purposely misrepresent Plato on this point? Did he misunderstand Plato? This latter hypothesis seems hardly tenable. How could a brilliant mind like that of Aristotle, having been in almost daily contact with Plato for twenty years, misconceive such a basic point as this? Perhaps the answer may be that Aristotle was so exclusively concerned with the ontological problem as such, that the spatio-temporality of all entities seemed to him an inescapable conclusion. Whereas in contrast, Plato's interest in epistemology and axiology leads him to hold the non-spatiotemporal and absolutely unconditioned existence of the great aesthetic and ethical principles in Reality. Plato's conviction in this respect would in a sense provide him with a ground for postulating Ideas of "things" in the same way. When all is said and done, it must be admitted that no really satisfactory theory to explain Aristotle's criticism of Plato has as yet been evolved. It may be that this very lack of a theory is itself evidence that we are dealing with a radical philosophical quarrel. Perhaps it was literally impossible for

Aristotle to attach any meaning to Plato's non-spatial and non-temporal realm of Being.

Aristotle, then, rejects the Platonic Theory of Ideas primarily on ontological grounds, and in the rejection pays no attention to the axiological function of the Theory. The whole burden of the present book is to examine the philosophical consequences of the rejection of the Theory of Ideas with its fourfold function. Broadly speaking, Aristotle introduced a new and substitute ontology, the ontology of the τόδε τι or οὐσία as substance. This asserts, to all intents and purposes, the ultimate reality of the individual particular thing, whether it be a stick or a stone, a plant or an animal or a man. With this ontology he was able to couple a new epistemology, which is generally empirical in character, as the opening sentences of the first book of the *Metaphysics* more than amply indicate. As for the logical function, Aristotle was able to preserve this aspect of the Theory of Ideas virtually unchanged. To use the terminology of the medieval Schoolmen, all he needed to do was to change the *universalia ante rem*, i.e., the Platonic Ideas, into *universalia in re*. By changing, so to speak, the "location" of the Idea or Universal from the non-spatial and non-temporal realm of Being, and by placing the universal in each and every particular instance, the logical function of the Theory of Ideas is preserved, and made to blend with the ontology which maintains the ultimate reality of the individual particular thing. By thus changing the "locus" of the universal and making it inhere in particulars Aristotle feels he has overcome the two major hazards of the Theory of Ideas. No longer need he be worried about the metaphorical verbiage involved in the conception of "participation." Nor is he bothered by the difficulty of efficiency. There is no question of efficiency if one is dealing with *universalia in re*. And at the same time, so Aristotle would affirm, in this context predication can be shown to be a valid procedure. He writes in the *Analytica Posteriora*, "So demonstration does not necessarily imply the being of Ideas, nor a one beside a Many, but it does necessarily imply the possibility of truly predicating one of many; since without this possibility we cannot save the universal, and if the universal goes, the middle term goes with it, and so demonstration

55

becomes impossible. We conclude, then, that there must be a single identical term unequivocally predicable of a number of individuals."[65]

In summary, then, Aristotle, after having repudiated the Theory of Ideas, develops a new ontology and a new epistemology. By shifting the location of the universal, he can preserve the Platonic logic. But the important question remains concerning the nature of Aristotle's theory of value. What steps did he take in this aspect of his thought to repair the loss which he sustained when in effect he removed from his metaphysics the Ideas in their normative function? Aristotle, by the very nature of his new ontology had permitted the separate consideration of being apart from value. As we proceed, we shall see the price which Aristotle paid from the axiological point of view, since it can be shown, we hope, that he never developed a consistent or coherent theory of value. And further, it might even be urged that the baffling difficulty of understanding many passages in Aristotle results from his attempt to concentrate on ontology to the exclusion of value theory. These passages might be far easier to comprehend, were there a coherent value theory underlying them. In other words, our task will be to describe the results which Aristotle produced in the sphere of value thinking in the new philosophical setting which he created for himself by rejecting the Theory of Ideas.

But first we must bring before us the general nature of the newly forged Aristotelian position, so that the contrast between it and Plato's Theory of Ideas may be unmistakable. Though to a degree the rational methods of Plato and Aristotle are the same (after all, Aristotle absorbed Plato's logic), the real difference between the two positions may be reduced to a radical difference between the mind and temperament of the two men. A phrase from the early philosopher of Christianity, Origen, may illustrate

---

[65] 77 a 5-9. The translation is that of G. R. G. Mure, *The Works of Aristotle Translated into English*, vol. I (Oxford, Clarendon Press, 1928). I have altered Mure's translation of εἴδη, Forms, to Ideas, in order to be consistent with my usage in this book. The Greek text runs: εἴδη μὲν οὖν εἶναι ἢ ἕν τι παρὰ τὰ πολλὰ οὐκ ἀνάγκη, εἰ ἀπόδειξις ἔσται, εἶναι μέντοι ἓν κατὰ πολλῶν ἀληθὲς εἰπεῖν ἀνάγκη· οὐ γὰρ ἔσται τὸ καθόλου, ἂν μὴ τοῦτο ᾖ· ἐὰν δὲ τὸ καθόλου μὴ ᾖ, τὸ μέσον οὐκ ἔσται, ὥστ' οὐδ' ἀπόδειξις. δεῖ ἄρα τι ἓν καὶ τὸ αὐτὸ ἐπὶ πλειόνων εἶναι μὴ ὁμώνυμον.

the point.[66] Celsus has brought the reproach that the Christians make this demand, μὴ ἐξέταζε, ἀλλὰ πίστευσον, "Don't examine or investigate, but believe."[67] Origen admits the reproach in a way, by observing that few men have the time or the inclination for investigation. But, Origen goes on to say that the gentiles really do the same thing: "For it is not by waiting to hear the arguments of all the philosophers and of the different sects, and by learning how some may be upset and others established, that a man chooses to be a Stoic, or a follower of Plato or a Peripatetic, or an Epicurean . . .; but it is by a certain unreasoning impulse (ἀλόγῳ τινὶ φορᾷ), though they will not admit the fact." One way to express the difference between Plato and Aristotle may be this: whereas the ἄλογος φορά of Plato led him to feel the reality of the other-world and the illusion of phenomena, the ἄλογος φορά of Aristotle led him in the opposite direction. To him the individual concrete thing is that which is ulitmately real, and it is now that we must turn to consider the imposing philosophical structure which he erected from this initial conviction.

[66] *Contra Celsum*, I, 9–10. This illustration was suggested by P. E. More in a series of lectures delivered in the Graduate School of Princeton University in 1930–1931.
[67] Cf. Plato, *Apology*, 38 a, where Socrates makes his famous statement that "for man the unexamined life is not worth living." ὁ δὲ ἀνεξέταστος βίος οὐ βιωτὸς ἀνθρώπῳ.

CHAPTER III

ARISTOTLE'S METAPHYSICS
OF THE INDIVIDUAL PARTICULAR:
THE STATIC APPROACH

ARISTOTLE'S postulate that the concrete particular is ultimately real, that is, the τόδε τι, or the οὐσία αἰσθητή, dictates his whole method of metaphysical analysis. He must begin his investigation into the nature of reality with that which surely exists. The thing of sense, the object of sense-perception thus becomes the starting point of his thinking. But before considering Aristotle's inquiries in this direction, three fundamental axioms of his thought must be kept clearly in mind: the axiom of contradiction, the axiom of correspondence, and the axiom of finality.

Nowhere obviously does or can Aristotle demostrate the principle of contradiction, but in the *Metaphysics* he introduces it explicitly as an axiom, and confirms its validity by pointing to the impossible consequences which accrue if the principle is denied.[1] If the axiom of contradiction is not true, and a thing can be and not be at the same time, in the same place, and in the same relation, then there is no coherence in our thought, no meaning in our words, and so on. All things will be one, says Aristotle, and we will come to the position of Anaxagoras, that "all things are mingled together." The net result of this view will be that "nothing in any true sense will exist."[2] Of the three axioms, that of contradiction is the only one which is specifically formulated and treated as such. And, it goes without saying, the whole structure of Aristotle's logic is based upon the acceptance of the axiom of contradiction.

The whole of Aristotle's epistemology depends in turn upon the acceptance of the axiom of correspondence. It amounts simply

---

[1] *Metaphysics* Γ, chapters 3 and 4.
[2] *Metaphysics*, 1007 b 25–26.

to this. When we analyze an object, a particular, a τόδε τι,, with respect to what it is and the various reasons or "causes" why it has come to be what it is, Aristotle assumes that our analysis, the structure we have erected in our λόγος or our reason, and the structure in the objective thing *correspond*. In other words, our apprehension of a thing, and our reflection upon it are "true." As we shall see later, when Aristotle works out in detail his theory of knowledge, he formulates a doctrine maintaining that in the knowing process, somehow or other the thing known and the knower merge and become one.[3] Such a conclusion depends ultimately upon an extension of the fundamental axiom of correspondence.

Each time Aristotle rejects an infinite regress, he asserts the axiom of finality. Nothing to infinity, οὐκ εἰς ἄπειρον, is a phrase frequently employed by Aristotle, and its implications and influence are to be seen largely in his metaphysical and theological thinking. The axiom might be called the "law of limitation," and in this sense can easily be connected with Aristotle's fundamental belief in the reality of the individual particular thing. After all, the οὐσία αἰσθητή, the concrete object of perception, is, as Aristotle would say, a πεπερασμένον, a thing limited and apart from other things. For him there is no existing unlimited *thing*, no ἄπειρον. Typical of Aristotle's use of the axiom of finality is a passage in which he argues that there must be a first principle, and that there is not an infinite series of causes: "Evidently there is a first principle, and the causes of things are neither an infinite series nor infinitely various in kind. For (1), on the one hand, one thing cannot proceed from another, as from matter, *ad infinitum*, e.g., flesh from earth, earth from air, air from fire, and so on without stopping; nor on the other hand can the efficient causes form an endless series, man for instance being acted on by air, air by the sun, the sun by Strife, and so on without limit. Similarly the final causes cannot go on *ad infinitum*—walking for the sake of health, this for the sake of happiness, happiness for the sake of something else, and so one thing always for

---

[3] Cf., for example, *De Anima*, 425 b 26 ff., 431 a 1. Cf. also *De Interpretatione*, 16 a 1 ff. and *Analytica Posteriora*, 71 a 1 ff.

the sake of another. And the case of the formal cause is similar."⁴

When Aristotle asks himself "the eternal question: What is Being?"⁵ he answers that "being" first and foremost is the individual particular thing, the τόδε τι, in the sense that it is that which ultimately is real. His analysis of the τόδε τι, (and it should be noted, the terms of the analysis exclude the problem of value) which he carries on in the context of the three axioms of contradiction, correspondence, and finality, provides the same kind of core to this thought as does the Theory of Ideas for Plato. No aspect of Aristotle can be fully understood without reference to his notions concerning οὐσία, substance, as τόδε τι, whether the subject be logic, biology, ethics, or poetics. Hence, as the Theory of Ideas was discussed with respect to its implications for the problems of logic, ontology, epistemology, and axiology, so must Aristotle's metaphysics of οὐσία, "substance" be explored in detail, so that subsequently we shall be able to see the nature of Aristotle's positively developed and interrelated logic, ontology, and epistemology, when in fact axiology is neglected. The following scheme indicates in outline the character of Aristotle's thought on substance, οὐσία:⁶

A. οὐσία (τόδε τι)
Substance as the individual particular thing

	B. εἶδος	ὕλη . . . B'.	Principle of
Static	Form	Matter	Individuation
	C. οὐσία (τί ἦν εἶναι)	συμβεβηκότα C'.	Definition
	Substance as essence	Accidents	

	D. ἐντελέχεια	στέρησις
	Complete actuality	Privation

	E. ἐνέργεια	δύναμις . . E'.	Motion and change
Dynamic	Actuality as activity	Potentiality	
	F. αἰτίαι [οὐσιώδεις]	αἰτία ὑλική . F'.	Causality
	"Essential" Causes	Material Cause	

G. οὐσία (τέλος)
Substance as "end"

⁴ *Metaphysics*, 994 a 1–11. Ἀλλὰ μὴν ὅτι γ' ἔστιν ἀρχή τις καὶ οὐκ ἄπειρα τὰ αἴτια τῶν ὄντων οὔτ' εἰς εὐθυωρίαν οὔτε κατ' εἶδος, δῆλον. οὔτε γὰρ ὡς ἐξ ὕλης τόδ' ἐκ τοῦδε δυνατὸν ἰέναι εἰς ἄπειρον (οἷον σάρκα μὲν ἐκ γῆς, γῆν δ' ἐξ ἀέρος, ἀέρα δ' ἐκ πυρός, καὶ τοῦτο μὴ ἵστασθαι), οὔτε ὅθεν ἡ ἀρχὴ τῆς κινήσεως

Aristotle's analysis and his method of investigation will emerge as we proceed. He asks, "What is this particular thing (which we know, by the way, is ultimately real) and how can we break it down into its constituent elements?" In the opening chapter of the *Physics*, he has given a very specific statement of his method of procedure, "The natural path of investigation starts from what is more readily knowable and more evident *to us*, and proceeds towards what is more *self*-evident and intrinsically more intelligible; for it is one thing to be knowable to us and quite another to be intelligible objectively. This, then, is the method prescribed: to advance from what is clearer to us, though intrinsically more obscure, towards what is intrinsically clearer and more intelligible.

"The things that stand out as plain and obvious at first glance are τὰ συγκεχυμένα, 'confused mixtures,' whose elements and principles become known only on subsequent analysis. Accordingly we must proceed from the 'general character of a thing' (ἐκ τῶν καθόλου) to its constituent factors; for what the senses discern most readily are 'concrete wholes,' and a thing's general character is a kind of concrete whole, embracing as it does a number of constitutent factors or aspects."[7] The starting point is thus clearly fixed as the individual concrete whole, the particular thing which is, apparently, "more readily knowable and more evident to us." In this light the first term to consider is:

(οἷον τὸν μὲν ἄνθρωπον ὑπὸ τοῦ ἀέρος κινηθῆναι, τοῦτον δ' ὑπὸ τοῦ ἡλίου, τὸν δὲ ἥλιον ὑπὸ τοῦ νείκους, καὶ τούτου μηδὲν εἶναι πέρας)· ὁμοίως δὲ οὐδὲ τὸ οὗ ἕνεκα εἰς ἄπειρον οἷόν τε ἰέναι, βάδισιν μὲν ὑγιείας ἕνεκα, ταύτην δ' εὐδαιμονίας, τὴν δ' εὐδαιμονίαν ἄλλου, καὶ οὕτως ἀεὶ ἄλλο ἄλλου ἕνεκεν εἶναι· καὶ ἐπὶ τοῦ τί ἦν εἶναι δ' ὡσαύτως. I have followed both the text and translation of W. D. Ross.

[5] Cf. above, chapter I, p. 6.

[6] This scheme is taken from the notes of P. E. More.

[7] *Physics*, 184 a 16–26. πέφυκε δὲ ἐκ τῶν γνωριμωτέρων ἡμῖν ἡ ὁδὸς καὶ σαφεστέρων ἐπὶ τὰ σαφέστερα τῇ φύσει καὶ γνωριμώτερα· οὐ γὰρ ταὐτὰ ἡμῖν τε γνώριμα καὶ ἁπλῶς. διόπερ ἀνάγκη τὸν τρόπον τοῦτον προάγειν ἐκ τῶν ἀσαφεστέρων μὲν τῇ φύσει ἡμῖν δὲ σαφεστέρων ἐπὶ τὰ σαφέστερα τῇ φύσει καὶ γνωριμώτερα. ἔστι δ' ἡμῖν τὸ πρῶτον δῆλα καὶ σαφῆ τὰ συγκεχυμένα μᾶλλον· ὕστερον δ' ἐκ τούτων γίγνεται γνώριμα τὰ στοιχεῖα καὶ αἱ ἀρχαὶ διαιροῦσι ταῦτα. διὸ ἐκ τῶν καθόλου ἐπὶ τὰ καθ' ἕκαστα δεῖ προϊέναι· τὸ γὰρ ὅλον κατὰ τὴν αἴσθησιν γνωριμώτερον, τὸ δὲ καθόλου ὅλον τί ἐστι· πολλὰ γὰρ περιλαμβάνει ὡς μέρη τὸ καθόλου. The text is that of W. D. Ross, *Aristotle's Physics* (Oxford, Clarendon Press, 1936). The translation is taken from P. Wheelwright, *Aristotle* (New York, Doubleday, Doran and Co., 1935), pp. 3–4. Cf. also *Physics*, 189 a 5–9.

A. οὐσία (τόδε τι), *substance as the individual particular thing.* The regular English rendering for οὐσία is substance, but every reader of Aristotle knows that he must be constantly on his guard lest he be confused by the ambiguities that are always possible in the case of Aristotle's basic terms.[8] Substance in this first and most important use means the independently existing concrete particular. In this sense, it is that which is really an existent. Aristotle, for example, remarks, when he is struggling with a problem of classification, that the real existences, the οὐσίαι, are the individuals which fall within a species, such as Socrates and Coriscus, who are individual particular men within the species man.[9]

Many such illustrations could be adduced, but the most important for our present purposes occur in the *Categories*, the work which appears first in the Aristotelian corpus. The categories themselves, are, according to Ross,[10] ultimate unanalyzable notions, which are set up to cover the existential use of the verb "to be" and the nine different kinds of predication. Aristotle lists the ten as follows: substance, quantity, quality, relation, place, time, position, possession, activity, and passivity.[11] No

---

[8] It is interesting to compare Plato and Aristotle with respect to their use of technical terminology. Plato seems, in characteristic fashion, to have attempted to avoid the use of a technical terminology in so far as he could. To be sure, he has a few such terms which he employs regularly, for example, when he wants to discuss the Theory of Ideas with maximum precision. But, on the whole, Plato struggles against the tendency to have his thought become imprisoned in a particular set of words or terms. Aristotle in a sense then may be considered as prime founder of technical terminology. But his task was so great, and his rôle was so much that of a pioneer, that he uses often the same word for a variety of technical meanings. Despite the fact that he makes every effort to avoid ambiguity (in the main he does this by adding explanatory tags or making the context explicit), still in many instances the reader may be at a loss to know which of a number of technical meanings Aristotle wishes to suggest by a given technical term. It is hoped that the present discussion will be of some assistance in this connection. Frequent reference to Book Δ of the *Metaphysics*, Aristotle's philosophical lexicon, is always helpful.

[9] *De Partibus Animalium*, 644 a 23–25. The words τὰ ἔσχατα εἴδη must mean the individuals within the species. W. Ogle, the Oxford translator, in a note *ad loc.*, so believes, but would prefer to emend the text by eliminating the word εἴδη.

[10] W. D. Ross, *Aristotle*[2] (London, Methuen, 1930), pp. 21 ff.

[11] *Categories*, 1 b 25–27. τῶν κατὰ μηδεμίαν συμπλοκὴν λεγομένων ἕκαστον ἤτοι οὐσίαν σημαίνει ἢ ποσὸν ἢ ποιὸν ἢ πρός τι ἢ ποῦ ἢ ποτὲ ἢ κεῖσθαι ἢ ἔχειν ἢ πάσχειν. Position and possession are omitted in all but one other passage when the list of the categories is given. Cf. Ross, *Aristotle*, p. 22, and the passages there cited.

doubt he owed much to the speculation devoted to the problem by the Academy and Plato, when Aristotle compiled this list, and so far as his own thinking is concerned, it cleared up once and for all the difficulties inherent in predication.[12] But in his discussion of the first of the categories, substance, Aristotle expresses the views which are fundamental to all his subsequent metaphysical thought.

Perhaps the most illuminating passage occurs when Aristotle discusses what he calls "primary" and "secondary" substances, οὐσίαι. "Substance, in the most authoritative and primary and accurate sense of the word, is that which *is not predicable of* any subject and *is not present in* (i.e., does not have its real existence in) any subject; e.g., the individual man, or the individual horse. Those species are called secondary substances in which the primary substances are included; similarly with the genera of those species: e.g., the individual man falls within the species man, and the genus of this species is animal. These, therefore—i.e., the species 'man' and the genus 'animal'—are called secondary substances."[13]

The two phrases italicized above are most significant. When Aristotle says that substance in its most precise meaning "is not predicable of" of any subject, he not only in logical terms distinguishes it from the other nine categories, but also he unequivocally asserts its independent, separate, and ultimate existence. Socrates is such a primary, independent substance. Socrates can never be predicated of another subject. Thus logically and ontologically, Socrates as a primary substance is on a par with all other primary substances, i.e., all other individual particulars.

---

[12] On the doctrine of the categories, cf. especially the introduction in J. Burnet, *The Ethics of Aristotle* (London, Methuen, 1900) pp. xlviii–lii and O. Apelt, *Kategorienlehre des Aristoteles* in Beiträge zur Geschichte der Griechischen Philosophie (Leipzig, 1891), pp. 191–216.

[13] *Categories*, 2 a 11–19. οὐσία δέ ἐστιν ἡ κυριώτατά τε καὶ πρώτως καὶ μάλιστα λεγομένη, ἢ μήτε καθ᾽ ὑποκειμένου τινὸς λέγεται μήτ᾽ ἐν ὑποκειμένῳ τινί ἐστιν, οἷον ὁ τὶς ἄνθρωπος ἢ ὁ τὶς ἵππος. δεύτεραι δὲ οὐσίαι λέγονται, ἐν οἷς εἴδεσιν αἱ πρώτως οὐσίαι λεγόμεναι ὑπάρχουσι, ταῦτά τε καὶ τὰ τῶν εἰδῶν τούτων γένη, οἷον ὁ τὶς ἄνθρωπος ἐν εἴδει μὲν ὑπάρχει τῷ ἀνθρώπῳ, γένος δὲ τοῦ εἴδους ἐστὶ τὸ ζῷον. δεύτεραι οὖν αὗται λέγονται οὐσίαι, οἷον ὅ τε ἄνθρωπος καὶ τὸ ζῷον. The text is that of Bekker in the Prussian Academy edition of Aristotle. The translation is my own, with some indebtedness to E. M. Edghill's rendering in the Oxford translation of Aristotle.

Now all the other nine categories comprise predicates. The quality "bald" is an example of that which can be predicated of a primary substance. The other italicized phrase, "is not present in," which is the equivalent of "does not have its real existence in," Aristotle takes care to explain specifically: "By 'present in a subject' I do not mean as a part is present in a whole, but 'present in' in the sense of being unable to exist apart from that in which it is present."[14] Thus a quality "bald" is present in a subject not in the way, for example, that a chemical element is present in a chemical compound, but rather in the sense that no existence is possible for it apart from a given subject. In the light of this conception, the independent existence of a primary substance is emphasized.

If, according to Aristotle, everything other than primary substances does not have a separate existence, but rather is present in such primary substances, then all the other predicables, such as quantity and quality, as well as the secondary substances, i.e., the species and genera, can have only a dependent existence.[15] Thus the other nine categories and the secondary substances are placed in, so to speak, an inferior ontological position, since Aristotle attributes full, "substantial," and independent existence alone to primary substances. Indeed, he does suggest some sort of ontological scale, or "hierarchy of substantiality" when he maintains that "of the secondary substances, the species is 'more substance' (i.e., more truly a substance) than the genus, for it is nearer to primary substance."[16] But, among primary substances, he insists that all are on a plane with one another. In other words, on the top ontological level are all primary substances, and there is no difference to be seen among them, as is clear in this statement: "Similarly, of the primary substances no one is more truly a substance than another; an individual man is not more truly a substance than an individual ox."[17] However, Aristotle takes pains

---

[14] Categories, 1 a 24–25. ἐν ὑποκειμένῳ δὲ λέγω, ὃ ἔν τινι μὴ ὡς μέρος ὑπάρχον, ἀδύνατον χωρὶς εἶναι τοῦ ἐν ᾧ ἐστίν. Bekker's text.

[15] Categories, 2 a 34–35. τὰ δ' ἄλλα πάντα ἤτοι ὑποκειμένων λέγεται τῶν πρώτων οὐσιῶν ἢ ἐν ὑποκειμέναις αὐταῖς ἐστίν. Bekker's text.

[16] Categories, 2 b 7–8. τῶν δὲ δευτέρων οὐσιῶν μᾶλλον οὐσία τὸ εἶδος τοῦ γένους. ἔγγιον γὰρ τῆς πρώτης οὐσίας ἐστίν. Bekker's text.

[17] Categories, 2 b 26–28. ὡσαύτως δὲ καὶ τῶν πρώτων οὐσιῶν οὐδὲν μᾶλλον ἕτερον ἑτέρου οὐσία ἐστίν· οὐδὲν γὰρ μᾶλλον ὅτις ἄνθρωπος οὐσία ἢ ὁ τὶς βοῦς. Bekker's text.

to establish the greater importance of "secondary substances" than the rest of the predicables in the other nine categories, as when he points out, "Very reasonably, alone of everything else after primary substances, species and genera are called secondary substances; for these alone of the predicates 'throw light upon' or 'clarify' primary substances."[18]

A primary substance, then, is the independently existing individual particular, the τόδε τι, and the other predicables, including the secondary substances—i.e., species and genera—really comprise, broadly speaking, the Aristotelian universals, which exist, to be sure, but never exist apart from primary substances. They are all "present in" or "have their real existence in" primary substances. Now, in the main, the passages which have been cited are those which have a primarily logical connotation, but their combined logical and ontological significance is unmistakable. And it is safe to say that throughout the Aristotelian corpus there is consistently the same attitude towards the individual particular, that entity which exists in complete separation from other things, but which has within it all these other constituent elements which are of such an order that they are incapable of independent or separate existence. All the universals are elements of this sort. But the exclusive ontological and logical nature of the analysis here cannot be overlooked. It is as if Aristotle were asked "What is real?" or "What has being in the full sense of the word;" and he answered, "These things which I have called 'primary substances.' My reasons for this are clear. In the first place, all we need do is look about us, and we see them. It makes no difference whether they are sticks or stones or trees or horses or men or stars. They are all primary substances, particular things, and no one is more of a primary substance than another. My reflections on the problems of logic confirm my view. For there are various subordinate notions which in our speech and thought we attach to them, such notions as to how they may be classified, what qualities they may have, and the like."[19] No

---

[18] *Categories*, 2 b 29–31. εἰκότως δὲ μετὰ τὰς πρώτας οὐσίας μόνα τῶν ἄλλων τὰ εἴδη καὶ τὰ γένη δεύτεραι οὐσίαι λέγονται· μόνα γὰρ δηλοῖ τὴν πρώτην οὐσίαν τῶν κατηγορουμένων. Bekker's text.

[19] By way of anticipation, I should like to underscore Aristotle's remark that a man is no more truly a substance than an ox. This bespeaks the fact that

more and no less is Aristotle's initial answer to the eternal question, "What is Being?"[20]

Aristotle here is engaging in philosophical isolationism. In a logical context, to be sure, he has emerged with an exclusively ontological pronouncement. He is keeping strictly to the sphere of being, and there is no question or possibility that value will obtrude itself. Whatever may be the explanation, so far as his analysis of substance as τόδε τι is concerned, his approach here in the *Categories* and throughout is always ontological. Being and Value, which are obviously apart in the *Categories*, remain apart. But someone may urge that, from the point of view of logic, there is no difference between an ox and a man and that we should wait until later when Aristotle will have plenty to say about such great differences as do obtain between men and oxen. To a degree, this is, of course, true but it is likewise true that the whole Aristotelian position, however ramified, is still dominated to its detriment by the implications of this proposition that a man is no more truly a substance than an ox.

[20] A word must be said about Werner Jaeger's thesis concerning the development or evolution of Aristotle's thought. In his well-known book, *Aristoteles* (Berlin, Weidmann, 1923; English translation by Richard Robinson, *Aristotle* [Oxford, Clarendon Press, 1934]), Jaeger has formulated his theory that Aristotle as a younger man was a Platonist, and that, by gradual steps, he departed from the Platonic position and developed his own contrasting system. Jaeger's evidence depends in considerable measure upon his reconstruction of some of Aristotle's earlier lost writings which were composed in the dialogue form. The theory thus gives Jaeger a chronological testing instrument. For example, if a passage in Aristotle smacks strongly of Platonic influence, Jaeger is permitted to say that it derives from an earlier stratum of Aristotle's thought.

Now it is no doubt true that Aristotle as a younger man must have been profoundly affected by his master, and, as we have already remarked, there is scarcely a page of his that does not have some Platonic vestige upon it. But—and this is the important point—there was that crucial moment when Aristotle said to himself that he could not accept the Theory of Ideas. Now we do not know, nor can we ever discover precisely, when that moment occurred. But from that time on, the *philosophical* significance of everything he wrote has to be *fundamentally* anti-Platonic, however much the subsidiary features of his thought may bear a Platonic colour. The crucial moment of the rejection must have come before the composition of any of the genuine works of Aristotle which are now preserved, because they all presuppose the conviction that Ideas as separate and non-spatiotemporal entities do not exist. And, throughout the corpus there is assumed this metaphysics of substance which we are attempting here to outline. From the philosophical point of view, then, the developmental hypothesis of Jaeger is not a matter of concern. In other words, the decreasing incidence of Platonic influence in the subsidiary features of Aristotle's thought is an important fact to know, but it does not alter the basic meaning of that thought.

Therefore, in discussing Aristotle's metaphysics of substance, it is perfectly sound methodologically to derive our evidence indiscriminately from the entire corpus. That this is sound method is borne out by the generally accepted view of the nature of Aristotle's writings as we have them. They seem to be, in broad terms, the "lecture notes" from which Aristotle worked in presenting his system to his pupils in the Lyceum. These he kept in a more or less fluid condition and, so to speak, "up to date." This hypothesis seems to explain quite plausibly the several peculiarities of the corpus. In its terms we can understand the frequent cross-references, the alternative treatments of the same problem which sometimes

The whole direction of Aristotle's analysis is therefore turned towards primary substance, and, as if he were burrowing into these objects, he emerges first with an initial dualism of form and matter. First, then to consider:

B. εἶδος, *form*. Aristotle's attitude towards form is typically indicated in the opening words of the *Historia Animalium:* "Of the parts of animals some are uncompounded; such as are divided into parts uniform with themselves [and with the wholes of which they themselves are parts]; e.g., flesh is divided into flesh. Others are compounded, such as are divided into parts not uniform with themselves [and with the wholes of which they themselves are parts]; e.g., a hand is not divided into hands nor a face into faces."[21] In the light of this remark, man, as an animal, has two types of organic parts, and they may be differentiated by the presence or absence of form in them. Those parts which are brought together into the form of man are ultimate units because of form. If one divides man by form, the division results in face, hands, and so on—in general units which are not further divisible upon the basis of form. But if one divides flesh into smaller bits of flesh, the division is on a basis of matter. If, in other words, the unit which is ultimate in form is further

---

appear, and places where an insertion has been made (cf. the familiar instance of chapter 8 in Book Λ of the *Metaphysics*). Also differences in style are understandable. We can assume that passages written in short, cryptic, and choppy sentences were really bare notes upon which Aristotle would expand extemporaneously when he was in the process of an oral presentation of the material. Other passages Aristotle chose to work out more completely as though he were preparing them for publication. This hypothesis also would explain the contiguity of so-called "Platonic" passages and later treatments. For example, Jaeger (*Aristoteles*, pp. 229 ff.) argues for an early date for *Metaphysics* Λ, but would insist that chapter 8 is a late insertion.

But if this general hypothesis as to the nature of Aristotle's writings is sound, the important point is that for Aristotle himself the whole corpus would represent a statement of his system made as coherent as he possibly could at any given moment. Such must have been his attitude towards these "lecture notes" when they left his hand for the last time. Hence, since the entire body of writings, as we have argued, is a systematic account of an entire philosophical system, it is fair to draw from any part of it in order to elucidate the metaphysics of substance which lies at its core.

[21] *Historia Animalium*, 486 a 5–8. τῶν ἐν τοῖς ζῴοις μορίων τὰ μέν ἐστιν ἀσύνθετα, ὅσα διαιρεῖται εἰς ὁμοιομερῆ, οἷον σάρκες εἰς σάρκας, τὰ δὲ σύνθετα, ὅσα εἰς ἀνομοιομερῆ, οἷον ἡ χεὶρ οὐκ εἰς χεῖρας διαιρεῖται οὐδὲ τὸ πρόσωπον εἰς πρόσωπα. Bekker's text.

divided, then the divisions are uncompounded parts, *i.e.*, mere matter—flesh, bone, and the like. As a result of this type of analysis Aristotle sees οὐσία (τόδε τι), *i.e.*, primary substance, as a compound of form and matter. To take another random example, Aristotle says, "The whole, then, a certain form of such and such a nature, in this flesh and these bones, is Callias and Socrates."[22]

The other member of this initial dualism is more difficult to treat, because the subtleties of Aristotle's analysis are reflected much more clearly in those passages which deal with matter than in those which consider form, εἶδος, in its more superficial significance, let us say, of external configuration. And, at the moment, in the present discussion it is necessary to limit the meaning of form to this more superficial sense. So then to turn to:

ὕλη, *matter*. A passage which takes the reader very suddenly into the complete complexity of Aristotle's thought on the nature of matter occurs in *Metaphysics* Z: "I mean by matter that which by itself is spoken of as neither a particular thing, nor a quantity, nor any other thing by which being is determined. For there is something of which each of these categories is predicated so that its mode of existence is different even from each one of the categories, for all the other [nine] categories are predicated of substance [οὐσία], while substance is predicated [in a certain sense] of matter. The result is that this ultimate entity [*i.e.*, matter] by itself is neither a particular thing nor a quantity nor anything else; nor further, is it the negations of these, for even these will belong to it accidentally."[23] The important implication of this passage is that Aristotle employs at times a conception of ὕλη, matter, as some kind of ultimate whose "mode of existence" is really different from that of everything else, and different in this way, that οὐσία, in its meaning of primary substance, can in a sense

[22] *Metaphysics* Z, 1034 a 5–7. τὸ δ' ἅπαν ἤδη, τὸ τοιόνδε εἶδος ἐν ταῖσδε ταῖς σαρξὶ καὶ ὀστοῖς, Καλλίας καὶ Σωκράτης. Ross's text.

[23] *Metaphysics* Z, 1029 a 20–26. λέγω δ' ὕλην ἣ καθ' αὑτὴν μήτε τὶ μήτε ποσὸν μήτε ἄλλο μηδὲν λέγεται οἷς ὥρισται τὸ ὄν. ἔστι γάρ τι καθ' οὗ κατηγορεῖται τούτων ἕκαστον, ὥστε τὸ εἶναι ἕτερον καὶ τῶν κατηγοριῶν ἑκάστῃ (τὰ μὲν γὰρ ἄλλα τῆς οὐσίας κατηγορεῖται, αὕτη δὲ τῆς ὕλης), ὥστε τὸ ἔσχατον καθ' αὑτὸ οὔτε τὶ οὔτε ποσὸν οὔτε ἄλλο οὐδέν ἐστιν· οὐδὲ δὴ αἱ ἀποφάσεις, καὶ γὰρ αὗται ὑπάρξουσι κατὰ συμβεβηκός. Ross's text. I have read ὥστε in 1029 a 22 instead of ᾧ, thus following the text which Ross preferred when he was making his translation of the *Metaphysics*.

"be predicated" of it. Aristotle, perhaps, by this can mean only that this ultimate "matter" is a kind of thing, which is absolutely characterless in itself, and which at the same time provides the indispensable condition for the very existence of οὐσία, primary substance—that which in the full sense is real.[24]

In order to understand the conception of matter as an ultimate "substratum," the term which is used conventionally in this connection, it is necessary to know what Aristotle believes to be the intervening stages between it and the ordinary matter of our sense experience. In his treatise *On Coming-to-be and Passing-away*, he remarks, "But we say that there is a matter of perceptible bodies, but this is never separate but always along with a contrariety [*i.e.*, hot, cold, moist, dry] out of which come-to-be the so-called elements [*i.e.*, fire, air, water, earth]."[25] The matter referred to here is the ultimate substratum, but it has no separate existence; that is, before it comes to be recognized as the matter of our ordinary sense experience, it is seen in its inseparable association with one of the contraries, and thus it is that from which one of the fundamental elements, fire, air, etc., can come into existence. In this way, we get the picture of Aristotle's conception of matter as a combination of "substratum" matter with the contraries and the elements. The distinction between matter as substratum and sensible matter is brought out more clearly (and in typically Aristotelian fashion, with an additional distinction) in a passage from the *Metaphysics*, where Aristotle says, "But matter is unknowable by itself. There is on the one hand sensible matter, and on the other intelligible matter. Sensible matter is, for example, bronze and wood, and whatever matter that is changeable; whereas intelligible matter belongs

---

[24] The difficulty here may be in the ambiguity inherent in Aristotle's use of οὐσία, the multiple connotations of which, as they appear in Aristotle's Greek text, are impossible to reproduce in English. In the passage just quoted οὐσία does have the connotation of primary substance, and yet at the same time, so far as "matter" is concerned οὐσία seems to have a strong existential force. Aristotle seems to want us to believe beyond any doubt that there is an "is-ness" (οὐσία) about this matter even though it may be in itself utterly characterless.

[25] *De Generatione et Corruptione*, 329 a 24–26. ἡμεῖς δὲ φαμὲν μὲν εἶναι τινα ὕλην τῶν σωμάτων τῶν αἰσθητῶν, ἀλλὰ ταύτην οὐ χωριστὴν ἀλλ᾽ ἀεὶ μετ᾽ ἐναντιώσεως, ἐξ ἧς γίνεται τὰ καλούμενα στοιχεῖα. Bekker's text.

to sensible things, not in their specific character as sensible things, for example, the objects of mathematics."[26]

For the present, there is no need to take up the question of what Aristotle means by "intelligible matter." It should be enough to remark that it is one of the conceptions which appear in Aristotle as part of his unending battle to settle the problem of the ontological status of the objects of mathematics—a battle, it may be said, from which Aristotle hardly emerges with the laurels of victory upon his brow. But so far as the whole passage is concerned, Ross's note on the passage is illuminating, particularly in its concluding remark, "We thus get a scale of matters, each of which implies all that precedes it:

1) ὕλη νοητή (intelligible matter)
2) ὕλη αἰσθητή (sensible matter)
   a) κινητή (τοπική) (changeable in respect of place)
   b) ἀλλοιωτή (changeable in respect of alteration)
   c) αὐξητὴ καὶ φθιτή (changeable in respect of increase and diminution)
   d) γεννητὴ καὶ φθαρτή (changeable in respect of generation and corruption)."[27]

In other words, as Ross indicates, "Everything that has sensible matter has intelligible matter, while the converse is not the case." Therefore, the conception of matter which implies the most is sensible matter which is changeable in respect of generation and corruption. To throw light on this conception Ross cites a passage from the treatise *On Coming-to-be and Passing-away:* "Matter, in the most proper and accurate sense of the word, is the substratum receptive of coming-to-be and passing-away, but

---

[26] *Metaphysics* Z, 1036 a 8–12. ἡ δ᾽ ὕλη ἄγνωστος καθ᾽ αὑτήν. ὕλη ἡ μὲν αἰσθητή ἐστιν ἡ δὲ νοητή, αἰσθητὴ μὲν οἷον χαλκὸς καὶ ξύλον καὶ ὅση κινητὴ ὕλη, νοητὴ δὲ ἐν τοῖς αἰσθητοῖς ὑπάρχουσα μὴ ᾗ αἰσθητά, οἷον τὰ μαθηματικά. Ross's text.

[27] In the text Aristotle has referred to sensible matter as "changeable." Ross in his "scale of matters" has simply introduced the standard Aristotelian analysis of motion and change into the four types: locomotion, alteration, change in size, and coming-into-being and passing-out-of-being. Subsequently Aristotle's views on motion and change will be examined in detail. At the moment, it is useful here, in order to get a sense of the complexity of Aristotle's basic conceptions in his metaphysics of substance.

also in a certain sense it is the substratum in the other types of change since the substrata are all receptive of certain contraries."[28]

To summarize Aristotle's doctrine on matter, it can be said that it is in one sense even more ultimate than οὐσία, primary substance. It is the "ground" wherein the basic contraries—hot and cold, dry and moist—find their being, and from which the time-honoured four elements come into existence. Matter also has an intelligible aspect in so far as it has to do with the objects of mathematics. And too there is sensible matter, in the ordinary use of the term, matter as the material cause, the wood and bronze, the stuff out of which the ordinary objects of sense-experience are made. But then, too, Aristotle makes certain that we do not forget matter in its sense of substratum, as that entity which is always underlying the phenomena of change, whether it be a case of the most fundamental category of change, that of coming into existence or passing out of existence, or whether it be a case of change of place, of quantity, or of alteration. Furthermore, Aristotle warns that matter, really in every sense, is unknowable by itself. It can only be "known" when some form, εἶδος, has been imposed upon it, i.e., when it has been informed. In general, the two main uses, matter as substratum and matter as material cause, should suffice as guide-posts in grasping this Aristotelian conception.

The conception of the individual particular as a compound of form and matter[29] raises, as a corollary problem to Aristotle's metaphysics of substance, the question of:

B'. *The Principle of Individuation.* In the light of the conclusion that primary substances are compounded of form and matter, what really is it that individuates each particular thing? What is the principle of individuation—the διαφορά as Aristotle calls it, the principle which marks off one thing from another? Now in Aristotelian terms, there are many things which have the same form. These fall into groups by virtue of the common formal elements in respect to which they resemble one another. In this

---

[28] *De Generatione et Corruptione*, 320 a 2–5. ἔστι δὲ ὕλη μάλιστα μὲν καὶ κυρίως τὸ ὑποκείμενον γενέσεως καὶ φθορᾶς δεκτικόν, τρόπον δέ τινα καὶ τὸ ταῖς ἄλλαις μεταβολαῖς, ὅτι πάντα δεκτικὰ τὰ ὑποκείμενα ἐναντιώσεών τινων. Bekker's text.

[29] i.e., οὐσία (τόδε τι) as a σύνθετον of εἶδος and ὕλη.

situation, form (εἶδος) is not only the principle of individuation of an individual particular, but it is also the principle which marks off or distinguishes one species from another within the same genus. To take a simple example, horse and dog are species within the genus, animal. The horse is differentiated from the dog, according to this aspect of the Aristotelian analysis, solely upon the basis of form. If, then, form is that which individuates on the level of particulars, and likewise on the level of species, then matter seems to be the common element, the κοινόν.[30]

Now the problem is really never satisfactorily resolved in Aristotle, as can clearly be seen in examining the implications of a passage in the De Anima: "Now we call one class of existent things substance, including under the term, firstly, matter, which by itself is not a particular thing, [i.e., a this or that]; secondly, 'shape' and 'form,' in virtue of which the term indicating a particular thing is at once applied; and thirdly, the compound of the two, [i.e., the whole made up of matter and form].[31] The obvious major meaning of this quotation refers to the multiple use of the term οὐσία, substance, a point which will be elaborated in the discussion of substance as essence. However, before going into the problem of individuation, it is well to be reminded that in terms of the analysis which produced the intitial dualism, i.e., primary substance viewed as a compound of matter and form, Aristotle permits himself to use the same term, οὐσία, to refer to matter, form, and the compound of the two. But, so far as the problem of individuation is concerned, the relevance of the passage appears in the ambiguity latent in the term "form." To some extent, Aristotle has tried to clarify the ambiguity by introducing the term "shape," μορφή, i.e., external configuration. At all events, the term "form," εἶδος, means individual form, the "form" which permits something to be called a particular this or that, but at the same time "form," εἶδος, means "species." Now when form means species, it becomes the common element,

---

[30] Anyone familiar with the history of philosophy knows the endless debate which the problem of the principle of individuation precipitated among the Medieval Schoolmen.

[31] De Anima, 412 a 6–9. λέγομεν δὴ γένος ἕν τι τῶν ὄντων τὴν οὐσίαν, ταύτης δὲ τὸ μὲν ὡς ὕλην, ὃ καθ' αὑτὸ μὲν οὐκ ἔστι τόδε τι, ἕτερον δὲ μορφὴν καὶ εἶδος, καθ' ἣν ἤδη λέγεται τόδε τι, καὶ τρίτον τὸ ἐκ τούτων. Bekker's text.

the κοινόν, and as a result, matter constitutes the principle of individuation, the διαφορά, which distinguishes individuals within a
species.

In the discussion of primary substance, reference was made to
the passage from the *Metaphysics* which asserted that a whole,
made up of a form in the matter of flesh and bones, constituted
the primary substances, such as Callias and Socrates.[32] The
succeeding remark bears explicitly upon the problem of individuation, "They [*i.e.*, Callias and Socrates] are different by virtue of
their matter, for it is different, but they are the same in form,
for their 'form' [*i.e.*, εἶδος = species = man] is indivisible."[33]
Perhaps, Aristotle's attitude can be summarized by pointing out
that "form" functions as the principle of individuation if we look
at things by ascent from primary substance to genus. All things
have matter as a common substratum, but they can be distinguished
by form into primary substances, species, and genera. But matter
becomes the principle of individuation if we are differently
oriented in our analysis, and begin with the genus, and descend
to primary substance. The genus, after all, is a class of things
which have a common form, really the same indivisible form,
and hence can only be differentiated from one another by the
particular "segment," so to speak, of matter in which the common
form inheres.[34]

There can be no doubt that this unresolved problem concerning
the principle of individuation constituted a real difficulty for
Aristotle as he worked out his ontology. Not unrelated and, in
a sense, parallel to it, is the epistemological dilemma into which
his ontology leads him, a fact which may be mentioned here
briefly by way of anticipation. As Aristotle indicated in his description of his own method, we proceed from what is more
readily knowable to us to that which is intrinsically more intelligible.[35] This implies that we really never can come to know
these primary substances, these particulars that are compounded

---

[32] Cf. above, p. 68, and note 22.

[33] *Metaphysics* Z, 1034 a 7–8. καὶ ἕτερον μὲν διὰ τὴν ὕλην (ἑτέρα γάρ),
ταὐτὸ δὲ τῷ εἴδει (ἄτομον γὰρ τὸ εἶδος). Ross's text.

[34] This treatment of the principle of individuation I owe largely to P. E. More's
notes on Aristotle.

[35] Cf. above, p. 61.

of form and matter, even though they are apparently so readily available to us as knowing subjects. The dilemma may be stated in this way: On the one hand, Aristotle holds that the individual particular is that which is ultimately real; yet, on the other hand, we can never know this real individual particular, for the general, the universal, is the genuine object of our knowledge, something we abstract from particulars.[36] In other words, the ultimately real is unknowable. What we know has only a secondary status among the orders of existence. And, to return to the relation of this problem to the principle of individuation, if it is true that we know the universal, then we know things classified according to universals or generals, things, that is, which are differentiated by form. But what we do not know is the individual particular which is differentiated from other particulars by matter, and in one sense matter is the ultimate differentiation.

The next step in the analysis of primary substance, which has been carried on thus far by Aristotle within strictly ontological and epistemological limits, leads to the first member of a new dualism in the conception of:

C. οὐσία (τὸ τί ἦν εἶναι), *substance as essence.* We have already had occasion to refer to the ambiguity in the term εἶδος, in that it can mean either form or species. Also in the discussion of the principle of individuation, it was observed that εἶδος, form, could function as that principle. Perhaps Aristotle is led deeper into his analysis of primary substance, of the concrete whole, the σύνθετον, by this ambiguity in the term εἶδος. If form is taken

---

[36] This point is stated specifically in the *Rhetoric*, 1356 b 31–32. "The individual particular is infinitely complex, and cannot be known." τὸ δὲ καθ' ἕκαστον ἄπειρον καὶ οὐκ ἐπιστητόν. (Bekker's text.) Lane Cooper, in *The Rhetoric of Aristotle* (New York, Appleton, 1932) translates, "Particulars being infinite, the individual fact cannot be scientifically known." W. R. Roberts in the Oxford translation renders it, "Individual cases are so infinitely various that no systematic knowledge of them is possible." In the context, Aristotle is asserting that the arts do not investigate (σκοπεῖ) the particular. Medicine does not investigate what will cure the individuals, Socrates or Callias, but rather a class of persons who are in such-and-such condition. Now, both Cooper and Roberts make a plural out of τὸ καθ' ἕκαστον, and, in my opinion, they are not justified in so doing. I believe rather that here is a direct reference to the standard epistemology of Aristotle in which the particular is not knowable, but only the universal. I have rendered ἄπειρον as "infinitely complex." It might be translated as "infinitely inexhaustible." I would hold no brief for either rendering. The point is that there is some kind of infinitude about a particular which makes it unknowable.

as the principle of individuation, and if we ask, for example, why is Socrates this particular individual, *i.e.*, this primary substance, there seems to be some decisively determining factor of reality here besides form, εἶδος; or else it is εἶδος in a more profound sense than mere visible external shape. So, in Aristotle's thought, form, εἶδος takes on an internal significance, and seems to designate that something inside the individual particular which gives it its form. It seems to be in this way that Aristotle arrives at the conception of essence, and to make his meaning as precise as possible he uses the phrase, τὸ τί ἦν εἶναι (literally, the being precisely what a thing is and not something else). Because the conception of essence points to the central reality in a particular, Aristotle in a sense can call essence the "substance," the οὐσία of a thing. In other words, by the conception of essence, Aristotle can account for that which makes this primary substance, as a compound *(οὐσία as a σύνθετον)*, to be what it is. Thus substance, οὐσία, as essence, is not another name for a primary substance, a σύνθετον, but rather designates that which differentiates one particular primary substance from all other primary substances. It is in some such terms as these that this first term in the second dualism should be understood, substance as essence, which soon will be contrasted with the conception of "accidents." A short phrase in the *Metaphysics*, in a section which discusses the problem of becoming (and thus is not a matter of immediate concern) sums up tersely Aristotle's attitude concerning essence. Aristotle says, "When I speak of substance without matter I mean the essence."[37]

There are few terms in Aristotle which are more confusing than substance, οὐσία. Hence, the several uses of the term, which in their meanings have a habit of blurring into one another, should be clearly distinguished now, before considering the conception of "accidents," συμβεβηκότα. Early in the first book of the *Metaphysics*, Aristotle lists his familiar four causes, material, formal, efficient, and final, but his manner of characterizing the formal cause is relevant in the present connection. He observes,

---

[37] This is Ross's translation as he gives it in a note in his edition to *Metaphysics* Z, 1032 b 14, λέγω δὲ οὐσίαν ἄνευ ὕλης τὸ τί ἦν εἶναι. Ross's text.

"One of the causes we say is substance as essence."[38] Now Ross in a note to this passage refers to a later book of the *Metaphysics*, where Aristotle writes, "Substance [*i.e.*, οὐσία] is used, if not in more ways, at least especially in four: the substance of each thing seems to be the essence, the universal, the genus, and fourthly, the substratum."[39] The note, within which is the reference to this latter passage, is worth quoting in full: "Though οὐσία is properly a non-committal word, meaning the most real element in a thing, wherever that is to be found—in the essence of the thing, the universal or class under which it falls, or its material substratum (Z, 1028 b 33)—yet Aristotle tends constantly to use it in the sense of that which he himself believes (Z, 1041 b 7–9) to be the most real element in a thing, *viz.*, its form or essence." In order to make more complete the crucial evidence in Aristotle for this conception, the second passage from *Metaphysics* Z must be given: "Therefore we seek the reason why the matter is some definite thing (and this is its form); and this is its substance."[40]

Out of this group of quotations taken together with passages which have already been cited, the following several meanings of substance (οὐσία) can be distinguished, even though some of the meanings tend to run into one another:

1. Substance = the individual particular; *i.e.*, primary substance.
2. Substance = form, in the sense of species or genus; *i.e.*, secondary substance.
3. Substance = the universal.
4. Substance = matter as substratum.
5. Substance = essence; the formal cause.

Of these five meanings, numbers 2, 3, and 5 exhibit the closest interconnection. In other words, to call form (*i.e.*, species), the universal, the essence, and the formal cause, all by the same

---

[38] *Metaphysics* A, 983 a 27–28. ὧν μίαν μὲν αἰτίαν φαμὲν εἶναι τὴν οὐσίαν καὶ τὸ τί ἦν εἶναι. Ross's text.

[39] *Metaphysics* Z, 1028 b 33–36. λέγεται δ᾽ ἡ οὐσία, εἰ μὴ πλεοναχῶς, ἀλλ᾽ ἐν τέτταρσί γε μάλιστα· καὶ γὰρ τὸ τί ἦν εἶναι καὶ τὸ καθόλου καὶ τὸ γένος οὐσία δοκεῖ εἶναι ἑκάστου, καὶ τέταρτον τούτων τὸ ὑποκείμενον. Ross's text.

[40] *Metaphysics* Z, 1041 b 7–9. ὥστε τὸ αἴτιον ζητεῖται τῆς ὕλης (τοῦτο δ᾽ ἐστὶ τὸ εἶδος) ᾧ τί ἐστιν· τοῦτο δ᾽ ἡ οὐσία. Ross's text.

term, substance (οὐσία), is to underscore the fact that in Aristotle's mind the objects of these various designations are very close together, or if not close together they may even be reduced to a single entity, variously called, to differentiate among three distinguishable modes of approach to this same entity. As a matter of fact, in a single sentence in the *Metaphysics*, Aristotle indicates the tight inter-relationship in his thought between form and essence: "By form I mean the essence of each thing and its primary substance."[41] Here, of course, there is a possibility of confusion arising from the fact that Aristotle uses the same phrase, "primary substance," to refer both to the individual particular and to that within it which makes it be what it is, namely, its essence.[42] Essence, then, as a term with rich associations, may be taken to be that constant factor in a thing, which, by way of contrast, leads to the other member of the dualism:

συμβεβηκότα, *accidents*.[43] The reason should be clear why substance as essence falls within the left-hand column of the scheme which was submitted to indicate Aristotle's metaphysics of substance.[44] It is simply because of the close relation obtaining between form and essence. Similarly, accidents, in a sense, are more closely connected with matter, whether one takes matter in its more metaphysical meaning of substratum, or in its more obvious meaning, that is, in the sense that bronze is the matter of a statue. "Accidents," in Aristotle's sense, are those attributes which come to be attached to an individual particular, not out of necessity, and in turn are of a nature which in no way affects or modifies the essence of that particular. To take an example, the substance as essence of Socrates, the thing about Socrates which causes him to be essentially the man that he is, is abiding, remains unchanged. But the "accidents" of Socrates, the fact that he is bald, the amount which he weighs, etc., all may change. This

---

[41] *Metaphysics* Z, 1032 b 1–2. εἶδος δὲ λέγω τὸ τί ἦν εἶναι ἑκάστου καὶ τὴν πρώτην οὐσίαν. Ross's text.

[42] In using the word πρώτη here with οὐσία to refer to essence, Aristotle seems merely to be insisting upon the "primary" importance of essence in each individual particular thing.

[43] For a relatively concise statement which embodies Aristotle's views on συμβεβηκότα, cf. *Metaphysics* Δ, 1025 a 14–34.

[44] Cf. above, p. 60.

distinction between essence and accidents is reflected in a short, almost parenthetical, phrase in the first book of the *Metaphysics*, "with the substance abiding, while there are changes in affections."[45] In passing, and in order to fix the nature of the distinction, we can recall the metaphysical basis of the Roman Catholic doctrine of transubstantiation. There it is maintained that on the consecration of the Host there enters into it a new essence—the body and blood of Christ—while the accidents—that is, the physical attributes or characteristics of the bread and wine—remain the same.

Finally, in connection with the dualism of essence and accidents, the relation between the two can be seen in Aristotle's doctrine of the categories. The first category, substance, is related to the nine others, *i.e.*, the predicables of quantity, quality, and so on, as essence is related to accidents. Perhaps this point should not be stated as a proportion, but rather as a pair of equivalences. Substance, the first category, comes to be virtually the equivalent of substance as essence, whereas the other nine categories are completely the equivalent of accidents. In this connection, the tendency on Aristotle's part to identify primary substance, the τόδε τι, and substance as essence is not only typical, but also one of the reasons why it is difficult to fix firmly the meanings of some of his most basic terms. It is easy to see why Aristotle, given the mode and temper of his analytical approach, should tend to identify that mysterious individual particular with its essence. Perhaps he was led to do so under the pressure of the epistemological dilemma, about which comment has already been made, because, though the particular cannot be known,

---

[45] *Metaphysics* A, 983 b 9–10. τῆς μὲν οὐσίας ὑπομενούσης τοῖς δὲ πάθεσι μεταβαλλούσης. Ross's text. It may be objected that this passage does not properly illustrate the distinction between essence and accidents. As a matter of fact, in the context, Aristotle is talking about the early philosophers who saw in the nature of matter the principles of all things, and held that things came to be as a result of modifications of this primordial substratum. This would suggest that οὐσία here is used in the sense of οὐσία as substratum. To a degree this is true. But the only and, I trust, sufficient justification for citing the passage here lies in the presence of the term πάθη. "Affections" are the equivalent of accidents, and as such, the οὐσία with which πάθη are coupled must take on some fraction of the connotation of essence. Whether or not the passage is aptly chosen, at least it should suggest the nature of the dualism of essence and accidents in Aristotle's thought.

the essence can be known, closely identified as it is with form and the universal. But, whatever may be the reason for Aristotle's making an equivalence of primary substance and essence, he actually does so on occasions, and thus it is justifiable to consider the first of the categories as essence and the other nine as accidents.[46]

In connection with the dualism of essence and accidents, it is necessary to touch at least briefly upon the Aristotelian attitude towards:

C'. *Definition.* In definition, it is necessary to pass from the area or operation of mere predication, to the attempt to find in reason or rational formula *(λόγος)* that which corresponds to substance. In other words, definition has as its goal the transference of the essence of a thing to *λόγος*,—and it may be remembered that the validity of the whole enterprise depends ultimately upon the acceptance of the Aristotelian "axiom of correspondence." For Aristotle, the predication of accidents does not define. For example, to say of Socrates that "he sits" is by no means a definition.[47] But, the identification of the genus or species or the "universal" of a thing helps on the way to definition.[48] Yet, if one wants to arrive at the essence of a particular, let us say, of Socrates, it is necessary to move from the general to the particular. And hence, Aristotle drives in this opposite direction. He argues that since a genus does not exist apart from the species which go to make it up, a definition must be the formula *(λόγος)* which consists of differentiae. The process, then, must continue until the species that is without differentiae is reached. So in pursuance of this line of analysis, Aristotle concludes that the last differentia *(ἡ τελευταία διαφορά)* will

---

[46] The equivalence of primary substance and essence is explicitly stated in *Metaphysics* Z, 1032 a 4–6: ὅτι μὲν οὖν ἐπὶ τῶν πρώτων καὶ καθ᾽ αὑτὰ λεγομένων τὸ ἑκάστῳ εἶναι καὶ ἕκαστον τὸ αὐτὸ καὶ ἕν ἐστι, δῆλον. Ross's text. "Clearly, then, in the case of those things which are primary, and are said to exist by themselves, essence and 'primary' substance are one and the same." It should be noted that the chapter from which this passage is taken examines the sense in which primary substance and essence are the same, and the sense in which they are not.

[47] The reader is referred to Aristotle's *Topica*, Book I, chapter 4 and ff. for material on the problem of definition.

[48] Cf. *Metaphysics* Z, 1036 a 28–29. τοῦ γὰρ καθόλου καὶ τοῦ εἴδους ὁ ὁρισμός. Ross's text. "For definition is of the universal and the form."

be the essence and the definition of a thing.[49] In terms of this approach, in order to "define" Socrates one must proceed from the genus, "animate," to the species, "animal"; from the genus, "animal," to the species, "man"—that is, until one reaches that "class" which contains no differences within itself. This, according to Aristotle in the present context, would constitute the definition, the last item which differentiates the thing to be defined from the next larger class above. But it is hardly necessary to point out that to say "Socrates is a man" is far from being a satisfactory "definition" of Socrates.

Definition obviously raises the familiar problem of the relation of the particular to the general. Aristotle does not believe that "accidents" can define, and, to some extent at least, is not satisfied with definition which identifies the final differentia. Perhaps, in the effort to find something that "belongs to" an individual particular and yet is not an accident, he introduces the conception of a "property," ἴδιον. Aristotle means by a "property" that which is not the equivalent of a thing's essence, but which pertains to that thing alone, and as a consequence is predicated convertibly of it. An illustration of a property submitted by Aristotle is man's ability to learn grammar. The ability to learn grammar and man can be predicated convertibly. If a particular "thing" can learn grammar, "it" must be a man. If a particular thing is a man, then he has the ability to learn grammar. In this respect, of course, a property is different from an accident, for an accident is not predicated convertibly. For example, man is capable of being asleep, but it does not follow that if a thing is capable of being asleep, it is a man.[50]

But actually it is fair to ask how far this additional notion of a property is helpful in facing the problem of definition. The conventional form of definition by genus and differentia, for example, "man is a rational animal," is satisfactory enough if the *definiendum* is on the level of a species or a genus. But if the thing to be defined is a particular, the conception of a property does not add anything to the admittedly unsatisfactory methods involving accidents, or genus and final differentia. A property

---

[49] I have here paraphrased Aristotle's argument in *Metaphysics* Z, 1038 a 5–20.
[50] *Topica*, 102 a 18–30.

certainly does not designate the last differentia of Socrates, that which finally differentiates him from Callias. Aristotle insists upon the relation between definition and essence, when he asserts, "Definition is the formula, or rational account which points out or signifies essence."[51] Now, as it will be recalled, essence is that in a particular which causes it to be precisely what it is and not something else. Hence, this Aristotelian view of definition as that which states precisely the essence of the *definiendum* represents perhaps his deepest and best thought on the problem. For Aristotle, the conception of essence is, in a way, his means of resolving the problem of the relation of the universal and the particular. Essence does, or should fuse the most universal conception of a thing *and* the complete individuality of it. But it may be doubted that Aristotle's conception of essence actually accomplished this reconciliation. Aristotle insists that it is that which causes a thing to be what it is, *i.e.*, it designates its individuality. But when Aristotle is asked to say exactly what essence is, he is immediately forced from the level of the particular, and talks in terms of universals, form, genus, species, or class. In other words, the tight association of essence with species, form, and universal prevents essence from performing its function in particulars. Hence it would appear that, for Aristotle, as, particulars are unknowable, so they are undefinable. Thus this outcome of the Aristotelian doctrine of definition reflects, or is another manifestation of, his epistemological-ontological dilemma that he cannot know the particulars which are ultimately real. In Aristotle, then, is definition anywhere near so final a thing as he so often makes us believe? Can it be that definition in an absolute sense is impossible, and that actually definitions are merely clarificatory organizations of universals, useful working formulae, of no absolute worth in and of themselves, but rather workable instruments to be employed by the speculative mind?

In a sense, the discussion of the dualism of essence and accidents brings to a conclusion the sketch of Aristotle's analysis of the metaphysics of substance, studied exclusively from the static point of view. However, before undertaking the analysis from

---

[51] *Topica*, 101 b 6. ἔστι δ' ὅρος μὲν λόγος ὁ τὸ τί ἦν εἶναι σημαίνων. Bekker's text.

the dynamic point of view, there is still another pair of terms, not explicitly related to each other in Aristotle, which occupy a kind of transitional position between the static and dynamic approaches. The ensuing observations, then, should be regarded as a rounding off of the static analysis, and at the same time, as an introduction to the dynamic analysis. These two terms are "complete actuality" and "privation."

D. ἐντελέχεια, *complete actuality*. Entelechy, or as it might be expressed, actuality as *perfectio*, is a term introduced into the vocabulary of philosophy by Aristotle, and in a sense is an extension of the notions already discussed, where "form" (εἶδος) conceived as "essence" (οὐσία) designated the actuality of a thing. The conception of entelechy carries actuality further, for it takes into account the phenomenon that some things fulfill the notion of "complete actuality" far better than others. To take a simple example, Socrates seems to be more of a man than a low-grade moron, that is, he comes far closer to the complete perfection or complete actuality or entelechy of a man. The meaning of the term perhaps may become clearer by employing some amateurish etymologizing, which is not totally without scientific support. The following sequence of equations suggests itself: ἐν + τέλει + ἔχειν = τελείως ἔχειν (*i.e.*, ἐν τέλει = τελείως) = to be τέλειον = complete = perfect. Therefore, ἐν + τέλος + ἔχειν may be the equivalent of ἐν ἑαυτῷ τὸ τέλος ἔχειν, *i.e.*, "having its telos in itself." However faulty this etymology may be, at any rate it does indicate the significance of entelechy as the *perfectio*, the actuality of a thing that possesses its perfect οὐσία as τέλος, and is thus τέλειον. Aristotle's view of the term is revealed in a passage in the *Metaphysics* where he is discussing the relation of substance or essence to number. He remarks, "and substance or essence thus is one, but not as some maintain, that it is a kind of a monad or point, but that each substance or essence is an entelechy, an actuality and a certain particular nature."[52]

If we analyse the term entelechy further, it immediately becomes clear that it, as the complete and actual perfection of a thing, would have to do not only with a thing's form or essence,

[52] *Metaphysics* H, 1044 a 7–9. καὶ ἡ οὐσία ἐν οὕτως, ἀλλ' οὐχ ὡς λέγουσί τινες οἷον μονάς τις οὖσα ἢ στιγμή, ἀλλ' ἐντελέχεια καὶ φύσις τις ἑκάστη. Ross's text.

but also with those attributes which contribute to the actualization of the thing's τέλος, or perfection or completeness. But, at the same time, as the passage just quoted seems to indicate, there is an intimate connection between a thing's entelechy and its essence. For this point, as well as to indicate Aristotle's conception of entelechy in animate things, the following passage from the *De Anima* may be illuminating: "*Οὐσία* is used in three different ways, as we have already pointed out: One, form, two, matter, and three, the combination of the two; one of these, *i.e.*, matter, is potentiality, and the second, form, is entelechy (actuality as *perfectio*). Now when the combination of the two is animate, the body is not the entelechy of the soul, but the soul is the entelechy of a particular body."[53] It is now possible to turn to the term which has been paired with entelechy:

στέρησις, *privation*. At the outset it should be noted that this dualism is not explicit in Aristotle. Normally he contrasts entelechy either with δύναμις, potentiality, or with ὕλη, matter. But there is a reasonable and philosophical justification for introducing στέρησις at this point, for after all, a thing's entelechy is known and recognized by what the thing *has*, whereas στέρησις denotes the lack of that which a thing might have. In chapter 22 of *Metaphysics* Δ Aristotle gives a full account of the meaning of στέρησις coupled with copious illustrations, but the same general material, in a more compressed form, is repeated in *Metaphysics* Θ :

"Privation has several meanings:

1) not having a quality,
2) not having a quality when it is natural to have it,
   a) from the point of view of circumstance:
      α) either in general, or
      β) whenever natural
   b) from the point of view of manner:
      α) either in a particular way, *e.g.*, lacking it completely, or
      β) if it lacks the quality in any degree whatsoever.

---

[53] *De Anima*, 414 a 14–19. τριχῶς γὰρ λεγομένης τῆς οὐσίας, καθάπερ εἴπομεν, ὧν τὸ μὲν εἶδος, τὸ δὲ ὕλη, τὸ δὲ ἐξ ἀμφοῖν, τούτων δ' ἡ μὲν ὕλη δύναμις, τὸ δὲ εἶδος ἐντελέχεια, ἐπεὶ τὸ ἐξ ἀμφοῖν ἔμψυχον, οὐ τὸ σῶμά ἐστιν ἐντελέχεια ψυχῆς, ἀλλ' αὕτη σώματός τινος. Bekker's text. Cf. note 31 above.

3) In certain connections, we say that a thing has been deprived of a quality if it possesses the quality by nature and does not have it because of violence."[54] Perhaps some of the examples from *Metaphysics* Δ may be helpful. To illustrate 1 above, Aristotle cites the "privation" of eyes in a plant, whereas for 2, a, α, he points out that a mole in general is blind, but naturally according to the mole's genus, animal, it would have sight. Under 2, a, β, an example is found in the case of a man born blind who lacks sight, though it is natural for him to possess sight. For 2, b, α, Aristotle cites the instance that by "privation" of sight, a man is totally blind, while, for 2, b, β, by "privation" of sight, a man is blind in one eye, or has imperfect vision. Aristotle illustrates 3 by the simple instance of a man deprived of sight if he has lost his vision in an accident.

The foregoing treatment of στέρησις should afford ample justification for coupling the term with entelechy with its con-notation of perfect completeness. But it should be remembered that Aristotle uses privation most frequently in connection with opposition and its various kinds. In fact, στέρησις is named as one of the four regular kinds of opposition, Now, the opposites and the problem of opposition are most important for Aristotle for two reasons. First is the connection of opposition with his formal logic. As is well known, Aristotle's so-called "square of opposition" is at the very root of his logical theory. Secondly, opposition is important for his theories of "coming-to-be" and "passing-away," and for that matter, for his whole treatment of motion and change. This latter problem will be considered in detail, but for the moment it should be sufficient to note that Aristotle's theory of motion and change is at the root of his physics and metaphysics.

In the *Categories*, Aristotle takes pains to formulate a simple statement and explanation of the phenomenon of opposition: "One thing is said to be opposed to another in four different ways: in respect of relation, of contrariety, of privation and possession, and of affirmation and denial. To speak in outline

---

[54] *Metaphysics* Θ, 1046 a 31–35. ἡ δὲ στέρησις λέγεται πολλαχῶς· καὶ γὰρ τό μὴ ἔχον καὶ τὸ πεφυκὸς ἂν μὴ ἔχῃ, ἢ ὅλως ἢ ὅτε πέφυκεν, καὶ ἢ ὡδί, οἷον παντελῶς, ἢ κἂν ὁπωσοῦν. ἐπ᾽ ἐνίων δέ, ἂν πεφυκότα ἔχειν μὴ ἔχῃ βίᾳ, ἐστε-ρῆσθαι ταῦτα λέγομεν. Ross's text.

of each of these types of opposition: (1) in respect of relation, *e.g.*, as double is opposed to half; (2) in respect of contrariety, *e.g.*, as evil is opposed to good; (3) in respect of privation and possession, *e.g.*, as blindness is opposed to sight; and (4) in respect of affirmation and denial, *e.g.*, as 'he sits' is opposed to 'he does not sit.' "[55] Another passage, this from the *Metaphysics*, extends the analysis somewhat further: "If indeed the kinds of opposition are contradiction, privation, contrariety, and relation, and if the first of these is contradiction, and if there is no middle term in contradiction, whereas there may be a middle term in contraries, it is clear that contradiction and contrariety are not the same."[56] The relationship of the several terms in these two passages can therefore be represented as follows:

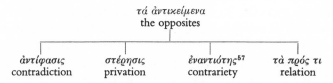

One of the more important points of the passages is the familiar distinction between contradiction and contrariety, along with the reference to the "excluded middle," a conception well known to students of elementary logic. All these terms should be clearly understood, in order to grasp Aristotle's theory of privation and its relation to opposition in general. Now, if we take the two statements, "Mr. Jones is here" and "Mr. Jones is not here," it is obvious that they are in contradictory opposition. Either one or the other of the propositions must be true; the second is merely a denial of the first. But there is absolutely no middle

[55] *Categories*, 11 b 17–23. λέγεται δὲ ἕτερον ἑτέρῳ ἀντικεῖσθαι τετραχῶς, ἢ ὡς τὰ πρός τι, ἢ ὡς τὰ ἐναντία, ἢ ὡς στέρησις καὶ ἕξις, ἢ ὡς κατάφασις καὶ ἀπόφασις. ἀντίκειται δὲ ἕκαστον τῶν τοιούτων ὡς τύπῳ εἰπεῖν ὡς μὲν τὰ πρός τι, οἷον τὸ διπλάσιον τῷ ἡμίσει, ὡς δὲ τὰ ἐναντία, οἷον τὸ κακὸν τῷ ἀγαθῷ, ὡς δὲ τὰ κατὰ στέρησιν καὶ ἕξιν, οἷον τυφλότης καὶ ὄψις, ὡς δὲ κατάφασις καὶ ἀπόφασις, οἷον κάθηται—οὐ κάθηται. Bekker's text.
[56] *Metaphysics* I, 1055 a 38–b 3. εἰ δὴ ἀντίκειται μὲν ἀντίφασις καὶ στέρησις καὶ ἐναντιότης καὶ τὰ πρός τι, τούτων δὲ πρῶτον ἀντίφασις, ἀντιφάσεως δὲ μηδέν ἐστι μεταξύ, τῶν δὲ ἐναντίων ἐνδέχεται, ὅτι μὲν οὐ ταὐτὸν ἀντίφασις καὶ τἀναντία δῆλον. Ross's text.
[57] The word ἐναντίωσις is sometimes the equivalent of ἐναντιότης, but it is also used as the general word for "opposition."

ground, no middle term, between them. It is possible to argue from the truth of one proposition to the falsity of the other, as well as from the falsity of one to the truth of the other. But the situation is different if we take the propositions, "Mr. Jones is good" and "Mr. Jones is bad." These are in contrary opposition. Either one or the other of them may be true. Thus, if one is true, the other must be false. Furthermore, they may both be false, and therefore it is not possible to argue from the falsity of one propostion to the truth of the other. This is because there is a middle ground, or a "middle term" here, as if one were to say, "Mr. Jones is fairly good." In other words, contradiction merely denies, whereas contrariety denies *and* asserts something in addition. Hence if we take the contrariety, "Mr. Jones is good" and "Mr. Jones is bad," the second proposition could be expanded, in order to give its full meaning, to read, "No, Mr. Jones is not only not good, but also in addition he is bad."

Aristotle, in the full context in the *Metaphysics* from which the last passage was quoted,[58] treats in detail the relationship of privation to opposition. He points out that στέρησις is a kind of contradiction, though in certain senses it admits of a middle term, *i.e.*, in the case of partial privation. Also he points to the relation of privation to contrariety when he says, "All contrariety would be privation, but not all privation in like manner would be contrariety."[59] Again the explanation lies in the fact that privation can be partial. For example, good is a privation of bad, and bad is a privation of good. Good and bad are contraries. But "partially good" is a privation and "partially bad" is a privation. However, "partially good" is not the contrary of "partially bad."

Though perhaps privation is not completely integrated into the right-hand column of the scheme given above,[60] still it is not unrelated to the material constituents in things. At one point Aristotle does distinguish explicitly between privation and matter. In the *Metaphysics*, he says, "Since that which is coming into being comes into being by some agency—and from something (but

---

[58] *Metaphysics* I, 1055 a 35–b 29.
[59] *Metaphysics* I, 1055 b 14–15. ἡ μὲν ἐναντίωσις στέρησις ἂν εἴη πᾶσα, ἡ δὲ στέρησις ἴσως οὐ πᾶσα ἐναντιότης. Ross's text.
[60] Cf. above, p. 60.

let this not be the privation, but the matter [*i.e.*, as ultimate substratum]), etc."[61] Now in one sense the phrase "from something" (ἔκ τινος) does refer to the coming-into-being of one thing from its opposite as privation. For example, health comes from or out of its opposite, disease, and in this sense health may be considered as a privation of disease.[62] But, as this passage and the preceding chapter in the *Metaphysics* indicate, "from something" refers to "matter," ὕλη. Hence Aristotle never quite identifies "privation" and "matter." Furthermore, the whole question of the position of privation in Aristotle's thought takes on an additional significance when we see how Plotinus uses the conception of privation considerably under the influence of Aristotle's analysis. Privation for Plotinus is an all-important element in his cosmic scheme. In contrast to Aristotle's refusal to identify completely privation and matter, Plotinus virtually makes the identification since for him matter is that which is at the extremity of the emanations from The One, and thus really amounts to the "privation" of all those qualities which things nearer The One possess.

The analysis of the dualism of entelechy and privation concludes the study of the individual particular, the τόδε τι, from the static point of view. But we should not overlook the fact that this dualism, though involving an essentially static approach, compels us through the notion of opposition to look forward to the question of "coming-into-being" and "passing-away," and thence to all the problems of motion and change. It is in this way that the dualism of entelechy and privation occupies a pivotal position and forms a natural transition to our analysis from the dynamic point of view.

---

[61] *Metaphysics* Z, 1033 a 24–26. Ἐπεὶ δὲ ὑπό τινός τε γίγνεται τὸ γιγνόμενον ... καὶ ἔκ τινος (ἔστω δὲ μὴ ἡ στέρησις τοῦτο ἀλλ᾽ ἡ ὕλη) κτλ. (Cf. 1033 a 8 ff.) Ross's text.

[62] In this connection, one cannot fail to be reminded of the famous "cyclic" argument for the immortality of the soul in Plato's *Phaedo*, 70 d ff.

CHAPTER IV

ARISTOTLE'S METAPHYSICS
OF THE INDIVIDUAL PARTICULAR:
THE DYNAMIC APPROACH

IN one sense the transition from the static approach to the dynamic involves moving from the more theoretical to the more practical, though in Aristotle the method of attack and the mode of analysis remain the same. It is easy to see why a consideration of the individual particular, the τόδε τι, as static is more theoretical. Actually, from Aristotle's point of view, no individual particular, whether it be a stone, a chair, a tree, an animal, or a man, as we observe it through our senses, is ever static. Rather, our senses reveal it to be dynamic, *i.e.*, it is always subject to motion and change. It comes into being and it passes out of being. Therefore, the analysis from the static point of view in Aristotle is merely a necessary theoretical propaedeutic to embark upon his description of man.

That this is explicitly Aristotle's mode of procedure is corroborated by the opening pages of the *Historia Animalium*. We have already had occasion to refer to the introduction to this work, which deals with simple and composite parts, as this topic bears upon Aristotle's conception of εἶδος, form.[1] After discussing the meaning of parts, he turns to the question of the species and genera of the various animals, their organs, and so on, until he is about to embark upon his description of man. Thus far he has assumed the static point of view, but at precisely this juncture he makes a remark which completely reveals how he is thinking, *i.e.*, how he moves from the static to the dynamic: "These statements have been made now in this way, more or less in outline form, in order to give us a taste of the number of things we must examine, and concerning the characteristics of which we must

[1] Cf. above, p. 67.

investigate, so that we may grasp first the underlying differentiae and attributes or 'accidents' for all things. Later we shall speak of them more accurately. After this we must try to discover their causes. For thus our further investigation can be carried out naturally, with the detailed account of each object already at hand before we continue. From these remarks it becomes apparent what are the subjects of our demonstration and what are the premisses upon which our demonstration must rest."[2]

The indispensable first step in investigation in Aristotle's mind is to explore the differentiae and attributes or properties of things. But these matters are actually those which permit of adequate analysis from the static point of view. After such preliminaries it is appropriate to take up causes, and of course, causes in their very operation presuppose an approach from the dynamic point of view which looks at things as they move and change. Aristotle sums up his whole attitude towards this method by saying that it will proceed "naturally," for only in this way can satisfactory "demonstration" be produced.

The conception of entelechy leads easily into an analysis of Aristotle's dynamic terms. The postulate that there is such a thing as complete and perfect actuality in a man, for example, takes us inevitably to the notion of a man's developing towards that completeness, that *telos*; in other words, we must now consider his motion and change as he undergoes this process of development. Therefore, the next pair of terms we must take up are thus closely related to the conception of entelechy:

E. *ἐνέργεια, actuality as activity.* Perhaps here more than with any other of the dualisms it is difficult to discuss one member of the pair separately from the other. Hence, at this point, only a few preliminary remarks may be in order concerning actuality as activity. In the static approach, Aristotle suggests that a thing is determined by its form or essence; but now in a dynamic

---

[2] *Historia Animalium*, 491 a 7–14. Ταῦτα μὲν οὖν τοῦτον τὸν τρόπον εἴρηται νῦν ὡς ἐν τύπῳ, γεύματος χάριν περὶ ὅσων καὶ ὅσα θεωρητέον· δι' ἀκριβείας δ' ὕστερον ἐροῦμεν, ἵνα πρῶτον τὰς ὑπαρχούσας διαφορὰς καὶ τὰ συμβεβηκότα πᾶσι λάβωμεν. Μετὰ δὲ τοῦτο τὰς αἰτίας τούτων πειρατέον εὑρεῖν. Οὕτω γὰρ κατὰ φύσιν ἐστὶ ποιεῖσθαι τὴν μέθοδον, ὑπαρχούσης τῆς ἱστορίας τῆς περὶ ἕκαστον· περὶ ὧν τε γὰρ καὶ ἐξ ὧν εἶναι δεῖ τὴν ἀπόδειξιν, ἐκ τούτων γίνεται φανερόν. Bekker's text.

context, ἐνέργεια invites us to think of this "form" as *doing* something. Actuality as activity emphasizes the process of development, of actualization. It bids us look at that process of transition, let us say, from boyhood to manhood, and at the same time keeps reminding us to fix our attention on the goal or *telos* of that development, *i.e.*, the state of being a man, in actuality. The other member of the dualism must now be introduced:

δύναμις, *potentiality*. At the outset, this term can best be understood as it is used in such sentences as "In a boy is the potentiality of becoming a man," or "The boy already is a man potentially." He may or may not become a man actually, or as the Greek has it, ἐνεργείᾳ.[3] Now actuality finds its place in the left-hand column of the scheme because of its close relation with form, essence, and entelechy. Potentiality is in the right-hand column for the very basic reason that it is "matter" which has the potentiality of becoming something.

Before going into further detail in the analysis of this dualism, it is essential to point out that Aristotle did not believe it possible for any of the objects, the individual particulars of this earth, of the "sublunary realm," to reach its full actuality. For example, we may believe that Socrates is more *actually* a man than any other with whom we may be acquainted, yet it is possible that Socrates may not have reached his own full actuality or entelechy. But this point in turn raises the question of the difference between actuality as activity and entelechy. It seems clear that in most contexts Aristotle does not make any distinction between the terms, but on occasion he does pause to differentiate them. One such passage occurs in the *Metaphysics*, "The name 'actuality as activity,' which we think of as connected with 'complete actuality,' has been extended from movements particularly to other things. For strictly speaking, 'actuality as activity' seems to be movement."[4] To grasp completely the distinction made here, we

---

[3] The dative singulars of these two words, ἐνεργείᾳ and δυνάμει are regularly translated into English by the adverbs, "actually" and "potentially."

[4] *Metaphysics* Θ, 1047 a 30–32. ἐλήλυθε δ' ἡ ἐνέργεια τοὔνομα, ἡ πρὸς τὴν ἐντελέχειαν συντιθεμένη, καὶ ἐπὶ τὰ ἄλλα ἐκ τῶν κινήσεων μάλιστα· δοκεῖ γὰρ ἡ ἐνέργεια μάλιστα ἡ κίνησις εἶναι. Ross's text. The non-kinetic meaning of ἐνέργεια will be taken up later in the discussion of change and motion, μεταβολή and κίνησις.

need to be aware of what Aristotle says a few pages later in the *Metaphysics*: "For the 'action' is the end, but the 'actuality as activity' is the 'action'; therefore even the name 'actuality as activity' comes from 'action' and tends towards 'entelechy, complete actuality.' "[5]

Ross's note on the first of these passages is most illuminating: "From 1050 a 21 it appears that strictly speaking ἐνέργεια means activity or actualization while ἐντελέχεια means the resulting actuality or perfection. *Yet ἐνέργεια is not a movement towards something other than itself; this is the difference between it and κίνησις.*[6] . . . In Λ. 6, 7, where God is viewed as the prime mover of the universe, He is called ἐνέργεια, activity, but in 8. 1074 a 36, where the immateriality and perfection of His being is insisted on, He is described as ἐντελέχεια."[7] Perhaps we can boil the distinction down to this: that entelechy, complete actuality, is essentially a static term, while "energy," actuality as activity, is essentially a dynamic conception.

Now it is necessary to follow Aristotle as he probes deeper into his conception of potentiality. In the philosophical lexicon of *Metaphysics* Δ, he presents a characteristically penetrating definition: "Potentiality means the principle of movement or change which is in something other than the thing changed, or in the thing changed *quâ* other. For example, the science of building is a potentiality which is not inherent in the thing built, the science of healing (medicine), being a potentiality, may be in the person healed, but not *quâ* healed. Then, in general, potentiality means the principle of movement or of change which is in something other or in itself *quâ* other, *i.e.*, where the change is brought about by something other or by itself *quâ* other."[8]

---

[5] *Metaphysics* Θ, 1050 a 21–23. τὸ γὰρ ἔργον τέλος, ἡ δὲ ἐνέργεια τὸ ἔργον, διὸ καὶ τοὔνομα ἐνέργεια λέγεται κατὰ τὸ ἔργον καὶ συντείνει πρὸς τὴν ἐντελέχειαν. Ross's text.

[6] The italics are mine. The full import of Ross's statement will become clear as we carry on our analysis of potentiality, motion, and change.

[7] We shall, of course, have much to say about the value overtones of these Aristotelian conceptions. To raise the value question at this point is not apposite to our present purpose of delineating at length Aristotle's metaphysics of the individual particular.

[8] *Metaphysics* Δ, 1019 a 15–20. Δύναμις λέγεται ἡ μὲν ἀρχὴ κινήσεως ἢ μεταβολῆς ἡ ἐν ἑτέρῳ ἢ ᾗ ἕτερον, οἷον ἡ οἰκοδομικὴ δύναμίς ἐστιν ἢ οὐχ ὑπάρχει ἐν τῷ οἰκοδομουμένῳ, ἀλλ᾽ ἡ ἰατρικὴ δύναμις οὖσα ὑπάρχοι ἂν ἐν τῷ ἰατρευομένῳ,

Aristotle could not be more explicit in identifying the fundamental meaning of potentiality as the principle or source which is capable of producing motion or change, either actively or passively, and it is not too much to say that all other uses of the term are related to this principal meaning.

There is one further point to be observed at this stage of our analysis which is most important for Aristotle's thought in general. This has to do with the reasons why Aristotle is careful to insert the phrase "*quâ* other" into his definition. If potentiality is merely the principle of motion or change in something other than the thing changed, then the phenomenon, for example, of a doctor healing himself would invalidate the definition. A rock has the "potentiality" of being moved by something outside itself. Here, of course, there is no need of the idea, "*quâ* other." However, if the entity under consideration is a complex being like a man, then "*quâ* other" is essential. Hence Aristotle's primary conception of potentiality really presupposes or asserts an agent-patient dualism within the human being. The consequences of this presupposition are obvious for ethics, and here indeed is one crucial point at which Aristotelian metaphysics and ethics come together. In fact, without the agent-patient dualism necessitated by the notion of potentiality, Aristotelian ethics would have no metaphysical ground. Perhaps the relationship will be clearer if we consider the problem in this way: An individual boy, who is potentially a man, actualizes that state of being a man by his "potentiality" of manhood, by that power to produce change in himself "*quâ* other," in his moral choices

---

ἀλλ' οὐχ ᾗ ἰατρευόμενος. ἡ μὲν οὖν ὅλως ἀρχὴ μεταβολῆς ἢ κινήσεως λέγεται δύναμις ἐν ἑτέρῳ ἢ ᾗ ἕτερον, ἡ δ' ὑφ' ἑτέρου ἢ ᾗ ἕτερον. Ross's text. It may be interesting here to quote Aristotle's definition of rhetoric: Ἔστω δὴ ῥητορικὴ δύναμις περὶ ἕκαστον τοῦ θεωρῆσαι τὸ ἐνδεχόμενον πιθανόν. *Rhetoric*, 1355 b 25-26. Ross's text. This may be translated in a somewhat expanded form as follows: "Let rhetoric then be the potentiality, *i.e.*, as a capacity to produce change, involved in observing concerning each particular that which is capable of being persuasive." W. R. Roberts renders it thus: "Rhetoric may be defined as the faculty of observing in any given case the available means of persuasion," while Lane Cooper's version is: "So let rhetoric be defined as the faculty [power] of discovering in the particular case what are the available means of persuasion." Neither Roberts nor Cooper appears to give to the translation of δύναμις enough of its primary meaning as a principle capable of producing movement or change.

which will contribute to the actualization, ἐνέργεια, of himself as a man.

Two further quotations should suffice to round out our understanding of the dualism of actuality as activity and potentiality. They both occur in Book Θ of the *Metaphysics* in a context in which Aristotle is arguing for the priority of actuality over potentiality in respect of substantiality.[9] At one juncture Aristotle remarks, "Since everything that is coming into being moves towards a first principle and a goal, *telos* (for this principle is the purpose, and the coming-into-being is for the sake of the goal, or end)—the actuality is the goal, and the potentiality is assumed for this purpose."[10] Here actuality as activity is identified as the goal or purpose of things, and potentiality is delineated as somehow preliminary to this goal.[11] The same general attitude towards the relation of actuality to potentiality appears when a little later on in the same chapter he takes up the question of the existential status of matter. "Further, matter exists potentially since it *might be informed*; whenever it exists actually, then it is *informed*."[12]

Before going into the whole problem of Aristotle's treatment of motion and change, it is obviously necessary to make some comment on his theory of time. All would agree that the problem of time is one of the most difficult in metaphysics, and thus here we can perhaps do no more than take comfort from Saint Augustine's often-quoted remark, "What is time? If nobody asks me, I know. If I want to explain it to a questioner, I don't know."[13] Aristotle closely associates time and motion, as is apparent in

---

[9] We shall have occasion later to discuss the argument of Book Θ.

[10] *Metaphysics* Θ, 1050 a 7–10. ὅτι ἅπαν ἐπ᾽ ἀρχὴν βαδίζει τὸ γιγνόμενον καὶ τέλος (ἀρχὴ γὰρ τὸ οὗ ἕνεκα, τοῦ τέλους δὲ ἕνεκα ἡ γένεσις), τέλος δ᾽ ἡ ἐνέργεια, καὶ τούτου χάριν ἡ δύναμις λαμβάνεται. Ross's text.

[11] It might be noticed that Aristotle's teleological attitude of mind, has begun to appear in the quotations which characterize his analysis from the dynamic point of view.

[12] *Metaphysics* Θ, 1050 a 15–16. ἔτι ἡ ὕλη ἔστι δυνάμει ὅτι ἔλθοι ἂν εἰς τὸ εἶδος. ὅταν δέ γε ἐνεργείᾳ ᾖ, τότε ἐν τῷ εἴδει ἐστίν. Ross's text.

[13] *Confessions*, XI. 14. In recent years, two remarkable contributions to the metaphysical speculation on time have been made by the late Professor A. A. Bowman of Glasgow University. Cf. his article, "Spirit-Time," *Proceedings of the Aristotelian Society*, XXIII, N. S. (1932–1933) pp. 295–332, as well as his book, *A Sacramental Universe* (Princeton, Princeton University Press, 1939).

his famous definition of time, "For this is time: the number of motion in respect of before and after."[14] The obvious, and indeed unanswerable criticism of this definition is its circularity. After all, the conception of time is reused in the definition, since "before" and "after" are themselves time words. Hence the definition actually tells us nothing about time in and of itself.[15] In fact, it may very well be that Aristotle's general empirical approach as well as the close association which he felt to exist between time and motion, plus in addition the fundamental position in reality which he assigned to motion, prevented him from obtaining any genuinely fruitful results in his thought about time. Aristotle's general inconclusiveness on the matter can perhaps be seen when he says in the *Metaphysics*: "But it is impossible for motion either to have come into being, or to have passed out of being (for it is everlasting), nor time. For 'before' and after' cannot exist if time does not exist. And thus then motion is continuous just as time is. For time is either the same thing as motion or some kind of affection of it."[16] But, quite apart from his view of time, Aristotle devotes almost unlimited attention to:

E'. *Motion and Change*. A passage from the *Physics* expresses compactly Aristotle's basic thinking on the problem of motion and change:

"Since we have marked off class by class that which exists actually, and that which exists potentially, the actualization of that which exists potentially is motion: the kind of motion being the kind whereby the process of actualization is brought about: for example:

---

[14] *Physics*, 219 b 1-2. τοῦτο γάρ ἐστιν ὁ χρόνος, ἀριθμὸς κινήσεως κατὰ τὸ πρότερον καὶ ὕστερον. Ross's text.

[15] Aristotle's view can be contrasted with Kant's conclusion that time and space are not objects of perception, but rather are modes of perceiving objects. J. F. Callahan in his book, *Four Views of Time in Ancient Philosophy* (Cambridge, Harvard University Press, 1948), has devoted a long chapter to Aristotle's theory of time, but unfortunately he never adequately criticizes the circularity of the Aristotelian definition.

[16] *Metaphysics* Λ, 1071 b 6-10. ἀλλ' ἀδύνατον κίνησιν ἢ γενέσθαι ἢ φθαρῆναι (ἀεὶ γὰρ ἦν), οὐδὲ χρόνον. οὐ γὰρ οἷόν τε τὸ πρότερον καὶ ὕστερον εἶναι μὴ ὄντος χρόνου· καὶ ἡ κίνησις ἄρα οὕτω συνεχὴς ὥσπερ καὶ ὁ χρόνος· ἢ γὰρ τὸ αὐτὸ ἢ κινήσεώς τι πάθος. Ross's text. As we shall see later, Aristotle's notion that time and motion are everlasting—in other words, that he holds no doctrine of creation—has profound implications for his teleology, as well as for his value theory in general. Cf. below, pp. 247–253.

1) the actualization of that which exists potentially and is alterable, *quâ* alterable, is called alteration.

2) the actualization of that which exists potentially and grows and does its opposite, diminishes (there is no common name for the two) *quâ* growing and diminishing, is called growth and diminution.

3) the actualization of that which exists potentially and comes into being and passes out of being, *quâ* coming into being and passing out of being, is called coming into being and passing out of being.

4) the actualization of that which exists potentially and admits of locomotion, *quâ* admitting of change of place, is called locomotion."[17] In a later passage of the *Physics*, Aristotle expresses his point even more succinctly: "We maintain that motion is the actualization of the movable, *quâ* movable."[18] And a little later, and in a somewhat different context, he gives another summary statement of his view, "In our books on physics, nature was set up as the source alike of motion and of rest, but nevertheless, motion is natural [or as Hardie and Gaye, the Oxford translators render it, 'motion is the characteristic fact of nature']."[19]

Aristotle thus identifies motion as a process of actualization, and has analyzed motion and change into four different kinds. So far as the terms motion and change are concerned, he

[17] *Physics*, 201 a 9–15. διῃρημένου δὲ καθ᾽ ἕκαστον γένος τοῦ μὲν ἐντελεχείᾳ τοῦ δὲ δυνάμει ἡ τοῦ δυνάμει ὄντος ἐντελέχεια, ᾗ τοιοῦτον, κίνησίς ἐστιν, οἷον τοῦ μὲν ἀλλοιωτοῦ, ᾗ ἀλλοιωτόν, ἀλλοίωσις, τοῦ δὲ αὐξητοῦ καὶ τοῦ ἀντικειμένου φθιτοῦ (οὐδὲν γὰρ ὄνομα κοινὸν ἐπ᾽ ἀμφοῖν) αὔξησις καὶ φθίσις, τοῦ δὲ γεννητοῦ καὶ φθαρτοῦ γένεσις καὶ φθορά, τοῦ δὲ φορητοῦ φορά. Ross's text. In my English rendering I have expanded the Greek, and at the cost of some awkward repetition, have repeated the Aristotelian formula for each kind of motion, in the hope that Aristotle's position might thereby be made perfectly clear. It should also be noted in passing that in this quotation we have an instance of the interchangeable use of ἐντελέχεια and ἐνέργεια.

[18] *Physics*, 251 a 9–10. φαμὲν δὴ τὴν κίνησιν εἶναι ἐνέργειαν τοῦ κινητοῦ ᾗ κινητόν. Ross's text.

[19] *Physics*, 253 b 7–9. ἐτέθη γὰρ ἡ φύσις ἐν τοῖς φυσικοῖς ἀρχὴ καθάπερ κινήσεως καὶ ἠρεμίας, ὅμως δὲ φυσικὸν ἡ κίνησις. Ross's text. In this context, Aristotle is dissenting from the opinions held by the Heracliteans and the Parmenideans, *i.e.*, the apostles of the flux and the apostles of rest. He rejects, I think, both these theories basically because of the difficulties raised by the data of sense perception for both. In other words, for Aristotle, in so far as he can see by using his senses, some things are in motion, others at rest, and others are now in motion and now at rest.

sometimes regards them as synonymous, as can be seen in a short parenthetical sentence which he injects into an argument in the *Physics*: "Let there be no difference for the present as to whether we speak of motion or change."[20] At other times, of the four kinds (*i.e.*, alteration, growth and diminution, generation and corruption, and locomotion) locomotion is considered to be the primary motion, as when he writes, "If, then, it is necessary that there always be motion, it is also necessary that locomotion always be the primary one of the motions."[21] Here, locomotion, and thus indirectly motion, seems to be at the head of the list, and is that to which all other forms of change can be reduced. In other words, if we take the cosmos as a whole, from the Prime Mover on down, locomotion holds the first position and produces all the other forms of change.

Ordinarily, however, "change" is the more inclusive term, as in the passage in the *Physics*, "Every motion is a kind of change."[22] Or again, in a more extended passage in the *Metaphysics*, "But if the kinds of change be four in number, either in respect of the 'what,' *i.e.*, substance, or of quality or of quantity or of place (the change in respect of substance being called simple generation and corruption; in respect of quantity being called growth and diminution; in respect of affection, *i.e.*, quality, being called alteration; and in respect of place being called locomotion) the changes would be into opposites in these several respects."[23] But though change is regularly the inclusive term, Aristotle definitely makes a distinction between change and motion. For

---

[20] *Physics*, 218 b 19–20. μηδὲν δὲ διαφερέτω λέγειν ἡμῖν ἐν τῷ παρόντι κίνησιν ἢ μεταβολήν. Ross's text.

[21] *Physics*, 260 b 4–6. εἰ ἄρα ἀνάγκη ἀεὶ κίνησιν εἶναι, ἀνάγκη καὶ φορὰν ἀεὶ εἶναι πρώτην τῶν κινήσεων. Ross's text.

[22] *Physics*, 225 a 34. πᾶσα κίνησις μεταβολή τις. Ross's text.

[23] *Metaphysics* Λ, 1069 b 9–14. εἰ δὴ αἱ μεταβολαὶ τέτταρες, ἢ κατὰ τὸ τί ἢ κατὰ τὸ ποῖον ἢ πόσον ἢ ποῦ, καὶ γένεσις μὲν ἡ ἁπλῆ καὶ φθορὰ ἡ κατὰ τόδε, αὔξησις δὲ καὶ φθίσις ἡ κατὰ τὸ ποσόν, ἀλλοίωσις δὲ ἡ κατὰ τὸ πάθος, φορὰ δὲ ἡ κατὰ τόπον, εἰς ἐναντιώσεις ἂν εἶεν τὰς καθ' ἕκαστον αἱ μεταβολαί. Ross's text. It should be noted that Ross in the Oxford translation gives ἐναντιώσεις the force of "contrary." This can hardly be accurate as subsequent quotations will show. Change in respect of substance, *i.e.*, generation and corruption, is between the opposites, being and not-being, which in turn are in contradictory opposition. The other three forms of change occur between contrary opposites.

example, in the *Metaphysics*, he says, "The changes in respect of generation and corruption are not motions."[24]

In articulating the distinction between motion and change, or rather, their relation, Aristotle refers back to his doctrine of the categories. He argues, then, in this way: "If then the categories are marked off into the following: substance, quality, place, activity and passivity, relation, and quantity, it is necessary that there be three kinds of motion, *viz.*, in respect of quality, or quantity, and of place. There cannot be motion in respect of substance, since there is nothing contrary to substance; nor can there be motion in respect of relation (for when one member of a relation changes, it is not possible for the relation to be true, if the other member does not change: therefore their motion is accidental); nor can there be motion in respect of activity and passivity."[25] This passage perhaps may demand some further explanation. Only seven of the original ten categories are listed, and here as six, since activity and passivity are lumped together as one.[26] Also possession and position are apparently subsumed under activity and passivity, while time *(ποτέ)* is omitted as not involving a separate kind of motion, since it is inherent in all motion by Aristotle's definition, "Time is the number of motion."[27] Thus of the six remaining categories, Aristotle can see motion only in connection with the three, quantity, quality, and place. He rules out motion in the category of substance, for substance has no contrary. Not-being, or if you like, "non-substance" is in contradictory opposition to substance. Therefore, in the case of generation and corruption Aristotle insists that there is change but not motion.

Ross explains why Aristotle does not admit motion in respect of relation: "There is no movement of, *i.e.*, in respect of, relation,

---

[24] *Metaphysics* K, 1068 a 2–3. αἱ κατὰ γένεσιν καὶ φθορὰν ⟨*sc.* μεταβολαὶ⟩ οὐ κινήσεις. Ross's text.

[25] *Metaphysics* K, 1068 a 8–14. Εἰ οὖν αἱ κατηγορίαι διήρηνται οὐσίᾳ, ποιότητι, τόπῳ, τῷ ποιεῖν ἢ πάσχειν, τῷ πρός τι, τῷ ποσῷ, ἀνάγκη τρεῖς εἶναι κινήσεις, ποιοῦ, ποσοῦ, τόπου· κατ᾽ οὐσίαν δ᾽ οὔ, διὰ τὸ μηδὲν εἶναι οὐσίᾳ ἐναντίον, οὐδὲ τοῦ πρός τι (ἔστι γὰρ θατέρου μεταβάλλοντος μὴ ἀληθεύεσθαι θάτερον μηδὲν μεταβάλλον, ὥστε κατὰ συμβεβηκὸς ἡ κίνησις αὐτῶν), οὐδὲ ποιοῦντος καὶ πάσχοντος. Ross's text.

[26] Cf. the discussion of the categories above, pp. 62 ff.

[27] Cf. above, p. 94.

because A may change in respect of its relation to B when A itself does not change at all but only B. Then the movement of A in respect of relation is only incidental to a change of B in some other respect—in size, quality, or place."[28] In other words, when A equals 60 miles per hour and B equals 20 miles per hour, the relation of A to B is triple. If B changes from 20 miles per hour to 30 miles per hour, and A remains 60 miles per hour, the relation of A to B has changed from triple to double; but the change of A in respect of relation is incidental to a change in quantity in B.

Ross's explanation of Aristotle's failure to admit motion in respect of activity and passivity is not equally clear. He comments, "There is not besides movement in size, quality, and place, another kind of movement in respect of action or passivity. Movement from one activity to another or from one passivity to another, or from activity to passivity or *vice versa* is, as Aristotle will try to show in lines 22–23, merely incidental to alteration, increase or diminution, or locomotion."[29] As a matter of fact, in so far as one can grasp Aristotle's argument here, activity and passivity are ruled out because this category, like time, pertains to all motions indifferently. In other words, anything that moves, of whatever sort its motion may be, is "doing" something and "suffering" something.

The interrelation of the various terms employed by Aristotle in his analysis of motion and change can perhaps best be understood by the help of a diagrammatic scheme:

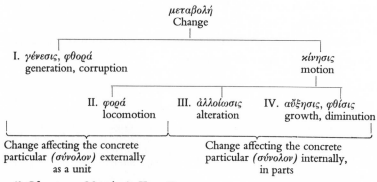

$\mu\varepsilon\tau\alpha\beta o\lambda\dot{\eta}$
Change

I. $\gamma\acute{\varepsilon}\nu\varepsilon\sigma\iota\varsigma$, $\varphi\theta o\varrho\acute{\alpha}$
generation, corruption

$\varkappa\acute{\iota}\nu\eta\sigma\iota\varsigma$
motion

II. $\varphi o\varrho\acute{\alpha}$
locomotion

III. $\dot{\alpha}\lambda\lambda o\acute{\iota}\omega\sigma\iota\varsigma$
alteration

IV. $a\breve{\upsilon}\xi\eta\sigma\iota\varsigma$, $\varphi\theta\acute{\iota}\sigma\iota\varsigma$
growth, diminution

Change affecting the concrete particular *($\sigma\acute{\upsilon}\nu o\lambda o\nu$)* externally as a unit

Change affecting the concrete particular *($\sigma\acute{\upsilon}\nu o\lambda o\nu$)* internally, in parts

[28] Cf. note on *Metaphysics* K, 1068 a 11.
[29] Cf. note on *Metaphysics* K, 1068 a 13.

As we have seen, Aristotle separates I, as concerned with substance, from II, III, and IV, as concerned with accidents. The grouping of I and II together as over against III and IV will be particularly significant when we come to deal with Aristotle's doctrine of the four causes.

Before leaving the pair of terms under consideration, actuality as activity and potentiality, appropriate notice must be given to Aristotle's method of resolving the problem of evil. In the discussion of his conception of δύναμις, the bearing of this notion upon the problems of ethics should have become clear.[30] Aristotle not only relied upon δύναμις as a metaphysical ground for his ethics (where moral evil is involved), but also used it to help him to account for cosmic evil as well. In connection with the eighth chapter of Metaphysics Θ, where Aristotle attempts to demonstrate his doctrine of the priority of actuality to potentiality, Ross has some remarks which must be quoted at length:[31] "Aristotle's doctrine of the priority of actuality leads him to deny the existence of any evil principle in the world.[32] That which is potential is as much superior to bad actuality as it is inferior to good. If that which is eternal can have no element of potentiality, a fortiori it can have no element of evil. 'There is no evil apart from particular things.'[33] Evil in other words is not a necessary feature of the universe but a by-product of the world-process, something that casually emerges in the course of the endeavour of individual things to reach such perfection as is open to them, and thus to approximate as nearly as they can to the divine life, 'to become immortal as far as they can.'[34] That they to a large extent fail is due to matter or necessity, but this is not an evil principle but a principle indifferent to good and evil. And for Aristotle the world-process is so much a striving after form or good that matter itself is sometimes described as so striving."[35]

[30] Cf. above, pp. 92–93.

[31] Ross, Aristotle, p. 178.

[32] Cf. Metaphysics Θ, 1051 a 4–21.

[33] Metaphysics Θ, 1051 a 17–18. δῆλον ἄρα ὅτι οὐκ ἔστι τὸ κακὸν παρὰ τὰ πράγματα. Ross's text.

[34] Nicomachean Ethics X, 1177 b 33. ἐφ' ὅσον ἐνδέχεται ἀθανατίζειν. Bywater's text.

[35] Ross here cites Physics I, 192 a 16–25. This rather curious passage runs as follows: "For admitting with them that there is something divine, good and

Clearly this theory will have to be examined later at considerable length, but for the present it will suffice to call attention to the passage in the tenth book of the *Nicomachean Ethics* to which Ross alludes. It is, of course, a famous text, one of the few in the Aristotelian corpus of great eloquence. Full of Platonic fervour and overtones, it is important because it reveals the way in which Aristotle's mind works, the quality of his teleology, and, most important of all, it shows how according to our theory the Aristotelian metaphysics of Being is found wanting as a ground for value judgments at those points when matters of supreme value for man are under consideration. In the present context Aristotle presents actuality as the *telos* or goal, but it seems to be tacitly assumed that this *telos* is a good actuality; in fact, nothing is said of the possibility of the *telos* being the equivalent of a bad actualization. Thus, the analysis of actuality and potentiality, at first undertaken in the spirit of neutrality with respect to value, becomes loaded with value overtones when *telos* is equated with actuality, whereas in fact the neutral nature of the analytical process provides no compelling reason for being concerned more with good actuality than with a bad. In other words a neutral ontological analysis cannot, without some kind of metaphysical legerdemain, provide an adequate set of criteria with which to identify confidently the "good actuality" or the "good *telos*."

Despite the undeniable emotional power of his words, Aristotle in this passage opens himself to this kind of criticism. As anyone

---

desirable, we hold that there are two other principles, the one contrary to it, the other such as of its own nature to desire and yearn for it. But the consequence of their view is that the contrary desires its own extinction. Yet the form cannot desire itself, for it is not defective; nor can the contrary desire it, for contraries are mutually destructive. The truth is that what desires the form is matter, as the female desires the male and the ugly the beautiful—only the ugly or the female not *per se* but *per accidens*." The Greek text reads: ὄντος γὰρ θείου καὶ ἀγαθοῦ καὶ ἐφετοῦ, τὸ μὲν ἐναντίον αὐτῷ φαμεν εἶναι, τὸ δὲ ὃ πέφυκεν ἐφίεσθαι καὶ ὀρέγεσθαι αὐτοῦ κατὰ τὴν αὐτοῦ φύσιν. τοῖς δὲ συμβαίνει τὸ ἐναντίον ὀρέγεσθαι τῆς αὐτοῦ φθορᾶς. καίτοι οὔτε αὐτὸ αὑτοῦ οἷόν τε ἐφίεσθαι τὸ εἶδος διὰ τὸ μὴ εἶναι ἐνδεές, οὔτε τὸ ἐναντίον (φθαρτικὰ γὰρ ἀλλήλων τὰ ἐναντία), ἀλλὰ τοῦτ' ἔστιν ἡ ὕλη, ὥσπερ ἂν εἰ θῆλυ ἄρρενος καὶ αἰσχρὸν καλοῦ. πλὴν οὐ καθ' αὑτὸ αἰσχρόν, ἀλλὰ κατὰ συμβεβηκός, οὐδὲ θῆλυ, ἀλλὰ κατὰ συμβεβηκός. Ross's text. Throughout this text as well as the others which bear upon Aristotle's theory of evil, it is interesting to note how his failure to see the relation between the ontological and the axiological orders has resulted in confusion.

with even the slightest acquaintance with Aristotle will recall, he is describing the contemplative life as the life which provides the highest happiness: "If then reason is something divine when compared with man as a whole, therefore the life of reason or intellect is divine in comparison to ordinary human life. One need not follow the precepts of those who praise things human, namely, that a man, being a man, should think merely human thoughts, and that, being a mortal, should think on mortal things, but rather in so far as he is able, he must strive to be immortal and do all things with a view towards living according to the best that is in him; for even though this divine part be little in bulk, it far overpasses everything else in power and in value. This divine part would seem to be the ⟨essence of⟩ each individual man, if indeed it is that which is master, and that which is better. It would be strange indeed if a man should not follow this life which is essentially his own, but rather one [that is] guided by something other than that which is his essential self."[36] Here are many assertions which seem to rest not upon any metaphysically rigorous conception of "actuality," but rather upon standard conventional ways of contrasting the human with the divine.

Ross has one further notable observation on Aristotle's view of evil, which perhaps will emphasize the difficulty, or perhaps even the anomaly, involved in the foregoing plea for men "to become immortal, in so far as they can." Ross remarks, "He (Aristotle) has no serious beliefs in divine rewards and punishments; he has no interest as Plato has in justifying the ways of God to man."[37] To this he has appended a footnote, part of which runs, "Not that matter has any predisposition towards evil; but, being a potentiality of opposites, it is a potentiality of evil as well as good."

[36] *Nicomachean Ethics* X, 1177 b 30–1178 a 4: εἰ δὴ θεῖον ὁ νοῦς πρὸς τὸν ἄνθρωπον, καὶ ὁ κατὰ τοῦτον βίος θεῖος πρὸς τὸν ἀνθρώπινον βίον. οὐ χρὴ δὲ κατὰ τοὺς παραινοῦντας ἀνθρώπινα φρονεῖν ἄνθρωπον ὄντα οὐδὲ θνητὰ τὸν θνητόν, ἀλλ᾽ ἐφ᾽ ὅσον ἐνδέχεται ἀθανατίζειν καὶ πάντα ποιεῖν πρὸς τὸ ζῆν κατὰ τὸ κράτιστον τῶν ἐν αὐτῷ· εἰ γὰρ καὶ τῷ ὄγκῳ μικρόν ἐστι, δυνάμει καὶ τιμιότητι πολὺ μᾶλλον πάντων ὑπερέχει. δόξειε δ᾽ ἂν καὶ εἶναι ἕκαστος τοῦτο, εἴπερ τὸ κύριον καὶ ἄμεινον. ἄτοπον οὖν γίνοιτ᾽ ἄν, εἰ μὴ τὸν αὐτοῦ βίον αἱροῖτο ἀλλά τινος ἄλλου. Bywater's text. The translation is purposely expanded in the hope of achieving greater clarity.
[37] Ross, *Aristotle*, p. 186.

This brief consideration of the problem of evil in Aristotle is justified at this point in our discussion, because it raises emphatically the questions: How does Aristotle know or identify what is good or evil? What are precisely his philosophical grounds? Can a rationalistic or logical analysis of such conceptions as actuality and potentiality lead to an adequate theory of value or to any kind of intelligible hypothesis with respect to the supreme and heartbreaking problem at the centre of any value theory, the problem of evil?

We are now in a position to take up the remaining pair of terms to be discussed:

F. αἰτίαι [οὐσιώδεις], "*essential*" *causes*, and αἰτία ὑλική, *the material cause*. In the consideration of the other pairs of terms, it was possible for the most part to analyze them spearately, but such is not the case with the celebrated Aristotelian doctrine of the four causes. Now the subject of causality has been looming larger in our investigation of Aristotle's metaphysics of being and was particularly apparent in the study of motion and change. As a preliminary, two quotations should be before us, which occur in the last chapter of *Metaphysics* Z, where Aristotle is discussing οὐσία, substance or essence, as it bears upon the problem of causality. In one of the passages, he says, "But this then is the substance or essence of each particular, for this is the primary cause of its existence."[38] The other passage has already been quoted in connection with the treatment of substance as essence, "Therefore we seek the reason why the matter is some definite thing (and this is its form); and this is its substance."[39] It should be noted that here οὐσία as essence is equated with the formal cause or causal determinant.[40] This same point is made in the section of Book A of the *Metaphysics* which states in full Aristotle's conception of the four causes.[41]

[38] *Metaphysics* Z, 1041 b 27–28. οὐσία δὲ ἑκάστου μὲν τοῦτο (τοῦτο γὰρ αἴτιον πρῶτον τοῦ εἶναι). Ross's text.

[39] *Metaphysics* Z, 1041 b 7–9. ὥστε τὸ αἴτιον ζητεῖται τῆς ὕλης (τοῦτο δ' ἐστὶ τὸ εἶδος) ᾧ τί ἐστιν· τοῦτο δ' ἡ οὐσία. Ross's text. Cf. above, pp. 75–76.

[40] Cf. P. Wheelwright, *Aristotle from Natural Science, Psychology, The Nicomachean Ethics* (New York, Doubleday, Doran and Co., 1935) *e.g.*, p. xxxv, where he uses "causal determinant" or "determinant," in preference to the simple word "cause" on the ground that these renderings reflect more precisely the meaning of the Greek word αἰτία than does the conventional translation, "cause."

[41] Cf. above, pp. 75–76.

This passage, one of the most notable in the Aristotelian corpus, runs as follows: "Since it is apparent that we must obtain knowledge of the fundamental causes (for then we say that we have knowledge of each thing, when we think we recognize its primary cause), causal determinants or the causes are used in four different ways:

1. First of these we maintain is the substance or essence of a thing (for the question 'why' takes us back to the ultimate formula, or definition, and a cause and principle is the primary reason 'why' of a thing),

2. Secondly, there is the matter and/or the substratum,

3. Thirdly, there is that from which comes the source of the motion,

4. And fourthly, there is the causal determinant which is opposed to this, the purpose and the good (for this is a goal, or end, of all generation and motion).

We have examined this problem sufficiently in our works on Natural Science."[42]

The doctrine of the four causal determinants can be, and usually is, illustrated by citing the example of such an object as a house.[43] A house, i.e., a work produced by any "art" (τέχνη) will reveal the four causal determinants thus:

---

[42] *Metaphysics* A, 983 a 24-b 1. Ἐπεὶ δὲ φανερὸν ὅτι τῶν ἐξ ἀρχῆς αἰτίων δεῖ λαβεῖν ἐπιστήμην (τότε γὰρ εἰδέναι φαμὲν ἕκαστον, ὅταν τὴν πρώτην αἰτίαν οἰώμεθα γνωρίζειν), τὰ δ' αἴτια λέγεται τετραχῶς, ὧν μίαν μὲν αἰτίαν φαμὲν εἶναι τὴν οὐσίαν καὶ τὸ τί ἦν εἶναι (ἀνάγεται γὰρ τὸ διὰ τί εἰς τὸν λόγον ἔσχατον, αἴτιον δὲ καὶ ἀρχὴ τὸ διὰ τί πρῶτον), ἑτέραν δὲ τὴν ὕλην καὶ τὸ ὑποκείμενον, τρίτην δὲ ὅθεν ἡ ἀρχὴ τῆς κινήσεως, τετάρτην δὲ τὴν ἀντικειμένην αἰτίαν ταύτῃ, τὸ οὗ ἕνεκα καὶ τἀγαθόν (τέλος γὰρ γενέσεως καὶ κινήσεως πάσης τοῦτ' ἐστίν), τεθεώρηται μὲν οὖν ἱκανῶς περὶ αὐτῶν ἡμῖν ἐν τοῖς περὶ φύσεως. Ross's text. We should note here in passing the phrase τὸ οὗ ἕνεκα καὶ τἀγαθόν. Aristotle frequently puts together "the purpose" and "the good" and seems to use them as though they were synonymous. This may reflect the vestigial Platonism in Aristotle's thought, and those who are bent upon seeing little difference between the two thinkers attempt to make much of Aristotle's use of this phrase. However, the reader should not forget that "the good" mentioned here is "the good" of an individual particular thing and should be thought of in connection with the conception of a particular thing's entelechy. There should be no need to point out that "the good" as the entelechy of a particular is philosophically worlds apart from Plato's transcendent Idea of the Good, a notion which Aristotle always repudiates.

[43] The most complete exposition of the doctrine of the four cause is found in the *Physics*, Book II, 194 b 15 ff. This passage is repeated almost word for word in the second chapter of *Metaphysics* Δ.

1) The material determinant *(ὕλη)* = stone, brick, wood, etc.;

2) The formal determinant *(εἶδος)* = the plan;

3) The efficient determinant *(ὅθεν ἡ ἀρχὴ τῆς μεταβολῆς ἡ πρώτη ἢ ἠρεμήσεως)* = the builder;

4) The final or telic determinant *(τέλος, οὗ ἕνεκα)* = to provide a home and shelter for human beings.

When Aristotle analyzes such objects from the static point of view, he tries to answer the question "what?" or "what is a house?" Now with the dynamic approach, the question shifts to "why?" or "why is this house here?" Aristotle's answer is the doctrine of the four causal determinants.

Ross, in a note on the passage from *Metaphysics* A quoted above, remarks, "Here as in the *Physics*, 194 b 23, the doctrine of the four causes is introduced quite abruptly. Aristotle nowhere shows us how he reached it, nor offers any logical deduction of it. The best that he does is to show—what it is the main object of Book A to show—that these four causes are those that one after another came to light in the earlier history of philosophy, and that no others had come to light, cf. 993 a 11." It is of course a commonplace of Aristotelian criticism that the assumption underlying the writing of Book A is Aristotle's conviction, first, that the doctrine of the four causes is an absolutely exhaustive analysis of the problem of causation, and second, that as such the doctrine can be used definitely as a criterion for evaluating the views of all the thinkers who had preceded him. Of course, for Aristotle, the more precise the approximation to his own view produced by a predecessor, the brighter and sounder the predecessor.

The causes, material, formal, efficient, and final, can be analyzed further in two ways. From one point of view the material and the formal causes can be grouped together, for they are static and, in a sense, passive determinants, whereas the efficient and the final causes, taken together, are dynamic and active determinants. The other mode of grouping them is revealed in our general scheme where the material cause alone appears in the right-hand column, while the formal, efficient, and final causes are put together and appear in the left-hand column with the label, "essential causes."[44] The textual support for this grouping will be discussed presently, but for the moment we should recall Aristotle's notion of potentiality. We have already noted that δύναμις was defined in *Metaphysics* Δ as a source or principle of movement or motion, ἡ ἀρχὴ κινήσεως.[45] This definition would certainly answer the question involved in the efficient cause or derterminant. We might even set up a series of equations in this fashion: efficient cause = whence motion = source or principle of motion = potentiality.[46] Therefore, it is easy to see that only in a special sense does potentiality belong in the right-hand column, that is, when it is conceived passively. Curiously and paradoxically, potentiality passively conceived is almost the equivalent of a privation of potentiality. For example, from the passive point of view, a large stone is potentially a heap of gravel, *i.e.*, it would become a heap of gravel if it were submitted to a rock-crusher. It has not the power of itself to become a heap of gravel. Similarly, an undeveloped child is potentially a man, though he may not become one because of a certain lack of power physically or spiritually. Hence, potentiality in this passive sense properly belongs in the right-hand column under matter, privation, and the rest. But potentiality, δύναμις, as efficient cause, leads us to the left-hand column, and serves in a sense as a bridge between the columns. Perhaps it can be regarded in this way: potentiality viewed as lack of actuality belongs in the right-hand column, whereas potentiality viewed as a source or principle of motion looks to actuality, for after all Aristotle does regard motion as a process of actualization.

The crucial passage for considering the formal, efficient, and final causes together appears in the second book of the *Physics*: "It is clear then that these are the causal determinants, and that they are this many in number. Since the causes are four, it is the business of the natural scientist to know about them all, and referring to them all, he will render an answer to the question 'why?' after the manner of natural science, in the following terms: the

---

[44] αἰτίαι [οὐσιώδεις]. οὐσιώδεις is here bracketed because Aristotle never used it to modify αἰτία in his writings.
[45] *Metaphysics* Δ, 1019 a 15. Cf. above, p. 91.
[46] The efficient cause = ὅθεν ἡ κίνησις = ἡ ἀρχὴ κινήσεως = δύναμις.

matter, the form, the mover, the purpose. Often the latter are reduced to one: for the essence and the purpose are one, while the primary source of motion is the same in species as these, *i.e.*, the essence and the purpose: for man begets man. Likewise in general this is the case with whatever things which, when moved, produce motion. (But whatever, when not moved, produces motion, is no longer a legitimate subject of natural science. For such things produce motion, not having motion in themselves nor a principle of motion ⟨with which to move themselves⟩, but rather as unmoved or immobile. Therefore there are three subjects of investigation involved here: one, concerning the unmoved; second, concerning those things which are moved, but are indestructible; and third, concerning those things which are destructible.)"[47]

There are a number of important implications in this passage. As to the whole nature of its argument, O. Hamelin[48] reasonably points out that the chapter in its entirety urges the view that the natural scientist must take into consideration all the four causal determinants. Because the final cause as such is supposed to be the subject of "First Philosophy," there might be the argument that therefore the natural scientist should have nothing to do with the "Final Cause," but only with the material, formal, and efficient causes. Aristotle, Hamelin contends, by pointing out that the formal, efficient, and final causes reduce themselves to one, demonstrates that the natural scientist cannot avoid including the final cause within his study. And of course the best example for the purpose of his argument is the one Aristotle chooses, man. Man, the form or essence, is the same as man, the *telos* or goal. Man, the *telos*, is the efficient cause of man, *i.e.*, man begets man. And man, the form or essence, is the same as man, the efficient

---

[47] Physics II, 198 a 21–31. ὅτι μὲν οὖν τὰ αἴτια ταῦτα καὶ τοσαῦτα, φανερόν· ἐπεὶ δ' αἱ αἰτίαι τέτταρες, περὶ πασῶν τοῦ φυσικοῦ εἰδέναι, καὶ εἰς πάσας ἀνάγων τὸ διὰ τί ἀποδώσει φυσικῶς, τὴν ὕλην, τὸ εἶδος, τὸ κινῆσαν, τὸ οὗ ἕνεκα. ἔρχεται δὲ τὰ τρία εἰς [τὸ] ἕν πολλάκις· τὸ μὲν γὰρ τί ἐστι καὶ τὸ οὗ ἕνεκα ἕν ἐστι, τὸ δ' ὅθεν ἡ κίνησις πρῶτον τῷ εἴδει ταὐτὸ τούτοις· ἄνθρωπος γὰρ ἄνθρωπον γεννᾷ— καὶ ὅλως ὅσα κινούμενα κινεῖ· (ὅσα δὲ μή, οὐκέτι φυσικῆς· οὐ γὰρ ἐν αὑτοῖς ἔχοντα κίνησιν οὐδ' ἀρχὴν κινήσεως κινεῖ, ἀλλ' ἀκίνητα ὄντα. διὸ τρεῖς αἱ πραγματεῖαι, ἡ μὲν περὶ ἀκινήτων, ἡ δὲ περὶ κινουμένων μὲν ἀφθάρτων δέ, ἡ δὲ περὶ τὰ φθαρτά). Ross's text

[48] Aristote, Physique II (Paris, Alcan, 1907) pp. 143–144.

cause, *i.e.*, it is the man *quâ* form or essence which operates as efficient cause.[49]

A word might be added in explanation of the three subjects of investigation or the three branches of study to which Aristotle alludes. The first of these has as its "subject matter" those things which are unmoved. Here we meet for the first time Aristotle's conception of the "Unmoved Mover" or "unmoved movers" which we will examine again when we come to our analysis of substance (*οὐσία*) as *telos*. This branch of study concerns itself with that which is subject to no type of change. This is "First Philosophy," or "metaphysics" in its most rigorously defined sense. The second branch of study has as its subject matter that which is susceptible to only three kinds of motion or change, namely, of place, quality, and size. This is "astronomy," and of course for Aristotle astronomical bodies are not subject to the type of change involved in coming into being and passing out of being. The third branch of study concerns itself with that which is destructible, *i.e.*, with things which are subject to all four types of change. These are "natural" things and the study therefore is "natural science."

Further comment is perhaps necessary on Aristotle's words, "Likewise in general this is the case with whatever things which, when moved, produce motion." This passage refers, one can assume, to those natural movements wherein the formal, efficient, and final causes reduce themselves to one. Ross has an interesting comment on the point in question.[50] After noting that the formal-final cause is really the efficient cause in the case of *artefacta*, since the form of the object to be produced is imaginatively apprehended in the artist's or artisan's mind and sets him to work to produce the object, Ross goes on to say, "And in nature, the form which is to find fresh embodiment is already present and is the cause of movement.

"The leading type of this natural movement is that involved in reproduction. Here the male parent, whose function in reproduction is treated as being purely that of form, finds in the matter

---

[49] It should be noted that in this argument Aristotle actually identifies cause and effect, and therefore perhaps casts little or no light on the basic problem of causality.

[50] Ross, *Aristotle*, pp. 74–75.

contributed by the female parent a new embodiment for the form of the species.

"But natural movement or process has forms less radical than the production of a new individual substance. There is change of place, quality, and of size. In what sense is the formal-final cause here also the efficient cause? Each type of material thing has, according to Aristotle, a natural movement, which it will make when not interfered with; it tends towards a definite region of the universe—fire towards the circumference, earth towards the centre. To be in that region is part of its very form,[51] and this fact operates both as final and as efficient cause. In change of quality and in growth or decay the same principle applies. The quality and size which accompany a thing's attainment of its complete development are included in its form and operate as a final and thereby as an efficient cause."[52]

We have already indicated that the English word "cause" does not properly connote what Aristotle means by αἰτία in Greek, and hence to correct for this situation we have used from time to time the phrase "causal determinant." Ross's comments on this question are illuminating, "It will be noted that of Aristotle's four causes only two, the efficient and the final, answer to the meaning of 'cause' in English. We think of matter and form not as relative to an event which they cause but as static

[51] Ross here cites De Caelo IV, 311 a 1–8. I believe that it is worth while to give the passage in full: "Whenever air comes into being out of water, i.e., light out of heavy, it moves upwards. Immediately it is light, and no longer is coming into being, but exists there. It is clear then that first it exists potentially, and then as it proceeds towards its actualization it moves to that place and to that size and to that quality which are involved in that actualization in respect of place, size and quality. The same reason explains why already existing earth and fire move to their proper places, when nothing prevents them." The Greek runs as follows: ὅταν μὲν οὖν γίγνηται ἐξ ὕδατος ἀὴρ καὶ ἐκ βαρέος κοῦφον, ἔρχεται εἰς τὸ ἄνω. ἅμα δ' ἐστὶ κοῦφον, καὶ οὐκέτι γίνεται, ἀλλ' ἐκεῖ ἔστιν. φανερὸν δὴ ὅτι δυνάμει ὄν, εἰς ἐντελέχειαν ἰὸν ἔρχεται ἐκεῖ καὶ εἰς τοσοῦτον καὶ τοιοῦτον, οὗ ἡ ἐντελέχεια καὶ ὅσου καὶ οἵου (omitting καὶ ὅπου with F and J. L. Stocks, the Oxford translator). τὸ δ' αὐτὸ αἴτιον καὶ τοῦ ἤδη ὑπάρχοντα καὶ ὄντα γῆν καὶ πῦρ κινεῖσθαι εἰς τοὺς αὐτῶν τόπους μηδενὸς ἐμποδίζοντος. Prantl's text as modified by J. L. Stocks.

[52] It is rather tantalizing to observe that in this process of putting together the formal, efficient, and final causes, Aristotle really is providing himself with some kind of metaphysical ground on the basis of which he could relate Being and Value—the final cause in its way being a clue to value. But the fact is that Aristotle does not exploit the possibilities of his metaphysical situation in this direction.

elements which analysis discovers in a complex thing. This is because we think of cause as that which is both necessary and sufficient to produce a certain effect. But for Aristotle none of the four causes, is sufficient to produce an event; and speaking generally we may say that in his view all four are necessary for the production of any effect. We have, then, to think of his 'causes' as conditions necessary but not separately sufficient to account for the existence of a thing; and if we look at them in this way we shall cease to be surprised that matter and form are called causes. For certainly without them no natural thing can be or come into being. Aristotle is in fact bringing together here under the general head of 'cause,' i.e., necessary condition, the two internal or constituent elements already discovered by the analysis of becoming (privation, which was a precondition but not a constituent, being omitted) and the two external conditions which naturally suggest themselves, the efficient cause or *vis a tergo* and the final cause or *vis a fronte*."[53]

The introduction in this paragraph of the conception "event" demands further discussion. If we take as an example of an "event" the phenomenon of "taking a walk" or "exercise," in Aristotle's terms exercise is the efficient cause of health, whereas health is the final cause of exercise.[54] In this connection we see Aristotle applying his doctrine of the causes to entities of quite a different sort, i.e., to purposeful events (e.g., exercise) and to states (e.g., health). There are also for Aristotle "accidental" events, things which occur by spontaneity or by chance, and these two are scrutinized carefully to determine how they bear upon the problem of causation.[55] With the inclusion of such entities as these, it can be shown that, though illuminating in certain respects, Aristotle's theory of the four causes is confusing and leaves much to be desired.

Thus far we have seen Aristotle applying his causal doctrine to five categories of entities:

1) Natural processes of a higher order: e.g., man begets man;

[53] Ross, *Aristotle*, p. 73.
[54] Ross, *Aristotle*, p. 72.
[55] Aristotle devotes chapters 4–6 of Book II of the *Physics* to a discussion of τὸ αὐτόματον and τύχη.

2) natural processes of a lower order: *e.g.*, air moves up;

3) *artefacta*: *e.g.*, a statue or a table;

4) events: (a) teleological: *e.g.*, exercise; (b) accidental: *e.g.*, a certain man is struck by lightning;

5) states, relations and the like: *e.g.*, health is the final cause of exercise; or, as Aristotle says in the *Physics*, "The causes of the octave are said to be the double and number."[56]

Let us put the case this way. Aristotle apparently starts with his doctrine of the four causes, which, as we have seen from Ross's comment, he introduces abruptly,[57] and then proceeds to illustrate the theory by citing examples indiscriminately from all sorts of sources. In certain ways, this appears to be the very antithesis of the solid empirical method for which Aristotle is so justly noted. It does not seem unwarranted to assert that a more empirical approach in the case of the problem of causation, *i.e.*, to start by analyzing the material in the illustrations, and then to develop a theory, would perhaps have yielded less confusing results for Aristotle.

In certain respects, as the doctrine of the four causes now stands, Aristotle appears to leave the central problem of causation untouched. After all, how helpful is it to say that a tree grows because of its "final cause"? Or do we learn much from giving the same answer in connection with the growth and development of a man? Why does one moving billiard ball impart motion to a second? To answer that the motion of the first is the "efficient cause" of the motion of the second merely amounts to a restatement of the event in different terms, and inevitably throws no light on the basic philosophical puzzle. What of the "cause" which every man knows from his inner experience, that he is able to "cause" the motion of his own body, or "cause" his thoughts to flow in a certain direction? Why he can or how he can (the Behaviourists to the contrary notwithstanding) are questions lying in the region of insoluble or unsolved philosophical problems. It is such areas as these that disclose the inadequacy,

[56] *Physics* II, 195 a 31. ⟨τὰ αἴτια⟩ τοῦ διὰ πασῶν τὸ διπλάσιον καὶ ἀριθμός. Ross's text.

[57] Cf. above, p. 104.

or at best the incompleteness, of Aristotle's causal thinking. But whatever may be its shortcomings, it is relatively easy to identify it and to understand how it functions within the general scheme of Aristotle's philosophy.[58]

Now to return to the two ways in which the four causes may be divided—one, where the material and formal were taken together as static, and the efficient and final were taken together as dynamic; and the other mode of division with the material cause set over against the formal, efficient, and final taken together as essential causes—it should be noted that according to either division the efficient and final causes are found together. A great deal in the understanding and appraisal of Aristotle's philosophy depends upon the likeness, difference, and perhaps the ultimate confusion of the two. They are obviously alike in the respect that they both produce change. But their differences are apparent when they are viewed in the perspective of our scheme for presenting Aristotle's views on motion and change.[59] The efficient cause works in two ways: in producing generation and in producing locomotion. In the case of generation, the efficient cause is not in the individual but in an individual of the same species; e.g., man begets man. In the case of locomotion, the efficient cause may be in the individual as a dualism of soul and body; e.g., the soul effects the locomotion of the body. However, it may be between two bodies; e.g., when one thing, when moved (κινούμενον), moves another thing. Yet in both cases there is change which affects the concrete particular externally and as a whole, i.e., either in coming to be a concrete particular, or when it is in locomotion as a concrete particular. On the other hand, the final cause operates to bring matter or potentiality (here conceived largely in its passive sense) to its full form or substance (οὐσία), or its entelechy. Here the final cause works internally and by alteration or by growth-diminution.

At this point let us refer back to the scheme which has provided the framework for our analysis of Aristotle's "metaphysics of

[58] For a concise treatment of the general problem of causality, cf. A. E. Taylor, *Elements of Metaphysics* (7th edition, London, Methuen, 1924) pp. 164–190, and pp. 320 ff.

[59] Cf. above, p. 98.

the individual particular."[60] The right-hand column is definitely subordinate in Aristotle's attack on the problem of reality. All these terms—matter, accidents, privation, potentiality, and the material cause—in one sense or another are not much more than various names for the same constituent in reality, *i.e.*, the material as the necessary condition of existence. But, in contrast, the terms in their order in the left-hand column denote in one form or another the increasingly active elements in the investigation. Note the intensification of significance of the successive terms:

1. Form *(εἶδος)* in one sense at least is a relatively superficial conception.

2. Essence *(οὐσία):* it is clear that we penetrate more deeply into the reality of a thing when we regard the form as the essence *(τὸ τί ἦν εἶναι).*

3. Actuality as perfection *(ἐντελέχεια)*: we become still more definite when we regard a thing as possessing in itself its end, as having that which gives it its perfection.

4. Actuality as activity *(ἐνέργεια)*: we go still further when we regard entelechy as dynamic, as an "energy" in the thing which is working to its end.

5. Essential causes *(αἰτίαι [οὐσιώδεις])*: here we see "energy" as causality, *i.e.*, there is a definite endeavour to explain the "why" of a thing.

In other words, the five terms not only indicate a deepening penetration into reality, but also in a sense signify a scale of realities, a hierarchy in things themselves. To put it alternatively, all things have mere form—but all things do not possess the essential causes in the same way. For example, a lump of bronze has form but it has no entelechy in the sense that a bronze statue of a man has. The bronze statue has entelechy, but no "energy" in the sense that a living man has. The moron has "energy," but his "energy" is not directed and controlled as is the "energy" of Socrates. In any fundamental sense one is not interested in asking why the moron does thus and so. His activity is "caused," but

[60] Cf. above, p. 60.

on the whole the causality operates chiefly from without—or, in so far as it is within, it is not dominated by "final cause" as conscious purpose. Thus in this sense, the lump of bronze represents a lower and less complex mode of reality than the statue, the statue than the living man, and one living man more than another according to the degree to which final cause is dominant within him.[61]

In the light of this example we are now ready to turn to the last of the Aristotelian terms to be discussed:

G. οὐσία (τέλος), *substance as "end."* As we advanced in the left-hand column of the general scheme, more and more those terms tended to dominate the corresponding material constituents. One reaches something very close to perfection, according to Aristotle, in Socrates in his full development. But obviously, that complete perfection can never be reached; in the world we know, things will approach it. But such a situation becomes an instance of infinite regression, unless actually there is postulated a goal or end or limit—a *telos*. As we have seen, Aristotle cannot accept infinite regression because of his axiom of finality, οὐκ εἰς ἄπειρον.[62] According to his thought, we cannot think of the process of refinement going on to infinity. There must be a *telos*, and this "end" must be absolute. Actually, what we do have is the absolute dominance of the left-hand column, and in this the absolute emergence of the highest of these terms, the final cause which becomes οὐσία as *telos*.[63]

A simple way to communicate the essential nature of this supreme Aristotelian conception is to point out that, in the general scheme, all the right-hand terms have been dropped, with the remaining left-hand terms used to describe a monistic finality. Think of it in this way—οὐσία (τέλος), substance as "end," as:

a) pure form with no matter
b) pure essence with no accidents

[61] If this example is at all sound, it should reinforce the point made above in note 52, to the effect that in the conception of final cause there is potentially but never actually the germ of an adequate value theory for Aristotle.

[62] Cf. above, pp. 59–60.

[63] For obvious reasons, there is no need to go into great detail at this juncture. Aristotle's discussion of the problem can be found in *Metaphysics* Λ.

   c) pure entelechy with no privation
   d) pure "energy" with no potentiality
   e) pure essential causes with no material cause

—all these together become pure final cause. But as we have seen, the formal, efficient, and final causes are reduced to one, with the result that the *telos*, as embodying the three causes, is the equivalent of the Unmoved Mover, Aristotle's God. And here, as we shall see in greater detail later, Aristotle's rationalistic procedure seems to run away with him. God is pure "energy," pure activity. But what activity? It must be the highest and best activity. If not, some element of the material constituents would creep in, some taint of potentiality. This highest and best activity is the activity of contemplation. But contemplation must have an object. What object? It too must be highest and best, or the taint of the material or the potential again cannot be avoided. Therefore, this highest and best object must be contemplation. Thus, Aristotle's God, the Unmoved Mover, the pure Final Cause, as a result of this strange logical analysis, is defined as "contemplation of contemplation," νόησις νοήσεως. Needless to say, this Aristotelian conception of God creates profound difficulties for him whenever he faces any kind of a value situation. Naturally, we shall have much more to say about the implications of this doctrine in a later chapter.

With this presentation of Aristotle's conception of "substance as end," the account of the terms basic to his "metaphysics of the individual particular" is completed. One further diagram may well be introduced here to show the various relations between the specific subjects studied in the Aristotelian corpus, and how they in turn are grouped into the three general "subjects of investigation" or "branches of study" to which we already have had occasion to refer.[64] The diagram attempts to suggest a complex set of general relationships, for which, to be sure, there is no explicit textual support in Aristotle's writings, but on the other hand it is fair to say that the diagram is implicitly grounded in the text as a whole.[65]

---

[64] Cf. above, p. 107.
[65] The scheme here reproduced was originally worked out by P. E. More.

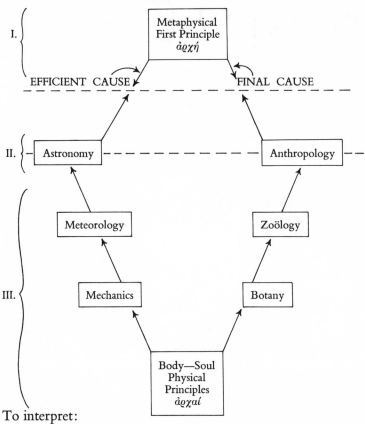

To interpret:

Category I includes the theoretical study of the immutable absolute, and is usually called Metaphysics.

Category II includes the study of the mutable but eternal. On the one hand there is Astronomy in its aspect as a "hyperphysical" science, so to speak. On the other, there is Anthropology, considered as the study of anything having to do with man, with particular emphasis upon the Humanities at their summit, *i.e.*, where they deal, according to Aristotle, with that which is mutable but eternal, for example, the νοῦς in ethics.

Category III includes the study of the mutable and the perishable, whether animate or inanimate. These are the Natural or the "Physical" Sciences.

Aristotle seems to begin at the bottom of this scale and to work upwards. In other words, he appears to take his start from "physics" and psychology. In the scheme, the lower broken line which runs through Astronomy and Anthropology indicates that in these fields there is a lower aspect which is a legitimate subject for the natural or "physical" sciences, whereas the upper aspect has to be dealt with by "hyperphysical" science, which treats the subject matter *quâ* eternal and mutable.

The upper broken line raises the most basic question, or the gravest problem in Aristotelian metaphysics: What is the connection between the metaphysical first principle or ἀρχή and the lower subjects of study? The diagram quite properly indicates a gap, for indeed the gap is there. We already have some idea of Aristotle's method of leaping the gap, for example, in his notion that the Unmoved Mover causes motion by "being an object of love," ὡς ἐρώμενον. This, indeed, for Aristotle, is a philosophical difficulty completely analogous to the problem of "participation" in Plato's Theory of Ideas, which Aristotle himself never tired of criticizing. How valid is Aristotle's mode of leaping the gap? Can the gap be closed on more valid and more cogent grounds? These questions are absolutely fundamental to our inquiry into the metaphysical problem of the relation of being and value. They should never be far from the centre of our attention as we proceed to explore the implications of Aristotle's "metaphysics of the individual particular" for the general problem of value and its relation to being.

APPENDIX A

There is one difficulty of interpretation raised by Aristotle's theory of motion as between contraries. The particular problem occurs in connection with motion in respect of quantity. In the *Categories*, Aristotle states flatly, "Quantity has no opposite."[1] He then goes on to develop the notion that "great" and "small" are not contrary opposites, but rather are terms expressing relation. For example, I can say that Mr. Jones, height five feet eight, is "great" and Mr. Smith, height five feet four is "small." However, I can also say that Mr. Brown, height six feet, is "great," and

---

[1] *Categories*, 5 b 11. ἔτι τῷ ποσῷ οὐδέν ἐστιν ἐναντίον. Bekker's text.

Mr. Jones, height five feet eight, is "small." Hence I have called Mr. Jones both "great" and "small," even though he is still five feet eight in height, *i.e.*, the same quantity in respect of height. But this violates the axiom of contradiction, for Mr. Jones cannot be both great and small at the same time. Hence, the only way out of this dilemma is to conclude that "great" and "small" are relative terms and not quantitative contraries. As Aristotle puts it in the *Categories*, "For if the great is contrary to the small, and if the same thing is at the same time great and small, it would be contrary to itself. But for anything to be contrary to itself is one of the impossibilities. Therefore the great is not contrary to the small, nor the many to the few."[2]

The resolution of this difficulty can be found by recalling, first, that Aristotle in the *Categories* is approaching the problem from the static point of view. Secondly, it seems appropriate to apply the distinction indicated above between the types of change which affect the concrete particular externally (*viz.*, generation-corruption and locomotion) and the types of change which affect it internally (*viz.*, alteration and growth-diminution). In the *Categories*, Aristotle is simply saying that one large particular thing cannot be the opposite or contrary of one small particular thing. In other words, in this context "large" and "small" are relative terms when one concrete particular is put over against another concrete particular externally. After all, "large" and "small" for Aristotle could only be contrary if there were an Absolute Large and an Absolute Small, and, of course, Aristotle will never admit the existence of such absolutes. However, in the context of motion and change, and more specifically in the context of motion in respect of quantity, *i.e.*, growth-diminution, such motion applies to change from "large" to "small" internally within the concrete particular. This does not involve putting one concrete particular over against another, and hence does not raise the issue of postulating absolutes. Change in size affects the concrete particular internally: when it is "large" it is in a

---

[2] *Categories*, 6 a 5–9. εἰ γάρ ἐστι τὸ μέγα τῷ μικρῷ ἐναντίον, τὸ δ' αὐτό ἐστιν ἅμα μέγα καὶ μικρόν, αὐτὸ ἑαυτῷ εἴη ἂν ἐναντίον. ἀλλὰ τῶν ἀδυνάτων ἐστὶν αὐτὸ ἑαυτῷ εἶναί τι ἐναντίον. οὐκ ἔστιν ἄρα τὸ μέγα τῷ μικρῷ ἐναντίον, οὐδὲ τὸ πολὺ τῷ ὀλίγῳ. Bekker's text. Cf. the treatment of the same problem by Plato in the *Republic*, 523 c 4 ff.

state contrary to that in which it was when it was "small"—but only within the limits of the particular thing, and thus no appeal to any external standard is necessitated. Hence the change in respect of quantity is internal, from one state to a contrary state.[3]

By way of confirming the foregoing argument, one can refer to a passage in the *Categories* which definitely explains why Aristotle regards "large" and "small" as relative terms. As they are used in connection with growth-diminution, they are not externally relative, but rather internally relative, which after all is the equivalent of being internally contrary. So Aristotle says, "Furthermore, two cubits and three cubits and each example of things of this sort signifies quantity, but great and small do not signify quantity but rather relation; for great and small look to something else, *i.e.*, something external: or 'to an external standard.' "[4]

---

[3] A simple illustration may clarify the point, if indeed it needs clarification. If one took a bladder and blew it up to one foot in diameter (stage 1) and then blew it up to two feet in diameter (stage 2), one could say there had been motion (change) in respect of size. Stage 1 is contrary to stage 2. Stage 1 is "small," while stage 2 is "large." First it was "small" and then it was "large." It should be noted that, according to the Aristotelian analysis, in neither stage can it be both "large" and "small," simply because nothing besides the bladder is being considered.

[4] *Categories,* 5 b 26–29. ἔτι τὸ μὲν δίπηχυ καὶ τρίπηχυ καὶ ἕκαστον τῶν τοιούτων ποσὸν σημαίνει, τὸ δὲ μέγα ἢ μικρὸν οὐ σημαίνει ποσὸν ἀλλὰ μᾶλλον πρός τι· πρὸς γὰρ ἕτερον θεωρεῖται τὸ μέγα καὶ τὸ μικρόν. Minio-Paluello's text.

CHAPTER V

THE PROBLEM OF VALUE IN
ARISTOTLE'S LOGICAL, PHYSICAL,
PSYCHOLOGICAL, AND BIOLOGICAL
TREATISES

A. THE *ORGANON*

ACCORDING to Ross, Aristotle's work in logic, as it is embodied in the *Organon*, has actually four main divisions. The *Categories* and the *De Interpretatione* deal with terms and propositions respectively and serve as a general introduction to the study of logic. The *Prior Analytics* presents the syllogism in "its formal varieties" and "may fairly be called a formal logic or logic of consistency." Next there is the *Posterior Analytics*, "in which Aristotle discusses the further characteristics which reasoning must have if it is to be not merely self-consistent but in the full sense scientific. This is emphatically a logic interested not in mere consistency but in truth." And finally there are the *Topics* and the *Sophistic Elenchi* wherein "he studies those modes of reasoning which are syllogistically correct, but fail to satisfy one or more of the conditions of scientific thought." Ross further points out that, for Aristotle, logic is "a study not of words but of the thought of which words are signs; of thought not with reference to its natural history but with reference to its success or failure in attaining truth; of thought not as constituting but as apprehending the nature of things."[1]

Ross's description of logic should make clear that in this discipline the "problem of value" as we understand it, or the phenomena of evaluation, will of necessity not obtrude themselves. The study of reasoning and the structure of language that will reflect essentially the structure of the thought it represents, and

---

[1] This paragraph is based upon Ross, *Aristotle*, pp. 20–21. N.B. how Ross in effect expresses exactly what we have meant by the "axiom of correspondence" and the relation of the discipline of logic to it. Cf. above, pp. 58–59.

its relation to "Being," can evoke only the value criteria of self-consistency and correspondence, that is to say, truth.[2] For this reason, there is little or nothing in the texts of the *Categories*, the *De Interpretatione*, and the two *Analytics* which will throw light upon the problem of the relation of Being and Value in Aristotle's thought. To be sure, from time to time he will use value words in his illustrations of terms, propositions, opposites, and syllogisms, but in the context of logic these words function virtually as mathematical *x*s and *y*s. Generally speaking, the same point may be made with respect to the *Topics* and the *Sophistic Elenchi*. The latter, as is well known, incorporates Aristotle's study and classification of fallacies, whereas the former is a kind of handbook for those who find themselves involved in dialectical argument.

Because the *Topics* is less concerned with the formal structures of logic and by the same token faces the concrete situations of practical argument, it is not surprising to find in this work an extended passage which has a direct bearing on the question of value. This passage, the first four chapters of the third book,[3] is particularly important for our purposes and must be examined in detail since it supplies vivid evidence that even in the *Organon*, which presents logic as the indispensable instrument for the analysis of Being and its modes, it is impossible for Aristotle to maintain, so to say, a scientific neutrality with respect to value.[4]

---

[2] Cf. *e.g.*, *Posterior Analytics*, 85 a 20–86 a 30.

[3] *Topics*, III, chapters 1–4, 116 a 1–119 a 11. The general connection between the *Topics* and the *Rhetoric* should not be overlooked.

[4] Ross, *Aristotle*, p. 19, note 1, writes: "The *Topics* may have been composed in the order . . . II.–VII. 2, VII. 3–5, I., VIII. . . . The main part of the work, II.–VII. 2, moves for the most part within the Platonic circle of ideas." It is difficult to understand precisely what Ross means by "the Platonic circle of ideas." The *Topics* as it stands seems to have a clear organic unity of its own, and at the same time possesses a well-defined relation to the rest of the *Organon*. It is quite true that in the *Topics* Aristotle treats notions that are to be found in Plato, but cannot this be said of the large majority of Aristotle's works? Here, as in so many places, the real question seems to be: Is Aristotle dealing with Platonic subjects within the framework of a fundamentally non-Platonic metaphysics? From the critical point of view it is dangerous to conclude that Platonic subject matter presupposes a basic Platonic metaphysic, yet this seems to be the tendency of scholars who are Aristotelians and interpret Plato from the Aristotelain point of view. Their whole drive is to minimize the difference between Plato and Aristotle, and to forget the supreme *philosophical* significance of Aristotle's radical critique of the Theory of Ideas.

:e first book of the *Topics*, Aristotle
intends to accomplish in the work:
a line of inquiry whereby we shall
ns that are generally accepted about
ɔ us, and also shall ourselves, when
, avoid saying anything that will
ceeds to distinguish between four
:here is demonstration *(ἀπόδειξις)*
and "primary" premises. Next is
·ικὸς συλλογισμός)* which proceeds
·ally accepted. The third species is
ning *(ἐριστικὸς συλλογισμός)* which
apparently generally accepted but in
are "misreasonings" *(παραλογισμοί)*
fic premises. Dialectical reasoning,
that is, the subject matter of the *Topics*, differs from demonstration
in this way. Things (the premises in demonstration) are true
and primary if they command belief on the basis of self-evidence,
for, as Aristotle says, "There is no need in the case of scientific
first principles to search out the 'why.' "[6] In contrast, the premisses of dialectical reasoning are generally accepted opinions *(ἔνδοξα)*
which are defined by Aristotle as "those opinions which seem
good to everybody or to the majority or to the wise, and in the
case of the latter, either to all of them or the majority, or to those
who are especially well-known or honoured."[7] In other words,
in distinction to the realm of "science" where the criterion of
validity is self-evidence, in the realm of practical argument the
criterion of validity has become universal acceptance, majority
acceptance, or acceptance by the experts.

Now this conception of the probable as the context for

---

[5] *Topics*, 100 a 18–21. Ἡ μὲν πρόθεσις τῆς πραγματείας μέθοδον εὑρεῖν, ἀφ᾽
ἧς δυνησόμεθα συλλογίζεσθαι περὶ παντὸς τοῦ προτεθέντος προβλήματος ἐξ
ἐνδόξων καὶ αὐτοὶ λόγον ὑπέχοντες μηθὲν ἐροῦμεν ὑπεναντίον. Strache-Wallies'
text.

[6] *Topics*, 100 b 19–20. οὐ δεῖ γὰρ ἐν ταῖς ἐπιστημονικαῖς ἀρχαῖς ἐπιζητεῖσθαι
τὸ διὰ τί. Strache-Wallies' text.

[7] *Topics*, 100 b 21–23. ἔνδοξα δὲ τὰ δοκοῦντα πᾶσιν ἢ τοῖς πλείστοις ἢ τοῖς
σοφοῖς, καὶ τούτοις ἢ πᾶσιν ἢ τοῖς πλείστοις ἢ τοῖς μάλιστα γνωρίμοις καὶ
ἐνδόξοις. Strache-Wallies' text. Can it be that the repetition ἔνδοξα-ἐνδόξοις
reveals a certain circularity in Aristotle's definition?

dialectical reasoning is satisfactory as Aristotle treats the nature of arguments, problems connected with predication, with the genus, with the notion of property, with definition and the like, but in the crucial (that is, crucial for us) passage at the opening of the third book, the situation is somewhat different. In his outline of the text, Pickard-Cambridge calls this section, "Comparative predications of Value-predicates of A or B." This title for a sub-section has admittedly very little glamour, but it is precisely here, as has already been indicated, that Aristotle does come face to face with the question of value.

Aristotle begins the third book with the air of an amiable debating coach. In deciding which of two or more things is preferable or better (αἰρετώτερον ἢ βέλτιον), he specifies as a preliminary condition that the investigation should not be concerned with things that differ widely from each other, "for no one is at a loss as to whether happiness is more desirable than wealth,"[8] but rather should deal with things that are closely akin. For example, we argue about which person we are going to vote for[9] when we cannot see any superiority of one over against another. A single instance of superiority in one or the other in any situation should convince us that it is the preferable or better.

Having laid down this restriction on his sphere of inquiry, Aristotle proceeds to examine the various criteria which can be invoked to help us resolve the question of desirability or superiority. His list is most interesting: "First, then, that which is more lasting or secure is more desirable than that which is less so: and so is that which is more likely to be chosen by the prudent or by the good man or by the right law, or by men who are good in any particular line, when they make their choice as such, or by the experts in regard to any particular class of things . . .; e.g., in medicine or in carpentry those things are more desirable which most, or all, doctors would choose; or in general, whatever most men or all men or all things would choose, e.g., the good: for everything aims at the good. You should direct the argument

---

[8] *Topics*, 116 a 6-7. οὐδεὶς γὰρ ἀπορεῖ πότερον ἡ εὐδαιμονία ἢ ὁ πλοῦτος αἰρετώτερον. Strache-Wallies' text.

[9] Pickard-Cambridge translates προσθέσθαι in this way.

you intend to employ to whatever end is useful to you. Of what is 'better' or 'more desirable' the absolute standard is the verdict of the better science, though relatively to a given individual the standard may be his own particular science."[10]

Note the line of Aristotle's argument. He first mentions the capacity to last or security as symptoms of superiority. This seems merely to be an appeal to a conventional value standard. Then, as he did in establishing the criterion of the "probable" at the beginning of the first book, Aristotle invokes the principle of the φρόνιμος, or the "good" man, or the "right" law. Obviously, this does not help us very much because he does not tell us how we know a φρόνιμος when we see one, or how a "good" man is good, or how a "right" law is right. All these value terms are in fact unkeyed. The general line of thought seems to be that a good man is one whom everybody or the majority or a group of other "good" men deem to be good. Next, he adds the principle of the expert, a familiar enough criterion on a fairly superficial level from the time of Plato to the present. We are all deeply trained to accept without question the principle of the expert. But it must be said that in the present passage Aristotle does not leave the argument with the principle of the expert, for he adds the point in a generalized form that "the good" is a criterion and he defines "the good" as that which the majority of men or all men or all things would choose. Furthermore, he backs up his definition by repeating the familiar dictum that "all things aim at the good."

Now, of course, it is possible to say that in this last remark and in many other similar ones, Aristotle is talking like a Platonist, or, as Ross says, is moving within "the Platonic circle of ideas." But there is nothing here to indicate that Aristotle has in mind anything like Plato's transcendental Idea of the Good. Rather

---

[10] *Topics*, 116 a 13–22. Πρῶτον μὲν οὖν τὸ πολυχρονιώτερον ἢ βεβαιότερον αἱρετώτερον τοῦ ἥττον τοιούτον. καὶ ὃ μᾶλλον ἂν ἕλοιτο ὁ φρόνιμος ἢ ὁ ἀγαθὸς ἀνὴρ ἢ ὁ νόμος ὁ ὀρθὸς ἢ οἱ σπουδαῖοι περὶ ἕκαστα αἱρούμενοι ᾗ τοιούτοί εἰσιν ἢ οἱ ἐν ἑκάστῳ γένει ἐπιστήμονες, . . . οἷον ἐν ἰατρικῇ ἢ τεκτονικῇ ἃ οἱ πλείους τῶν ἰατρῶν ἢ πάντες, ἢ ὅσα ὅλως οἱ πλείους ἢ πάντες ἢ πάντα, οἷον τἀγαθόν· πάντα γὰρ τἀγαθοῦ ἐφίεται. δεῖ δ' ἄγειν πρὸς ὅ τι ἂν ᾖ χρήσιμον τὸ ῥηθησόμενον. ἔστι δ' ἁπλῶς μὲν βέλτιον καὶ αἱρετώτερον τὸ κατὰ τὴν βελτίω ἐπιστήμην, τινὶ δὲ τὸ κατὰ τὴν οἰκείαν. Strache-Wallies' text. The Oxford translation has been slightly modified.

he seems to be asserting his standard view which identifies "the good" with the Final Cause of any "man" or any "thing." The good for a thing resides in its own perfection, but the difficulty lies in discovering the relation between these infinitely numerous final causes or "goods," with one for each individual particular thing.

In many ways, the paragraph which we are now studying exhibits in concentrated form the typical Aristotelian attitude *vis-à-vis* the value question. The points made are blurred about the edges as Aristotle moves from talking about the capacity to last as a means of detecting worth, on to his use of the principle of the expert, and next to the notion of "the good" as that at which everything aims. And even in the concluding sentence of the paragraph, the force of his notion of the good as a thing's Final Cause is impaired by his adding the view that the absolute standard in determining what is "better" or "more desirable" is "the verdict of the better science." Again, we are justified in asking how we are to identify the "better" science.

It is in much the same fashion that Aristotle continues in the pages which follow. His next gambit consists in using the conception of genus as a touchstone. Accordingly, something that is within a genus is preferable to something that falls outside it. His illustration is curious, *viz.*, "Justice is better than a just man."[11] Aristotle argues that justice is within the genus "good" whereas "a just man" falls within the genus "animal," we may suppose; hence justice is preferable because of its inclusion under the genus "good." Here apparently we have a strictly logical argument which assigns "genus" as a criterion of value, but when the illustration involves value terms, it is difficult to get much meaning out of Aristotle's reasoning. And furthermore, it should be noted that Aristotle in no way appears to regard these species and genera under discussion as having a separate or hypostatized existence.

A list of Aristotle's next points is very illuminating:[12]

1. A thing chosen for itself is preferable to that which is chosen for something else. For example, health is more desirable than gymnastics.

2. The desirable in itself is to be preferred to that which is

---

[11] *Topics*, 116 a 23–24. ἡ δικαιοσύνη τοῦ δικαίου.
[12] *Topics*, 116 a 29 ff.

desired "accidentally" *(κατὰ συμβεβηκός)*. For example, justice in our friends is more desirable than justice in our enemies.

3. The cause in itself of good is better than that which causes good accidentally. For example, virtue is better than luck.[13]

4. The good absolutely *(τὸ ἁπλῶς ἀγαθόν)* is better than the good for some particular person. For example, becoming healthy is better than undergoing an operation.

5. The good by nature *(φύσει)* is better than the good not by nature *(μὴ φύσει)*. For example, justice is better than the just man. Justice is good by nature, but in the case of the just man, his quality of justice has not come to him by nature, but he has acquired it.

6. That which belongs to something that is better or more honourable is better. For example, what belongs to a god is better than what belongs to a man. Also what belongs to a soul is better than what belongs to a body.[14]

7. That which is in things that are better or prior or more honoured is better. For example, health is better than strength or beauty. For health is to be found in the moist and dry and hot and cold, that is, from the primary elements out of which the living being is constituted, whereas strength and beauty lie in secondary constituents. Strength is to be found in sinew and bone, while beauty seems to be in some kind of proportion of the limbs.

8. An end is preferable to the means, and of two means, the one nearer the end is better. And in general the means that looks towards the end of life is preferable to that which looks towards something else. For example, that which makes for happiness is better than that which makes for practical wisdom.[15]

9. The "potent" is better than the "impotent."[16] Of two things that can produce ends the one is better which produces the better end.[17]

[13] Aristotle here cites the contrary situation, namely, that the cause of evil in itself is more to be avoided than that which causes evil accidentally, *e.g.*, vice *(κακία)* is more to be avoided than luck *(τύχη)*.

[14] "What belongs to" is a translation of the Greek phrase τὸ ὑπάρχον. Aristotle makes the same point with respect to "property," τὸ ἴδιον. Cf. *Topics*, 116 b 13–15. Cf. above, p. 80.

[15] On this point, cf. above, Chapter IV, note 52.

[16] *Topics*, 116 b 26. καὶ τὸ δύνατον τοῦ ἀδυνάτου.

[17] Aristotle goes on to show how by the use of a mathematical proportion one can determine whether or not that which produces an end is better than an

10. The intrinsically fairer, more honoured, and more praise-worthy are better than those things which are intrinsically less so. For example, friendship is better than wealth, and justice than strength.

11. In the case of things that are very much alike, a clue to superiority can be found in the consequences of each.

12. More goods are preferable to fewer goods; *i.e.*, number or quantity is the clue to the more desirable.

13. The same things are better if pleasure occurs with them than if there is no attendant pleasure. Likewise in the case of freedom from pain and the painful.

14. Things are better if they come at the right time. For example, freedom from pain is better in old age than in youth. Practical wisdom is better in old age, while courage is better in youth, as well as self-control.

15. What is more useful at all or most times is better. For example, justice and self-control are always useful, and hence are superior to courage which is only useful at times.[18]

16. If there are two things and if all possess one and there is no need of the other, the one which all possess is better. For example, justice is better than courage, for courage is not needed if all are just, whereas if all men were courageous justice would still be useful.

17. Preferability can be calculated from destructions, losses, generations, seizures, and contraries. In general, if one wants more to avoid the destruction of a thing, then the thing in question is to be preferred. And the situation also prevails in the case of the other categories mentioned.

18. What is nearer the good is better.

19. Something is better than something else if it is more like something better than itself. For example, Ajax was better than Odysseus because he was more like Achilles.[19]

20. What is more conspicuous is better than what is less so.

---

end. In his illustration, he argues that that which is productive of happiness is better than health. *Topics*, 116 b 27–36.

[18] Note how crude the results of this analysis are when it depends ultimately on conventional value responses.

[19] *Topics*, 117 b 12–14. καὶ τὸ τῷ βελτίονι αὐτοῦ ὁμοιότερον, καθάπερ τὸν Αἴαντα τοῦ Ὀδυσσέως φασὶ βελτίω τινὲς εἶναι, διότι ὁμοιότερος τῷ Ἀχιλλεῖ. Strache-Wallies' text.

21. What is more difficult is better than what is less so.

22. What is one's own personally is better than what is more commonly shared.

23. What is more free from the taint of evil things is preferable.

24. If one genus is better than another genus, then the best member of the first class is better than the best member of the second class.

25. Things in which it is possible for one's friends to have a share are better than things in which it is not possible.

26. What we like to do to a friend is better than what we would do to any chance person.

27. That which arises from abundance is better than that which is a necessity, and sometimes it is likewise preferable. For living well is better than living. Living well comes from abundance, but living itself is a necessity. Sometimes things can be better but not preferable. For example, being a philosopher is *better* than being a money-maker, but it is not *preferable* for the man who is in need of the necessities.[20]

28. What cannot be acquired from something else is better than what can also be acquired from something else, as is the case with justice in relation to courage.

29. One thing is better than another if the former is worth choosing without the latter while the latter is not worth choosing without the former. For example, power is not choice-worthy without practical wisdom, while practical wisdom is choice-worthy without power.

30. If we decline one thing in order to seem to possess another, the latter—that is, the thing we wish to have the reputation of possessing —is preferable. For example, if we decline to be lovers of hard work, in order that we may have the reputation of being clever.[21]

31. Something is preferable if people are not so much to be blamed for being annoyed by the absence of it. And the converse is also the case.

---

[20] Note how the moral tone of this passage is identical with that of the remark in the *Nicomachean Ethics*, which has already been quoted, where Aristotle says that a man to be happy needs the goods of the body, external goods, and the goods of fortune. Cf. above, Chapter II, note 7.

[21] *Topics*, 118 a 22–23. οἷον φιλοπονεῖν ἀρνούμεθα, ἵν᾽ εὐφυεῖς εἶναι δόξωμεν. Strache-Wallies' text.

And so Aristotle carries on his exhaustive listing of handy helps to the debater.[22] To be sure, we should not forget that the context is in a sense that of compiling commonplaces or τόποι for immediate and practical application to the procedures of argument. And perhaps we should not cavil at the fact that the whole passage is pervaded with a banal, conventional, and by no means completely coherent attitude towards the question of value judgments. Yet at the same time, in the introduction to the *Topics*, which we have already discussed, Aristotle distinguishes between pure reasoning which will result in demonstration and "scientific truth" on the one hand, and dialectical reasoning (διαλεκτικὸς συλλογισμός) on the other. Even though dialectical reasoning, as it deals with the probable, will not produce results that will achieve a full measure of "scientific truth" in Aristotle's sense, still we are invited to believe that through dialectical reasoning conclusions will emerge which will have some definite validity. They will be "true" as compared to the results of eristic or fallacious argument, which will of necessity be "false." In other words, because Aristotle has taken pains to relate specifically the subject matter of the *Topics* to the rest of the *Organon* and implicitly to his whole basic metaphysical position, it is fully justifiable to take these pages from the third book of the *Topics* with full seriousness in their bearing upon the whole problem of Being and Value.

If we roughly classify the items listed above, we can see that evaluation is based on "intrinsic desirability" in at least four of them.[23] But in this connection if we search for the sanction of this evaluation it seems to be again merely the common or majority opinion of men. Two items can be put in a second class, in which the "good absolutely" or the "good by nature" are cited as sanctions.[24] Here it should be noted that something extrinsic to the evaluator is cited, and hence implies a scheme of evaluation very different from the subjectivism postulated in the notion of majority opinion. Another classification suggests that decisions

---

[22] Chapter 3 of the third book of the *Topics* continues very much in the same vein as prevails in the two chapters which we have just been analyzing.

[23] Cf. numbers 1, 2, 3, and 10.

[24] Cf. numbers 4 and 5.

concerning the better or the more desirable can be made by discovering some kind of association or connection with something
"good."[25] Quite obviously, these passages really beg the question,
since they assume that we will all agree on what is good. Numbers
8 and 9, however, are somewhat different because they invoke
the conception of end as a value criterion, and here happiness is
explicitly named as the supreme end of life for man. The tone
of these passages is virtually identical with that of the opening
pages of the *Nicomachen Ethics*.[26] But again here, though the
value system implicit in the conception of happiness as the end
of life can be constructed with complete coherence, the difficulty
in this extended section of the *Topics* is to discover how this
principle may be related to such notions as "intrinsic desirability"
or the "good by nature." And indeed, if it be true that one of
the basic problems in value theory involves an attempt to face
the issue of "objectivism" *versus* "subjectivism," one cannot help
realizing how a value theory based on a happiness principle actually must leave the relation of the objective and the subjective
unclear.[27]

The remaining items adduce a wide variety of sanctions for
value judgments. Are the consequences of something "good"?
Is the thing "useful"? Is it attended by pleasure? Is it associated
with friendship? Is it conspicuous? Is it difficult? How is its
timing? And so on. It should be perfectly clear that the germs
of many different value theories are present here: hedonistic
and pragmatic in particular. Of course, it can be argued that
Aristotle in a logical work does not intend to construct a "value
theory," and hence we should not be surprised at the amorphous
character of these pages in the *Topics*. But the startling point

---

[25] Cf. 6, 7, 18, and 19. Number 23 involves the same principle, though it is
expressed negatively.

[26] We shall, of course, examine the whole question of happiness as a value
sanction when we discuss Aristotle's *Nicomachean Ethics*.

[27] Is it possible that a "happiness ethic" or value theory may not ultimately
be subject to the same kind of refutation as Plato advances against hedonism in
the *Gorgias*? Presumably that which is good will make us happy, but Aristotle
would not have us believe that our own so-called "happiness reaction" is the true
and exclusive means of identifying what is good. There is an objective dimension
to Aristotle's ethical thought, but in the long run he fails to provide us with any
sure guides as to the nature and structure of that objective dimension.

remains that we shall find the same kind of amorphousness in other treatises, particularly the ethical works, where the problem of value is supremely important.

B. THE PHYSICAL TREATISES

In these works, which include the *Physics*, *De Caelo*, *De Generatione et Corruptione*, and the *Meteorologica*,[28] Aristotle develops his philosophy of nature. The general character of Aristotle's thought on this subject has been covered, we hope adequately, in the chapters above on his Metaphysics of Being. Such topics as the first principles of nature, the problem of motion and change, time, the Unmoved Mover, the heavenly and sublunary bodies, and the like, are obviously essential to any sufficient comprehension of the basic Aristotelian position. But, as is the case with the logical works, the analytical and descriptive treatment of this kind of subject matter precludes for the most part any direct contact with what we have called the phenomena of evaluation. Yet there are various passages which by implication give us hints concerning the several different ways employed by Aristotle when a question of evaluation is unavoidable. That such passages occur bears out our fundamental contention that Being and Value are actually copresent in human experience. In other words, Aristotle, when he expounds his philosophy of nature as a part of his full analysis of Being, cannot avoid completely the question of value. It is therefore most important for us to examine a representative few of these passages as part of the task of comprehending the variegated character of Aristotle's thought in the field of axiology.

In the second book of the *Physics*, where Aristotle is discussing "chance" and "spontaneity," he remarks: "Chance or fortune is called 'good' when the result is good, 'evil' when it is evil. The terms 'good fortune' and 'ill fortune' are used when either result is of considerable magnitude."[29] And after pointing out

---

[28] I am omitting *De Mundo*, which, as Ross says, "has no claim to be regarded as Aristotle's." Cf. *Aristotle*, p. 11.

[29] *Physics*, 197 a 25–27. τύχη δὲ ἀγαθὴ μὲν λέγεται ὅταν ἀγαθόν τι ἀποβῇ, φαύλη δὲ ὅταν φαῦλόν τι, εὐτυχία δὲ καὶ δυστυχία ὅταν μέγεθος ἔχοντα ταῦτα. Ross's text. The same thought is expressed in *Metaphysics* K, 1065 a 35–b 1.

that "spontaneity" is the more inclusive term, he continues: "Chance and what results from chance are appropriate to agents that are capable of good fortune and of moral action generally. Therefore chance is in the sphere of moral actions. This is indicated by the fact that good fortune is thought to be the same, or nearly the same, as happiness, and happiness to be a kind of moral action, since it is well-doing. Hence what is not capable of moral action cannot do anything by chance. Thus an inanimate thing or a lower animal or a child cannot do anything by chance, because it is incapable of deliberate intention; nor can 'good fortune' or 'ill fortune' be ascribed to them except metaphorically."[30]

Now for the moment we are not concerned with the relation of chance or spontaneity to the other types of cause, but rather to the attitude towards value which underlies Aristotle's obervations. Luck is good or bad according to its results, but the most interesting point is that "luck" or "fortune" can only be appraised by, or even can only "happen to" human beings who are capable of moral action or activity, *i.e.*, πρᾶξις. And then Aristotle sets up the proposition that good fortune is the equivalent, or virtually so, of happiness, for they are both actions, πράξεις, of the highest order. Nothing inanimate, no beast or child can have good luck or happiness, since they are not capable of exercising "deliberate intention," choice, προαίρεσις. Values, then, or value judgments, are implicitly regarded as human phenomena on the highest level, and, at least in this context, they are related to happiness which is explicitly described as a supreme moral activity. The passage invites us to suppose that the touchstone of evaluation is to be found subjectively in the humanly actualized moral agent who alone is capable of happiness.

Thus far the position in this section of the *Physics* seems to be perfectly clear, but in almost the same fashion as we observed in the third book of the *Topics*, Aristotle proceeds to blur his own

---

[30] *Physics*, 197 b 1–9. ἡ μὲν γὰρ τύχη καὶ τὸ ἀπὸ τύχης ἐστὶν ὅσοις καὶ τὸ εὐτυχῆσαι ἂν ὑπάρξειεν καὶ ὅλως πρᾶξις. διὸ καὶ ἀνάγκη περὶ τὰ πρακτὰ εἶναι τὴν τύχην (σημεῖον δ' ὅτι δοκεῖ ἤτοι ταὐτὸν εἶναι τῇ εὐδαιμονίᾳ ἡ εὐτυχία ἢ ἐγγύς, ἡ δ' εὐδαιμονία πρᾶξίς τις· εὐπραξία γάρ), ὥσθ' ὁπόσοις μὴ ἐνδέχεται πρᾶξαι, οὐδὲ τὸ ἀπὸ τύχης τι ποιῆσαι. καὶ διὰ τοῦτο οὔτε ἄψυχον οὐδὲν οὔτε θηρίον οὔτε παιδίον οὐδὲν ποιεῖ ἀπὸ τύχης, ὅτι οὐκ ἔχει προαίρεσιν· οὐδ' εὐτυχία οὐδ' ἀτυχία ὑπάρχει τούτοις, εἰ μὴ καθ' ὁμοιότητα. Ross's text.

point of view.[31] At the very end of his treatment of chance and spontaneity we have a perfect illustration of the shift in attitude towards the question of value which results from Aristotle's concentration on the problem of Being. The revealing words are: "Spontaneity and chance, therefore, are posterior to intelligence and nature. Hence, however true it may be that the heavens are due to spontaneity, it will still be true that intelligence and nature will be prior causes of this All and of many things in it besides."[32] In this passage, the perspective is changed from that of man to that of the Universe. In the context of the problem of causation, Aristotle evaluates spontaneity and chance over against intelligence and nature, and gives the palm to the latter pair. They are the "cause" of the Universe and much that is in it, and hence "intelligence and nature" cosmically must be regarded as sources of value. It is scarcely necessary to point out that the implied value theory here is quite different from the one based on the principle of the happiness of the moral agent which Aristotle advances in the immediately preceding page. Of course, much elaboration is necessary in order to determine exactly in what sense intelligence and nature can be taken as the "cause" of the Universe.

As we move along in the second book of the *Physics*, we come to another and rather closely related implied value system which is based upon the notion that the end or goal or τέλος is that from which value derives. There, of course, are many passages in Aristotle, particularly in the *Metaphysics*, in which this situation obtains and therefore we can take the present section of the *Physics* as a typical example of this characteristic Aristotelian attitude of mind. At the conclusion of a chapter in which he is discussing whether nature acts for an end, he says: "Therefore action for an end is present in things which come to be and are by nature." And then he continues: "Further, where a series has a completion, all the preceding steps are for the sake of that. Now surely as in intelligent action, so in nature; and as in nature, so

[31] Cf. above, pp. 128–129, and especially note 27.
[32] *Physics*, 198 a 9–13. ὕστερον ἄρα τὸ αὐτόματον καὶ ἡ τύχη καὶ νοῦ καὶ φύσεως· ὥστ᾽ εἰ ὅτι μάλιστα τοῦ οὐρανοῦ αἴτιον τὸ αὐτόματον, ἀνάγκη πρότερον νοῦν αἴτιον καὶ φύσιν εἶναι καὶ ἄλλων πολλῶν καὶ τοῦδε τοῦ παντός. Ross's text.

it is in each action, if nothing interferes. Now intelligent action is for the sake of an end; therefore the nature of things also is so. Thus if a house, *e.g.*, had been a thing made by nature, it would have been made in the same way as it is now by art; and if things made by nature were made also by art, they would come to be in the same way as by nature. Each step in the series is for the sake of the next; and generally art partly completes what nature cannot bring to a finish, and partly imitates her. If, therefore, artificial products are for the sake of an end, so clearly also are natural products. The relation of the later to the earlier terms of the series is the same in both."[33]

To use the terminology of the Oxford translators, intelligent action, that which is produced by nature and that which is produced by art—all may be evaluated by the goal or τέλος for which the processes of becoming have been undertaken. And Aristotle continues his argument by pointing out that in other animate beings, in plants, birds, insects, and the like, the final cause or purpose or τέλος operates in nature. The concluding sentence of the passage rounds out the evidence for the value system based upon the conception of τέλος which we have been attempting to reconstruct: "And since 'nature' means two things, the matter and the form, of which the latter is the end, and since all the rest is for the sake of the end, the form must be the cause in the sense of 'that for the sake of which.' "[34]

---

[33] *Physics*, 199 a 7–20. ἔστιν ἄρα τὸ ἕνεκά τοῦ ἐν τοῖς φύσει γιγνομένοις καὶ οὖσιν. ἔτι ἐν ὅσοις τέλος ἔστι τι, τούτου ἕνεκα πράττεται τὸ πρότερον καὶ τὸ ἐφεξῆς. οὐκοῦν ὡς πράττεται, οὕτω πέφυκε, καὶ ὡς πέφυκεν, οὕτω πράττεται ἕκαστον, ἂν μή τι ἐμποδίζῃ. πράττεται δ' ἕνεκά του· καὶ πέφυκεν ἄρα ἕνεκά του οἷον εἰ οἰκία τῶν φύσει γιγνομένων ἦν, οὕτως ἂν ἐγίγνετο ὡς νῦν ὑπὸ τῆς τέχνης· εἰ δὲ τὰ φύσει μὴ μόνον φύσει ἀλλὰ καὶ τέχνῃ γίγνοιτο, ὡσαύτως ἂν γίγνοιτο ᾗ πέφυκεν. ἕνεκα ἄρα θατέρου θάτερον. ὅλως δὲ ἡ τέχνη τὰ μὲν ἐπιτελεῖ ἃ ἡ φύσις ἀδυνατεῖ ἀπεργάσασθαι, τὰ δὲ μιμεῖται. εἰ οὖν τὰ κατὰ τέχνην ἕνεκά του, δῆλον ὅτι καὶ τὰ κατὰ φύσιν· ὁμοίως γὰρ ἔχει πρὸς ἄλληλα ἐν τοῖς κατὰ τέχνην καὶ ἐν τοῖς κατὰ φύσιν τὰ ὕστερα πρὸς τὰ πρότερα. Ross's text. Cf. Ross's note *ad loc.* where Simplicius is quoted as saying that τέλος in this passage should be taken in a temporal but not a teleological sense. A fair reading of the passage seems to justify fully taking it in the teleological sense, particularly in the light of other similar passages. One notable instance is *De Partibus Animalium*, 639 b 13ff.

[34] *Physics*, 199 a 30–32. καὶ ἐπεὶ ἡ φύσις διττή, ἡ μὲν ὡς ὕλη ἡ δ' ὡς μορφή, τέλος δ' αὕτη, τοῦ τέλους δὲ ἕνεκα τἆλλα, αὕτη ἂν εἴη ἡ αἰτία, ἡ οὗ ἕνεκα. Ross's text. Ross in a note *ad loc.* calls attention to the earlier point in the *Physics* where the same question is discussed, *viz.*, especially 193 a 28–31. On the question of identifying the formal and the final cause, cf. above, pp. 105–108.

The equation of form and goal or purpose in things of all orders, then, presupposes a kind of value system which is fundamentally objective in character. However, here it refers only to each of the infinite number of individual particular things in which the form, considered as the equivalent of its purpose, reveals its value or worth. Now there is a sense in which this value system does recognize our postulate in regard to the co-presence of Being and Value, but Aristotle does not explicitly give any indication that he was engaging in a different kind of value thinking when he invoked his happiness principle or when he talked about "intelligence" and "nature" as sources of value in the perspective of the Universe. Furthermore, though Being and Value do come together in a way in the notion that the form of a thing is the equivalent of its purpose, yet there seems to be nothing in the thought of Aristotle, at least in the present context, which would help us to determine the *relative* value of each of these particular things.

This whole point becomes extremely clear in the concluding paragraph of the chapter immediately preceding the one with which we have just been dealing in the second book of the *Physics*. We therefore should examine it in full. "Now the principles which cause motion in a physical way are two, of which one is not physical, as it has no principle of motion in itself.[35] Of this kind is whatever causes movement, not being itself moved, such as (1) that which is completely unchangeable, the primary reality, and (2) the essence of that which is coming to be, *i.e.*, the form; for this is the end or 'that for the sake of which.' Hence, since nature is for the sake of something, we must know this cause also. We must explain the 'why' in all the senses of the term, namely (1) that from this that will necessarily result ('from this' either without qualification or in most cases); (2) that 'this must be so if that is to be so' (as the conclusion presupposes the premises); (3) that this was the essence of the thing; and (4) because it is better thus (not without qualification, but with reference to the essential nature in each case)."[36]

[35] As Aristotle points out immediately, the Unmoved Mover would fall under this category.

[36] *Physics*, 198 a 35-b 9. διτταὶ δὲ αἱ ἀρχαὶ αἱ κινοῦσαι φυσικῶς, ὧν ἡ ἑτέρα οὐ φυσική· οὐ γὰρ ἔχει κινήσεως ἀρχὴν ἐν αὐτῇ. τοιοῦτον δ' ἐστὶν εἴ τι κινεῖ μὴ

In the first place, we should not fail to notice the very succinct way in which Aristotle here reexpresses his doctrine of the four causes, listing them in the order of efficient, material, formal, and final. It is also interesting that form is placed in the category of "whatever causes movement, not being itself moved." But the final phrase of the quotation completely supports our contention that form or purpose is confined to individual particular things internally, and thus cannot provide us with any ground for comparative evaluation. In other words, when he describes the purpose of a thing by saying, "because it is better thus, not without qualification (or absolutely) but with reference to the essential nature in each case," "better" has only an internal significance. That is, the particular thing is "better" the more closely it approximates its essential form and purpose. In no way can "better" mean that one thing is "better" than another. It should be needless to add that this point is extremely important if we are to grasp clearly the nature of Aristotle's teleology.

Ross in his notes on this passage[37] inadvertently reveals the ultimate confusion and obscurity inherent in this teleological doctrine. He says, "There are two types of ἀρχή that produce natural movement—natural, as distinct from the changes imposed on things by τέχνη or προαίρεσις."[38] He goes on to say that one of these types is found in "what when moved produces motion."[39] The other type "is found in (1) the unmoved first mover, and in (2) the formal cause of each natural thing. Both (1) and (2) are final causes of natural process, the one its transcendent, the other its immanent end." There does not seem to be one shred of

---

κινούμενον, ὥσπερ τό τε παντελῶς ἀκίνητον καὶ τὸ πάντων πρῶτον καὶ τὸ τί ἐστιν καὶ ἡ μορφή· τέλος γὰρ καὶ οὗ ἕνεκα· ὥστε ἐπεὶ ἡ φύσις ἕνεκά του, καὶ ταύτην εἰδέναι δεῖ, καὶ πάντως ἀποδοτέον τὸ διὰ τί, οἷον ὅτι ἐκ τοῦδε ἀνάγκη τόδε (τὸ δὲ ἐκ τοῦδε ἢ ἁπλῶς ἢ ὡς ἐπὶ τὸ πολύ), καὶ εἰ μέλλει τοδὶ ἔσεσθαι (ὥσπερ ἐκ τῶν προτάσεων τὸ συμπέρασμα), καὶ ὅτι τοῦτ᾽ ἦν τὸ τί ἦν εἶναι, καὶ διότι βέλτιον οὕτως, οὐχ ἁπλῶς, ἀλλὰ τὸ πρὸς τὴν ἑκάστου οὐσίαν. Ross's text, though I have not bracketed the τὸ at the end of line 198 b 1.

[37] Cf. Ross, *Physics*, notes on 198 a 35–b 4 and 198 b 5–9.
[38] Cf. above, pp. 132–133, where the identity of the operation of final cause was shown in the case of the results of intelligent action, art, and of "coming-to-be" by nature. Hence the distinction here marked by Ross is not significant for our argument. In other words, it may apply just as well in the area of τέχνη and προαίρεσις.
[39] *Physics*, 198 a 27. Cf. above, pp. 105 ff. where this passage is discussed.

evidence here to warrant Ross's assertion that the unmoved first mover should be regarded as a transcendent end. In fact, one of the major difficulties in the Aristotelian position is to understand how he would relate the Prime Mover or God to particular things.[40] Ross's rather cavalier use of the terms "transcendent" and "immanent" does not resolve the inherent conflict raised by Aristotle's statement, "because it is better thus, not without qualification, but with reference to the essential nature in each case."

Ross's own note on this line seems to indicate the fact that he has forgotten what he said on the preceding page: " 'That the thing is so because it is better thus,' refers to the final cause, and Aristotle points out that in explaining natural process the physicist must not be content, as a Platonist might, to say 'this is so, because it subserves the end of the whole universe,' but he must be able to show that the attributes each thing has are better with a view to the nature of that particular thing." In other words, in this whole context, not only the text of Aristotle but also Ross's own note go to show that it is not possible here to use validly the term "transcendent."[41]

Another representative passage which implies a value theory occurs in the seventh book of the *Physics*. At this particular point Aristotle is concerned to show that "acquired states" are not "alterations," that is, they are not the products of this type of motion or change. The general temper of his argument appears in his opening sentences: "Again, acquired states, whether of the body or of the soul, are not alterations. For some are excellences and others are defects, and neither excellence nor defect is an alteration: excellence is a perfection (for when anything acquires its proper excellence we call it perfect, since it is then if ever that a thing exists in its natural state: *e.g.*, we have a perfect circle whenever it becomes a circle in the full sense of the term and whenever it is best), while defect is a perishing of or departure from this condition."[42]

---

[40] Cf. above, pp. 115–116.

[41] Obviously, we shall have more to say on the nature of Aristotle's cosmic teleology when we come to deal with Book Λ of the *Metaphysics* and Book X of the *Nicomachean Ethics*.

[42] *Physics*, 246 a 10–17. ἀλλὰ μὴν οὐδ' αἱ ἕξεις οὔθ' αἱ τοῦ σώματος οὔθ' αἱ τῆς ψυχῆς ἀλλοιώσεις. αἱ μὲν γὰρ ἀρεταὶ αἱ δὲ κακίαι τῶν ἕξεων· οὐκ ἔστι δὲ

Aristotle goes on to point out that "excellences" *(ἀρεταί)* are a result of relations. Health, for example, depends on a mixture in proper proportion of the elements of hot and cold in the body. The case is the same with respect to beauty, strength, and the other excellences and defects of the body. "Each of them exists in virtue of a particular relation and puts that which possesses it in a good or bad condition with regard to its proper affections, where by 'proper' affections I mean those influences that from the natural constitution of a thing tend to promote or destroy its existence."[43]

Clearly, for the purposes of our analysis, the important terms are excellence, defect, perfection, and the notion of the natural or nature. Excellence, ἀρετή, is regarded as the equivalent of perfection or completion *(τελείωσις)*. And next, when a thing is perfect, Aristotle asserts, "Then if ever a thing exists in its natural state," so that in a sense here "nature" and "perfection" are equated. Also we should not overlook his remarks about "proper affections" *(τὰ οἰκεῖα πάθη)*. "Proper" here appears to describe something which can have a profound effect on the very existence of anything, and the "condition" of a thing is labelled as "good" or "bad" depending upon whether these "proper affections" are or are not making for the thing's completion or perfection or arriving at its full natural state. Interestingly enough the implied value theory of this passage amounts to a restatement in different

---

οὔτε ἡ ἀρετὴ οὔτε ἡ κακία ἀλλοίωσις, ἀλλ' ἡ μὲν ἀρετὴ τελείωσίς τις (ὅταν γὰρ λάβῃ τὴν αὑτοῦ ἀρετήν, τότε λέγεται τέλειον ἕκαστον—τότε γὰρ ἔστι μάλιστα [τὸ] κατὰ φύσιν—ὥσπερ κύκλος τέλειος, ὅταν μάλιστα γένηται καὶ ὅταν βέλτιστος), ἡ δὲ κακία φθορὰ τούτου καὶ ἔκστασις. Ross's text. The Oxford translation has been modified slightly to conform with Ross's reading of 246 a 16. In his note to the passage Ross cites the definition of ἀρετή in *Metaphysics* Δ, 1021 b 20–23. ἡ ἀρετὴ τελείωσίς τις· ἕκαστον γὰρ τότε τέλειον καὶ οὐσία πᾶσα τότε τελεία, ὅταν κατὰ τὸ εἶδος τῆς οἰκείας ἀρετῆς μηδὲν ἐλλείπῃ μόριον τοῦ κατὰ φύσιν μεγέθους. "And excellence is a completion; for each thing is complete and every substance is complete, when in respect of its proper kind of excellence it lacks no part of its natural magnitude." Ross's text. Note that the whole doctrine in chapter 16 of *Metaphysics* Δ (1021 b 12–1022 a 3) is exactly the same as that of the passage of the *Physics* which we are now examining.

[43] *Physics*, 246 b 8–10. ἑκάστῃ γάρ ἐστι τῷ πρός τι πῶς ἔχειν, καὶ περὶ τὰ οἰκεῖα πάθη εὖ ἢ κακῶς διατίθησι τὸ ἔχον· οἰκεῖα δ' ὑφ' ὧν γίγνεσθαι καὶ φθείρεσθαι πέφυκεν. Ross's text.

terms, and with a different emphasis, of the scheme which associates value with a thing's goal or purpose. Also it should be noted that "good," "bad," "perfection," "natural state," and the like are terms bearing only upon the internal condition of the particular thing in question—and in turn do not afford any bases for what we called above "comparative evaluation." But there is the further important point that the evaluative dimension of this analysis becomes much more explicit when among the terms used we find excellence, defect, and perfection, which are loaded with value connotations.[44] And as the value overtones become more explicit, the more difficult it is to discover the relation of Being and Value in this particular aspect of Aristotle's thought, and in turn to relate it to the other value schemes we have already discussed.

But to return to the passage in the seventh book of the *Physics*, after having dealt with bodily excellences, Aristotle turns to the problem in connection with the soul. He asserts that the case of the states of the soul is similar to that of the body. The states of the soul depend upon certain relations with "the excellences being perfections of nature and the defects departures from it."[45] He then makes the same point about the good and bad condition of the soul with respect to proper affections. Next, since the particular point of the argument is to show that "states" are not "alterations," Aristotle reaffirms his position, but he does admit that the coming into being of these states "is necessarily the result of an alteration of the sensitive part of the soul, and this is altered by sensible objects."[46] Then immediately follows the sentence which is most significant for our own argument: "For all moral excellence is concerned with bodily pleasures and pains, which

---

[44] ἀρετή, κακία, and τελείωσις. One may properly be reminded here of the well-known argument of St. Thomas, where by some kind of metaphysical sleight of hand he moves from a pure ontological conception of full Being to the notion of perfection, a primarily axiological conception. In other words value emerges after or posterior to the fact of being. Cf. E. Gilson, *The Philosophy of St. Thomas Aquinas* (St. Louis, Herder, 1929) pp.106–107. We shall have more to say about this problem when we treat *Metaphysics* Λ.

[45] *Physics*, 247 a 2–3. αἱ μὲν ἀρεταὶ τελειώσεις, αἱ δὲ κακίαι ἐκστάσεις. Ross's text.

[46] *Physics*, 247 a 6–7. γίγνεσθαι δ' αὐτὰς ἀναγκαῖον ἀλλοιουμένου τοῦ αἰσθητικοῦ μέρους. ἀλλοιωθήσεται δ' ὑπὸ τῶν αἰσθητῶν. Ross's text.

again depend upon acting or upon remembering or upon anticipating."[47]

We are not here concerned with Aristotle's argument about "states" and "alterations" but when, in the course of it, he says that "all moral excellence is concerned with bodily pleasures and pains," we obviously have a passage that is extremely relevant for us in our inquiry into Aristotle's attitude towards the question of value. Here we have a phenomenon much like the one we met in the very first passage from the *Physics* which we took up.[48] There we were invited to suppose (or, at least, such was our argument) that "the touchstone of evaluation is to be found subjectively in the humanly actualized moral agent who alone is capable of happiness." In our present passage the same sort of limitation to the moral sphere is apparent, but the value scheme, though also subjective in character, invokes the criteria of pleasure and pain rather than happiness. So we must add to our list of the various implied value systems in the *Physics* another which is explicitly hedonistic.

Ross, in commenting on this passage, says, "Aristotle is led to give an excessively physiological account of the genesis of virtue and vice. He speaks as if it were due merely to a waxing or waning insusceptibility to bodily pleasures and pains. In the *Nicomachean Ethics* he corrects this account by allowing for the fact that a man's attitude to pleasure and pain may be modified by such a motive as love of country or of friends, or by desire to realize the καλόν."[49] No doubt, Aristotle's treatment of pleasure in the *Nicomachean Ethics* does represent a more refined view of the problem, but the question still remains there concerning the relation between eudaemonism and hedonism as it does in this chapter of the *Physics*, Book VII.[50]

There is one further representative passage from the physical treatises which may serve to round out our grasp of the question

---

[47] *Physics*, 247 a 7-9. ἅπασα γὰρ ἡ ἠθικὴ ἀρετὴ περὶ ἡδονὰς καὶ λύπας τὰς σωματικάς, αὗται δὲ ἢ ἐν τῷ πράττειν ἢ ἐν τῷ μεμνῆσθαι ἢ ἐν τῷ ἐλπίζειν. Ross's text.

[48] Cf. above, pp. 130-131.

[49] Cf. Ross, *Physics*, note on 247 a 6-19.

[50] Naturally, this matter will be explored fully in the treatment of Aristotle's ethical position.

of evaluation as it appears in this general section of the Aristotelian corpus. It occurs near the end of the second book of the *De Generatione et Corruptione* where Aristotle is more or less bringing together the results of the treatise. The significant paragraph for us reads as follows: "As we have said, coming-into-being and passing-away will always be continuous and will never fail by virtue of the cause which we have already mentioned.[51] And this has happened very reasonably, for we have asserted that in all things Nature ever desires the better, and 'being' is better than 'non-being' (the various senses in which we use the term 'being' have been discussed elsewhere). But it is impossible that this be equally present in all things because of the distance by which they are removed from the first principle. By using a method that was left open to Him, God completed the universe by making coming-into-being continual, for thus most especially would being go on continually because of the close proximity of everlasting coming-into-being and passing-away to Being in the full sense of the word. The cause of this, as we have often remarked, is circular motion, for it alone is continuous."[52]

In connection with this passage we should first always be aware of the fact that Aristotle is discussing coming-into-being and passing-away as one of the four types of motion and change.[53] So far as one can see the whole argument is a fine illustration of Aristotelian rational procedure. Fundamentally "reason" (*e.g.*, as it is embedded in the word, εὐλόγως) provides the validation for his mode of analysis. Then we are surely justified in asserting that in the passage Being[54] is postulated as the source of value.

---

[51] This is the material cause, with matter considered as substratum. Joachim in his Oxford translation refers here to *De Generatione et Corruptione*, 318 a 9 ff.

[52] *De Generatione et Corruptione*, 336 b 25–337 a 1. ἀεὶ δ᾽, ὥσπερ εἴρηται, συνεχὴς ἔσται ἡ γένεσις καὶ ἡ φθορά, καὶ οὐδέποτε ὑπολείψει δι᾽ ἣν εἴπομεν αἰτίαν. τοῦτο δ᾽ εὐλόγως συμβέβηκεν· ἐπεὶ γὰρ ἐν ἅπασιν ἀεὶ τοῦ βελτίονος ὀρέγεσθαί φαμεν τὴν φύσιν, βέλτιον δὲ τὸ εἶναι ἢ τὸ μὴ εἶναι (τὸ δ᾽ εἶναι ποσαχῶς λέγομεν, ἐν ἄλλοις εἴρηται), τοῦτο δ᾽ ἀδύνατον ἐν ἅπασιν ὑπάρχειν διὰ τὸ πόρρω τῆς ἀρχῆς ἀφίστασθαι, τῷ λειπομένῳ τρόπῳ συνεπλήρωσε τὸ ὅλον ὁ θεός, ἐνδελεχῆ ποιήσας τὴν γένεσιν· οὕτω γὰρ ἂν μάλιστα συνείροιτο τὸ εἶναι διὰ τὸ ἐγγύτατα εἶναι τῆς οὐσίας τὸ γίνεσθαι ἀεὶ καὶ τὴν γένεσιν. τούτου δ᾽ αἴτιον, ὥσπερ εἴρηται πολλάκις, ἡ κύκλῳ φορά· μόνη γὰρ συνεχής. Prantl's text. The translation is mine.

[53] Cf. above, pp. 94–98.

[54] Being, i.e., οὐσία in 336 b 33, is clearly used in the sense of οὐσία, as τέλος, as we described it above, pp. 113–114.

Hence when Aristotle says that "Nature always desires the better," and when he says that "being is better than non-being," and further when he employs the notion that things are better the more closely they approach the "first principle" or "Being in the full sense of the word," he clearly is maintaining that this supreme ontological entity is something from which value may be derived, so to speak, after the fact of Being itself has been totally established.

The passage also is notable because Aristotle inserts the notion of God. It must be said that the three terms, Nature, God, and Being are not sharply differentiated, and it might even be urged they are merely alternative designations of the same thing. But one temptation perhaps should be firmly resisted, namely, to take the thought that "God completed the Universe by making coming-into-being continual" in any sense as a doctrine of creationism. That is to say, though there may be some verbal similarities between this passage and the famous pages of Plato's *Timaeus*,[55] the context in Aristotle is the analysis of coming-into-being and passing-away as a type of motion and change. Furthermore, coming-into-being and passing-away are continual, everlasting, eternal—caused, as he says, by circular motion, which is alone continuous. In this perspective God, as final cause, or we even might call Him Being, is the everlasting source of this type of motion or change in perpetuity. Therefore God here cannot be regarded as a creator even in the limited sense of the Demiurge in the *Timaeus*.

By way of recapitulation, on the basis of these several representative passages which we have analyzed, we have been able to identify the following different implied value schemes:

1) values, as human phenomena, related to and authenticated by happiness, regarded as a supreme moral activity and viewed subjectively.

2) values derived from intelligence and nature, viewed as the causes of the universe;

3) values derived from a thing's end or τέλος, viewed objectively with its form and end equated, but relevant only to the thing internally, and forming no basis for comparative evaluation;

4) values derived from a thing's excellence or nature, viewed

---

[55] Cf. above, pp. 23–25.

as its completion or perfection (this is closely related to the preceding scheme);

5) values derived in the sphere of moral excellence subjectively from bodily pleasures and pains;

6) values derived objectively from Nature, God, Being—but becoming "values" after the fact of Being has been established.

Now it is perfectly apparent that these six sample schemes have some elements in common, e.g., numbers 3 and 4 approximate each other as to a lesser degree do numbers 2 and 6. But finally there are several unresolved questions, viz.: What is the relation between the objective and the subjective? What is the relation between the happiness principle and the pleasure principle? What is the basis of comparative evaluation? What is the relation between nature internally conceived, and Nature or Being or God from the cosmic point of view? And so on. As we move through the corpus towards the crucial metaphysics, ethics, politics, and literary criticism, the consequences of these unresolved questions will become more and more striking.

C. THE *DE ANIMA*

In many ways, the value implications for Aristotle's thought in his psychological treatises differ very little from those to be found in the logical and physical works. For our purposes, we perhaps need only to consider briefly the framework or the point of view which appears to be inherent in the *De Anima*, the most fundamental of the psychological writings, in order to understand how Aristotle handles questions of evaluation in this field. Soul is regarded by Aristotle as something to which the highest value is regularly assigned, and which by the same token can be used as a ground for making value judgments. This point and the argument for it can be found in the opening words of the *De Anima*, which, like all of Aristotle's introductions, sets the tone for the whole treatise.

He begins with the following observation: "Since we assume that in our knowledge of fair and honourable fields of learning, one type is to be preferred to another either because of its precision or its concern with better or more marvelous objects, on both these scores we would very reasonably place among the foremost the results of an inquiry concerning the soul. For solid knowledge about it seems to contribute greatly to truth in every sense, but in particular to our grasp of Nature, for the soul is, as it were, a first principle of living beings."[56]

Let us examine with care the terms in this passage which connote or suggest value. "Fair and honourable things" (I have rendered the unkeyed neuter as "fields of learning") as a phrase suggests that we all know what is "fair" or "honourable" and hence it would amount to Aristotle's use here of conventional value responses as a value criterion. "Precision" really raises the whole epistemological question, but fundamentally we may suppose that truth as a value is being invoked. Then the terms "better" and "more marvelous" in turn depend on conventional thinking. Soul, so to speak, as an area of inquiry or a subject matter, Aristotle seems to say, falls into the category of the "fair," the "honourable," the "better," and the "more marvelous," as everyone will agree. It is that kind of subject, and we are invited to believe that it can be investigated with an appropriate degree of precision. But next there seems to be a shift in Aristotle's value criterion. Up to this point, conventional value thinking has served to support the notion of the high importance of the soul. Now the soul and knowledge of it are regarded as superior because they contribute to "truth in every sense" and to "our grasp of Nature," for the soul is a "first principle of living beings." In other words, instead of the criterion of conventional value response, we now have "truth in every sense" and "Nature" submitted as the bases for determining the actual value of soul. Then when the soul is thus evaluated, it itself becomes not a thing evaluated but a criterion of value, so that, with a curious kind of circularity, the argument invites us to see in the soul as value criterion something of what is meant by "fair," "honourable," "better," and "more marvelous."

---

[56] De Anima, 402 a 1–7. τῶν καλῶν καὶ τιμίων τὴν εἴδησιν ὑπολαμβάνοντες, μᾶλλον δ' ἑτέραν ἑτέρας ἢ κατ' ἀκρίβειαν ἢ τῷ βελτιόνων τε καὶ θαυμασιωτέρων εἶναι, δι' ἀμφότερα ταῦτα τὴν περὶ τῆς ψυχῆς ἱστορίαν εὐλόγως ἂν ἐν πρώτοις τιθείημεν. δοκεῖ δὲ καὶ πρὸς ἀλήθειαν ἅπασαν ἡ γνῶσις αὐτῆς μεγάλα συμβάλλεσθαι, μάλιστα δὲ πρὸς τὴν φύσιν· ἔστι γὰρ οἷον ἀρχὴ τῶν ζῴων. Biehl's text. The translation is mine.

An analysis of this brief passage then seems to indicate that Aristotle in this context does not give any clear evidence of a firm point of approach to the question of value. He does not seem to be aware of the all-important distinction between the thing valued and the criterion by which it is valued. And in addition, he manages to compound the confusion by introducing such varied notions as conventional value reactions, truth, and Nature. Obviously, from the point of view of our own argument, this passage is most significant. That is, if one sets out to investigate the soul—to discover its essence and its attributes[57]—in the perspective of a philosopher of Being, it seems to be an inevitable consequence that he will be without solid points of reference not only with respect to the worth of his own enterprise but also with respect to the values involved in the area of his investigation.

If we follow Aristotle's introductory argument a little further, it is possible to get additional confirmation of our contention. Characteristically he proceeds to enumerate the various difficulties or problems which face an investigator of the soul (we perhaps could call him a psychologist) and in the course of his discussion he observes, "Accidents (*i.e.*, attributes or affections) contribute in large measure to our knowledge of what a thing is essentially, for whenever we can give an account, according to appearances, of a thing's accidents, either all or most of them, then we shall also be able to say something worth while about the thing itself."[58] This, of course, is a thoroughly familiar Aristotelian way of looking at things,[59] but at this point in our argument it is sufficient to note that here Aristotle, without departing from his standard position on the relation of essence and accidents, is showing how a grasp of a thing's accidents may contribute to our sound knowledge of its essence. But it is most important to remember that in the whole situation *essence* is primary and accidents are secondary and of lesser significance.

---

[57] Cf. *De Anima*, 402 a 7–10.

[58] *De Anima*, 402 b 21–25. . . . τὰ συμβεβηκότα συμβάλλεται μέγα μέρος πρὸς τὸ εἰδέναι τὸ τί ἐστιν· ἐπειδὰν γὰρ ἔχωμεν ἀποδιδόναι κατὰ τὴν φαντασίαν περὶ τῶν συμβεβηκότων, ἢ πάντων ἢ τῶν πλείστων, τότε καὶ περὶ τῆς οὐσίας ἕξομέν τι λέγειν κάλλιστα. Bielh's text. The translation is mine.

[59] Cf. above, pp. 74–81, where we discussed the terms essence and accidents as well as the problem of definition.

Next Aristotle applies this general principle to the specific problem of the soul. He asks whether the affections (i.e., τὰ πάθη, the equivalent of accidents) of the soul are peculiar to it alone or in effect does the soul have to be in a body, that is, be embodied, in order to be able to have "affections" of any sort. He insists that on the face of it most "affections" need the body—for example, "being angry, being courageous, feeling desire, and perceiving in general."[60] He adds that "thinking" (τὸ νοεῖν) may be an "affection" peculiar to the soul alone, but tends to conclude that all "affections" of the soul definitely need to be grounded in a complex of soul and body.

For the moment we are not immediately concerned with the question of the soul's separate existence, but rather with Aristotle's identification of the "affections" of the soul. For this reason, the following sentence is particularly relevant to our purpose: "But it seems then that all the affections of the soul exist in conjunction with a body: anger, gentleness, fear, pity, courage, and likewise joy and loving and hating, for in these the body simultaneously experiences an affection of some sort or other."[61] It will be noticed that the list of "affections" incorporates both moral states and emotions or feelings—in other words, the very material which Aristotle analyzes in detail in his ethical treatises. For example, anger, fear, and pity in the *Nicomachean Ethics* are presented as emotional states or states of feeling deeply bound up with moral states or virtues (or could we say moral values?) like gentleness and courage.[62] But the main point is that these moral states or moral values are located metaphysically, so to speak, as "affections" or "attributes" or "accidents." That is to say, they are secondary to or posterior to essence or essential nature, and are therefore fundamentally dependent. The situation here is much the same as it is in the context of the doctrine of the ten categories. The first category is οὐσία in the sense of the individual particular

---

[60] *De Anima*, 403 a 7. οἷον ὀργίζεσθαι, θαρρεῖν, ἐπιθυμεῖν, ὅλως αἰσθάνεσθαι. Biehl's text.

[61] *De Anima*, 403 a 16–19. ἔοικε δὲ καὶ τὰ τῆς ψυχῆς πάθη πάντα εἶναι μετὰ σώματος, θυμός, πραότης, φόβος, ἔλεος, θάρσος, ἔτι χαρὰ καὶ τὸ φιλεῖν τε καὶ μισεῖν· ἅμα γὰρ τούτοις πάσχει τι τὸ σῶμα. Biehl's text. The translation is mine.

[62] Cf. the very useful table in Ross, *Aristotle*, p. 203, which indicates the relations between states of feeling, actions, and moral states, as they are analyzed in the *Nicomachean Ethics*.

—the most precise meaning of Being, while the other nine categories comprise accidents. There is a sense in which this doctrine of the categories would dictate that "values" as we normally understand them would be subsumed under ποιόν, quality. In other words, they would be subsidiary to and dependent on the first category of Being.[63] Similarly here in the *De Anima*, moral states are described as "affections" of the soul.

Now to present "values" as attributes or qualities of things, and in some sense posterior to or derivative from the full ontological status of things—all this is a perfectly understandable and indeed a time-honoured way of resolving the problem of value and its relation to Being. But in Aristotle we are faced with this question, among others: How can we make this value theory expressed in the opening pages of the *De Anima* cohere, for example, with the view that a thing's form or essence is the same as its completion or perfection or purpose which Aristotle, as we have already seen, postulates so often as a source or sanction of value?[64] It is perfectly obvious that these two modes of attacking the problem of value are not only radically different from each other but also are in fact mutually exclusive. And when two such opposing views are promulgated by the same thinker, along with other equally different attitudes, the result can only be a basic puzzlement in the mind of the reader, and perhaps he may be well justified in urging that these confusions arise ultimately from the assumption that Being can be validly explored apart from Value. Perhaps it can be, but the thinker who does so must be prepared to accept the consequence of that decision for the question of value. In a sense, this is what Aristotle could not do because the influence of Plato was too strong in him—and hence he has given us the confusions which we have been attempting to point out. Plato's anchor with respect to Being and Value is always basically the Theory of Ideas. Several of the implied or explicit value theories in Aristotle individually can be derived from a metaphysics of Being—but our main argument is that not all of them can be asserted simultaneously without profound philosophical loss. And yet this is what we are finding in the text of Aristotle.

[63] Cf. our discussion of the *Categories* above, pp. 62–64, and 78–79.
[64] Cf. above, pp. 123–124, 129, 132–136, 136–138, 139–141.

So far as the general psychological doctrine is concerned, there is not much that will bear sharply upon our argument. But as we proceed, and in particular when we come to treat the *Metaphysics* and the *Nicomachean Ethics*, we should keep in mind some of the basic notions which Aristotle submits in the *De Anima*. For example, there is the conception that νοῦς or mind is an οὐσία embedded in the soul and incapable of being destroyed.[65] Then too there is the argument that soul is related to body as form is to matter. And if we consider form as essence, then the soul must be regarded as the actuality or entelechy (the Greek word is in fact ἐντελέχεια) of a body.[66] Aristotle takes pains to elaborate this last point, when he announces that the soul is the cause and first principle or source of the living body. It is the source of movement of all sorts; it is the final cause or end of the living body and it is the essence of the living body.[67] Further, there is the interesting theory regarding the mean and its function in the phenomena of sensation.[68] Other psychological theories expressed in the *De Anima* might be mentioned, but for our purposes the foregoing are clearly the most important.

Before we leave Aristotle's psychology, we should glance at three more passages which merit our attention. The first occurs after Aristotle has advanced his conception of the three parts of soul—the nutritive, the sensory and appetitive, and the rational—and made clear that plants possess only the first part, while animals have the first and second, and man has all three. He then says that his analysis must begin with the nutritive part, for it is the most fundamental and widespread element of the soul. It is in his description of this part of the soul that we find an expression of another characteristic Aristotelian attitude towards value: "The acts in which it [*i.e.*, the nutritive soul] manifests itself are reproduction and the use of food—reproduction, I say, because for any living thing that has reached its normal development and which is unmutilated, and whose mode of generation is not spontaneous, the most natural act is the production of another

---

[65] Cf. *De Anima*, 408 b 18–19.
[66] Cf. *De Anima*, 412 a 19–22.
[67] Cf. *De Anima*, 415 b 8–28.
[68] Cf. my article on "The Doctrine of the Mean," *The Philosophical Review*, XLV (1936) pp. 382–398. See especially pp. 393–396.

like itself, an animal producing an animal, a plant a plant, in order that, as far as its nature allows, it may partake in the eternal and divine. That is the goal towards which all things strive, that for the sake of which they do whatsoever their nature renders possible. The phrase 'for the sake of which' is ambiguous; it may mean either (a) the end to achieve which, or (b) the being in whose interest, the act is done. Since then no living thing is able to partake in what is eternal and divine by uninterrupted continuance (for nothing perishable can for ever remain one and the same), it tries to achieve that end in the only way possible to it, and success is possible in varying degrees; so it remains not indeed as the self-same individual but continues its existence in something *like* itself—not numerically but specifically one."[69]

In this passage once again Aristotle sets up the eternal and divine as the goal for which all things strive—in other words, as an ultimate criterion of value. This, to be sure, is an extension of the value theory which we have just been discussing, that is, when a thing's worth is measured by the degree of its completion or perfection. But when Aristotle introduces a "transcendental" conception like the "eternal and the divine" we are surely faced with a markedly different situation in so far as questions of value are concerned, where the final sanction seems to be eternity which seems almost to be a synonym for the divine. Furthermore, it is quite startling here to see Aristotle using the terms κοινωνεῖν and μετέχειν, "to have a share in" and "to partake in," the Platonic "technical" words to explain the relation between particulars and the Ideas. Aristotle's dilemma is again apparent. On the one hand, by rejecting the theory of Ideas he has in effect rejected the divine and the transcendental, has in fact called κοινωνεῖν and μετέχειν "empty verbiage,"[70] and yet on the

---

[69] *De Anima*, 415 a 25–b 7. ἧς ἐστιν ἔργα γεννῆσαι καὶ τροφῇ χρῆσθαι· φυσικώτατον γὰρ τῶν ἔργων τοῖς ζῶσιν, ὅσα τέλεια καὶ μὴ πηρώματα, ἢ τὴν γένεσιν αὐτομάτην ἔχει, τὸ ποιῆσαι ἕτερον οἷον αὐτό, ζῷον μὲν ζῷον, φυτὸν δὲ φυτόν, ἵνα τοῦ ἀεὶ καὶ τοῦ θείου μετέχωσιν ᾗ δύνανται· πάντα γὰρ ἐκείνου ὀρέγεται, καὶ ἐκείνου ἕνεκα πράττει ὅσα πράττει κατὰ φύσιν. τὸ δ᾽ οὗ ἕνεκα διττόν, τὸ μὲν οὗ, τὸ δὲ ᾧ. ἐπεὶ οὖν κοινωνεῖν ἀδυνατεῖ τοῦ ἀεὶ καὶ τοῦ θείου τῇ συνεχείᾳ, διὰ τὸ μηδὲν ἐνδέχεσθαι τῶν φθαρτῶν ταὐτὸ καὶ ἓν ἀριθμῷ διαμένειν, ᾗ δύναται μετέχειν ἕκαστον, κοινωνεῖ ταύτῃ, τὸ μὲν μᾶλλον τὸ δ᾽ ἧττον· καὶ διαμένει οὐκ αὐτὸ ἀλλ᾽ οἷον αὐτό, ἀριθμῷ μὲν οὐχ ἕν, εἴδει δ᾽ ἕν. Biehl's text.
[70] Cf. *Metaphysics* A, 991 a 20–22.

other, he introduces these very conceptions and all they imply for a value theory in this very serious and in many ways crucial passage in the *De Anima*.

The second passage which we should not overlook in the *De Anima* has to do with the priority of actuality over potentiality. This is a standard Aristotelian doctrine and we shall have more to say about it in our treatment of the *Metaphysics*.[71] We should introduce it here not only because the notion pervades Aristotle's thought but also because in it we find another way in which he consciously or unconsciously establishes a ground for making value judgments. The passage runs as follows: "Actual knowledge is identical with its object: potential knowledge in the individual is in time prior to actual knowledge but in the universe it has no priority even in time; for all things that come into being arise from what actually is. In the case of sense clearly the sensitive faculty already was potentially what the object makes it to be actually; the faculty is not affected or altered. This must therefore be a different kind from movement; for movement is, as we saw, an actualization of what is imperfect, activity or actuality in the unqualified sense, *i.e.*, that of what has been perfected, is different from movement."[72] Obviously this passage is most significant for the theory of knowledge and sensation or perception which it contains, but for our purposes it is useful because it shows how Aristotle typically attaches greater emphasis to actuality than to potentiality. And we should underline the point that the implied value theory here is one which has an ontological ground. That is to say, the higher the degree of reality or "reification" a thing achieves, the more valuable it is. But, note, the converse is not implied, as we have seen to be the case in Plato's metaphysic of the Ideas.

The other passage in the *De Anima* appears immediately after the one we have just been discussing. Aristotle here is elaborating

[71] Cf. especially *Metaphysics* Θ, chapter 8.
[72] *De Anima*, 431 a 1–7. τὸ δ' αὐτό ἐστω ἡ κατ' ἐνέργειαν ἐπιστήμη τῷ πράγματι. ἡ δὲ κατὰ δύναμιν χρόνῳ προτέρα ἐν τῷ ἑνί, ὅλως δὲ οὐδὲ χρόνῳ. ἔστι γὰρ ἐξ ἐντελεχείᾳ ὄντος πάντα τὰ γιγνόμενα. φαίνεται δὲ τὸ μὲν αἰσθητὸν ἐκ δυνάμει ὄντος τοῦ αἰσθητικοῦ ἐνεργείᾳ ποιοῦν· οὐ γὰρ πάσχει οὐδ' ἀλλοιοῦται. διὸ ἄλλο εἶδος τοῦτο κινήσεως. ἡ γὰρ κίνησις τοῦ ἀτελοῦς ἐνέργεια ἦν, ἡ δ' ἁπλῶς ἐνέργεια ἑτέρα ἡ τοῦ τετελεσμένου. Biehl's text. The Oxford translation has been slightly modified.

on his theory of perception and the rôle which the so-called "sensitive mean" plays in it, but again we are more interested in the light it may throw on the nature of his value thinking. Aristotle writes: "To perceive then is like bare asserting or knowing; but when the object is pleasant or painful, the soul makes a quasi-affirmation or negation, and pursues or avoids the object. To feel pleasure or pain is to act with the sensitive mean towards what is good or bad as such."[73] The full implications of this passage are very difficult to determine. Evidently it is attempting to describe the reactions of pursuit and avoidance on the part of the perceiving soul to pleasant or painful objects. But the meaning of this sentence is not clear: "To feel pleasure and pain is to act with the sensitive mean towards what is good or bad as such." Does he wish us to identify the good by the fact of our pleasurable reaction to it, that is, is pleasure the key to the good? Or does Aristotle wish us to hold the converse, *viz.*, that the good is the key to pleasure? And further, what is the significance of the phrase "as such"? So far as we can see, there is no way to answer adequately these questions, because Aristotle does not maintain a sufficiently firm attitude towards the inter-relation of the terms in this sentence, nor does he ever give us a consistent enough generalized value framework in the perspective of which we could formulate an appropriate reply.

So much for the evidence in the *De Anima*. In this treatise to a greater degree than in any of the others which have been examined up to this point, there are the perplexing contradictions and puzzles which can arise from a multiple and shifting attitude towards value. But as we proceed, we shall see the same notions repeated and our hope will be that before we are through we may be able to delineate sharply the precise nature of this multiplicity.

D. THE BIOLOGICAL TREATISES

Since Aristotle in his investigation of biology is primarily interested in problems of classification and description, that is,

---

[73] *De Anima*, 431 a 8–12. τὸ μὲν οὖν αἰσθάνεσθαι ὅμοιον τῷ φάναι μόνον καὶ νοεῖν· ὅταν δὲ ἡδὺ ἢ λυπηρόν, οἷον καταφᾶσα ἢ ἀποφᾶσα, διώκει ἢ φεύγει· καὶ ἔστι τὸ ἥδεσθαι καὶ λυπεῖσθαι τὸ ἐνεργεῖν τῇ αἰσθητικῇ μεσότητι πρὸς τὸ ἀγαθὸν ἢ κακόν, ᾗ τοιαῦτα. Biehl's text. For a special discussion of this passage, cf. my article, "The Doctrine of the Mean" (see note 68 above) pp. 395–396.

since he wishes to bring order into a vast amount of empirical data, it is not surprising that there are few passages which will be helpful to us in our inquiry into his attitudes towards the question of value. Again for the most part we will be dealing with matters of implication, and again we shall find repeated some of the points of view we have already discussed in the earlier sections of this chapter.

Typical of the kind of evidence which is to be found in the biological treatises is a passage from the first chapter of the first book of the *Historia Animalium*. At the outset Aristotle is concerned with the various means whereby animals may be classified and how they may be distributed into their several species and genera. In this connection he discusses differences in form, character, and habits. Of some interest to us are his remarks on the characters of animals: "Animals also differ from one another in regard to character in the following respects. Some are good-tempered, sluggish, and little prone to ferocity, as the ox; others are quick-tempered, ferocious, and unteachable, as the wild boar; some are intelligent and timid, as the stag and the hare; others are mean and treacherous, as the snake; others are noble and courageous and high-bred, as the lion; others are thorough-bred and wild and treacherous, as the wolf; for by the way, an animal is high-bred if it comes from noble stock, and an animal is thorough-bred if it does not deflect from its racial characteristics. Further some are crafty and mischievous, as the fox; some are spirited and affectionate and fawning, as the dog; others are easy-tempered and easily domesticated, as the elephant; others are cautious and watchful, as the goose; others are jealous and self-conceited, as the peacock. But of all animals man alone is capable of deliberation. Many animals have memory, and are capable of instruction; but no other creature except man can recall the past at will."[74]

[74] *Historia Animalium*, 488 b 11-27. διαφέρουσι δὲ ταῖς τοιαῖσδε διαφοραῖς κατὰ τὸ ἦθος. τὰ μὲν γὰρ ἐστι πρᾶα καὶ δύσθυμα καὶ οὐκ ἐνστατικά, οἷον βοῦς, τὰ δὲ θυμώδη καὶ ἐνστατικὰ καὶ ἀμαθῆ, οἷον ὗς ἄγριος, τὰ δὲ φρόνιμα καὶ δειλά, οἷον ἔλαφος, δασύπους, τὰ δ' ἀνελεύθερα καὶ ἐπίβουλα, οἷον οἱ ὄφεις, τὰ δ' ἐλεύθερα καὶ ἀνδρεῖα καὶ εὐγενῆ, οἷον λέων, τὰ δὲ γενναῖα καὶ ἄγρια καὶ ἐπίβουλα, οἷον λύκος· εὐγενὲς μὲν γάρ ἐστι τὸ ἐξ ἀγαθοῦ γένους, γενναῖον δὲ τὸ μὴ ἐξιστάμενον ἐκ τῆς αὑτοῦ φύσεως, καὶ μὲν πανοῦργα καὶ κακοῦργα, οἷον ἀλώπηξ, τὰ δὲ θυμικὰ καὶ φιλητικὰ καὶ θωπευτικά, οἷον κύων, τὰ δὲ πρᾶα καὶ τιθασσευτικά,

Apart from the fairly amusing way in which this passage reflects the pathetic fallacy, it is noteworthy to see how Aristotle uses conventional designations of moral characteristics in much the same way as he does in the *Nicomachean Ethics* in his analysis of virtues and vices as means and extremes.[75] And though it is far from explicit, the animals are surely evaluated by implication by these conventional moral norms, for example, when the lion is called "noble, courageous, and high-bred," or when snakes are called "mean and treacherous." Furthermore, man is given the highest rank because he is "capable of deliberation" and because he has the capacity to "recall the past at will."

In the *De Partibus Animalium* there are a few passages which we do not need to quote or analyze in detail for they merely afford additional illustrations of implied value theories with which we are already familiar. For example, when he is discussing generation in nature, or natural generation, final cause or the good end functions as a value sanction.[76] Or again, to take a sentence like the following: "Let us now consider the character of the material nature whose necessary results have been made available by rational nature for a final cause,"[77] we can readily see how

---

οἷον ἐλέφας, τὰ δ' αἰσχυντηλὰ καὶ φυλακτικά, οἷον χήν, τὰ δὲ φθονερὰ καὶ φιλόκαλα, οἷον ταώς. βουλευτικὸν δὲ μόνον ἄνθρωπός ἐστι τῶν ζῴων. καὶ μνήμης μὲν καὶ διδαχῆς πόλλα κοινωνεῖ, ἀναμιμνήσκεσθαι δ' οὐδὲν ἄλλο δύναται πλὴν ἄνθρωπος. Dittmeyer's text with the brackets removed from δασύπους in line 16. For other places where Aristotle refers to the characters of animals, cf., for example, *Historia Animalium*, 588 a 15–b 4, and 612 b 18 ff.

[75] In Books III, IV, and V of the *Nicomachean Ethics*.

[76] Cf. *De Partibus Animalium*, 639 b 11–21. Note especially this phrase, τὸ οὗ ἕνεκα καὶ τὸ καλὸν ἐν τοῖς τῆς φύσεως ἔργοις. Another good instance of this kind of thinking occurs in chapter 5 of the first book of the *De Partibus Animalium*. He is defending the study of biology and in particular his interest in the lower animals. He insists that in all the objects of Nature there is something marvelous and tells the story of Heracleitus, who was warming himself in the kitchen when some unexpected visitors called and were reluctant to enter. He urged them to come in, for, said he, "even here there are gods present." Aristotle then continues, "For each and all animals will reveal to us something natural and something beautiful . Absence of haphazard and conduciveness of everything to an end are to be found in Nature's works in the highest degree, and the resultant end of her generations and her combinations is a form of the beautiful." *De Partibus Animalium*, 645 a 23–26. ὡς ἐν ἅπασιν ὄντος τινὸς φυσικοῦ καὶ καλοῦ. τὸ γὰρ μὴ τυχόντως ἀλλ' ἕνεκά ἐν τοῖς τῆς φύσεως ἔργοις ἐστὶ καὶ μάλιστα· οὗ δ' ἕνεκα συνέστηκεν ἢ γέγονε τέλους, τὴν τοῦ καλοῦ χώραν εἴληφεν. Langkavel's text.

[77] *De Partibus Animalium*, 663 b 22–24. πῶς δὲ τῆς ἀναγκαίας φύσεως ἐχούσης τοῖς ὑπάρχουσιν ἐξ ἀνάγκης ἡ κατὰ τὸν λόγον φύσις ἕνεκά του κατακέχρηται,

Aristotle is asking us to accept the conceptions of nature, reason, and final cause not only as interrelated but also as guarantors of the validity of the ensuing argument. In this sense they are value sanctions.

Another rather unusual passage bespeaks a curious kind of naive value thinking, if we can call it that. In the context Aristotle is trying to explain why the various parts of the body are located as they are. He observes that the heart is in the front and center of the body, presumably the best position, because it is the first principle of the living being and of all motion and perception.[78] A little further on he makes this somewhat strange remark: "And it is a universal law that, as regards above and below, front and back, right and left, the nobler and more honourable part invariably is placed uppermost, in front, and on the right, rather than in the opposite positions, unless some more important object stands in the way."[79] Anyone is free to conjecture why the "nobler and more honourable" parts of the body should be associated with above, front, and right rather than with below, back, and left. Perhaps this may come from a kind of instinctive value reaction to a certain amount of physiological empirical evidence.

A passage of much greater significance occurs in the sixth chapter of the *De Motu Animalium*. Here Aristotle undertakes to investigate "how the soul moves the body and what is the source or first principle of motion in a living being."[80] He refers back to the *De Anima* as having covered the subject of the soul's motion, and he refers also to the *Metaphysics* in which the Prime Mover

---

λέγωμεν. Langkavel's text. Ogle apparently bases his Oxford translation of ἀναγκαίας φύσεως as "material nature" on the ground of the argument which follows. For our purposes, the word "material" should not be taken technically.

[78] Cf. *De Partibus Animalium*, 665 a 11–13.

[79] *De Partibus Animalium*, 665 a 22–25. ὅλως δ' ἀεὶ τὸ βέλτιον καὶ τιμιώτερον, ὅπου μηδὲν μεῖζον ἕτερον ἐμποδίζει, τοῦ μὲν ἄνω καὶ κάτω ἐν τοῖς μᾶλλόν ἐστιν ἄνω, τοῦ δ' ἔμπροσθεν καὶ ὄπισθεν ἐν τοῖς ἔμπροσθεν, τοῦ δεξιοῦ δὲ καὶ ἀριστεροῦ ἐν τοῖς δεξιοῖς. Langkavel's text. Perhaps he is justified in translating ὅλως by "it is a universal law" but in my opinion it should be rendered much less sharply. For other places where he invokes this "universal law," cf. *De Partibus Animalium*, 665 b 18–21; 667 b 33–668 a 1; 672 b 19–24.

[80] *De Motu Animalium*, 700 b 10–11. πῶς ἡ ψυχὴ κινεῖ τὸ σῶμα, καὶ τίς ἡ ἀρχὴ τῆς τοῦ ζῴου κινήσεως. Jaeger's text.

and that which is first moved and moved eternally are discussed.[81] He then proceeds to point out that besides the motion of the cosmos or universe animate objects cause all other movements save those that derive from things coming into contact with one another. Those motions caused by animate objects are limited since the animate objects themselves are limited. "For all living beings both move and are moved on account of something, so that this is the limit for all their motions, that is, the purpose or goal."[82] Next he lists the forces that move the living being as intelligence, imagination, choice, wish, and appetite.[83] These may be summed up under the two terms, mind and desire.[84]

Following a brief argument to show why the five notions may be reduced to two, there comes a passage which must be quoted in full: "Therefore the object of desire or of intellect first initiates movement, not, that is, every object of intellect, only the end in the domain of conduct. Accordingly among goods that which moves is a practical end, not the good in its whole extent. For it initiates movement only so far as something else is for its sake, or so far as it is the object of that which is for the sake of something else. And we must suppose that a seeming good may take the room of actual good, and so may the pleasant, which is itself a seeming good. From these considerations it is clear that in one regard that which is eternally moved by the eternal mover is moved in the same way as every living being, in another regard differently, and so while some things are moved eternally, the movement of living beings has a term. Now the eternal beautiful, and the truly and primarily good (which if not at one time good, at another time not good), is too divine and precious to be relative to anything else. The prime mover then moves, itself being unmoved, whereas desire and its faculty are moved and so move."[85]

---

[81] Note this typical instance of the way in which Aristotle cross-references his treatises.

[82] De Motu Animalium, 700 b 15–16. πάντα γὰρ τὰ ζῷα καὶ κινεῖ καὶ κινεῖται ἕνεκά τινος, ὥστε τοῦτ᾽ ἔστιν αὐτοῖς πάσης τῆς κινήσεως πέρας, τὸ οὗ ἕνεκα. Jaeger's text. The translation is mine.

[83] His terms are: διάνοια, φαντασία, προαίρεσις, βούλησις, and ἐπιθυμία.

[84] i.e., νοῦς and ὄρεξις.

[85] De Motu Animalium, 700 b 23–701 a 1. ὥστε κινεῖ πρῶτον τὸ ὀρεκτὸν καὶ τὸ διανοητόν. οὐ πᾶν δὲ διανοητόν, ἀλλὰ τὸ τῶν πρακτῶν τέλος. διὸ τὸ τοιοῦτόν

This is, of course, another instance of an implied value theory which finds its validation in the notion of goal or end or final cause. But we should not overlook the point that at the very outset in this analysis of the movement of living beings Aristotle limits the conception of end to "the domain of conduct" or of practical activity, τῶν πρακτῶν. This "practical end" is regarded as a source of movement and is to be found among "things that are good," τῶν ἀγαθῶν. Note here that Aristotle in no sense thus far makes explicit any way by which we may determine what these "goods" are, except perhaps by conjuring up some form or other of his famous catch-word that all things by Nature strive for the good. And by now in our argument it should be clear how circular and therefore ultimately unsatisfactory this catch-word is when it is brought face to face with the complexities of the problem of value. But the most important point for our argument is the sharp dissociation the passage makes between the good conceived as a practical end and "the good in its whole extent," i.e., between τὸ τῶν πρακτῶν τέλος and πᾶν τὸ καλόν.

This dissociation should be submitted to very careful scrutiny. In the first place, there are certain times in Aristotle when he apparently wants us to see a connection between the final cause or purpose that is operative in individual things and the Prime Mover as Final Cause for the Universe. But here he explicitly separates the two in such a way that it becomes difficult to see how, if at all, Aristotle ever did conceive of their interrelation. Next, in the passage as a kind of parenthesis, in connection with the notion of good as a practical end he inserts the notion of the "seeming good" which takes the place of an "actual good," yet again without much specification as to the difference between them. He does announce rather flatly that "the pleasant" (τὸ ἡδύ)

ἐστι τῶν ἀγαθῶν τὸ κινοῦν, ἀλλ' οὐ πᾶν τὸ καλόν· ἢ γάρ ἕνεκα τούτου ἄλλο, καὶ ἢ τέλος ἐστὶ τῶν ἄλλου τινὸς ἕνεκα ὄντων, ταύτῃ κινεῖ. δεῖ δὲ τιθέναι καὶ τὸ φαινόμενον ἀγαθὸν ἀγαθοῦ χώραν ἔχειν, καὶ τὸ ἡδύ· φαινόμενον γάρ ἐστιν ἀγαθόν. ὥστε δῆλον ὅτι ἔστι μὲν ἢ ὁμοίως κινεῖται τὸ ἀεὶ κινούμενον ὑπὸ ἀεὶ κινοῦντος καὶ τῶν ζῴων ἕκαστον, ἔστι δ' ἢ ἄλλως, διὸ καὶ τὰ μὲν ἀεὶ κινεῖται, ἡ δὲ τῶν ζῴων κίνησις ἔχει πέρας. τὸ δὲ ἀΐδιον καλόν, καὶ τὸ ἀληθῶς καὶ τὸ πρώτως ἀγαθὸν καὶ μὴ ποτὲ μὲν ποτὲ δὲ μή, θειότερον καὶ τιμιώτερον ἢ ὥστ' εἶναι πρὸς ἕτερον. τὸ μὲν οὖν πρῶτον οὐ κινούμενον κινεῖ, ἡ δ' ὄρεξις καὶ τὸ ὀρεκτικὸν κινούμενον κινεῖ. Jaeger's text, except I have read πρὸς ἕτερον for πρότερόν ⟨τι⟩ in 700 b 35. The Oxford translation has been modified slightly.

is a seeming good, but then again Aristotle is by no means consistent in maintaining this attitude towards pleasure or the pleasant.[86]

After the parenthesis Aristotle returns to the relation between the final cause as a practical end and "the good in its whole extent" and does suggest that the relation may be one of analogy, namely, that there is a respect in which the eternal mover moves certain things eternally in the same way as living beings are moved, that is, we may suppose, by the operation of a mover that is itself unmoved.[87] But, after advancing this analogical relation, he appears to drive the two members even farther apart by underscoring the difference in this way: the movement caused by the Eternal Mover is eternal, whereas "the movement of living beings has a term." And then, in almost more glowing language than is to be found in *Metaphysics* Λ, and even in phrases that recall the words of Diotima's description of the Idea of Beauty in the *Symposium*,[88] he affirms that the "eternal beautiful," the "truly and primarily good" is "too divine and too precious to be relative to anything else." In other words, the cosmic Prime Mover which causes cosmic motion is denoted by a series of value terms, *viz.*, eternal beautiful, truly and primarily good, divine, precious—terms which would suggest that somehow or other Being and Value do from the cosmic point of view coincide —as they do in Plato's Idea of the Good. But there is absolutely no connection suggested as to how this cosmic Prime Mover may be related to the good as a practical end which is a prime unmoved mover for the movement of living beings, by stimulating their desires and appetitive faculties which both move and are moved.

[86] Farquharson in his Oxford translation cites in connection with these lines the following passages: De Anima, 433 a 28, Nicomachean Ethics, 1113 a 16, Eudemian Ethics, 1227 a 39, Rhetoric 1369 b 18. The problem of Aristotle's view of pleasure will be discussed at length when we deal with his ethical treatises.

[87] Cf. Farquharson's note in the Oxford translation on De Motu Animalium, 700 b 35, τὸ μὲν οὖν πρῶτον οὐ κινούμενον κινεῖ: "i.e., the good aimed at or achieved in act. Cf. De Anima, 433 b 16, τὸ ὀρεκτόν is τὸ κινοῦν οὐ κινούμενον (433 b 12), i.e., τὸ πρακτὸν ἀγαθόν, here called τὸ πρῶτον οὐ κινούμενον κινοῦν."

[88] Cf. Symposium, 210 e 2–211 d 1. Note especially the words οὐδὲ τοτὲ μέν, τοτὲ δὲ οὔ in 211 a 3 and cf. Aristotle's μὴ ποτὲ μὲν ποτὲ δὲ μή in 700 b 34; or Plato's οὐδὲ πρὸς μὲν τὸ καλόν, πρὸς δὲ τὸ αἰσχρόν in 211 a 3–4 and cf. Aristotle's ὥστ' εἶναι πρὸς ἕτερον in 700 b 34–35.

The key phrase, it seems, that really marks out the nature of Aristotle's philosophical or metaphysical failure at this point is "too divine and too precious to be relative to anything else—πρὸς ἕτερον." Would it not be fair to say that the inveterate drive of reason or rationalism in Aristotle's mind has resulted in something like this: The eternal beautiful, the real Prime Mover must not be qualified in any way at all—it may, to be sure, be described by the most potent value terms, and if it is so described then what results is a potentially geniune Platonic situation. But when Aristotle adds that it cannot be related to anything else, and thus cannot be related to the "practical end" which causes the movement of living beings, then by this divorce, it—as cosmic Prime Mover—cannot be used as a ground for explaining the phenomena of evaluation in the world in which living beings exists. For Plato, as we have seen, this is the world of "sights and sounds," and in the passage from the *Symposium* cited above he uses explicitly the conception of "participation" to account for the relation of the "beauties" we see in the world of sights and sounds to the supreme Idea of Beauty.[89] But, in sharp contrast, Aristotle, at least in this passage of the *De Motu Animalium*, rules out the possibility of any connection at all, with the exception of the vague one involved in the suggested analogy between the movement caused by the real Prime Mover and those caused by a prime mover conceived as the good as a practical end.

In the diagram which appears at the end of the fourth chapter above, we indicated the gap which seems to exist in Aristotle's thought between the supreme First Cause and all the rest of the constituent elements in Reality as Aristotle sees them.[90] There can be no doubt that this most interesting section of the *De Motu Animalium* provides us with striking evidence that the gap is really there and with fairly clear notions about the reasons for its being there. And finally this detailed examination of the passage should show how difficult it is, in the context of Aristotle's basic metaphysical position, for him to bridge the gap in any satisfactory fashion.

[89] Cf. *Symposium*, 211 b 1–3, the description of the Idea of Beauty as: αὐτὸ καθ' αὑτὸ μεθ' αὑτοῦ μονοειδὲς ἀεὶ ὄν, τὰ δὲ ἄλλα πάντα καλὰ ἐκείνου μετέχοντα τρόπον τινὰ τοιοῦτον. Burnet's text.

[90] Cf. above, pp. 115–116.

There is one further section in the *De Motu Animalium* which serves to complicate the picture we derive from it concerning Aristotelian value thinking. In the eighth chapter he starts out to discuss changes in temperature in the body. This particular problem, of course, need not concern us, but the words Aristotle uses by way of introducing the question are of some interest. He says: "But to return, the object we pursue or avoid in the field of action is, as has been explained, the orginal of movement, and upon the conception and imagination of this there necessarily follows a change in the temperature of the body. For what is painful we avoid, what is pleasing we pursue."[91] We can readily see that we are back with the question of the source or cause of the movement of living beings. In the passage which we have just been discussing the source of movement was identified as the object of desire or of thought within in the limited field of practical action. It then appeared that these objects were to be regarded as examples of the good as a practical end, although, as we pointed out, Aristotle does not help us very much if we try to discover exactly what this good or these goods are. But here in the next quotation we are told that the source of movement on the level of practical action is what we pursue or avoid. And, of course, as is so typical of Aristotle, he equates the painful with what we avoid and the pleasant with what we pursue. In other words, in the earlier passage we were met with a value situation in which the notions of pleasure and pain were certainly not regarded as central to the argument (in fact, the pleasant was referred to as a "seeming" good) whereas a few pages later, we find Aristotle announcing that pleasure and pain reactions are really the source of the movement of living beings, and hence really must be at the heart of their scheme of values. There should be no need to labour the point further that the value notions of these two passages cannot be made consistent with each other.

The *De Generatione Animalium* gives us further evidence of Aristotle's use of Nature and Final Cause as key conceptions in

[91] *De Motu Animalium*, 701 b 33–36. ἀρχὴ μὲν οὖν, ὥσπερ εἴρηται, τῆς κινήσεως τὸ ἐν τῷ πρακτῷ διωκτὸν καὶ φευκτόν. ἐξ ἀνάγκης δ᾽ ἀκολουθεῖ τῇ νοήσει καὶ τῇ φαντασίᾳ αὐτῶν θερμότης καὶ ψύξις. τὸ μὲν γὰρ λυπηρὸν φευκτόν, τὸ δ᾽ ἡδὺ διωκτόν. Jaeger's text.

evaluation. In the introduction to the treatise he points out that he will be primarily concerned with the efficient and the material causes. Elsewhere in the essay he in effect identifies these two causes with "that which is of necessity" and contrasts them with the Final Cause. For example, in accounting for the existence of the testes in males, he makes this characteristic statement: "Now if Nature makes everything either because it is necessary or because it is better so, this part also must be for one of these two reasons."[92] Nature here seems to be the over-arching conception, and it is also clear that "the better" is the equivalent of Final Cause. And furthermore, here again we should note that "better" has only a significance that can be applied internally to the individual particular involved.[93]

At the beginning of the second book of the *De Generatione Animalium*, Aristotle returns again to discuss the broad metaphysical framework within which he is carrying on his inquiry into this subject. As we shall see, he repeats with certain modifications the view he expressed of the First Cause or Prime Mover in the *De Anima* in a passage which we have already analyzed.[94] In the section now under consideration Aristotle first specifies the nature of the problem he is facing. Male and female have already been identified as principles of generation. The next task is to show how they come to be and exist from necessity and from the first efficient cause that moves them and also to show the nature of their matter. Though the following passage is long, its importance as such warrants our quoting it in full:

"That they exist (*i.e.*, male and female) because it is better and on account of the final cause, takes us back to a principle still

---

[92] *De Generatione Animalium*, 717 a 15–17. εἰ δὴ πᾶν ἡ φύσις ἢ διὰ τὸ ἀναγκαῖον ποιεῖ ἢ διὰ τὸ βέλτιον, κἂν τοῦτο τὸ μόριον εἴη διὰ τούτων θάτερον. Peck's text. This attitude towards Nature is reflected by the frequency with which Aristotle repeats in the *De Generatione Animalium* his familiar dictum that Nature does nothing that is in vain or superfluous. Cf. 739 b 20, 741 b 4, 744 a 36, 788 b 20. Cf. also 770 b 9–27, where Aristotle discusses monstrosities as "contrary to Nature" and defines precisely the sense in which he means this phrase to be taken. On the relation of Nature, Necessity, and final cause Aristotle makes some further comments in 778 a 29–b 19.

[93] For much of the material in this paragraph, I am indebted to A. L. Peck's introduction to his translation of Aristotle's *Generation of Animals* in the Loeb Classical Library (Cambridge, Harvard University Press, 1943) pp. xli–xlii.

[94] Cf. above, pp. 147–149, the discussion of *De Anima*, 415 a 25–b 7.

further remote. Now (1) some existing things are eternal and divine while others admit of both existence and non-existence. But (2) that which is noble and divine is always, in virtue of its own nature, the cause of the better in such things as admit of being better or worse, and what is not eternal does admit of existence and non-existence, and can partake in the better and the worse. And (3) soul is better than body, and the living, having soul, is thereby better than the lifeless which has none, and being is better than not being, living than not living. These, then, are the reasons of the generation of animals. For since it is impossible that such a class of things as animals should be of an eternal nature, therefore that which comes into being is eternal in the only way possible. Now it is impossible for it to be eternal as an individual (though of course the real essence of things is in the individual— were it such it would be eternal—but it is possible for it as a species. This is why there is always a class of men and animals and plants. But since the male and female essences are the first principles of these, they will exist in the existing individuals for the sake of generation. Again, as the first efficient or moving cause, to which belong the definition and the form, is better and more divine in its nature than the material on which it works, it is better that the superior principle should be separated from the inferior."[95]

Aristotle closes this phase of his argument by making the male the equivalent of the formal and efficient cause and thus superior to the female, the material cause. At the moment we may disregard this familiar substantiation of his belief in the superiority of

[95] *De Generatione Animalium*, 731 b 23–732 a 6. ὡς δὲ διὰ τὸ βέλτιον καὶ τὴν αἰτίαν τὴν ἕνεκά τινος, ἄνωθεν ἔχει τὴν ἀρχήν· ἐπεὶ γάρ ἐστι τὰ μὲν ἀίδια καὶ θεῖα τῶν ὄντων, τὰ δ' ἐνδεχόμενα καὶ εἶναι καὶ μὴ εἶναι, τὸ δὲ καλὸν καὶ τὸ θεῖον αἴτιον ἀεὶ κατὰ τὴν αὑτοῦ φύσιν τοῦ βελτίονος ἐν τοῖς ἐνδεχομένοις, τὸ δὲ μὴ ἐνδεχόμενόν ἐστι καὶ εἶναι ‹καὶ μὴ εἶναι› καὶ μεταλαμβάνειν καὶ τοῦ χείρονος καὶ τοῦ βελτίονος, βέλτιον δὲ ψυχὴ μὲν σώματος, τὸ δ' ἔμψυχον τοῦ ἀψύχου διὰ τὴν ψυχήν, καὶ τὸ εἶναι τοῦ μὴ εἶναι καὶ τὸ ζῆν τοῦ μὴ ζῆν, διὰ ταύτας τὰς αἰτίας γένεσις ζῴων ἐστίν· ἐπεὶ γὰρ ἀδύνατος ἡ φύσις τοῦ τοιούτου γένους ἀίδιος εἶναι, καθ' ὃν ἐνδέχεται τρόπον, κατὰ τοῦτόν ἐστιν ἀίδιον τὸ γινόμενον. ἀριθμῷ μὲν οὖν ἀδύνατον, ἡ γὰρ οὐσία τῶν ὄντων ἐν τῷ καθ' ἕκαστον· τοιοῦτον δ' εἴπερ ἦν, ἀίδιον ἂν ἦν· εἴδει δ' ἐνδέχεται. διὸ γένος ἀεὶ ἀνθρώπων καὶ ζῴων ἐστὶ καὶ φυτῶν. ἐπεὶ δὲ τούτων ἀρχὴ τὸ θῆλυ καὶ τὸ ἄρρεν, ἕνεκα τὴν γενέσεως ἂν εἴη τὸ θῆλυ καὶ τὸ ἄρρεν ἐν τοῖς οὖσιν ἑκάτερον τούτων· βελτίονος δὲ καὶ θειοτέρας τὴν φύσιν οὔσης τῆς αἰτίας τῆς κινούσης πρώτης, ᾗ ὁ λόγος ὑπάρχει καὶ τὸ εἶδος, τῆς ὕλης, βέλτιον καὶ τὸ κεχωρίσθαι τὸ κρεῖττον τοῦ χείρονος. Peck's text.

the male, but it is important to observe how Aristotle argues to show that the phenomenon (in this case, the existence of the two sexes) exists because it is "better" and the result of a "final cause," and therefore must be referred to a more ultimate principle. Then we are immediately placed in the context of the Prime Mover, we may suppose, as one of those things whose existence is eternal and divine, but actually the Prime Mover as such is not named. According to the argument, we are told that the "noble" and "divine" (τὸ καλόν and τὸ θεῖον) always cause what is "better" in things that are not "eternal," but can be better or worse, and in fact can "be" or "not be." But Aristotle does not tell us how or why this comes about, and at the same time uses the terms "noble" and "divine" and "eternal" just as though he were in total agreement with Plato. Then he launches into a series of comparative evaluations—soul is better than body, living than being lifeless, being than not being—just as though he had established a valid relation, on the one hand, between "noble," "divine," and "eternal," and on the other, all those existing things which can be or not be, or can be better or worse. This, in sum, says Aristotle, is the reason why there is generation of animals.

The next aspect of the analysis is quite arresting when we come to think about it. We are really made to assume that being "eternal" is a final and ultimate goal for things. Individual perishable things by definition cannot be eternal individually, but the species to which they belong can be; therefore animals propagate to perpetuate the species, and in this way get their share of this ultimate value, "eternality." All of this, as is perfectly obvious, is understandable in the eyes of a Platonist, but it becomes difficult to comprehend Aristotle when he talks in this fashion if we remember how vehement he is in denying that the "noble" and the "divine" and the "eternal" can function in this essentially Platonic way. And even in this very passage we have concrete evidence that Aristotle has not forgotten his metaphysical quarrel with Plato when he remarks parenthetically "though of course the real essence of things is in the individual."[96] And finally he closes the analysis by invoking the argument that the male as form and definition and efficient cause is therefore

[96] Cf. *De Generatione Animalium*, 731 b 34.

better and more divine than the female which is the material. When all is said and done, we can only insist that this passage constitutes another important item of evidence in our case that it is most difficult for Aristotle to be a Platonic anti-Platonist. It is surely not without significance that the passages where he reveals his own dilemma, in the psychological and biological works, for example, occur when he is setting up the broad metaphysical frame within which he will carry on the inquiry at hand. In other words, these are the key points where the implications of the relation of Being and Value are supremely relevant. Is it too much to say that in these situations Aristotle cannot have it both ways?

As we move now from the treatises which have dealt with logic, physics, psychology, and biology to the absolutely central metaphysics, we shall be reaching the most critical point of our entire study, and the one which will provide the ground for our argument in those areas where the phenomena of evaluation are supremely important—in ethics, politics, and literary criticism.[97]

[97] Since the so-called *Opuscula* and *Problemata* are not the genuine works of Aristotle, we shall omit any reference to them. In so far as they reflect the general Peripatetic point of view, there are several passages similar in content to those which we already have examined or will examine subsequently.

CHAPTER VI

BEING AND VALUE IN THE
METAPHYSICS

THE first book of Aristotle's *Metaphysics* is perhaps as famous as any other section of his writings of comparable length. By many and most often traditionally, it has been regarded as the first explicit "history of philosophy" ever written, and in fact much valuable information about the Pre-Socratics in particular is preserved for us in these pages. But a more careful reading of the book and a check of its contents against evidence derived from other sources, including the rest of the Aristotelian corpus, have led scholars in some instances to question the reliability of Aristotle's testimony,[1] as well as to doubt the historical intent of the author. The book is certainly not a "history" in our sense of the word. Rather, it is an attempt by Aristotle to demonstrate the definitive character of his own position by an examination of his philosophical predecessors and their doctrines. In other words, the underlying assumption of the book is that Aristotle's own metaphysics of Being, his own conception of first principles and "First Philosophy," and above all, his doctrine of the four causes, are exhaustive and final and in no sense susceptible of improvement or extension.

In this spirit he indicates how and in what degree various of the Pre-Socratics anticipated or adumbrated his own doctrine of the four causes, dispensing praise or dispraise according to the closeness with which each one of them approximated the Aristotelian view. The outcome of the book then is that in one way or another the several causes had been more or less vaguely touched upon, but no one of his predecessors had succeeded in arriving at a doctrine of four causes. Furthermore no one had been able to suggest another additional type of cause, so that Aristotle, via this excursion into the philosophical tradition which

[1] Cf. notably, H. F. Cherniss, *Aristotle's Criticism of Presocratic Philosophy* (Baltimore, Johns Hopkins Press, 1935).

he had inherited, invites us to accept his own conviction concerning the finality of his position.

It is obviously not to our purpose to analyze and appraise the nature of Aristotle's treatment of his tradition, but rather, so far as the first book of the *Metaphysics* is concerned, and particularly in the earlier chapters, we should be aware of those elements in this introduction which go far to set the speculative tone of the whole treatise. This tone quite naturally will be all important for us in our efforts to descry the implications of the *Metaphysics* for Aristotle's position *vis-à-vis* the question of value.

A. THE "CLIMATE" CREATED BY *METAPHYSICS* A

"All men by nature desire to know."[2] It takes little imagination to feel how much is contributed to the "value climate" by this famous opening sentence. The supreme worth of knowledge, sanctioned by nature, reinforced by the desires of all men, when it is thus announced, creates the context which will condition all that follows. Then, in this truly remarkable first chapter, Aristotle with astonishing economy, outlines his theory of knowledge and its empirical base. We are introduced to all of the essential terms: sense ($\alpha\check{\iota}\sigma\theta\eta\sigma\iota\varsigma$), in which men take delight; memory ($\mu\nu\acute{\eta}\mu\eta$) which is not possessed by all animals; experience ($\dot{\epsilon}\mu\pi\epsilon\iota\varrho\acute{\iota}\alpha$) possessed for the most part by men, which is created for them by many memories of the same thing; "reasonings" ($\lambda o\gamma\iota\sigma\mu o\acute{\iota}$) which are instrumental in producing: art ($\tau\acute{\epsilon}\chi\nu\eta$)— "and art arises when from many notions gained by experience one universal judgement about a class of objects is produced."[3] Art, Aristotle continues, is not here to be distinguished from "science" or knowledge ($\dot{\epsilon}\pi\iota\sigma\tau\acute{\eta}\mu\eta$) and involves a grasp of universals ($\tau\grave{\alpha}$ $\varkappa\alpha\theta\acute{o}\lambda o\upsilon$) while experience is a "knowledge" ($\gamma\nu\tilde{\omega}\sigma\iota\varsigma$) of particulars ($\tau\grave{\alpha}$ $\varkappa\alpha\theta$' $\check{\epsilon}\varkappa\alpha\sigma\tau o\nu$). In this sense, then, art leads to wisdom ($\sigma o\varphi\acute{\iota}\alpha$), that state or activity of mind which Aristotle places at the summit of the hierarchy he has so carefully constructed. And so he concludes this first chapter of Book A

---

[2] *Metaphysics* A, 980 a 21. Πάντες ἄνθρωποι τοῦ εἰδέναι ὀρέγονται φύσει.

[3] *Metaphysics* A, 981 a 5–7. γίγνεται δὲ τέχνη ὅταν ἐκ πολλῶν τῆς ἐμπειρίας ἐννοημάτων μία καθόλου γένηται περὶ τῶν ὁμοίων ὑπόληψις. Ross's text.

with these words: "The point of our present discussion is this, that all men suppose what is called Wisdom to deal with the first causes and the principles of things. This is why, as has been said before, the man of experience is thought to be wiser than the possessors of any perception whatever, the artist wiser than the men of experience, the master-worker than the mechanic, and the theoretical kinds of knowledge to be more of the nature of Wisdom than the productive. Clearly then Wisdom is knowledge about certain causes and principles."[4]

This atmosphere which asserts the primacy of causes, principles, the universal, and wisdom, is maintained in the following chapter. The wise man, Aristotle asserts, knows all things in so far as possible, though he does not know each of them as particulars, or in detail. He has the capacity to master things that are difficult (τὰ χαλεπά); he operates more accurately, and he is better able to teach causes; and he knows those subjects (or sciences—i.e., ἐπιστῆμαι) which are ends in themselves, rather than those which subserve some further end.[5] The "sciences" which deal with first principles, the universal, are the most difficult, the most important, and the most communicable.[6] "For he who chooses to know for the sake of knowing will choose most readily that which is most truly knowledge, and such is the knowledge of that which is most knowable; and the first principles and the causes are most knowable; for by reason of these, and from these, all other things are known, but these are not known by means of the things subordinate to them. And the science which knows to what end each thing must be done is the most authoritative of the sciences, and more authoritative than any ancillary science; and this end is the good in each class, and in general the supreme good in the whole of nature. Judged by all the tests we have mentioned, then, the name in question ['Wisdom'] falls to the same science; this must be a science that investigates the first

<hr />

[4] *Metaphysics* A, 981 b 27–982 a 3. οὗ δ' ἕνεκα νῦν ποιούμεθα τὸν λόγον τοῦτ' ἐστίν, ὅτι τὴν ὀνομαζομένην σοφίαν περὶ τὰ πρῶτα αἴτια καὶ τὰς ἀρχὰς ὑπολαμβάνουσι πάντες· ὥστε, καθάπερ εἴρηται πρότερον, ὁ μὲν ἔμπειρος τῶν ὁποιανοῦν ἐχόντων αἴσθησιν εἶναι δοκεῖ σοφώτερος, ὁ δὲ τεχνίτης τῶν ἐμπείρων, χειροτέχνου δὲ ἀρχιτέκτων, αἱ δὲ θεωρητικαὶ τῶν ποιητικῶν μᾶλλον. ὅτι μὲν οὖν ἡ σοφία περί τινας ἀρχὰς καὶ αἰτίας ἐστὶν ἐπιστήμη, δῆλον. Ross's text.

[5] *Metaphysics* A, 982 a 8–19.

[6] *Metaphysics* A, 982 a 21 ff.

principles and causes; for the good, *i.e.*, the end and aim is one of the causes."[7]

The implications of this passage for our argument are easy to point out. "Wisdom" is related closely to causes, universals, principles. These are intrinsically most knowable.[8] And Aristotle gives the palm to that "science which knows to what end each thing must be done," with this "end" being specified as "the good in each class" as well as "in general the supreme good *(τὸ ἄριστον)* in the whole of nature." And finally, in the concluding sentence, one of the causes, *i.e.*, the Final Cause, is identified with the good. So Wisdom is definitely concerned, according to Aristotle, with "good" (and hence, we can say, with "the problem of value") and we get the impression that he is thinking here to all intents and purposes like a Platonist. Certainly we are already fully familiar with Aristotle's characteristic way of identifying the good and the Final Cause.[9] Though, of course, we shall return to this problem in a later section[10] of this chapter, for the present it is worth noting the implied dichotomy in the phrase, ". . . this end is the good in each class, and in general the supreme good in the whole of nature."[11]

Perhaps two more passages from Book A will serve to indicate what we have called the "value climate" which this introductory section sets for the whole *Metaphysics*. In the third chapter, Aristotle begins his apparently historical treatment of the problem of causation in the earlier philosophers. After discussing Thales briefly, he mentions several others, Hippo, Anaximenes, Diogenes, Hippasus, Heraclitus, Empedocles, Anaxagoras, and Parmenides— mainly with respect to their views on the prime principle or

---

[7] *Metaphysics* A, 982 a 32–b 10. (ὁ γὰρ τὸ ἐπίστασθαι δι᾽ αὑτὸ αἱρούμενος τὴν μάλιστα ἐπιστήμην μάλιστα αἱρήσεται, τοιαύτη δ᾽ ἐστὶν ἡ τοῦ μάλιστα ἐπιστητοῦ) μάλιστα δ᾽ ἐπιστητὰ τὰ πρῶτα καὶ τὰ αἴτια (διὰ γὰρ ταῦτα καὶ ἐκ τούτων τἆλλα γνωρίζεται ἀλλ᾽ οὐ ταῦτα διὰ τῶν ὑποκειμένων), ἀρχικωτάτη δὲ τῶν ἐπιστημῶν, καὶ μᾶλλον ἀρχικὴ τῆς ὑπηρετούσης, ἡ γνωρίζουσα τίνος ἕνεκέν ἐστι πρακτέον ἕκαστον· τοῦτο δ᾽ ἐστὶ τἀγαθὸν ἑκάστου, ὅλως δὲ τὸ ἄριστον ἐν τῇ φύσει πάσῃ. ἐξ ἁπάντων οὖν τῶν εἰρημένων ἐπὶ τὴν αὐτὴν ἐπιστήμην πίπτει τὸ ζητούμενον ὄνομα· δεῖ γὰρ ταύτην τῶν πρώτων ἀρχῶν καὶ αἰτιῶν εἶναι θεωρητικήν· καὶ γὰρ τἀγαθὸν καὶ τὸ οὗ ἕνεκα ἓν τῶν αἰτίων ἐστίν. Ross's text.

[8] Cf. above, Chapter III, p. 61.

[9] Cf. above, Chapter V, pp. 123–124, 132–136, 137–138, 141–142, 147–149, 153–157, 159–161.

[10] Cf. below, Chapter VI, sections H and K.

[11] Cf. above, Chapter V, especially pp. 153–157.

principles underlying matter, *i.e.*, the material cause. Aristotle then closes the chapter in this way: "When these men and the principles of this kind had had their day, as the latter were found inadequate to generate the nature of things, men were again *forced by the truth itself*, as we said, to inquire into the next kind of cause. For surely it is not likely either that fire or earth or any such element should be the reason why things manifest goodness and beauty both in their being and in their coming to be, or that those thinkers should have supposed it was; nor again could it be right to ascribe so great a matter to spontaneity and luck. When one man[12] said, then, that reason was present— as in animals, so throughout nature—as the cause of the world and of all its order, he seemed like a sober man in contrast with the random talk of his predecessors, . . . Those who thought thus stated that there is a principle of things which is at the same time the cause of beauty, and that sort of cause from which things acquire movement."[13]

Whatever may be the merits of Aristotle's observations on the earlier philosophers or however accurate or inaccurate his testimony, the passage quoted does give us some important insight into Aristotle's own thinking with respect to values. First, when he uses the phrase, "forced by the truth itself," we can readily recognize Aristotle's characteristic attitude towards this "value," truth, and the compelling force and power inherent in it. Furthermore, we are entitled to point to a considerable awareness, on Aristotle's part, of the "problem of value." This is particularly evident when he criticizes the thinkers who assert fire or earth as first principles, on the ground that it is impossible to account for the goodness and beauty of things by appealing to such

---

[12] *i.e.*, Anaxagoras.

[13] *Metaphysics* A, 984 b 8–18; 20–22. μετὰ δὲ τούτους καὶ τὰς τοιαύτας ἀρχάς, ὡς οὐχ ἱκανῶν οὐσῶν γεννῆσαι τὴν τῶν ὄντων φύσιν, πάλιν ὑπ' αὐτῆς τῆς ἀληθείας, ὥσπερ εἴπομεν, ἀναγκαζόμενοι τὴν ἐχομένην ἐζήτησαν ἀρχήν. τοῦ γὰρ εὖ καὶ καλῶς τὰ μὲν ἔχειν τὰ δὲ γίγνεσθαι τῶν ὄντων ἴσως οὔτε πῦρ οὔτε γῆν οὔτ' ἄλλο τῶν τοιούτων οὐθὲν οὔτ' εἰκὸς αἴτιον εἶναι οὔτ' ἐκείνους οἰηθῆναι· οὐδ' αὖ τῷ αὐτομάτῳ καὶ τύχῃ τοσοῦτον ἐπιτρέψαι πρᾶγμα καλῶς εἶχεν. νοῦν δή τις εἰπὼν ἐνεῖναι, καθάπερ ἐν τοῖς ζῴοις, καὶ ἐν τῇ φύσει τὸν αἴτιον τοῦ κόσμου καὶ τῆς τάξεως πάσης οἷον νήφων ἐφάνη παρ' εἰκῇ λέγοντας τοὺς πρότερον. . . . οἱ μὲν οὖν οὕτως ὑπολαμβάνοντες ἅμα τοῦ καλῶς τὴν αἰτίαν ἀρχὴν εἶναι τῶν ὄντων ἔθεσαν, καὶ τὴν τοιαύτην ὅθεν ἡ κίνησις ὑπάρχει τοῖς οὖσιν. Ross's text. The italics are mine.

principles. The same attitude is apparent in his approval of the Anaxagorean principle of νοῦς as the cause of the κόσμος and its order *(τάξις)*, and of those who posited a principle which could be a cause of beauty and at the same time a cause of motion. Clearly Aristotle reveals his concern to account philosophically for the presence of "values" in things in nature or in the cosmos.

The other passage, which might even be called a *locus classicus* for Aristotle's comprehension of the basic questions of value, occurs when he reintroduces Empedocles into his discussion: "But since the contraries of various goods were also perceived to be present in nature—not only order and the beautiful, but also disorder and the ugly, and bad things in greater number than good, and ignoble things than beautiful, therefore another thinker[14] introduced friendship and strife, each of the two cause of one of these two sets of things. For if we were to follow out the view of Empedocles, and interpret it according to its meaning and not to its lisping expression, we should find that friendship is the cause of good things, and strife of bad. Therefore, if we said that Empedocles in a sense both mentions, and is the first to mention, the bad and the good as principles, we should perhaps be right, if that is to say the cause of all the goods is the good itself, and of the evils evil itself."[15]

[14] *i.e.*, Empedocles.

[15] *Metaphysics* A, 984 b 32–985 a 10. ἐπεὶ δὲ καὶ τἀναντία τοῖς ἀγαθοῖς ἐνόντα ἐφαίνετο ἐν τῇ φύσει, καὶ οὐ μόνον τάξις καὶ τὸ καλὸν ἀλλὰ καὶ ἀταξία καὶ τὸ αἰσχρόν, καὶ πλείω τὰ κακὰ τῶν ἀγαθῶν καὶ τὰ φαῦλα τῶν καλῶν, οὕτως ἄλλος τις φιλίαν εἰσήνεγκε καὶ νεῖκος, ἑκάτερον ἑκατέρων αἴτιον τούτων. εἰ γάρ τις ἀκολουθοίη καὶ λαμβάνοι πρὸς τὴν διάνοιαν καὶ μὴ πρὸς ἃ ψελλίζεται λέγων Ἐμπεδοκλῆς, εὑρήσει τὴν μὲν φιλίαν αἰτίαν οὖσαν τῶν ἀγαθῶν τὸ δὲ νεῖκος τῶν κακῶν· ὥστ' εἴ τις φαίη τρόπον τινὰ καὶ λέγειν καὶ πρῶτον λέγειν τὸ κακὸν καὶ τὸ ἀγαθὸν ἀρχὰς Ἐμπεδοκλέα, τάχ' ἂν λέγοι καλῶς, εἴπερ τὸ τῶν ἀγαθῶν ἁπάντων αἴτιον αὐτὸ τἀγαθόν ἐστι καὶ τῶν κακῶν τὸ κακόν. Ross's text except that I have removed the brackets from καὶ τῶν κακῶν τὸ κακόν. I have also modified the Oxford translation in the following places: In 984 b 2–333, I have rendered τοῖς ἀγαθοῖς as "the various goods" instead of Ross's "forms of good," which has a somewhat different philosophical meaning in English; in 985 a 3–4, I have rendered ἑκατέρων . . . τούτων as "these two sets of things," instead of Ross's "these two sets of qualities," again because in this passage the philosophical implications of the term "quality" in English are not supported by the neuter plural, τούτων, of the Greek text; and finally, I believe it an error to translate εἴπερ in 985 a 9 as "since." I have used "if that is to say," following Liddell and Scott, s.v. I notice that Cherniss, in commenting on this passage understands εἴπερ as "since," which, it seems to me, definitely changes the sense

Beyond doubt Aristotle shows in this analysis that it is incumbent upon a philosopher not only to explain the presence of "order" and the "beautiful" in things, but also to take into account their opposites, "disorder" and "the ugly." He even goes on to remark, somewhat ruefully, that men have observed in the world the numerical superiority of "bad things" over "good," and "ignoble things" *(τὰ φαῦλα)* over "beautiful things" *(τῶν καλῶν)*. In other words, Aristotle here explicitly recognizes what modern thinkers might call the problem of value and disvalue. But in his ensuing comments Aristotle seems to forget this question of the "cause of good and evil." He rather reverts to his ontological preoccupation, as he concentrates on the two causes, the material and the efficient, which these earlier thinkers had more or less clearly identified. Here at least the value question drops out of sight.

In the rest of Book A, there is very little which bears definitely on our main interest. To be sure, at the very end of the sixth chapter,[16] where Aristotle first turns his attention to the views of Plato and the Theory of Ideas, he gives a slight indication of the axiological function of the theory. Aristotle here observes that Plato has employed only two of the four causes, *viz.*, the material and the formal. Plato, he asserts, maintains that the Ideas are the "causes" of the "essence" *(τί ἐστιν)* of all else, whereas the One *(τὸ ἕν)* is the cause of the essence of the Ideas. Aristotle then continues: "And it is evident what the underlying matter is, of which the Ideas are predicated in the case of sensible things, and the One in the case of Ideas, *viz.*, that this is a dyad, the great and the small. Further, he has assigned the cause of good and that of evil to the elements, one to each of the two, as

---

of Aristotle's comment on this Empedoclean doctrine. In other words, if εἴπερ is rendered as "since," the implication is that Aristotle is plumping for the view that "the cause of all the goods is the good itself," whereas when εἴπερ is rendered as "if really," "if indeed," or "if that is to say," one preserves the basic view of Aristotle which would deny both the existence of the "good itself" *(αὐτὸ τἀγαθόν)* and its power to cause "all the goods." For Cherniss' reference to the passage, cf. *Aristotle's Criticism of Presocratic Philosophy*, pp. 222–223. In support of my view, cf. J. D. Denniston, *The Greek Particles*² (Oxford, Clarendon Press, 1954) pp. 487–489.

[16] *Metaphysics* A, 988 a 7–17.

we say some of his predecessors sought to do, *e.g.*, Empedocles and Anaxagoras."[17]

This is obviously and fortunately not the place to go into the vexed question of the One and the Indeterminate Dyad of the Great and Small, or to explore the reasons why Aristotle attributes this doctrine to Plato, or where in Plato's thought, either written or unwritten, Aristotle found his evidence for this ascription, or what finally is the relation between Ideas and Numbers in the Platonic position. Suffice it to say that neither in this chapter nor in the ninth, where a full-length attack on the Theory of Ideas appears, is there any other mention of the axiological function of the theory than this single concluding sentence which assigns the view to Plato that the One is the cause of good and the Indeterminate Dyad is the cause of evil. This fact is astonishing in itself, as we have already noted,[18] when we remember how the Ideas for Plato provide him simultaneously with the metaphysical grounds for his ontological as well as his value thinking. But the fact that Aristotle overlooks this supremely important dimension of Plato's thought in this very crucial Book A, the introduction to the *Metaphysics*, indicates not only the extent of Aristotle's preoccupation with the problem of Being but also how far from the center of his interests the investigation of the phenomena of evaluation lies.

The only other place in Book A where the question of value obtrudes is found in the brief seventh chapter, which Ross describes as a "summary account of the treatment of the four causes by earlier thinkers."[19] Here Aristotle maintains that several philosophers have denominated the material cause variously, "but certain others have mentioned the source of movement, *e.g.*, those who make friendship and strife, or reason, or love, a principle."[20] He goes on to say that, though no one has

[17] *Metaphysics* A, 988 a 11–17. [φανερὸν] καὶ τίς ἡ ὕλη ἡ ὑποκειμένη καθ᾽ ἧς τὰ εἴδη μὲν ἐπὶ τῶν αἰσθητῶν τὸ δ᾽ ἓν ἐν τοῖς εἴδεσι λέγεται, ὅτι αὕτη δυάς ἐστιν, τὸ μέγα καὶ τὸ μικρόν, ἔτι δὲ τὴν τοῦ εὖ καὶ τοῦ κακῶς αἰτίαν τοῖς στοιχείοις ἀπέδωκεν ἑκατέροις ἑκατέραν, ὥσπερ φαμὲν καὶ τῶν προτέρων ἐπιζητῆσαί τινας φιλοσόφων, οἷον Ἐμπεδοκλέα καὶ Ἀναξαγόραν. Ross's text. In the translation, I have used "Ideas" instead of "Forms" for τὰ εἴδη.

[18] Cf. above, Chapter II, pp. 52–56.

[19] Cf. Ross, *Metaphysics*, vol. I, p. 177.

[20] *Metaphysics* A, 988 a 33–34. ἕτεροι δέ τινες ὅθεν ἡ ἀρχὴ τῆς κινήσεως (οἷον ὅσοι φιλίαν καὶ νεῖκος ἢ νοῦν ἢ ἔρωτα ποιοῦσιν ἀρχήν) Ross's text.

treated the formal or "essential" cause satisfactorily, the Platonists have been the most successful. But his remarks on the treatment of the Final Cause by his predecessors are very relevant to our general argument: "That which is the end for which actions and changes and movements take place, they assert to be a cause in a way, but not in this way, *i.e.*, not in the way in which it is its *nature* to be a cause. For those who speak of reason or friendship class these causes as goods; they do not speak, however, as if anything that exists either existed or came into being for the sake of these, but as if movement started from these. In the same way those who say the One or the existent is the good, say that it is the cause of substance, but not that substance either is or comes to be for the sake of this. Therefore, it turns out that in a sense they both say and do not say the good is a cause; for they do not call it a cause *quâ* good but only incidentally."[21]

This statement is notable perhaps for two reasons. First, it indicates how, whenever he does think of the question of value, Aristotle links it with his conception of Final Cause. And second, the passage constrains us to wonder how in the world Aristotle could have so described Platonism, when he knew Plato and knew his writings. Even Ross, confirmed Aristotelian that he is, is compelled to say in a footnote, "The Platonists, who say the One or the existent is the good, are making goodness an accident of the formal cause as Anaxagoras and Empedocles make it an

[21] *Metaphysics* A, 988 b 6–16. τὸ δ' οὗ ἕνεκα αἱ πράξεις καὶ αἱ μεταβολαὶ καὶ αἱ κινήσεις τρόπον μέν τινα λέγουσιν αἴτιον, οὕτω δὲ οὐ λέγουσιν οὐδ' ὅνπερ πέφυκεν. οἱ μὲν γὰρ νοῦν λέγοντες ἢ φιλίαν ὡς ἀγαθὸν μὲν ταύτας τὰς αἰτίας τιθέασιν, οὐ μὴν ὡς ἕνεκά γε τούτων ἢ ὂν ἢ γιγνόμενόν τι τῶν ὄντων ἀλλ' ὡς ἀπὸ τούτων τὰς κινήσεις οὔσας λέγουσιν· ὡς δ' αὕτως καὶ οἱ τὸ ἓν ἢ τὸ ὂν φάσκοντες εἶναι τὴν τοιαύτην φύσιν τῆς μὲν οὐσίας αἴτιόν φασιν εἶναι, οὐ μὴν τούτου γε ἕνεκα ἢ εἶναι ἢ γίγνεσθαι, ὥστε λέγειν τε καὶ μὴ λέγειν πῶς συμβαίνει αὐτοῖς τἀγαθὸν αἴτιον· οὐ γὰρ ἀπλῶς ἀλλὰ κατὰ συμβεβηκὸς λέγουσιν. Ross's text. Perhaps τὸ ὄν of 988 b 12 might be better translated by "being" than by "the existent." Also I cannot get away from the feeling that it is inaccurate in this context to render τῆς μὲν οὐσίας (988 b 12–13) by the term "substance." Admittedly it is virtually impossible in many instances to find any adequate English equivalent for οὐσία. Perhaps here what is meant is the total being (essence + existence?) of any particular thing that is. Maybe "substance" in its technical sense conveys this notion. In any event, it is always very troublesome when Aristotle uses one of his own technical or semi-technical terms in the interpretation of the doctrine of another thinker. Witness how in Chapter 9 of Book A he speaks of Plato's Ideas as οὐσίαι. Certainly, according to Plato's philosophy, an Idea is not an οὐσία, in any sense of the senses in which Aristotle uses that term.

accident of the efficient cause; in neither case is the good made a cause in its own right, as the end of being and becoming. Aristotle ignores the distinctly teleological view which Plato expresses in some dialogues."[22] In any event, it is perfectly and completely clear that in the *Metaphysics*, as introduced by Book A, Aristotle's dominant interest is ontological, and in the ways in which his causal theory can illuminate ontology. And it may be that this over-riding interest is one of the main reasons why his treatment of Plato's Ideas seems so distorted, particularly in their value aspect.

So much then for a brief characterization of the "value climate" of Book A. Perhaps the most important conclusion we can draw is that implicit in this book is an awareness on Aristotle's part of the various basic issues raised by the question of value.

B. KNOWLEDGE, TRUTH, AND UNIVERSALS

As a preliminary to further discussion of the nature of Aristotle's value thinking in the *Metaphysics*, it will be desirable to examine a few passages in which we can observe the relationships obtaining between the Aristotelian conceptions of knowledge, universals and truth. In particular, of course, we shall be most interested in identifying the ways in which truth functions as a value.

Perhaps the best introduction to a consideration of these conceptions can be found in the opening lines of *Metaphysics* α,[23] where Aristotle remarks: "The investigation of the truth is in one way hard, in another easy. An indication of this is found in the fact that no one is able to attain the truth adequately, while, on the other hand, no one fails entirely, but everyone says something true about the nature of things, and while individually they contribute little or nothing to the truth, by the union of all a considerable amount is amassed. Therefore, if indeed the truth seems to be like the proverbial door, which no one can fail to

[22] *Metaphysics*, vol. I, p. 179, note on 988 b 11–14. Ross refers also to an earlier note on 988 a 9 where he cites several passages in Plato's *Phaedrus, Laws, Sophist, Timaeus* and *Philebus*. I wonder why he omits any reference to the *Phaedo* or the *Republic*.

[23] On the nature of this book and the question of its authenticity, cf. Ross, *Metaphysics*, vol. I, p. 213. I personally see no compelling reason for not regarding it as genuine.

hit, in this way it is easy, but the fact that we can have a whole truth and not the particular part we aim at shows the difficulty of it.

"Perhaps, as difficulties are of two kinds, the cause of the present difficulty is not in the facts but in us. For as the eyes of bats are to the blaze of day, so is the reason in our soul to the things which are by nature most evident of all."[24]

It may be, as Ross has suggested,[25] that *Metaphysics α* was "an introduction not to metaphysics but to physics or to theoretical philosophy in general," but in any case it is worth noting that Aristotle sets up the conception truth, *(ἀλήθεια)* as the ultimate objective of the person who speculates about "the nature of things" *(φύσις)* and therefore will be *the* value, or sanction of value, which is omnipresent throughout the speculative context. Though it may seem otiose or platitudinous to labour this point here, nevertheless it does seem necessary to emphasize every significant instance where Aristotle makes his own attitude explicit. Also in this passage, it should not escape our notice that Aristotle tempers his more usual view that in matters of first principles and through the use of syllogistic or "scientific" demonstration it is possible to arrive at certain truth. No one, he says, can "attain the truth adequately," but we all are in some measure successful. And finally in the passage, we get another expression of Aristotle's belief that reason *(νοῦς)* within our souls is the instrument which we employ in our efforts to attain truth.

The concluding paragraph of the first chapter of *Metaphysics α* gives us more precise evidence on Aristotle's conception of truth: "It is right also that philosophy should be called knowledge of the truth. For the end of theoretical knowledge is truth, while

[24] *Metaphysics α*, 993 a 30–b 11. Ἡ περὶ τῆς ἀληθείας θεωρία τῇ μὲν χαλεπὴ τῇ δὲ ῥαδία. σημεῖον δὲ τὸ μήτ᾽ ἀξίως μηδένα δύνασθαι θιγεῖν αὐτῆς μήτε πάντας ἀποτυγχάνειν, ἀλλ᾽ ἕκαστον λέγειν τι περὶ τῆς φύσεως, καὶ καθ᾽ ἕνα μὲν ἢ μηθὲν ἢ μικρὸν ἐπιβάλλειν αὐτῇ, ἐκ πάντων δὲ συναθροιζομένων γίγνεσθαί τι μέγεθος· ὥστ᾽ εἴπερ ἔοικεν ἔχειν καθάπερ τυγχάνομεν παροιμιαζόμενοι, τίς ἂν θύρας ἁμάρτοι; ταύτῃ μὲν ἂν εἴη ῥαδία, τὸ δ᾽ ὅλον τι ἔχειν καὶ μέρος μὴ δύνασθαι δηλοῖ τὸ χαλεπὸν αὐτῆς. ἴσως δὲ καὶ τῆς χαλεπότητος οὔσης κατὰ δύο τρόπους, οὐκ ἐν τοῖς πράγμασιν ἀλλ᾽ ἐν ἡμῖν τὸ αἴτιον αὐτῆς· ὥσπερ γὰρ τὰ τῶν νυκτερίδων ὄμματα πρὸς τὸ φέγγος ἔχει τὸ μεθ᾽ ἡμέραν, οὕτω καὶ τῆς ἡμετέρας ψυχῆς ὁ νοῦς πρὸς τὰ τῇ φύσει φανερώτατα πάντων. Ross's text. In the translation, I have used "if indeed" instead of "since" for εἴπερ in 993 b 4. Cf. above, note 15.

[25] Cf. above, note 23.

that of practical knowledge is action (for even if they consider how things are, practical men do not study the eternal, but in some relation and at some time). Now we do not know a truth without its cause; and each thing, in virtue of which a common nature belongs to the other things that have that nature, itself is (*i.e.*, has that nature) in a higher degree than the other things (*e.g.*, fire is the hottest of things; for it is the cause of the heat of all other things); so that that which causes derivative truths to be true is most true. Therefore the principles of eternal things must be always most true; for they are not merely sometimes true, nor is there any cause of their being, but they themselves are the cause of the being of other things, so that as each thing is in respect of being, so is it in respect of truth."[26] Throughout this passage, truth, we may suppose, has its most general meaning.[27] Philosophy is knowledge of truth in this sense. The pursuit of theoretical knowledge has truth as its goal, while "action" (ἔργον) is the goal of practical knowledge. So much is familiar enough Aristotelian doctrine, but what follows is particularly important for our discussion. Aristotle announces that truth or a truth or that which is true (τὸ ἀληθές) without the, or its, cause (τῆς αἰτίας) is something which we do not know. In other words, here in an epistemological setting truth and cause are linked tightly or almost functionally together. Truth leads to cause; no truth without cause.

What follows is even more significant. Truths, regarded as causes, are conceived as hierarchically arranged. That which

[26] *Metaphysics* α, 993 b 19–31. ὀρθῶς δ' ἔχει καὶ τὸ καλεῖσθαι τὴν φιλοσοφίαν ἐπιστήμην τῆς ἀληθείας. θεωρητικῆς μὲν γὰρ τέλος ἀλήθεια πρακτικῆς δ' ἔργον· καὶ γὰρ ἂν τὸ πῶς ἔχει σκοπῶσιν, οὐ τὸ ἀίδιον ἀλλὰ πρός τι καὶ νῦν θεωροῦσιν οἱ πρακτικοί. οὐκ ἴσμεν δὲ τὸ ἀληθὲς ἄνευ τῆς αἰτίας· ἕκαστον δὲ μάλιστα αὐτὸ τῶν ἄλλων καθ' ὃ καὶ τοῖς ἄλλοις ὑπάρχει τὸ συνώνυμον (οἷον τὸ πῦρ θερμότατον· καὶ γὰρ τοῖς ἄλλοις τὸ αἴτιον τοῦτο τῆς θερμότητος)· ὥστε καὶ ἀληθέστατον τὸ τοῖς ὑστέροις αἴτιον τοῦ ἀληθέσιν εἶναι. διὸ τὰς τῶν ἀεὶ ὄντων ἀρχὰς ἀναγκαῖον ἀεὶ εἶναι ἀληθεστάτας (οὐ γάρ ποτε ἀληθεῖς, οὐδ' ἐκείναις αἴτιόν τί ἐστι τοῦ εἶναι, ἀλλ' ἐκεῖναι τοῖς ἄλλοις), ὥσθ' ἕκαστον ὡς ἔχει τοῦ εἶναι, οὕτω καὶ τῆς ἀληθείας. Ross's text. I have modified the translation in two places: in 993 b 22 Ross's text reads οὐ τὸ ἀίδιον ἀλλὰ instead of οὐ τὸ αἴτιον καθ' αὑτὸ ἀλλὰ which he adopted when he originally made his translation; and for the rendering of ἕκαστον . . . συνώνυμον, 993 b 24–25, I have substituted Ross's translation given in his note *ad loc.*, since it is a great improvement over his earlier version in the Oxford translation.

[27] Cf. Ross, *Metaphysics*, vol. I, note on A, 983 b 2.

causes a derivative truth to be true is most true. As a consequence, the principles *(τὰς ἀϱχάς)*, and we can call these causes, of things that "always are" *(τῶν ἀεὶ ὄντων)* are the truest of all. Why? First, because they are not true at times and untrue at others. And second, because nothing causes them, *i.e.*, their being, but they are the cause of the being of other things. Note here how the additional conception of "being" is introduced into the argument. We now have three terms, *viz.*, cause, truth, being. They are interrelated, are all in a sense components of "things." The whole is summed up in the concluding phrase, a clause of result, "so that as each thing is in respect of being, so is it in respect of truth." So the result is that in the hierarchical order of things the degrees of truth and the degrees of being correspond precisely. They are uniformly copresent; the highest being, therefore, would seem to be the equivalent of the highest truth.

The foregoing doctrine naturally gives great comfort to the critic who wishes to minimize the differences between Plato and Aristotle. They can, and within certain limits, with perfect justification urge that here Aristotle is giving expression to the fundamental insight of the Theory of Ideas, and, indeed, in so far as truth is a value, and of course it is, he is in effect saying the more "real" a thing is, the more "valuable "it is. But a demurrer must be entered at this point, because "truth," as any one would agree, is *sui generis* among the range of values. Throughout our ensuing argument, as we deal now with the *Metaphysics*, and later when we come to the works on ethics, politics, and literary criticism, we will be faced with the problem of the relation of the value "truth" with values of the aesthetic and ethical orders. But for the moment perhaps it will be sufficient to point out that "truth" is marked off from other values because of its supreme ontological bearing. It inevitably centers on "being," whether it is taken in its broad sense, as we have it in this particular passage of *Metaphysics a*, or whether it is used in connection with propositions. At any rate, at this point in the *Metaphysics*, the doctrine of Aristotle is clear that "things" are true in proportion to the degree to which they "are." So it can be urged that we should look at the conception of truth in the *Metaphysics* in the perspective of the phrase from Book E, which we have already had occasion to quote, "The eternal question: What is Being?"[28] The really difficult problem is to see how Aristotle will move from this context of "Knowledge, Truth, and Universals" to that of "The Good, The Beautiful, and the *Telos*" to which we shall devote a later section of this chapter.[29]

Perhaps no other portion of the *Metaphysics* asserts the primacy of Being and knowledge of it in Aristotle's thought more explicitly than Book E. This is clearly announced in the opening sentence: "We are seeking the principles and the causes of things that are, and obviously of things *quâ* being."[30] By way of elaboration he proceeds to speak of various sciences which involve reasoning *(διάνοια)* and have to do with causes and principles, either simply or more precisely formulated. This leads him ultimately to distinguish among three kinds of thought, practical, productive, and theoretical. Physics, he avers, is a theoretical science, "but it will theorize about such being as admits of being moved, and only about that kind of substance which in respect of its definition is for the most part not separable from matter."[31] And a little further on, he completes his analysis of the three "theoretical philosophies": "For physics deals with things which are separable but not immovable, and some parts of mathematics deal with things which are immovable, but probably not separable, but embodied in matter; while the first science deals with things which are both separable and immovable. Now all causes must be eternal, but especially these; for they are the causes of so much of the divine as appears to us. There must then be three theoretical philosophies, mathematics, physics, and what we may call theology, since it is obvious that if the divine is present anywhere, it is present in things of this sort. And the highest science must deal with the highest genus, so that the theoretical sciences are superior to the other sciences, and this to the other theoretical sciences. One might indeed raise the

---

[28] Cf. above, Chapter I, p. 6 and note 3.

[29] Cf. below, Chapter VI, section H.

[30] *Metaphysics* E, 1025 b 3–4. Αἱ ἀρχαὶ καὶ τὰ αἴτια ζητεῖται τῶν ὄντων, δῆλον δὲ ὅτι ᾗ ὄντα. Ross's text. Cf. the similar thought expressed in the first sentence of Book Γ, 1003 a 21–22.

[31] *Metaphysics* E, 1025 b 26–28. ἀλλὰ θεωρητικὴ περὶ τοιοῦτον ὂν ὅ ἐστι δυνατὸν κινεῖσθαι, καὶ περὶ οὐσίαν τὴν κατὰ τὸν λόγον ὡς ἐπὶ τὸ πολὺ ὡς οὐ χωριστὴν μόνον. Ross's text.

question whether first philosophy is universal, or deals with one genus, *i.e.*, some one kind of being . . . . We answer that if there is no substance other than those which are formed by nature, natural science will be the first science; but if there is an immovable substance, the science of this must be prior and must be first philosophy, and universal in this way, because it is first. And it will belong to this to consider being *quâ* being—both what it is and the attributes which belong to it *quâ* being."[32]

There are a number of interesting points for us in this quotation. Among the three types of "theoretical science" or philosophy, it is of course standard Aristotelian doctrine to call "first philosophy" that which deals with both the "separable and immovable," *i.e.*, that which is absolutely without change and which possesses separate or independent existence. Perhaps we should pass over the difficulty involved in the meaning of Arisotle's opening proposition that "all causes must be eternal," upon which his subsequent argument is based.[33] At any rate, we can assume that the particular causes, or perhaps we had better say First Cause, he has in mind is eternal and separate, and is "the cause of so much of the divine as appears to us." This, of course, refers to the movement of the heavenly bodies, as Ross has pointed out.[34] The introduction of the notion of the divine gives to the passage a powerful value overtone, and we should note how Aristotle employs it. Why, in other words, does he call these causes, or

[32] *Metaphysics* E, 1026 a 13–25 and 27–32. ἡ μὲν γὰρ φυσικὴ περὶ χωριστὰ μὲν ἀλλ᾽ οὐκ ἀκίνητα, τῆς δὲ μαθηματικῆς ἔνια περὶ ἀκίνητα μὲν οὐ χωριστὰ δὲ ἴσως ἀλλ᾽ ὡς ἐν ὕλῃ· ἡ δὲ πρώτη καὶ περὶ χωριστὰ καὶ ἀκίνητα. ἀνάγκη δὲ πάντα μὲν τὰ αἴτια ἀίδια εἶναι, μάλιστα δὲ ταῦτα· ταῦτα γὰρ αἴτια τοῖς φανεροῖς τῶν θείων. ὥστε τρεῖς ἂν εἶεν φιλοσοφίαι θεωρητικαί, μαθηματική, φυσική, θεολογική (οὐ γὰρ ἄδηλον ὅτι εἴ που τὸ θεῖον ὑπάρχει, ἐν τῇ τοιαύτῃ φύσει ὑπάρχει), καὶ τὴν τιμιωτάτην δεῖ περὶ τὸ τιμιώτατον γένος εἶναι. αἱ μὲν οὖν θεωρητικαὶ τῶν ἄλλων ἐπιστημῶν αἱρετώταται, αὕτη δὲ τῶν θεωρητικῶν. ἀπορήσειε γὰρ ἄν τις πότερόν ποθ᾽ ἡ πρώτη φιλοσοφία καθόλου ἐστὶν ἢ περί τι γένος καὶ φύσιν τινὰ μίαν. . . . εἰ μὲν οὖν μὴ ἔστι τις ἑτέρα οὐσία παρὰ τὰς φύσει συνεστηκυίας, ἡ φυσικὴ ἂν εἴη πρώτη ἐπιστήμη· εἰ δ᾽ ἔστι τις οὐσία ἀκίνητος, αὕτη προτέρα καὶ φιλοσοφία πρώτη, καὶ καθόλου οὕτως ὅτι πρώτη· καὶ περὶ τοῦ ὄντος ᾗ ὂν ταύτης ἂν εἴη θεωρῆσαι, καὶ τί ἐστι καὶ τὰ ὑπάρχοντα ᾗ ὄν. Ross's text. The rendering is also that of Ross except in 1026 a 14, where in the translation he read ἀχώριστα, where in his text he has, and I think correctly, accepted Schwegler's emendation, χωριστά. Cf. Ross's note *ad loc*. At the end of the passage, Ross invites the reader to refer to two places in Book B, where Aristotle discusses this same problem, *viz.*, 995 b 10–13, and 997 a 15–25.

[33] Ross's note on 1026 a 16–18 may be helpful.

[34] Cf. his note to 1026 a 18 in his translation.

this First Cause, divine? Because he asserts that they are eternal, *i.e.*, ἀΐδια, a notion, it must be said, which has a primary onto-logical bearing.[35] In a sense, everything else in the argument derives from or is developed out of this assertion. First Philosophy is denominated theology, because it deals with this "divine," *i.e.*, eternal and separate, subject matter.

Then let us observe carefully how Aristotle builds his various hierarchies. He has set up his supreme ontological entity, First Cause, highest Being. Next he says, "The highest science must deal with the highest genus," and note that the words which Ross translates as "highest" are τιμιωτάτην and τιμιώτατον, that is, something which is most honoured, or to which most "value" can be assigned. So then, having indicated that the highest value is a derivative from the highest Being, he can assert that the theoretical sciences are to be preferred either to the practical or productive sciences, because their subject matter is "closer" to Being, so theology is to be preferred to physics or mathematics, for its subject matter is Being *quâ* Being. In other words again the degree of Being achieved by anything gives us a clue as to its worth. But let us not overlook the fact that this is not a two-way street, for the converse, that is, that value is a clue to the degree of Being, is not asserted. For evidence, all we need do is to look at the concluding sentences of the quotation, which answer the difficulty as to whether first philosophy is universal or not. Aristotle bases his argument here on the ontological notion of "substance" (οὐσία). If there are no other substances than natural οὐσίαι, then natural science will achieve "top billing." But "if there is an immovable substance," then its science will have priority. But the case on this point has already been decided, for the discussion began with the postulate that there was such an "immovable substance." As we have already urged, both "immovable" and "substance" are ontological conceptions, and here, decidedly, value judgments are based upon them. So then, this "science of the immovable substance" is called "first philosophy," and "universal because it is first." And so Aristotle

---

[35] Ross, in his note *ad loc.*, maintains that this assertion must be made if we are to avoid infinite regress, and refers us back to the argument of *Metaphysics* a, chapter 2.

concludes by saying, "And it will belong to this to consider being *quâ* being." It would be difficult to find a clearer expression of the degree to which ontology, pure and simple, is dominant in Aristotle's thought.[36]

There is one other section of Book E of the *Metaphysics* which demands our attention in the present context. In the fourth and final chapter, Aristotle takes up again the conception of truth, this time relating it precisely to propositions and the principle of contradiction. And in this connection he makes the following very interesting observation: "For falsity and truth are not in things—it is not as if the good were true and the bad were itself false—but in thought; while with regard to simple objects and essences falsity and truth do not exist even in thought. We must consider later[37] what has to be discussed with regard to that which is or is not in this sense; but since the combination and the separation are in thought and not in the things, and that which is in this sense is a different sort of 'being' from the things that are in the full sense (for the thought attaches or removes either the 'what' or quality or quantity or one of the other categories), that which *is* accidentally and that which *is* in the sense of being true must be dismissed. For the cause of the former is indeterminate, and that of the latter is some affection of the thought, and both are related to the remaining genus of being, and do not indicate any separate class of being."[38]

It is completely clear that Aristotle is introducing a different notion of "truth" from the one we have been considering thus

---

[36] I expect we should not leave this passage without commenting on the cautious way in which Aristotle speaks of the objects of mathematics as "things which are immovable but probably not separable, but embodied in matter." It seems impossible to see how the "metaphysics of the τόδε τι" can ever deal with *mathematica* to any very satisfactory degree. It also should be noted that the same argument of *Metaphysics* E, 1026 a 13–32 is found in *Metaphysics* K, 1064 a 28–b 14.

[37] Here Ross in his translation refers us to *Metaphysics* Θ, chapter 10.

[38] *Metaphysics* E, 1027 b 25–1028 a 2. οὐ γάρ ἐστι τὸ ψεῦδος καὶ τὸ ἀληθὲς ἐν τοῖς πράγμασιν, οἷον τὸ μὲν ἀγαθὸν ἀληθὲς τὸ δὲ κακὸν εὐθὺς ψεῦδος, ἀλλ' ἐν διανοίᾳ, περὶ δὲ τὰ ἁπλᾶ καὶ τὰ τί ἐστιν οὐδ' ἐν διανοίᾳ . . . ὅσα μὲν οὖν δεῖ θεωρῆσαι περὶ τὸ οὕτως ὄν καὶ μὴ ὄν, ὕστερον ἐπισκεπτέον· ἐπεὶ δὲ ἡ συμπλοκή ἐστιν καὶ ἡ διαίρεσις ἐν διανοίᾳ ἀλλ' οὐκ ἐν τοῖς πράγμασι, τὸ δ' οὕτως ὄν ἕτερον τῶν κυρίως (ἢ γὰρ τὸ τί ἐστιν ἢ ὅτι ποιὸν ἢ ὅτι ποσὸν ἢ τι ἄλλο συνάπτει ἢ διαιρεῖ ἡ διάνοια), τὸ μὲν ὡς συμβεβηκὸς τὸ ὡς ἀληθὲς ὄν ἀφετέον. . . . τὸ γὰρ αἴτιον τοῦ μὲν ἀόριστον τοῦ δὲ τῆς διανοίας τι πάθος, καὶ ἀμφότερα περὶ τὸ λοιπὸν γένος τοῦ ὄντος, καὶ οὐκ ἔξω δηλοῦσιν οὐσάν τινα φύσιν τοῦ ὄντος. Ross's text. As a translation of τὰ ἁπλᾶ in 1027 b 27, I have substituted "objects" for "concepts."

far in this section of our discussion, that is, the "truth" with regard to "simple objects and essences" where "falsity and truth do not exist even in thought." As Ross quite correctly remarks, "The only alternatives are apprehension of them and non-apprehension."[39] Aristotle here is dealing, as we indicated above, with the truth and falsity of propositions where, by the activity of "thought," statements are forged by abstracting from the "objects" quantity, quality, and so on, and by weaving these together either correctly or incorrectly. But is it too much to ask why Aristotle in his parenthetical comment says "It is not as if the good were true and the bad were itself false"? Apart from equating the good with "true" and the bad with "false," which is puzzling enough in itself, the whole phrase suggests some kind of value system which exists not objectively, but somehow subjectively, ἐν διανοίᾳ, "in thought."

Far more typical of Aristotle's attitude towards "truth" and how we may validate our judgements about it is a brief comment in *Metaphysics* K: "In general, it is absurd to make the fact that the things of this earth are observed to change and never to remain in the same state, the basis of our judgement about the truth. For in pursuing the truth one must start from the things that are always in the same state and suffer no change. Such are the heavenly bodies; for these do not appear to be now of one nature and again of another, but are manifestly always the same and share in no change."[40] Here Aristotle sees in the permanences of the heavenly bodies that objective element in the Universe which can provide us with a solid basis for our "judgement about the truth."

In concluding this present section, let us turn to two passages from the *Metaphysics* which can give us the essential character of Aristotle's conception of ἐπιστήμη, knowledge, and its relation to its object. And here we should recall our previous remarks concerning the dilemma of the Aristotelian metaphysics of the τόδε τι, which asserts that one cannot "know" the ultimately real

---

[39] Cf. Ross's note on 1027 b 28.

[40] *Metaphysics* K, 1063 a 10–17. ὅλως δὲ ἄτοπον ἐκ τοῦ φαίνεσθαι τὰ δεῦρο μεταβάλλοντα, καὶ μηδέποτε διαμένοντα ἐν τοῖς αὐτοῖς, ἐκ τούτου περὶ τῆς ἀληθείας τὴν κρίσιν ποιεῖσθαι· δεῖ γὰρ ἐκ τῶν ἀεὶ κατὰ ταὐτὰ ἐχόντων καὶ μηδεμίαν μεταβολὴν ποιουμένων τἀληθὲς θηρεύειν, τοιαῦτα δ᾽ ἐστὶ τὰ κατὰ τὸν κόσμον· ταῦτα γὰρ οὐχ ὁτὲ μὲν τοιαδὶ πάλιν δ᾽ ἀλλοῖα φαίνεται, ταὐτὰ δ᾽ ἀεὶ καὶ μεταβολῆς οὐδεμιᾶς κοινωνοῦντα. Ross's text.

τόδε τι, but only the universals which inhere in it and thus have an inferior ontological status. Also we should not forget that aspect of Aristotle's epistemology which maintains that somehow in the knowing process the thinking intelligence and the object of its thought become one and the same.

The first passage for our consideration occurs in *Metaphysics* K, where Aristotle explicitly recognizes his epistemological dilemma: "A further difficulty is raised by the fact that all knowledge is of universals and of the 'such,' but substance does not belong to universals, but is rather a 'this'—a separable thing, so that if there is knowledge about the first principles, the question arises, how. are we to suppose the first principle to be substance?"[41] It seems safe to say that Aristotle was never able to resolve this difficulty. The individual particular is unknowable, though it "harbours" many knowable universals. But what of the ontological status of the "first principles," the ἀρχαί? Can they ever be regarded as οὐσίαι, on a par with the individual particular, the τόδε τι? Within the Aristotelian framework this appears not to be possible. Yet, the alternative would be to view the ἀρχαί as hypostatizations, but this is equally unacceptable to Aristotle in view of his rejection of the Platonic Theory of Ideas. We can only conclude that the difficulty is an inevitable consequence of the ontology and epistemology entailed by the Aristotelian metaphysics of the individual particular.

We cannot leave this problem without looking at Aristotle's extra, and unsuccessful, effort to solve it. In the final chapter of *Metaphysics* M, he writes: "The statement that all knowledge is of the universal, so that the principles of things must also be universal and not separate substances, presents indeed, of all the points we have mentioned, the greatest difficulty, but yet the statement is in a sense true, although in a sense it is not. For knowledge, like the verb 'to know,' means two things, of which one is potential and one actual. The potency, being, as matter,

---

[41] *Metaphysics* K, 1060 b 19–23. παρέχει δ' ἀπορίαν καὶ τὸ πᾶσαν μὲν ἐπιστήμην εἶναι τῶν καθόλου καὶ τοῦ τοιουδί, τὴν δ' οὐσίαν μὴ τῶν καθόλου εἶναι, μᾶλλον δὲ τόδε τι καὶ χωριστόν, ὥστ' εἰ περὶ τὰς ἀρχάς ἐστιν ἐπιστήμη, πῶς δεῖ τὴν ἀρχὴν ὑπολαβεῖν οὐσίαν εἶναι; Ross's text. Cf. *Metaphysics* B, 1003 a 5–17, where the same difficulty is stated at somewhat greater length. For further discussion of the problem see *Metaphysics* Z, chapters 13–15.

universal and indefinite, deals with the universal and indefinite; but the actuality, being definite, deals with a definite object— being a 'this,' it deals with a 'this.' But *per accidens* sight sees universal colour, because this individual colour which it sees is colour; and this individual *a* which the grammarian investigates is an *a*. For if the principles must be universal, what is derived from them must also be universal, as in demonstrations; and if this is so, there will be nothing capable of separate existence—*i.e.*, no substance. But evidently in a sense, knowledge is of the universal, and in a sense it is not."[42]

As far as one can grasp the import of this passage, Aristotle by invoking his familiar notions of actuality and potentiality is attempting to extricate himself from the toils of the problem. Nowhere else in his writing does he offer this current solution, which is not consistent with his regularly held position, *viz.*, (1) the ultimate reality of the τόδε τι; (2) the unknowability or indefinability of the τόδε τι;[43] and (3) knowledge, ἐπιστήμη, is of universals. But one is constrained to wonder how much Aristotle really has accomplished by invoking a distinction between "potential" ἐπιστήμη and "actual" ἐπιστήμη. We gather that the former refers to the standard conception that knowledge is of universals. By the latter we are invited to believe that, when knowledge is "in act," it grasps its objects as a kind of universal and particular rolled into one. This solution finally fails to satisfy, for even when knowledge is "in act," what it apprehends are still the universals that inhere in the particular, and the particular in all its infinite complexity continues to remain beyond the reach of knowledge.

---

[42] *Metaphysics* M, 1087 a 10–25. τὸ δὲ τὴν ἐπιστήμην εἶναι καθόλου πᾶσαν, ὥστε ἀναγκαῖον εἶναι καὶ τὰς τῶν ὄντων ἀρχὰς καθόλου εἶναι καὶ μὴ οὐσίας κεχωρισμένας, ἔχει μὲν μάλιστ' ἀπορίαν τῶν λεχθέντων, οὐ μὴν ἀλλὰ ἔστι μὲν ὡς ἀληθὲς τὸ λεγόμενον, ἔστι δ' ὡς οὐκ ἀληθές. ἡ γὰρ ἐπιστήμη, ὥσπερ καὶ τὸ ἐπίστασθαι, διττόν, ὧν τὸ μὲν δυνάμει τὸ δὲ ἐνεργείᾳ. ἡ μὲν οὖν δύναμις ὡς ὕλη [τοῦ] καθόλου οὖσα καὶ ἀόριστος τοῦ καθόλου καὶ ἀορίστου ἐστίν, ἡ δ' ἐνέργεια ὡρισμένη καὶ ὡρισμένου, τόδε τι οὖσα τοῦδέ τινος, ἀλλὰ κατὰ συμβεβηκὸς ἡ ὄψις τὸ καθόλου χρῶμα ὁρᾷ ὅτι τόδε τὸ χρῶμα ὃ ὁρᾷ χρῶμά ἐστιν, καὶ ὃ θεωρεῖ ὁ γραμματικός, τόδε τὸ ἄλφα ἄλφα· ἐπεὶ εἰ ἀνάγκη τὰς ἀρχὰς καθόλου εἶναι, ἀνάγκη καὶ τὰ ἐκ τούτων καθόλου, ὥσπερ ἐπὶ τῶν ἀποδείξεων· εἰ δὲ τοῦτο, οὐκ ἔσται χωριστὸν οὐθὲν οὐδ' οὐσία. ἀλλὰ δῆλον ὅτι ἔστι μὲν ὡς ἡ ἐπιστήμη καθόλου, ἔστι δ' ὡς οὔ. Ross's text. I have slightly modified the translation in 1087 a 11 by inserting the definite article before "universal," following Tredennick in the Loeb translation.

[43] This is the burden of *Metaphysics* Z, chapter 15.

Aristotle might have offered a slightly more convincing resolution of the difficulty had he invoked his view of the identity or near-identity of οὐσία as "primary substance" and οὐσία as τὸ τί ἦν εἶναι, "substance as essence."[44] But even though such an approach might have been more fruitful, it still would fail for the same reason that the distinction between "potential knowledge" and "knowledge in act," failed. After all, in Aristotle's view, οὐσία as τόδε τι cannot be made identical with οὐσία as τὸ τί ἦν εἶναι, essence. The doctrine of the indefinability and the unknowability of the τόδε τι remains to block any solution.[45]

It may be thought that we have spent too much time in discussing what we have called Aristotle's "ontological and epistemological dilemma." The answer to such a criticism would be to the effect that if one is interested in the problem of the relation of Being and Value one has to pay particular attention to the consequences for a thinker who is predominantly preoccupied with ontology. Aristotle's ontology declares that the individual particular is ultimately real, and, as we have remarked before, he had to devise an epistemology which would accord with his ontology. The epistemology he developed is basically empiricist and Aristotle becomes, at least in many aspects of his thought what Santayana called him, "a naturalist through and through."[46] But finally there is too much of Plato in Aristotle to permit him to be a "naturalist through and through." In so far as he is not a naturalist, he falls victim to the ontological and epistemological dilemma. In so far as he is a naturalist, he is not able to develop an adequate theory of value.

C. THE PLACE OF THE RELATIVE AND THE NECESSARY

Aristotle's view of the relative, πρός τι, in the *Metaphysics* should be briefly examined because of its obvious implications

---

[44] Cf. the discussion of this view above, pp. 75 ff.

[45] Ross in his note on *Metaphysics* M, 1087 a 13, somewhat reluctantly admits the inconsistency between the doctrine here advanced and the standard Aristotelian conception of knowledge. Cf. J. Tricot, *Aristote. La Métaphysique* (Paris, J. Vrin, 1953), who in his note on *Metaphysics* M, 1087 a 18 remarks, "Cette conception de la science est, dans l'esprit même de l'Aristotélisme, inadmissible." Cf. also Tricot's note on *Metaphysics* Z, 1040 b 4.

[46] Cf. J. H. Randall, Jr., *Aristotle* (New York, Columbia University Press, 1960) pp. 103 and 138–40.

for the question of value. One typical reference should suffice for us at this point. In *Metaphysics* Γ, we read "But if not all things are relative, but some are self-existent, not everything that appears will be true; for that which appears appears to some one; so that he who says that all things that appear are true, makes all things relative."[47] Here Aristotle succinctly declares himself as a non-relativist, while at the same time in the sentences which follow he takes fully into account those aspects of the human condition which are inescapably relative. In other words, because of the objective stability of certain elements in reality, Aristotle will never become a thoroughgoing relativist. In fact, this short passage can be regarded as Aristotle's anwer to the Protagorean doctrine of Man the Measure. And it should be added that the attitude here expressed gives a certain degree of coherence to Aristotle's treatment of value at various points in his works.

The conception of the Necessary, τὸ ἀναγκαῖον, in Aristotle's thought can also be analyzed briefly with respect to its relevance to the question of value. In *Metaphysics* Δ, he devotes a chapter to this notion, of which one section is important for us: "[The necessary means] . . . the conditions without which good cannot be or come to be, or without which we cannot get rid or be freed of evil, *e.g.*, drinking the medicine is necessary in order that we may be cured of disease, and sailing to Aegina is necessary in order that we may get our money."[48] It is interesting to note that of the several meanings of "necessary" Aristotle singles out one to define the term in a value context, as a "necessary condition" for the achieving of good and the being freed of evil. This notion appears to have possibilities, but we perhaps may be a little disappointed at the common-sensical tone introduced by the illustrations of disease as an evil and money as a good.

In the famous seventh chapter of *Metaphysics* Λ, Aristotle employs this sense of the Necessary as he argues to establish the

---

[47] *Metaphysics* Γ, 1011 a 17–20. εἰ δὲ μὴ ἔστι πάντα πρός τι, ἀλλ᾽ ἔνιά ἐστι καὶ αὐτὰ καθ᾽ αὐτά, οὐκ ἂν εἴη πᾶν τὸ φαινόμενον ἀληθές· τὸ γὰρ φαινόμενον τινί ἐστι φαινόμενον· ὥστε ὁ λέγων ἅπαντα τὰ φαινόμενα εἶναι ἀληθῆ ἅπαντα ποιεῖ τὰ ὄντα πρός τις. Ross's text.

[48] *Metaphysics* Δ, 1015 a 22–26. [Ἀναγκαῖον λέγεται] . . . ὧν ἄνευ τὸ ἀγαθὸν μὴ ἐνδέχεται ἢ εἶναι ἢ γενέσθαι, ἢ τὸ κακὸν ἀποβαλεῖν ἢ στερηθῆναι (οἷον τὸ πιεῖν τὸ φάρμακον ἀναγκαῖον ἵνα μὴ κάμνῃ, καὶ τὸ πλεῦσαι εἰς Αἴγιναν ἵνα ἀπολάβῃ τὰ χρήματα). Ross's text.

existence and worth of the Unmoved Mover. "The first mover, then, of necessity exists; and in so far as it is necessary, it is good, and in this sense a first principle. For the necessary has all these senses—that which is necessary perforce because it is contrary to the natural impulse, that without which the good is impossible, and that which cannot be otherwise but is *absolutely* necessary."[49] The text here is probably as important as any for the light it throws on Aristotle's thinking in the realm of value. Earlier in the chapter, fundamentally by invoking his axiom οὐκ εἰς ἄπειρον, "nothing to infinity" he postulates a Mover who is himself unmoved, and whom he calls ἀΐδιον καὶ οὐσία καὶ ἐνέργεια, "being eternal, substance, and actuality."[50] A few lines later Aristotle advances his view that this Unmoved Mover moves by being loved. But how can this Mover be an object of love or desire? Aristotle in some way must show him to be good.[51] The method employed is interesting, to say the least. Remaining clearly within the limits of ontology, Aristotle asserts that the heavenly bodies, the first things moved by the Unmoved Mover, are only otherwise than they are with respect to their primary circular motion, *i.e.*, they are "changed" only with respect to place. Since the Unmoved Mover must move them, he must *necessarily* exist. Having then introduced the notion of the necessary, Aristotle can now use it to move from the domain of ontology to that of axiology. After all, has he not insisted that one of the meanings of the necessary is that without which the good is impossible? Hence if the Prime Mover exists of necessity, he therefore must be good and as such certainly can qualify as an object of love.

M. Tricot, in his French translation of the *Metaphysics*, calls this argument *délicate*.[52] It is probably all of that. Surely one

---

[49] *Metaphysics* Λ, 1072 b 10–13. ἐξ ἀνάγκης ἄρα ἐστὶν ὄν· καὶ ᾗ ἀνάγκη, καλῶς, καὶ οὕτως ἀρχή. τὸ γὰρ ἀναγκαῖον τοσαυταχῶς, τὸ μὲν βίᾳ ὅτι παρὰ τὴν ὁρμήν, τὸ δὲ οὗ οὐκ ἄνευ τὸ εὖ, τὸ δὲ μὴ ἐνδεχόμενον ἄλλως ἀλλ' ἁπλῶς. Ross's text. Cf. J. Chevalier, *La Notion du Necessaire chez Aristote* (Paris, 1915) pp. 141–142. For further study of this passage in context, see below, Chapter VI, section I, especially pp. 232 ff.

[50] *Metaphysics* Λ, 1072 a 25.

[51] For the way in which Aristotle had already sought to establish the goodness of the Unmoved Mover, see below, Chapter VI, section I, pp. 228–232.

[52] *op. cit.*, p. 679.

cannot help but feel a certain circularity in it, for out of the postulation of the Prime Mover on the basis of the οὐκ εἰς ἄπειρον axiom, we suddenly find that He exists of necessity, and as a result of this situation, we are told that He is good. Is one justified in calling this metaphysical legerdemain? Is it correct to assert that Aristotle's ontological preoccupation produces for him a Prime Mover, a God, who, from the point of view of value, in this context, is neutral until the notion of the Necessary permits Aristotle to argue that He is good. Can it be that Aristotle wishes us to think of τὸ ἀναγκαῖον, Necessity, as the matrix of value?

In conclusion, it is not unimportant to observe how Aristotle proceeds after he has established the existence and worth of his Prime Mover. He appears to be relieved, for he writes with unction the famous lines (1072b 13–30)[53] which are at the heart of his theology and which have been built into the thought of Saint Thomas Aquinas. Listen to the closing words of this passage: "And life also belongs to God; for the actuality of thought is life, and God is that actuality; and God's essential actuality is life most good and eternal. We say therefore that God is a living being, eternal, most good, so that life and duration continuous and eternal belong to God; for this *is* God."[54]

D. PARENTHESIS: THE "NORMAL MAN"
AS A VALUE SANCTION

Before dealing with values as they appear under the category "quality," it is appropriate to mention one typical passage in which the so-called "normal man" is to be trusted, according to Aristotle, in questions involving value judgements. In *Metaphysics* K he writes: "But to lend oneself equally to the opinions and the fancies of disputing parties is foolish; for clearly one of them must be mistaken. And this is evident from what happens

---

[53] For a further treatment of this passage, see below, pp. 232 ff.

[54] *Metaphysics* Λ, 1072 b 26–30. καὶ ζωὴ δέ γε ὑπάρχει· ἡ γὰρ νοῦ ἐνέργεια ζωή, ἐκεῖνος δὲ ἡ ἐνέργεια· ἐνέργεια δὲ ἡ καθ᾽ αὑτὴν ἐκείνου ζωὴ ἀρίστη καὶ ἀΐδιος. φαμὲν δὴ τὸν θεὸν εἶναι ζῷον ἀΐδιον ἄριστον, ὥστε ζωὴ καὶ αἰὼν συνεχὴς καὶ ἀΐδιος ὑπάρχει τῷ θεῷ. τοῦτο γὰρ ὁ θεός. Ross's text. For further discussion of God as the Unmoved Mover, see below, section I of the present chapter.

in sensation; for the same thing never appears sweet to some and bitter to others, unless in the one case the sense organ which discriminates the aforesaid flavours has been perverted and injured. And if this is so the one party must be taken to be the measure, and the other must not. And I say the same of good and bad, and beautiful and ugly, and all other such qualities."[55]

In the chapter from which this quotation is taken Aristotle is attacking the Protagorean doctrine of Man the Measure. It is not surprising to find the argument built upon an analogy with sensation. The same thing never appears sweet to one man and bitter to another under normal circumstances. If such a situation should arise, it can only be explained on the ground that the sense organ of one of the parties in the "dispute" has been damaged, *i.e.*, is "abnormal." Hence the person with the "normal" un-damaged sense organ is to be trusted. It is indeed tantalizing that Aristotle has not developed further his meaning when he adds, "I say the same of good and bad, and beautiful and ugly, and all other such qualities." We can only infer that in disputes about "values" Aristotle is recommending that we side with the "normal" man in such a situation. But who is the "normal" man in a value dispute? On the analogy with sensation, he can only be the person who possesses unimpaired the moral and aesthetic instruments by which he forges his value judgements.

It may not be fanciful to suggest that in this "value" context Aristotle is thinking of the "normal man," as we have called him, in much the same way as he thinks of the $\varphi\varrho\acute{o}\nu\iota\mu\sigma\varsigma$, the man of practical wisdom. Consider the famous definition of virtue: "Virtue, then, is a state of character concerned with choice, being in a mean which is relative to us, and which is determined by

---

[55] *Metaphysics* K, 1062 b 33–1063 a 6. τό γε μὴν ὁμοίως προσέχειν ταῖς δόξαις καὶ ταῖς φαντασίαις τῶν πρὸς αὐτοὺς διαμφισβητούντων εὔηθες· δῆλον γὰρ ὅτι τοὺς ἑτέρους αὐτῶν ἀνάγκη διεψεῦσθαι. φανερὸν δὲ τοῦτ' ἐκ τῶν γιγνομ-ένων κατὰ τὴν αἴσθησιν· οὐδέποτε γὰρ τὸ αὐτὸ φαίνεται τοῖς μὲν γλυκὺ τοῖς δὲ τοὐναντίον, μὴ διεφθαρμένων καὶ λελωβημένων τῶν ἑτέρων τὸ αἰσθητήριον καὶ κριτήριον τῶν λεχθέντων χυμῶν. τούτου δ' ὄντος τοιούτου τοὺς ἑτέρους μὲν ὑποληπτέον μέτρον εἶναι τοὺς δ' ἄλλους οὐχ ὑποληπτέον. ὁμοίως δὲ τοῦτο λέγω καὶ ἐπὶ ἀγαθοῦ καὶ κακοῦ, καὶ καλοῦ καὶ αἰσχροῦ, καὶ τῶν ἄλλων τῶν τοιούτων. Ross's text. The same point is covered in *Metaphysics* Γ, 1010 b 1–26, but it is interesting to note that in this earlier passage Aristotle says nothing of "good and bad and beautiful and ugly."

reason or that by which the man of practical wisdom would define it."[56] We shall of course treat in detail the rôle of the φρόνιμος when we come to discuss the question of value in Aristotle's ethical thinking. At that time it will be important to recall the present passage from *Metaphysics* K.

E. VALUE AS QUALITY

In our study of the relation of Being and Value, Aristotle's view of the category, ποιόν, quality, is highly significant. Nowhere does he express more clearly his commitment to the primacy of Being and his more or less conscious conviction that Value must be assigned a secondary status. We shall analyze several passages from the *Metaphysics* in the effort to establish this point. Perhaps the best section to consider at the outset is the fourteenth chapter of the philosophical lexicon, *Metaphysics* Δ, which Aristotle devotes to a discussion of "quality." He suggests that the term has four meanings: (1) the essential differentia, ἡ διαφορὰ τῆς οὐσίας, e.g., man is two-footed; (2) the essence of the objects of mathematics; (3) the attributes of substances in motion; and (4) virtue and vice, and in general, evil and good.

Let us examine the remainder of the chapter in full: "Quality, then, seems to have practically two meanings, and one of these is the more proper. The primary quality is the essential differentia, and of this the quality in numbers is a part; for it is a differentia of essences, but either not of things in motion or not of them *quâ* in motion. Secondly, there are the modifications of things in motion *quâ* in motion, and the differentiae of movements. Virtue and vice fall among these modifications; for they indicate differentiae of the movement or activity, according to which the things in motion act or are acted on well or badly; for that which can be moved or act in one way is good, and that which can do so in another—the contrary—way is vicious. Good and evil indicate quality especially in living things, and among these

---

[56] *Nicomachean Ethics* II, 1106 b 36–1107 a 2. Ἔστιν ἄρα ἡ ἀρετὴ ἕξις προαιρετική, ἐν μεσότητι οὖσα τῇ πρὸς ἡμᾶς, ὡρισμένη λόγῳ καὶ ᾧ ἂν ὁ φρόνιμος ὁρίσειεν. Bywater's text. The rendering is mine.

especially in those which have purpose [or purposive choice]."[57]

We should first note that in this second paragraph of the chapter Aristotle reduces the four kinds of "quality" to two more general classes. These two general classes are to be distinguished by the fact that in the former Aristotle's approach to his problem is from the "static" point of view, while in the latter he is conducting his analysis from a "dynamic" stance, that is, he is looking at things as they are subject to motion and change.[58] Secondly, in his conception of quality, Aristotle's emphasis is overwhelmingly ontological and logical. "The primary quality is the essential differentia." In other words, "quality" and what we could call "value" coincide only in the fourth type in the first analysis, and in a subdivision of the second general class when the approach is dynamic. This passage then constitutes another instance of Aristotle's asserting the primacy of ontology with the consequence that questions of value are reduced to a rôle of secondary or derivative importance.

The concluding sentences of the chapter deserve further consideration. Here "virtue" and vice" (ἀρετή and κακία) are regarded as "modifications" or "affections" (παθήματα) of "things in motion" (τὰ ἐν κινήσει ὄντα) and are to be applied to these "things in motion," "virtue" if the things act or are acted upon "well" (καλῶς) and "vice" if the things act or are acted upon "badly" (φαύλως). Then in the next sentence Aristotle substitutes "good" (ἀγαθόν) and "vicious" (μοχθηρόν) for "virtue" and "vice." Apparently, we are invited to believe that "things in motion" (certainly this is an all-inclusive designation for everything that can act or be acted upon) can have attached to them the qualitative terms "virtuous" or "vicious" depending upon whether they act

---

[57] *Metaphysics* Δ, 1020 b 13–25. σχεδὸν δὴ κατὰ δύο τρόπους λέγοιτ' ἂν τὸ ποιόν, καὶ τούτων ἕνα τὸν κυριώτατον· πρώτη μὲν γὰρ ποιότης ἡ τῆς οὐσίας διαφορά (ταύτης δέ τι καὶ ἡ ἐν τοῖς ἀριθμοῖς ποιότης μέρος· διαφορὰ γάρ τις οὐσίων, ἀλλ' ἢ οὐ κινουμένων ἢ οὐχ ᾗ κινούμενα), τὰ δὲ πάθη τῶν κινουμένων ᾗ κινούμενα, καὶ αἱ τῶν κινήσεων διαφοραί. ἀρετὴ δὲ καὶ κακία τῶν παθημάτων μέρος τι· διαφορὰς γὰρ δηλοῦσι τῆς κινήσεως καὶ τῆς ἐνεργείας, καθ' ἃς ποιοῦσιν ἢ πάσχουσι καλῶς ἢ φαύλως τὰ ἐν κινήσει ὄντα· τὸ μὲν γὰρ ὡδὶ δυνάμενον κινεῖσθαι ἢ ἐνεργεῖν ἀγαθὸν τὸ δ' ὡδὶ καὶ ἐναντίως μοχθηρόν. μάλιστα δὲ τὸ ἀγαθὸν καὶ τὸ κακὸν σημαίνει τὸ ποιὸν ἐπὶ τῶν ἐμψύχων, καὶ τούτων μάλιστα ἐπὶ τοῖς ἔχουσι προαίρεσιν. Ross's text.

[58] Cf. the distinction made above in our study of the metaphysics of the individual particular, Chapters III and IV.

or are acted upon "well or badly." It is needless to point out that these observations do not help us very much in coping with the question of value, for there is nothing here to indicate what the criteria may be in terms of which we might determine that any given "action" or "passion" is virtuous or vicious. Perhaps this is an unfair stricture, since it could be argued that in a short chapter of a philosophical lexicon devoted to working definitions of important terms, Aristotle could hardly be expected to elaborate a "value theory" even though the term under consideration was "quality." Yet on the other hand, it might be urged that this chapter is just another instance where Aristotle's ontological preoccupation results in a pervasive vagueness when the question of value obtrudes itself.

The very last sentence of the chapter is not without interest, for here Aristotle does indicate the special sphere of morality in which the terms "good" and "evil" (τὸ ἀγαθόν and τὸ κακόν) signify quality. The repetition of μάλιστα shows how Aristotle wishes to delineate as sharply as possible this moral domain where the words "good" and "evil" will have their fullest meaning. They are *especially* applicable in the area of "living things" and among these *especially* to those "living things" which are capable of "purposive choice," that is, to men. But it must be added that the moral qualities of "good" and "evil" are in a secondary status when they are "attached" to an individual particular man when he puts into action his purposive choice.

The opening chapter of *Metaphysics* Z expresses this same attitude towards the secondary or dependent status of "quality" which Aristotle consistently maintains as a consequence of his doctrine of the categories. He opens the book with a consideration of the various meanings of "Being" (τὸ ὄν), and then immediately goes on to say: "While 'being' has all these senses, obviously that which 'is' primarily is the 'what,' which indicates the substance of the thing. For when we say of what quality a thing is, we say that it is good or bad, but not that it is three cubits long or that it is a man; but when we say *what* it is, we do not say 'white' or 'hot' or 'three cubits long,' but 'man' or 'God.' "[59]

---

[59] *Metaphysics* Z, 1028 a 13–18. τοσαυταχῶς δὲ λεγομένου τοῦ ὄντος φανερὸν ὅτι τούτων πρῶτον ὂν τὸ τί ἐστιν, ὅπερ σημαίνει τὴν οὐσίαν (ὅταν μὲν γὰρ

A few lines later Aristotle makes his position even more explicit: "Now these [*i.e.*, qualities, quantities, affections, etc.] are seen to be more real because there is something definite which underlies them; and this is the substance or individual, which is implied in such a predicate; for 'good' or 'sitting' apart from that which sits or is good has no meaning."[60]

Two points here are worth noting. In the first place, Aristotle introduces a "degrees of reality" theory when he uses the phrase μᾶλλον ὄντα, "more real," to describe the qualities and affections under discussion. They are so designated, their ontological status specified, because of their indissoluble relation with an individual particular, the τόδε τι which is fully real and capable of separate existence. Secondly, values as qualities belong to or are subsumed under the general class of attributes, affections, and the like, so that a "value" conceived as a quality is incapable of separate existence. Thus τὸ ἀγαθόν, "the good," is asserted to have no meaning without something that is good.

In this connection, it is necessary to refer again to a passage which we have already discussed in part when we were analyzing Aristotle's views with respect to the nature or "problem" of evil:[61] "Clearly, then, the bad does not exist apart from bad things; for the bad is in its nature posterior to the potency. And therefore we may also say that in the things which are from the beginning, *i.e.*, in eternal things, there is nothing bad, nothing defective, nothing perverted (for perversion is something bad)."[62] At this juncture it is enough to note that

---

εἴπωμεν ποῖόν τι τόδε, ἢ ἀγαθὸν λέγομεν ἢ κακόν, ἀλλ' οὐ τρίπηχυ ἢ ἄνθρωπον· ὅταν δὲ τί ἐστιν, οὐ λευκὸν οὐδὲ θερμὸν οὐδὲ τρίπηχυ, ἀλλὰ ἄνθρωπον ἢ θεόν). Ross's text. The text in line 16 reads κακόν, while Ross in his translation read καλόν. He also in his note *ad loc.* points to the irrelevancy of τρίπηχυ in line 16. Aristotle possibly was careless here, but I suppose that he could be defended by saying that τρίπηχυ denotes a quantity, and so could be used here where the discussion is centered on quality.

[60] *Metaphysics* Z, 1028 a 25–29. ταῦτα δὲ μᾶλλον φαίνεται ὄντα, διότι ἔστι τι τὸ ὑποκείμενον αὐτοῖς ὡρισμένον (τοῦτο δ' ἐστὶν ἡ οὐσία καὶ τὸ καθ' ἕκαστον), ὅπερ ἐμφαίνεται ἐν τῇ κατηγορίᾳ τῇ τοιαύτῃ· τὸ ἀγαθὸν γὰρ ἢ τὸ καθήμενον οὐκ ἄνευ τούτου λέγεται. Ross's text.

[61] Cf. above, Chapter IV, p. 99.

[62] *Metaphysics* Θ, 1051 a 17–21. δῆλον ἄρα ὅτι οὐκ ἔστι τὸ κακὸν παρὰ τὰ πράγματα· ὕστερον γὰρ τῇ φύσει τὸ κακὸν τῆς δυνάμεως. οὐκ ἄρα οὐδ' ἐν τοῖς ἐξ ἀρχῆς καὶ τοῖς ἀϊδίοις οὐθὲν ἔστιν οὔτε κακὸν οὔτε ἁμάρτημα οὔτε διεφθαρμένον (καὶ γὰρ ἡ διαφθορὰ τῶν κακῶν ἐστίν). Ross's text.

"bad" *(τὸ κακόν)* is viewed as a quality, incapable of separate existence— it cannot be said to be unless it inheres in something which is bad. Furthermore, Aristotle, as we have remarked in Chapter IV above, relates this conception of "bad" with "potency" *(δύναμις)*. By its nature it is posterior to potency. On the basis of this contention, that is, that "bad" can emerge only from a potency or potentiality that is capable of either a good or a bad actualization, Aristotle can argue that in the case of "eternal things" (we may suppose here that Aristotle has in mind the Unmoved Mover and the heavenly bodies) there is no trace of potentiality and therefore in them there can be "nothing bad, nothing defective, nothing perverted."

But at this point we must examine with great care the portion of chapter 9 of *Metaphysics* Θ which immediately precedes the passage which we have just quoted. This chapter is indeed as important as any other in connection with the basic thesis with respect to Being and Value which we have been attempting to develop.[63] Let us then have the full text of the passage before us.

"That the [good] actuality is better and more valuable than the good potency is evident from the following argument. Everything of which we say that it can do something, is alike capable of contraries, *e.g.*, that of which we say that it can be well is the same as that can be ill, and has both potencies at once; for one and the same potency is a potency of health and illness, of rest and motion, of building and throwing down, of being built and of being thrown down. The capacity for contraries is present at the same time; but contraries cannot be present at the same time, and the actualities also cannot be present at the same time, *e.g.*, health and illness. Therefore one of them must be the good, but the capacity is both the contraries alike, or neither; the actuality, then, is better. And in the case of bad things, the end or actuality must be worse than the potency; for that which 'can' is both contraries alike."[64]

[63] Again cf. above, Chapter IV, pp. 99-101. At this point we shall try to expand the argument contained in those pages.

[64] *Metaphysics* Θ, 1051 a 4-17. Ὅτι δὲ καὶ βελτίων καὶ τιμιωτέρα τῆς σπουδαίας δυνάμεως ἡ ἐνέργεια, ἐκ τῶνδε δῆλον. ὅσα γὰρ κατὰ τὸ δύνασθαι λέγεται, ταὐτόν ἐστι δυνατὸν τἀναντία, οἷον τὸ δύνασθαι λεγόμενον ὑγιαίνειν ταὐτόν ἐστι καὶ τὸ νοσεῖν, καὶ ἅμα· ἡ αὐτὴ γὰρ δύναμις τοῦ ὑγιαίνειν καὶ κάμνειν, καὶ ἠρεμεῖν καὶ κινεῖσθαι, καὶ οἰκοδομεῖν καὶ καταβάλλειν, καὶ οἰκοδομεῖσθαι

On the surface of it, this argument seems to be clear. We have presented to us a kind of scale of worth or value which could be represented as follows:

1. The "good actuality" = that which is valuable.
2. Potentiality = neutral in the value scale.
3. The "bad actuality" = that which is "disvaluable."

In other words the "good actuality" is as much better than potency or potentiality as potency is better than the "bad actuality." But on closer inspection the passage is puzzling and appears to be rather carelessly written. In the first place, the phrase, τῆς σπουδαίας δυνάμεως, is strange in that a potency is called good or excellent (σπουδαία) in the first sentence whereas at a later stage potencies are considered to be neutral from the point of view of value since they are capable of becoming either one or the other of a pair of opposites, e.g., "good" or "bad." Furthermore, the sentence, "Therefore one of them must be the good, but the capacity is both the contraries alike, or neither; the actuality, then, is better," is not without difficulty.

Part of Ross's note on these lines may help us in understanding the problem: "Bonitz complains that Aristotle suggests that of any two contraries one must be good, and thus introduces good and evil into regions where they are inappropriate. But Aristotle does not make this mistake. He takes only the δυνάμεις which *would* be called good (1.4), and shows that they are really neutral, and are called good only because we forget the bad actualizations of which they are capable; and that therefore the good actualization is better than the potentiality. His only mistake is in calling one thing better than another when the other is strictly speaking not good at all but neutral."[65]

καὶ καταπίπτειν. τὸ μὲν οὖν δύνασθαι τἀναντία ἅμα ὑπάρχει· τὰ δ' ἐναντία ἅμα ἀδύνατον, καὶ τὰς ἐνεργείας δὲ ἅμα ἀδύνατον ὑπάρχειν (οἷον ὑγιαίνειν καὶ κάμνειν), ὥστ' ἀνάγκη τούτων θάτερον εἶναι τἀγαθὸν, τὸ δὲ δύνασθαι ὁμοίως ἀμφότερον ἢ οὐδέτερον· ἢ ἄρα ἐνέργεια βελτίων. ἀνάγκη δὲ καὶ ἐπὶ τῶν κακῶν τὸ τέλος καὶ τὴν ἐνέργειαν εἶναι χεῖρον τῆς δυνάμεως· τὸ γὰρ δυνάμενον ταὐτὸ ἄμφω τἀναντία. Ross's text. I have bracketed "good" as the qualifier of ἐνέργεια in 1051 a 5 since it is not to be found in the Greek, but I suppose is to be inferred from 1051 a 15–16, ἀνάγκη through δυνάμεως.

[65] Note on 1051 a 13–15.

This note surely indicates the nature of the tangle which results from Aristotle's failure to face the problem of the relation of Being and Value. Bonitz' complaint is understandable, if one holds the position he evidently does, namely, that "good" and "evil" should not be "introduced into regions that are inappropriate." If one concentrates exclusively on ontology, as evidently Bonitz thinks that Aristotle should, then the introduction of "good" and "evil" at this point is indeed inappropriate. But the fact of the matter is that in this passage Aristotle does introduce "good" and "evil," and, I should argue, because his thinking is not clear on Being and Value, his commentators are sorely put to it to explain the difficulty. Ross's additional thought does not seem to be very helpful either. What is his real evidence that Aristotle "takes only the δυνάμεις which *would* be called good and shows that they are really neutral, and are called good only because we forget the bad actualizations of which they are capable?" How in the world does Ross know that we forget the "bad actualizations?" Aristotle was not forgetting them. After all, towards the end of the passage under study, does he not say: "And in the case of bad things, the end or actuality must be worse than the potency?" Furthermore, the whole notion that "neutrality" has no place in a value scale, as Ross would have us believe, is rather strange. Certainly, when Aristotle gives us the sequence "good actuality," "potentiality," and "bad actuality," he is inviting us to look at these three as being perfectly able to be compared with one another from the point of view of value.

It is clear that the difficulty arises because Aristotle's theory of potentiality and actuality simply does not accommodate itself as a ground for a theory of value or worth. It must be said that it does so in part for we have already noted instances where end or goal or actuality (τέλος and ἐνέργεια) have been deeply associated with "good," and have therefore taken on unmistakeable value overtones. But in the present passage we are thrown off by the introduction of the notion of a "bad actuality" and Aristotle does not vary his terms when he speaks of it: "And in the case of bad things, the end or actuality (τὸ τέλος καὶ τὴν ἐνέργειαν) must be worse than the potency."

The concluding paragraph of Ross's note on 1051 a 17–21 is

relevant at this juncture. "The reasoning in ll. 17–19 involves, as Bonitz shows, a fallacy of equivocation. For actuality is prior to potentiality, according to Aristotle's view, in *reality* or substantiality (this was what was argued in 1050 a 4–1051 a 3), while potentiality is prior to the bad in *worth* (this was what was argued) in 1051 a 15–17). When the bad is shown to be posterior to the potentiality (in worth), it is treated as one of the contrary actualizations of the potentiality. But then it must be prior to the potentiality in reality, according to the argument of 1050 a 4–1051 a 3)." The consequence of it all is that, given the implications for the relation of Being and Value inherent in the Aristotelian conceptions of potentiality and actuality, one cannot deal with a question of worth in the context of potentiality and actuality without equivocation. In other words, the passage we have been studying suggests some kind of "parity" relation between Being and Value and we have seen that such a relation cannot be made to cohere with the Aristotelian view of potentiality and actuality. When all is said and done, the question of worth for Aristotle must remain subordinate to and dependent upon the question of Being.

There is one other feature of this passage that is troublesome. It derives, I think, from the illustrations which Aristotle employs. He begins by remarking that a thing that can be well also can be ill, and possesses both potencies at once. He then asserts that "one and the same potency is a potency of health and illness, of rest and motion, of building and throwing down, of being built and being thrown down." Note that the various "actualites" or "actualizations" mentioned are all "states" or "affections" of some one given thing. A man can be sick or well. Every individual particular can be at rest or in motion. A man can build or tear down. A structure can be built or torn down. So here Aristotle is not thinking of the actualization of a "thing" as he often does (*e.g.*, an acorn becoming an oak) but of the actualizations of affections. The contraries he lists are familiar enough, but it is noteworthy that rest, motion, building, tearing down, being built, and being torn down are only ontologically significant. We then cannot fail to be startled when Aristotle announces, "Therefore one of them must be the good," when only one of his pairs of contraries, "health and illness," could be subsumed under the axiological contraries of good and evil. Is this just carelessness, or can it be that Aristotle's ingrained ontological habit of mind prevents him from dealing adequately with situations which have simultaneously ontological and axiological dimensions?

F. SUBSTANCE AND PRIORITY

Aristotle's treatment of "priority" and its close affiliation with οὐσία in the sense of substance as individual particular exhibits once again the complete dominance of ontology in his thought. For example in chapter 11 of *Metaphysics* Δ, which he devotes to the terms "prior" and "posterior," he discusses three ways in which they can be used, and then adds a fourth to which the other three may ultimately be reduced:[66] "Some things then are called prior and posterior in this sense, others in respect of nature and substance, *i.e.*, those which can be without other things, while the others cannot be without them."[67] There could be no more explicit statement of Aristotle's conviction with respect to the priority of an οὐσία capable of separate existence. To cite one more example of this attitude: "For neither in formula nor in time nor in generation can the affections be prior to the substance; for then they would be separable from it."[68]

Implicit in the view thus set forth is that any axiological question can have, so to say, only a secondary status. However, in *Metaphysics* B, Aristotle makes a casual remark which does relate "prior" to "better." In his discussion of species, genera, and principles, he makes this observation: "But in the indivisible

---

[66] Cf. *Metaphysics* Δ, 1019 a 11–12.

[67] *Metaphysics* Δ, 1019 a 1–4. τὰ μὲν δὴ οὕτω λέγεται πρότερα καὶ ὕστερα, τὰ δὲ κατὰ φύσιν καὶ οὐσίαν, ὅσα ἐνδέχεται εἶναι ἄνευ ἄλλων, ἐκεῖνα δὲ ἄνευ ἐκείνων μή. Ross's text. Incidentally, Aristotle concludes the sentence here quoted by adding ᾗ διαιρέσει ἐχρήσατο Πλάτων, "a distinction which Plato used." Scholars cannot discover a passage in the Platonic corpus in which this distinction is made. Ross, in his note *ad loc.*, concludes that "Aristotle is thinking doubtless of an oral utterance of his master."

[68] *Metaphysics* Z, 1038 b 27–29. οὔτε λόγῳ γὰρ οὔτε χρόνῳ οὔτε γενέσει οἶόν τε τὰ πάθη τῆς οὐσίας εἶναι πρότερα· ἔσται γὰρ καὶ χωριστά. Ross's text. In the translation, I have changed "knowledge" to "generation." When he did the translation, Ross had accepted Lord's emendation γνώσει for γενέσει.

species one member is not prior and another posterior. Further, where one is better and another worse, the better is always prior; so that of these also no genus can exist."[69] Such passing comments, which are potentially important from the point of view of value, are, to say the least, tantalizing for Aristotle does not expand upon them. We are left to wonder about the criteria upon the basis of which a thing may be validly judged to be better or worse. Nor are we helped very much in this connection by a relevant passage in the *Categories*. In chapter 12 Aristotle is discussing the meaning of "prior" and gives the following as one of the senses in which the term may be used: "That which is better and more honourable is said to have a natural priority. In common parlance men speak of those whom they honour and love as 'coming first' with them. This sense of the word is perhaps the most far-fetched."[70] So far as the question of value is concerned Aristotle here is obviously at his most perfunctory. The passage reduces the matter of worth to the conventional responses of men, "what the many usually say." The Greek, as the Oxford translator has managed to convey, is colloquial and even slangy. And when he calls this sense of the word "prior" ἀλλοτριώτταος, "the most far-fetched" or "alien," "strange" or "foreign," Aristotle can hardly be said to be seriously involved in the question at issue.

One more passage remains to be discussed before leaving the conception of priority. It occurs in the famous seventh chapter of *Metaphysics* Λ, and, though it does not mention specifically the term "prior," the notion is clearly present by implication. "For the thinking is the starting point. And thought is moved by the object of thought, and one side of the list of opposites is in itself the object of thought; and in this, substance is first, and in substance, that which is simple and exists actually. . . . But the good, also, and that which is in itself desirable are on this same side of the list; and the first in any class is always best, or analogous

---

[69] *Metaphysics* B, 999 a 12–14. ἐν δὲ τοῖς ἀτόμοις οὐκ ἔστι τὸ μὲν πρότερον τὸ δ' ὕστερον. ἔτι ὅπου τὸ μὲν βέλτιον τὸ δὲ χεῖρον, ἀεὶ τὸ βέλτιον πρότερον· ὥστ' οὐδὲ τούτων ἂν εἴη γένος. Ross's text.

[70] *Categories* 14 a 4–8. τὸ βέλτιον καὶ τὸ τιμιώτερον πρότερον εἶναι τῇ φύσει δοκεῖ. εἰώθασι δὲ καὶ οἱ πολλοὶ τοὺς ἐντιμοτέρους καὶ μᾶλλον ἀγαπωμένους ὑπ' αὑτῶν προτέρους φάσκειν παρ' αὑτοῖς εἶναι. ἔστι μὲν δὴ καὶ σχεδὸν ἀλλοτρι-ώτατος τῶν τρόπων οὗτος. Bekker's text.

to the best."[71] Just exactly what Aristotle means by "one side" or "one column of the list of opposites" must remain enigmatic though in all probability it must go back in some way to the ten principles, arranged in pairs, of the Pythagorean school.[72] And, as Ross has pointed out in the note just referred to, Aristotle "recognizes a positive συστοιχία or column including such terms as being, unity, substance, and a negative συστοιχία including not-being, plurality, not-substance." Some such conception as this must have been in his mind. In any event, in our quotation Aristotle begins with reality, *i.e.*, with ontology. There is thought and the object of thought, and that which is primary (or ultimately "prior," we can say) is substance, οὐσία generally conceived, and within substances thus generally conceived is that which is absolutely primary, namely, substance or οὐσία which "is simple and exists actually." This is our οὐσία as τέλος, discussed above in Chapter IV, "substance as end."[73] And it is at this point that Aristotle does his familiar shift into the area of value, even though here the ground for the shift seems to be slight indeed. At any rate, Aristotle announces that "on the same side of the list" as substance are to be found τὸ καλόν (which Ross translates as "the good") and "that which is in itself desirable." And so he concludes by asserting that this "first" (it is difficult to determine exactly what Aristotle means here by τὸ πρῶτον) is "always the best" or "analogous" to it.

I suppose that the most one can do with this passage is to cite it as a typical instance of Aristotle's moving from an initial ontological analysis in the context of the Prime Mover into the area of value which it must have if the Aristotelian "system" is to stand.

G. ACTUALITY AND POTENTIALITY: DISVALUE

Having now seen how the conceptions of substance and priority reflect the dominance of ontology in Aristotle's thought, we may

---

[71] *Metaphysics* Λ, 1072 a 30–b 1. ἀρχὴ γὰρ ἡ νόησις. νοῦς δὲ ὑπὸ τοῦ νοητοῦ κινεῖται, νοητὴ δὲ ἡ ἑτέρα συστοιχία καθ' αὑτήν· καὶ ταύτης ἡ οὐσία πρώτη, καὶ ταύτης ἡ ἁπλῆ καὶ κατ' ἐνέργειαν. . . . ἀλλὰ μὴν καὶ τὸ καλὸν καὶ τὸ δι' αὑτὸ αἱρετὸν ἐν τῇ αὐτῇ συστοιχίᾳ· καὶ ἔστιν ἄριστον ἀεὶ ἢ ἀνάλογον τὸ πρῶτον. Ross's text. I have omitted the parenthesis, 1072 a 32–34, as not germane to the matter in hand.

[72] Cf. *Metaphysics* A, 986 a 22–26. See Ross's note on *Metaphysics* Λ, 1072 a 31 where he gives other references on Aristotle's use of the conception of συστοιχία.

[73] Cf. above, pp. 113 ff.

return with profit to consider actuality and potentiality with a view particularly to consider further how "potentiality" or "potency" functions as a source of "disvalue." We have discussed at length the very significant passage in the ninth chapter of *Metaphysics* Θ[74] where potency is identified as that from which a "bad actualization" may arise. Our present purpose is to review other places in the *Metaphysics* where the same point of view is either expressed or implied.[75]

For example, in the fourth chapter of *Metaphysics* Δ, which is devoted to potentiality, δύναμις, Aristotle describes the term in its passive sense as follows: "The case of passivity is similar. . . . The states in virtue of which things are absolutely impassive or unchangeable, or not easily changed for the worse, are called potencies."[76] Here the potency which can, though with difficulty, be "changed for the worse" is clearly the origin of the state of "disvalue" that will ensue after the change has taken place. We must add that we are not enlightened as to how or by what standard the thing can be said to have become worse. And, furthermore, it is curious that Aristotle should have chosen to mention "worse" rather than "better," for according to the theory the potency is capable of becoming the one just as much as the other.

In the discussion of "the complete" (τέλειον) a little later in *Metaphysics* Δ we have further evidence of the way in which Aristotle's mind works in this matter. He remarks that "the complete" means: "That which in respect of excellence and goodness cannot be excelled in its kind, *e.g.*, a doctor is complete and a flute-player is complete, when they lack nothing in respect of their proper kind of excellence. And thus we transfer the word to bad things, and speak of a complete scandal-monger and a complete thief; indeed we even call them *good*, *i.e.*, a good thief and a good scandal-monger. . . . Moreover, the things which have attained a good end are called complete; for things are

---

[74] 1051 a 4–21. Cf. above, pp. 191–196.

[75] The reader should bear in mind here our discussion of Aristotle's treatment of Empedocles, *Metaphysics* A, 984 b 32–985 a 10. See above, pp. 168–169.

[76] *Metaphysics* Δ, 1019 a 26–28. ὁμοίως δὲ καὶ ἐπὶ τοῦ πάσχειν. ἔτι ὅσαι ἕξεις καθ' ἃς ἀπαθῆ ὅλως ἢ ἀμετάβλητα ἢ μὴ ῥᾳδίως ἐπὶ τὸ χεῖρον εὐμετακίνητα, δυνάμεις λέγονται. Ross's text.

complete in virtue of having attained their end. Therefore, since the end is something ultimate, we transfer the word to bad things and say a thing has been completely spoilt, and completely destroyed, when it in no way falls short of destruction and badness, but is at its last point. This is why death is by a figure of speech called the end, because both are last things. The ultimate purpose is also an end."[77]

We already have had occasion to refer to this quotation when we were discussing a passage of similar import above.[78] But here our attention must fall upon the way in which Aristotle deals with what we surely are entitled to call a "bad actualization." We certainly have no difficulty in understanding his notion of the excellence of the complete and good doctor or flute-player. But then, almost in the manner of certain of our own contemporary philosophers who make so much of "ordinary speech" or how we talk normally, Aristotle points to the conventional transfer of the conception "complete" to "bad things." So we meet the "complete scandal-monger" and the "complete thief" and these become the equivalent of the "good thief" and the "good scandal-monger." And then after he goes on to mention the use of the word "complete" to refer to things "which have attained a good end," he similarly introduces the notion of transference to "bad things." Things are "completely spoilt" or "completely destroyed" when the job is really done to perfection. Also he refers to the "figure of speech" *(μεταφορά)* by which death *(τελευτή)* is called the end *(τέλος)*. Perhaps it may not be unfair to say that Aristotle in the present passage is not facing squarely the difficulty

---

[77] *Metaphysics* Δ, 1021 b 14–20 and 1021 b 23–30. καὶ τὸ κατ' ἀρετὴν καὶ τὸ εὖ μὴ ἔχον ὑπερβολὴν πρὸς τὸ γένος, οἷον τέλειος ἰατρὸς καὶ τέλειος αὐλητὴς ὅταν κατὰ τὸ εἶδος τῆς οἰκείας ἀρετῆς μηθὲν ἐλλείπωσιν (οὕτω δὲ μεταφέροντες καὶ ἐπὶ τῶν κακῶν λέγομεν συκοφάντην τέλειον καὶ κλέπτην τέλειον, ἐπειδὴ καὶ ἀγαθοὺς αὐτούς, οἷον κλέπτην ἀγαθὸν καὶ συκοφάντην ἀγαθόν. . . . ἔτι οἷς ὑπάρχει τὸ τέλος, σπουδαῖον ‹ὄν›, ταῦτα λέγεται τέλεια· κατὰ γὰρ τὸ ἔχειν τὸ τέλος τέλεια, ὥστ' ἐπεὶ τὸ τέλος τῶν ἐσχάτων τί ἐστι, καὶ ἐπὶ τὰ φαῦλα μεταφέροντες λέγομεν τελείως ἀπολωλέναι καὶ τελείως ἐφθάρθαι, ὅταν μηδὲν ἐλλείπῃ τῆς φθορᾶς καὶ τοῦ κακοῦ ἀλλ' ἐπὶ τῷ ἐσχάτῳ ᾖ· διὸ καὶ ἡ τελευτὴ κατὰ μεταφορὰν λέγεται τέλος, ὅτι ἄμφω ἔσχατα· τέλος δὲ καὶ τὸ οὗ ἕνεκα ἔσχατον. Ross's text with 1021 a 20–23 omitted.

[78] Cf. the treatment of *Physics*, 246 a 10–17, above pp. 136–138. See especially note 42, where we had occasion to quote *Metaphysics* Δ, 1021 a 20–23, the passage omitted in note 77.

involved in a "bad actualization."[79] In each instance he resorts to, or, one might even say, hides behind either the conception of metaphor or the conventional habits of normal speech.

That Aristotle continues to be worried by this question is evident in various passages in his great book, *Metaphyscs* Θ, which is devoted to a searching analysis of potentiality and actuality. For example, in the very first chapter, after mentioning the relation of being or substance to the other categories, Aristotle turns to the subject of his book, *viz.*, how "being" can be looked at in the perspective of potentiality and actuality. He then repeats the primary definition of potentiality as a principle or beginning (ἀρχή) of change in something else or in the thing itself *quâ* other.[80] But a rather strange statement follows: "And another kind is a state of insusceptibility to change for the worse and to destruction by another thing or by the thing itself *quâ* other, *i.e.*, by a principle of change. In all these definitions is implied the formula of potency in the primary sense. . . . And again these so-called potencies are potencies either of acting merely or of being acted on, or of acting or being acted on *well*, so that even in the formulae of the latter the formulae of the prior kinds of potency are somehow implied."[81] It appears to be strange for here, in the midst of a context which analytically is strictly ontological, Aristotle twice introduces a value notion. One, the reference to the "state of insusceptibility to change for the worse and to destruction," is puzzling in that it refers only to the possibility of change "for the worse" with no reference to the opposed possibility of improvement. A contrary puzzle is in the succeeding observation which distinguishes between the potencies of acting and being acted upon and acting and being acted upon *well*. Again, we may be just in asking why Aristotle omits to mention the

[79] Aristotle did seem to face the problem squarely in his discussion in *Metaphysics* Θ, 1051 a 4–21. See our argument above, pp. 192–196, where we maintained in effect that, even if he grapples with the question with utmost seriousness, the approach via the pair of terms, actuality and potentiality, prevents him from resolving the difficulty without equivocation.

[80] Cf. above, Chapter IV, pp. 91 ff.

[81] *Metaphysics* Θ, 1046 a 13–19. ἡ δ᾽ ἕξις ἀπαθείας τῆς ἐπὶ τὸ χεῖρον καὶ φθορᾶς τῆς ὑπ᾽ ἄλλου ἢ ᾗ ἄλλο ὑπ᾽ ἀρχῆς μεταβλητικῆς. ἐν γὰρ τούτοις ἔνεστι πᾶσι τοῖς ὅροις ὁ τῆς πρώτης δυνάμεως λόγος. πάλιν δ᾽ αὗται δυνάμεις λέγονται ἢ τοῦ μόνον ποιῆσαι ἢ [τοῦ] παθεῖν ἢ τοῦ καλῶς, ὥστε καὶ ἐν τοῖς τούτων λόγοις ἐνυπάρχουσί πως οἱ τῶν προτέρων δυνάμεων λόγοι. Ross's text.

alternative of acting and being acted upon badly. Perhaps the passage may be an example of the cryptic character which so often marks Aristotle's text. In the oral presentation of a lecture, he may very well have elaborated on the value implications of his analysis, or, as has been suggested, he may have been worried, uneasy, or not quite clear on the whole problem. In any event, whatever else may be the import of the passage, it does fix on potency, δύναμις, as somehow the ground of either emergent good or evil.

As Book Θ of the *Metaphysics* moves on, Aristotle's meaning for the terms "potentiality and actuality" begins to sharpen. Even though his approach is characteristically ontological, we still should be aware of the light that it throws on Aristotle's mode of coping with the question of value. One passage in particular is revealing: "The name 'actuality as activity,' which we think of as connected with 'complete actuality,' has been extended from movements particularly to other things. For strictly speaking, 'actuality as activity' seems to be movement. Therefore also men do not assign movement to non-existent things but they do assign certain other predicates, as for example they assert that non-existent things are objects of thought and of desire. They do not say that they are 'moved,' and this because, though not existing actuality, they would have to exist actually, if they were to be moved. For among non-existent things some exist potentially, but they do not exist, since they do not exist in complete actuality."[82] Apart from the distinction between "actuality as activity" and "complete actuality," the passage has some significance for us when we examine what is implied by the various terms introduced. Not only do we have "actuality as activity," "complete actuality" and their relation to movement, but also

---

[82] *Metaphysics* Θ, 1047 a 30–b 2. ἐλήλυθε δ᾽ ἡ ἐνέργεια τοὔνομα, ἡ πρὸς τὴν ἐντελέχειαν συντιθεμένη, καὶ ἐπὶ τὰ ἄλλα ἐκ τῶν κινήσεων μάλιστα· δοκεῖ γὰρ ἡ ἐνέργεια μάλιστα ἡ κίνησις εἶναι, διὸ καὶ τοῖς μὴ οὖσιν οὐκ ἀποδιδόασι τὸ κινεῖσθαι, ἄλλας δέ τινας κατηγορίας, οἷον διανοητὰ καὶ ἐπιθυμητὰ εἶναι τὰ μὴ ὄντα, κινούμενα δὲ οὔ, τοῦτο δὲ ὅτι οὐκ ὄντα ἐνεργείᾳ ἔσονται ἐνεργείᾳ. τῶν γὰρ μὴ ὄντων ἔνια δυνάμει ἐστίν· οὐκ ἔστι δέ, ὅτι οὐκ ἐντελεχείᾳ ἐστίν. Ross's text. The rendering is my own, with some indebtedness to that of the Oxford translation. We have already examined 1047 a 30–32 above, Chapter IV, pp. 90–91 and note 4 where we were discussing the distinction between ἐνέργεια and ἐντελέχεια.

potentiality and those "non-existent" things, some of which exist potentially, though never in the full sense of complete actuality. The point to be noted is that implicit in the passage is a "degrees of reality" theory, ranging from the "non-existent things" on through to "complete actuality." It should be unnecessary to add that, whenever one meets with a "degrees of reality" theory, there is always attendant upon it some kind of suggested scale of value. The highest value seems to be attached to actuality with lesser values inhering in potentiality on down to the "non-existent things." But again, the value implication is posterior to and a function of the ontological analysis.

The same general significance is to be found in chapter 8 of *Metaphysics* Θ. Here we meet Aristotle's well-known argument to establish the priority of actuality over potentiality which he expresses in summary form as follows: "To all such potency, then, actuality is prior both in formula and in substance; and in time it is prior in one sense, and in another not."[83] After producing his arguments for this thesis and explaining that "in time an actual member of a species precedes any potential member, though the individual is potential before it is actual,"[84] Aristotle proceeds to identify "actuality" with end or τέλος.[85] And this finally permits him to reach in turn his climactic position with respect to actuality: "Obviously, therefore, the substance or form is actuality. From this argument it is obvious that actuality is prior in substantial being to potency; and as we have said, one actuality always precedes another in time right back to the actuality of the eternal prime mover."[86] It is in this way that Aristotle

[83] *Metaphysics* Θ, 1049 b 10–12. πάσης δὴ τῆς τοιαύτης προτέρα ἐστὶν ἡ ἐνέργεια καὶ λόγῳ καὶ τῇ οὐσίᾳ· χρόνῳ δ' ἔστι μὲν ὥς, ἔστι δὲ ὡς οὔ. Ross's text. One might even give as equivalents of the terms λόγος, οὐσία, and χρόνος in some such version as this: "Actuality is prior logically (or in definition), ontologically, and chronologically at least in one sense."

[84] This is quoted from Ross's explanatory comment on 1049 b 17.

[85] *Metaphysics* Θ, 1050 a 9.

[86] *Metaphysics* Θ, 1050 b 2–6. ὥστε φανερὸν ὅτι ἡ οὐσία καὶ τὸ εἶδος ἐνέργειά ἐστιν. κατά τε δὴ τοῦτον τὸν λόγον φανερὸν ὅτι πρότερον τῇ οὐσίᾳ ἐνέργεια δυνάμεως, καὶ ὥσπερ εἴπομεν, τοῦ χρόνου ἀεὶ προλαμβάνει ἐνέργεια ἑτέρα πρὸ ἑτέρας ἕως τῆς τοῦ ἀεὶ κινοῦντος πρώτως. Ross's text. Incidentally one should not overlook the immediately preceding sentence where Aristotle, in the midst of an ontological analysis, makes an unexpected and brief sally into the area of value in much the same way as he did in the passage we discussed above, pp. 201–202. In the present instance, he has observed that when nothing else results

to all intents and purposes brings his analysis of potentiality and actuality to a conclusion, and sets the stage for his discussion of the Unmoved Mover in Metaphysics Λ, where, as is well known, he is much more explicit with respect to the question of value. Certainly from the cosmic point of view this is the case. But when we come to consider specifically the nature of the Unmoved Mover as τέλος and complete actuality we must not forget the argument of the ninth chapter of *Metaphysics* Θ, which produced the conception of "bad actuality."

There is one further passage, this time from *Metaphysics* Λ, which we should examine for it will serve as a transition from the topic of actuality and potentiality to the subject matter of the next two sections, "The Good, the Beautiful, and the Telos," and "God, the Unmoved Mover." During the course of chapter 7 of the book, Aristotle has occasion to make this remark: "Those who suppose, as the Pythagoreans and Speusippos do, that supreme beauty and goodness are not present in the beginning, because the beginnings both of plants and of animals are *causes*, but beauty and completeness are in the *effects* of these, are wrong in their opinion. For the seed comes from other individuals which are prior and complete, and the first thing is not seed but the complete being, *e.g.*, we must say that before the seed there is a man—not the man produced from the seed, but another from whom the seed comes."[87] For the moment, we are not concerned

---

besides the actualization, then the actualization is in the person who acts. His illustrations are: "The act of seeing is in the seeing subject and that of theoriz-ing in the theorizing subject and the life is in the soul (and therefore well-being [or happiness] also; for it is a certain kind of life)." Ross's text in the Greek runs: οἷον ἡ ὅρασις ἐν τῷ ὁρῶντι καὶ ἡ θεωρία ἐν τῷ θεωροῦντι καὶ ἡ ζωὴ ἐν τῇ ψυχῇ, διὸ καὶ ἡ εὐδαιμονία· ζωὴ γὰρ ποιά τίς ἐστιν. (1050 a 35–b 2) Ross, in his note *ad loc.*, calls the reference to εὐδαιμονία a digression. I would rather call it something which Aristotle definitely thought was relevant in the context, but for some reason or other was not willing to expand upon it. It surely can be taken to be evidence that Aristotle was more or less consciously aware of the value implications of his analysis.

[87] *Metaphysics* Λ, 1072 b 30–1073 a 3. ὅσοι δὲ ὑπολαμβάνουσιν, ὥσπερ οἱ Πυθαγόρειοι καὶ Σπεύσιππος τὸ κάλλιστον καὶ ἄριστον μὴ ἐν ἀρχῇ εἶναι, διὰ τὸ καὶ τῶν φυτῶν καὶ τῶν ζῴων τὰς ἀρχὰς αἴτια μὲν εἶναι τὸ δὲ καλὸν καὶ τέλειον ἐν τοῖς ἐκ τούτων, οὐκ ὀρθῶς οἴονται. τὸ γὰρ σπέρμα ἐξ ἑτέρων ἐστὶ προτέρων τελείων, καὶ τὸ πρῶτον οὐ σπέρμα ἐστὶν ἀλλὰ τὸ τέλειον· οἷον πρό-τερον ἄνθρωπον ἂν φαίη τις εἶναι τοῦ σπέρματος, οὐ τὸν ἐκ τούτου γενόμενον ἀλλ' ἕτερον ἐξ οὗ τὸ σπέρμα. Ross's text. Cf. also *Metaphysics* Λ, 1075 a 36; N, 1091 a 29–36; and N, 1092 a 11–15.

with the precise nature of the views attributed to the Pythagoreans and Speusippos,[88] but rather we should notice that the argument of the quotation depends upon the acceptance of Aristotle's view that actuality is prior to potentiality. Supreme beauty, goodness, and completeness must be "in the beginning," must be associated with the complete reality of the "beginning" or of the first principle. Aristotle then is identifying "complete actuality" as the source or origin of supreme beauty and goodness.[89]

H. THE GOOD, THE BEAUTIFUL, AND THE TELOS

In the present section we shall attempt to discuss a certain number of selections from the *Metaphysics* in which Aristotle has seen fit to address himself to the specific conceptions of value embodied in the terms "The Good" and "The Beautiful." Our purpose will be to examine these passages in order to determine what kind or kinds of value theory may be said to be suggested by them. We shall also try to discover the ways in which Aristotle sees "The Good" and "The Beautiful" in their relation to his conception of goal or end, or Telos. It is to be hoped that we will thereby be better provided with the necessary background for our specific analysis of the Unmoved Mover. As one might well imagine, our task will not be without difficulty for when Aristotle begins to talk about the Good and the Beautiful, he is bound to sound as though he were echoing the views of his master, Plato. For the searcher after chronological layers in the *Metaphysics*, the problem is easy. If Aristotle seems to be uttering a Platonic sentiment, the passage in question can automatically be labelled "early," as having come from Aristotle's "Platonic period." We have already expressed our own position on this question.[90] Our approach rather must be to take these so-called "Platonic

---

[88] Cf. the very interesting note of Tricot, *Aristote. La Métaphysique*, on 1072 b32.

[89] In the final sentences of chapter 8 of *Metaphysics* Θ, it is interesting to observe how Aristotle uses the doctrine of the priority of actuality in his running fight to discredit Plato's Theory of Ideas. Aristotle in essence argues that particular instances of Ideas will be more of the nature of actualities *(ἐνέργειαι μᾶλλον)* than the Ideas. Therefore the Ideas will be potentialities or potencies of the particular instances *(δυνάμεις τούτων)*, and thus as posterior entities are effectively discredited. 1050 b 34–1051 a 2.

[90] Cf. above, Chapter III, note 20.

passages" as instances of those aspects of Aristotle's thought which are in fact inheritances from Plato and which Aristotle strove to assimilate to his own position.

Typical of the kind of passage with which we shall be dealing is a short sentence in *Metaphysics* α. Aristotle has been arguing for the existence of a final cause on the basis of his axiom of finality, οὐκ εἰς ἄπειρον.[91] He then adds: "But those who maintain the infinite series destroy the Good without knowing it."[92] Slight though this remark apparently may be, it is nonetheless most useful to us, for it expresses Aristotle's view of the profound consequences for the thought of those who deny the axiom of finality, *i.e.*, those who posit τὸ ἄπειρον. They do away with the "nature of the Good." This, for Aristotle, is completely unacceptable. We can therefore conclude that in this passage Aristotle reveals not only his own concern for his axiom and the attendant principle of the ultimate Final Cause, but also his belief that in some way final cause entails a conception of the nature of the Good which is closely tied in with it.

The foregoing remark may be said to reflect Aristotle's regular attitude concerning the absolute Final Cause and the question of the Good. But in *Metaphysics* B, chapter 2, we are confronted with a somewhat different point of view. In the very first of the difficulties *(ἀπορίαι)* which the study of metaphysics must face, Aristotle asks whether it is the task of one or more "sciences" to study all the kinds of causes. He then goes on to say: "Further, there are many things to which not all the principles pertain. For how can a principle of change or the nature of the good be present in unchangeable things, if indeed everything that in itself and by its own nature is good is an end, and a cause in the sense that for its sake the other things both come to be and are, and since an end or purpose is the end of some action, and all actions imply change; so that in unchangeable things this principle could not exist nor could there be a good-in-itself. This is why in mathematics nothing is proved by means of this kind of cause, nor is there any demonstration of this kind—'because it is better, or

---

[91] Cf. above, Chapter III, pp. 59–60.
[92] *Metaphysics* α, 994 b 12–13. ἀλλ᾽ οἱ τὸ ἄπειρον ποιοῦντες λανθάνουσιν ἐξαιροῦντες τὴν τοῦ ἀγαθοῦ φύσιν. Ross's text.

worse'; indeed no one even mentions anything of the kind. And so for this reason some of the Sophists, *e.g.*, Aristippus, ridiculed mathematics; for in the arts, even in the industrial arts, *e.g.*, in carpentry and cobbling, the reason always given is 'because it is better, or worse,' but the mathematical sciences take no account of goods and evils.'"[93]

This doctrine, if I have understood it aright, is somewhat surprising, and of course, it must be admitted that the very nature of *Metaphysics* B, that is, a review of all the difficulties which beset the student of metaphysics, makes it very trying for an individual to interpret excerpts from it. Does the argument amount to something like this? Among immovables there can be no principle of motion nor no nature of the good. Why? A thing that is good is an end and a final cause which brings other things into being. As an end it is an end of an action and this entails the presence of motion. If this be so, then among immovables there is no principle of change nor no "principle" of the "good." It should be unnecessary to point out that this view is in direct conflict with the normal Aristotelian position which assimilates the notion of "the good" into the Final Cause. And certainly no one could argue that the Final Cause as the Unmoved Mover is not among those things which can be called immovable.

The rest of the quotation deals with the objects of mathematics that are posited as things which are immovable. These, Aristotle asserts, do not involve any proof or demonstration into which the terms "better" or "worse" can be injected. In fact, he maintains that no one ever makes any mention of such value terms in

---

[93] *Metaphysics* B, 996 a 22–b 1. ἔτι δὲ πολλοῖς τῶν ὄντων οὐχ ὑπάρχουσι πᾶσαι· τίνα γὰρ τρόπον οἷόν τε κινήσεως ἀρχὴν εἶναι τοῖς ἀκινήτοις ἢ τὴν τἀγαθοῦ φύσιν, εἴπερ ἅπαν ὃ ἂν ᾖ ἀγαθὸν καθ᾽ αὐτὸ καὶ διὰ τὴν αὐτοῦ φύσιν τέλος ἐστὶ καὶ οὕτως αἴτιον ὅτι ἐκείνου ἕνεκα καὶ γίγνεται καὶ ἔστι τἆλλα, τὸ δὲ τέλος καὶ τὸ οὗ ἕνεκα πράξεώς τινός ἐστι τέλος, αἱ δὲ πράξεις πᾶσαι μετὰ κινήσεως; ὥστ᾽ ἐν τοῖς ἀκινήτοις οὐδ᾽ ἂν ἐνδέχοιτο ταύτην εἶναι τὴν ἀρχὴν οὐδ᾽ εἶναί τι αὐτοαγαθόν. διὸ καὶ ἐν τοῖς μαθήμασιν οὐθὲν δείκνυται διὰ ταύτης τῆς αἰτίας, οὐδ᾽ ἔστιν ἀπόδειξις οὐδεμία διότι βέλτιον ἢ χεῖρον, ἀλλ᾽ οὐδὲ τὸ παράπαν μέμνηται οὐθεὶς οὐθενὸς τῶν τοιούτων, ὥστε διὰ ταῦτα τῶν σοφιστῶν τινὲς οἷον Ἀρίστιππος προεπηλάκιζεν αὐτάς· ἐν μὲν γὰρ ταῖς ἄλλαις τέχναις, καὶ ταῖς βαναύσοις, οἷον ἐν τεκτονικῇ καὶ σκυτικῇ, διότι βέλτιον ἢ χεῖρον λέγεσθαι πάντα, τὰς δὲ μαθηματικὰς οὐθένα ποιεῖσθαι λόγον περὶ ἀγαθῶν καὶ κακῶν. Ross's text. Once again I have changed the translation of εἴπερ (996 a 23) from "since" to "if indeed."

the procedures of mathematics. He then goes on to explain the rather extreme position of some Sophists, like Aristippus, who do not take mathematics seriously, in fact, they "bespatter it with mud" as not a worthy activity since it does not deal with terms like "better" or "worse" as the arts, even the "banausic" arts consistently do. In other words, Aristotle seems to be saying that, while Aristippus and his associates are quite correct in their view that mathematics does not involve terms like "better" or "worse," this still does not permit them to "bespatter" the subject "with mud." If they only remembered the intrinsic nature of the objects of mathematics which Aristotle has just been seeking to elucidate, namely that they simply cannot be concerned with "better" or "worse," then they would realize that this charge against mathematics is irrelevant and hence provides no ground for the rejection of mathematics as a legitimate subject of study.[94] So Aristotle concludes by reaffirming his view that the mathematical sciences, since they are concerned with immovables, "take no account of goods and evils."

Ross, in his note on the passage, observes that Aristotle in the first chapter of *Metaphysics* Γ does answer the initial question raised. Metaphysics does "study all the causes or principles of being *quâ* being." But Ross goes on to say, "The precise difficulties raised here, however, are not solved." Nor in the rest of his notes does he pay any attention to the problem arising from the assertion that in immovables there is no principle of the good. However, Ross does mention an argument in *Metaphysics* M, in which he says, "Aristotle shows that τὸ καλόν, if not τὸ ἀγαθόν, has a place in mathematics."

Let us examine in full this excerpt from *Metaphysics* M, because it brings out with considerable clarity the conflict to which we have pointed, a conflict, we would urge, which arises from Aristotle's consistent uncertainty when he confronts questions of value as they relate to being. "Now since the good and the beautiful are different (for the former always implies conduct as its subject, while the beautiful is found also in motionless things), those who assert that the mathematical sciences say nothing of the

---

[94] This interpretation rests ultimately upon the tone introduced by the word προεπηλάκιζεν, to "besmirch," to "spatter with mud."

beautiful or the good are in error. For these sciences say and prove a very great deal about them; for if they do not expressly mention them, but prove attributes which are their results or their defining formulae, it is not true to say that they tell us nothing about them. The chief forms of beauty are order and symmetry and definiteness, which the mathematical sciences demonstrate in a special degree. And since these (*e.g.*, order and definiteness) are obviously causes of many things, evidently these sciences must treat this sort of causative principle also (*i.e.*, the beautiful) as in some sense a cause. But we shall speak more plainly elsewhere about these matters."[95]

We must compare very carefully these two passages from *Metaphysics* B and M. In the first place, in B the substance of the argument is to deny the presence of "the nature of the good" in immovables. And it is on this ground, as I have suggested, that Aristotle agrees with the Sophists like Aristippus who recognize this fact about the immovables like the objects of mathematics, but he does not agree with their rejection of the mathematical sciences. Further, it should be noted that there is no mention of the beautiful in the B passage. But in the quotation from M the first point established is the difference between the good (τὸ ἀγαθόν) and the beautiful (τὸ καλόν) on the ground that the good is "always in an action" (or, as Ross renders it, "always implies conduct") while "the beautiful is found also in motionless things." This can mean only the following: (1) the good is in conduct (ἐν πράξει); (2) the beautiful is involved "in conduct"; (3) the good is not to be found in motionless things, this being implied in the distinction between the good and the beautiful; and (4) the beautiful is *also* in motionless things (καὶ ἐν τοῖς ἀκινήτοις). The second, third, and fourth conclusions must be inferred because of the presence of *also* (καὶ) in the fourth proposition.

[95] *Metaphysics* M, 1078 a 31–b 6. ἐπεὶ δὲ τὸ ἀγαθὸν καὶ τὸ καλὸν ἕτερον (τὸ μὲν γὰρ ἀεὶ ἐν πράξει, τὸ δὲ καλὸν καὶ ἐν τοῖς ἀκινήτοις), οἱ φάσκοντες οὐδὲν λέγειν τὰς μαθηματικὰς ἐπιστήμας περὶ καλοῦ ἢ ἀγαθοῦ ψεύδονται. λέγουσι γὰρ καὶ δεικνύουσι μάλιστα· οὐ γὰρ εἰ μὴ ὀνομάζουσι τὰ δ' ἔργα καὶ τοὺς λόγους δεικνύουσιν, οὐ λέγουσι περὶ αὐτῶν. τοῦ δὲ καλοῦ μέγιστα εἴδη τάξις καὶ συμμετρία καὶ τὸ ὡρισμένον, ἃ μάλιστα δεικνύουσιν αἱ μαθηματικαὶ ἐπιστῆμαι. καὶ ἐπεί γε πολλῶν αἴτια φαίνεται ταῦτα (λέγω δ' οἷον ἡ τάξις καὶ τὸ ὡρισμένον), δῆλον ὅτι λέγοιεν ἂν καὶ τὴν τοιαύτην αἰτίαν τὴν ὡς τὸ καλὸν αἴτιον τρόπον τινά. μᾶλλον δὲ γνωρίμως ἐν ἄλλοις περὶ αὐτῶν ἐροῦμεν. Ross's text.

If the foregoing interpretation be correct—and, given the text, no other seems possible—we are bound to be dismayed by the next statement: "Those who assert that the mathematical sciences say nothing of the beautiful or the good are in error."[96] We have already been told that the mathematical sciences are concerned with the beautiful, but we were told in the passage in B and in the first part of this specific sentence that there is no place for "the good" in mathematics. We can suppose that the thinkers referred to are "some Sophists like Aristippus" mentioned in the quotation from B and we have suggested the way in which Aristotle's attitude in that passage must be understood. But now in the excerpt from M, Aristotle is unqualified in his criticism of these thinkers. Simply stated, then, the conflict or contradiction in Aristotle comes to this: in B, concern with the good is denied to mathematics, and, within a single sentence from the passage in M concern for the good is first denied to mathematics and then affirmed to it.

Aristotle's next statement in the latter quotation is vague. "The mathematical sciences say and prove a very great deal about them" (*i.e.*, the beautiful and the good). We are urged not to be worried by the fact that the beautiful and the good are not explicitly mentioned. If their results (*τὰ ἔργα*), or "their defining formulae" (*τοὺς λόγους*) are proved, the mathematical sciences do tell us something about the good and the beautiful. From this point on, Aristotle says nothing more about the good, but he does specify the "chief forms of beauty" as "order, symmetry, and definiteness," and goes on to suggest, again somewhat vaguely, how, because of the presence of these forms of beauty in the mathematical sciences, they must treat "the beautiful as in some sense a cause." The passage concludes with Aristotle's promise that he will speak "more knowledgeably" (*μᾶλλον δὲ γνωρίμως*) about these problems elsewhere.

Ross's note on our quotation from *Metaphysics* M needs correction. He quite rightly begins by observing that the thinkers criticized here are "some Sophists like Aristippus" of B, 996 a 32, and goes on to point out, as we have done, that there we find no

---

[96] The translation "are in error" is surely a palpable softening of the sense of *ψεύδονται*, a really rough word, the primary meaning of which is "to lie."

mention of the beautiful. In M, Ross continues, these thinkers are said to assert that mathematics has nothing to do with either the good or the beautiful. Ross then adds: "Aristotle replies that it uses the latter though not the former." But, as we have just seen, Aristotle actually says that "the mathematical sciences say and prove a very great deal about the good and the beautiful." Ross comments that the distinction here offered between the good and the beautiful is not found elsewhere in Aristotle.[97] He admits he is surprised at Aristotle's assertion that the good is "always in conduct" *(ἀεὶ ἐν πράξει)* when "it is found in every category and can be applied to God and to reason."[98] Ross then continues by discussing somewhat irrelevantly the Aristotelian theory that the beautiful is primarily applicable to the physically beautiful and the good to the morally good. I have said "irrelevantly" because Ross seems to forget that he is interpreting a passage which has to do with the involvement of the good and the beautiful in the mathematical sciences. Ross concludes somewhat lamely to this effect: "Or at any rate for the sake of argument Aristotle is willing to admit this restriction of the meaning of *ἀγαθόν.*"

It is to be hoped that the foregoing discussion has given ample evidence that, in this very tricky problem which at bottom presents the question of the relation of Being and Value, Aristotle has fallen into contradiction, has appeared to be uncertain or off-balance, and has introduced a distinction which does not appear elsewhere in his writings. The reader who has been puzzled by the two passages from B and M may feel lifted in spirit when he discovers, at the conclusion of the latter, Aristotle's promise that he will "speak more plainly about these matters elsewhere." But he will be doomed to disappointment, for as Ross rather sadly notes, the other possible places in the Aristotelian corpus where further clarity might be expected[99] actually do not fill the bill. And so Ross is compelled to say: "It seems best to treat it as one of Aristotle's unfulfilled promises."

---

[97] Ross suggests that a trace of the distinction might be found in *De Motu Animalium,* 700 b 25. Cf. our discussion of this passage above, Chapter V, pp. 153–157.

[98] Here Ross cites *Nicomachean Ethics,* 1096 a 23.

[99] Ross and other commentators cite *Metaphysics* Λ, 7 (1072 a 34), 8, 10, N, 4, and the *De Caelo.*

Perhaps it may be rightly conjectured that Aristotle did not fulfill his promise because he could not speak more clearly on this particular matter in which Being and Value confront each other, given his original decision that he will undertake his philosophizing from an ontological point of view. So far as one can see, in the two passages from B and M which we have been studying, the real underlying difficulty lies in Aristotle's inability to move from his conception of an absolute Final Cause to the conception of a specific final cause or goal or end or purpose for each individual particular. We have become accustomed to Aristotle's association of value with his absolute Final Cause, but this is not the first time in which we have seen his failure to integrate this notion with the teleology which he invites us to accept as applicable to individual particulars. And in these passages from the *Metaphysics*, the problem is made no easier for Aristotle because the objects of mathematics or the mathematical sciences are at the center of the discussion. One only needs to recall Aristotle's continual struggle with the question of the ontological status of the objects of mathematics and his consistent inability finally to resolve the question. Lack of certainty in this area has unquestionably contributed to the difficulties which we have disclosed in the excerpts from *Metaphysics* B and M. At all events, if we do see in these passages an instance of Aristotle's inability to relate Final Cause to individual final cause, then our present discussion should be read along with our observations concerning the very interesting passage from the *De Motu Animalium*, for there, it was our contention, precisely the same difficulty emerges.[100]

Shortly after the section in *Metaphysics* B which we have just been considering comes another that we must have before us. Aristotle is asking which of the sciences might be called Wisdom (σοφία). He has just enumerated the four causes and observes that there is some reason for giving the study of each of them this name. He continues: "For inasmuch as it is most architectonic and authoritative and the other sciences, like slave-women, may not even contradict it, the science of the *end* and of the *good* is of the nature of Wisdom (for the other things are for the sake of

---

[100] Cf. Chapter V above, pp. 153–157, on *De Motu Animalium*, 700 b 23–701 a 1.

the end). But inasmuch as it was described as dealing with the first causes and that which is in the highest sense object of knowledge, the science of *substance* must be of *the nature of Wisdom*."[101]

Aristotle in this way explains why the study of the final cause and the formal cause deserve the name of Wisdom.[102] Our concern is not so much for this argument nor for the claim put forward a few lines later that the study of the efficient cause also deserves the name of Wisdom. Rather we should see in the passage two points which are characteristic of Aristotle's normal position. First, as a result of his decisive emphasis on ontology, he gives a high place to the science of substance as essence and repeats his view that substance as essence "is in the highest sense object of knowledge."[103] And second, we should be aware of the extravagant language he uses in describing the study of Final Cause. Hear his superlatives, "most architectonic" and "most authoritative," and could there even be a slight touch of humour when Aristotle in defining the subordinate status of the other sciences says they cannot contradict the science of Final Cause and likens them to "slave-women"? But most important for us is the fact that he characterizes this science of Final Cause as concerned with the *end* and the *good*, and, of course, we shall see these two, end and good, frequently linked together.[104] At the same time we should also note that Aristotle does not make clear whether he is talking about absolute Final Cause or about the final cause of an individual particular.

In the second chapter of *Metaphysics* Δ Aristotle takes up the several meanings of "cause" and includes a statement concerning "final cause" which is germane to our purpose. He has just been

---

[101] *Metaphysics* B, 996 b 10–14. ᾗ μὲν γὰρ ἀρχικωτάτη καὶ ἡγεμονικωτάτη καὶ ᾗ ὥσπερ δούλας οὐδ᾽ ἀντείπειν τὰς ἄλλας ἐπιστήμας δίκαιον, ἡ τοῦ τέλους καὶ τἀγαθοῦ τοιαύτη (τούτου γὰρ ἕνεκα τἆλλα), ᾗ δὲ τῶν πρώτων αἰτίων καὶ τοῦ μάλιστα ἐπιστητοῦ διωρίσθη εἶναι, ἡ τῆς οὐσίας ἂν εἴη τοιαύτη. Ross's text.

[102] It is clear that οὐσίας in 996 b 14 means "substance as essence," that is to say, the formal cause.

[103] We should be reminded here of Aristotle's epistemological dilemma, as I have called it, *viz.*, that what one can know, form, substance as essence, or universal has a secondary ontological status as compared to the fully real, the individual particular τόδε τι, which remains ultimately unknowable. Cf. above, Chapter III, pp. 73–74, note 36, and Chapter VI, pp. 181–183.

[104] Cf., for example, *Metaphysics* K, 1059 a 35–38 where the same connection is made.

giving illustrations of what he means by the material, formal, and efficient causes, and then continues: "The remainder are causes as the end and the good of the other things; for that, for the sake of which other things are, is naturally the best and the end of the other things; let us take it as making no difference whether we call it good or apparent good."[105] Noteworthy in the first place is the collocation again of the end and the good as a means of defining the final cause. The other causes are subordinated and at least in this context they do not have any implied value attached to them. Value enters only with the emergence of the final cause. More literally, "The purpose (τὸ οὗ ἕνεκα) wills to be the best and the end of the other things." Here Aristotle is not thinking of the absolute Final Cause, but of the final causes of things which are met in ordinary experience. The last sentence to the effect that it makes no difference whether we call this end the real good or the apparent good is puzzling. In the present argument, perhaps Aristotle means to suggest that in the analysis of the final cause in the world of practical affairs it is not a matter of moment whether the good involved is actual or apparent.

As we have already become aware, very often in the various arguments in the *Metaphysics* references which have some kind of value implications occur in a specific illustration of a point or an analysis which Aristotle is seeking to elucidate. An instance of this sort occurs in chapter 18 of *Metaphysics* Δ, where the term, "that in virtue of which" is being explained. The first meaning to which he turns his attention is expressed as follows: " 'That in virtue of which' has several meanings, (1) the form or substance of each thing, *e.g.*, that in virtue of which a man is good is the good itself."[106] We first should note that the phrase "form or substance" refers to the essence of an individual particular or, as Ross frequently expresses it, "substance as essence." Perhaps there is no clear answer to the question why Aristotle uses the value term "good" as his illustration. But since he has done so, it is

---

[105] *Metaphysics* B, 1013 b 25–28. τὰ δ᾽ ὡς τὸ τέλος καὶ τἀγαθὸν τῶν ἄλλων· τὸ γὰρ οὗ ἕνεκα βέλτιστον καὶ τέλος τῶν ἄλλων ἐθέλει εἶναι· διαφερέτω δὲ μηδὲν αὐτὸ εἰπεῖν ἀγαθὸν ἢ φαινόμενον ἀγαθόν. Ross's text.

[106] *Metaphysics* Δ, 1022 a 14–16. τὸ καθ᾽ ὃ λέγεται πολλαχῶς, ἕνα μὲν τρόπον τὸ εἶδος καὶ ἡ οὐσία ἑκάστου πράγματος, οἷον καθ᾽ ὃ ἀγαθός, αὐτὸ ἀγαθόν. Ross's text.

fair to try to identify the theory with respect to value that can be inferred. Ross's note in this connection is interesting: "The statement is curiously Platonic, and Δ may well belong to the Platonic period of Aristotle's thought."[107] Ross apparently would have us believe that "the good itself" is the equivalent of the Idea of the Good with the consequence that a man is good "in virtue of" some kind of sharing in or participation in the Idea. The passage does not have to be read in this un-Aristotelian fashion. In fact, it is thoroughly Aristotelian. The form or essence of the man (in this case the example offered of any particular) is made the equivalent of the good itself, not the Idea of the Good. If this equation be accepted, then, since the form or essence is incapable of separate existence (*i.e.*, the unwavering view of Aristotle) the "good itself" must likewise be incapable of separate existence. (And, of course, an outstanding characteristic of Plato's Idea of the Good, as well as all other Ideas, is that it does exist "apart" or separately.) Hence the good itself must inhere in the individual particular just like the form or essence. So then we will have to conclude that the situation here is something like the view of value as a "quality." However, the status assigned to value is somewhat "higher," if indeed we have been right in seeing a virtual equivalence between form or essence and the value "good" in the illustration.

Another instance of injecting a value notion in an illustration can be found in the third chapter of *Metaphysics* Z. "For it is an advantage to advance to that which is more intelligible. For learning proceeds for all in this way—through that which is less intelligible by nature to that which is more intelligible; and just as in conduct our work is to start from what is good for each and make what is good in itself good for each, so it is our work to start from what is more intelligible to oneself and make what is intelligible by nature intelligible to oneself."[108] We are already familiar with Aristotle's method as outlined here and its

---

[107] Cf. Tricot, *Aristote. La Métaphysique*, note ad loc., where substantially the same point is made.

[108] *Metaphysics*, Z, 1029 b 3–8. ἡ γὰρ μάθησις οὕτω γίγνεται πᾶσι διὰ τῶν ἧττον γνωρίμων φύσει εἰς τὰ γνώριμα μᾶλλον· καὶ τοῦτο ἔργον ἐστίν, ὥσπερ ἐν ταῖς πράξεσι τὸ ποιῆσαι ἐκ τῶν ἑκάστῳ ἀγαθῶν τὰ ὅλως ἀγαθὰ ἑκάστῳ ἀγαθά, οὕτως ἐκ τῶν αὐτῷ γνωριμωτέρων τὰ τῇ φύσει γνώριμα αὐτῷ γνώριμα. Ross's text.

importance for his theory of knowledge.[109] But what concerns us at the moment is the ethical analogy which Aristotle introduces in order to illuminate his epistemological mode of procedure. Let us therefore look at the ethical analogy a little more carefully. It perhaps could be translated somewhat more literally as follows: "As in actions, beginning with those goods for each individual, it is our task to make the goods that are wholly so good for each individual,"[110] There is, I believe, some virtue in being reminded that the Greek text contains the plural "goods" in each instance. It appears then that in this ethical analogy Aristotle is operating on a common-sense conventional plane. It is as if he were saying that anyone can tell you what "the goods that are wholly so" actually are. Also we are supposed to be able to identify "the goods for each individual." In other words, the kind of value theory that is suggested here is one which has no metaphysical sanction but rather is based upon the normal conventional reactions of men.

There is no need to dwell on the fact that this ethical analogy based on conventional ethical notions does not help us very much in understanding the epistemological analysis which asserts that learning proceeds from what is apparently intelligible, though intrinsically not so, to that which is apparently not intelligible, though intrinsically it is so. This Aristotelian view is thoroughly anchored in his metaphysics as is clear from the parallel passage in the *Physics*, 184 a 16–26, to which we have already referred. Ross's note on the ethical analogy attempts (I believe, with in-different success) to defend its application. He writes: "The passage is to some extent explained by *Nicomachean Ethics* 1129 b 5, where we learn that we should choose what is good for us (*i.e.*, what aids *us* towards the good life) and pray that what is good in itself (*i.e.*, external goods) may be good for us. Here he simply says 'make' instead of 'pray.' Originally, owing to some defect in us, what is good in itself may not be good for us; but we must (starting by choosing the things that *are* good for us) transform ourselves till this is no longer so. So too what is intelligible in

---

[109] Cf. above, Chapter III, p. 61, where *Physics* 184 a 16–26 is discussed.

[110] Tricot, *op. cit.*, translate τὰ ὅλως ἀγαθά by "*le bien général*" while Tredennick's version in the Loeb Classical Library is "absolute good."

itself is originally not intelligible to us; but we must clarify our minds until it *is* intelligible to us, by starting with the apprehension of what is already intelligible to us."

The concluding sentence of the note is fairly satisfactory, though it would have been more precise had Ross said that we should start with what is apparently more intelligible. But, be that as it may, the rest of the comment can well bear examination. An aura of conventionalism is obviously pervasive. We are told we must choose what is good for us which will aid and abet us in our quest for the good life. The implication, of course, is that we can easily discover what is good for us. We are then given to understand that the wretched part of the problem lies in what is good in itself, and we are urged to pray that this "good in itself" may be good for us. But then Ross equates "good in itself" with "external goods." In the passage from the *Nicomachean Ethics* which Ross is paraphrasing these goods are identified as those which make for "prosperity." They are also sometimes called the "goods of fortune."[111] Ross's next remarks are no less than astonishing. Having equated the "good in iteslf" with "external goods," Ross observes that this good in itself may not be good for us, owing to some defect. Well, then, what are we to do? We must get rid of that pestiferous defect so that we can make these external goods good for us and thus can advance merrily on the way to prosperity. How do we shake the pest? We must start by choosing the things that *are* good for us and then we must "transform ourselves till this is no longer so." Can Ross really mean that we should no longer choose things that *are* good for us in order to assimilate external goods? Whatever may be Ross's intention, the whole note reveals that no ingenuity can remove the conventional and almost banal ethical context which marks Aristotle's thought in this passage.

In our discussion of the Good, and the Beautiful, the Telos, we have seen the Telos or end or purpose being identified with the Final Cause on several occasions. In this connection we are forced to face the question of the nature of Aristotle's teleology. We shall of course have more to say about this problem when we come to deal below with the implications for Aristotle's thought

[111] *e.g., Nicomachean Ethics*, 1153 b 18.

that emerge from his not having any doctrine of creation.[112] For the moment we can say this much in summary: Aristotle's teleology has two aspects, one a cosmic teleology where the absolute Final Cause operates as End or Purpose, and the other the final cause or purpose which operates for an individual particular. And more than once we have noted Aristotle's inability to make these two aspects cohere with each other. Furthermore in our discussion of the so-called doctrine of the four causes,[113] we observed that Aristotle applies the doctrine to various "categories of entities," as is revealed by the examples he submits. We listed the following five: natural processes of a higher order (*e.g.*, man begets man); natural processes of a lower order (*e.g.*, air moves up); *artefacta* (*e.g.*, a statue or a table); events, either teleological (*e.g.*, exercise) or accidental (*e.g.*, a man struck by lightning); and states, relations, and the like (*e.g.*, health is the final cause of exercise).

Now it is evident that the doctrine of the four causes "works" best in the categories of natural processes of a higher order and of *artefacta*. Here it is easy to identify the material, formal, and efficient causes, as well as to specify precisely the final cause or purpose. In the other categories the situation is considerably blurred. In the case of the final cause, it simply cannot be named, except in the category of what we have called teleolgical events. One's first question might well be: Was Aristotle aware of this difficulty? The fact of the matter is that he was aware of it, although, to my knowledge, on only one occasion did he express himself on the problem in so many words. The occasion is in the fourth chapter of *Metaphysics* H, the subject of which Ross describes as "the various causes of generable natural substances, eternal natural substances, and natural events." The passage of particular importance to us occurs in connection with the discussion of "natural events." Aristotle writes: "Nor does matter belong to those things which exist by nature but are not substances; their substratum is the *substance*. E.g., what is the cause of an eclipse? What is its matter? There is none; the *moon* is

---

[112] Cf. below, section J of this chapter.

[113] Cf. above, Chapter IV, pp. 102–111. In particular note pp. 105–106 on the basis for regarding the formal, efficient, and final causes as capable of being reduced to one. Also note the critique of the doctrine of the four causes on pp. 109–111.

that which suffers eclipse. What is the moving cause which extinguishes the light? The earth. The final cause perhaps does not exist. The formal principle is the definitory formula, but this is obscure if it does not include the [efficient] cause. E.g., what is eclipse? Deprivation of light. But if we add 'by interposition of the earth,' this is the formula which includes the [efficient] cause."[114]

Aristotle here admits that in an eclipse, a natural event but not a substance, there is a formal cause and an efficient cause closely interinvolved, but there is no material cause and "perhaps the final cause does not exist." Ross's note on this remark is illuminating. "This is a serious admission in view of Aristotle's identification in line 1[115] of the formal with the final cause. His teleology is in fact not complete. There is not always a final cause. But where there is, it is the formal cause as well. In the absence of a final cause, the thing is defined by reference to its efficient cause, as in lines 14, 15. Eclipse is for Aristotle an example of ταὐτόματον. The sun's motion is no doubt ἕνεκά του and so is that of the moon, but the two acting together may produce a result which is not ἕνεκά του."

For the moment, it may be best for us to make the suggestion that this admitted incompleteness in Aristotle's teleological thinking is basically the reason for his difficulties not only in relating the absolute Final Cause to the final causes of particulars, but also with respect to developing a coherent set of relationships between final cause in any sense and the various notions of value which he

---

[114] *Metaphysics* H, 1044 b 8–15. οὐδ᾿ ὅσα δὴ φύσει μέν, μὴ οὐσίαι δέ, οὐκ ἔστι τούτοις ὕλη, ἀλλὰ τὸ ὑποκείμενον ἡ οὐσία. οἷον τί αἴτιον ἐκλείψεως, τίς ὕλη; οὐ γὰρ ἔστιν, ἀλλ᾿ ἡ σελήνη τὸ πάσχον. τί δ᾿ αἴτιον ὡς κινῆσαν καὶ φθεῖραν τὸ φῶς; ἡ γῆ. τὸ δ᾿ οὗ ἕνεκα ἴσως οὐκ ἔστιν. τὸ δ᾿ ὡς εἶδος ὁ λόγος, ἀλλὰ ἄδηλος ἐὰν μὴ μετὰ τῆς αἰτίας ᾖ ὁ λόγος. οἷον τί ἔκλειψις; στέρησις φωτός. ἐὰν δὲ προστεθῇ τὸ ὑπὸ γῆς ἐν μέσῳ γιγνομένης, ὁ σὺν τῷ αἰτίῳ λόγος οὗτος. Ross's text. The rendering is that of the Oxford translation, though I have inserted "efficient" before the αἰτίας of 1044 b 13, as is suggested by Ross's note. I have also inserted "efficient" before the αἰτίῳ of 1044 b 15, following the lead of Tredennick in his version in the Loeb Classical Library. We also might take note of Tricot's translation (*op. cit.*) of τὸ δ᾿ οὗ ἕνεκα ἴσως οὐκ ἔστιν (1044 b 12): "*Quant à la cause finale, sans doute n'y en a-t-il pas.*" Also in discussing the importance of the efficient cause Tricot, *op. cit.*, note on 1044 b 12, refers to *Posterior Analytics*, Book II, chapter 2, and chapter 8, 93 a 23 ff.

[115] That is, *Metaphysics* H, 1044 b 1, where, after mentioning the formal cause and the final cause, Aristotle says: ἴσως δὲ ταῦτα ἄμφω τὸ αὐτό. "Perhaps these two are the same."

wishes to assimilate thereto. Or to put it another way, if teleology is to provide a solid clue as to the nature of value (and, I should add, its relation to being), then the teleology must be "complete" (to use Ross's word). Otherwise, if in some sense we are faced with the problem of the way in which value (and disvalue) permeate reality, and if we choose to seek our solution teleologically, we are doomed to failure, unless we develop a teleology commensurate with the task.[116]

One more example might well be cited to illustrate Aristotle's characteristic method of employing a value term to designate the Final Cause as Telos. The passage occurs early in chapter 8 of Metaphysics Λ: "For the apparent good is the object of appetite, and the real good is the primary object of rational desire."[117] "The real good" or "the really beautiful" (τὸ ὂν καλόν) is that which inspires rational desire, and so it can function as the Unmoved Mover, *i.e.*, the Final Cause.

One final quotation can fittingly serve as a conclusion for our discussion of the Good, the Beautiful, and the Telos, mainly because in it we find Aristotle being reasonably explicit. In the fourth chapter of *Metaphysics* N, he raises the question of "how the elements and the principles are related to the good and the beautiful."[118] After reviewing briefly the positions of the "mythologists," the Pythagoreans, Plato, Speusippus, the old poets, the Magi, Empedocles, and Anaxagoras, Aristotle expresses his own position in the following words: "It would be strange if to that which is primary and eternal and most self-sufficient this very quality—self-sufficiency and self-maintenance—belongs primarily in some other way than *as a good*. But indeed it can be for no other reason indestructible or self-sufficient than because its nature is good. Therefore to say that the first principle is good

---

[116] As I have already suggested, there seems to be a profound interconnection between teleology and a doctrine of creation.

[117] *Metaphysics* Λ, 1072 a 27–28. ἐπιθυμητὸν μὲν γὰρ τὸ φαινόμενον καλόν, βουλητὸν δὲ πρῶτον τὸ ὂν καλόν. Ross's text. It should not be necessary to point out that this passage is one among others which is being quoted not for the rôle it plays in the development of Aristotle's particular argument there in progress, but rather because it does exhibit his use of value terms in relation to the Final Cause.

[118] *Metaphysics* N, 1091 a 30–31. πῶς ἔχει πρὸς τὸ ἀγαθὸν καὶ τὸ καλὸν τὰ στοιχεῖα καὶ αἱ ἀρχαί. Ross's text.

is probably correct."[119] Ross has this to say about the passage: "Aristotle establishes the goodness of the first principle in two ways: (1) the self-sufficiency and eternality which it is assumed to possess are good qualities. It could not have these if it were not in itself good."

In the first place it is fair to hold that Tricot's use of the phrase "le Souverain Bien" does not appear to be warranted by the Aristotelian text. Such a rendering really equates the first principle of the present passage with the Idea of the Good of Plato's *Republic*. If evidence were needed to show that Aristotle here is expressing a position distinctively his own and one different from that of Plato, one would only have to point out that Aristotle immediately after our present quotation launches an attack against Plato and the Theory of Ideas. Secondly, I believe we are justified in asserting that Ross himself in his version has to a degree over-translated the Greek, as I have tried to indicate in my alternative rendering. But what seems to be unmistakable about the purport of the passage is that Aristotle's first principle has "goodness" as an attribute. And in so far as we can make out from a careful scrutiny of the Greek words, we have here a congeries of characteristics or attributes or qualites of this first principle, *viz.*, eternity, self-sufficiency, "safety" or self-mainten-ance, indestructibility, and goodness. Surely the statement that the first principle is "well-disposed" or "in good condition" designates "goodness" as an attribute. Furthermore Aristotle by his argument establishes a thoroughgoing intercompatibility of this series of attributes. But the final conclusion cannot be avoided that the "first principle" primarily *exists* and therefore there is a secondary status inevitably assigned to all of these attributes including goodness.

[119] *Metaphysics* N, 1091 b 16–20. θαυμαστὸν δ᾽ εἰ τῷ πρώτῳ καὶ ἀϊδίῳ καὶ αὐτ-αρκεστάτῳ τοῦτ᾽ αὐτὸ πρῶτον οὐχ ὡς ἀγαθὸν ὑπάρχει, τὸ αὔταρκες καὶ ἡ σωτηρία. ἀλλὰ μὴν οὐ δι᾽ ἄλλο τι ἄφθαρτον ἢ διότι εὖ ἔχει. οὐδ᾽ αὔταρκες, ὥστε τὸ μὲν φάναι τὴν τοιαύτην εἶναι εὔλογον ἀληθὲς εἶναι. Ross's text. An alternative version might run as follows: "It would be astonishing if this very primary characteristic, *viz.*, self-sufficiency and safety, did not belong as a good to that which is first and eternal and most self-sufficient. But indeed it is neither indestructible nor self-sufficient for any other reason than that it is well-disposed (or in good condition), with the result that to assert the first principle to be of such a sort is reasonable and true." Tricot, *op. cit.*, translates the last clause thus: "*Par conséquent, dire que le principe est le Souverain Bien, c'est parler selon la vérité et la raison.*"

So we may conclude this section with this further statement of the normal Aristotelian position with respect to the Final Cause. Our background now should be adequate for our analysis in the next section.

I. GOD, THE UNMOVED MOVER

The material which we must review in this section of our investigation is most familiar not only to students of Aristotle but as well to all who have even the slightest interest in theology. Our purpose will be to examine this material once again with a view to discovering first the nature of the arguments Aristotle uses to establish the existence of God, the Unmoved Mover. Second, we must have before us the various ways in which he describes this God. And finally, we must try to analyze and appraise Aristotle's effort to delineate God, the Unmoved Mover, as the source of value. And in this latter connection we must continually bear in mind what we have already said about the Final Cause.

We can most easily introduce our discussion by citing a notable passage in the second chapter of *Metaphysics* A: "But the divine power cannot be jealous (nay, according to the proverb,[120] 'bards tell many a lie'), nor should any science be thought more honourable than one of this sort. For the most divine science is also most honourable; and this science alone is, in two ways, most divine. For the science, which it would be most meet for God to have is a divine science, and so is any science that deals with divine objects; and this science alone has both these qualities; for (1) God is thought to be among the causes of all things and to be a first principle, and (2) such a science either God alone can have, or God above all others. All the sciences, indeed, are more necessary than this, but none is better."[121] Here Aristotle, at

[120] Ross notes here that this already had become a proverb for Solon, fr. 26 Hiller.

[121] *Metaphysics* A, 983 a 2–11. ἀλλ' οὔτε τὸ θεῖον φθονερὸν ἐνδέχεται εἶναι, ἀλλὰ κατὰ τὴν παροιμίαν πολλὰ ψεύδονται ἀοιδοί, οὔτε τῆς τοιαύτης ἄλλην χρὴ νομίζειν τιμιωτέραν. ἡ γὰρ θειοτάτη καὶ τιμιωτάτη· τοιαύτη δὲ διχῶς ἂν εἴη· μόνη· ἥν τε γὰρ μάλιστ' ἂν ὁ θεὸς ἔχοι, θεία τῶν ἐπιστημῶν ἐστί, κἂν εἴ τις τῶν θείων εἴη. μόνη δ' αὕτη τούτων ἀμφοτέρων τετύχηκεν· ὅ τε γὰρ θεὸς δοκεῖ τῶν αἰτίων πᾶσιν εἶναι καὶ ἀρχή τις, καὶ τὴν τοιαύτην ἢ μόνος ἢ μάλιστ' ἂν ἔχοι ὁ θεός. ἀναγκαιότεραι μὲν οὖν πᾶσαι ταύτης, ἀμείνων δ' οὐδεμία. Ross's text.

least to some extent, is speaking with the unmistakable awe of a devout monotheist. The divine is without jealousy. The science of things divine, *i.e.*, theology, is the most honourable, and this must be peculiarly God's own "science." It is fitting for Him to have it, for God "seems" or "is thought" to be one of the causes of all things, and is in some sense a first principle. Either God alone can possess this "divine science," this theology, or if others can have it, God would have to remain in a preeminent position with respect to it. All other "sciences," by which Aristotle, we can assume, means all other subjects of study, are more immediately useful, but "none is better." Note that three times Aristotle uses the singular "God," ὁ θεός. It is almost with unction that Aristotle uses words rich with value connotations such as "divine," "honourable," and "better." But somehow when he comes to speak more explicitly about God, the monotheistic enthusiasm is diminished to a degree. God "*is thought* to be among the causes of all things" and He is "*a* first principle," we can presume, I suppose, among others.

In a note Ross has caught at least in part this tone in the passage: "In assigning to God knowledge of the causes of existing things, Aristotle is inconsistent with his account in Book Λ, in which God's thought has no object but Himself. He is speaking of God as commonly conceived."[122] It could be argued that God is described as not only having knowledge of existing things but also as among the causes of them and a first principle. But Ross is clearly right in seeing that God's "divine science" is infinitely rich and variegated in content as compared with the content assigned to His thought in Book Λ. Nonetheless, we can be justified in refusing to accept Ross's explanation of the inconsistency. Is Aristotle here actually speaking of God "as commonly conceived"? May we not ask "commonly conceived" by whom? How widespread was this kind of monotheistic view? For the present, let us hazard the suggestion that Ross is pointing to a real inconsistency which remained unresolved in Aristotle's thought It may well be that Aristotle never reconciled this God of *Metaphysics* A with the God of Book Λ whose "thought had no object but Himself." If this be true, then any attempt on Aristotle's

[122] Note on 983 a 6.

part to see God as a source of value will always be handicapped by the inconsistency of his view of God.[123]

Let us now review rapidly the decisive passages in *Metaphysics* Λ in which Aristotle develops his argument for the existence of God, the Unmoved or Prime Mover.

In chapter 6, he begins with this flat assertion: "It is necessary that there should be an eternal unmovable substance."[124]

Aristotle immediately supports his assertion with the following reason: "For substances are the first of existing things, and if they are all destructible, all things are destructible."[125] Here he repeats his ultimate conviction with respect to the primacy of οὐσία, the thing or "substance" which is capable of separate and independent existence, and, as Ross has pointed out, Aristotle has taken pains to restate his position in this respect in the very opening words of Book Λ.[126] So the argument insists that if substances are primary, it is impossible or unthinkable that all

---

[123] Before proceeding to our consideration of God, the Unmoved Mover, of Book Λ, it may be useful to have before us an example of the kind of Aristotelian argumentation which looms so large in that book. This is purportedly an excerpt from the lost dialogue, "On Philosophy," and runs as follows:

"In general, where there is a better there is a best. Since, then, among existing things one is better than another, there is also something that is best, which will be the divine. Now that which changes is changed either by something else or by itself, and if by something else, either by something better or by something worse, and if by itself, either to something worse or through desire for something better; but the divine has nothing better than itself by which it may be changed (for that other would then have been more divine), nor on the other hand is it lawful for the better to be affected by the worse; besides, if it were changed by something worse, it would have admitted some evil into itself, but nothing in it is evil. On the other hand, it does not change itself through desire for something better, since it lacks none of its own excellences; nor again does it change itself for the worse, since even a man does not willingly make himself worse, nor has it anything evil such as it would have acquired from a change to the worse. (This proof, too, Aristotle took over from the second book of Plato's *Republic*.)" *On Philosophy*, Fragment 16, in Ross's translation of *Select Fragments, The Works of Aristotle Translated into English*, vol. XII. For the Greek text, see Simplicius, *In De Caelo* 289. 1–15.

Note how the argument hangs on the acceptance of the axiom of finality, οὐκ εἰς ἄπειρον, as well as on the acceptance of the equation the best = the divine. The reader might also be referred to *Metaphysics* Γ, 1008 b 31–1009 a 5.

[124] *Metaphysics* Λ, 1071 b 4–5. ἀνάγκη εἶναι ἀΐδιόν τινα οὐσίαν ἀκίνητον. Ross's text.

[125] *Metaphysics* Λ, 1071 b 6–7. αἵ τε γὰρ οὐσίαι πρώτων ὄντων, καὶ εἰ πᾶσαι φθαρταί, πάντα φθαρτά. Ross's text.

[126] *Metaphysics* Λ, 1069 a 19–26.

things should be destructible which would be a consequence of the destructibility of all *substances*.

Aristotle next introduces his view that motion is everlasting:[127] "But it is impossible for motion either to have come into being or to have passed out of being (for it is everlasting), nor time. For 'before' and 'after' cannot exist if time does not exist. And thus then motion is continuous just as time is. For time is either the same thing as motion or some kind of an affection of it."[128] Ross in his notes on this passage reveals clearly how the argument is articulated. "If all substances are perishable, everything else is perishable (since everything else is posterior to and depends on substance). But movement and time are not perishable.[129] Therefore not all substances are perishable."[130] Ross then continues his anlysis by observing: "If you say time comes into being, you imply that before that there was no time; but the very word 'before' implies time."[131] So we have Ross's conclusion: "Having used the eternity of movement to prove that there must be an eternal substance, Aristotle now draws from it a further inference, that movement must be continuous, and from this he develops his whole astronomical theory."

We may now proceed to the next decisive passage in the unfolding argument. As Aristotle continues after the discussion of

---

[127] We have already had occasion to quote this passage above, Chapter IV, pp. 93–94 and note 16, where we were discussing briefly Aristotle's theory of time.

[128] *Metaphysics* Λ, 1071 b 6–10. ἀλλ' ἀδύνατον κίνησιν ἢ γενέσθαι ἢ φθαρῆναι (ἀεὶ γὰρ ἦν), οὐδὲ χρόνον. οὐ γὰρ οἷόν τε τὸ πρότερον καὶ ὕστερον εἶναι μὴ ὄντος χρόνου· καὶ ἡ κίνησις ἄρα οὕτω συνεχὴς ὥσπερ καὶ ὁ χρόνος· ἢ γὰρ τὸ αὐτὸ ἢ κινήσεώς τι πάθος. Ross's text. The translation is mine. For comparison, here is Ross's version: "But it is impossible that movement should either come into being or cease to be; for it must always have existed. Nor can time come into being or cease to be; for there could not be a before and an after if time did not exist. Movement also is continuous, then, in the sense in which time is; for time is either the same thing as movement or an attribute of movement." For Aristotle's argument *in extenso* for the eternity of motion, cf. *Physics*, Book VIII, chapters 1–3, and, of course, the rest of this book discusses the Prime Mover.

[129] To complete the chain of reasoning, we should insert the Aristotelian view that movement and time themselves are not substances, but are posterior to and dependent upon substance.

[130] In other words, there must be some non-perishable substances to which non-perishable movement and time may be attached. This seems to be the way in which Aristotle wishes us to understand the argument.

[131] Here Ross asks, "But does not Aristotle's view that *space* is finite contain the same difficulty?"

the eternity of motion, he insists that this motion must be locomotion, and the only kind of such motion that is continuous is
circular. He next remarks on the implications of his conception
of potentiality, and then concludes: "There must, then, be such
a principle, whose very essence is actuality. Further, then, these
substances must be without matter; for they must be eternal, at
least if anything else is eternal. Therefore they must be actuality."[132] The first sentence of the quotation is a legitimate conclusion to this phase of the argument, if one has been persuaded
by the preceding steps. However, the shift to the plural, "substances," is unexpected. We are not surprised that the eternal
"substance," the existence of which Aristotle has been seeking to
establish, should be "without matter," but we have thus far not
been too well prepared to entertain the notion of a plurality of
such eternal substances. Ross explains the shift in this way: "So
far Aristotle has spoken of the necessity of one unmoved mover
of the universe. He now refers by anticipation to the unmoved
movers of the several celestial spheres, for which cf. 1074 a 15."
It is enough for us to note the presence of Aristotle's theory
advanced in the eighth chapter of *Metaphysics* Λ to the effect that
there are fifty-five "unmoved movers" which are instrumental
in bringing about the motions of the celestial spheres. Since this
theory has no bearing on our present problem of God, the Unmoved Mover as a source of value, we fortunately do not need to
become involved in the controversy concerning Λ, chapter 8,
its position in the Aristotelian corpus, and the complicated and
detailed cosmology it suggests. Our task rather is to concentrate on
what Ross has just called "one unmoved mover of the universe."[133]

---

[132] *Metaphysics* Λ, 1071 b 19–22. δεῖ ἄρα εἶναι ἀρχὴν τοιαύτην ἧς ἡ οὐσία
ἐνέργεια. ἔτι τοίνυν ταύτας δεῖ τὰς οὐσίας εἶναι ἄνευ ὕλης· ἀϊδίους γὰρ δεῖ, εἴπερ
γε καὶ ἄλλο τι ἀΐδιον. ἐνέργεια ἄρα. Ross's text. Incidentally, we should observe that Ross here translates, I believe correctly, εἴπερ by "at least if." Cf.
above, Chapter VI, note 15, where I argued against rendering εἴπερ as "since."

[133] For a summary and critique of Aristotle's theology, see Ross, *Aristotle's
Metaphysics*, vol. I, Introduction, pp. cxxx–xliv. As for the position of chapter 8
of Book Λ, it has long been noted that it interrupts the argument of chapters 6,
7, and 9 which are devoted exclusively to the subject of God, the Unmoved
Mover. Furthermore, whereas the style of chapter 8 is very carefully worked
out, that of the other three seems to be abbreviated, choppy, and cryptic. Jaeger
(*Aristotle*, 2nd edition, Oxford, Clarendon Press, pp. 342 ff.) argues vigorously that
chapter 8 was written late in Aristotle's life while most of the rest of Book Λ is early.

The concluding section of chapter 6 of Book Λ should be before us as a necessary extension of the argument thus far: "Therefore chaos or night did not exist for an infinite time, but the same things have always existed (either passing through a cycle of changes or obeying some other law), since actuality is prior to potency. If, then, there is a constant, something must always remain, acting in the same way. And if there is to be generation and destruction, there must be something else which is always acting in different ways. This must, then, act in one way in virtue of itself, and in another in virtue of something else—either of a third agent, therefore, or of the first. But it must be in virtue of the first. For otherwise this again causes the motion both of the third agent and of the second. Therefore it is better to say 'the first.' For it was the cause of eternal movement; and something else is the cause of variety, and evidently both together are the cause of eternal variety. This, accordingly, is the character which the motions actually exhibit. What need then is there to seek for other principles"?[134] So, having established the existence of the immovable substance, and the eternity of motion, Aristotle now shows how the motion of the sphere of the fixed stars and

---

Though it must be admitted that the so-called early and late passages have not been made to cohere completely with each other, we should not overlook the fact that Aristotle must have had some such intention in mind. The use of the plural, "substances," in 1071 b 21 in chapter 6 is evidence for this if Ross indeed is right that it anticipates the content of chapter 8. Also the passage in chapter 8, 1074 a 31–38, which argues for the existence of "one heaven" *(εἷς οὐρανός)* seems to have been inserted, and is actually more relevant to the subject matter of chapters 6, 7, and 9 than to that of chapter 8. On the basis of data such as these we can be the more confident of our theory as to the nature of Aristotle's writings. Some passages are typical lecture notes. Others are carefully wrought. The whole was kept in a fluid condition, with Aristotle continually striving to eliminate internal inconsistencies. When the corpus left his hands for the last time by no means all of these inconsistencies had been ironed out. Cf. above, Chapter III, note 20.

[134] *Metaphysics* Λ, 1072 a 7–18. ὥστ' οὐκ ἦν ἄπειρον χρόνον χάος ἢ νύξ, ἀλλὰ ταὐτὰ ἀεὶ ἢ περιόδῳ ἢ ἄλλως, εἴπερ πρότερον ἐνέργεια δυνάμεως. εἰ δὴ τὸ αὐτὸ ἀεὶ περιόδῳ, δεῖ τι ἀεὶ μένειν ὡσαύτως ἐνεργοῦν. εἰ δὲ μέλλει γένεσις καὶ φθορὰ εἶναι, ἄλλο δεῖ εἶναι ἐνεργοῦν ἄλλως καὶ ἄλλως. ἀνάγκη ἄρα ὡδὶ μὲν καθ' αὑτὸ ἐνεργεῖν ὡδὶ δὲ κατ' ἄλλο· ἤτοι ἄρα καθ' ἕτερον ἢ κατὰ τὸ πρῶτον. ἀνάγκη δὴ κατὰ τοῦτο· πάλιν γὰρ ἐκεῖνο αὐτῷ τε αἴτιον κἀκείνῳ. οὐκοῦν βέλτιον τὸ πρῶτον· καὶ γὰρ αἴτιον ἦν ἐκεῖνο τοῦ ἀεὶ ὡσαύτως· τοῦ δ' ἄλλως ἕτερον, τοῦ δ' ἀεὶ ἄλλως ἄμφω δηλονότι. οὐκοῦν οὕτως καὶ ἔχουσιν αἱ κινήσεις. τί οὖν ἄλλας δεῖ ζητεῖν ἀρχάς; Ross's text.

of the sun derive from the initial postulates. As Ross indicates, the phrase "something must always remain, acting in the same way" refers to the sphere of the fixed stars. Likewise, when Aristotle says "There must be something else which is always acting in different ways," he means the spheres of the sun, moon, and planets, for to these motions can be attributed the presence of generation and destruction in the world in which we live. With these points at the very end of the sixth chapter of Book Λ added to the argument, we have now been given a fair preliminary sketch of Aristotle's views of the Unmoved Mover and how it functions in relation not only to the motions of the astronomical bodies but also to the motions involved in generation and destruction on the earth.[135]

Now we come to the seventh chapter of Book Λ which is devoted exclusively to the Unmoved Mover. Some of the passages which we shall quote have already been discussed but they need to appear again in order that we may have as complete a sense of the present argument as we possibly can. So we meet the following assertion: "Therefore the first heavens must be eternal. There is therefore also something which moves them. And since that which is moved and moves is intermediate, there is a mover which moves without being moved, being eternal, substance, and actuality. And the object of desire and the object of thought move in this way; they move without being moved. The primary objects of desire and of thought are the same."[136] The eternal first "heavens" must have something to move them and so again by a suppressed reliance upon the axiom of finality (οὐκ εἰς ἄπειρον) the existence of the Unmoved Mover is the more thoroughly established. Now Aristotle must explain why this Mover moves, and so he introduces the notion that the objects of desire and thought cause motion in precisely this way, i.e., without being moved. He then goes on to assert that "the primary objects of

---

[135] For fuller details on the argument of this passage, see Ross's notes on 1072 a 7–18.

[136] *Metaphysics* Λ, 1072 a 23–27. ὥστ᾽ ἀΐδιος ἂν εἴη ὁ πρῶτος οὐρανός. ἔστι τοίνυν τι καὶ ὃ κινεῖ. ἐπεὶ δὲ τὸ κινούμενον καὶ κινοῦν μέσον, † τοίνυν † ἔστι τι ὃ οὐ κινούμενον κινεῖ, ἀΐδιον καὶ οὐσία καὶ ἐνέργεια οὖσα. κινεῖ δὲ ὧδε τὸ ὀρεκτὸν καὶ τὸ νοητόν· κινεῖ οὐ κινούμενα. τούτων τὰ πρῶτα τὰ αὐτά. Ross's text except I have eliminated [καὶ] in 1072 a 24. For a brief discussion of the textual problems in the passage, cf. Ross, note *ad loc.*

desire and of thought are the same." So far as one can see, Aristotle
has apparently no basis or evidence for making this assertion.
At least, there is none up to this point in the argument.

But let us see how Aristotle attempts to exploit the consequences
of his assertion. The next sentence reads: "For the apparent
good is the object of appetite, and the real good is the primary
object of rational desire."[137] We already have had occasion to
quote this passage in our discussion of the Good, the Beautiful,
and the Telos, where we cited it as an illustration of the way in
which Aristotle often uses a value term as description of the Final
Cause. On that occasion we took pains to say that we were considering the passage as an illustration of a characteristic Aristotelian
method and were not looking at it as part of an argument.[138]
But now we are concerned with it as a step in the argument.
What we must emphasize is that here *for the first time* in *Metaphysics*
Λ do we meet value terms, *viz.*, "the apparent good or beautiful"
(*τὸ φαινόμενον καλόν*) and "the real good or really beautiful"
(*τὸ ὂν καλόν*). Why it should come here is perhaps easy to explain.
Let us remember that up to this point the argument has been
strictly ontological in that it has been concerned with an explanation of motion, which, as we have had occasion to observe,
Aristotle regarded as "the characteristic fact of nature."[139] The
Unmoved Mover has been introduced, and, as we have said, he
has to explain why it causes motion. He had cited objects of
thought and of desire as causing motion without being moved.
And he has made the unsupported claim that the primary objects
of desire and thought are the same. If they are, and mind you,
we have as yet been given no evidence that they are, then Aristotle
has one way out. "The real good is the primary object of rational
desire." He simply introduces the value "the real good," and
having done so, he can set up this series of equations: The
Unmoved Mover = the primary object of thought = the primary object of desire = the real good (*τὸ ὂν καλόν*). And so
Aristotle has laid the ground-work for his coming answer to the

[137] For the Greek text, cf. above, note 117.
[138] Cf. above, Chapter VI, p. 220, and note 117.
[139] Cf. above, Chapter IV, p. 95 and note 19 where we were discussing
Physics, 253 b 7–9.

question: How does the Unmoved Mover cause motion? But let us not forget that he would have been unable to do so, had he not inserted value into the argument.[140]

Let us move on to the next step in the Aristotelian text where he goes back to his statement that "the primary objects of desire and of thought are the same." He now clearly wants to present some support for this proposition which, as we have noted, has remained unsubstantiated. He writes: "For the thinking is the starting-point. And thought is moved by the object of thought and one side of the list of opposites is in itself the object of thought; and in this substance is first, and in substance, that which is simple and exists actually.. . . . But the good, also, and that which is in itself desirable are on this same side of the list; and the first in any class is always best or analogous to the best."[141] We studied this passage in a preliminary way in the section on Substance and Priority.[142] There our interest was primarily in the consistent way in which Aristotle assigns priority to substance. We commented on the meaning of the phrase "one side of the list of opposites" and quoted Ross's note thereon. We also observed (and this is important in our present context) that the argument begins ontologically. The start is thinking, and the prime object of thought is substance, as part of that which is to be found on the "one side of the list of opposites." Furthermore, within substance, the completely primary as an object of thought is substance or that substance "which is simple and exists actually." (Note that we are still in the ontological domain.) We also pointed out that this simple and actually existing substance is οὐσία as τέλος, just another name for absolute Final Cause, the Unmoved Mover. And, in studying the conception of priority, we called attention to the shift into the area of value, apparently unsupported, which occurs when Aristotle asserts that on the same side of the "list" as substance is "the good or the beautiful," *(τὸ καλόν)* and "that

---

[140] Ross in his note *ad loc.* in his translation calls the argument "not very clearly stated." Tricot, *op. cit.*, note *ad loc.*, calls it *"fort difficile."* Neither of these scholars has noticed the implications of the fact that late in an ontological argument a value notion has been introduced to cut a Gordian knot. It is to be hoped that the approach to the analysis of this argument from the point of view of Being and Value will prove to be illuminating.

[141] For the Greek text, cf. above, note 71.

[142] Cf. above, Chapter VI, pp. 197–198.

which is in itself desirable."[143] So in our earlier discussion it had to suffice us to say that the shift from "being" to "value" was a typical instance of Aristotelian procedure.

How then does the passage attempt to support the contention that "the primary objects of desire and of thought are the same"? And let us not forget that Aristotle's whole theory of the way in which the Unmoved Mover causes motion depends ultimately upon the validity of this contention. The answer, it must be confessed, is not very convincing. Aristotle simply says that the object of thought, *i.e.*, substance, and the object of desire, *i.e.*, the good (τὸ καλόν), appears on the "same side of the list of opposites." This hardly seems to be a sufficient ground to establish the identity between the object of thought and the object of desire which is essential to Aristotle's argument. So to summarize: (a) Throughout, Aristotle exhibits his characteristic ontological emphasis. There is no doubt about the primacy of substance in the argument. (b) Aristotle needs a notion of value, for without it he cannot possibly explain how the Unmoved Mover causes motion. (c) The only argument for the so-called "identity" of substance as object of thought and good as object of desire is to the effect that they both appear on the same side of the list of opposites. (d) No matter what he may say, Aristotle, because of his general metaphysical approach, cannot avoid having value in a secondary status.[144]

Whatever may be the weakness of his case, Aristotle now proceeds on the assumption that he is on firmer ground. At any rate he does feel justified in making this claim: "The final cause, then, produces motion by being loved, and by that which it moves, it moves all other things."[145] This is Aristotle's theory to explain

---

[143] I should like to suggest that, in 1072 a 34–35, ἀλλὰ μὴν καὶ τὸ καλὸν καὶ τὸ δι᾽ αὑτὸ αἱρετὸν ἐν τῇ αὐτῇ συστοιχίᾳ, the second καί could be better translated as "that is." So the "good" or "beautiful" should be understood as "that which in itself is desirable."

[144] It is respectfully requested at this point that the reader compare Plato's Theory of Ideas, where at the apex of the hierarchy of Ideas stands the Idea of the Good, that which at the same time is most real and most valuable. See the argument of Chapter II, above.

[145] *Metaphysics* Λ, 1072 b 3–4. κινεῖ δὴ ὡς ἐρώμενον, κινούμενα δὲ τἆλλα κινεῖ. Ross's text. He offers the emendation κινούμενα for κινουμένῳ which is found in several MSS. Ross is followed, *e.g.*, by the translators Tricot, *op. cit.*, and Tredennick in the Loeb Classical Library. However, Jaeger, *Aristotelis Metaphysica*

the way in which the Unmoved Mover causes motion, that "characteristic fact of nature." Because of the goodness imputed to the Unmoved Mover, he has become a legitimate object of desire or love. In short, for Aristotle this is what makes the world go round.

Perhaps because he felt that he needed another reason for attributing goodness to the Unmoved Mover, Aristotle turns now to rely on his conception of Necessity: "The First Mover, then, of necessity exists; and in so far as it is necessary, it is good, and in this sense a first principle."[146] It will be recalled that we analyzed this passage when we were discussing the place of the Relative and the Necessary.[147] There we insisted that the text was very significant for our understanding of Aristotle's attitude towards the question of value. We resumed very briefly the argument of Book Λ, chapter 7, and we pointed out how the goodness of the Unmoved Mover is established on the basis of one of the meanings of the necessary, *viz.*, "that without which the good is impossible." Aristotle's reasoning apparently is as follows: If necessity can mean the *sine qua non* of the good, and if the Unmoved Mover exists of Necessity, the Unmoved Mover must be good (and, of course, can as a consequence be an object of love). But there is a difficulty here. Can Aristotle argue, from the *sine qua non* as a ground for the good, that this same *sine qua non* can be the sufficient reason for the good? This is clearly not possible and hence the Aristotelian argument must stand convicted. The foregoing point, I believe, reinforces our contention in our earlier treatment of the Necessary. As we argued then, the necessary existence of the Prime or Unmoved Mover depends upon the axiom of finality. It is the case, as we suggested before, that an ontological approach produces an Unmoved Mover who is really neutral in the area of value, until in the present context the notion of Necessity lets Aristotle assert that He is good. (And we have seen why this step cannot withstand scrutiny.) We now repeat

---

(Oxford Classical Texts, 1957), reads κινουμένῳ and suggests that it modifies τῷ οὐρανῷ which is to be supplied.

[146] For the Greek text of *Metaphysics* Λ, 1072 b 10–11, cf. above, Chapter VI, note 49. Also in 1072 b 12, the Greek for the sense of necessity which is relevant here runs: τὸ δὲ οὗ οὐκ ἄνευ τὸ εὖ.

[147] Cf. above, Chapter VI, pp. 184–186.

our earlier question: "Can it be that Aristotle wishes us to think of τὸ ἀναγκαῖον, Necessity, as the matrix of value?" This may be his wish (at least to make us think of Necessity as *a* matrix of value), but if it is, the argument he has adduced fails to compel assent.[148]

The following description of the Unmoved Mover is one of the most notable passages in the Aristotelian corpus. Though it is somewhat lengthy, still it must be quoted in full, so that we

[148] Ross, in the Oxford translation of the *Metaphysics*, adds this note on 1072 b 10–11: "*i.e.*, it is necessary in the sense of οὗ οὐκ ἄνευ τὸ εὖ, and is ∴. good." It is, of course, this argument which we have been criticizing. And this also is Alexander's view of the passage. However Ross, in his annotated edition of the *Metaphysics* (see notes on 1072 b 10–11) has a most curious series of observations. He first offers this expanded paraphrase of the text: "Since it is not subject even to the minimal change (and therefore, *a fortiori*, is not subject to generation and destruction) it is a thing that exists of necessity; and inasmuch as it exists of necessity, its existence is good, and it is in this way (*sc.* as good or object of desire) that it is a principle, *i.e.*, the principle of movement of the universe." Thus far it would seem that Ross was relying on the sense of necessary defined as τὸ οὗ οὐκ ἄνευ τὸ εὖ. But in the next note he refers to *Metaphysics* Δ, 1015 b 14, εἰ ἄρα ἔστιν ἄττα ἀΐδια καὶ ἀκίνητα, οὐδὲν ἐκείνοις ἐστι βίαιον οὐδὲ παρὰ φύσιν. (Ross renders this sentence as follows: "If, then, there are certain eternal and unmovable things, nothing compulsory or against their nature attaches to them.") Ross then adds that "that which admits of no contingency of any kind" (A reference here is made to 1072 b 8 where no value term is present) "καλῶς ἔχει because nothing contrary to its nature can happen to it."

There seems to be no justification in the text for Ross to say that these "certain eternal and unmovable things" are "faring well" or "are in good condition" or "are doing fine"—however one wishes to render καλῶς ἔχει. All we do have is the flat ontological statement, that because of their non-contingent character these things necessarily exist. But Ross argues that since they are "in good condition," then they, and among them the Unmoved Mover, are good, and hence the Unmoved Mover is a valid object of desire. So, in short, the goodness of the Unmoved Mover is made to derive from the fact that He is necessary in the sense of τὸ μὴ ἐνδεχόμενον ἄλλως ἔχειν (1072 b 13), *i.e.*, "of not being able to be otherwise." It need hardly be added that "not being able to be otherwise" cannot suffice as a source of goodness. Ross then goes on to assert that the sense of necessary, *viz.*, τὸ οὗ οὐκ ἄνευ τὸ εὖ is not the one which Aristotle means in the passage. (Incidentally, Ross does not refer to the fact that when he did his translation of the *Metaphysics*, he believed that Aristotle was relying on the sense of necessary as τὸ οὗ οὐκ ἄνευ τὸ εὖ.)

He then convicts the sense of τὸ οὗ οὐκ ἄνευ τὸ εὖ in substantially the same way as we have attempted to do. Ross says that this sense "is simply the condition of the good, and may be a necessary evil, οἷον τὸ πιεῖν τὸ φάρμακον ἀναγκαῖον ἵνα μὴ κάμνῃ (*e.g.*, the drinking of a drug is necessary in order not to be sick), Δ, 1015 a 24; it is evidently not in this sense that the life of God is necessary." The outcome of the whole matter is this: the goodness of the Unmoved Mover cannot derive from his non-contingency, τὸ μὴ ἐνδεχόμενον ἄλλως ἔχειν; τὸ οὗ οὐκ ἄνευ τὸ εὖ is merely the condition of the good but cannot be its sufficient cause.

may grasp the sequence of its thought and the cryptic and assertive character of its language.[149] "On such a principle, then, depend the heavens and the world of nature. And its life is such as the best which we enjoy, and enjoy for but a short time. For it is ever in this state (which we cannot be), since its actuality is also pleasure. (And therefore are waking, perception, and thinking most pleasant, and hopes and memories are so because of their reference to these.) And thought in itself deals with that which is best in itself, and that which is thought in the fullest sense with that which is best in the fullest sense. And thought thinks itself because it shares the nature of the object of thought; for it becomes an object of thought in coming into contact with and thinking its objects, so that thought and object of thought are the same. For that which is *capable* of receiving the object of thought, *i.e.*, the essence, is thought. And it is *active* when it *possesses* this object. Therefore the latter [possession] rather than the former [receptivity] is the divine element which thought seems to contain, and the act of contemplation is what is most pleasant and best. If, then, God is always in that good state in which we sometimes are, this compels our wonder; and if in a better, this compels it yet more. And God *is* in a better state. And life also belongs to God; for the actuality of thought is life most good and eternal. We say therefore that God is a living being, eternal, most good, so that life and duration continuous and eternal belong to God; for this *is* God."[150]

We can now see what Aristotle is able to say about his principle, the Unmoved Mover, once he has established it, to his own

---

[149] We had occasion to quote the last five lines above, p. 186.

[150] *Metaphysics* Λ, 1072 b 13–30. ἐκ τοιαύτης ἄρα ἀρχῆς ἤρτηται ὁ οὐρανὸς καὶ ἡ φύσις. διαγωγὴ δ' ἐστὶν οἵα ἡ ἀρίστη μικρὸν χρόνον ἡμῖν. οὕτω γὰρ ἀεὶ ἐκεῖνο (ἡμῖν μὲν γὰρ ἀδύνατον), ἐπεὶ καὶ ἡδονὴ ἡ ἐνέργεια τούτου (καὶ διὰ τοῦτο ἐγρήγορσις αἴσθησις νόησις ἥδιστον, ἐλπίδες δὲ καὶ μνῆμαι διὰ ταῦτα). ἡ δὲ νόησις ἡ καθ' αὑτὴν τοῦ καθ' αὑτὸ ἀρίστου, καὶ ἡ μάλιστα τοῦ μάλιστα. αὑτὸν δὲ νοεῖ ὁ νοῦς κατὰ μετάληψιν τοῦ νοητοῦ· νοητὸς γὰρ γίγνεται θιγγάνων καὶ νοῶν, ὥστε ταὐτὸν νοῦς καὶ νοητόν. τὸ γὰρ δεκτικὸν τοῦ νοητοῦ καὶ τῆς οὐσίας νοῦς, ἐνεργεῖ δὲ ἔχων, ὥστ' ἐκείνου μᾶλλον τοῦτο ὃ δοκεῖ ὁ νοῦς θεῖον ἔχειν, καὶ ἡ θεωρία τὸ ἥδιστον καὶ ἄριστον. εἰ οὖν οὕτως εὖ ἔχει, ὡς ἡμεῖς ποτέ, ὁ θεὸς ἀεί, θαυμαστόν· εἰ δὲ μᾶλλον, ἔτι θαυμασιώτερον. ἔχει δὲ ὧδε. καὶ ζωὴ δέ γε ὑπάρχει· ἡ γὰρ νοῦ ἐνέργεια ζωή, ἐκεῖνος δὲ ἡ ἐνέργεια· ἐνέργεια δὲ ἡ καθ' αὑτὴν ἐκείνου ζωὴ ἀρίστη καὶ ἀΐδιος. φαμὲν δὴ τὸν θεὸν εἶναι ζῷον ἀΐδιον ἄριστον, ὥστε ζωὴ καὶ αἰὼν συνεχὴς καὶ ἀΐδιος ὑπάρχει τῷ θεῷ· τοῦτο γὰρ ὁ θεός. Ross's text.

satisfaction, as the source of motion, as pure and immaterial activity, as eternal, and above all as good. It is as if he can give his reasoning powers free rein to make a series of deductions about this principle. What must its life *(διαγωγή)* be like? Where can we turn to obtain a clue for answering this question? Aristotle simply cites human life and asserts that the best human activity is engaging in or experiencing *νόησις*, which Ross calls "immediate or intuitive knowledge."[151] Because man is a thoroughly contingent being he can experience this activity of *νόησις* for only a short time, but since it is best for man, it *must* be best for the completely non-contingent Being—the Unmoved Mover. Clearly this conclusion depends upon an assumption on Aristotle's part, *viz.*, that it is *really* best for man.

At any rate, the next assertion is to the effect that the Unmoved Mover's activity of *νόησις* is everlasting, and in support of this contention Aristotle identifies the activity or actuality with pleasure.[152] Again he seems to be arguing from the most pleasant experiences or activities of human beings, *e.g.*, waking, perception, and thinking *(νόησις)* as well as hopes and dreams of these, with the conclusion that the *νόησις* of the Unmoved Mover must be correspondingly pleasant in a superlative degree.

When we get to the bottom of it the ensuing passage on the nature of *νόησις*, the activity of immediate or intuitive knowledge, seems to be sheer assertion, or could we say assertive ratiocination, supported from time to time by reference to human experience. Take the claim, "thought in itself deals with that which is best in itself." Evidently we are meant to suppose that when a man experiences immediate or intuitive knowledge, he deals with what is best in itself. Why this should be so we are not told, but we are exhorted to believe that thought "in its fullest sense" deals with "what is best in the fullest sense." Here the reference must be to the *νόησις* of the Unmoved Mover. How can this *νόησις* be further delineated? Aristotle's answer in summary lies in

---

[151] Cf. Ross, note on *Metaphysics* Λ, 1072 b 14–24. At several points during my discussion of our long quotation I am indebted to his notes.

[152] Ross in his note *ad loc.* invites comparison with *Nicomachean Ethics*, 1153 a 14, where the identity of pleasure and activity is promulgated. He also refers to *Nicomachean Ethics*, 1175 a 15, where in "exacter language" Aristotle argues that "pleasure inevitably accompanies and completes activity."

obliterating the distinction of thought and its object, or to put it the other way, in insisting upon the identity of thought and its object. Here we do have ratiocination unalloyed. Only by establishing this identity of νόησις and its object can the actuality of the Unmoved Mover, *viz.*, νόησις, become completely relieved of any shred of potentiality. When it *has* its object, or alternatively, when it *is* its object, we are then confronted with pure actuality or activity.

Once Aristotle has announced that the taint of potentiality has been totally eliminated, he forthwith for the first time in *Metaphysics* Λ introduces the conception of the divine, θεῖον, i.e., pure activity is what is divine for νοῦς. This is all translated into another form of the announcement, "The act of contemplation *(θεωρία)* is most pleasant and best." And now all the names for the first principle, Unmoved Mover, Final Cause, eternal substance, and so on, have substituted for them the one name, God. He is *always* engaged in the supreme activity of contemplation. He supremely commands our wonder. He "has" life, for again Aristotle pronounces his conviction that the "actuality of thought is life," and now comes the reiteration of the superlative value term "most good" to characterize God.

After a short interlude in which Aristotle injects another argument for associating supreme beauty and goodness with the first principle,[153] he presents the following summary description of the Prime Mover: "It is clear then from what has been said that there is a substance which is eternal and unmovable and separate from sensible things. It has been shown also that this substance cannot have any magnitude, but it is without parts and indivisible. For it produces movement through infinite time, but nothing finite has infinite power. And, while every magnitude is either infinite or finite, it cannot, for the above reason, have finite magnitude, and it cannot have infinite magnitude because there is no infinite magnitude at all. But it is also clear that it is impassive and unalterable; for all the other changes are posterior to change of place. It is clear, then, why the first mover has these attributes."[154]

[153] We briefly glanced at this passage in section G, Chapter VI, where we were studying actuality and potentiality. Cf. above, pp. 204–205.

[154] *Metaphysics* Λ, 1073 a 3–13. ὅτι μὲν οὖν ἔστιν οὐσία τις ἀΐδιος καὶ ἀκίνητος καὶ κεχωρισμένη τῶν αἰσθητῶν, φανερὸν ἐκ τῶν εἰρημένων· δέδεικται δὲ καὶ

There are several striking aspects in this summary description. No longer does the name God appear. The Prime Mover or the Unmoved Mover is referred to as a "substance," an οὐσία. There is no talk of God's everlasting "good state" nor of his "most pleasant and best" activity of contemplation. We are not told that He compels our wonder, nor does Aristotle restate in different language that God is "a living being, eternal, most good." Rather the terms now employed are those of abstract metaphysics and of strictly ontological import. The "substance" is eternal, unmovable, separate from sensibles.[155] It has no magnitude, it is without parts, it is indivisible, it causes motion through infinite time, it is impassive and unalterable.[156] Each of these characteristics or attributes of the Prime Mover has already been affirmed of "it" save its impassivity.[157] *Why, one can well ask, is there no mention of goodness in the list?* It does seem as though the more Aristotle turns loose his ratiocinative powers in developing his description of this "substance," the more abstract it becomes, and the more it becomes emptied of any humanly understandable meaning or content.

In our study of God, the Unmoved Mover, the title we chose to give to the present section of our inquiry, there remains to consider Aristotle's additional argument in chapter 9 of *Metaphysics* Λ. This is by way of being a companion piece or a completion of chapter 7. The two chapters together (and perhaps even to a greater degree the latter) have precipitated unlimited comment on the part of classicists, philosophers, and theologians from the

---

ὅτι μέγεθος οὐδὲν ἔχειν ἐνδέχεται ταύτην τὴν οὐσίαν ἀλλ' ἀμερὴς καὶ ἀδιαίρετός ἐστιν (κινεῖ γὰρ τὸν ἄπειρον χρόνον, οὐδὲν δ' ἔχει δύναμιν ἄπειρον πεπερασμένον· ἐπεὶ δὲ πᾶν μέγεθος ἢ ἄπειρον ἢ πεπερασμένον, πεπερασμένον μὲν διὰ τοῦτο οὐκ ἂν ἔχοι μέγεθος, ἄπειρον δ' ὅτι ὅλως οὐκ ἔστιν οὐδὲν ἄπειρον μέγεθος)· ἀλλὰ μὴν καὶ ὅτι ἀπαθὲς καὶ ἀναλλοίωτον· πᾶσαι γὰρ αἱ ἄλλαι κινήσεις ὕστεραι τῆς κατὰ τόπον. ταῦτα μὲν οὖν δῆλα διότι τοῦτον ἔχει τὸν τρόπον. Ross's text.

[155] When one recalls Aristotle's scathing invective against Plato's Ideas as hypostatizations, as existing apart, χωριστά, one cannot help but feel that those same criticisms could be directed just as well at this super-hypostatization, this "substance" which exists "separate from sensibles," κεχωρισμένη τῶν αἰσθητῶν.

[156] Note the *a fortiori* character of this argument. The Prime Mover is not capable of φορά, locomotion. Since φορά is the first of motions and if the Prime Mover does not have it, then it cannot experience a posterior form of motion, ἀλλοίωσις, alteration. Hence it is unalterable.

[157] Its lack of magnitude or extension is simply another way of expressing the immateriality of the first principle.

fourth century before Christ to the present day, and one can suppose that this situation will continue into the indefinite future. We can only hope that our approach which attempts to discover the relation between ontology and axiology in these two famous Aristotelian chapters may throw some new light on their significance. With respect to chapter 9, we should like to urge that here Aristotle's major motive is to establish more firmly the ways in which value may be associated with the Unmoved Mover. If this indeed be his major motive, let us try to determine the extent to which he has been successful in his effort.

The chapter opens with this statement: "Matters having to do with thought present certain problems; for while it does seem to be the most divine of phenomena, how it comes to be such as it is involves difficulties."[158] It must be admitted that the meaning of this passage is not completely unambiguous. Aristotle appears to begin with the generalized notion of thought under which, I take it, both human thought and divine thought may be subsumed. Again the argument seems to work from what is considered to be most valuable and important in human affairs to that which *must* be, therefore, most valuable and important, in an absolute sense, in divine thought. In other words, the suggestion seems warranted that we have here a parallel argument to that advanced in chapter 7 when Aristotle is describing the "life"of his "first principle" *(διαγωγή)*.[159] There, it will be recalled, it was asserted that "its life is such as the best which we enjoy, and enjoy for but a short time."

After this opening argument in chapter 9, the center of Aristotle's attention begins to focus more sharply on the nature of divine thought, though always the nature of human thought is present for purposes of comparison. It is as if Aristotle were proceeding to analyze non-contingent divine thought in the light of contingent human thought. So, to paraphrase his reasoning, it is urged that thought cannot be very important if it has nothing

---

[158] *Metaphysics* Λ, 1074 b 15–17. Τὰ δὲ περὶ τὸν νοῦν ἔχει τινὰς ἀπορίας· δοκεῖ μὲν γὰρ εἶναι τῶν φαινομένων θειότατον, πῶς δ' ἔχων τοιοῦτος ἂν εἴη, ἔχει τινὰς δυσκολίας. Ross's text. The rendering is my own. Ross, I believe, is not warranted in translating the opening words as "The nature of the divine thought." Incidentally, his version of δοκεῖ through θειότατον runs: ". . . for while thought is held to be the most divine of things observed by us."

[159] Cf. *Metaphysics* Λ, 1072 b 14–15. See above, Chapter VI, pp. 233–235.

for its object. Aristotle next observes: "And if it thinks, but this depends on something else, then (as that which is its substance [or essence] is not the act of thinking, but a potency) it cannot be the best substance [or essence]; for it is through thinking that its value belongs to it."[160] What are we supposed to understand by this statement? It must be something like this: If thought thinks, and if its thinking is somehow subservient to something else, the thought as subservient cannot have as its essence the "best" essence. Thought, so regarded, is really a potentiality of thinking. Thought must in the full sense be actually engaged in the activity of thinking if it is to lose its subservient status and if its essence is properly to be called best. And, Aristotle insists, thought really becomes valuable (*τίμιον*) only when it is actively thinking. The argument rests on two bases: (1) the priority or superiority of actuality over potentiality, and (2) the assertion of Book Λ, chapter 9, that thinking is the best activity.[161] It will of course be recalled that on examination this latter assertion was found to rest on rather tenuous support. And in the former point we should not fail to notice this very decisive instance of the characteristic Aristotelian habit of deriving value from actuality, the axiological from the ontological.

As he moves on in his analysis, Aristotle drops the question of the location of the "essence" in the problem, *i.e.*, whether it be thought or the act of thinking,[162] and asks abruptly, "What does thought think?" His answer is categorical: "Either it thinks itself or something else."[163] The tone now takes on a ring of eloquence as Aristotle continues: "Does it matter, then, or not, whether it thinks the good [or beautiful] or any chance thing? Are there not some things about which it is incredible that it should think? Evidently, then, it thinks that which is most divine

---

[160] *Metaphysics* Λ, 1074 b 18–21. εἴτε νοεῖ, τούτου δ᾽ ἄλλο κύριον, οὐ γάρ ἐστι τοῦτο ὅ ἐστιν αὐτοῦ ἡ οὐσία νόησις, ἀλλὰ δύναμις, οὐκ ἂν ἡ ἀρίστη οὐσία εἴη· διὰ γὰρ τοῦ νοεῖν τὸ τίμιον αὐτῷ ὑπάρχει. Ross's text. In the translation I have inserted in brackets twice the phrase "or essence." This clearly is the sense of οὐσία which Aristotle has in mind in the present context.

[161] Again cf. above, Chapter VI, pp. 233–235.

[162] *i.e.*, νοῦς or νόησις.

[163] *Metaphysics* Λ, 1074 b 22–23. τί νοεῖ;; ἢ γὰρ αὐτὸς αὑτὸν ἢ ἕτερόν τι. Ross's text. We do not need to pay any attention to the next phrase: καὶ εἰ ἕτερόν τι, ἢ τὸ αὐτὸ ἀεὶ ἢ ἄλλο (and if something else, either that which is always the same or something different), as it is not essential to the argument.

and precious, and it does not change; for change would change for the worse, and this would be already a movement."[164] He really manages to lend elevation to a rather common-sense argument. We are now supposed to be convinced that the divine act of thinking is best. How could it then have a chance thing as its object and not the good or beautiful? No one, Aristotle would argue, could imagine the divine act of thinking contemplating things—horrible, we might guess, among others. No, comes the conclusion, for because the activity of divine thinking is best, its object must be "most divine and most precious" or valued. Further, this divine act of thinking does not change,[165] for if it is most divine and most precious, any change must be for the worse, and on top of this, such a change would entail motion. But, this has long since been ruled out, for the actuality, *i.e.*, the divine activity of thinking, has been established as unmovable. So Aristotle is arguing from the excellence of the act of divine thinking to the conclusion that its object must be equally excellent.

We next are confronted again with the consequences of maintaining that the activity of thinking be regarded as a potentiality. Aristotle first holds that if it is not a pure act or activity, but rather a process of bringing some potency into an actuality, undoubtedly this continuous process would prove to be very wearisome or laborious for the divine thought. Obviously, it is unthinkable that the divine thought, that best entity, could ever be in a state of getting tired out. And in the second place, if the divine thinking is in some sense a potency, then the object of thought would be more valuable or more precious than thought itself. Under such circumstances, thinking will be engaged in even by a man who has the worst object of thought, with the result that this worst actualization, the object, will be better than the potentiality, *viz.*, thinking (remember in this argument thinking is

---

[164] *Metaphysics* Λ, 1074 b 23–27. πότερον οὖν διαφέρει τι ἢ οὐδὲν τὸ νοεῖν τὸ καλὸν ἢ τὸ τυχόν; ἢ καὶ ἄτοπον τὸ διανοεῖσθαι περὶ ἐνίων; δῆλον τοίνυν ὅτι τὸ θειότατον καὶ τιμιώτατον νοεῖ, καὶ οὐ μεταβάλλει· εἰς χεῖρον γὰρ ἡ μεταβολή, καὶ κίνησίς τις ἤδη τὸ τοιοῦτον. Ross's text. In the translation I have inserted in brackets, "or beautiful," as, I think, a necessary gloss on τὸ καλόν..

[165] Tricot, *op. cit.*, suggests in his translation that the divine act of thinking does not change the object of its thought, making μεταβάλλει transitive, and not intransitive as do Ross and Tredennick. The suggestion may have some merit.

regarded as a potentiality), and so Aristotle specifies the results: "Therefore if this is to be avoided (as it is, since it is better not to see some things than to see them), thinking cannot be the supreme good."[166] Once more we find him using the theory that a potentiality is a potentiality of opposites with the resultant notion that a potentiality is capable of producing a "bad actualization." We have already explored the consequences of this essentially self-contradictory conception, and what difficulties it gives Aristotle when he finds himself faced with a situation where something must be done with the problem of value.[167] In all events, so far as this problem is concerned, thus far in Book Λ, chapter 9, the prime emphasis has been upon the activity or actuality of thinking, νόησις, and whatever terms connoting value which have been associated with it have consistently been in a secondary or derivative relation to it. In other words, Aristotle's stance here towards the value question seems to be much the same as the one we studied above when we were considering "Value as Quality."

What is in many ways the dramatic and climactic conclusion of *Metaphysics* Λ follows immediately: "Therefore it must be itself that thought thinks (since [or if indeed] it is the most excellent of things), and its thinking is a thinking on thinking."[168] Given certain Aristotelian premises as well as some of his more or less vaguely supported assertions, there is an inexorability about the reasoning which leads to this conclusion.[169] To put it in slightly colloquial form, if indeed thinking is the best thing that there is, and if it has to be thinking about something that is the very best thing that there is (and, mind you, this condition

---

[166] *Metaphysics* Λ, 1074 b 32–33. ὥστ᾽ εἰ φευκτὸν τοῦτο (καὶ γὰρ μὴ ὁρᾶν ἔνια κρεῖττον ἢ ὁρᾶν), οὐκ ἂν εἴη τὸ ἄριστον ἡ νόησις. Ross's text. The rendering is that of Tredennick in the Loeb Classical Library.

[167] Cf. above, Chapter VI, section E, "Value as Quality," pp. 192–196, where we were exploring the implications of *Metaphysics* Θ, 1051 a 4–17.

[168] *Metaphysics* Λ, 1074 b 33–35. αὐτὸν ἄρα νοεῖ, εἴπερ ἐστὶ τὸ κράτιστον, καὶ ἔστιν ἡ νόησις νοήσεως νόησις. Ross's text. In the translation, I have added in brackets "or if indeed" for εἴπερ in order to suggest the widest possible range of meaning for the word. Also one should not fail to note the superlative which Aristotle chooses here to express the supreme worth of νόησις or divine thought, τὸ κράτιστον, the most excellent and with the inevitable extra connotation of the extreme in power.

[169] Cf. our summary treatment of this argumentation above, Chapter IV, pp. 113–114.

rules out anything that might be in any way second-rate), one cannot get away from it, thinking must be thinking about itself, *viz.*, thinking. As has been frequently pointed out, the process of this reasoning has produced a God who is the pure activity of unalloyed and contentless self-consciousness. At any rate, from the human point of view, it appears impossible to see how this divine thinking, or as I have called it, self-consciousness, can be anything other than contentless. And, too, we should be aware that in this chapter Aristotle does not call thinking, νόησις, God, but only asserts that it is most divine and most precious. We must repeat that the more this type of reasoning tries to expand upon just exactly what this principle, this Prime Mover, this God, this divine thinking is, the more the terms lose meaning, and so we end with the abstraction "Its thinking is a thinking on thinking." Repeatedly the question has been asked: "How can this principle, or whatever name you wish to call it, so void of content, be asserted to be supremely good, *le souverain Bien*, the phrase used so often by Tricot, and as such be the object of love, ultimately the source of all motion in the universe?" As we have been attempting to show by our close scrutiny of the text, Aristotle has been able to produce little by way of coercive evidence, but rather has had to rely for the most part on his flat pronouncements that this is the way it is, because he says that this is the way it is.

Aristotle has only two or three more points to add to his discussion. Once again he takes us back to the realm of the contingent, to set up another analogical argument from the contingent to the non-contingent, and as we have noted before, the evidence of the contingent is about all by way of supporting data which he has been able to bring to bear in making his case. At this present juncture, he cites the illustrations of "science" or "knowledge," perception, opinion, and understanding.[170] All these operations of the human intellect, he maintains, always are concerned with something other than themselves as their object, and only incidentally have themselves as object. In other words, they are only incidentally self-conscious, or aware of what it is that they are doing. Ross suggests the example that "the medical man

---

[170] The Greek terms are: ἐπιστήμη, αἴσθησις, δόξα, and διάνοια.

knows primarily about health."[171] Aristotle then goes on to ask how value or worth or goodness *(τὸ εὖ)* may be discovered in or be found to belong in the activity of thinking, if the act of thinking and the object of thought are different, *i.e.*, in that they do not have the same essence. The answer follows immediately: "We answer that in some cases the knowledge is the object. In the productive sciences (if we abstract from the matter) the substance in the sense of essence, and in the theoretical sciences the formula or the act of thinking, *is* the object. As, then, thought and the object of thought are not different in the case of things that have not matter, they will be the same, *i.e.*, the divine thinking will be one with the object of its thought."[172] In this way Aristotle completes his analogical argument. By calling attention to the productive sciences and the theoretical sciences, which are contingent human affairs and under certain circumstances are concerned with objects that are without matter, he reminds the reader of his view that in such instances the activity of thinking and the object of thought are the same.[173] If this is the case in these areas of the contingent, by analogy it must be the case in the domain of the non-contingent, where the divine thinking certainly must be dealing with the non-material. So Aristotle can confidently announce his conclusion that divine thinking will be one with its object, and this of course explains to his satisfaction how goodness or worth *(τὸ εὖ)* is found in the activity of divine thinking. It is good. It is identical with its object. Therefore its object is good.

Aristotle has only one more question to ask and the effort to answer it involves him in still another analogical argument. Is the object of divine thought a composite? If it were, this would entail change for the divine thinking as it moves from one part to another of its object.[174] Here is Aristotle's resolution: "We

---

[171] Cf. note on *Metaphysics* Λ, 1074 b 36.

[172] *Metaphysics* Λ, 1074 b 38–1075 a 5. ἢ ἐπ᾽ ἐνίων ἡ ἐπιστήμη τὸ πρᾶγμα, ἐπὶ μὲν τῶν ποιητικῶν ἄνευ ὕλης ἡ οὐσία καὶ τὸ τί ἦν εἶναι, ἐπὶ δὲ τῶν θεωρητικῶν ὁ λόγος τὸ πρᾶγμα καὶ ἡ νόησις; οὐχ ἑτέρου οὖν ὄντος τοῦ νοουμένου καὶ τοῦ νοῦ, ὅσα μὴ ὕλην ἔχει, τὸ αὐτὸ ἔσται, καὶ ἡ νόησις τῷ νοουμένῳ μία. Ross's text.

[173] This whole problem is discussed at length in the *De Anima*, Book III, chapters 4–6. Ross calls particular attention to *De Anima*, 430 a 2 ff. and 430 a 19 ff. as well as to *Metaphysics* Z, 1032 a 32–b 14.

[174] One may wonder why Aristotle saw a special difficulty *(ἀπορία)* in this problem with respect to the object of divine thought. If divine thought is another

answer that everything which has not matter is indivisible. As human thought, or rather the thought of composite objects, is in a certain period of time (for it does not possess the good at this moment or at that, but its best, being something *different* from it, is attained only in a whole period of time), so throughout eternity is the thought which has *itself* for its object."[175] The analogy is clear. Human thought (or thought of composite beings) is designated as contingent. At its very best, it is able to lay hold on the very best *(τὸ ἄριστον)* which is extrinsic to it, *i.e.*, this is the condition of being contingent, "in a whole period of time" or "in an organized life of activity." Aristotle suggests that this is a considerable achievement for a contingent being and all of us can understand fairly well what it means. And so, by analogy, we are invited to attempt to grasp its significance when we are translated into the realm of the non-contingent. When all contingency is banished, because divine thought thinks itself, such is its situation, divine thought thinking itself, identical with itself, throughout all eternity. Aristotle merely repeats his dictum that divine thinking is thinking on thinking, a dictum, as we said before, from which all humanly comprehensible meaning has been drained. And yet, at the same time, Aristotle is asking us to believe that this divine thinking is the absolute best.

To recapitulate briefly the results of our analysis of God, the Unmoved Mover, we saw first how the remarks about God in *Metaphysics* A, in particular, when He was described as a cause of all things, are inconsistent with the doctrine advanced in

---

name for Prime Mover, God, etc., then its indivisibility has already been asserted (1073 a 6–7). And if divine thinking is one with its object (the result of the immediately preceding argument) then the object must be indivisible and not a composite. It might be suggested that the raising of this final difficulty permitted him to introduce one more analogical argument.

[175] *Metaphysics* Λ, 1075 a 6–10. ἢ ἀδιαίρετον πᾶν τό μὴ ἔχον ὕλην—ὥσπερ ὁ ἀνθρώπινος νοῦς ἢ ὅ γε τῶν συνθέτων ἔχει ἔν τινι χρόνῳ (οὐ γὰρ ἔχει τὸ εὖ ἐν τῳδὶ ἢ ἐν τῳδί, ἀλλ᾽ ἐν ὅλῳ τινὶ τὸ ἄριστον, ὂν ἄλλο τι)—οὕτως δ᾽ ἔχει αὐτὴ αὑτῆς ἡ νόησις τὸν ἄπαντα αἰῶνα; Ross's text. It might have been more precise if Ross had translated ὅ γε τῶν συνθέτων as "the thought of composite beings." That is, it is the thinker who is composite not the object of his thought. Also Ross's notes in his annotated text reveal that he changed his mind concerning the meaning of ἐν τῳδὶ ἢ ἐν τῳδί ἐν ὅλῳ τινί. and χρόνῳ τῳδί, τῳδί, ὅλῳ τινί. Instead of understanding χρόνῳ as the noun which τῳδί, τῳδί, and ὅλῳ τινί qualify, he suggests the meaning to be: ". . . for it does not possess the good in this particular activity or in that, but it possesses the *summum bonum* in an organized life of activity."

Metaphysics Λ. We then moved to this later book and saw Aristotle constructing his argument to establish the existence of a "first principle," as he reaffirmed his theories of the primacy of substance and of the eternity of motion, with the consequence that there must be a cause of this motion. The cause of motion was designated as the Unmoved Mover, and we attempted to show that Aristotle was somewhat less than successful in the ensuing stage of the reasoning. In order that the Unmoved Mover could in fact cause motion, He had to be set up as simultaneously the object of thought and of desire. If He is to cause motion by being loved, He must be good. Our contention was that Aristotle actually was unable to demonstrate convincingly the goodness of the Unmoved Mover. We argued that the emphasis on ontology proves to be a serious handicap when it becomes necessary to introduce some kind of conception of value, as clearly was the case when it had to be shown that somehow the Unmoved Mover must be good. After noting the presence of analogical arguments based on the experience of men, we observed how Aristotle shifted his nomenclature, and began to refer to the first principle as divine, as God, though it also became apparent that Aristotle thereafter quickly reverted to the terms of abstract metaphysics. We concluded our study with a discussion of the ninth chapter of Book Λ and attempted to demonstrate that Aristotle was trying again to strengthen his case for the goodness of his first principle. Here he concentrated on the divine thought or act of thinking and again relied upon the persuasive power of analogical argument. The result was the emergence of the famous doctrine that divine thinking is thinking on thinking. We felt constrained to affirm again, as has often been done, that this "principle" so described is from the human point of view without content or meaning. No matter how strenuously Aristotle urges us to regard it as the most excellent, best, and most precious, it is very difficult for a human being to grasp why this must be so on the grounds which have been submitted.

In summary, we may justifiably contend that the greatest force in Aristotle's reasoning lies in his use of arguments from analogy. But, even though much store has been set by such arguments, in Aristotle, when such arguments are advanced for the purpose of establishing a value, their usefulness is impaired, according to our theory, because of the inadequacy of his view of the relation of Being and Value. In other words, as we have repeatedly argued, Aristotle's too exclusive stress upon ontology has prevented him from constructing a consistent value theory. A consistent value theory in the area of human action is essential if analogical arguments are going to function with maximum effectiveness in the situation with which Aristotle is faced, *viz.*, to establish the goodness of the first principle, the Prime Mover or God.

A passage in Ross's introduction to the *Metaphysics* illustrates in some degree the point which we have been trying to make. "Aristotle's characteristic philosophical virtue of faithfulness to the given facts made this [*i.e.*, to regard motion as illusory] impossible for him; he had to allow the reality of motion. But he could not regard it as not needing explanation. He therefore tried to explain it as due to something which was itself exempt from motion. *It is exclusively as first mover that a God is necessary to his system.* Aristotle does not, indeed, succeed in explaining movement; we are left with the question how a non-physical activity of desire can produce movement in space. But, apart from this difficulty, the God whom he sets up is inadequate to meet the demands of the religious consciousness."[176] Ross here explicitly recognizes the fact that God enters the Aristotelian picture in order to answer the ontological question: What causes motion? If this be the case, and it unquestionably is, there is no wonder that Aristotle should have difficulty in showing how goodness may attach to God. We can only come to the conclusion that Aristotle's doctrine of God, the Unmoved Mover, cannot explain satisfactorily why this God is good, and how goodness can find its way into the universe, and how such goodness in the universe may be identified.[177]

[176] Ross, *op. cit.*, vol. I, p. cliii. (The italics are mine.) See also above, Chapter VI, note 133. It may have been observed that in our discussion we have not mentioned Aristotle's much debated doctrine of the "active reason." It has been omitted since after careful reflection it does not seem really to bear upon our central problem.

[177] Ross, *op. cit.*, vol. I, Introduction, p. clii, has made the following very pertinent remark: "But the deeper defects of his [Aristotle's] theology arise not from its being based on a particular physical theory, but from its being based on physics to the exclusion of other possible bases." In other words the base on physics is strictly ontological.

J. PARENTHESIS: CREATION AND VALUE

Aristotle repeatedly makes it clear that he holds no doctrine of creation. For evidence we need only cite such passages as the extended argument in the *De Caelo*,[178] or the pronouncement that there is no genesis or generation of form or essence,[179] nor is there any generation of the categories.[180] Or there is the instance where he remarks: "It is strange also to attribute generation to eternal things, or rather this is one of the things that are impossible."[181] And, of course, there is the decisive testimony of the passage on the eternality of motion, and of time, to which we have already referred on two former occasions: "But it is impossible for motion either to have come into being or to have passed out of being (for it is everlasting), nor time. For 'before' and 'after' cannot exist if time does not exist. And thus then motion is continuous just as time is. For time is either the same thing as motion or some kind of an affection of it."[182]

Furthermore, there are two interesting places where Aristotle is critical of Plato's doctrine of creation, and be it noted, Aristotle clearly attributes such a doctrine to his master. The first occurs in the eighth book of the *Physics*, where it is remarked: "Plato alone asserts the creation of time, saying that it had a becoming together with the universe, the universe according to him having had a becoming."[183] The second passage appears in the *De Caelo*: "For

---

[178] *De Caelo*, 279 b 12 ff. See also 301 b 31.

[179] *Metaphysics* Z, 1033 a 5–7. φανερὸν ἄρα ὅτι οὐδὲ τὸ εἶδος, ἢ ὁτιδήποτε χρὴ καλεῖν τὴν ἐν τῷ αἰσθητῷ μορφήν, οὐ γίγνεται, οὐδ' ἔστιν αὐτοῦ γένεσις, οὐδὲ τὸ τί ἦν εἶναι. Ross's text. "It is clear then that neither the form nor whatever one should call the external configuration of a sensible, comes into being nor is there any generation of it, neither is there any generation of the essence." The translation is mine.

[180] *Metaphysics* Z, 1034 b 7–10. οὐ μόνον δὲ περὶ τῆς οὐσίας ὁ λόγος δηλοῖ τὸ μὴ γίγνεσθαι τὸ εἶδος, ἀλλὰ περὶ πάντων ὁμοίως τῶν πρώτων κοινὸς ὁ λόγος, οἷον ποσοῦ ποιοῦ καὶ τῶν ἄλλων κατηγοριῶν. Ross's text. "But not only regarding substance does our argument prove that its form does not come to be, but the argument applies to all the primary classes alike, *i.e.*, quantity, quality, and the other categories."

[181] *Metaphysics* N, 1091 a 12–13. ἄτοπον δὲ καὶ γένεσιν ποιεῖν ἀϊδίων ὄντων, μᾶλλον δ' ἔν τι τῶν ἀδυνάτων. Ross's text.

[182] Cf. above, Chapter VI, p. 225, and notes 127 and 128.

[183] *Physics*, 251 b 17–19. (Democritus has just been quoted as having said that there was no generation of time.) Πλάτων δὲ γεννᾷ μόνος. ἅμα μὲν γὰρ αὐτὸν τῷ οὐρανῷ γεγονέναι, τὸν δ' οὐρανὸν γεγονέναι φησίν. Ross's text, except that I have removed the brackets from γεγονέναι in 251 b 18. As Ross points out,

there are some who think it possible both for the ungenerated to be destroyed and for the generated to persist undestroyed. (This is held in the *Timaeus*, where Plato says that the heaven, though it was generated, will nonetheless exist to eternity.)"[184] Even if we had only the evidence of these two quotations there would be no doubt as to the extent to which Aristotle had dissociated himself from Plato's doctrine of the creation of the universe and of time, and held rather to the view that the universe is uncreated, that it exists from everlasting to everlasting, and is characterized by an eternity of motion and of time.[185]

It is my conviction that Aristotle's lack of a doctrine of creation has affected very profoundly his complicated and in many ways inconsistent attitude towards questions of value. If one is a thoroughgoing naturalist, with no commitment to any transcendent element in Reality, it is perfectly possible to construct a coherent theory of value. A basic hedonism or the "greatest happiness" principle of the utilitarian produce views of value

---

Aristotle has in mind the *Timaeus*, 28 b and 38 b. Scholars are familiar with A. E. Taylor's contention, followed by Cornford, that Plato was speaking metaphorically, and did not hold a doctrine of creation. I am not convinced by Taylor's argument. Furthermore, we should note that Taylor has not been persuaded by the testimony of Aristotle, for certainly Aristotle does *not* think that Plato was speaking metaphorically. For my own view of the doctrine in the *Timaeus*, cf. above, Chapter II, pp. 23–25.

[184] De Caelo, 280 a 28–32. εἰσὶ γάρ τινες οἷς ἐνδέχεσθαι δοκεῖ καὶ ἀγένητόν τι ὂν φθαρῆναι καὶ γενόμενον ἄφθαρτον διατελεῖν, ὥσπερ ἐν τῷ Τιμαίῳ. ἐκεῖ γάρ φησι τὸν οὐρανὸν γενέσθαι μέν, οὐ μὴν ἀλλ᾽ ἔσεσθαί γε τὸν ἀεὶ χρόνον. Bekker's text. The passages referred to in the *Timaeus* is 31.

[185] Some may be worried by the phrase which Aristotle does use from time to time, as, for example, in *De Caelo*, 271 a 34, ὁ δὲ θεὸς καὶ ἡ φύσις οὐδὲν μάτην ποιοῦσιν. "God and nature make [or "create"] nothing in vain." That this should be taken as reflecting a serious Aristotelian view that God is to be regarded as a Creator seems hardly possible. As Ross has remarked (*op. cit.*, vol. I, Introduction, p. clii), "For the one passage in which he says that God and nature do nothing in vain, there are many in which he says that nature does nothing in vain." [For examples of the latter expression, cf. *De Anima*, 432 b 21; 434 a 30; *De Partibus Animalium*, 661 b 24; *De Incessu Animalium*, 704 b 15; 708 a 9; *Politics*, 1253 a 9 ; 1256 b 20-21. For passages where nature seems to be almost personified, cf. *De Partibus Animalium*, 663 a 31 ff.; 686 a 7 ff.; 687 a 15 ff.; 694 b 14; *De Generatione Animalium*, 755 a 31. For variations on the general theme, cf. *De Partibus Animalium*, 691 b 4 [nature makes nothing superfluous, περίεργον]; *De Generatione Animalium*, 717 a 15-16 [nature makes everything either because it is necessary or because it is better]; 731 a 24 [nature acts like a craftsman, δημιουργεῖ]; 744 b 16 [nature is compared to a good house-manager, οἰκονόμος ἀγαθός]. It may be added that Aristotle's conception of φύσις in its many aspects well repays serious study.

that emerge inevitably from the acceptance of their respective prior assumptions. Similarly, such theisms as Judaeism or Christianity, with their shared doctrine of Creation, possess coherent systems of value—in which God as Creator of all things is also and simultaneously the source of all the values and the things valued in the created universe as well as the human spirits who function as evaluating agents in the world which surrounds them. The difficulty of the Aristotelian position might be expressed in this way: On the one hand, Aristotle has set up a theism, or more precisely, a quasi-theism or quasi-deism, with God, the Unmoved Mover at its head; and on the other, he has so contrived it that God is far removed from the world of men and can exert nothing but a most indirect influence upon it. Furthermore, God conceived as the act of thought thinking upon itself means that He cannot have in His consciousness the universe and its contents, of which He is the Prime Mover. In other words, the theist stance would invite the construction of a value system emanating from God as its source, but this is rendered impossible by the absolute and exclusive self-consciousness of God. It might be argued that Aristotle has asserted that God is good. Quite apart from the fact that Aristotle's case for the goodness of God proves to be far from convincing, as we have attempted to show, it is difficult to see how this goodness defined as thought thinking upon itself could ever function as a sanction for value. And this difficulty is exacerbated further by the Aristotelian view that God is related in no way to the universe and to men as a Creator.[186]

Inevitably Aristotle's conception that the universe is uncreated raises the question of the nature of his teleology. Let us begin by examining a statement by Ross concerning the problem: "Apart from occasional sports and coincidences all that exists and all that happens exists or happens for an end. But it is not so clear what interpretation is to be put on this view. Does he mean

---

[186] The following summary comment by Ross (*op. cit.*, vol. I, Introduction, p. (liii) is well worth quoting: "The prime mover is not the creator of the universe, for both matter and the subordinate forms are uncreated and eternal; nor is He a providential ruler, since His thought is of Himself alone; nor is He a God of love, since emotion of any sort would mar His life of pure contemplation. Still less does He meet the other set of demands [*sc.* of the religious consciousness], since His relation to the universe and to human spirits is (in Λ) described as one of transcendence alone."

(1) that the whole structure and history of the universe is the fulfillment of a divine plan? Or (2) that it is due to the conscious
working towards ends of individual beings? Or (3) that there is
in nature an unconscious striving towards ends?"[187] The first
alternative is rejected basically because "the sole activity of God
is self-knowledge."[188] Ross rejects the second because "the
teleology in nature is definitely opposed to the working of
thought."[189] He therefore plumps for the third alternative on
which he proceeds to comment as follows: "The notion of
unconscious teleogy is, it is true, profoundly unsatisfactory. If
we are to view action not merely as producing a result but as being
aimed at producing it, we must view the doer of it either as
imagining the result and aiming at reaching it, or as merely the
agent of some other intelligence which through it is realizing its
conscious purposes. *Unconscious teleology implies a purpose which
is not the purpose of any mind, and hence not a purpose at all.* But
Aristotle's language suggests that he (like many modern thinkers)
did not feel this difficulty, and that, for the most part, he was
content to work with the notion of an unconscious purpose in
nature itself."[190]

So far as one can see, Ross's analysis is unassailable. No one
can take objection to his rejection of the first two alternative ways
of explaining the meaning of Aristotle's teleology. Ross is quite
correct in seeing that "unconscious teleology" is in fact a contradiction in terms. For teleology to have meaning, as every one
would agree, a mind fully conscious of the purpose in view and

---

[187] Ross, *op. cit.*, vol. I, Introduction, p. cli.

[188] Ross does mention traces of a different mode of thought in the Aristotelian
corpus. He cites first the comparison of God to the captain of an army who is
responsible for the "order" of the army. (In Chapter VI, section K, below, we
shall treat this whole notion advanced by Aristotle in *Metaphysics* Λ, chapter 10.)
On the basis of this passage it might be possible to think of the world's history
being controlled by God's will, so Ross suggests. To conclude thus, in my
opinion, really stretches the imagination. Similarly Ross cites the *De Generatione
et Corruptione*, 336 b 31, where Aristotle argues that for things which are incapable
of permanent existence, God has contrived the next best expedient and has seen
to it that generation shall be continual. (For our interpretation of this passage,
see above, Chapter V, pp. 139–141.) Finally Ross refers to Aristotle's praise of
Anaxagoras for his notion that "reason" *(νοῦς)* is the cause of the world and its
order (*Metaphysics* A, 984 b 15–18).

[189] Ross here refers to *Physics*, 199 b 26.

[190] Ross, *op. cit.*, vol. I, Introduction, p. clii. The italics are mine.

capable in some sense as an agent to do something about achieving the purpose is absolutely essential. The best one can do for the conception of "unconscious teleology" is to call it a metaphor, which involves almost despite itself a quasi-personification of Nature, with the result that through the personification a "mind" is introduced into the picture.

For the moment, let us look at Aristotle's teleology from a different point of view. Can it be that this most teleological of all thinkers, at least by reputation and upon the basis of many texts in his corpus, has not produced a genuine teleology at all, but rather one that is truncated, or, if you will, to a degree spurious? May we put it this way?[191] Aristotle presents us with a universe in which there are untold myriads of individual particulars, all of which come into being and pass out of being, and all of which are dominated by the final cause, or end, or purpose they seek to achieve. In the realm of the animate, the acorn strives to become as complete an oak tree as it can, and the boy seeks to become as much of a man as he can. Even in the realm of the inanimate, it is through the operation of the formal, efficient, and final causes viewed as one that things seek to find their proper region in the universe.[192] Also in the realm of artefacts, final cause or purpose is dominant. The builder, looking at the plans, moulds the wood, brick, and stone, for the *purpose* of constructing a house for the shelter of human beings. So much in summary for the teleology of particulars in the universe. At the same time, Aristotle tells us that there is an absolute cosmic Final Cause, which operates also as an efficient cause, since as the object of thought and desire it sustains the eternally existent motion in the universe. And do not forget that the other names for this absolute Final Cause are Prime Mover, Unmoved Mover, God who is the act of thought thinking upon itself.

Let us ask again in what sense are we to understand the teleology of this Final Cause. We have examined the contention advanced by Ross that Aristotle on the whole "explains" cosmic teleology by postulating the existence of an "unconscious teleology" in

---

[191] Cf. our preliminary discussion of Aristotle's teleology, Chapter VI, section H, pp. 217–220.

[192] Cf. above, Chapter IV, pp. 107–108.

nature, and we agreed with Ross that an "unconscious teleology" is in fact no teleology at all. When you come right down to it, the real question is this: How can the Aristotelian Final Cause produce a genuine cosmic teleology, particularly if there is no attendant doctrine of creation? All the Final Cause can "produce" is motion, and in reality it cannot even be said to "produce" motion; more precisely, it can only "sustain" motion, for motion is uncreated. In other words, the Aristotelian universe is essentially static. At its core sits God, the so-called Final Cause, thinking unmoved upon Himself, and around Him whirl ceaselessly the heavenly bodies in circular motion. Such a universe cannot have a history. There can only be "histories" of the myriads of particulars within the universe which come into being and pass out of being. Furthermore, value cannot enter the universe from the Final Cause as a source if there be no doctrine of creation. Without a doctrine of creation, how in Aristotelian terms can you answer the question: What is the purpose of the universe? This question the conception of a cosmic Final Cause inevitably entails.

To repeat the point which we have already tried to make: One does not need to have a God or a transcendental element in Reality or a doctrine of creation in order to fashion a self-consistent theory of value. If, however, a view of Reality postulates a God *and* a doctrine of creation, then it is possible also to formulate a coherent cosmic theory of value by maintaining that God through his creative activity has brought value into the world of space and time. As we have observed, such is the case with Judaeism and Christianity, as well as with the kind of creationism attributed by Plato to the Demiurge in the *Timaeus*.[193] But if, as in Aristotle, one is faced with a "system" in which there is a God *without* a doctrine of creation, it is our contention that it is impossible to fashion a thoroughly coherent and self-consistent theory of value. Such a conclusion is substantiated by our estimate of Aristotle's teleology. His cosmic Final Cause really is based upon another argument from analogy. The "final cause" or conscious purpose of the boy is to become a man. The "final cause" of the house, through the conscious purpose of the architect and

---

[193] Plato's is, of course, not *creatio ex nihilo*, as in Judaeism and Christianity.

builder, is to become a shelter for human beings. In each case something is "created." But the analogical argument fails in two respects: the cosmic Final Cause does not possess conscious purpose and it cannot engage in creative activity.

K. ENVOI: GOOD IN THE UNIVERSE

Aristotle takes his leave of his study of theology in the rather curious tenth and concluding chapter of *Metaphysics* Λ. Much of it need not concern us, for it consists of a series of critiques of his Pre-Socratic and Platonic predecessors in somewhat the spirit of *Metaphysics* A. He points to the impossibilities and strange notions of some of them as well as to the utterances of thinkers of the more refined sort and to those views which involve the fewest difficulties.[194] But the chapter opens with two fairly elaborate images which are designed to illuminate the way in which "the good" is in the universe. It seems as though (perhaps this suggestion is fanciful) he may still be somewhat uneasy about the case he has made for the "goodness" of the Prime Mover and for the nature of "good" as a principle. In any event, in the light of our concern to discover how Being and Value are related in Aristotle's thought, it is most important to examine with care these two images.

The chapter opens as follows: "We must consider also in which of two ways the nature of the universe contains the good or the best [or most excellent], whether as something separate and by itself, or as the order of the parts. Or does it in both ways, as in an army? For the good is found both in the order and in the leader, and more in the latter; for he does not depend on the order but it depends on him."[195] In the first place, and perhaps

---

[194] The key words are: ἀδύνατα, ἄτοπα, οἱ χαριεστέρως λέγοντες, and ἐλάχισται ἀπορίαι, *Metaphysics* Λ, 1075 a 25-27.

[195] *Metaphysics* Λ, 1075 a 11-15. Ἐπισκεπτέον δὲ καὶ ποτέρως ἔχει ἡ τοῦ ὅλου φύσις τὸ ἀγαθὸν καὶ τὸ ἄριστον, πότερον κεχωρισμένον τι καὶ αὐτὸ καθ' αὑτό, ἢ τὴν τάξιν. ἢ ἀμφοτέρως ὥσπερ στράτευμα; καὶ γὰρ ἐν τῇ τάξει καὶ ὁ στρατηγός, καὶ μᾶλλον οὗτος· οὐ γὰρ οὗτος διὰ τὴν τάξιν ἀλλ' ἐκείνη διὰ τοῦτόν ἐστιν. Ross's text. In the translation, I have substituted "the best or most excellent" instead of "the highest good" for τὸ ἄριστον. Also I have preserved the interrogative form of the original for ἢ through στράτευμα. καὶ γὰρ through διὰ τοῦτόν ἐστιν perhaps could be translated more precisely than Ross has done in the Oxford version. Could it in more extended form run something like this: "And the reason I say this is that (= the expansion of καὶ γὰρ) the good of the

incidentally, we should not fail to notice the language Aristotle employs to express the first of the two ways in which "the nature of the universe contains the good '*viz.*,' as something separate and by itself 'or' self-substantiating."[196] No one needs to be reminded that this is exactly the terminology which Plato uses in order to describe the existence "apart" of a Platonic Idea. In other words, Aristotle here is postulating the existence of an entity, in fact an hypostatized entity, in exactly the same fashion as he has repeatedly declared to be illegitimate when he finds the same thing happening in Plato.[197]

But be this as it may, let us attempt to see as accurately as we can what meaning can be derived from the image of the army. There can be no doubt that order in an army is a good for the army, and it is surely sound military theory that this order ultimately derives from the commanding general. The better the general the better will be the order of the troops under him. So much is the clear meaning of the concluding sentence, "The general does not exist by reason of the order of the army, but rather the order exists by reason of the general." Similarly, because of the derivative nature of the order, we can understand why the general is "more of a good" than the order. But the Greek text is not completely clear so far as the "goodness" of the general is concerned.[198] Is he "the good" or "the best"? Are they identical? Or is he "good" and "best," *i.e.*, are these his primary attributes? The latter would look to be the case, on the grounds of the phrase, $\mu\tilde{\alpha}\lambda\lambda o\nu$ $o\tilde{\upsilon}\tau o\varsigma$, *i.e.*, *he* is more of a good than the order which comes from him.

Now for the application of the image as an answer to the question how "the nature of the universe contains the good and the

---

army is in its order and its good is its general likewise; and the general is even more so its good. For the general does not exist by reason of the order of the army, but rather the order exists by reason of the general."

[196] *i.e.*, $\varkappa\varepsilon\chi\omega\rho\iota\sigma\mu\acute{\varepsilon}\nu o\nu$ $\tau\iota$ $\varkappa\alpha\grave{\iota}$ $\alpha\grave{\upsilon}\tau\grave{o}$ $\varkappa\alpha\vartheta'$ $\alpha\grave{\upsilon}\tau\acute{o}$.

[197] Aristotle would doubtless counter that his $\varkappa\varepsilon\chi\omega\rho\iota\sigma\mu\acute{\varepsilon}\nu o\nu$ $\tau\iota$ was an immaterial "substance," $o\grave{\upsilon}\sigma\acute{\iota}\alpha$, and as a "substance" capable of "separate existence." And we all remember how Aristotle insists that the Platonic Ideas cannot be "substances," $o\grave{\upsilon}\sigma\acute{\iota}\alpha\iota$. It should be needless to point out that the Aristotelian conception of $o\grave{\upsilon}\sigma\acute{\iota}\alpha$ as substance simply has no place in Platonic metaphysics.

[198] It might be observed that a general is isolated enough $(\varkappa\varepsilon\chi\omega\rho\iota\sigma\mu\acute{\varepsilon}\nu o\nu)$, but is he self-substantiating $(\alpha\grave{\upsilon}\tau\grave{o}$ $\varkappa\alpha\vartheta'\alpha\grave{\upsilon}\tau\acute{o})$?

best." Again there would be no argument that the universe is ordered, and that this in the overwhelming opinion of men is a good. As for how it comes to be in the universe, are we to understand from the image that it comes from some self-subsistent principle, The Good? But Aristotle nowhere else recognizes the existence of such a separately existing principle. It does seem sometimes that enthusiastic admirers of Aristotle may make too much of the image. Ross, for example, writes in an extravagant manner: "The doctrine here stated is that goodness exists not only immanently in the world but transcendently in God, and even more fundamentally in Him, since He is the source of the good in the world, which is produced by the desire for Him as the order in an army is produced by its striving to do the will of its leader."[199] Observe that under Ross's hand the "general" has become God. God is transcendent and the order of the universe that comes from "desire for Him" becomes the ground for adding to the doctrine of theological transcendentalism a doctrine of theological immanentism. Such an interpretation, of course, ignores the lack of clarity, if not ambiguity, in the Greek text to which we have already called attention.

In his introduction to the text of the *Metaphysics* Ross seems to temper his views to a degree. He quotes the image of the army as a passage which "at first sight" seems to indicate that God is both transcendent and immanent. He then goes on to say: "But, though Aristotle says that the good exists both as a transcendent spirit, and as an immanent order, he does not say that *God* exists in both these ways. God is essentially for him, in Λ, the first cause; and in view of his often-repeated doctrine of the priority of substance, the cause must for him be a substance and not an abstraction such as order is. Yet he treats the order as due to God, so that his God may truly be said to be at work in the world, and in *this* sense immanent."[200] Ross's statement is open to criticism.

---

[199] Note on *Metaphysics* Λ, 1075 a 11–15. Observe how Ross picks up the notion that the Final Cause moves by being an object of love (κινεῖ δὴ ὡς ἐρώμενον, 1072 b 3), a passage on which we have commented above, Chapter VI, pp. 231–232 (see also the pages immediately preceding and following). I suppose that "the order in an army is produced by its striving to do the will of its leader," but there may be many disenchanted military men who would disagree.

[200] Ross, *op. cit.*, vol. I, Introduction, p. cl.

To be absolutely precise, in the Greek text Aristotle does not mention God, nor does he call "the good" a "transcendent spirit." Furthermore, he does not say that "the good" exists as an immanent order, but rather he says that it is "in the order" (ἐν τῇ τάξει).[201] It is true, Aristotle "does not say that *God* exists in both these ways." *i.e.*, transcendently and immanently. To repeat, he does not mention God, though, or course, the introduction of God is justified as an easy inference from the "general" of the image. Yet, as we should recall, the text does not tell us whether we are talking about "the good" which is the "general" or the "good general." In addition, it does not help matters to refer to order as an abstraction, when in fact it is presented to us as an attribute of the universe as it is an attribute of the army. And finally, it is hard to see how Ross is warranted in affirming that, owing to the order in the world which supposedly derives from God, He "may be truly said to be at work in the world."

The upshot of it all seems to be this: Aristotle faces in his theology these difficulties, as we have been insisting: (1) What is the nature and status of goodness or "the good"? (2) How can it be said that goodness inheres in the Final Cause, the Unmoved Mover, God? (3) How in fact does God (under God must be subsumed all the other names which Aristotle gives to his first principle) affect the universe? We have seen that he has failed to answer these three questions with fully compelling argument. The good is presented in a rather blurred fashion, now vaguely as a kind of principle,[202] and now as a quality or attribute. We have seen Aristotle struggle to convince us that the Final Cause must be good, and we have seen that, when all is said and done, the Final Cause really affects the universe only as a sustainer of its everlasting motion. These three answers to these three questions reveal sharply the relation between Being and Value in Aristotle's thought in the realm of "First Philosophy" or

[201] Perhaps my stricture here is overly nice, but I do believe that Ross is straining every nerve, and over-straining the evidence, in order to attribute some kind of theological immanentism to Aristotle.

[202] Cf., for example, the statement a little later in the tenth book of *Metaphysics* Λ, 1075 a 37. καίτοι ἐν ἅπασι μάλιστα τὸ ἀγαθὸν ἀρχή. (Ross's text.) "And yet in all things the good is especially a principle."

256

theology. Therefore we must conclude that the so-called "image of the army" really does not serve to strengthen Aristotle's case, for it can in no way be designated as an argument. Could it be that the image expresses in some degree the way in which Aristotle would have liked to articulate his theology, but which he was unable to accomplish owing to the fundamentally ontological character of his metaphysical prior assumptions?

We shall see that the other image elaborates the conception of order contained in the image of the army, which immediately precedes it. The text and the context in which it appears run as follows: "And all things are ordered together somehow, but not all alike—both fishes and fowls and plants; and the world is not such that one thing has nothing to do with another, but they are connected. For all are ordered together to one end. (But it is as in a house, where the freemen are least at liberty to act at random, but all things or most things are already ordained for them, while the slaves and the beasts do little for the common good, and for the most part live at random; for this is the sort of principle that constitutes the nature of each.) I mean, for instance, that all must at least come to be dissolved into their elements and there are other functions similarly in which all share for the good of the whole."[203] Aristotle announces that all things have some kind of order, which may vary according to the nature of the particular thing involved. He then notes the interconnectedness of all things and that they are arranged for one purpose.[204] (All we need do here is to remind the reader that the nature of Aristotle's teleology cannot resolve the question of the purpose of the universe.) Next comes the comparison with the house. Ross's note is interesting: "The freemen in the house answer to the heavenly bodies, which are bound by necessity, the slaves and animals to mankind and indeed all sublunary

---

[203] *Metaphysics* Λ, 1075 a 16–25. πάντα δὲ συντέτακταί πως, ἀλλ᾽ οὐχ ὁμοίως, καὶ πλωτὰ καὶ πτηνὰ καὶ φυτά· καὶ οὐχ οὕτως ἔχει ὥστε μὴ εἶναι θατέρῳ πρὸς θάτερον μηδέν, ἀλλ᾽ ἔστι τι. πρὸς μὲν γὰρ ἓν ἅπαντα συντέτακται, ἀλλ᾽ ὥσπερ ἐν οἰκίᾳ τοῖς ἐλευθέροις ἥκιστα ἔξεστιν ὅ τι ἔτυχε ποιεῖν, ἀλλὰ πάντα ἢ τὰ πλεῖστα τέτακται, τοῖς δὲ ἀνδραπόδοις καὶ τοῖς θηρίοις μικρὸν τὸ εἰς τὸ κοινόν, τὸ δὲ πολὺ ὅ τι ἔτυχεν· τοιαύτη γὰρ ἑκάστου ἀρχὴ αὐτῶν ἡ φύσις ἐστίν. λέγω δ᾽ οἷον εἴς γε τὸ διακριθῆναι ἀνάγκη ἅπασιν ἐλθεῖν, καὶ ἄλλα οὕτως ἐστιν ὧν κοινωνεῖ ἅπαντα εἰς τὸ ὅλον. Ross's text.

[204] I believe Ross is right in seeing this to be the sense of the phrase πρὸς μὲν γὰρ ἕν.

creatures, which are much less divine (*Nicomachean Ethics*, 1141 a 34 ff.) and whose actions are largely contingent."[205]

I expect that Ross is probably correct in joining other commentators in making the freemen in the house stand for the heavenly bodies in the universe. As freemen have the greatest responsibility for organizing the household and thus can ill-afford to act at random, so do the heavenly bodies function in the ordering of the universe. At any rate, we do have the image of the house to illustrate how the components of the universe must be arranged for the sake of the whole. It must be in this spirit that Aristotle adds his final sentence. Even the humblest component can make its contribution to the whole by being separated into its elements, so that out of them presumably something better may be able to come into being. He concludes very vaguely by stating that there are other similar "functions" in which everything has a share for the sake of the whole. So the image of the house upon examination, although it does elaborate somewhat Aristotle's notion of the order in the universe, can scarcely be said to have added much by way of an answer to the questions we raised in connection with our analysis of the image of the army.

"But the world must not be governed badly. 'The rule of many is not good; let one be the ruler.' "[206] These are the words which Aristotle chooses as the conclusion of *Metaphysics* Λ. He has just been criticizing Speusippus and his mathematicizing

---

[205] Note on *Metaphysics* Λ, 1075 a 19–22. Ross goes on to quote Alexander Grant, who remarks that Aristotle assumes freedom for man, "not so much from a sense of the deep importance of morality, but rather from an idea of the slightness of man and of his actions in comparison with nature, and with what he would call the 'diviner parts' of the universe." If this be so, then freedom and contingency become equivalent. The greater the freedom of the agent, the more contingent or random become his actions. If one follows this reasoning further, then the less contingent, *e.g.*, the heavenly bodies, act from necessity, *i.e.*, with the least freedom, and thus God, the absolutely non-contingent, has no freedom at all. Something seems to be amiss in this interpretation of Ross and Grant, possibly in the understanding of what Aristotle means by the "freemen" in the house. Only in a very superficial sense can freedom be equated with contingent or random behavior.

[206] *Metaphysics* Λ, 1076 a 3–4. τὰ δὲ ὄντα οὐ βούλεται πολιτεύεσθαι κακῶς. "οὐκ ἀγαθὸν πολυκοιρανίη. εἷς κοίρανος ἔστω." Ross's text. I have modified the translation, to include the ἔστω of Ross's text, which he omitted, following several manuscripts, when he did his translation. Perhaps "the world" is fair enough as a rendering of τὰ ὄντα. Tricot, *op. cit.*, translates by *les êtres*. However, I have a feeling that "things that exist" might have been better. The quotation is from the *Iliad*, II. 204.

followers for postulating many first principles.[207] Such a situation
in the universe is intolerable for Aristotle, for it entails bad
government for "the things that exist." So the authority of
Homer is invoked: "Let one be the ruler." It seems as though
Aristotle here is making one final plea that we think of God, the
Prime Mover, as the κοίρανος of the universe.[208] Our study of
this Aristotelian God should have revealed the radical ways in
which we must understand that His "rule" is limited.

[207] Cf. Ross, *op. cit.*, note on *Metaphysics* Λ, 1076 a 3. "The word πολιτεύεσθαι
and the quotation from Homer show that ἀρχή is used with reference to its
meaning of 'rule' as well as to its ordinary Aristotelian sense of 'originative
source.' For a similar play on the meaning of ἀρχή cf. *Analytica Posteriora*,
100 a 13."

[208] Cf. the comment of Pseudo-Alexander: εἷς κοίρανος, μία αρχή, εἷς θεός.

CHAPTER VII

THE EVIDENCE OF THE
NICOMACHEAN ETHICS AND THE *POLITICS*

AFTER having studied our problem of the relation of Being and Value in Aristotle, first in his logical, physical, psychological, and biological thinking, and second and more fundamentally in the text of his *Metaphysics*, there remains to consider the relevant evidence to be found in the *Nicomachean Ethics* and *Politics*, and in the two treatises which deal broadly with what we might call literary criticism, the *Rhetoric* and the *Poetics*.[1] In taking up the *Ethics*, we shall try first to get an impression of the way in which Aristotle approaches this subject where questions of value are absolutely central, a situation which has not been the case in any of the documents thus far before us. To this end we shall examine his conception of "Wisdom," σοφία, in the sixth book. We shall then turn back to the first book and review rapidly Aristotle's view of the "good" and happiness in his ethical thinking. Our next task will be to analyze the famous Doctrine of the Mean in the second book and its

---

[1] In our investigation, we do not propose to deal with the *Eudemian Ethics*, the *Magna Moralia*, the *De Virtutibus et Vitiis*, the *Constitution of Athens*, and the *Rhetorica ad Alexandrum*. The second, third, and fifth of these treatises are being omitted because they are not genuine works of Aristotle. We are not treating the *Constitution of Athens*, since it does not bear explicitly on our study of the question of value. The omission of the *Eudemian Ethics* poses a somewhat different problem. If it is genuine and if it is in the direct line of the development of Aristotle's ethical thinking from the *Protrepticus* to the *Eudemian Ethics* and finally to the *Nicomachean Ethics*, as Jaeger has argued (*Aristotle*, translated by R. Robinson, 2nd Edition, Oxford, Clarendon Press, 1948, pp. 228–258), it has seemed best to concentrate on the *Nicomachean Ethics* as the maturest statement of Aristotle's ethical position. To have examined in detail the *Eudemian Ethics* would have led to a certain amount of needless repetition. Also, from the point of view of the question of value, such aspects of the *Eudemian Ethics* which differ from the position of the *Nicomachean Ethics*, differ only in the matter of degree. For example, the conception of God as a value sanction in *Eudemian Ethics* VII, is perhaps more explicitly theological than the similar doctrine of *Nicomachean Ethics* X. In other words, so far as the determination of Aristotle's attitude towards value is concerned, all his characteristic modes are found in the *Nicomachean Ethics*, so that nothing essential will be lost by our omission of a specific study of the *Eudemian Ethics*.

implications. We shall then attempt to identify the several different or differing "value schemes" which seem to be at work in the *Ethics*.[2] In each instance we shall examine carefully only one or two illustrative passages and cite in a footnote several other representative sections where the "value scheme" in question appears to be functioning. And finally we shall follow much the same method in presenting the less extensive evidence to be found in the *Politics*.

Throughout our discussion two familiar points must be kept constantly in mind: (1) Aristotle did not regard ethics and politics as discrete, but rather as two aspects of a single subject of study.[3] Hence the positions of the *Ethics* all have implications for his political thinking. (2) Aristotle believed that complete accuracy and precision were not possible in ethics: "We must be content, then, in speaking of such subjects and with such premises to indicate the truth roughly and in outline, and in speaking about things which are only for the most part true and with premises of the same kind to reach conclusions that are no better. In the same spirit, therefore, should each type of statement be *received*: for it is the mark of an educated man to look for precision in each class of things just so far as the nature of the subject admits; it is evidently foolish to accept probable reasoning from a mathematician and to demand from a rhetorician scientific proofs."[4]

---

[2] Cf. our effort above, Chapter V, pp. 141–142, to identify six variant "value schemes" which can be found in Aristotle's physical treatises.

[3] Cf. the conclusion of the *Nicomachean Ethics*, 1181 b 12–24.

[4] *Nicomachean Ethics* I, 1094 b 19–27. ἀγαπητὸν οὖν περὶ τοιούτων καὶ ἐκ τοιούτων λέγοντας παχυλῶς καὶ τύπῳ τἀληθὲς ἐνδείκνυσθαι, καὶ περὶ τῶν ὡς ἐπὶ τὸ πολὺ καὶ ἐκ τοιούτων λέγοντας τοιαῦτα καὶ συμπεραίνεσθαι. τὸν αὐτὸν δὴ τρόπον καὶ ἀποδέχεσθαι χρεὼν ἕκαστα τῶν λεγομένων· πεπαιδευμένου γάρ ἐστιν ἐπὶ τοσοῦτον τἀκριβὲς ἐπιζητεῖν καθ᾽ ἕκαστον γένος, ἐφ᾽ ὅσον ἡ τοῦ πράγματος φύσις ἐπιδέχεται· παραπλήσιον γὰρ φαίνεται μαθηματικοῦ τε πιθανολογοῦντος ἀποδέχεσθαι καὶ ῥητορικὸν ἀποδείξεις ἀπαιτεῖν. Bywater's text. Immediately before the quotation Aristotle has been commenting on things that are fair and just—those objects which concern the political scientist, about which there is such difference of opinion that one might think they arose from convention and not by nature. Similar differences arise in connection with goods because they cause hurt to many people. He illustrates the point by observing that some men are ruined by their wealth while others are ruined by their courage. Note Aristotle's selection of wealth and courage as examples of goods. With respect to precision the same point is made in 1098 a 26 ff. Cf. also *Nicomachean Ethics* II, 1103 b 34–1104 a 10, where Aristotle introduces his partial "relativism" in ethics.

PART I

THE *NICOMACHEAN ETHICS*

A. PROLOGUE: THE INTELLECTUAL VIRTUE, WISDOM

At the very end of the first book of the *Nicomachean Ethics*, Aristotle makes his well-known distinction between the moral and the intellectual virtues, citing liberality, ἐλευθεϱότης, and temperance, σωφϱοσύνη, as examples of the former, while for the latter he instances wisdom, σοφία, understanding, σύνεσις, and practical wisdom, φϱόνησις.[5] As will be recalled, the second book begins the investigation of the moral virtues and it is not until the sixth book that Aristotle turns specifically to the intellectual virtues. The principal ones among these he lists as art, τέχνη, scientific knowledge, ἐπιστήμη, practical wisdom, φϱόνησις, philosophic wisdom, σοφία, and intuitive reason, νοῦς.[6] It is to the account of wisdom or philosophic wisdom that we can well turn our attention as an introduction to our study of the ethical thinking of Aristotle.

At the outset of his discussion, he indicates that he has a precise meaning in mind for wisdom, σοφία, and this is not the one of ordinary Greek parlance which would call master artists like Phidias or Polycleitus wise. He makes his point clear when he says: "Therefore wisdom must plainly be the most finished of the forms of knowledge. It follows that the wise man must not only know what follows from the first principles, but must also possess truth about the first principles. Therefore wisdom must be intuitive reason combined with scientific knowledge—scientific knowledge of the highest objects which has received as it were its proper completion."[7] This is the wisdom, the wisdom or

---

[5] *Nicomachean Ethics* I, 1103 a 4–10.

[6] *Nicomachean Ethics* VI, 1139 b 16–17. I have followed Ross's translation of the terms, and will continue to do so for the sake of clarity in so far as this is possible. There are, of course, many variant English versions. Cf., for example, that of the recent translation of J. A. K. Thomson, *The Ethics of Aristotle* (London, Allen and Unwin, 1953), "art, science, practical wisdom, speculative wisdom, pure intelligence." Cf. also Rackham in the Loeb Classical Library, "Art or technical skill, Scientific Knowledge, Prudence, Wisdom, and Intelligence."

[7] *Nicomachean Ethics* VI, 1141 a 16–20. ὥστε δῆλον ὅτι ἀκϱιβεστάτη ἂν τῶν ἐπιστήμων εἴη ἡ σοφία. δεῖ ἄϱα τὸν σοφὸν μὴ μόνον τὰ ἐκ τῶν ἀϱχῶν εἰδέναι, ἀλλὰ καὶ πεϱὶ τὰς ἀϱχὰς ἀληθεύειν. ὥστ' εἴη ἂν ἡ σοφία νοῦς καὶ ἐπιστήμη, ὥσπεϱ κεφαλὴν ἔχουσα ἐπιστήμη τῶν τιμιωτάτων. Bywater's text.

"First Philosophy" which Aristotle delineated for us in the first chapter of *Metaphysics* A. But let us see how he elaborates his conception of wisdom in the context of ethics. Thus far we have been told that it is the most precise of the modes of the mind, that it has a firm grasp on first principles and their implications, that in some way it involves in its operation both scientific knowledge and intuitive reason, and finally that it concerns itself with the highest or most valuable objects. Aristotle's next comment asserts that political science or practical wisdom can only be regarded as the most serious activities of the intellect if man is the best and most important thing in the universe.

Note how he proceeds to disparage the status of man: "Now if what is healthy or good is different for men and for fishes, but what is white or straight is always the same, any one would say that what is wise is the same but what is practically wise is different for it is to that which observes well the various matters concerning itself that one ascribes practical wisdom, and it is to this that one will entrust such matters."[8] Man is thus assigned exclusively to the realm of the variable and contingent (along with the fish). Practical wisdom is capable of coping with this realm and let the reader observe that "values," of which health and good are offered as examples, are also found within the variable and contingent. Wisdom, in contrast, has as its object the invariable and constant, as illustrated by "white" and "straight." The implication, of course, is that wisdom has nothing to do with "values." One is inevitably reminded here of an earlier remark of Aristotle when he was discussing the differing ways in which a carpenter and geometrician look at a right angle. The former attempts to see how it may be useful, while the latter, as "a spectator of truth," tries to discover what a right angle is or what sort of thing it is. Aristotle then adds: "It is enough in some cases that the *fact* be well established, as in the case of the first principles; the fact is the primary thing or first principle."[9] We seem to have here a

---

[8] *Nicomachean Ethics* VI, 1141 a 22–26. εἰ δὴ ὑγιεινὸν μὲν καὶ ἀγαθὸν ἕτερον ἀνθρώποις καὶ ἰχθύσι, τὸ δὲ λευκὸν καὶ εὐθὺ ταὐτὸν ἀεί, καὶ τὸ σοφὸν ταὐτὸ πάντες ἂν εἴποιεν, φρόνιμον δὲ ἕτερον· τὰ γὰρ περὶ αὑτὸ ἕκαστα τὸ εὖ θεωροῦν φησὶν εἶναι φρόνιμον, καὶ τούτῳ ἐπιτρέψει αὐτά. Bywater's text.

[9] *Nicomachean Ethics* I, 1098 b 1–3. ἀλλ᾽ ἱκανὸν ἔν τισι τὸ ὅτι δειχθῆναι καλῶς, οἷον καὶ περὶ τὰς ἀρχάς· τὸ δ᾽ ὅτι πρῶτον καὶ ἀρχή. Bywater's text.

radical disjunction between reality or being or fact conjoined with wisdom on the one hand, with value and practical wisdom on the other.

But let us see how Aristotle carries on his discussion of wisdom. He points to the custom of saying that some animals possess "practical wisdom" if they exhibit the capacity to take forethought with respect to their own lives. He next shows why wisdom and political science cannot be the same. The outcome of his argument is that wisdom is basically unified or one, *i.e.*, there cannot be many "philosophic wisdoms," while political science must be concerned with all the varying goods in the contingent world. He seems to be saying that in the realm of values there cannot be a unified science (could we say the philosophic wisdom is a unified science of being?) any more than there can be "one art of medicine for all existing things."[10] And so he continues: "But if the argument be that man is the best of the animals, this makes no difference; for there are other things much more divine in their nature even than man, *e.g.*, most conspicuously, the bodies of which the heavens are framed."[11]

There is definitely a curious twist here. Aristotle is clearly of the opinion that philosophic wisdom ranks above practical wisdom since it deals with the non-contingent (being) while practical wisdom focuses upon the contingent and contingent human values. Yet he places an appraisal on man by using a value term, *viz.*, by referring to something "more divine than man." So philosophic wisdom comes out by having to do with beings that are more valuable. Could we put it this way? Aristotle disjoins Being and Value in developing his distinction between philosophic wisdom and practical wisdom, but as he talks further about philosophic wisdom he is unable to keep it free of a value dimension—but the trouble is that there is no relation between the value dimension of that with which philosophic wisdom is concerned and the values upon which practical wisdom concentrates. That this is the case is clear from what follows in the text. Aristotle

[10] *Nicomachean Ethics* VI, 1141 a 32–33. ἰατρικὴ μία περὶ πάντων τῶν ὄντων. Bywater's text.

[11] *Nicomachean Ethics* VI, 1141 a 33–1141 b 2. εἰ δ᾽ ὅτι βέλτιστον ἄνθρωπος τῶν ἄλλων ζῴων, οὐδὲν διαφέρει· καὶ γὰρ ἀνθρώπου ἄλλα πολὺ θειότερα τὴν φύσιν, οἷον φανερώτατά γε ἐξ ὧν ὁ κόσμος συνέστηκεν. Bywater's text.

repeats his definition of philosophic wisdom as combining scientific knowledge and intuitive reason "of the things that are the highest, or most honoured, or most precious, or most valuable by nature."[12] He then goes on to point out that we call Anaxagoras, Thales, and their ilk wise but not practically wise since they are ignorant of what will advantage them. This is "why we say that they know things that are remarkable, admirable, difficult, and divine, but useless; *viz.*, because it is not human goods that they seek."[13] In other words, philosophic wisdom is again asserted to have nothing to do with human goods or values. The radical disjunction of Being and Value,—at least human value, is repeated.

The succeeding few lines have to do further with practical wisdom and from the passage we perhaps can infer that the characteristics attributed to practical wisdom are not to be attributed to philosophic wisdom. "Practical wisdom on the other hand is concerned with things human and things about which it is possible to deliberate; for we say this is above all the work of the man of practical wisdom, to deliberate well, but no one deliberates about things invariable, nor about things which have not an end, and that a good that can be brought about by action. The man who is without qualification good at deliberating is the man who is capable of aiming in accordance with calculation at the best for man of things attainable by action."[14] Our inference may then be with respect to philosophic wisdom, σοφία: Not being concerned with "things human" (including human values), it never becomes involved in deliberation. It *is* concerned with things which cannot be otherwise about which it is impossible to deliberate. But the next remark is strange, for it asserts that no one deliberates about things which have no τέλος or goal, and

---

[12] *Nicomachean Ethics* VI, 1141 b 3. τῶν τιμιωτάτων τῇ φύσει. Bywater's text.

[13] *Nicomachean Ethics* VI, 1141 b 6–8. καὶ περιττὰ μὲν καὶ θαυμαστὰ καὶ χαλεπὰ καὶ δαιμόνια εἰδέναι αὐτούς φασιν, ἄχρηστα δ᾽, ὅτι οὐ τὰ ἀνθρώπινα ἀγαθὰ ζητοῦσιν. Bywater's text.

[14] *Nicomachean Ethics* VI, 1141 b 8–14. ἡ δὲ φρόνησις περὶ τὰ ἀνθρώπινα καὶ περὶ ὧν ἔστι βουλεύσασθαι· τοῦ γὰρ φρονίμου μάλιστα τοῦτ᾽ ἔργον εἶναί φαμεν, τὸ εὖ βουλεύεσθαι, βουλεύεται δ᾽ οὐδεὶς περὶ τῶν ἀδυνάτων ἄλλως ἔχειν, οὐδ᾽ ὅσων μὴ τέλος τι ἔστι, καὶ τοῦτο πρακτὸν ἀγαθόν. ὁ δ᾽ ἁπλῶς εὔβουλος ὁ τοῦ ἀρίστου ἀνθρώπῳ τῶν πρακτῶν στοχαστικὸς κατὰ τὸν λογισμόν. Bywater's text.

this a goal or good entailing action. Thus, according to the present passage, philosophic wisdom cannot address itself to questions of human goals or goods that are realized in human action.

The remainder of the section[15] adds the point that practical wisdom not only must be thoroughly acquainted with universals but also must know particulars, for this is "practical," in the sense that "action has to do with particulars."[16] Aristotle concludes on this note of giving a bit of an accolade to the "empirics" who often in practical affairs may be more successful than their more knowledgeable or philosophic friends. For illustration, he cites the man who knows that light meat is easily digestible but does not know which meats are light, as one who will be less successful in producing health than the man of experience who simply knows that chicken is good for you.[17]

We have chosen this comparison or contrast of philosophic widom and practical wisdom as a prologue to our study of the *Nicomachean Ethics* to indicate how deeply in Aristotle's ethical thinking is this split between the realms of the non-contingent and the contingent. On the one hand, as everyone knows, the practical or down-to-earth aspect of the Aristotelian ethic has given it its widespread appeal. But, on the other hand, as we have attempted to suggest, Aristotle cannot as a thinker, given, if you will, his Platonic inheritance, abide by or live with the consequences of the split. Values obtrude themselves in the non-contingent realm of Being, and ontology never ceases to be an over-riding consideration in the contingent and variable realm of human values. To put it in another way, human action, πρᾶξις, does not appear totally unrelated to the activity or actuality, ἐνέργεια, which characterizes Aristotle's metaphysical thinking, let alone the pure actuality in the domain of the non-contingent, the Unmoved Mover. It will be our hope in the following pages to indicate the results in Aristotle's ethical thinking of his uncertainty or lack of clarity in facing questions of value and how it must be related to "fact" or being.

---

[15] *Nicomachean Ethics* VI, 1141 b 14–23.

[16] *Nicomachean Ethics* VI, 1141 b 16. ἡ δὲ πρᾶξις περὶ τὰ καθ᾽ ἕκαστα.

[17] The same point is made with respect to the "empirics" in *Metaphysics* A, 981 a 12–24. Cf. a recent definition of the physicist as one who knows why the door-bell does not ring, but cannot fix it.

B. THE ANALYSIS IN *NICOMACHEAN ETHICS*, BOOK I

"Every art and every inquiry, and similarly every action and pursuit, is thought to aim at some good; and for this reason the good has rightly been declared to be that at which all things aim"[18]. These are the well-known words with which Aristotle opens his ethical investigation. It will be our purpose to reconstruct as rapidly as possible the argument of this opening book against which all that follows in the rest of the treatise must in one way or another be understood. After pointing out the relation between his inquiry and the art of politics, and their concern for the good for man as a goal or end,[19] Aristotle notices that both ordinary folk as well as people of cultivation believe happiness, εὐδαιμονία, to be that good, though there is dispute concerning the precise nature of happiness. Pleasure, wealth, honour, and health are mentioned, as well as Plato's conception that these goods are somehow "caused" by the Idea of the Good.[20] We need not concern ourselves with the ensuing critique of the Platonic doctrine,[21] save to note that for the most part the attack is based on strictly logical considerations.

Aristotle carries forward his argument by seeking to establish happiness as a complete and final goal, as something which is always pursued for its own sake and never for the sake of something else.[22] Presently, then, he finds himself able to offer his preliminary sketch of happiness as the ultimate human good which he wishes to identify: "If this is the case, we state the function of man to be a certain kind of life, and this to be an activity or actions of the soul implying a rational principle, and the function of a good man to be the good and noble performance and any action is well performed when it is performed in accordance with the

---

[18] *Nicomachean Ethics* I, 1094 a 1–3. Πᾶσα τέχνη καὶ πᾶσα μέθοδος, ὁμοίως δὲ πρᾶξίς τε καὶ προαίρεσις, ἀγαθοῦ τινὸς ἐφίεσθαι δοκεῖ· διὸ καλῶς ἀπεφήναντο τἀγαθόν, οὗ πάντ᾽ ἐφίεται. Bywater's text.

[19] *Nicomachean Ethics* I, 1094 a 27–b 7.

[20] *Nicomachean Ethics* I, 1095 a 17–28. Shortly hereafter Aristotle lists three kinds of life, with differing conceptions of happiness: the life of pleasure, political life the good of which is honour, and the contemplative life. He deals briefly with the first two, but postpones any treatment of the βίος θεωρητικός, 1095 b 14–1096 a 5.

[21] *Nicomachean Ethics* I, 1096 a 11–1097 a 11 (= chapter 6).

[22] *Nicomachean Ethics* I, 1097 a 30–b 6.

appropriate excellence: if this is the case, human good turns out to be activity of soul in accordance with virtue, and if there are more than one virtue, in accordance with the best and most complete. But we must add 'in a complete life.' For one swallow does not make a summer, nor does one day; and so too one day, or a short time, does not make a man blessed and happy."[23]

Aristotle's next move is to bring forward data in support of the conception of happiness thus proffered. He first cites the three-fold classification of goods, *viz.*, external goods, goods of the soul, and goods of the body, of which it is generally agreed that those of the soul are in the highest sense goods. So Aristotle has the philosophers who hold this view behind him.[24] Such is likewise the case with those who hold that the happy man lives well and fares well.[25] After mentioning those who have asserted that happiness has something to do with virtue or practical wisdom or philosophic wisdom or pleasure or prosperity, he pauses for the moment to dwell on virtue. He makes the point that an emphasis on virtue is compatible with his own view of happiness, entails virtuous activity, and not merely the possession of virtue. The Olympic victor gets the prize not by simply looking handsome and strong but by the activity of competition.[26] It is in this way that Aristotle introduces the conviction which is so important for his ethical thinking that activity, ἐνέργεια, is of the highest worth, as compared to the state, ἕξις.

He next turns to the question of pleasure and insists that the life of the happy man will also be pleasant.[27] In this connection Aristotle makes an observation which is important as an anticipation of his detailed discussion of pleasure in the seventh and tenth

[23] *Nicomachean Ethics* I, 1098 a 12–20. εἰ δ' οὕτως, ἀνθρώπου δὲ τίθεμεν ἔργον ζωήν τινα, ταύτην δὲ ψυχῆς ἐνέργειαν καὶ πράξεις μετὰ λόγου, σπουδαίου δ' ἀνδρὸς εὖ ταῦτα καὶ καλῶς, ἕκαστον δ' εὖ κατὰ τὴν οἰκείαν ἀρετὴν ἀποτελεῖται· εἰ δ' οὕτω, τὸ ἀνθρώπινον ἀγαθὸν ψυχῆς ἐνέργεια γίνεται κατ' ἀρετήν, εἰ δὲ πλείους αἱ ἀρεταί, κατὰ τὴν ἀρίστην καὶ τελειοτάτην. ἔτι δ' ἐν βίῳ τελείῳ. μία γὰρ χελιδὼν ἔαρ οὐ ποιεῖ, οὐδὲ μία ἡμέρα· οὕτω δὲ οὐδὲ μακάριον καὶ εὐδαίμονα μία ἡμέρα οὐδ' ὀλίγος χρόνος. Bywater's text. I have removed Bywater's brackets from ἀνθρώπου to εἰ δ' οὕτω (following H. H. Joachim's commentary on the *Nicomachean Ethics* [Oxford, Clarendon Press, 1951] in his note on 1098 a 12–16) and have adjusted the translation accordingly.

[24] *Nicomachean Ethics* I, 1098 b 12–20.
[25] *Nicomachean Ethics* I, 1098 b 20–22.
[26] *Nicomachean Ethics* I, 1098 b 22–1099 a 7.
[27] *Nicomachean Ethics* I, 1099 a 7.

books of the treatise: "Now for most men their pleasures are in conflict with one another because these are not by nature pleasant, but the lovers of what is noble find pleasant the things that are by nature pleasant; and virtuous actions are such, so that these are pleasant for such men as well as in their own nature. Their life, therefore, has no further need of pleasure as a sort of adventitious charm, but has its pleasure in itself."[28] It is clear that this preliminary view is affiliated with the doctrine of the tenth book in particular, where pleasure is regarded as a concomitant and completion of an activity.[29] And so Aristotle concludes this section of his analysis by affirming: "Happiness then is the best, noblest, and most pleasant thing in the world."[30] But he adds in a practical or "realistic" spirit that external goods are needed as well.[31] No doubt it is hard to be happy in the Aristotelian sense of engaging in virtuous activity, if one is poor, ill-born, ugly, lonely and childless, but, as we shall see, it is the "realistic" and this-wordly character of Aristotle's thought which injects into his ethic on numerous occasions what can only be called unelevated and banal.

The foregoing to all intents and purposes contains the essence of Aristotle's view of happiness as the ultimate human good, a view which he summarizes in the following words: "To us it is clear from what has been said that happiness is among the things that are prized and perfect. It seems to be so also from the fact that it is a first principle; for it is for the sake of this that we do all that we do, and the first principle and cause of things good is, we claim, something prized and divine."[32] One cannot fail to

---

[28] *Nicomachean Ethics* I, 1099 a 11–16. τοῖς μὲν οὖν πολλοῖς τὰ ἡδέα μάχεται διὰ τὸ μὴ φύσει τοιαῦτ᾽ εἶναι, τοῖς δὲ φιλοκάλοις ἐστὶν ἡδέα τὰ φύσει ἡδέα· τοιαῦται δ᾽ αἱ κατ᾽ ἀρετὴν πράξεις, ὥστε καὶ τούτοις εἰσὶν ἡδεῖαι καὶ καθ᾽ αὑτάς. οὐδὲν δὴ προσδεῖται τῆς ἡδονῆς ὁ βίος αὐτῶν ὥσπερ περιάπτου τινός. ἀλλ᾽ ἔχει τὴν ἡδονὴν ἐν ἑαυτῷ. Bywater's text.
[29] *Nicomachean Ethics* X, chapters 4 and 5.
[30] *Nicomachean Ethics* I, 1099 a 24–25. ἄριστον ἄρα καὶ κάλλιστον καὶ ἥδιστον ἡ εὐδαιμονία. Bywater's text.
[31] *Nicomachean Ethics* I, 1099 a 31–b 8.
[32] *Nicomachean Ethics* I, 1101 b 35–1102 a 4. ἡμῖν δὲ δῆλον ἐκ τῶν εἰρημένων ὅτι ἐστὶν ἡ εὐδαιμονία τῶν τιμίων καὶ τελείων. ἔοικε δ᾽ οὕτως ἔχειν καὶ διὰ τὸ εἶναι ἀρχή· ταύτης γὰρ χάριν τὰ λοιπὰ πάντα πάντες πράττομεν, τὴν ἀρχὴν δὲ καὶ τὸ αἴτιον τῶν ἀγαθῶν τίμιόν τι καὶ θεῖον τίθεμεν. Bywater's text. In the translation, I have substituted Rackham's "things good" (Loeb Classical Library) for τῶν ἀγαθῶν (1102 a 4) instead of Ross's "goods."

note how similar this language and this thought concerning happiness is to that which Aristotle used in connection with the Prime Mover. We can hear the echo in the words, "prized," "perfect," "first principle," "divine," and the "cause of things good." But we are not told in the present passage exactly how happiness, that is, human happiness (we are definitely in the contingent realm of the human) can function as a cause of things good.[33]

The remainder of the first book of the *Nicomachean Ethics* really constitutes a transition to the subject matter of the second book which is devoted to the study of moral virtue. Having stated his position that happiness is an activity in accordance with virtue, Aristotle now turns to the question of the nature of virtue. He quickly makes it explicit that he intends to confine himself to the domain of the human: "But it is clear that we must investigate human virtue. I say this because we were seeking the human good, that is, human happiness. But we maintain that human virtue is not that of the body, but rather that of the soul. And we say that happiness is an activity of the soul."[34] Since it does concern the soul, Aristotle reminds his readers of his psychological doctrine. Of the three parts of the soul, the vegetative, the appetitive, and the rational, the vegetative is clearly irrational and hence must be disregarded in any ethical inquiry. The appetitive in a sense is irrational, but in another sense is rational, so that ethics must concentrate upon the appetitive and the rational

[33] We shall have occasion to return to this question when we discuss below the latter portion of the tenth book of the *Nicomachean Ethics* where the subject of νοῦς and the life of contemplation is being treated by Aristotle. In the meantime we may ask how far we should be persuaded by the following comment of J. A. Stewart, *Notes on the Nicomachean Ethics* (Oxford, Clarendon Press, 1892) on 1102 a 2: "The τέλος, or perfect adult form, is the ἀρχή which determines the growth, through all its stages, of a plant or animal (see *Metaphysics* Λ, chapter 8, 1073 a 1, τὸ πρῶτον οὐ σπέρμα ἐστὶν ἀλλὰ τὸ τέλειον); similarly εὐδαιμονία—the τέλος, or perfect form of human nature, is, as καλόν, the ἀρχή, or principle of attraction, which moves states and individuals to the performance of noble actions." Here Stewart makes the analogy between happiness and the cosmic Prime Mover explicit.

[34] *Nicomachean Ethics* I, 1102 a 13–18. περὶ ἀρετῆς δὲ ἐπισκεπτέον ἀνθρωπίνης δῆλον ὅτι. καὶ γὰρ τἀγαθὸν ἀνθρώπινον ἐζητοῦμεν καὶ τὴν εὐδαιμονίαν ἀνθρωπίνην. ἀρετὴν δὲ λέγομεν ἀνθρωπίνην οὐ τὴν τοῦ σώματος ἀλλὰ τὴν τῆς ψυχῆς. καὶ τὴν εὐδαιμονίαν δὲ ψυχῆς ἐνέργειαν λέγομεν. Bywater's text. The translation is mine. It seems unquestioned to me that καί of 1102 a 15 should be rendered as "that is."

parts of the soul.[35] The book concludes with Aristotle making the distinction between the moral and intellectual virtues in a passage to which we have already referred,[36] and with the suggestion that the moral and intellectual virtues are related to each other as the appetitive is related to the rational part of the soul.

As we move now to our discussion of the cardinal doctrine of the mean, let us take note of the fact that the introductory analysis of this first book has laid down the following points which are significant for us: (1) the inquiry is to be confined to the contingent realm of the human; (2) the human good, happiness, a value, is an activity, and thus is subordinate to, dependent upon, an attribute of—however one wishes to phrase it—a being—a human being. How can Aristotle relate these points to the doctrine of his First Philosophy? Or does he believe that ethical inquiry is in fact independent of First Philosophy?

C. THE DOCTRINE OF THE MEAN

Aristotle opens his treatment of moral virtue or the moral virtues by arguing that they derive from habit and do not arise either by nature or by teaching. However, men naturally have the capability of developing them, and they do bring them to completion by habit.[37] After reemphasizing the practical purpose of his ethical investigation ("For we are inquiring not in order to know what virtue is, but in order to become good, since otherwise our inquiry would have been of no use"),[38] he introduces in a preliminary way his all-important conception of the mean and the extremes of excess and defect.[39] Next he glances at the relation of virtue to pleasures and pains,[40] and he repeats his contention that we become virtuous by performing virtuous acts.[41] Virtue is then asserted to be a state of character, since it

---

[35] Cf. *Nicomachean Ethics* I, 1102 a 26–1103 a 3. Note especially 1102 b 28–31.

[36] Cf. above, Chapter VII, p. 262.

[37] *Nicomachean Ethics* II, 1103 a 14–26.

[38] *Nicomachean Ethics* II, 1103 b 27–29. οὐ γὰρ ἵνα εἰδῶμεν τί ἐστιν ἡ ἀρετὴ σκεπτόμεθα, ἀλλ᾽ ἵν᾽ ἀγαθοὶ γενώμεθα, ἐπεὶ οὐδὲν ἂν ἦν ὄφελος αὐτῆς. Bywater's text.

[39] *Nicomachean Ethics* II, 1104 a 10–27.

[40] Cf. the summary statement, *Nicomachean Ethics* II, 1105 a 13–16.

[41] Cf., *e.g.*, *Nicomachean Ethics* II, 1105 b 5–12.

must be one of the three kinds of things which make up the "contents" of the soul, *viz.*, passions, faculties, and states of character.[42]

Aristotle proceeds to elaborate further what he signifies by the mean and the extremes of excess and defect in the context of ethics, and he now is prepared to submit his carefully contrived and justly famous definition of virtue: "Virtue, then, is a state of character concerned with choice, being in a mean which is relative to us, and which is determined by reason or that by which the man of practical wisdom would define it."[43] It can readily be seen how this definition completes or complements the definition of the human good, happiness, as an activity of soul in accordance with virtue. Virtue is a state of the soul from which choice of action emanates. But now let us examine what Aristotle means by his statement "being in a mean which is relative to us." Several considerations are important.[44]

1. The mean and extremes constitute a mathematical image.

2. The mean can be said to be the "locus" of value (virtue), while the extremes of excess and defect are the "loci" of disvalue (vice).

3. This mean is not to be considered in rigid objective arithmetical terms, as 6 is the mean between 10 and 2. Rather it is "relative to us," in that in any situation involving moral choice, the individual and the circumstances in which he finds himself must be taken fully into consideration.[45]

4. The mean is of the nature of an extreme: "Hence in respect of its substance and the definition which states its essence virtue is a mean, with regard to what is best and right an extreme."[46]

---

[42] πάθη, δυνάμεις, and ἕξεις. The whole argument is developed in the fifth chapter of *Nicomachean Ethics* II, 1105 b 19–1106 a 13.

[43] *Nicomachean Ethics* II, 1106 b 36–1107 a 2. Ἔστιν ἄρα ἡ ἀρετὴ προαιρετική, ἐν μεσότητι οὖσα τῇ πρὸς ἡμᾶς, ὡρισμένῃ λόγῳ καὶ ᾧ ἂν ὁ φρόνιμος ὁρίσειεν. Bywater's text. The translation is mine. It may be recalled that we quoted this passage above, Chapter VI, pp. 187–188.

[44] For a fuller treatment of what follows, cf. my article, "The Doctrine of the Mean," *The Philosophical Review*, XLV (1936) pp. 382–398. See especially pp. 383–384 and 389–393. Note in particular the diagram on p. 390.

[45] *Nicomachean Ethics* II, 1106 a 26–b 7.

[46] *Nicomachean Ethics* II, 1107 a 6–8. διὸ κατὰ μὲν τὴν οὐσίαν καὶ τὸν λόγον τὸν τὸ τί ἦν εἶναι λέγοντα μεσότης ἐστὶν ἡ ἀρετή, κατὰ δὲ τὸ ἄριστον καὶ τὸ εὖ ἀκρότης. Bywater's text. In the article referred to above, note 44, I criticized a diagram offered by M. L. von Kohoutek (unpublished Marburg dissertation, 1923)

Furthermore it is explicitly affirmed that "there is no mean of excess itself or defect itself, nor is there any excess of the virtue."[47] Or to quote Aristotle's words: "For in general there is neither a mean of excess and deficiency, nor excess and deficiency of a mean."[48] Or as I tried to express it, "One can be more rash or less rash, but there is no mean state of rashness and likewise there can be no such thing as excess of courage."[49] By way of further elucidation, it could be pointed out that in terms of the Aristotelian analysis of the mean, it simply does not make sense to say that "so-and-so is *too* honest." For Aristotle, the conduct which prompted such a statement was somehow of the sort that had lost the essential quality of the virtue honesty.

The rest of the definition of virtue is likewise significant for our purpose. The mean "is determined by reason or that by which the man of practical wisdom would define it." Aristotle's line of argument seems to run something like this: Asked what is the highest human good, he answers, "Happiness." What is happiness? "An activity of soul." What kind of activity? "One in accordance with virtue." What is virtue? "A state of character, concerned with choice, lying in a mean relative to us." Where can one find this mean, which holds the key to the whole problem? Aristotle answers, "It can be identified if one appeals to one's 'reason,' and if this fails, one can always ask the φρόνιμος,

---

which had a horizontal line to represent the mean "ontologically," κατὰ τὴν οὐσίαν καὶ τὸν λόγον τὸν τὸ τί ἦν εἶναι λέγοντα, and a line perpendicular to it to represent the mean "axiologically." My objection was to the effect that the mean and extremes of the mathematical image signify value (and disvalue) so that there is some basic confusion on Aristotle's part in inserting the ontological phrase κατὰ τὴν οὐσίαν κτλ in an essentially axiological situation. In the image the mean is a "mean" position, and, as may be suggested, qualifies or illuminates or locates or establishes the context of virtue, which in turn is an attribute of the activity happiness. This series of dependencies, I believe, more precisely describes the ontological ground of the axiological situation. At the same time, we should not overlook the importance of the phrase κατὰ τὸ ἄριστον καὶ τὸ εὖ ἀκρότης. As I tried to indicate in my article (p. 390, note 16 and p. 393), the conception of the mean as an extreme really answers the criticism that Aristotle conceived of the difference between right and wrong as purely quantitative.

[47] Cf. my article, *op. cit.*, pp. 390–391.
[48] *Nicomachean Ethics* II, 1107 a 25–27. ὅλως γὰρ οὔθ' ὑπερβολῆς καὶ ἐλλείψεως μεσότης ἐστιν, οὔτε μεσότητος ὑπερβολὴ καὶ ἔλλειψις. Bywater's text. This text, of course, establishes the fact that the extremes of excess and defect are infinite tendencies.
[49] Cf. my article, *op. cit.*, p. 391.

the man of practical wisdom, and he will produce a definition."[50]
What then are the implications for the question of value in the
argument? The highest human value, *i.e.*, the highest human
good, is happiness. At the outset the major support for this contention lies in the fact that most people think so, at least most good
or refined or cultivated people hold the view. Why do they
think so? Because it is an activity of soul. Here Aristotle brings
in "activity" and "soul," both of which he consistently associates
with highest worth, as compared with "potentiality" and the
"body," respectively. He then introduces the notion of "virtue,"
a human value, which is used to fortify us and to help us to understand the highest human value, happiness. What is this virtue
and what is its sanction? By using the mathematical image of the
mean, Aristotle can answer that reason, λόγος, or the man of
practical wisdom, are the sanctions. Reason, the φρόνιμος, and
the collective opinions of good people, support the value scheme
that is promulgated in this analysis. Note above all that there is
nothing here which suggests any need for any kind of transcendent sanction for ethical value. Aristotle within the present
context is living up to his promise that he is investigating
human virtue and its relation to human good, that is, human
happiness.[51]

So much then for our treatment of the doctrine of the mean
and the light which it throws on Aristotle's characteristic thinking
in the realm of value. That the doctrine is absolutely central to
his conception of ethical values is made abundantly clear by his
extensive analyses of numerous specific virtues which he begins
right after his enunciation of the definition of virtue and does not
end until he has dealt with justice at the close of the fifth book of
the *Nicomachean Ethics*.[52] In our next three sections we shall
attempt to illustrate briefly how Aristotle characteristically uses

---

[50] In tracing the chain of argumentation in this way, I have, of course, confined
myself to the matter of moral virtue. Intellectual virtue, as has been indicated
above, Chapter VII, section A, presents a different problem.
[51] *Nicomachean Ethics* I, 1102 a 13–18. Cf. above, Chapter VII, pp. 270–271.
[52] Ross, in his version of the *Nicomachean Ethics* in the Oxford translation, note
on 1108 b 7–9, lists the following passages which deal with the distinction between
the two kinds of justice, "distributive" and "corrective," and the way in which
each of them is a mean: 1129 a 26–b 1, 1130 a 14–b 5, 1131 b 9–15, 1132 a 24–30,
1133 b 30–1134 a 1.

the conceptions of activity *(ἐνέργεια)*, reason *(λόγος)*, and the man of practical wisdom or the good man *(ὁ φρόνιμος* or *ὁ σπουδαῖος)* in the text of the *Nicomachean Ethics*.[53]

D. ACTIVITY

Perhaps little more need be said concerning the way in which Aristotle associates activity with value. We have, of course, the definition of happiness, the highest human good, as an activity of soul.[54] We also have been made aware of Aristotle's view that we are virtuous not by the mere possession of the virtuous state but rather by the performance of virtuous *acts*.[55] One further passage should suffice to exemplify the importance of activity in Aristotle's ethical thinking. In the ninth book of the *Nicomachean Ethics*, which along with the eighth book is devoted to the topic of friendship, he endeavours to explain why bene-factors are likely to be fonder of those who receive the bene-factions than the recipients are of the benefactors. In the course of the argument Aristotle remarks, "The reason is that everything desires and loves just *to be*. Now we realize our being in action (for we exist by living and acting), and the man who has made something may be said to exist in a manner through his activity. So he loves his handiwork because he loves existence. It is part of the nature of things. What is potential becomes actual in the work which gives it expression."[56] It should be observed that Aristotle reveals here once again his conviction with respect to the primacy of being—his familiar ontological preoccupation. Being in the highest sense lies in activity. Why should this be so? Because it is *φυσικόν*, "part of the nature of things." The implica-tion is clear that in this particular argument we are to understand

---

[53] We shall not pause to consider Aristotle's discussion in the first five chapters of the third book of the *Nicomachean Ethics*, where he analyzes the conceptions of voluntary and involuntary actions, choice, deliberation, wish, desire, and responsibility. All these have to do, one could say, with the "mechanics" of moral decision. They therefore are incidental to the value scheme or schemes which it is our purpose to explore and do not demand our specific attention.

[54] *Nicomachean Ethics* I, 1098 a 12–20. Cf. above, Chapter VII, pp. 267–268.

[55] *Nicomachean Ethics* II, 1103 a 14–26. Cf. above, Chapter VII, p. 271.

[56] *Nicomachean Ethics* IX, 1168 a 5–9. τούτου δ' αἴτιον ὅτι τὸ εἶναι πᾶσιν αἱρετὸν καὶ φιλητόν, ἐσμὲν δ' ἐνεργείᾳ (τῷ ζῆν γὰρ καὶ πράττειν), ἐνεργείᾳ δὲ ὁ ποιήσας τὸ ἔργον ἔστι πως· στέργει δὴ τὸ ἔργον, διότι καὶ τὸ εἶναι. τοῦτο δὲ φυσικόν· ὃ γάρ ἐστι δυνάμει, τοῦτο ἐνεργείᾳ τὸ ἔργον μηνύει. Bywater's text.

worth or value as somehow deriving from being, activity, and nature.

One cannot refrain from quoting still another passage, somewhat lighter in tone, which likewise bespeaks the great store set upon activity by Aristotle. This also is taken from his discussion of friendship. "As in regard to the virtues some men are called good in respect of a state of character, others in respect of an activity, so too in the case of friendship; for those who live together delight in each other and confer benefits, but those who are asleep or locally separated are not performing, but are disposed to perform, the activities of friendship; distance does not break off the friendship absolutely, but only the activity of it. But if the absence is lasting, it seems actually to make men forget their friendship; hence the saying 'out of sight, out of mind' "[57]

E. LOGOS

". . . a mean which is determined by reason or that by which the man of practical wisdom would define it."[58] Nowhere else has Aristotle so succinctly expressed his belief in reason as somehow an ultimate sanction for moral values. We submit "reason" as a proper translation for λόγος in the present context, and if we had nothing of Aristotle's ethical writings other than his analysis of moral virtue, we would be justified in classifying him as fundamentally a proponent of a rationalistic ethic.[59]

---

[57] *Nicomachean Ethics* VIII, 1157 b 5–13. "Ὥσπερ δ᾽ ἐπὶ τῶν ἀρετῶν οἱ μὲν καθ᾽ ἕξιν οἱ δὲ κατ᾽ ἐνέργειαν ἀγαθοὶ λέγονται, οὕτω καὶ ἐπὶ τῆς φιλίας. οἱ μὲν γὰρ συζῶντες χαίρουσιν ἀλλήλοις καὶ πορίζουσι τἀγαθά, οἱ δὲ καθεύδοντες ἢ κεχωρισμένοι τοῖς τόποις οὐκ ἐνεργοῦσι μέν, οὕτω δ᾽ ἔχουσιν ὥστ᾽ ἐνεργεῖν φιλικῶς. οἱ γὰρ τόποι οὐ διαλύουσι τὴν φιλίαν ἁπλῶς, ἀλλὰ τὴν ἐνέργειαν. ἐὰν δὲ χρόνιος ἀπουσία γίνηται, καὶ τῆς φιλίας δοκεῖ λήθην ποιεῖν. ὅθεν εἴρηται "πολλὰς δὴ φιλίας ἀπροσηγορία διέλυσεν." Bywater's text. For further illustrations of ἐνέργεια functioning in the same way, cf. *Nicomachean Ethics* X, 1173 a 13–15 and 1173 b 2–4. Numerous other passages obviously could be cited.

[58] *Nicomachean Ethics* II, 1107 a 1–2. Cf. above, Chapter VII, p. 272.

[59] The following passages illustrate how Aristotle offers "reason" or "right reason" as a value sanction: *Nicomachean Ethics*: II, 1103 b 31–32; III, 1115 b 17–20; III, 1119 b 15–18; VI, 1139 a 31–33; VI, 1144 b 1–1145 a 6 [especially on the relation of "right reason," ὁ ὀρθὸς λόγος, and practical wisdom, φρόνησις and the bearing of both upon virtue]; VII, 1147 a 35–b 5; VII, 1151 a 12 [παρὰ τὸν ὀρθὸν λόγον]. It should be noted that Ross regularly translates the phrases as "rule" or "right rule," whereas Rackham and Thomson tend to use "principle" and "right principle."

The texts cited in the foregoing note may be regarded as reflecting the normal Aristotelian attitude towards "reason" in the analysis of value, but there is evidence that he wished to go as far as he could to establish his assertion with respect to the ultimacy of reason in the realm of ethics. One cannot fail to be impressed in this connection by the review of the doctrine of the mean with which the sixth book of the *Nicomachean Ethics* opens. This must be quoted in full. "Since we have previously said that one ought to choose that which is intermediate, not the excess nor the defect, and that the intermediate is determined by the dictates of 'right reason' [the right rule], let us discuss the nature of these dictates. In all the states of character we have mentioned, as in all other matters, there is a mark to which the man who has 'reason' [the rule] looks and heightens or relaxes his activity accordingly, that is, there is a certain standard which determines the mean states which we say are intermediate between excess and defect, being in accordance with 'right reason' [the right rule]. But such a statement, though true, is by no means clear; for not only here but in all other pursuits which are objects of knowledge it is indeed true to say that we must not exert ourselves nor relax our efforts too much nor too little, but to an intermediate extent and as 'right reason' [the right rule] dictates; but if a man had only this knowledge he would be none the wiser— *e.g.*, we should not know what sort of medicines to apply to our body if some one were to say 'all those which the medical art prescribes, and which agree with the practice of one who possesses the art.' Hence it is necessary with regard to the states of the soul also not only that this true statement should be made, but also that it should be determined what is 'right reason' [right rule] and what is the standard that fixes it."[60]

---

[60] *Nicomachean Ethics* VI, 1138 b 18–34. Ἐπεὶ δὲ τυγχάνομεν πρότερον εἰρηκότες ὅτι δεῖ τὸ μέσον αἱρεῖσθαι, μὴ τὴν ὑπερβολὴν μηδὲ τὴν ἔλλειψιν, τὸ δὲ μέσον ἐστὶν ὡς ὁ λόγος ὁ ὀρθὸς λέγει, τοῦτο διέλωμεν. ἐν πάσαις γὰρ ταῖς εἰρημέναις ἕξεσι, καθάπερ καὶ ἐπὶ τῶν ἄλλων, ἔστι τις σκοπὸς πρὸς ὃν ἀποβλέπων ὁ τὸν λόγον ἔχων ἐπιτείνει καὶ ἀνίησιν, καί τις ἔστιν ὅρος τῶν μεσοτήτων, ἃς μεταξύ φαμεν εἶναι τῆς ὑπερβολῆς καὶ τῆς ἐλλείψεως, οὔσας κατὰ τὸν ὀρθὸν λόγον. ἔστι δὲ τὸ μὲν εἰπεῖν οὕτως ἀληθὲς μέν, οὐθὲν δὲ σαφές· καὶ γὰρ ἐν ταῖς ἄλλαις ἐπιμελείαις, περὶ ὅσας ἐστὶν ἐπιστήμη, τοῦτ' ἀληθὲς μὲν εἰπεῖν, ὅτι οὔτε πλείω οὔτε ἐλάττω δεῖ πονεῖν οὐδὲ ῥᾳθυμεῖν, ἀλλὰ τὰ μέσα καὶ ὡς ὁ ὀρθὸς λόγος· τοῦτο δὲ μόνον ἔχων ἄν τις οὐδὲν ἂν εἰδείη πλέον, οἷον ποῖα δεῖ προσφέρεσθαι πρὸς τὸ σῶμα, εἴ τις εἴπειεν ὅτι ὅσα ἡ ἰατρικὴ κελεύει καὶ ὡς ὁ ταύτην ἔχων.

A close inspection of this text should be rewarding. After repeating at the outset that "reason" identifies or locates the mean, as he had done in the definition of virtue, Aristotle affirms that there is "a mark" (σκοπός) on which the man who possesses "reason" has his eyes fixed in guiding his actions. He then proceeds to state more precisely what he means by "a mark." There is a certain "standard," ὅρος, presumably the equivalent of "mark," "which determines the mean states." One can only conclude that Aristotle has introduced a new element into his definition of virtue. The earlier argument ran to the effect that virtue was in a mean, and that this mean could be discovered by "reason." Now evidently there is something more ultimate to which the reason must look, *i.e.*, the "mark" or "standard" which "fixes" the mean. This, Aristotle explains, is why we say that mean states "are intermediate between excess and defect, being in accordance with right reason." In other words, we can use the conception of right reason here, because the man who possesses it has looked to the "mark" or "standard," has apprehended it accurately, and hence has been able to make his "reason" "right." Obviously, at this point we are eager to find out more about this new element, the "mark" or "standard."

We cannot then fail to be impressed by the next remark to the effect that, in talking as he has about the mean, his statements have been true but they have been not at all clear. It is perfectly well to say that in many fields one should avoid extremes and aim at the mean as "right reason" directs, but this does not leave one in fact very much better off. Aristotle here introduces an illustration from the field of medicine. He asks, in effect, how much wiser you are if you want to know what kind of medicine to take merely to be told in the vaguest general terms that you should take whatever the art of medicine bids you to, or whatever the man who possesses this art suggests. So in the realm of moral

---

διὸ δεῖ καὶ περὶ τὰς τῆς ψυχῆς ἕξεις μὴ μόνον ἀληθῶς εἶναι τοῦτ᾽ εἰρημένον, ἀλλὰ καὶ διωρισμένον τίς ἐστιν ὁ ὀρθὸς λόγος καὶ τούτου τίς ὅρος. Bywater's text. In the translation, I have substituted "reason" and "right reason", λόγος and ὁ ὀρθὸς λόγος, for "the rule" and "the right rule" of Ross's version. I have included the latter in brackets at the appropriate points. Also I have translated the second καί of 1138 b 23 as "that is" instead of Ross's "and." I have also, following Rackham, inserted "certain" to convey the force of τις in the same line.

virtue one must not stop with simply the true enough statement of the doctrine of the mean, but one must go further and find out exactly what "right reason" is and "what is the standard that fixes it." But at this juncture Aristotle launches directly into his analysis of the intellectual virtues and says no more for the moment about "right reason" or the "standard."[61] Let us see if we can discover the rationale of this somewhat strange transition.

Some light may be forthcoming if we examine with equal care a passage near the close of the sixth book of the *Nicomachean Ethics*. Aristotle has brought up the view of some persons who affirm that all the virtues are "practical wisdoms" (φρονήσεις) or "forms of practical wisdom," as Ross translates it. He criticizes Socrates for holding this opinion, but on the other hand applauds him for maintaining that virtues "are not without practical wisdom."[62] He then continues his argument in the following words: "This is confirmed by the fact that even now all men, when they define virtue, after naming the state of character and its objects add 'that (state) which is in accordance with "right reason" [the right rule]'; now 'right reason' [the right rule] is that which is in accordance with practical wisdom. All men, then, seem somehow to divine that this kind of state is virtue, *viz.*, that which is in accordance with practical wisdom. But we must go a little further. For it is not merely the state in accordance with 'right reason' [the right rule], but the state that implies the *presence* of 'right reason' [the right rule], that is virtue; and practical wisdom is 'right reason' [a right rule] about such matters."[63]

---

[61] The notes of Stewart, *op. cit.*, Burnet, *The Ethics of Aristotle* (London, Methuen, 1904), and Joachim, *op. cit.*, on *Nicomachean Ethics* VI, 1138 b 18-34 are most instructive. The abrupt transition to the subject of the intellectual virtues has led some scholars to hold that 1138 b 18-34 is a later and non-Aristotelian addition. I agree with Burnet and Joachim that this is not the case.

[62] *Nicomachean Ethics* VI, 1144 b 17-21. διόπερ τινές φασι πάσας τὰς ἀρετὰς φρονήσεις εἶναι, καὶ Σωκράτης τῇ μὲν ὀρθῶς ἐζήτει τῇ δ᾽ ἡμάρτανεν· ὅτι μὲν γὰρ φρονήσεις ᾤετο εἶναι πάσας τὰς ἀρετάς, ἡμάρτανεν, ὅτι δ᾽ οὐκ ἄνευ φρονήσεως, καλῶς ἔλεγεν. Bywater's text.

[63] *Nicomachean Ethics* VI, 1144 b 21-28. σημεῖον δέ· καὶ γὰρ νῦν πάντες, ὅταν ὁρίζωνται τὴν ἀρετήν, προστιθέασι, τὴν ἕξιν εἰπόντες καὶ πρὸς ἅ ἐστι, τὴν κατὰ τὸν ὀρθὸν λόγον. ὀρθὸς δ᾽ ὁ κατὰ τὴν φρόνησιν. ἐοίκασι δὴ μαντεύεσθαι πως ἅπαντες ὅτι ἡ τοιαύτη ἕξις ἀρετή ἐστιν, ἡ κατὰ τὴν φρόνησιν. δεῖ δὲ μικρὸν

In the first place, I believe we are justified in maintaining that this present quotation constitutes an effort on Aristotle's part to fill the need he brought up in the introduction to the sixth book of the *Nicomachean Ethics*, *viz.*, that we must determine precisely what "right reason" is.[64] We can therefore say that there can be no doubt about the genuineness of that introduction, for when Aristotle submits that "right reason" is in accordance with practical wisdom he is clearly tying together his analysis of the moral virtues with that of the intellectual virtues.[65] But what of the merits of this theory that "right reason" which determines the "mean" of moral virtue is "in accordance with practical wisdom?" How far, may we assert with candour, has Aristotle actually advanced his case? Is he really in any better position than he was when he complained, "But such a statement, though true, is by no means clear?"[66] Furthermore, it must not escape our notice that here in the conclusion of the sixth book he makes no mention of the "mark" or "standard" of the introduction, which we, I believe, legitimately called a new element in the analysis of the moral mean. The introduction would surely have us believe that the "standard," ὅϱος, is really that than which there is nothing more ultimate in a man's search for moral virtue. The "standard" is the navigational "fix" for "right reason." This in turn determines the mean, and it is in the mean that virtue lies. And we must repeat, we are not helped very much by being told in the conclusion of the book that "right reason" is as it is because it is "in accordance with practical wisdom." We might suppose that practical wisdom or the man who possesses it would have full information about this all-important "standard," but Aristotle does not tell us so, nor does he tell us anything more about the "standard," at least for the present.[67]

μεταβῆναι. ἔστι γὰϱ οὐ μόνον ἡ κατὰ τὸν ὀϱθὸν λόγον, ἀλλ' ἡ μετὰ τοῦ ὀϱθοῦ λόγου ἕξις ἀϱετή ἐστιν. ὀϱθὸς δὲ λόγος πεϱὶ τῶν τοιούτων ἡ φϱόνησίς ἐστιν. Bywater's text. Again I have substituted "right reason" for "the right rule" of Ross's version, but have included the latter in brackets at the appropriate points. As may be recalled, we cited the long passage of which this is a part in note 59 of Chapter VII above.

[64] *Nicomachean Ethics* VI, 1138 b 32–34.

[65] Cf. Chapter VII, note 61 above.

[66] *Nicomachean Ethics* VI, 1138 b 25–26.

[67] Burnet, *op. cit.*, note on *Nicomachean Ethics* VI, 1138 b 26, ἀληθὲς μέν, οὐθὲν δὲ σαφές, answers the scholars who say that this phrase is a criticism of Aristotle

What finally can we say about "reason" or "right reason" as an arbiter or determinant for value in the light of our examination of these two passages in the sixth book of the *Nicomachean Ethics*? One surely must be impressed by the fact that Aristotle is seeking to refine and make more solid his doctrine of the mean as it was delineated in the second book. His attempt, which eventuates in the appearance of the new element, "mark" or "standard," is a laudable effort to get to the bottom of the problem. Also it is noteworthy to see how Aristotle establishes the connection between his theory of moral virtue and the intellectual virtue of practical wisdom. But we are forced to conclude that not much ground has in fact been gained by the introduction of the conception of "standard," upon which he did not elaborate.

---

by Eudemus. In concluding his argument, he observes, "In Book X Aristotle explains what the ὅρος or σκοπός is much more fully than Eudemos ever does. We there learn that it is the θεωρητικὸς βίος on which the φρόνιμος keeps his eye, and the meaning of this is thoroughly worked out, while Eudemos dismisses in half a page his corresponding doctrine that the ὅρος τῆς καλοκἀγαθίας (i.e., τῆς ἠθικῆς ἀρετῆς) is τὸν θεὸν θεραπεύειν καὶ θεωρεῖν."

Here we are not concerned with the problem of the status of the *Eudemian Ethics*. (Incidentally, Burnet believes that Eudemus was the author, and calls it "the most authoritative commentary on the *Nicomachean Ethics*," *op. cit.*, Introduction, p. xiv.) Our purpose is rather with Burnet's solution in regard to the nature of the ὅρος or σκοπός. It is an easy inference to identify this "standard" with the contemplative life expatiated upon in the tenth book of the *Nicomachean Ethics*, but there is no explicit statement in that book that Aristotle had such an identification in mind, and if he did, he is certainly by no means clear about it. In the first place, the contemplative life is the unconditioned activity of "thinking upon thinking" of the Prime Mover. By definition, it is possible only for the σοφός, the man of philosophic wisdom, to have the contemplative life as a legitimate object of his thought. Secondly and on the other hand, the φρόνιμος, the man of practical wisdom, again by definition, can have only "things human" as the object of his thought. How then can he hold before his eyes a "standard," ὅρος, which is the non-contingent contemplative life? Aristotle, it must be admitted, does say that the contemplative life of the philosopher can be taken as a human analogy for the contemplative life of the Prime Mover. The trouble, at bottom, seems to be this: First, the notion of "standard" suggests some kind of externally existing norm, but Aristotle on metaphysical grounds cannot admit the separate existence of such an entity as a sanction or guarantor for moral values. Second, he has sharply separated the activity of the φρόνιμος from that of the σοφός, as we saw above in section A of this Chapter.

We can only conclude that the doctrine of the sixth book of the *Nicomachean Ethics* and that of the tenth have not been fully coordinated. And I should argue, the metaphysical frame within which Aristotle has chosen to operate precludes by its very nature the possibility of articulating any such full coordination. We shall have more to say on this question when we discuss the contemplative life in section I below.

Yet, as he is setting up the relations between "right reason" and practical wisdom, he speaks in a spirit of full confidence in his theory when he says, "All men, when they define virtue, after naming the state of character and its objects add 'that (state) of character which is in accordance with right reason.' "[68] But on the other hand, when he says that the definition of virtue is true but is "by no means clear,"[69] it is difficult to avoid getting the impression that Aristotle himself is a little uncertain, and perhaps lacks full conviction that "right reason" in and of itself is a sufficient sanction for moral values.

The same spirit may be detected in the second passage at the conclusion of the sixth book when he remarks, "*All men*, then, seem somehow to divine that this kind of state is virtue, *viz.*, that which is in accordance with practical wisdom. But we must go a little further."[70] Confidence exudes from the reference to "all men," but it is blunted by the use of the verb "to divine" and the qualifying adverb "somehow." Also the statement that "we must go a little further" bespeaks a lack of satisfaction on Aristotle's part with the results of his argument thus far. The additional point he then makes is interesting when he says that the virtuous state is not only "in accordance with" right reason (the preposition is κατά) but also it "implies the presence of right reason" or it goes "along with" right reason or right reason is "inherent in it." This time the preposition is μετά. Burnet[71] may be correct in saying that "in accordance with" seems to imply a kind of Platonic external standard only, while it is important for Aristotle to insist that moral goodness "is inseparably bound up with 'practical wisdom.'" It is to convey this meaning that the preposition μετά has been used. Again we may ask how much further have we actually gone by this shift in prepositions. And if Burnet is right in his interpretation, the problem raised by the nature of the "mark" or "standard" is only aggravated. For the moment, we should be aware that in this study of reason, right reason, practical wisdom, and virtue, Aristotle has kept

[68] *Nicomachean Ethics* VI, 1144 b 21–23.
[69] *Nicomachean Ethics* VI, 1138 b 25–26.
[70] *Nicomachean Ethics* VI, 1144 b 24–26.
[71] *op. cit.*, note on *Nicomachean Ethics* VI, 1144 b 25–26.

within the limits of "things human," whatever he may have in mind to suggest by the introduction of the conception of "standard."[72]

E. APPENDIX

There is a passage in the seventh book of the *Nicomachean Ethics* which gives us a somewhat different insight into Aristotle's conception of the rôle of "reason" or λόγος in ethical situations. In his general discussion of continence and incontinence, Aristotle is contrasting the profligate or self-indulgent man with the incontinent or unrestrained man. At one point in the argument he makes this observation: "For virtue and vice respectively preserve and destroy the first principle, and in actions the final cause is the first principle, as the hypotheses are in mathematics; neither in that case is it the reason that teaches the first principles, nor is it so here—virtue either natural or produced by habituation is what teaches right opinion about the first principle. Such a man as this, then, is temperate; his contrary is the self-indulgent."[73] Noteworthy here is the presence of the conception of the first principle, ἀρχή, which certainly has not obtruded itself in our discussions of moral values as they have centered around the doctrine of the mean. In the present passage a different set of interrelations is

[72] I do not believe that it helps very much to identify, as some scholars have, the "standard" with the "form *(εἶδος)* of goodness" which inheres in particulars. The argument runs that the λόγος of the φρόνιμος has grasped this "form" and acts accordingly. Such an analysis, it seems to me, leaves completely untouched the problem of the real nature of goodness, or to put it more broadly, the real nature of value. In the whole foregoing discussion, I realize that I may be criticized for translating λόγος and ὁ ὀρθὸς λόγος as "reason" and "right reason." On close study of the text, Ross's "rule" and "right rule" do not seem to reproduce the palpable meaning of the original. In my opinion, "rational principle" is somewhat more satisfactory. One finally has to ask oneself something like this: What are we to call this λόγος which operates in the inner being of the φρόνιμος? The simplest and the most direct answer seems to be "reason," for clearly the φρόνιμος is employing his "ratiocinative faculties." Certainly he is not being controlled by his passions. Hence I have opted for "reason" as the best translation, while at the same time being aware that λόγος in any context in Greek cannot be adequately reproduced by a single word in English.

[73] *Nicomachean Ethics* VII, 1151 a 15–20. ἡ γὰρ ἀρετὴ καὶ μοχθηρία τὴν ἀρχὴν ἢ μὲν φθείρει ἢ δὲ σώζει, ἐν δὲ ταῖς πράξεσι τὸ οὗ ἕνεκα ἀρχή, ὥσπερ ἐν τοῖς μαθηματικοῖς αἱ ὑποθέσεις· οὔτε δὴ ἐκεῖ ὁ λόγος διδασκαλικὸς τῶν ἀρχῶν οὔτε ἐνταῦθα, ἀλλ' ἀρετὴ ἢ φυσικὴ ἢ ἐθιστὴ τοῦ ὀρθοδοξεῖν περὶ τὴν ἀρχήν. σώφρων μὲν οὖν ὁ τοιοῦτος, ἀκόλαστος δ' ὁ ἐναντίος. Bywater's text. In the translation I have substituted "reason" for λόγος in 1151 a 17 in place of "argument."

put forward. Virtue preserves this first principle and vice destroys it. The first principle is defined as the final cause or purpose in actions, and "reason" is denied any function in teaching anything about first principles. Rather natural virtue or virtue inculcated by habit (I suppose Aristotle here means to suggest the intellectual and moral virtues) by the very act of being practiced produces right opinion about the first principle, in other words, about the purpose or final cause for which actions are undertaken. We are, of course, familiar with the notion that a man becomes just by performing just acts, but we cannot fail to be startled by the elimination of reason from playing any part at all in this analysis of the ethical situation. Perhaps Aristotle was careless in writing these lines. Perhaps we should not use "reason" as a translation for λόγος in this context, though it is difficult to see any sound evidence why we should not do so. Perhaps Aristotle was himself not clear in his own mind as to the rôle of reason, and its relation to first principles, in his theory of virtue. The thought underlying this passage, it seems, must remain obscure.

F. THE SPOUDAIOS AND THE PHRONIMOS

". . . a mean which is determined by reason or that by which the man of practical wisdom would define it."[74] We opened our discussion of "reason," λόγος, by quoting this part of Aristotle's definition of virtue, and it seems appropriate to repeat it here as we are about to take up the *phronimos* and the *spoudaios* and the functions they perform in Aristotle's scheme of moral values. In the preceding section it became abundantly clear that the man of practical wisdom (the *phronimos* is after all the person who possesses practical wisdom and acts upon it) has "right reason," which is "right" because it accords with practical wisdom, and hence is able to locate the mean wherein the moral value, virtue, lies. As such, the man of practical wisdom acts as a norm or sanction for moral values. It is in the light of this conviction that Aristotle, for example, can write, "Regarding practical wisdom we shall get at the truth by considering who are the persons we credit with it. Now it is thought to be the mark of a man of practical

[74] *Nicomachean Ethics* II, 1107 a 1–2.

wisdom to be able to deliberate well about what is good and expedient for himself, not in some particular respect, *e.g.*, about what sorts of thing conduce to health or to strength, but about what sorts of thing conduce to the good life in general. This is shown by the fact that we credit men with practical wisdom in some particular respect when they have calculated well with a view to some good end which is one of those that are not the object of any art."[75]

There can be no doubt that Aristotle had the *phronimos* and the *spoudaios* closely associated in his mind. The *phronimos*, the man of practical wisdom and in full possession of right reason, is never without ethical virtue,[76] and we have seen how he has served as a final court of appeal or ultimate sanction in ethical matters. But he is marked off because he is the particular individual who possesses and acts upon the intellectual virtue of practical wisdom. The conception of the *spoudaios*, on the other hand, seems to be much more generalized. He does not seem to be associated with any particular moral or intellectual virtue. He is simply *good*, no matter how one may look at him. To be sure, he is a human being, but Aristotle clearly wishes us to believe that he is preeminent in every way, and it is thus that this sober, serious, and excellent man too functions as some kind of an ultimate sanction in the Aristotelian ethical scheme.

Let us examine a lengthy passage, where, I believe, we shall be able to observe fairly accurately what happens when Aristotle

---

[75] *Nicomachean Ethics* VI, 1140 a 24–30. Περὶ δὲ φρονήσεως οὕτως ἂν λάβοιμεν, θεωρήσαντες τίνας λέγομεν τοὺς φρονίμους. δοκεῖ δὴ φρονίμου εἶναι τὸ δύνασθαι καλῶς βουλεύσασθαι περὶ τὰ αὑτῷ ἀγαθὰ καὶ συμφέροντα, οὐ κατὰ μέρος, οἷον ποῖα πρὸς ὑγίειαν, πρὸς ἰσχύν, ἀλλὰ πρὸς τὸ εὖ ζῆν ὅλως. σημεῖον δ᾽ ὅτι καὶ τοὺς περί τι φρονίμους λέγομεν, ὅταν πρὸς τέλος τι σπουδαῖον εὖ λογίσωνται, ὧν μή ἐστι τέχνη. Bywater's text. The last clause is present because Aristotle wishes to contrast φρόνησις with another intellectual virtue, τέχνη, art, which he has just been examining. We should note in particular the phrase "with a view to some good end," πρὸς τέλος τι σπουδαῖον. Could Aristotle's use of σπουδαῖον here invite us to associate the *phronimos* and the *spoudaios*? For other passages on practical wisdom and the *phronimos*, cf. the following: *Nicomachean Ethics*: VI, 1140 b 20–21; 1142 a 11–20 [why a young man cannot be a *phronimos*]; 1143 b 11–14 [why we should pay attention to the undemonstrated views of older people, experienced people and to men of practical wisdom no less than to proofs]; VII, 1152 a 6–9 [a *phronimos* cannot be incontinent; the same man is *phronimos* and *spoudaios*, good in character]; 1153 a 29–34 [the *phronimos* avoids bodily pleasures].

[76] *Nicomachean Ethics* VI, 1144 b 30–32.

actually comes face to face with the problem of value. In the
third book of the *Nicomachean Ethics,* as he is discussing what we
have had occasion to call the "mechanics" of moral decision,[77]
he has this to say about "wish," βούλησις: "That *wish* is for the
end has already been stated; some think it is for the good, others
for the apparent good. Now those who say that the good is
the object of wish must admit in consequence that that which
the man who does not choose aright wishes for is not an object
of wish (for if it is to be so, it must also be good; but it was, if
it so happened, bad); while those who say the apparent good is
the object of wish must admit that there is no natural object
of wish, but only what seems good to each man. Now different
things appear good to different people, and, if it so happens,
even contrary things. If these consequences are unpleasing, are
we to say that absolutely and in truth the good is the object of wish
but for each person the apparent good; that that which is in
truth an object of wish is an object of wish to the good man
(τῷ σπουδαίῳ), while any chance thing may be so to the bad man,
as in the case of bodies also the things that are in truth wholesome
are wholesome for bodies which are in good condition, while
for those that are diseased other things are wholesome—or bitter or
sweet or hot or heavy, and so on; since the good man *(ὁ σπουδαῖος)*
judges each class of things rightly, and in each the truth appears to
him? For each state of character has its own ideas of the noble
and the pleasant, and perhaps the good man *(ὁ σπουδαῖος)* differs
from others most by seeing the truth in each class of things, being
as it were the norm and measure of them."[78]

[77] Cf. above, Chapter VII, note 53.
[78] *Nicomachean Ethics* III, 1113 a 15–33. Ἡ δὲ βούλησις ὅτι μὲν τοῦ τέλους
ἐστὶν εἴρηται, δοκεῖ δὲ τοῖς μὲν τἀγαθοῦ εἶναι, τοῖς δὲ τοῦ φαινομένου ἀγαθοῦ.
συμβαίνει δὲ τοῖς μὲν [τὸ] βουλητὸν τἀγαθὸν λέγουσι μὴ εἶναι βουλητὸν ὃ βούλεται
ὁ μὴ ὀρθῶς αἱρούμενος (εἰ γὰρ ἔσται βουλητόν, καὶ ἀγαθόν· ἦν δ᾽, εἰ οὕτως ἔτυχε,
κακόν), τοῖς δ᾽ αὖ τὸ φαινόμενον ἀγαθὸν βουλητὸν λέγουσι μὴ εἶναι φύσει βουλητόν,
ἀλλ᾽ ἑκάστῳ τὸ δοκοῦν· ἄλλο δ᾽ ἄλλῳ φαίνεται, καὶ εἰ οὕτως ἔτυχε, τἀναντία. εἰ δὲ
δὴ ταῦτα μὴ ἀρέσκει, ἆρα φατέον ἁπλῶς μὲν καὶ κατ᾽ ἀλήθειαν βουλητὸν εἶναι
τἀγαθόν, ἑκάστῳ δὲ τὸ φαινόμενον· τῷ μὲν οὖν σπουδαίῳ τὸ κατ᾽ ἀλήθειαν εἶναι,
τῷ δὲ φαύλῳ τὸ τυχόν, ὥσπερ καὶ ἐπὶ τῶν σωμάτων τοῖς μὲν εὖ διακειμένοις ὑγιεινά
ἐστι τὰ κατ᾽ ἀλήθειαν τοιαῦτα ὄντα, τοῖς δ᾽ ἐπινόσοις ἕτερα, ὁμοίως δὲ καὶ πικρὰ
καὶ γλυκέα καὶ θερμὰ καὶ βαρέα καὶ τῶν ἄλλων ἕκαστα· ὁ σπουδαῖος γὰρ ἕκαστα
κρίνει ὀρθῶς, καὶ ἐν ἑκάστοις τἀληθὲς αὐτῷ φαίνεται. καθ᾽ ἑκάστην γὰρ ἕξιν ἰδιά
ἐστι καλὰ καὶ ἡδέα, καὶ διαφέρει πλεῖστον ἴσως ὁ σπουδαῖος τῷ τἀληθὲς ἐν
ἑκάστοις ὁρᾶν, ὥσπερ κανὼν καὶ μέτρον αὐτῶν ὤν. Bywater's text.

The substance of the argument seems to be something like this: If "wish" is always directed towards an end, is this the good or the apparent good? If one says that it is the apparent good, this would rule out the possibility of there being any real or actual good. Such a position leads to a relativism which Aristotle finds untenable. So he appears to be driven somewhat reluctantly to submit the *spoudaios*, the "good man", as the "norm" and "measure" of the "real" good or goods.[79] In other words, what we have here is Aristotle's repudiation of the *homo mensura* doctrine of Protagoras[80] and in place of it his substitution of a doctrine of *"spoudaios mensura."*[81] We must point out that here we have a value scheme which depends ultimately upon a *human* norm or sanction. We might remember at this point Jaeger's comment to the effect that Aristotle permitted Being and Value to fall apart.[82] It seems inescapable to conclude that when Aristotle did dissociate Being and Value from each other, he was forced in certain areas of the realm of value to introduce an expedient like the *spoudaios* to provide him with a base for a value scheme.[83]

[79] For a brief treatment of this passage, cf. my article, "Being and Value" in *Symbols and Society* (New York, Harper, 1955) p. 493.

[80] Cf. Burnet, *op. cit.*, note on *Nicomachean Ethics* III, 1113 a 33, where he remarks that μέτρον "is a clear reference to the dictum of Protagoras."

[81] In the present discussion the reader is invited to recall what we said about the so-called "normal man," Chapter VI, section D, pp. 186–188.

[82] Cf. above, Chapter I, pp. 16–17.

[83] For other passages where the σπουδαῖος is submitted as a "measure," cf. the following: *Nicomachean Ethics*: I, 1099 a 23; IX, 1166 a 12–13 [The succeeding lines, 1166 a 13–29, are devoted to the self-love, φιλαυτία, of the good man or σπουδαῖος where in effect Aristotle describes in detail how the good man gets along with himself. There are two interesting sentences in the passage. The one, a parenthesis, says, ἔχει γὰρ καὶ νῦν ὁ θεὸς τἀγαθόν, "for even now God possesses the good." This certainly is a sudden injection of ὁ θεός into the argument. The other is to the effect that τὸ νοοῦν, intellection, thinking, the activity of reason constitutes the essence of man]; IX, 1169 a 18–b 2 [a further description of the φιλαυτία of the σπουδαῖος, in fact, rather a romantic one for Aristotle]; IX, 1170 a 13–16 [the natural friendship of σπουδαῖος for σπουδαῖος, and the naturally good is good in the eyes of the σπουδαῖος. Is nature inserted here as a more ultimate norm than the σπουδαῖος?]; X, 1176 a 3–29 [the σπουδαῖος as the measure, μέτρον, or norm for pleasures]; X, 1176 b 24–1177 a 1 [the σπουδαῖος and the activity of happiness]. There are a number of places which mention ὁ ἀγαθός, the good man, ὁ δίκαιος, the just man, and the like, where they serve as value norms in the same way as does the *spoudaios*. Typical instances are the following: *Nicomachean Ethics*: II, 1104 b 30–1105 a 1; 1105 b 5–12; IX, 1168 b 25–31.

G. VALUES BASED ON CONVENTIONAL THINKING

John Burnet in the preface to his edition of the *Nicomachean Ethics* announces his belief that the treatise is "dialectical throughout," and that commentators have tended to approach it from a faulty point of view for failure to recognize this to be its character. He then describes the work of these commentators as follows: "They had tried to find in it (*i.e.*, the *Nicomachean Ethics*) the scientific and metaphysical basis of Aristotle's Moral Philosophy, and when they discovered instead that the foundations of the doctrine here set forth were of *the most shifting character*, taken as they are at one time from the opinions of ordinary people, at another from popular Platonism, they have been ready to accuse Aristotle of inconsistency, or to doubt the authenticity of the treatise in its present form."[84] Whatever may be the merits of the contention that the *Nicomachean Ethics* is "dialectical throughout" and whatever he may mean precisely by dialectic in this context,[85] it is nonetheless true that the foundations of the ethical doctrine *are* shifting in character, and they *are* often taken from the opinions of ordinary people. It is to this conventional aspect of the value thinking in the *Nicomachean Ethics* that we propose to devote the present section of our argument.

Early in the tenth book of the treatise, where Aristotle is taking up for a second time the problem of pleasure, there occurs a text which provides us with a suitable introduction to the analysis of his reliance upon conventional value thinking. "Those who object that that at which all things aim is not necessarily good are, we may surmise, talking nonsense. *For we say that that which every one thinks really is so;* and the man who attacks this belief will hardly have anything more credible to maintain instead."[86] This statement, of course, reflects Aristotle's characteristic empirical approach in all matters, but at the same time there could scarcely be a clearer expression of the Protagorean doctrine of *homo mensura*, this time not qualified by the notion of *spoudaios mensura*. It is surely not

---

[84] Burnet, *op. cit.*, pp. v–vi. Italics are mine.

[85] Cf. the instructive remarks of Joachim on dialectic, *op. cit.*, pp. 29–30.

[86] *Nicomachean Ethics* X, 1172 b 35–1173 a 2. οἱ δ' ἐνιστάμενοι ὡς οὐκ ἀγαθὸν οὗ πάντ' ἐφίεται, μὴ οὐθὲν λέγουσιν. ἃ γὰρ πᾶσι δοκεῖ, ταῦτ' εἶναί φαμεν· ὁ δ' ἀναιρῶν ταύτην τὴν πίστιν οὐ πάνυ πιστότερα ἐρεῖ. Bywater's text. The italics are mine.

profound philosophical speculation to maintain that what everybody thinks is the case must truly be the case. On the other hand,
Aristotle seems to be saying that it is plain common sense to
insist that an opinion on which there is unanimous agreement
must necessarily be true. *Everybody* simply cannot be wrong. In
any event, it is fair to say that Aristotle's frame of mind when he
writes these words gives us a clue as to the way in which he does
rely in his value thinking on "the opinions of ordinary people."

Nowhere is this conventional thinking more manifest than in
the descriptions of the various kinds of men who represent the
moral virtues in the mean and their related extremes of excess
and defect. These are praiseworthy in their effort to bring to
bear as much empirical evidence as possible in support of the
analysis of the moral states in question, yet at times the detail
is so great that one wonders whether Aristotle really would have
had to go to such lengths in the accumulation of data if his ethical
theory had been more adequately grounded. In any case, the conventional character of these descriptions could be illustrated by any
one of many, such as the delineations of liberality, magnificence,
ambition, good-temper, and the like. For our purposes, an examination of one of them should suffice as an exemplar. Let us
therefore take the treatment of μεγαλοψυχία as our typical instance.
It is admittedly difficult to find an adequate translation of the
term. It is *magnanimitas* in Latin and is generally rendered in
English as greatness of soul, pride, or lofty pride, and self-esteem.[87]

Aristotle devotes the third chapter of the fourth book of the
Nicomachean Ethics to his discussion of the virtue pride. Here are
some excerpts from the beginning of the presentation of pride.
"Pride seems even from its name to be concerned with great
things; what sort of great things, is the first question we must try
to answer . . . . Now the man is thought to be proud who thinks
himself worthy of great things, being worthy of them; for he
who does so beyond his deserts is a fool, but no virtuous man is
foolish or silly . . . . For pride implies greatness, as beauty implies

---

[87] Cf. Rackham, *op. cit.*, note on *Nicomachean Ethics* IV, 1123 a 34. Here he
warns that the term does not mean magnanimity or high-mindedness in our
sense of these words. Ross prefers "pride" as his rendering. We shall follow
him, and attempt to remember that μεγαλοψυχία does not carry the same set of
connotations in Greek as does "pride" in English.

a good-sized body and little people may be neat and well-proportioned but cannot be beautiful.. . . The proud man, then, is an extreme in respect of the greatness of his claims, but a mean in respect of the rightness of them; for he claims what is in accordance with his merits, while the others go to excess or fall short."[88] Thus far we should note that "pride," as a virtue, is to be associated with "great things" (what these "great things" are is as yet unspecified) and we are reminded that the proud man is correct in his self-appraisal that he deserves "great things." Furthermore, since he is virtuous, he cannot be either foolish or silly. But the conventionality of the thinking is revealed most clearly when Aristotle draws the analogy with beauty. Bigness, magnitude, is entailed by pride, as magnitude is entailed by the notion of beauty. We are told flatly that to be beautiful one has to have a big body. The poor little fellow may be neat, natty, and well-proportioned but cannot be beautiful.

Aristotle then proceeds to tell us what he means by "great things." "If, then, he [the proud man] deserves and claims great things, and above all the greatest things, he will be concerned with the one thing in particular. Desert is relative to external goods; and the greatest of these, we should say, is that which we render to the gods, and which people of position most aim at, and which is the prize appointed for the noblest deeds; and this is honour; that is surely the greatest of external goods. Honours and dishonours, therefore, are the objects with respect to which the proud man is as he should be."[89] The element of the

---

[88] *Nicomachean Ethics* IV, 1123 a 34–35; 1123 b 1–4; 1123 b 6–8; 1123 b 13–15. Ἡ δὲ μεγαλοψυχία περὶ μεγάλα μὲν καὶ ἐκ τοῦ ὀνόματος ἔοικεν εἶναι, περὶ ποῖα δ' ἐστὶ πρῶτον λάβωμεν· . . . δοκεῖ δὴ μεγαλόψυχος εἶναι ὁ μεγάλων αὑτὸν ἀξιῶν ἄξιος ὤν· ὁ γὰρ μὴ κατ' ἀξίαν αὐτὸ ποιῶν ἠλίθιος, τῶν δὲ κατ' ἀρετὴν οὐδεὶς ἠλίθιος οὐδ' ἀνόητος. . . . ἐν μεγέθει γὰρ ἡ μεγαλοψυχία, ὥσπερ καὶ τὸ κάλλος ἐν μεγάλῳ σώματι, οἱ μικροὶ δ' ἀστεῖοι καὶ σύμμετροι, καλοὶ δ' οὔ. . . .ἔστι δὴ ὁ μεγαλόψυχος τῷ μὲν μεγέθει ἄκρος, τῷ δὲ ὡς δεῖ μέσος· τοῦ γὰρ κατ' ἀξίαν αὑτὸν ἀξιοῖ· οἱ δ' ὑπερβάλλουσι καὶ ἐλλείπουσιν. Bywater's text. The second omission points out that the man who deserves little and thinks himself worth as much is "temperate," σώφρων, but not "proud." The third omission deals with the "vain" man, χαῦνος, who thinks he deserves much but does not.

[89] *Nicomachean Ethics* IV, 1123 b 15–22. εἰ δὴ μεγάλων ἑαυτὸν ἀξιοῖ ἄξιος ὤν, καὶ μάλιστα τῶν μεγίστων, περὶ ἓν μάλιστ' ἂν εἴη. ἡ δ' ἀξία λέγεται πρὸς τὰ ἐκτὸς ἀγαθά· μέγιστον δὲ τοῦτ' ἂν θείημεν ὃ τοῖς θεοῖς ἀπονέμομεν, καὶ οὗ μάλιστ' ἐφίενται οἱ ἐν ἀξιώματι, καὶ τὸ ἐπὶ τοῖς καλλίστοις ἆθλον· τοιοῦτον δὲ ἡ τιμή· μέγιστον γὰρ δὴ τοῦτο τῶν ἐκτὸς ἀγαθῶν. περὶ τιμὰς δὴ καὶ ἀτιμίας ὁ μεγαλόψυχός ἐστιν ὡς δεῖ. Bywater's text. Shades of the timocratic man of Plato's *Republic*!

conventional is not difficult to find. Honour, the greatest of external goods, what we offer to the gods, this is what "people of position most aim at," this is "the prize for the noblest deeds." This is *the* "great thing" with which the proud man is above all concerned. Such, if anything ever was, is the reflection of the opinions of ordinary people.

As the description proceeds there is a moment when Aristotle becomes slightly more philosophical and less conventional. "Now the proud man, since he deserves most, must be good in the highest degree; for the better man always deserves more, and the best man most. Therefore the truly proud man must be good. And greatness in every virtue would seem to be characteristic of a proud man."[90] He will never be cowardly, will never do injustice, nor will he ever act shamefully. "Pride, then, seems to be a sort of crown of the virtues; for it makes them greater, and it is not found without them. Therefore it is hard to be truly proud; for it is impossible without nobility and goodness of character."[91] However, the conventional tone tends to reassert itself as the description of the proud man becomes more and more detailed. "Yet he will also bear himself with moderation towards wealth and power and all good or evil fortune, whatever may befall him, and will be neither over-joyed by good fortune nor over-pained by evil. For not even towards honour does he bear himself as if it were a very great thing."[92] By now, we are beginning to get a picture of the proud man as someone completely virtuous in the conventional sense, who stands above all circumstance like some anticipatory Stoic hero, master of his fate and captain of his soul. He acts moderately in the face of wealth and power, good and evil fortune, all this as a manifestation of his

[90] *Nicomachean Ethics* IV, 1123 b 26–30. ὁ δὲ μεγαλόψυχος, εἴπερ τῶν μεγίστων ἄξιος, ἄριστος ἂν εἴη· μείζονος γὰρ ἀεὶ ὁ βελτίων ἄξιος, καὶ μεγίστων ὁ ἄριστος. τὸν ὡς ἀληθῶς ἄρα μεγαλόψυχον δεῖ ἀγαθὸν εἶναι. καὶ δόξειεν ⟨ἂν⟩ εἶναι μεγαλοψύχου τὸ ἐν ἑκάστῃ ἀρετῇ μέγα. Bywater's text.

[91] *Nicomachean Ethics* IV, 1124 a 1–4. ἔοικε μὲν οὖν ἡ μεγαλοψυχία οἷον κόσμος τις εἶναι τῶν ἀρετῶν· μείζους γὰρ αὐτὰς ποιεῖ, καὶ οὐ γίνεται ἄνευ ἐκείνων. διὰ τοῦτο χαλεπὸν τῇ ἀληθείᾳ μεγαλόψυχον εἶναι· οὐ γὰρ οἷόν τε ἄνευ καλοκαγαθίας. Bywater's text.

[92] *Nicomachean Ethics* IV, 1124 a 13–17. οὐ μὴν ἀλλὰ καὶ περὶ πλοῦτον καὶ δυναστείαν καὶ πᾶσαν εὐτυχίαν καὶ ἀτυχίαν μετρίως ἕξει, ὅπως ἂν γίνηται, καὶ οὔτ' εὐτυχῶν περιχαρὴς ἔσται οὔτ' ἀτυχῶν περίλυπος. οὐδὲ γὰρ περὶ τιμὴν οὕτως ἔχει ὡς μέγιστον ὄν. Bywater's text.

virtue. And yet he must be something of a master play-actor, for we are informed that he makes out as if honour were not of any particular significance, when we have already been told that this is the supreme of external goods with which as a proud man he must ultimately be concerned.

But let us continue with the portrait. "The goods of fortune also are thought to contribute towards pride. For men who are well-born are thought worthy of honour, and so are those who enjoy power or wealth; for they are in a superior position, and everything that has a superiority in something good is held in greater honour. Hence even such things make men prouder; for they are honoured by some for having them; but in truth the good man alone is to be honoured; he, however, who has both advantages is thought the more worthy of honour."[93] There is no doubt that the conventional goods or values of fortune, *viz.*, good birth, power, and wealth, are essential to support the virtue of pride. To be sure, the good man is worthy of honour, but he has to have something more if he is to achieve the crowning virtue of pride. The truly proud man must have both; goodness plus the goods of fortune. In this analysis it does seem as though Aristotle values external goods like birth, wealth, and power because of the extent to which he is conditioned by conventional thinking in his ethical inquiry.

As the description of the proud man is further elaborated, the implied ethic becomes less and less elevated. Take such a remark as this: "For the proud man despises justly (since he thinks truly), but the many do so at random."[94] One perhaps may wonder whether it is morally praiseworthy for a man to engage in the act of "despising."[95] Or again, after describing the high quality of the

---

[93] *Nicomachean Ethics* IV, 1124 a 20–26. Δοκεῖ δὲ καὶ τὰ εὐτυχήματα συμβάλλεσθαι πρὸς μεγαλοψυχίαν. οἱ γὰρ εὐγενεῖς ἀξιοῦνται τιμῆς καὶ οἱ δυναστεύοντες ἢ πλουτοῦντες· ἐν ὑπεροχῇ γάρ, τὸ δ᾽ ἀγαθῷ ὑπερέχον πᾶν ἐντιμότερον. διὸ καὶ τὰ τοιαῦτα μεγαλοψυχοτέρους ποιεῖ· τιμῶνται γὰρ ὑπό τινων· κατ᾽ ἀλήθειαν δ᾽ ὁ ἀγαθὸς μόνος τιμητός· ᾧ δ᾽ ἄμφω ὑπάρχει, μᾶλλον ἀξιοῦται τιμῆς. Bywater's text.

[94] *Nicomachean Ethics* IV, 1124 b 5–6. ὁ μὲν γὰρ μεγαλόψυχος δικαίως καταφρονεῖ (δοξάζει γὰρ ἀληθῶς), οἱ δὲ πολλοὶ τυχόντως. Bywater's text.

[95] It is admittedly difficult to criticize Aristotle's account of μεγαλοψυχία with complete justice for anyone who has been conditioned by a Christian or even a Platonic ethic. As is so obvious, much in the Aristotelian ethical atmosphere is antithetical to these two points of view.

proud man's courage, and his willingness to lay down his life if need be (here the ethical tone is raised), Aristotle continues, "And he is the sort of man to confer benefits, but he is ashamed of receiving them; for the one is the mark of a superior, the other of an inferior.. . . The proud man wishes to be superior."[96] Is it an error to see in this remark a reprehensible spirit of calculation and self-centeredness? Whatever may be the answer, there is no doubt that in the quotation the voice of convention can be heard.

More details are still forthcoming. "It is a mark of the proud man also to ask for nothing or scarcely anything, but to give help readily, and to be dignified towards people who enjoy high position and good fortune, but unassuming towards those of the middle class; for it is a difficult and lofty thing to be superior to the former, but easy to be so to the latter, and a lofty bearing over the former is no mark of ill-breeding, but among humble people it is as vulgar as a display of strength against the weak."[97] How this proud man has to watch his behaviour! How sensitive he has to be in recognizing the class of the people with whom he associates. He must establish his superiority over the people of high position, but how moderate he must be with his inferiors. What *noblesse oblige* must he contrive. How careful he must be in preserving the marks of his good breeding. Someone may object that Aristotle is simply describing the proud man as he is, but one could easily ask in turn how the proud man came to be as he is. At any rate, we cannot escape the conviction that the proud man is such in the eyes of ordinary people, and pride has been designated as the crown of the virtues.

"He must also be open in his hate and in his love (for to conceal one's feelings, *i.e.*, to care less for truth than for what people will think, is a coward's part), and must speak and act openly; for he

---

[96] *Nicomachean Ethics* IV, 1124 b 9–10; 1124 b 14. καὶ οἷος εὖ ποιεῖν, εὐεργετούμενος δ' αἰσχύνεται· τὸ μὲν γὰρ ὑπερέχονος, τὸ δ' ὑπερεχομένου. . . . βούλεται δ' ὑπερέχειν. Bywater's text.

[97] *Nicomachean Ethics* IV, 1124 b 17–23. μεγαλοψύχου δὲ καὶ τὸ μηδενὸς δεῖσθαι ἢ μόλις, ὑπηρετεῖν δὲ προθύμως, καὶ πρὸς μὲν τοὺς ἐν ἀξιώματι καὶ εὐτυχίαις μέγαν εἶναι, πρὸς δὲ τοὺς μέσους μέτριον· τῶν μὲν γὰρ ὑπερέχειν χαλεπὸν καὶ σεμνόν, τῶν δὲ ῥάδιον, καὶ ἐπ' ἐκείνοις μὲν σεμνύνεσθαι οὐκ ἀγεννές, ἐν δὲ τοῖς ταπεινοῖς φορτικόν, ὥσπερ εἰς τοὺς ἀσθενεῖς ἰσχυρίζεσθαι. Bywater's text.

is free of speech because he is contemptuous, and he is given to telling the truth, except when he speaks in irony to the vulgar."[98] Though it is, of course, laudable that the proud man speaks and acts openly, one may question the moral elevation of the notion that he should manifest hatred. We might also criticize his freedom of speech which rests upon the fact that he is contemptuous. Furthermore, though he is generally truthful, there is the important exception, for he is relieved of the responsibility of truthfulness when he may deal "ironically" with the many or the vulgar.[99]

And so the account goes on. The proud man is not slavish nor a flatterer. He anticipates Horace in following the dictum, *nil admirari*. He does not remember wrongs done to him. In conversation he does not deal in personalities. He speaks ill of no one, except, on occasion, of his enemies, because of his haughtiness (ὕβρις).[100] Also he is a man of culture. "He is one who will possess beautiful and profitless things rather than profitable and useful ones; for this is more proper to a character that suffices to itself."[101] The picture is completed with this final observation: "Further, a slow step is thought proper to the proud man, a deep voice, and a level utterance; for the man who takes few things seriously is not likely to be hurried, nor the man who thinks nothing great to be excited, while a shrill voice and a rapid gait are the results of hurry and excitement."[102]

What a portrait this is, even down to the details of his deliberate motion, his deep voice, and level utterance. Despite the numerous

---

[98] *Nicomachean Ethics* IV, 1124 b 26–31. ἀναγκαῖον δὲ καὶ φανερομισῆ εἶναι καὶ φανερόφιλον (τὸ γὰρ λανθάνειν φοβουμένου, καὶ ἀμελεῖν τῆς ἀληθείας μᾶλλον ἢ τῆς δόξης), καὶ λέγειν καὶ πράττειν φανερῶς (παρρησιαστὴς γὰρ διὰ τὸ καταφρονητικὸς εἶναι, καὶ ἀληθευτικός, πλὴν ὅσα μὴ δ' εἰρωνείαν [εἰρωνεία δὲ] πρὸς τοὺς πολλούς). Bywater's text, including his brackets around εἰρωνεία δέ.

[99] Cf. Burnet, *op. cit.*, note *ad loc.* Does he, as a Britisher, approve of irony when he writes, "The proud man affects a certain mock-humility in order to evade those who would trouble him with small matters. 'I fear that is not quite in my line.' "?

[100] The foregoing points are covered in *Nicomachean Ethics* IV, 1125 a 1–9.

[101] *Nicomachean Ethics* IV, 1125 a 11–12. καὶ οἷος κεκτῆσθαι μᾶλλον τὰ καλὰ καὶ ἄκαρπα τῶν καρπίμων καὶ ὠφελίμων· αὐτάρκους γὰρ μᾶλλον. Bywater's text.

[102] *Nicomachean Ethics* IV, 1125 a 12–16. καὶ κίνησις δὲ βραδεῖα τοῦ μεγαλοψύχου δοκεῖ εἶναι, καὶ φωνὴ βαρεῖα, καὶ λέξις στάσιμος· οὐ γὰρ σπευστικὸς ὁ περὶ ὀλίγα σπουδάζων, οὐδὲ σύντονος ὁ μηδὲν μέγα οἰόμενος· ἡ δ' ὀξυφωνία καὶ ἡ ταχυτὴς διὰ τούτων Bywater's text.

admirable qualities of the proud man, it is difficult to admire him. One could only do so if one accepted completely the conventional values which he is made to represent. Yet his virtue, pride, we repeat, is designated by Aristotle as the crowning virtue. It is to be hoped that the foregoing examination of the proud man will suffice to give us insight into this aspect of Aristotle's value thinking in the realm of ethics—the aspect that derives from convention, from the opinions of ordinary people.[103]

H. PLEASURE

It will not be our purpose in this present section to review in detail the much debated problem of pleasure in Aristotle's thought. Rather, we shall within as brief a compass as possible attempt to indicate the way or ways in which he regards pleasure either as a value or a sanction for value in the moral setting of the *Nicomachean Ethics*. He clearly regards the nature of pleasure as deeply relevant to his whole ethical inquiry as is so evident in the following passage taken from the second book of the treatise: "We must take as a sign of states of character the pleasure or pain that ensues on acts; for the man who abstains from bodily pleasures and delights in this very fact is temperate, while the man who is annoyed at it is self-indulgent, and he who stands his ground against things that are terrible and delights in this or at least is not pained is brave, while the man who is pained is a coward. For moral excellence is concerned with pleasures and pains; it is on account of the pleasure that we do bad things, and on account of the pain that we abstain from noble ones. Hence we ought to have been brought up in a particular way from our very youth, as Plato says, so as both to delight in and to be pained by the things that we ought; for this is the right education. Again, if the virtues are concerned with actions and passions, and

---

[103] I should like to cite the following passages in the *Nicomachean Ethics* which illustrate Aristotle's use of conventional value thinking or his dependence upon conventional reaction to support his views: II, 1105 a 9–10; III, 1110 a 4–11; 1112 b 12–15; 1115 a 10–11; 1116 a 12–15; 1117 b 11–13; V, 1132 b 33–1133 a 2; 1137 a 31–b 5; VII, 1145 b 2–20; 1150 a 33–b 1; VIII, 1155 a 3–b 16; 1158 b 11–28; 1159 a 12–33; 1163 a 1–23; 1163 a 24–b 28; IX, 1165 b 23–31; 1166 b 2–29; 1168 a 28–b 12; 1171 a 21–b 28.

every passion and every action is accompanied by pleasure and pain, for this reason also virtue will be concerned with pleasures and pains."[104]

The foregoing passage establishes, first of all, the fundamental interimplication, in Aristotle's thought, of the four conceptions: virtue, vice, pleasure, and pain. But we should be clear about the relationships. All ethical action, good or bad, entails some kind of pleasurable or painful reaction on the part of the agent. It is evident that attendant pleasure or pain both can function as a sanction or quasi-sanction for good or bad ethical action. For example, it is implied that the enjoyment of bodily pleasure is a "sign" of unsatisfactory ethical behaviour, for the man who delights in (takes pleasure in) abstention from bodily pleasures is virtuous. Here we have a "good" pleasure and a "bad" pleasure distinguished from each other, with the former being a quasi-sanction for good action, or at least attendant upon it, while the latter is a sign or symptom of evil action. Similarly the man who delights in (takes pleasure in) "terrible things," or at least is not pained by them, is brave, *i.e.*, virtuous, whereas the person who feels pain in the presence of "terrible things" is a coward, *i.e.*, vicious. But in the next observation, the rôles of pleasure and pain as quasi-sanctions or symptoms are reversed. Because of pleasure we act badly, and we are deterred from noble deeds because the performance of them would involve pain. And so Aristotle refers to Plato approvingly (something which he does not do very frequently) to the effect that one's early training should teach him to take pleasure in and be pained by "the things that we ought." This statement, of course, implies that there is some more ultimate value criterion than pleasure or pain, but,

---

[104] *Nicomachean Ethics* II, 1104 b 3–16. Σημεῖον δὲ δεῖ ποιεῖσθαι τῶν ἕξεων τὴν ἐπιγινομένην ἡδονὴν ἢ λύπην τοῖς ἔργοις· ὁ μὲν γὰρ ἀπεχόμενος τῶν σωματικῶν ἡδονῶν καὶ αὐτῷ τούτῳ χαίρων σώφρων, ὁ δ' ἀχθόμενος ἀκόλαστος, καὶ ὁ μὲν ὑπομένων τὰ δεινὰ καὶ χαίρων ἢ μὴ λυπούμενός γε ἀνδρεῖος, ὁ δὲ λυπούμενος δειλός. περὶ ἡδονὰς γὰρ καὶ λύπας ἐστὶν ἡ ἠθικὴ ἀρετή· διὰ μὲν γὰρ τὴν ἡδονὴν τὰ φαῦλα πράττομεν, διὰ δὲ τὴν λύπην τῶν καλῶν ἀπεχόμεθα. διὸ δεῖ ἦχθαί πως εὐθὺς ἐκ νέων, ὡς Πλάτων φησίν, ὥστε χαίρειν τε καὶ λυπεῖσθαι οἷς δεῖ· ἡ γὰρ ὀρθὴ παιδεία αὕτη ἐστιν. ἔτι δ' εἰ αἱ ἀρεταί εἰσι περὶ πράξεις καὶ πάθη, παντὶ δὲ πάθει καὶ πάσῃ πράξει ἕπεται ἡδονὴ καὶ λύπη, καὶ διὰ τοῦτ' ἂν εἴη ἡ ἀρετὴ περὶ ἡδονὰς καὶ λύπας. Bywater's text. Ross cites *Laws*, 653 a ff. and *Republic*, 401 e–402 a as the passages which Aristotle may have had in mind in his reference to Plato.

whatever the criterion by which actions are judged, there is always an attendant pleasurable or painful reaction.

There remains, however, the fact that, in Aristotle's view in the foregoing passage, a "good" act may be accompanied by either pleasure or pain, and at the same time a "bad" action also may be accompanied by either pleasure or pain. This is the clear meaning of a passage a few lines later, where we read: "But it is by reason of pleasures and pains that men become bad, by pursuing and avoiding these—either the pleasures and pains they ought not or when they ought not or as they ought not, or by going wrong in one of the other similar ways that may be distinguished."[105] And it should further be noted that Aristotle does not give us here any clue as to the nature of the ultimate value criterion implied in the phrase "they ought not or when they ought not or as they ought not." Again this lack of a clue is apparent when he says, "We assume, then, that this kind of excellence tends to do what is best with regard to pleasures and pains, and vice does the contrary."[106] In other words, we are given no hint as to the way in which we may identify "what is best." For the present, it is enough to say that these quotations from the second book of the *Nicomachean Ethics* indicate what I have called the "interimplication" of pleasure, pain, virtue, and vice in Aristotle's ethical analysis. Because of the suggestion that there is some kind of ultimate value criterion other than pleasure and pain, in this context one cannot see in Aristotle the posture of a thoroughgoing hedonist.[107]

In the seventh book of the *Nicomachean Ethics*, where the question of pleasure is specifically under consideration, there seems

[105] *Nicomachean Ethics* II, 1104 b 21-24. δι' ἡδονὰς δὲ καὶ λύπας φαῦλοι γίνονται, τῷ διώκειν ταύτας καὶ φεύγειν, ἢ ἃς μὴ δεῖ ἢ ὅτε οὐ δεῖ ἢ ὡς οὐ δεῖ ἢ ὁσαχῶς ἄλλως ὑπὸ τοῦ λόγου διορίζεται τὰ τοιαῦτα. Bywater's text.

[106] *Nicomachean Ethics* II, 1104 b 27-28. ὑπόκειται ἄρα ἡ ἀρετὴ εἶναι ἡ τοιαύτη περὶ ἡδονὰς καὶ λύπας τῶν βελτίστων πρακτική, ἡ δὲ κακία τοὐναντίον. Bywater's text.

[107] Other passages which reflect the same attitude towards pleasure and pain may be noted: *Nicomachean Ethics*: II, 1105 a 3-5; 1105 a 6-7; 1105 a 13-16; 1109 b 7-9; III, 1118 a 23-26. Cf. also VII, 1152 b 1-3, where Aristotle asserts that pleasure and pain are the concern of the political philosopher, for he is the one who devises the "end," to which we must refer whenever we judge each thing to be either good or bad in an absolute sense *(ἁπλῶς)*. Here τέλος functions as the criterion.

to be evidence that Aristotle approaches the issue tentatively and even in a gingerly fashion. After observing that the majority of people associate happiness with pleasure,[108] he reviews rapidly various points of view with respect to pleasure, ranging from the notion that no pleasure can be a good, or that some pleasures are good but the majority are bad, or that pleasure cannot be the *summum bonum*.[109] Aristotle then introduces his refutation of these positions with these words: "That it does not follow from these grounds that pleasure is not a good, or even the chief good, is plain from the following considerations."[110] There is no need to examine in detail the nature of the ensuing argument, but it is enough at the moment to point to the curiously negative way in which Aristotle opens the discussion of pleasure—"it does not follow . . . that pleasure is not a good."

The same tentative tone is apparent, for example, when the argument that some pleasures are bad is answered. "And if certain pleasures are bad, that does not prevent the chief good from being some pleasure, just as the chief good may be some form of knowledge though certain kinds of knowledge are bad. Perhaps it is even necessary, if each disposition has unimpeded activities, that, whether the activity (if unimpeded) of all our dispositions or that of some one of them is happiness, this should be the thing most worthy of our choice; and this activity is pleasure. Thus the chief good would be some pleasure, though most pleasures might perhaps be bad without qualification. And for this reason all men think that the happy life is pleasant and weave pleasure into their ideal of happiness—and reasonably too; for no activity is perfect when it is impeded, and happiness is a perfect thing."[111]

---

[108] *Nicomachean Ethics* VII, 1152 b 6–8.

[109] *Nicomachean Ethics* VII, 1152 b 8–24.

[110] *Nicomachean Ethics* VII, 1152 b 25–26. Ὅτι δ᾿ οὐ συμβαίνει διὰ ταῦτα μὴ εἶναι ἀγαθὸν μηδὲ τὸ ἄριστον, ἐκ τῶνδε δῆλον. Bywater's text.

[111] *Nicomachean Ethics* VII, 1153 b 7–17. τἄριστόν τ᾿ οὐδὲν κωλύει ἡδονήν τινα, εἰ ἔνιαι φαῦλαι ἡδοναί, ὥσπερ καὶ ἐπιστήμην τινὰ ἐνίων φαύλων οὐσῶν. ἴσως δὲ καὶ ἀναγκαῖον, εἴπερ ἑκάστης ἕξεώς εἰσιν ἐνέργειαι ἀνεμπόδιστοι, εἴθ᾿ ἡ πασῶν ἐνέργειά ἐστιν εὐδαιμονία εἴτε ἡ τινὸς αὐτῶν, ἂν ᾖ ἀνεμπόδιστος, αἱρετωτάτην εἶναι· τοῦτο δ᾿ ἐστὶν ἡδονή. ὥστε εἴη ἂν τις ἡδονὴ τὸ ἄριστον, τῶν πολλῶν ἡδονῶν φαύλων οὐσῶν, εἰ ἔτυχεν, ἁπλῶς. καὶ διὰ τοῦτο πάντες τὸν εὐδαίμονα ἡδὺν οἴονται βίον εἶναι, καὶ ἐμπλέκουσι τὴν ἡδονὴν εἰς τὴν εὐδαιμονίαν, εὐλόγως· οὐδεμία γὰρ ἐνέργεια τέλειος ἐμποδιζομένη, ἡ δ᾿ εὐδαιμονία τῶν τελείων. Bywater's text. Immediately following this quotation comes the famous passage (1153 b 17–21)

Though the tone at the outset is palpably tentative, and we do note the phrase "perhaps it is even necessary" that there is nothing to prevent pleasure from being the *summum bonum*, as Aristotle goes on, he appears to become more categorical, when he suggests that the unimpeded activity of pleasure, the equivalent of happiness, would be most choice-worthy. And, of course, he bolsters his argument characteristically by appealing to the beliefs of all men who "weave" pleasure into happiness.[112]

In a passage preceding the one we have just been studying, Aristotle appears to be even more categorical with respect to his view of pleasure. "Again, it is not necessary that there should be something else better than pleasure; for pleasures are not processes nor do they all involve process—they are activities and ends; nor do they arise when we are becoming something, but when we are exercising some faculty; and not all pleasures have an end different from themselves, but only the pleasures of persons who are being led to the perfecting of their nature. This is why it is not right to say that pleasure is perceptible process, but it should rather be called activity of the natural state, and instead of 'perceptible' 'unimpeded.' "[113] It might safely be observed that, although this argument is conditioned in part by its being an answer to the view of Speusippus,[114] we could use this passage as incontrovertible evidence for attributing hedonism to Aristotle, if we had nothing else upon which to rely, *i.e.*, if we did not possess

---

where Aristotle affirms that the happy man needs the goods of the body, external goods, and the goods of fortune, and goes on to say, "When men maintain that the man who is being broken on the wheel, or the man who is beset with great misfortunes, is happy if he is a good man, whether they mean to or not, they are talking nonsense." οἱ δὲ τὸν τροχιζόμενον καὶ τὸν δυστυχίαις μεγάλαις περιπίπτοντα εὐδαίμονα φάσκοντες εἶναι, ἐὰν ᾖ ἀγαθός, ἢ ἑκόντες ἢ ἄκοντες οὐδὲν λέγουσιν. Cf. above, Chapter II, note 7.

[112] Perhaps the use of the verb ἐμπλέκουσι may give some justification for my choice of "interimplication" above to express the relation between pleasure, pain, virtue, and vice. Obviously, I do not wish "interimplication" to be taken in a technical sense.

[113] *Nicomachean Ethics* VII, 1153 a 7–15. ἔτι οὐκ ἀνάγκη ἕτερόν τι εἶναι βέλτιον τῆς ἡδονῆς, ὥσπερ τινές φασι τὸ τέλος τῆς γενέσεως· οὐ γὰρ γενέσεις εἰσὶν οὐδὲ μετὰ γενέσεως πᾶσαι, ἀλλ᾽ ἐνέργειαι καὶ τέλος· οὐδὲ γινομένων συμβαίνουσιν ἀλλὰ χρωμένων· καὶ τέλος οὐ πασῶν ἕτερόν τι, ἀλλὰ τῶν εἰς τὴν τελέωσιν ἀγομένων τῆς φύσεως. διὸ καὶ οὐ καλῶς ἔχει τὸ αἰσθητὴν γένεσιν φάναι εἶναι τὴν ἡδονήν, ἀλλὰ μᾶλλον λεκτέον ἐνέργειαν τῆς κατὰ φύσιν ἕξεως, ἀντὶ δὲ τοῦ αἰσθητὴν ἀνεμπόδιστον. Bywater's text.

[114] Cf. Burnet, *op. cit.*, notes *ad loc.*

the various other places where pleasure is discussed. Here pleasure is identified with ἐνέργεια and τέλος, activity and goal. It is disassociated from γένεσις, becoming or process. Certain pleasures are denoted as ends in themselves. Only these pleasures which contribute to the natural perfecting of an individual may be said not to be ends in themselves. Pleasure is "an activity of the natural state." Such statements could hardly be made by someone other than a convinced hedonist.

But, as is well known, this is not the whole story, for it is not long before the tentative and hesitant tone reappears. Not only in the quotation we have already analyzed,[115] but also in another which merits our attention, we can find the requisite evidence for our contention. "And indeed the fact that all things, both brutes and men, pursue pleasure is an indication of its being somehow the chief good:

'No voice is wholly lost that many peoples . . .'

But since no one nature or state either is or is thought the best for all, neither do all pursue the same pleasure; yet all pursue pleasure. And perhaps they actually pursue not the pleasure they think they pursue nor that which they would say they pursue, but the same pleasure; for all things have by nature something divine in them."[116] Aristotle seems to be shrinking from categorical pronouncement. All animate beings pursue pleasure, and this is a sign that it is *somehow* (πως) the *summum bonum*. The line from Hesiod reflects Aristotle's familiar appeal to the opinions of many people as support for the proposition under discussion. But then the argument is blunted by the observation that, though all pursue pleasure, they do not pursue the same pleasure. Aristotle seems constrained to try to explain this phenomenon, but his attempt at explanation falters, to say the least. It opens with the

[115] *I.e., Nicomachean Ethics* VII, 1153 b 7–17.
[116] *Nicomachean Ethics* VII, 1153 b 25–33. καὶ τὸ διώκειν δ' ἅπαντα καὶ θηρία καὶ ἀνθρώπους τὴν ἡδονὴν σημεῖόν τι τοῦ εἶναί πως τὸ ἄριστον αὐτήν.
  φήμη δ' οὔτις πάμπαν ἀπόλλυται, ἥν τινα λαοὶ
  πολλοί . . .
ἀλλ' ἐπεὶ οὐχ ἡ αὐτὴ οὔτε φύσις οὔθ' ἕξις ἡ ἀρίστη οὔτ' ἔστιν οὔτε δοκεῖ, οὐδ' ἡδονὴν διώκουσι τὴν αὐτὴν πάντες, ἡδονὴν μέντοι πάντες. ἴσως δὲ καὶ διώκουσιν οὐχ ἣν οἴονται οὐδ' ἣν ἂν φαῖεν, ἀλλὰ τὴν αὐτήν· πάντα γὰρ φύσει ἔχει τι θεῖον. Bywater's text. The verse quotation is from Hesiod, *Works and Days*, l. 763.

word, "perhaps" (ἴσως), and then suggests that people may be confused about the pleasure they are pursuing and that actually the variations are illusory for it is indeed the same pleasure. And finally, to substantiate his view, he writes (rather surprisingly in the context), "For all things have by nature something divine in them."

How should we interpret this curious passage? It may be proper to suggest that Aristotle, at least at this point in his argument, really is divided in his mind with respect to the rôle of pleasure as a value criterion. In the face of a certain amount of empirical evidence (*e.g.*, all brutes and men pursue pleasure) he seems strongly tempted to adopt the hedonist position and make pleasure the *summum bonum*. But, on the other hand, he is bothered by the empirical fact of the wide variation in the choices of pleasures. He hardly succeeds in circumventing the difficulty by citing the confused state of the choosers as a possible solution. But why does he introduce the notion of the ubiquity of "something divine" as an argument in favour of the proposition that really everybody pursues the same pleasure? It seems almost as though Aristotle invokes the "divine element" in a desperate effort to shore up the validity of hedonism. At the same time, we cannot forget the presence of the tentative qualifiers, "somehow" and "perhaps." Is he moved by the claims and counter-claims of hedonism and do we have here in the seventh book of the *Nicomachean Ethics* the record of Aristotle's struggle to make up his own mind on the problem?

No matter what may be the answer to this question, we can hardly doubt the seriousness of Aristotle's conviction that pleasure is a good. That this is patently the case can be seen in the following passage: "And it is obvious that, unless pleasure is a good and an activity, it will not be possible for the happy man to live pleasantly for on account of what reason would he be in need of pleasure, if indeed it were not a good? But it is also possible for him to live painfully. For pain is neither good nor evil, if indeed pleasure is neither good nor evil. Therefore why should he avoid pain? Neither would the life of the good man be more pleasant, unless also his activities were more pleasant."[117]

---

[117] *Nicomachean Ethics* VII, 1154 a 1–7. φανερὸν δὲ καὶ ὅτι, εἰ μὴ ἡδονὴ ἀγαθὸν καὶ ἡ ἐνέργεια, οὐκ ἔσται ζῆν ἡδέως τὸν εὐδαίμονα . . . τίνος γὰρ ἕνεκα δέοι ἂν αὐτῆς, εἴπερ μὴ ἀγαθόν; . . . ἀλλὰ καὶ λυπηρῶς ἐνδέχεται ζῆν. οὔτε

Next comes a section on bodily pleasures, upon which we do not need to dwell save to note that bodily pleasures in moderation are considered to be good, while pain and bodily pleasures in excess are regarded as evil.[118] But we must review with care the concluding remarks of the seventh book. "There is no one thing that is always pleasant, because our nature is not simple but there is another element in us as well, inasmuch as we are perishable creatures, so that if the one element does something, this is unnatural to the other nature, and when the two elements are evenly balanced, what is done seems neither painful nor pleasant; for if the nature of anything were simple, the same action would always be most pleasant to it. This is why God always enjoys a single and simple pleasure; for there is not only an activity of movement but an activity of immobility, and pleasure is found more in rest than in movement. But 'change in all things is sweet,' as the poet says, because of some vice; for it is the vicious man that is changeable, so the nature that needs change is vicious; for it is not simple nor good."[119]

As can easily be seen, Aristotle is offering another explanation for the variation in choices of that which is pleasant, or in other words, an explanation for the fact that "no one thing is always pleasant." The argument opens by the assertion that the nature of man is not simple because he is perishable or corruptible—he passes out of existence. His nature then is postulated as a dualism—as containing two elements, each of which we are invited to look at as having a nature of its own, with somehow an opposition between the two natures. When one of the "elements" does

---

κακὸν γὰρ οὔτ' ἀγαθὸν ἡ λύπη, εἴπερ μηδ' ἡδονή· ὥστε διὰ τί ἂν φεύγοι; οὐδὲ δὴ ἡδίων ὁ βίος ὁ τοῦ σπουδαίου, εἰ μὴ καὶ αἱ ἐνέργειαι αὐτοῦ. Burnet's text. The translation is mine. The Greek seems to be so elliptical and compressed that in an oral presentation Aristotle may very well have expanded upon it.

[118] *Nicomachean Ethics* VII, 1154 a 8–b 20.

[119] *Nicomachean Ethics* VII, 1154 b 20–31. οὐκ ἀεὶ δ' οὐθὲν ἡδὺ τὸ αὐτὸ διὰ τὸ μὴ ἁπλῆν ἡμῶν εἶναι τὴν φύσιν, ἀλλ' ἐνεῖναί τι καὶ ἕτερον, καθὸ φθαρτοί, ὥστε ἄν τι θάτερον πράττῃ, τοῦτο τῇ ἑτέρᾳ φύσει παρὰ φύσιν, ὅταν δ' ἰσάζῃ, οὔτε λυπηρὸν δοκεῖ οὔθ' ἡδὺ τὸ πραττόμενον· ἐπεὶ εἴ του ἡ φύσις ἁπλῆ εἴη, ἀεὶ ἡ αὐτὴ πρᾶξις ἡδίστη ἔσται. διὸ ὁ θεὸς ἀεὶ μίαν καὶ ἁπλῆν χαίρει ἡδονήν· οὐ γὰρ μόνον κινήσεώς ἐστιν ἐνέργειαν ἀλλὰ καὶ ἀκινησίας, καὶ ἡδονὴ μᾶλλον ἐν ἠρεμίᾳ ἐστὶν ἢ ἐν κινήσει. μεταβολὴ δὲ πάντων γλυκύ, κατὰ τὸν ποιητήν, διὰ πονηρίαν τινά. ὥσπερ γὰρ ἄνθρωπος εὐμετάβολος ὁ πονηρός, καὶ ἡ φύσις ἡ δεομένη μεταβολῆς· οὐ γὰρ ἁπλῆ οὐδ' ἐπιεικής. Bywater's text. The poet quoted is Euripides, *Orestes*, l. 234.

something, the result will be pleasing to the nature of the element that does it, but will be presumably painful to the other and opposing element. Aristotle then makes the curious suggestion that, if anything is done when the two elements or natures are "evenly balanced," or are equal or equally powerful, there will be neither a pleasant nor a painful reaction on the part of either of the elements or natures. It is very difficult to see exactly what Aristotle means to convey by this unique (for him) dualistic theory of human nature. One may conjecture that his purpose can be explained in some such way as this: As something that is perishable, human nature is not simple but complex. The first degree of complexity in an entity consists in its being a dualism. This dualism is enough to account for the fact that "no one thing is always pleasant." Also, by postulating a situation in which the elements of the dualism are in balance, Aristotle can account for the human phenomenon which occurs when a man may have neither a pleasant nor a painful reaction to anything that may be done. All this is apparently preliminary to a consideration of not a complex nature, but a simple nature, to which "the same action will always be most pleasant."

What is this simple nature? There is only one answer to the question. It is God who has supremely a simple nature, and hence Aristotle can insist that He always enjoys a single pleasure. We are then told that there is an activity of motion as well as one of motionlessness, an obvious reference to the complete and unchanging actuality of God, as described in *Metaphysics* Λ. There follows a very strange argument to the effect that pleasure is to be found more in rest than in motion. To support the point Euripides is quoted as saying that change is sweet, and Aristotle adds, because of some kind of viciousness. The man who is easy to change is vicious, as well as the nature that needs change is vicious. Why? Simply because such a nature is neither simple nor good.

No one can fail to be somewhat surprised by the rather sudden introduction of God into this discussion of pleasure, and of course it does look forward to the point in the tenth book of the *Nicomachean Ethics* when the subject of God is taken up again. But if we are right in our theory that in the seventh book Aristotle is divided in his mind about the problem of pleasure and at the same time is doing his best to make the best case he can for a hedonism, it is easier to understand why he should bring in the nature of God as an argument in support of pleasure as a value. Pleasure has been specified as an activity and thus can be associated with the activity or actuality of God. Aristotle also exploits God's simple and unchanging nature by asserting that because of it He enjoys always a single and simple pleasure. It is, of course, the same kind of analogical argumentation which marks the theological sections of *Metaphysics* Λ. We move from the complexity of human nature to the simplicity of God's nature, from the variability in the human domain with regard to pleasure to the singleness and simplicity and perdurability of God's pleasure, and from the mutability of human affairs, whence in some way derives vice, to the immutability of God who is simple and good. One may have his doubts about the extent to which this line of reasoning is convincing, but the affiliation of God with pleasure indicates the seriousness of Aristotle's attitude towards the hedonistic point of view.[120]

The tenth book of the *Nicomachean Ethics* opens with a restatement of the relation of pleasure and pain to virtue and then reviews the position of Eudoxus as well as that of Plato in the *Philebus*. There is no need for us to look at this introductory section, but there is one passage near its close which is very revealing of the degree to which Aristotle appears to be uncertain in the face of the problem of pleasure. "In reply to those who bring forward the disgraceful pleasures one may say that these are not pleasant; if things are pleasant to people of vicious constitution, we must not suppose that they are also pleasant to others than these, just as we do not reason so about the things that are wholesome or sweet or bitter to sick people, or ascribe whiteness to the things that seem white to those suffering from a disease of the eye. Or one might answer thus—that the pleasures are desirable, but not from *these* sources, as wealth is desirable, but not as the reward of betrayal, and health, but not at the cost of eating anything and

---

[120] For other typical passages concerning pleasure, the reader may be referred to the following: *Nicomachean Ethics*: VII, 1153 a 23–25; 1153 b 1–4; VIII, 1155 b 18–21; 1157 b 16–17.

everything. Or perhaps pleasures differ in kind; for those derived from noble sources are different from those derived from base sources, and one cannot get the pleasures of the just man without being just, nor that of the musical man without being musical, and so on."121

The major point to be observed in this passage is Aristotle's way of meeting the powerful anti-hedonistic argument which inheres in the fact that admittedly there are such things as "disgraceful pleasures." One may recall Plato's use of the distinction between good and evil pleasures in his telling refutation of hedonism in the *Gorgias*. Aristotle's mood, however, is hesitant. He offers three alternatives: (a) disgraceful pleasures are really not pleasures; (b) the pleasures are themselves actually good but are tainted by the source whence they come; and (c) pleasures are in fact different in kind, this being a sort of variant of the second alternative. It must be confessed that none of these answers is particularly compelling and the impression is almost unavoidable that Aristotle here is again attempting to make out a strong case for some forms of hedonism but at the same time exhibits his inability to do so on the basis of such arguments as he has adduced thus far.

And so the stage is set for us to explore the final position which Aristotle takes with regard to pleasure. After completing the review of the problem included in the opening pages of the tenth book of the *Nicomachean Ethics*, Aristotle announces that he will take up the whole subject again from the beginning.122 His first step is to demonstrate that pleasure cannot be a "movement," a κίνησις, or a "process," a "coming-into-being," a γένεσις.123

---

121 *Nicomachean Ethics* X, 1173 b 20–31. πρὸς δὲ τοὺς προφέροντας τὰς ἐπονειδίστους τῶν ἡδονῶν λέγοι τις ἂν ὅτι οὐκ ἔστι ταῦθ' ἡδέα (οὐ γὰρ εἰ τοῖς κακῶς διακειμένοις ἡδέα ἐστίν, οἰητέον αὐτὰ καὶ ἡδέα εἶναι πλὴν τούτοις, καθάπερ οὐδὲ τὰ τοῖς κάμνουσιν ὑγιεινὰ ἢ γλυκέα ἢ πικρά, οὐδ' αὖ λευκὰ τὰ φαινόμενα τοῖς ὀφθαλμιῶσιν)· ἢ οὕτω λέγοι τις ἄν, ὅτι αἱ μὲν ἡδοναὶ αἱρεταί εἰσιν, οὐ μὴν ἀπό γε τούτων, ὥσπερ καὶ τὸ πλουτεῖν, προδόντι δ' οὔ, καὶ τὸ ὑγιαίνειν, οὐ μὴν ὁτιοῦν φαγόντι· ἢ τῷ εἴδει διαφέρουσιν αἱ ἡδοναί· ἕτεραι γὰρ αἱ ἀπὸ τῶν καλῶν τῶν ἀπὸ τῶν αἰσχρῶν, καὶ οὐκ ἔστιν·ἡσθῆναι τὴν τοῦ δικαίου μὴ ὄντα δίκαιον οὐδὲ τὴν τοῦ μουσικοῦ μὴ ὄντα μουσικόν, ὁμοίως δὲ καὶ ἐπὶ τῶν ἄλλων. Bywater's text. Thomson's (*op. cit.*) translation of οὐ μὴν ὁτιοῦν φαγόντι, "but not if it involves indiscriminate eating," may be better than Ross's rendering. At best, one is forced to say that the illustration is not a very good one.

122 *Nicomachean Ethics* X, 1174 a 13–14.

123 *Nicomachean Ethics* X, 1174 a 14–b 14.

We then come to the definitive passage for Aristotle's theory of pleasure. "Since every sense is active in relation to its object, and a sense which is in good condition acts perfectly in relation to the most beautiful of its objects (for perfect activity seems to be ideally of this nature; whether we say that *it* is active, or the organ in which it resides, may be assumed to be immaterial), it follows that in the case of each sense the best activity is that of the best-conditioned organ in relation to the finest of its objects. And this activity will be the most complete and pleasant. For, while there is pleasure in respect of any sense, and in respect of thought and contemplation no less, the most complete is pleasantest, and that of a well-conditioned organ in relation to the worthiest of its objects is the most complete; and the pleasure completes the activity.. . . Pleasure completes the activity not as the corresponding permanent state does, by its immanence, but as an end which supervenes as the bloom of youth does on those in the flower of their age. So long, then, as both the intelligible or sensible object and the discriminating or contemplative faculty are as they should be, the pleasure will be involved in the activity."[124]

Notice how the ground-work is laid. Aristotle first sets up the relation between sense and its object as a precondition for a pleasurable reaction. He then asserts that the best activity of any sense is when it is in its best condition and is in contact with its finest object. Under these circumstances, the activity will be most pleasant. We should not fail to observe here that Aristotle is actually begging the question of value. We may well understand how a sense organ may be in its very best condition when it functions perfectly (*e.g.*, 20–20 vision), but we are given no

---

[124] *Nicomachean Ethics* X, 1174 b 14–1175 a 1, with the omission of 1174 b 24–31. Αἰσθήσεως δέ πάσης πρὸς τὸ αἰσθητὸν ἐνεργούσης, τελείως δὲ τῆς εὖ διακειμένης πρὸς τὸ κάλλιστον τῶν ὑπὸ τὴν αἴσθησιν (τοιοῦτον γὰρ μάλιστ᾽ εἶναι δοκεῖ ἡ τελεία ἐνέργεια· αὐτὴν δὲ λέγειν ἐνεργεῖν, ἢ ἐν ᾧ ἐστί, μηθὲν διαφερέτω), καθ᾽ ἑκάστην δὴ βελτίστη ἐστὶν ἡ ἐνέργεια τοῦ ἄριστα διακειμένου πρὸς τὸ κράτιστον τῶν ὑπ᾽ αὐτήν. αὕτη δ᾽ ἂν τελειοτάτη εἴη καὶ ἡδίστη. κατὰ πᾶσαν γὰρ αἴσθησίν ἐστιν ἡδονή, ὁμοίως δὲ καὶ διάνοιαν καὶ θεωρίαν, ἡδίστη δ᾽ ἡ τελειοτάτη, τελειοτάτη δ᾽ ἡ τοῦ εὖ ἔχοντος πρὸς τὸ σπουδαιότατον τῶν ὑπ᾽ αὐτήν· τελειοῖ δὲ τὴν ἐνέργειαν ἡ ἡδονή. . . . τελειοῖ δὲ τὴν ἐνέργειαν ἡ ἡδονὴ οὐχ ὡς ἡ ἕξις ἐνυπάρχουσα, ἀλλ᾽ ὡς ἐπιγινόμενόν τι τέλος, οἷον τοῖς ἀκμαίοις ἡ ὥρα. ἕως ἂν οὖν τό τε νοητὸν ἢ αἰσθητὸν ᾖ οἷον δεῖ καὶ τὸ κρῖνον ἢ θεωροῦν, ἔσται ἐν τῇ ἐνεργείᾳ ἡ ἡδονή. Bywater's text.

criterion by means of which we can determine the finest of its objects. In any event this situation is asserted to be most complete and most pleasant. Aristotle next argues that an identical situation obtains in the realms of thought and contemplation, and, of course, at the mention of contemplation we are expected to think of the supreme norm, God, who is contemplation of contemplation. In the perspective of all of this Aristotle now can advance what is his final formula with regard to pleasure, *viz.*, it is pleasure which completes each and every one of these various perfect activities of sense, thought, and contemplation. And he explains this formula further by maintaining that the completion which pleasure performs is not like that contributed by an immanent state.[125] Rather, pleasure is held to be a supervenient end, a super-added goal, which automatically attends upon a perfect activity. It is in this way that we are to understand his illustration. The bloom of youth, that "supervenient perfection," as Burnet calls it,[126] inevitably attaches to the perfect activity of being in the flower of one's age. And so we can conclude that, in the light of this formula, Aristotle conceives of pleasure as a value of high importance, something that must be thought of as inextricably bound up with final cause. It is an activity, but it is not, so to say, an independent activity, for in the formula it does supervene upon an activity of sense or thought or contemplation. Because Aristotle in the end denies to pleasure an independent status, he cannot be considered a hedonist in any full sense of the word. But, on the other hand, his strong feelings for the claims of hedonism and his shifting attitudes towards the question of value as well as his lack of coherence in this area, permit him to assume the posture of a hedonist in a certain number of *ad hoc* situations.

Before leaving the subject of pleasure, we should glance briefly at two more passages. The first occurs shortly after the one which we have just been examining. "One might think that all men desire pleasure because they all aim at life; life is an activity, and each man is active about those things and with those faculties that he loves most; *e.g.*, the musician is active with his hearing in reference to tunes, the student with his mind in reference to

---

[125] By this we can presume that Aristotle means the formal cause.
[126] Cf. Burnet, *op. cit.*, note *ad loc.*

theoretical questions, and so in each case; now pleasure completes the activities, and therefore life, which they desire. It is with good reason, then, that they aim at pleasure too, since for every one it completes life, which is desirable. But whether we choose life for the sake of pleasure or pleasure for the sake of life is a question we may dismiss for the present. For they seem to be bound up together and not to admit of separation, since without activity pleasure does not arise, and every activity is completed by the attendant pleasure."[127] There is scarely any need to point out how this quotation strengthens and elaborates the formula of pleasure as a completion. Pleasure as an activity is allied with life as an activity, and it completes life, thus explaining why all men aim at pleasure. Aristotle could not have put the case more strongly than by saying that life and pleasure are indiscerptible.

Even though the position expressed in the foregoing passage is stated with clarity and vigour, in the last section which we must review, we find Aristotle again bothered by the phenomenon of disgraceful or bad pleasures. "Now since activities differ in respect of goodness and badness, and some are worthy to be chosen, others to be avoided, and others neutral, so, too, are the pleasures; for to each activity there is a proper pleasure. The pleasure proper to a worthy activity is good and that proper to an unworthy activity bad; just as the appetites for noble objects are laudable, those for base objects culpable. But the pleasures involved in activities are more proper to them than the desires; for the latter are separated both in time and in nature, while the former are close to the activities, and so hard to distinguish from them that it admits of dispute whether the activity is not the same as the pleasure. (Still, pleasure does not seem to *be* thought or perception—that would be strange; but because they are not found apart they appear to some people the same.) As activities are

<hr/>

[127] *Nicomachean Ethics* X, 1175 a 10–21. ὀϱέγεσθαι δὲ τῆς ἡδονῆς οἰηθείη τις ἂν ἅπαντας, ὅτι καὶ τοῦ ζῆν ἅπαντες ἐφίενται· ἡ δὲ ζωὴ ἐνέϱγειά τις ἐστί, καὶ ἕκαστος πεϱὶ ταῦτα καὶ τούτοις ἐνεϱγεῖ ἃ καὶ μάλιστ᾽ ἀγαπᾷ, οἷον ὁ μὲν μουσικὸς τῇ ἀκοῇ πεϱὶ τὰ μέλη, ὁ δὲ φιλομαθὴς τῇ διανοίᾳ πεϱὶ τὰ θεωϱήματα, οὕτω δὲ καὶ τῶν λοιπῶν ἕκαστος· ἡ δ᾽ ἡδονὴ τελειοῖ τὰς ἐνεϱγείας, καὶ τὸ ζῆν δή, οὗ ὀϱέγονται. εὐλόγως οὖν καὶ τῆς ἡδονῆς ἐφίενται· τελειοῖ γὰϱ ἑκάστῳ τὸ ζῆν, αἱϱετὸν ὄν. πότεϱον δὲ διὰ τὴν ἡδονὴν τὸ ζῆν αἱϱούμεθα ἢ διὰ τὸ ζῆν τὴν ἡδονήν, ἀφείσθω ἐν τῷ παϱόντι. συνεζεῦχθαι μὲν γὰϱ ταῦτα φαίνεται καὶ χωϱισμὸν οὐ δέχεσθαι. ἄνευ τε γὰϱ ἐνεϱγείας οὐ γίνεται ἡδονή, πάσάν τε ἐνέϱγειαν τελειοῖ ἡ ἡδονή. Bywater's text.

different, then, so are the corresponding pleasures. Now sight is superior to touch in purity, and hearing and smell to taste; the pleasures, therefore, are similarly superior, and those of thought superior to these, and within each of the two kinds some are superior to others."[128]

The implications of this quotation are noteworthy. The point which strikes us at the outset is Aristotle's introduction of the conception of a "bad" ἐνέργεια, activity or actuality. We have discussed at length the difficulty which this conception precipitates for Aristotle in our chapter on the *Metaphysics*.[129] There, it may be recalled, we invited attention to Aristotle's argument for a "scale of values" as an outgrowth of his analysis of potentiality and actuality. Potentiality was considered to be "neutral" from the point of view of value since as a potentiality it is capable of opposites and hence may become actualized in a good or a bad form. So the good actuality was ranked first, potentiality second, and the bad actuality third. So, in our passage from the tenth book of the *Nicomachean Ethics*, we have a similar scale propounded. Activities, or actualities (ἐνέργεια is the word in both the *Metaphysics* and the *Ethics*) are classified as either good, or bad, or neutral, and choice and avoidance are to be controlled accordingly. Since on the basis of the formula that pleasure completes an activity and is its inseparable "companion," there must be a pleasure "proper" to each activity. Hence the pleasure attaching to a good activity is good and that to a bad activity is bad. Aristotle next distinguishes between desires and pleasures, and presses further his argument for the close inter-association of activity and pleasure. He finally concludes by

---

[128] *Nicomachean Ethics* X, 1175 b 24–1176 a 3. διαφερουσῶν δὲ τῶν ἐνεργειῶν ἐπιεικείᾳ καὶ φαυλότητι, καὶ τῶν μὲν αἱρετῶν οὐσῶν τῶν δὲ φευκτῶν τῶν δ' οὐδετέρων, ὁμοίως ἔχουσι καὶ αἱ ἡδοναί· καθ' ἑκάστην γὰρ ἐνέργειαν οἰκεία ἡδονή ἐστιν. ἡ μὲν οὖν τῇ σπουδαίᾳ οἰκεία ἐπιεικής, ἡ δὲ τῇ φαύλῃ μοχθηρά. καὶ γὰρ αἱ ἐπιθυμίαι τῶν μὲν καλῶν ἐπαινεταί, τῶν δ' αἰσχρῶν ψεκταί. οἰκειότεραι δὲ ταῖς ἐνεργείαις αἱ ἐν αὐταῖς ἡδοναὶ τῶν ὀρέξεων· αἱ μὲν γὰρ διωρισμέναι εἰσὶ καὶ τοῖς χρόνοις καὶ τῇ φύσει, αἱ δὲ σύνεγγυς ταῖς ἐνεργείαις, καὶ ἀδιόριστοι οὕτως ὥστ' ἔχειν ἀμφισβήτησιν εἰ ταὐτόν ἐστιν ἡ ἐνέργεια τῇ ἡδονῇ. οὐ μὴν ἔοικέ γε ἡ ἡδονὴ διάνοια εἶναι οὐδ' αἴσθησις (ἄτοπον γάρ), ἀλλὰ διὰ τὸ μὴ χωρίζεσθαι φαίνεταί τισι ταὐτόν. ὥσπερ οὖν αἱ ἐνέργειαι ἕτεραι, καὶ αἱ ἡδοναί. διαφέρει δὲ ἡ ὄψις ἁφῆς καθαρειότητι, καὶ ἀκοὴ καὶ ὄσφρησις γεύσεως· ὁμοίως δὴ διαφέρουσι καὶ αἱ ἡδοναί, καὶ τούτων αἱ περὶ τὴν διάνοιαν, καὶ ἑκάτεραι ἀλλήλων. Bywater's text.

[129] Cf. above, Chapter VI, pp. 191–196.

postulating a scale of activities and, of course, of the corresponding pleasures. In the realm of sense, sight is affirmed to be superior to touch "in purity" (what in the world does Aristotle mean by "purity"?) and hearing and smell are similarly asserted to be superior to taste. Moving from the realm of sense to that of intellection, Aristotle insists upon the even greater superiority of the pleasures of thought.

What are we to make of this passage? In the first place, it is worth noting that in the concluding scale of activities and pleasures, *i.e.*, those involving the senses and thought, all the activities are put forward, at least by implication, as good. The activities of the senses are arranged in order of their "purity," and the resultant ranking in all probability reflects conventional opinion on the point. In other words, there is no mention of "bad" activities and pleasures, and, in fact, the difficulties that inescapably attach to the notion of a bad actuality or activity remain untouched. Furthermore, we should not forget how Aristotle, in his effort to build up the case for pleasure, keeps insisting that pleasure is an activity and not a process or a "becoming." How can activity function sometimes as a symptom of value or worth, and at the same time there be some such thing as a bad activity? It seems clear that Aristotle never resolves this dilemma. So far as this present passage is concerned, we are forced to conclude that no criterion has been submitted upon the basis of which one could say with confidence that such and such an activity-and-pleasure is good and choice-worthy, while such and such another is bad and should be avoided. It perhaps is no accident that in the passage which immediately follows and which brings to an end Aristotle's discussion of pleasure, the criterion of the *spoudaios* is introduced as the ultimate norm.[130]

I. NOUS AND THEORIA

We are now in a position to consider Aristotle's final argument in the *Nicomachean Ethics* where, as is well known, he expatiates upon νοῦς, reason or mind, the activity of θεωρία, contemplation

---

[130] *Nicomachean Ethics* X, 1176 a 3–29. This passage was cited above, Chapter VII, note 83.

and their relation to happiness. Every student of Aristotle, any reader of the *De Anima* or the *Metaphysics*, knows the high store which is set upon νοῦς. So it is, for example, in the ninth book of the *Nicomachean Ethics*, when the topic of self-love is being discussed, and νοῦς is singled out as the most authoritative component (τὸ κυριώτατον) in a man. Aristotle elaborates as follows: "Besides, a man is said to have or not to have self-control according as his reason has or has not the control, on the assumption that this is the man himself; and the things men have done on a rational principle are thought most properly their own acts and voluntary acts. That this is the man himself, then, or is so more than anything else, is plain, and also that the good man loves most this part of him."[131] Or we could cite his words a few lines later: "For reason in each of its possessors chooses what is best for itself, and the good man obeys his reason."[132]

At the conclusion of the sixth chapter of *Nicomachean Ethics* X, Aristotle reaffirms his position that the happy life is the one lived in accordance with virtue, that it is an activity, and that it does concern itself with serious matters, τὰ σπουδαῖα.[133] But the center of Aristotle's doctrine of reason, contemplation, and happiness is to be found in the seventh chapter whose contents we must examine with care. The opening of the discussion runs as follows: "If happiness is activity in accordance with virtue, it is reasonable that it should be in accordance with the highest virtue; and this will be that of the best thing in us. Whether it be reason or something else that is this element which is thought to be our natural ruler and guide and to take thought of things noble and divine, whether it be itself also divine or only the most divine element in us, the activity of this in accordance with its proper virtue will be perfect happiness. That this activity is contemplative we have already

---

[131] *Nicomachean Ethics* X, 1168 b 34–1169 a 3. καὶ ἐγκρατὴς δὲ καὶ ἀκρατὴς λέγεται τῷ κρατεῖν τὸν νοῦν ἢ μή, ὡς τούτου ἑκάστου ὄντος· καὶ πεπραγέναι δοκοῦσιν αὐτοὶ καὶ ἑκουσίως τὰ μετὰ λόγου μάλιστα. ὅτι μὲν οὖν τοῦθ' ἕκαστός ἐστιν ἢ μάλιστα, οὐκ ἄδηλον, καὶ ὅτι ὁ ἐπιεικὴς μάλιστα τοῦτ' ἀγαπᾷ. Bywater's text. Incidentally, the identification of νοῦς and λόγος in this passage may be taken as support for my contention that in appropriate contexts λόγος can best be translated as "reason." Cf. above, Chapter VII, note 72.

[132] *Nicomachean Ethics* IX, 1169 a 17–18. πᾶς γὰρ νοῦς αἱρεῖται τὸ βέλτιστον ἑαυτῷ, ὁ δ' ἐπιεικὴς πειθαρχεῖ τῷ νῷ. Bywater's text.

[133] *Nicomachean Ethics* X, 1177 a 1–11.

said."[134]   Aristotle invites us to consider some consequences of
his conception of happiness as an activity in accordance with
virtue. As we have already been told that happiness is the highest
human good, the virtue with which it must actively accord likewise must be the highest, and this must be the highest, and this
must be the virtue of the best thing in a man. The next phase of
the argument is interesting. Aristotle does not declare categorically here that this "best thing" is reason, but whatever it is, it
must be that which "by nature" (note the insertion of nature as
a value sanction) rules and guides a man, and causes him to fix
his attention on "things noble and divine." We should also note
here how Aristotle injects the notion of the divine into his reasoning. Now he goes on to suggest that this "best thing" may be
either divine itself or the most divine component in us, still
without stating specifically what it is. At any rate, the activity of
"it" according to its proper virtue is asserted to be complete
happiness. Aristotle finally tips his hand by saying that this
activity is contemplative, for what other than reason, νοῦς, can
have such an activity? It is impossible not to be aware of the
similarity of this opening argument to that concerning the
Unmoved Mover in *Metaphysics* Λ.

Let us review quickly the contents of the ensuing section in
which Aristotle states the claims for the primacy of reason and
contemplation.[135] He first points out that his position is consistent not only with what he has formerly asserted but also with
the truth. He then flatly announces that the activity of contemplation is the best, because it is the activity of reason, the best element
in us, which is also best because of the supreme value of the things
with which reason has to do, *i.e.*, the things it knows. Furthermore,
he argues, contemplation is the most continuous of any activity

---

[134] *Nicomachean Ethics* X, 1177 a 12–18. Εἰ δ' ἐστὶν ἡ εὐδαιμονία κατ' ἀρετὴν
ἐνέργεια, εὔλογον κατὰ τὴν κρατίστην· αὕτη δ' ἂν εἴη τοῦ ἀρίστου. εἴτε δὴ νοῦς
τοῦτο εἴτε ἄλλο τι, ὃ δὴ κατὰ φύσιν δοκεῖ ἄρχειν καὶ ἡγεῖσθαι καὶ ἔννοιαν ἔχειν
περὶ καλῶν καὶ θείων, εἴτε θεῖον ὂν καὶ αὐτὸ εἴτε τῶν ἐν ἡμῖν τὸ θειότατον, ἡ
τούτου ἐνέργεια κατὰ τὴν οἰκείαν ἀρετὴν εἴη ἂν ἡ τελεία εὐδαιμονία. ὅτι δ'
ἐστὶ θεωρητική, εἴρηται. Bywater's text. That it is contemplative has not strictly
been said, but, as Burnet, *op. cit.*, note *ad loc.*, points out, this follows from
Aristotle's view with respect to σοφία. Ross, in his translation, note *ad loc.*,
calls attention to the following: *Nicomachean Ethics*: 1095 b 14–1096 a 5; 1141
a 18–b 3; 1143 b 33–1144 a 6; 1145 a 6–11.
[135] *Nicomachean Ethics* X, 1177 a 18–b 26.

in which we may engage. The relation of pleasure to happiness is next exploited, for everyone, so he insists, simply admits that the activity of philosophic wisdom, σοφία, *i.e.*, contemplation, is the most pleasant of all virtuous activities. (Is this admittedly the case?) Philosophy is then praised in glowing terms for the marvelous pleasures which accrue from its practice, marvelous in their purity and their firmness. The "knowers" will have a more pleasant way of life than the "investigators." (It is fair to say that this argument makes the most of the degree to which Aristotle is a hedonist.)

He now proceeds much in the manner of a rhetorician composing an encomium as he moves on to his next τόπος, self-sufficiency. It is no surprise to learn that of all activities contemplation is the most self-sufficient. All virtuous men need the necessities for living, but when once these have been provided, people who are just or temperate or brave and so on need others of like sort with whom to practice their particular virtues. In contrast, the σοφός can engage in contemplation in solitude, and the better he is at it, the wiser he will become. Aristotle admits that such a man might do better if he had some coworkers in the enterprise, but nonetheless he is still the most self-sufficient. (Observe the rhetorician moving systematically through the four cardinal virtues, and distinguishing philosophic wisdom, σοφία, from the other three.)

Aristotle spends little time on the next topic, *viz.*, that contemplation is the one activity that is loved for its own sake, and passes on to the point that happiness is to be found in leisure. "For we are busy that we may have leisure, and make war that we may live in peace."[136] The activity involved in the practical virtues, he continues, in things political or military, is marked by lack of leisure. The activities inherent in war are completely devoid of it, whereas political activity, also lacking in leisure, is not pursued for its own sake, but for power and honour, and happiness for both political leader and citizen is pursued as something different from political activity itself. And we hear the rhetorician speaking again when we come to a summarizing passage. The

[136] *Nicomachean Ethics* X, 1177 b 4–6. ἀσχολούμεθα, γὰρ ἵνα σχολάζωμεν καὶ πολεμοῦμεν ἵν᾽ εἰρήνην ἄγωμεν. Bywater's text.

contemplative activity of reason is asserted to be superior in seriousness; it has no goal beyond itself; it possesses its own proper pleasure which enhances the activity and it is characterized by self-sufficiency, leisure, and perdurability, in so far as this is vouchsafed to man. Everything else good that might be considered as a part of the life of a blessed person comes to him through the contemplative activity of reason. Such is the complete happiness of man, and, Aristotle adds, it must be in a complete life, for none of the things which contribute to the happiness is incomplete. This is his encomium to reason, contemplation, and happiness. It is much more of a rhetorically designed statement of praise than a carefully constructed logical argument.

But Aristotle is not done with this impressive burst of eloquence, for he rises to even greater heights in his conclusion: "But such a life would be better than one accorded to a man, for he will not live in this way in his capacity as a man, but rather because there is something divine in him. As this is superior to the composite being which is a man, by so much is its activity better than the activity in accordance with virtue in its other forms. If then reason is something divine when compared with man as a whole, therefore the life of reason is divine in comparison to ordinary human life. One need not follow the precepts of those who praise things human, namely, that a man, being a man, should think merely human thoughts, and that, being a mortal, should think on mortal things, but rather, in so far as he is able, he must strive to be immortal and do all things with a view towards living according to the best that is in him; for even though this divine part be little in bulk, it far overpasses everything else in power and in value. This divine part would seem to be the [essence of] each individual man, if indeed it is that which is master and that which is better. It would be strange indeed if a man should not follow this life which is essentially his own, but rather one [that is] guided by something other than that which is his essential self. What we have said before will harmonize with the view now being advanced. For that which is proper to each particular thing is by nature the best and most pleasant for each particular thing. And such is the life according to reason for a man, if indeed it is the case that this is the [essence of a] man. Such a life too will therefore be the happiest."[137]

As has always been recognized, this passage is to be closely associated with Aristotle's doctrine of the Prime Mover as God. If the supreme human good is happiness, and it in turn is equated with the contemplative activity of reason, we have the life of God as the sanction and guarantor of this supreme human good or value. We are told again that our reason is something divine within us and we are fervently exhorted to become immortal in so far as may be. There is little need to point to the reflections of Platonic thought in these lines. But we are constrained to repeat some of the observations we made when we had occasion before to quote a part of this passage.[138] There we argued in effect that when the supreme human good, happiness, was called an activity or an actuality, ἐνέργεια, this term helped validate the claims of happiness as a good. We further noted that the passage from *Nicomachean Ethics* X was silent about the possibility of a bad actuality or activity. We then pointed to the fact that the analysis of potentiality and actuality or process and activity is strictly ontological and thus in Aristotle's terms it should be neutral from the point of view of value. And, finally, we insisted that the passage now before us did not, and, indeed, could not, argue from a basic notion of activity, but rather consisted of a moving appeal concerning happiness, contemplation, and pleasure, all sustained and undergirded by God and the life of God. Though the conception of God advanced or implied is put forward on a

---

[137] *Nicomachean Ethics* X, 1177 b 26–1178 a 8. ὁ δὲ τοιοῦτος ἂν εἴη βίος κρείττων ἢ κατ' ἄνθρωπον· οὐ γὰρ ᾗ ἄνθρωπός ἐστιν οὕτω βιώσεται, ἀλλ' ᾗ θεῖόν τι ἐν αὐτῷ ὑπάρχει· ὅσον δὲ διαφέρει τοῦτο τοῦ συνθέτου, τοσοῦτον καὶ ἡ ἐνέργεια τῆς κατὰ τὴν ἄλλην ἀρετήν. εἰ δὴ θεῖον ὁ νοῦς πρὸς τὸν ἄνθρωπον, καὶ ὁ κατὰ τοῦτον βίος θεῖος πρὸς τὸν ἀνθρώπινον βίον. οὐ χρὴ δὲ κατὰ τοὺς παραινοῦντας ἀνθρώπινα φρονεῖν ἄνθρωπον ὄντα οὐδὲ θνητὰ τὸν θνητόν, ἀλλ' ἐφ' ὅσον ἐνδέχεται ἀθανατίζειν καὶ πάντα ποιεῖν πρὸς τὸ ζῆν κατὰ τὸ κράτιστον τῶν ἐν αὐτῷ· εἰ γὰρ καὶ τῷ ὄγκῳ μικρόν ἐστι, δυνάμει καὶ τιμιότητι πολὺ μᾶλλον πάντων ὑπερέχει. δόξειε δ' ἂν καὶ εἶναι ἕκαστος τοῦτο, εἴπερ τὸ κύριον καὶ ἄμεινον. ἄτοπον οὖν γίνοιτ' ἄν, εἰ μὴ τὸν αὑτοῦ βίον αἱροῖτο ἀλλά τινος ἄλλου τὸ λεχθέν τε πρότερον ἁρμόσει καὶ νῦν· τὸ γὰρ οἰκεῖον ἑκάστῳ τῇ φύσει κράτιστον καὶ ἥδιστόν ἐστιν ἑκάστῳ· καὶ τῷ ἀνθρώπῳ δὴ ὁ κατὰ τὸν νοῦν βίος, εἴπερ τοῦτο μάλιστα ἄνθρωπος. οὗτος ἄρα καὶ εὐδαιμονέστατος. Bywater's text. The translation is mine.

[138] Cf. above, Chapter IV, pp. 100–101, where we discussed *Nicomachean Ethics* X, 1177 b 30–1178 a 4.

fairly high level of abstraction, still the appeal basically appears to rest on the conventionally received opinions with respect to the divine.

Two or three more observations could be made. Strangely enough there is no repetition of the notion advanced towards the close of the first book of the *Nicomachean Ethics* that happiness is a first principle and the cause of goods, and as such is something "prized and divine."[139] It is not too much to urge that the failure to develop the conception of happiness as cause can be taken as a symptom of Aristotle's not having succeeded in bringing the various aspects of his attitudes towards value into some kind of coherent interrelation. Take, for example, his insistence that the man of practical wisdom should have nothing to do with anything other than that which is specifically human. Hence he is divorced from the man of philosophic wisdom who is supposed to be absorbed in things higher than human and therefore will not be involved in the tensions of ethical inquiry. And yet, when Aristotle makes his final "argument" for the end of ethical endeavour, the contemplative activity of happiness, the man of philosophic wisdom appears as the king, and at least up to this point no mention has been made of the *phronimos*, the man of practical wisdom. When we put such failures of ultimate coherence together with what we have said about the value implications of Aristotle's use of pleasure, the *spoudaios*, and conventional value thinking, we may be able to arrive at some accurate conception of his varied and continually shifting position whenever he comes face to face with questions of value.

Aristotle evidently is bothered by the fact that he has not brought in the subject of practical wisdom and its relation to the moral virtues, so he has a few words to say about it in the next chapter of *Nicomachean Ethics* X.[140] He allows that men who live in accordance with the other virtues such as justice or courage can be happy in a secondary sense. This befits us—it is all so completely human, bound up as we are with passions, we poor

---

[139] *Nicomachean Ethics* I, 1101 b 35–1102 a 4. Cf. above, Chapter VII, pp. 269–270 and notes 32 and 33.
[140] *Nicomachean Ethics* X, 1178 a 9–b 7.

composite beings who can only be guided by practical wisdom. But he stops abruptly to return to his theme of reason: "The excellence of the reason is a thing apart; we must be content to say this much about it, for to describe it precisely is a task greater than our purpose requires."[141] Most noteworthy is Aristotle's categorical separation of the reason from the rest of the realm of ethics, and one may wonder why he chooses just at this point to say that a precise description of the excellence of the reason "is a task greater than our purpose requires." Instead, he repeats his view that reason needs little by way of external resources in order to engage in its activity, and indeed less than that required for the practice of the moral virtues. Everybody needs the absolute necessities in equal amount, but the liberal man, the just man, the brave man, and the temperate man do have greater need for external resources, than the σοφός, the man who engages in the contemplative activity of reason. (Note again the systematic coverage of the three cardinal virtues which are moral, according to Aristotle's analysis.) His final point is that only as a man will the man of philosophic wisdom need external resources, for as a man he may choose to engage in acts of moral virtue. The outcome of this whole section seems to be the great emphasis upon the separateness and the special character of νοῦς. This insistence certainly does not contribute to any kind of systematic unity for Aristotle's ethical value scheme.[142]

---

[141] *Nicomachean Ethics* X, 1178 a 22–23. ἡ δὲ τοῦ νοῦ κεχωρισμένη· τοσοῦτον γὰρ περὶ αὐτῆς εἰρήσθω· διακριβῶσαι γὰρ μεῖζον τοῦ προκειμένου ἐστίν. Bywater's text.

[142] One should be reminded at this point of our discussion above concerning the intellectual virtue of philosophic wisdom, σοφία, Chapter VII, pp. 262–266. There σοφία was distinguished from νοῦς, which in the context of the sixth book of the *Nicomachean Ethics* was translated as intuitive reason. There we tried to point to Aristotle's dilemma involved in positing that σοφία was concerned, so to say, with the non-contingent realm of Being while at the same time questions of value had a way of obtruding themselves into this realm. The same kind of dilemma appears in the tenth book, except that the contemplative activity of reason, *i.e.*, the supreme value of happiness is pushed as closely as possible to the non-contingent realm, and God and the divine are invoked as sanctions therefor, while the reason is sharply separated from the activities of the other moral virtues and practical wisdom. Here value is present in both areas, *i.e.*, of the contingent and the non-contingent. In many ways the differing attitudes towards σοφία of the sixth and the tenth books may be taken as prefiguring, if not inconsistency in Aristotle's value thinking, at least the degree to which it is inchoate.

But he has more to say that is revealing about the nature of God and contemplation in his view of things. "But that perfect happiness is a contemplative activity will appear from the following consideration as well. We assume the gods to be above all other beings blessed and happy; but what sort of actions must we assign to them? Acts of justice? Will not the gods seem absurd if they make contracts and return deposits, and so on? Acts of a brave man, then, confronting dangers and running risks because it is noble to do so? Or liberal acts? To whom will they give? It will be strange if they are really to have money or anything of the kind. And what would their temperate acts be? Is not such praise tasteless, since they have no bad appetites? If we were to run through them all, the circumstances of action would be found trivial and unworthy of gods. Still, every one supposes that they *live* and therefore that they are active; we cannot suppose them to sleep like Endymion. Now if you take away from a living being action, and still more production, what is left but contemplation? Therefore the activity of God, which surpasses all others in blessedness, must be contemplative; and of human activities, therefore, that which is most akin to this must be most of the nature of happiness."[143]

This passage again seems to be a piece of rhetorical special pleading, though at the same time there is a rationalistic argumentation that parallels that to be found in the account of the Prime Mover in *Metaphysics* Λ. As for the rhetoric, we can see Aristotle moving systematically through the catalogue of the principal moral virtues, *viz.*, justice, courage, liberality, and temperance. He begins with the conventionally received opinion about the

---

[143] *Nicomachean Ethics* X, 1178 b 7–23. ἡ δὲ τελεία εὐδαιμονία ὅτι θεωρητική τις ἐστιν ἐνέργεια, καὶ ἐντεῦθεν ἂν φανείη. τοὺς θεοὺς γὰρ μάλιστα ὑπειλήφαμεν μακαρίους καὶ εὐδαίμονας εἶναι· πράξεις δὲ ποίας ἀπονεῖμαι χρεὼν αὐτοῖς; πότερα τὰς δικαίας; ἢ γελοῖοι φανοῦνται συναλλάττοντες καὶ παρακαταθήκας ἀποδιδόντες καὶ ὅσα τοιαῦτα; ἀλλὰ τὰς ἀνδρείους ** ὑπομένοντας τὰ φοβερὰ καὶ κινδυνεύοντας ὅτι καλόν; ἢ τὰς ἐλευθερίους; τίνι δὲ δώσουσιν; ἄτοπον δ' εἰ καὶ ἔσται αὐτοῖς νόμισμα ἤ τι τοιοῦτον. αἱ δὲ σώφρονες τί ἂν εἶεν; ἢ φορτικὸς ὁ ἔπαινος, ὅτι οὐκ ἔχουσι φαύλας ἐπιθυμίας; διεξιοῦσι δὲ πάντα φαίνοιτ' ἂν τὰ περὶ τὰς πράξεις μικρὰ καὶ ἀνάξια θεῶν. ἀλλὰ μὴν ζῆν γε πάντες ὑπειλήφασιν αὐτοὺς καὶ ἐνεργεῖν ἄρα· οὐ γὰρ δὴ καθεύδειν ὥσπερ τὸν Ἐνδυμίωνα. τῷ δὴ ζῶντι τοῦ πράττειν ἀφαιρουμένου, ἔτι δὲ μᾶλλον τοῦ ποιεῖν, τί λείπεται πλὴν θεωρία; ὥστε ἡ τοῦ θεοῦ ἐνέργεια, μακαριότητι διαφέρουσα, θεωρητικὴ ἂν εἴη· καὶ τῶν ἀνθρωπίνων δὴ ἡ ταύτῃ συγγενεστάτη εὐδαιμονικωτάτη. Bywater's text. He believes that something has dropped out after ἀνδρείους in 1178 b 12.

happiness of the gods, and then argues that it would be ludicrous to attribute to them human actions which involve the moral virtues. It must be admitted that he contrives such a list of actions as to make these attributions to appear to be utterly silly to any one who has an enlightened conception of the gods. Making contracts and returning deposits, confronting dangers and running risks, carrying money around to give away, being temperate when by definition they can have no bad habits—to say that the gods act in these ways is ridiculous. Yet they live and must do something. By employing a method of "residues," Aristotle concludes that there is nothing left but contemplation. And here he shifts from the plural, "goods," and asserts that the activity of God is contemplative. The closest that man can approach to this activity, the happiest life he will have. Note that nothing is said about the objects of contemplation either for God or for man. Note also that in the rationalistic effort to purify the conception of God's activity, the more that conception becomes emptied of comprehensible content, and the same must be said of the human activity that approaches most closely to it. Such is the consequence for the human activity of happiness, when the activity of God is posited as the standard.

Let us now hear the final words of Aristotle's discourse in praise of *νοῦς*. "But while even such things (*sc.* the opinions of the wise) carry some conviction, the truth in practical matters is discerned from the facts of life; for these are the decisive factor. We must therefore survey what we have already said, bringing it to the test of the facts of life, and if it harmonizes with the facts we must accept it, but if it clashes with them we must suppose it to be mere theory. Now he who exercises his reason and cultivates it seems to be both in the best state of mind and most dear to the gods. For if the gods have any care for human affairs, as they are thought to have, it would be reasonable both that they should delight in that which was best and most akin to them (*i.e.*, reason) and that they should reward those who love and honour this most, as caring for the things that are dear to them and acting both rightly and nobly. And that all these attributes belong most of all to the philosopher is manifest. He, therefore, is the dearest to the gods. And he who is that will presumably be also the happiest; so that in this way too the philosopher will more than any other be happy."[144]

In many ways this is a curious passage. It opens by sounding a strong empirical note when Aristotle asserts that "the facts of life" are decisive in all matters. But then he reverts to a position which certain people would hardly regard as a fact of life, namely, that a man who engages in the activity of reason is the dearest of all to the gods. We find ourselves now being told that the gods care for human affairs, and that they delight in what is best and most akin to them, namely, the reason, and that they reward those who think highly of the reason, and so on. The philosopher is above all such a man. He is most loved by the gods and he is therefore the happiest of all. In other words, we were led to expect a tough-fibred empirical argument but we ended in listening to a repetition of some favorite Aristotelian assumptions with respect to *νοῦς* bolstered by the conventional opinion about the rôle of the gods as exercising care for human affairs.

Before we move on to examine the evidence for the problem of Being and Value in Aristotle's thought as revealed in the *Politics*, let us attempt to summarize our findings in the *Nicomachean Ethics*. May we advance the following conclusions:

1. The most consistent attitude towards value in the *Nicomachean Ethics* holds it to be in a secondary or dependent status in relation to being.

2. Practical wisdom and philosophic wisdom, so far as value is concerned, bear respectively on the contingent human realm and the domain of the non-contingent, though at the outset it was suggested that philosophic wisdom had to do only with

---

[144] *Nicomachean Ethics* X, 1179 a 17–32. πίστιν μὲν οὖν καὶ τὰ τοιαῦτα ἔχει τινά, τὸ δ' ἀληθὲς ἐν τοῖς πρακτικοῖς ἐκ τῶν ἔργων καὶ τοῦ βίου κρίνεται· ἐν τούτοις γὰρ τὸ κύριον. σκοπεῖν δὴ προειρημένα χρὴ ἐπὶ τὰ ἔργα καὶ τὸν βίον φέροντας, καὶ συναδόντων μὲν τοῖς ἔργοις ἀποδεκτέον, διαφωνούντων δὲ λόγους ὑποληπτέον. ὁ δὲ κατὰ νοῦν ἐνεργῶν καὶ τοῦτον θεραπεύων καὶ διακείμενος ἄριστα καὶ θεοφιλέστατος ἔοικεν. εἰ γάρ τις ἐπιμέλεια τῶν ἀνθρωπίνων ὑπὸ θεῶν γίνεται, ὥσπερ δοκεῖ, καὶ εἴη ἂν εὔλογον χαίρειν τε αὐτοὺς τῷ ἀρίστῳ καὶ συγγενεστάτῳ (τοῦτο δ' ἂν εἴη ὁ νοῦς) καὶ τοὺς ἀγαπῶντας μάλιστα τοῦτο καὶ τιμῶντας ἀντευποιεῖν ὡς τῶν φίλων αὐτοῖς ἐπιμελουμένους καὶ ὀρθῶς τε καὶ καλῶς πράττοντας. ὅτι δὲ πάντα ταῦτα τῷ σοφῷ μάλισθ' ὑπάρχει, οὐκ ἄδηλον. θεοφιλέστατος ἄρα. τὸν αὐτὸν δ' εἰκὸς καὶ εὐδαιμονέστατον· ὥστε κἂν οὕτως εἴη ὁ σοφὸς μάλιστ' εὐδαίμων. Bywater's text.

questions of being. In any event, the two forms of wisdom, φρόνησις and σοφία, are kept sharply apart.

3. Happiness, when it is set up as the supreme human good, is a value which can only be understood as "subjective."

4. The moral and the intellectual virtues (or values) must also, like happiness, be understood as "subjective."

5. Pleasure as a value, either in itself or viewed as that which completes the activity of happiness, also is thoroughly "subjective."

6. Aristotle, consciously or unconsciously aware of the difficulties inherent in "subjectivism," struggles hard to set up some kind of objective norm or criterion for his values. Witness the mean, and the λόγος in his definition of virtue, the appeal to the *spoudaios* and the *phronimos* as value sanctions, the frequent appeal to conventional value thinking, the effort to complete his definition of virtue by postulating the existence of an external mark or standard (σκοπός and ὅρος; recall that he failed to develop this notion successfully),[145] and the effort to exploit the value overtones in his conception of ἐνέργεια, activity or actuality, and the way in which the notion of a "bad" activity created a dilemma for him which he could not resolve.

7. Finally, there is the conception of happiness as the contemplative activity of reason. This is ultimately a subjective view, but again Aristotle attempts to interject an objective criterion by citing the divine, God, whose life is happy because it is His reason's contemplative activity. And remember, this God is incapable of any practical or productive activity (He can only contemplate) and hence cannot function as a really effective value sanction.

So much for our summary. We may now turn to the *Politics*.

PART II

THE *POLITICS*

As is well known, Aristotle did not believe that ethics and politics are separate and discrete disciplines, but are rather two closely related aspects of a single subject. Therefore, when we

[145] Cf. above, Chapter VII, pp. 276–283, and especially notes 67 and 72.

are now turning our attention to the *Politics*, it will, of course, not be our intention to review in detail Aristotle's political doctrine, but rather we shall seek to point to those passages which reflect the same attitudes towards value as we found in the *Nicomachean Ethics*. And so we are not surprised to see at the very beginning of the *Politics* a statement of the goal of the political enterprise: "But, if all communities aim at some good, the state or political community, which is the highest of all, and which embraces all the rest, aims at good in a greater degree than any other, and at the highest good."[146] This *telos*, or highest good, is soon specified to be "the good life."[147] Still continuing in a teleological mood, Aristotle quickly introduces for the state the goal or value of self-sufficiency. "Besides, the final cause and end of a thing is the best, and to be self-sufficing is the end and the best."[148]

This point of view on the goal of the good life and the value of self-sufficiency (recall the description of the activity of contemplation) are familiar to us in the *Nicomachean Ethics*. Similarly at the beginning of the seventh book of the *Politics*, where Aristotle addresses himself to the subject of the ideal state, he repeats his doctrine that the happy man needs external goods, the goods of the body, and the goods of the soul.[149] He then elaborates on the way in which happiness rests upon virtue, again the view of the *Nicomachean Ethics*, and calls on God as his witness in support of this view.[150] He summarizes his position explicitly by asserting that the doctrine in ethics applies fully in the domain of politics. "Let us assume then that the best life, both for individuals and states, is the life of virtue, when virtue has external goods enough for the performance of good actions."[151] He then proceeds to

---

[146] *Politics* I, 1252 a 3–7. δῆλον ὡς πᾶσαι μὲν ἀγαθοῦ τινος στοχάζονται, μάλιστα δὲ καὶ τοῦ κυριωτάτου πάντων ἡ πασῶν κυριωτάτη καὶ πάσας περιέχουσα τὰς ἄλλας. αὕτη δ᾽ ἐστὶν ἡ καλουμένη πόλις καὶ ἡ κοινωνία ἡ πολιτική. The text is that of W. D. Ross, *Aristotelis Politica* (Oxford, Clarendon Press, 1957.)

[147] *Politics* I, 1252 b 30. Cf. III, 1280 a 31–32 and 1280 b 39.

[148] *Politics* I, 1252 b 34–1253 a 1. ἔτι τὸ οὗ ἕνεκα καὶ τὸ τέλος βέλτιστον. ἡ δ᾽ αὐτάρκεια καὶ τέλος καὶ βέλτιστον. Ross's text. Cf. also II, 1261 b 10–15; VII, 1326 b 3 and 22–24.

[149] *Politics* VII, 1323 a 24–27.

[150] *Politics* VII, 1323 b 21–24.

[151] *Politics* VII, 1323 b 40–1324 a 2. νῦν δὲ ὑποκείσθω τοσοῦτον, ὅτι βίος μὲν ἄριστος, καὶ χωρὶς ἑκάστῳ καὶ κοινῇ ταῖς πόλεσιν, ὁ μετ᾽ ἀρετῆς κεχορηγημένης ἐπὶ τοσοῦτον ὥστε μετέχειν τῶν κατ᾽ ἀρετὴν πράξεων. Ross's text.

declare that happiness for the individual and the state is the same.[152] The outcome of it all is that, as in ethics, so in politics the supreme good and goal is happiness, the activity which must be in accord with virtue.

One point in Aristotle's argument is worth noting. In the light of the principle that happiness is the supreme good, what of the relative merits of the lives of the statesman and the philosopher? "Now it is evident that the form of government is best in which every man, whoever he is, can act best and live happily. But even those who agree in thinking that the life of virtue is the most eligible raise a question, whether the life of business and politics is or is not more eligible than one which is wholly independent of external goods, I mean than a contemplative life, which by some is maintained to be the only one worthy of a philosopher. For these two lives—the life of the philosopher and the life of the statesman—appear to have been preferred by those who have been most keen in the pursuit of virtue, both in our own and in other ages. Which is the better is a question of no small moment; for the wise man, like the wise state, will necessarily regulate his life according to the best end."[153] That Aristotle should feel the need to face the question as to which of these two lives is the superior is in no way surprising. It is, as he says, a matter "of no small moment." However, it is a little astonishing to find him describing the contemplative life as the life which *some* people maintain to be the only one worthy of a philosopher. This is hard to understand particularly when Aristotle's encomium of

---

[152] *Politics* VII, 1324 a 5–13. There are numerous other passages where happiness is asserted to be the *summum bonum*, the supreme good, and it is always associated with virtue. Cf., *e.g.*, VII, 1328 a 37–b 2; 1328 b 33–1329 a 2 [Note how Aristotle says here that mechanics, merchants, and farmers cannot become virtuous, because they lack the requisite leisure]; 1329 a 21–24; 1331 b 24–1332 a 27; 1332 a 29–b 11 [Note here that φύσις, ἔθος, and λόγος are cited as sources of virtue and goodness].

[153] *Politics* VII, 1324 a 23–35. ὅτι μὲν οὖν ἀναγκαῖον εἶναι πολιτείαν ἀρίστην ταύτην ⟨τὴν⟩ τάξιν καθ' ἣν κἂν ὁστισοῦν ἄριστα πράττοι καὶ ζῴη μακαρίως, φανερόν ἐστιν· ἀμφισβητεῖται δὲ παρ' αὐτῶν τῶν ὁμολογούντων τὸν μετ' ἀρετῆς εἶναι βίον αἱρετώτατον πότερον ὁ πολιτικὸς καὶ πρακτικὸς βίος αἱρετὸς ἢ μᾶλλον ὁ πάντων τῶν ἐκτὸς ἀπολελυμένος, οἷον θεωρητικός τις, ὃν μόνον τινές φασιν εἶναι φιλοσόφου. σχεδὸν γὰρ τούτους τοὺς δύο βίους τῶν ἀνθρώπων οἱ φιλοτιμότατοι πρὸς ἀρετὴν φαίνονται προαιρούμενοι, καὶ τῶν προτέρων καὶ τῶν νῦν. λέγω δὲ δύο τόν τε πολιτικὸν καὶ τὸν φιλόσοφον. διαφέρει δὲ οὐ μικρὸν ποτέρως ἔχει τὸ ἀληθές· ἀνάγκη γὰρ τόν γε εὖ φρονοῦντα πρὸς τὸν βελτίω σκοπὸν συντάττεσθαι, καὶ τῶν ἀνθρώπων ἕκαστον καὶ κοινῇ τὴν πολιτείαν. Ross's text.

theoria in the tenth book of the *Nicomachean Ethics* is still ringing freshly in one's ears. Why did he not say that he himself maintained the superiority of the contemplative life?[154] In any event, if we are looking for a decision on the question of which life is the better we are doomed to disappointment, for Aristotle permits himself to be diverted to other topics, and before long, he appears to have forgotten the problem entirely. He may very well be forgiven, since after all he is now writing a treatise on politics and should therefore be turning his attention to the more practical activity of the statesman rather than to that of the contemplative philosopher.

Throughout the *Politics*, we meet other familiar values or value sanctions. Nature, φύσις, appears with great frequency as a kind of ultimate sanction for an opinion. That which can use its intelligence to foresee, to look ahead, is "by nature" qualified to rule, and one oppositely disposed is by nature a slave.[155] The family or household exists "in accordance with nature" in order to supply the daily needs of men.[156] And, of course, it is well known that Aristotle bases his defense of slavery on the ground that "by nature" some men are slaves.[157] In a way the whole argument of the *Politics* depends on the famous declaration: "Hence it is evident that the state is a creation of nature and that man is by nature a political animal."[158] And finally, before we leave the conception of nature as it functions typically in the *Politics*, we should not be unaware of the kind of thinking which tends to eventuate from Aristotle's reliance on this conception. Take, for example, the following passage: "Now if nature makes nothing incomplete, and nothing in vain, the inference must be that she has made all animals for the sake of man. And so, in one point of view, the art of war is a natural art of acquisition, for the art of acquisition includes hunting, an art which we ought

[154] Perhaps Aristotle is making a little joke.

[155] *Politics* I, 1252 a 31–34.

[156] *Politics* I, 1252 b 12–14.

[157] Cf. the lengthy discussion of the subject in *Politics* I, chapters 4–7. See also the opening section of the third chapter of *Politics* VII. To take almost at random another instance of Aristotle's typical use of "nature," cf. *Politics* VII, 1329 a 14–16, where it is said that it is natural for the young to have power or strength, whereas the old naturally possess "practical wisdom," φρόνησις.

[158] *Politics* I, 1253 a 1–3. ἐκ τούτων οὖν φανερὸν ὅτι τῶν φύσει ἡ πόλις ἐστί, καὶ ὅτι ὁ ἄνθρωπος φύσει πολιτικὸν ζῷον. Ross's text.

to practice against wild beasts, and against men who, though intended by nature to be governed, will not submit; for war of such a kind is naturally just."¹⁵⁹ All we need do is to note these steps: War is "natural," a way of acquiring things, as hunting is, for it is a subdivision of the warlike art of acquisition. Nature validates our use of hunting against beasts. So nature validates our use of war against men who, according to the decree of nature, are fit only to be ruled, despite the fact that these men are so misguided as not to concur in nature's decree. Such a war is therefore confidently labelled as just. In this way, through a reliance upon nature as a sanction, Aristotle answers the knotty question, What is a just war? The argument, it must be said, gives the impression of being contrived to support a set of beliefs widely held by Arisotle's contemporaries.

Again, we are not surprised to find pleasure introduced into the *Politics* as a value or a sanction for value. For example, in his argument against Plato's view that private property should be eliminated for the guardian class in the state, Aristotle remarks, "Again, how immeasurably greater is the pleasure, when a man feels a thing to be his own; for surely the love of self is a feeling implanted by nature and not given in vain, although selfishness is rightly censured; this, however, is not the mere love of self, but the love of self in excess, like the miser's love of money; for all, or almost all, men love money and other such objects in a measure. And further, there is the greatest pleasure in doing a kindness or service to friends or guests or companions, which can only be rendered when a man has private property."¹⁶⁰ Not only should we observe here the rôle which is assigned to pleasure but also the specific reference to the treatment of love

---

¹⁵⁹ *Politics* I, 1256 b 20–26. εἰ οὖν ἡ φύσις μηθὲν μήτε ἀτελὲς ποιεῖ μήτε μάτην, ἀναγκαῖον τῶν ἀνθρώπων ἕνεκεν αὐτὰ πάντα πεποιηκέναι τὴν φύσιν. διὸ καὶ ἡ πολεμικὴ φύσει κτητική πως ἔσται (ἡ γὰρ θηρευτικὴ μέρος αὐτῆς), ᾗ δεῖ χρῆσθαι πρός τε τὰ θηρία καὶ τῶν ἀνθρώπων ὅσοι πεφυκότες ἄρχεσθαι μὴ θέλουσιν, ὡς φύσει δίκαιον τοῦτον ὄντα τὸν πόλεμον. Ross's text.

¹⁶⁰ *Politics* II, 1263 a 4–b 7. ἔτι δὲ καὶ πρὸς ἡδονὴν ἀμύθητον ὅσον διαφέρει τὸ νομίζειν ἴδιόν τι. μὴ γὰρ οὐ μάτην τὴν πρὸς αὐτὸν αὐτὸς ἔχει φιλίαν ἕκαστος, ἀλλ᾽ ἔστι τοῦτο φυσικόν. τὸ δὲ φίλαυτον εἶναι ψέγεται δικαίως· οὐκ ἔστι δὲ τοῦτο τὸ φιλεῖν ἑαυτόν, ἀλλὰ τὸ μᾶλλον ἢ δεῖ φιλεῖν, καθάπερ καὶ τὸ φιλοχρήματον, ἐπεὶ φιλοῦσί γε πάντες ὡς εἰπεῖν ἕκαστον τῶν τοιούτων. ἀλλὰ μὴν καὶ χαρίσασθαι καὶ βοηθῆσαι φίλοις ἢ ξένοις ἢ ἑταίροις ἥδιστον· ὃ γίνεται τῆς κτήσεως ἰδίας οὔσης. Ross's text.

of self or self-esteem found in the ninth book of the *Nicomachean Ethics*. Note too that self-esteem is said to be in man as something φυσικόν, or as Jowett renders it, "a feeling implanted by nature," and note further that Aristotle appeals to the principle of the mean (about which we shall have more to say in a moment) as the ground for censuring the excess of love of self, namely selfishness.

A familiar attitude towards pleasure, as found in the *Nicomachean Ethics*, can be seen in a passing remark on its relation to philosophy. "If any desire pleasures which depend on themselves, they will find the satisfaction of their desires nowhere but in philosophy; for all other pleasures we are dependent on others."[161] Here it is interesting to find again an expression of the view that philosophy (= contemplation) is above all self-sufficient, and furthermore, it is suggested that pleasure attends upon, or completes, the activity of philosophy. We might cite one more example of the rôle assigned to pleasure in the *Politics*. In the eighth book in the midst of his discussion of music, Aristotle has this revealing remark to make: "It sometimes happens that men make amusement the end, for the end probably contains some element of pleasure, though not any ordinary or lower pleasure; but they mistake the lower for the higher, and in seeking for the one find the other, since every pleasure has a likeness to the end of action. For the end is not eligible for the sake of any future good, nor do the pleasures we have described exist for the sake of any future good but of the past, that is to say, they are the alleviation of past toils and pains. And we may infer this to be the reason why men seek happiness from these pleasures."[162] And here Aristotle goes on to consider further the pleasures derivative from music. We, of course, can recognize the basic positions in the passage. Pleasure is related to the end of action, *i.e.*, there is a similarity or an affinity between a pleasure and the end of an action. We may

---

[161] *Politics* II, 1267 a 10–12. εἴ τινες βούλοιντο δι' αὑτῶν χαίρειν, οὐκ ἂν ἐπιζητοῖεν εἰ μὴ παρὰ φιλοσοφίας ἄκος. αἱ γὰρ ἄλλαι ἀνθρώπων δέονται. Ross's text.
[162] *Politics* VIII, 1339 b 31–40. συμβέβηκε δὲ τοῖς ἀνθρώποις ποιεῖσθαι τὰς παιδιὰς τέλος· ἔχει γὰρ ἴσως ἡδονήν τινα καὶ τὸ τέλος, ἀλλ' οὐ τὴν τυχοῦσαν, ζητοῦντες δὲ ταύτην λαμβάνουσιν ὡς ταύτην ἐκείνην, διὰ τὸ τῷ τέλει τῶν πράξεων ἔχειν ὁμοίωμά τι. τό τε γὰρ τέλος οὐθενὸς τῶν ἐσομένων χάριν αἱρετόν, καὶ αἱ τοιαῦται τῶν ἡδονῶν οὐθενός εἰσι τῶν ἐσομένων ἕνεκεν, ἀλλὰ τῶν γεγονότων, οἷον πόνων καὶ λύπης. δι' ἣν μὲν οὖν αἰτίαν ζητοῦσι τὴν εὐδαιμονίαν γίγνεσθαι διὰ τούτων τῶν ἡδονῶν, ταύτην εἰκότως ἄν τις ὑπολάβοι τὴν αἰτίαν. Ross's text.

suppose that his further remarks have to do with the particular pleasures attendant upon music, as peculiarly oriented towards the alleviation of past toils and pain. But we cannot overlook the close interdependence between happiness and pleasure which is postulated by Aristotle's assertion that "men seek happiness from these pleasures."

As we might expect, the virtues, both moral and intellectual, of the *Nicomachean Ethics*, find their way as values into the argument of the *Politics*. A short passage near the end of the first book may be taken as typical of Aristotle's point of view. "So it must necessarily be supposed to be with the moral virtues also; all [*sc.*, men, women, children, and slaves] should partake of them, but only in such manner and degree as is required by each for the fulfillment of his duty. Hence the ruler ought to have moral virtue in perfection, for his function, taken absolutely, demands a master artificer, and rational principle is such an artificer; the subjects, on the other hand, require only that measure of virtue which is proper to each of them. Clearly, then, moral virtue belongs to all of them; but the temperance of a man and of a woman, or the courage and justice of a man and of a woman, are not, as Socrates maintained, the same; the courage of a man is shown in commanding, of a woman in obeying."163 Quite apart from the standard discriminations made by Aristotle among men, women, children, and slaves, the quotation indicates the high importance or value placed upon the ethical virtues, as well as "rational principle," λόγος.164

---

163 *Politics* I, 1260 a 14–23. ὁμοίως τοίνυν ἀναγκαίως ἔχειν καὶ περὶ τὰς ἠθικὰς ἀρετὰς ὑποληπτέον, δεῖν μὲν μετέχειν πάντας, ἀλλ᾿ οὐ τὸν αὐτὸν τρόπον, ἀλλ᾿ ὅσον ‹ἱκανὸν› ἑκάστῳ πρὸς τὸ αὑτοῦ ἔργον· διὸ τὸν μὲν ἄρχοντα τελέαν ἔχειν δεῖ τὴν ἠθικὴν ἀρετήν (τὸ γὰρ ἔργον ἐστὶν ἁπλῶς τοῦ ἀρχιτέκτονος, ὁ δὲ λόγος ἀρχιτέκτων), τῶν δ᾿ ἄλλων ἕκαστον ἐπιβάλλει αὐτοῖς. ὥστε φανερὸν ὅτι ἔστιν ἠθικὴ ἀρετὴ τῶν εἰρημένων πάντων, καὶ οὐχ ἡ αὐτὴ σωφροσύνη γυναικὸς καὶ ἀνδρός, οὐδ᾿ ἀνδρεία καὶ δικαιοσύνη, καθάπερ ᾤετο Σωκράτης, ἀλλ᾿ ἡ μὲν ἀρχικὴ ἀνδρεία ἡ δ᾿ ὑπηρετική. Ross's text.

164 Other typical passages may be cited to illustrate Aristotle's use of the virtues as values in the *Politics*: II, 1261 a 30–31 [compensatory equality as related to justice. Cf. *Nicomachean Ethics* V, 1132 b 31–33]; 1262 b 7–9 [friendship as the greatest of the goods for states, a fine preventive against revolutions]; 1265 a 32–35 [temperance and liberality are relevant in connection with the use of property]; 1273 a 41–b 1 [virtue must be supreme in good government]; III, 1277 b 25–26 [practical wisdom is the sole peculiar virtue of a ruler]; 1282 b 14–18 [justice is the highest political good].

In the third and fourth chapters of *Politics* III, Aristotle engages in an interesting analysis of the question whether the good man and the good citizen are one and the same. The problem seems to give him considerable difficulty, mainly caused by the fact that "the virtue of the citizen must therefore be relative to the constitution of which he is a member."[165] There is a sense in which this relativity to the constitution may be considered to be analogous to the πρὸς ἡμᾶς, "relative to us," of the definition of virtue promulgated in the second book of the *Nicomachean Ethics*.[166] But, whereas in the definition of virtue the phrase "relative to us" indicates the need to take into consideration the individual and the circumstances in any situation involving the use of moral characteristics, the case is different in the context of politics. Here not only is there a wide variety of individuals to take into account, but also there is the wide variety of constitutions or forms of government, some of which Aristotle would call good and some bad. In other words, according to this "political relativism," a good citizen of a tyranny, the worst of the perverted forms of government in Aristotle's mind, could not be a good man. As we have said, the problem is troublesome, and after lengthy argument, Aristotle submits the following somewhat inconclusive summary statement: "As to the question whether the virtue of the good man is the same as that of the good citizen, the considerations already adduced prove that in some states the good man and the good citizen are the same, and in others different. When they are the same it is not every citizen who is a good man, but only the statesman and those who have or may have, alone or in conjunction with others, the conduct of public affairs."[167] While it must be conceded that this is an admirable statement in its effort to take into account the awesome complexity of any concrete political situation, one still does have the feeling that Aristotle's position

---

[165] *Politics* III, 1276 b 30–31. διὸ τὴν ἀρετὴν ἀναγκαῖον εἶναι τοῦ πολίτου πρὸς τὴν πολιτείαν. Ross's text.

[166] Cf. above, Chapter VII, p. 272.

[167] *Politics* III, 1278 a 40–b 5. πότερον μὲν οὖν ἑτέραν ἢ τὴν αὐτὴν θετέον, καθ' ἣν ἀνὴρ ἀγαθός ἐστι καὶ πολίτης σπουδαῖος, δῆλον ἐκ τῶν εἰρημένων, ὅτι τινὸς μὲν πόλεως ὁ αὐτὸς τινὸς δ' ἕτερος, κἀκεῖνος οὐ πᾶς ἀλλ' ὁ πολιτικὸς καὶ κύριος ἢ δυνάμενος εἶναι κύριος, ἢ καθ' αὐτὸν ἢ μετ' ἄλλων τῆς τῶν κοινῶν ἐπιμελείας. Ross's text.

might have been firmer, had he at his side a solider general scheme of values.

As was the case in the *Nicomachean Ethics*, the doctrine or principle of the mean is operative fundamentally in the *Politics*. For example, moderation or the mean is recommended in the case of property.[168]   Or, on another occasion, Aristotle says: "Hence it is evident that in seeking for justice men seek for the mean, for the law is the mean."[169] Or again, in praising the Greeks, he asserts: "But the Hellenic race, which is situated between them [*sc.*, the races of Europe and Asia], is likewise intermediate in character, being high-spirited and also intelligent."[170] But most important of all is Aristotle's application of the doctrine of the mean to the concrete problem of the forms of government. Actually it is this doctrine which is functioning in the ninth chapter of *Politics* IV where he is describing the genesis of the polity or constitutional government, the form that Aristotle on practical grounds considers to be superior. As may be recalled, he argues that polity is in a mean between oligarchy and democracy. The most decisive quotation follows: "For if what was said in the *Ethics* is true, that the happy life is the life according to virtue lived without impediment, and that virtue is a mean, then the life which is in a mean, and in a mean attainable by everyone, must be the best. And the same principles of virtue and vice are characteristic of cities and of constitutions, for the constitution is in a figure the life of the city."[171] Aristotle then goes on to describe this polity

[168] *Politics* II, 1266 b 24–28.

[169] *Politics* III, 1287 b 3–5. ὥστε δῆλον ὅτι τὸ δίκαιον ζητοῦντες τὸ μέσον ζητοῦσιν· ὁ γὰρ νόμος τὸ μέσον. Ross's text. In the translation, I have eliminated the phrase "or neutral" after the first "mean."

[170] *Politics* VII, 1327 b 29–31. τὸ δὲ τῶν Ἑλλήνων γένος, ὥσπερ μεσεύει κατὰ τοὺς τόπους, οὕτως ἀμφοῖν μετέχει. καὶ γὰρ ἔνθυμον καὶ διανοητικόν ἐστιν. Ross's text. Aristotle's point here is that Europeans are full of spirit and therefore have preserved their freedom, but they are not very intelligent. On the other hand, the Asians are intelligent but are wanting in spirit, and hence are prone to submit to slavery. It is in this sense that the Hellenes are in the mean. He goes on to observe that the Greeks are free and the best governed, and adds somewhat ruefully that they would be able to rule over everyone, if they could only become politically united. Cf. my essay, "The Ideal States of Plato and Aristotle," in *The Greek Political Experience* (Princeton, Princeton University Press, 1941) p. 205.

[171] *Politics* IV, 1295 a 35–b 1. εἰ γὰρ καλῶς ἐν τοῖς Ἠθικοῖς εἴρηται τὸ τὸν εὐδαίμονα βίον εἶναι τὸν κατ᾽ ἀρετὴν ἀνεμπόδιστον, μεσότητα δὲ τὴν ἀρετήν, τὸν μέσον ἀναγκαῖον εἶναι βίον βέλτιστον, ‹τὸ› τῆς ἑκάστοις ἐνδεχομένης τυχεῖν μεσότητος· τοὺς δὲ αὐτοὺς τούτους ὅρους ἀναγκαῖον εἶναι καὶ πόλεως ἀρετῆς καὶ κακίας καὶ πολιτείας· ἡ γὰρ πολιτεία βίος τίς ἐστι πόλεως. Ross's text.

and its advantages as a "mean" state, as one which depends heavily upon the health and vitality of its "mean" or middle class. We do not need to go into the details of this description. It should suffice to note that Aristotle explicitly bases his preference for the polity by introducing the fundamental doctrines of the *Nicomachean Ethics*, *viz.*, the happy life is lived in accordance with virtue which is in a mean; this is the supreme human good and is as applicable to states or constitutions as it is to individuals.

Towards the end of the discussion of the polity, the preferred "mean" state, in the eleventh chapter of *Politics* IV Aristotle permits himself a moment of historical reflection. For the superiority of the polity, he cites as evidence the fact that the best law-givers, such as Solon, Lycurgus, and Charondas, all were representatives of the middle or the "mean" class.[172] But he goes on to say that most governments actually tend to become either oligarchies or democracies. The mean is disregarded because in each case the middle class is weak. He sorrowfully records that never or practically never has the middling constitution been in existence. "One man alone of all who ever ruled in Hellas was induced to give this middle constitution to states. But it has now become a habit among the citizens of states, not even to care about equality; all men are seeking for dominion, or, if conquered, are willing to submit."[173] It is difficult not be to be moved by this disillusioned reaction on Aristotle's part to the political realities of fourth century Greece. In any event, despite his discouragement, he is satisfied that he has identified the best form of government as one based on the mean and he expresses his intention of using it, the polity, as a standard by which to appraise all other forms. And it is interesting to observe that he concludes this phase of his argument by repeating his doctrine of the necessity of political "relativism" when dealing with the concrete situations of politics. "For that which is nearest to the best must of necessity be better, and that which is furthest from it [the mean] worse, if we are judging absolutely and not relatively

---

[172] *Politics* IV, 1296 a 18–21.

[173] *Politics* IV, 1296 a 38–b 2. εἰς γὰρ ἀνὴρ συνεπείσθη μόνος τῶν πρότερον ἐφ' ἡγεμονία γενομένων ταύτην ἀποδοῦναι τὴν τάξιν, ἤδη δὲ καὶ τοῖς ἐν ταῖς πόλεσιν ἔθος καθέστηκε μηδὲ βούλεσθαι τὸ ἴσον, ἀλλ' ἢ ἄρχειν ζητεῖν ἢ κρατουμένους ὑπομένειν. Ross's text. The εἰς ἀνὴρ μόνος may possibly be Theramenes.

to given conditions: I say 'relatively to given conditions,' since a particular government may be preferable, but another form may be better for some people."[174]

Last among the criteria or sanctions for value which we must examine in the *Politics* is God or the divine. It must be said at the outset that the element of the divine does not play as extensive a rôle in Aristotle's discussion of politics as it does, for example, in the tenth book of the *Nicomachean Ethics*, but nonetheless it is present and seems to be invoked on a kind of *ad hoc* basis. We can see such an instance in the systematic inquiry into the nature of the ideal state with which the seventh book of the *Politics* opens. "Let us acknowledge then that each one has just so much of happiness as he has of virtue and wisdom, and of virtuous and wise action. God is a witness to us of this truth, for he is happy and blessed, not by reason of any external good, but in himself and by reason of his own nature."[175] Or again, there is a passage at the end of the third chapter of *Politics* VII. Aristotle has been talking about happiness as a virtuous activity and what this entails for both individuals and states. Here he is facing the problem that political activity must of necessity be practical, and this of course involves its relation to his view that the supreme activity of happiness is contemplation. He therefore attempts to show that states can be active in isolation, and that there is a contemplative aspect to a state's activity in so far as it is directed by intelligence. He concludes his argument in this way: "The same thing is equally true of every individual. If this were otherwise, God and the universe, who have no external actions over and above their own energies, would be far enough from perfection. Hence it is evident that the same life is best for each

[174] *Politics* IV, 1296 b 7–12. ἀεὶ γὰρ ἀναγκαῖον εἶναι βελτίω τὴν ἐγγύτατα ταύτης, χείρω δὲ ἀφεστηκυῖαν τοῦ μέσου πλεῖον, ἂν μὴ πρὸς ὑπόθεσιν κρίνῃ τις. λέγω δὲ πρὸς ὑπόθεσιν, ὅτι πολλάκις, οὔσης ἄλλης πολιτείας αἱρετωτέρας, ἐνίοις οὐδὲν κωλύει συμφέρειν ἑτέραν μᾶλλον εἶναι πολιτείαν. Ross's text. I have inserted "the mean" in the translation to bring out better the τοῦ μέσου of the Greek.

[175] *Politics* VII, 1323 b 21–26. ὅτι μὲν οὖν ἑκάστῳ τῆς εὐδαιμονίας ἐπιβάλλει τοσοῦτον ὅσον περ ἀρετῆς καὶ φρονήσεως καὶ τοῦ πράττειν κατὰ ταύτας, ἔστω συνωμολογημένον ἡμῖν, μάρτυρι τῷ θεῷ χρωμένοις, ὃς εὐδαίμων μέν ἐστι καὶ μακάριος, δ' οὐθὲν δὲ τῶν ἐξωτερικῶν ἀγαθῶν ἀλλὰ δι' αὐτὸν αὐτὸς καὶ τῷ ποιός τις εἶναι τὴν φύσιν. Ross's text. It is interesting to see how Aristotle in this quotation has linked happiness with virtue *and* practical wisdom *and* action, in accordance with the amplified definition of virtue in the sixth book of the *Nicomachean Ethics*. Cf. above, Chapter VII, pp. 276–283.

individual, and for states and for mankind collectively."[176] Here Aristotle adds "the universe" to God as the norm, and we see again the view that the activities of God and the universe are self-contained with no external involvements which might impair their perfection, with the consequence that from the human point of view they are emptied of content.

The foregoing is, of course, the familiar criticism leveled against the doctrine of the Unmoved Mover of *Metaphysics* Λ. There is, however, one further passage in the seventh book of the *Politics*, where God or the element of the divine appears as a sanction, but where it is implied that the rôle of God or the divine is in a real sense active in the universe. Aristotle has been holding that states should be limited in size. "We may argue on grounds of reason, and the same result will follow. For law is order, and good law is good order; but a very great multitude cannot be orderly: to introduce order into the unlimited is the work of a divine power—of such a power as holds together the universe. Beauty is realized in number and magnitude, and the state which combines magnitude with good order must necessarily be the most beautiful. To the size of states there is a limit, as there is to other things, plants, animals, implements; for none of these retain their natural power when they are too large or too small, but they either wholly lose their nature, or are spoiled."[177] There can

---

[176] *Politics* VII, 1325 b 27–32. ὁμοίως δὲ τοῦτο ὑπάρχει καὶ καθ᾽ ἑνὸς ὁτουοῦν τῶν ἀνθρώπων· σχολῇ γὰρ ἂν ὁ θεὸς ἔχοι καλῶς καὶ πᾶς ὁ κόσμος, οἷς οὐκ εἰσὶν ἐξωτερικαὶ πράξεις παρὰ τὰς οἰκείας τὰς αὐτῶν. ὅτι μὲν οὖν τὸν αὐτὸν βίον ἀναγκαῖον εἶναι τὸν ἄριστον ἑκάστῳ τε τῶν ἀνθρώπων καὶ κοινῇ ταῖς πόλεσι καὶ τοῖς ἀνθρώποις, φανερόν ἐστιν. Ross's text.

[177] *Politics* VII, 1326 a 29–40. τοῦτο δὲ δῆλον καὶ διὰ τῆς τῶν λόγων πίστεως. ὅ τε γὰρ νόμος τάξις τίς ἐστι, καὶ τὴν εὐνομίαν ἀναγκαῖον εὐταξίαν εἶναι, ὁ δὲ λίαν ὑπερβάλλων ἀριθμὸς οὐ δύναται μετέχειν τάξεως· θείας γὰρ δὴ τοῦτο δυνάμεως ἔργον, ἥτις καὶ τόδε συνέχει τὸ πᾶν· ἐπεὶ τό γε καλὸν ἐν πλήθει καὶ μεγέθει εἴωθε γίνεσθαι. διὸ καὶ πόλιν ᾗ μετὰ μεγέθους ὁ λεχθεὶς ὅρος ὑπάρχει, ταύτην εἶναι καλλίστην ἀναγκαῖον. ἀλλ᾽ ἔστι τι καὶ πόλεως μεγέθους μέτρον, ὥσπερ καὶ τῶν ἄλλων πάντων, ζῴων φυτῶν ὀργάνων· καὶ γὰρ τούτων ἕκαστον οὔτε λίαν μικρὸν οὔτε κατὰ μέγεθος ὑπερβάλλον ἕξει τὴν αὑτοῦ δύναμιν, ἀλλ᾽ ὁτὲ μὲν ὅλως ἐστερημένον ἔσται τῆς φύσεως ὁτὲ δὲ φαύλως ἔχον. Ross's text. The phrase "to introduce order into the unlimited," as can be seen, has no counterpart in the Greek text. It perhaps can be inferred, but there will be some who will feel that Jowett in the Oxford version has over-translated here. The same argument about size and beauty is offered in the *Poetics*, 1450 b 34–1451 a 6. It might also be added that the point made in the passage about reason, namely that it can be relied upon and can be regarded as a clue for the identification of things of superior value, is found frequently in the *Politics*. Cf., *e.g.*, VII, 1333 a 16–39.

be no doubt that the working of the divine power, something which holds together the universe, is not consistent with the normal Aristotelian conception of the complete impassivity of God or the Unmoved Mover. All one can say is that in this particular passage Aristotle is talking very much in the way in which Plato speaks of the activity of the Demiurge in the *Timaeus*.

Before we leave the *Politics*, there remains but one more passage which must be considered, this being the famous section which some have claimed was inspired by the career of Aristotle's distinguished tutee, Alexander the Great. "If, however, there be some one person, or more than one, although not enough to make up the full complement of a state, whose virtue is so pre-eminent that the virtues or the political capacity of all the rest admit of no comparison with his or theirs, he or they can no longer be regarded as part of a state; for justice will not be done to the superior, if he is reckoned only as the equal of those who are so far inferior to him in virtue and in political capacity. Such an one may truly be deemed a God among men. Hence we see that legislation is necessarily concerned only with those who are equal in birth and in capacity; and that for men of pre-eminent virtue there is no law—they are themselves a law."[178] Whether or not these words are meant to be associated with Alexander is not a problem with which we need be concerned. Rather we must attempt to explain why Aristotle is apparently willing to suspend virtually all his political principles in the face of an individual who is as a god among men. However, it must be noted that such a superman achieves his superiority because of his exceptional virtue, and because of his extraordinary "political capacity," whatever Aristotle wishes to connote by that term. Gone or forgotten is the principle of the mean which undergirds the excellence of the polity, and gone is Aristotle's conviction

---

[178] *Politics* III, 1284 a 3–14. εἰ δέ τις εἰς τοσοῦτον διαφέρων κατ' ἀρετῆς ὑπερβολήν, ἢ πλείους μὲν ἑνὸς μὴ μέντοι δυνατοὶ πλήρωμα παρασχέσθαι πόλεως, ὥστε μὴ συμβλητὴν εἶναι τὴν τῶν ἄλλων ἀρετὴν πάντων μηδὲ τὴν δύναμιν αὐτῶν τὴν πολιτικὴν πρὸς τὴν ἐκείνων, εἰ πλείους, εἰ δ' εἷς, τὴν ἐκείνου μόνον, οὐκέτι θετέον τούτους μέρος πόλεως· ἀδικήσονται γὰρ ἀξιούμενοι τῶν ἴσων, ἄνισοι τοσοῦτον κατ' ἀρετὴν ὄντες καὶ τὴν πολιτικὴν δύναμιν· ὥσπερ γὰρ θεὸν ἐν ἀνθρώποις εἰκὸς εἶναι τὸν τοιοῦτον. ὅθεν δῆλον ὅτι καὶ τὴν νομοθεσίαν ἀναγκαῖον εἶναι περὶ τοὺς ἴσους καὶ τῷ γένει καὶ τῇ δυνάμει, κατὰ δὲ τῶν τοιούτων οὐκ ἔστι νόμος· αὐτοὶ γὰρ εἰσι νόμος. Ross's text.

that in states law rather than men must be supreme. One might justifiably conjecture that he is willing to put the superman, if one should appear, above the law because of the degree to which his "political relativism" has tended to undermine the solidity of his political principles. This, of course, can be said with the full realization that the contingent nature of human affairs entails the admission of an inevitable element of relativism in this domain. However, it does not necessarily follow that this element of relativism should lead to the abandonment or suspension of firmly held principles. Perhaps if Aristotle had wrought more carefully and consistently his scheme of values, he would have been unwilling to suspend his principles in this way. One might add that he supports the suspension of principles by subtly invoking the sanction of God when he says that his superman would be "deemed a God among men." We can only observe that the activity imputed to God in this context cannot be made easily to conform with the impassivity of God, the Unmoved Mover.

To recapitulate briefly the evidence to be found in the *Politics* for Arisotle's views with respect to the question of value, we can say that the positions put forward in the *Nicomachean Ethics* are found again in its complementary treatise. Happiness is the highest human value for the state as well as for the individual. The conception of nature, φύσις, is present as it is throughout the Aristotelian corpus. The rôle of pleasure in the political context is to all intents and purposes the same as that revealed in the study of ethics. The virtues likewise appear as values, and they are supported by the principle of the mean, as is Aristotle's best form of government. And finally, as in the *Nicomachean Ethics*, God is introduced as a sanction for value on occasion, but it must be said that this conception of God partly reflects conventional thinking and partly a more sophisticated theological view, but one surely not wholly in accord with the doctrine of *Metaphysics* Λ. In sum, throughout the *Politics*, we find Aristotle again tending to shift his ground whenever he is called upon to engage in value judgements, that is, in those places where he must do more than analyze and describe.

334

CHAPTER VIII

THE EVIDENCE OF THE *RHETORIC* AND THE *POETICS*

PART I. THE *RHETORIC*

THE most striking characteristic of Aristotle's *Rhetoric*, from our point of view, is its ambivalence. On the one hand, it attempts to tie itself in with Aristotelian logic, ethics, and politics, while on the other it is a practical handbook for the instruction of public speakers in all the techniques and tricks of the trade. So far as the question of value is concerned, we can see in the *Rhetoric*, when the author has foremost in his mind his thought in logic, ethics, and politics, a reflection of the views expressed therein towards matters of value. But when he is in the mood of an author of a practical handbook,[1] any concern for value seems in some places to vanish, leaving us in a realm of amoralism, if not immoralism. Or, in other places, the point of view towards value reflects the most banal type of conventionalism. Perhaps the point about ambivalence can best be made by looking at Aristotle's definition of rhetoric submitted early in the work: "Let rhetoric then be the potentiality, *i.e.*, as a capacity to produce change, involved in observing concerning each particular that which is capable of being persuasive."[2] No one can read this without thinking of the famous passage in Plato's *Gorgias* where Socrates offers the following terse definition of rhetoric which is immediately accepted by his interlocutor of the moment, the great Gorgias himself: "Rhetoric is the artificer of persuasion."[3] As is well known, the whole argument of the dialogue is devoted to revealing the latent immoralism inherent in this definition. The Aristotelian definition, though it is slightly

[1] Cf. Ross, *Aristotle*, pp. 275–276.
[2] *Rhetoric* I, 1355 b 25–26. Ἔστω δὴ ἡ ῥητορικὴ δύναμις περὶ ἕκαστον τοῦ θεωρῆσαι τὸ ἐνδεχόμενον πιθανόν. Ross's text. The translation is mine, in a somewhat expanded form. Cf. above, Chapter IV, note 8, where the definition was quoted, and where also may be found the translations of Roberts and Cooper.
[3] Plato, *Gorgias*, 453 a 2. πειθοῦς δημιουργός ἐστιν ἡ ῥητορική. Burnet's text.

more extensive, really differs not at all in substance from the Platonic version, and therefore is vulnerable to the same kind of attack which is mounted by the Socrates of the dialogue.

That Aristotle does not wish to be vulnerable to such an attack is evident in a number of passages. He opens the treatise by announcing that rhetoric is the "counterpart" (ἀντίστροφος) of dialectic. As he takes pains to point out, as rhetoric in the field of oratory is akin to dialectic and not to scientific demonstration, so it is concerned not with certainties but with probabilities about which it is possible to deliberate. Also rhetoric is not confined to any one subject, but can be employed anywhere, no matter what the subject. As Ross observes, rhetoric in argument uses example, the rhetorical counterpart of induction, and enthymeme, the rhetorical counterpart of syllogism.[4] To take an example where Aristotle is clearly attempting to dignify rhetoric, one could cite the following: "The true and the approximately true are apprehended by the same faculty; it may also be noted that men have a sufficient natural instinct for what is true, and usually do arrive at the truth. Hence the man who makes a good guess at truth is likely to make a good guess at probabilities."[5] Or again, he tries to insist upon the natural affiliation of rhetoric for what is true when he says: "Further, we must be able to employ persuasion, just as strict reasoning can be employed, on opposite sides of a question, not in order that we may in practice employ it in both ways (for we must not make people believe what is wrong), but in order that we may see clearly what the facts are, and that, if another man argues unfairly, we on our part may be able to confute him. . . . Nevertheless, the underlying facts do not lend themselves equally well to the contrary views. No; things that are true and things that are better are, by their nature, practically always easier to prove and easier to believe in."[6] Notice how

---

[4] Cf. Ross, *Aristotle*, pp. 270–271. In general, an enthymeme has the basic form of a syllogism. Its premisses are probabilities, and in argument one of them may be suppressed.

[5] *Rhetoric* I, 1355 a 14–18. τό τε γὰρ ἀληθὲς καὶ τὸ ὅμοιον τῷ ἀληθεῖ τῆς αὐτῆς ἐστι δυνάμεως ἰδεῖν, ἅμα δὲ καὶ οἱ ἄνθρωποι πρὸς τὸ ἀληθὲς πεφύκασιν ἱκανῶς καὶ τὰ πλείω τυγχάνουσι τῆς ἀληθείας· διὸ πρὸς τὰ ἔνδοξα στοχαστικῶς ἔχειν τοῦ ὁμοίως ἔχοντος καὶ πρὸς τὴν ἀλήθειάν ἐστιν. Ross's text.

[6] *Rhetoric* I, 1355 a 29–38 (omitting 33–36). ἔτι δὲ τἀναντία δεῖ δύνασθαι πείθειν, καθάπερ καὶ ἐν τοῖς συλλογισμοῖς, οὐχ ὅπως ἀμφότερα πράττωμεν (οὐ

he protests that, though rhetorical persuasion may be used on either side of an argument, we should never do this in practical fact—"We must not make people believe what is wrong." After all, he insists, it is a fact of nature that the truth and the better are "easier to prove and easier to believe in." It does not seem wrong to detect in this passage a note of uneasy defensiveness, just as though Aristotle felt the presence of Aristophanes looking over his shoulder as he wrote and saying something about making the worse appear the better reason.

Another passage throws further light on Aristotle's attempt to make his conception of rhetoric philosophically grounded, and perhaps to answer in some measure the Platonic attacks upon the sophists and the rhetoric of a Gorgias. Aristotle's treatise, as is well known, owes much to the analysis of rhetoric in the *Phaedrus* of Plato, but Aristotelian metaphysics cannot provide the basis for a version of or an adaptation of Plato's "dialectical" rhetoric as "psychagogy" as developed in the *Phaedrus*. In brief, this Platonic conception holds rhetoric to be the instrument whereby the "soul" of man (*i.e.*, the totality of his inner being, including his cognitive faculties) is turned about, oriented towards, is "converted" to the "truth." In Platonic terms, this "truth" is the panoply of the Ideas or Forms dominated by the Idea of the Good. Because rhetoric can effect the reorientation of the soul, its awareness and comprehension of the eternal verities will be enhanced. As has been pointed out, since the Aristotelian metaphysics has denied the existence of these objective entities, the Ideas, it is plain that Aristotle's rhetorical theory is forced to be far vaguer with respect to the nature of truth, with which, so he says, the craft of persuasion has some concern.

But let us examine the passage which now perhaps can be better understood in the light of the foregoing remarks on the theory of the *Phaedrus*. "Furthermore, it is plain that it is the function of one and the same art to discern the real and the apparent means of persuasion, just as it is the function of dialectic to

---

γὰρ δεῖ τὰ φαῦλα πείθειν), ἀλλ᾽ ἵνα μὴ λανθάνῃ πῶς ἔχει, καὶ ὅπως ἄλλου χρωμένου τοῖς λόγοις μὴ δικαίως αὐτοὶ λύειν ἔχωμεν. . . . τὰ μέντοι ὑποκείμενα πράγματα οὐχ ὁμοίως ἔχει, ἀλλ᾽ ἀεὶ τἀληθῆ καὶ τὰ βελτίω τῇ φύσει εὐσυλ-λογιστότερα καὶ πιθανώτερα ὡς ἁπλῶς εἰπεῖν. Ross's text.

discern the real and the apparent syllogism. What makes a man a 'sophist' is not his faculty, but his moral purpose. In rhetoric, however, the term 'rhetorician' may describe either the speaker's knowledge of the art or his moral purpose. In dialectic it is different: a man is a 'sophist' because he has a certain kind of moral purpose, a 'dialectician' in respect, not of his moral purpose, but of his faculty."[7] It is perfectly obvious that here Aristotle does not wish the term "sophist" to have the unfavourable meaning which it has in the pages of Plato. For Aristotle here a "sophist" is a learned, "wise" man, someone whose distinction depends upon something more than his technical skill, let us say, as a dialectician, this something more being his προαίρεσις, his "moral purpose."[8] Aristotle apparently is disturbed by the fact that no such term as "sophist" is available to him in the field of oratory. The only word that can be used is "rhetorician," which can be applied both to the technically skilled speaker and to the speaker who has "moral purpose." In any event, the clear purport of the passage is to indicate, at least in the present circumstance, that Aristotle wishes us to see moral purpose as basic in his rhetorical theory.

There are other places where Aristotle appears to be attempting to relate rhetoric or persuasion to some form of accepted goodness. For example, when he asserts that in oral discourse, there are three ways in which belief is produced—by the character of the speaker, by his capacity to get his hearers into a proper frame of mind, and by the demonstration or apparent demonstration provided in his argument—Aristotle goes on to say: "Persuasion is achieved by the speaker's personal character when the speech is so spoken as to make us think him credible. We believe good men more fully and more readily than others. . . . It is not true,

---

[7] *Rhetoric* I, 1355 b 15–21. πρὸς δὲ τούτοις ὅτι τῆς αὐτῆς τό τε πιθανὸν καὶ τὸ φαινόμενον ἰδεῖν πιθανόν, ὥσπερ καὶ ἐπὶ τῆς διαλεκτικῆς συλλογισμόν τε καὶ φαινόμενον συλλογισμόν· ἡ γὰρ σοφιστικὴ οὐκ ἐν τῇ δυνάμει ἀλλ' ἐν τῇ προαιρέσει· πλὴν ἐνταῦθα μὲν ἔσται ὁ μὲν κατὰ τὴν ἐπιστήμην ὁ δὲ κατὰ τὴν προαίρεσιν ῥήτωρ, ἐκεῖ δὲ σοφιστὴς μὲν κατὰ τὴν προαίρεσιν, διαλεκτικὸς δὲ οὐ κατὰ τὴν προαίρεσιν ἀλλὰ κατὰ τὴν δύναμιν. Ross's text. The reader should be aware that "dialectic" in this passage has a different meaning from the "dialectic" of Plato's *Phaedrus*, to which we have just referred.

[8] Given the context, Roberts appears to be justified in translating προαίρεσις as "moral purpose." The primary meaning is simply "choice."

as some writers assume in their treatises on rhetoric, that the personal goodness revealed by the speaker contributes nothing to his power of persuasion; on the contrary, his character may almost be called the most effective means of persuasion he possesses."[9] And the same general spirit is evident, when a few lines later Aristotle remarks: "There are, then, these three means of effecting persuasion. The man who is to be in command of them must, it is clear, be able (1) to reason logically, (2) to understand human character and goodness in their various forms, and (3) to understand the emotions—that is, to name them and describe them, to know their causes and the way in which they are excited."[10]

Now we may turn to the other side of the ambivalence of the *Rhetoric*, as a practical handbook for the public speaker, in order to discover, if we can, the attitude towards value therein disclosed. Actually, Aristotle gets down to practical matters in the third chapter of the first book. After having distinguished between the three types of rhetoric or oratory, *viz.*, political, legal, and epideictic, or declamatory, he makes the following statement which gives us a clue as to what we may expect so far as the question of value is concerned: "Rhetoric has three distinct ends in view, one for each of its three kinds. The political orator aims at establishing the expediency or the harmfulness of a proposed course of action; if he urges its acceptance, he does so on the ground that it will do good; if he urges its rejection, he does so on the ground that it will do harm; and all other points, such as whether the proposal is just or unjust, honourable or dishonourable, he brings in as subsidiary and relative to this main consideration.

---

[9]. *Rhetoric* I, 1356 a 4–13 (omitting 7–10). διὰ μὲν οὖν τοῦ ἤθους, ὅταν οὕτω λεχθῇ ὁ λόγος ὥστε ἀξιόπιστον ποιῆσαι τὸν λέγοντα· τοῖς γὰρ ἐπιεικέσι πιστεύομεν μᾶλλον καὶ θᾶττον. . . . οὐ γάρ, ὥσπερ ἔνιοι τῶν τεχνολογούντων, ‹οὐ› τίθεμεν ἐν τῇ τέχνῃ καὶ τὴν ἐπιείκειαν τοῦ λέγοντος, ὡς οὐδὲν συμβαλλομένην πρὸς τὸ πιθανόν, ἀλλὰ σχεδὸν ὡς εἰπεῖν κυριωτάτην ἔχει πίστιν τὸ ἦθος. Ross's text.

[10] *Rhetoric* I, 1356 a 20–25. ἐπεὶ δ' αἱ πίστεις διὰ τούτων εἰσί, φανερὸν ὅτι ταύτας ἐστὶ λαβεῖν τοῦ συλλογίσασθαι δυναμένου καὶ τοῦ θεωρῆσαι περὶ τὰ ἤθη καὶ περὶ τὰς ἀρετὰς καὶ τρίτον [τοῦ] περὶ τὰ πάθη, τί τε ἕκαστόν ἐστιν τῶν παθῶν καὶ ποῖόν τι, καὶ ἐκ τίνων ἐγγίνεται καὶ πῶς. Ross's text. Other passages which might be cited in this connection are: *Rhetoric* III, 1404 b 1–4 [Style, or the "virtue of speaking," λέξεως ἀρετή, must be marked by clarity and by appropriateness, being neither too mean nor beyond what the subject merits.]; 1417 a 24–28 [the importance of moral purpose]; 1418 a 38–b 1.

Parties in a law case aim at establishing the justice or injustice of some action, and they too bring in all other points as subsidiary and relative to this one. Those who praise or attack a man aim at proving him worthy of honour or the reverse, and they too treat all other considerations with reference to this one."[11] The main point to observe in this passage is that there is an increasing emphasis upon the tactics of the orator as he engages in the activity of persuasion. The political speaker is advised to concentrate upon the expediency or advantageousness, τὸ συμφέρον, or the harmfulness "of a proposed course of action" and to regard as secondary matters of justice, injustice, honour, or dishonour. The situation is similar in the case of the trial-lawyer. Admittedly there is some lack of clarity in the advice, but the disturbing element is that nowhere is the speaker urged to say what is true about the point at issue. Perhaps we may be accused of being overly-sensitive on this question, but we are, I believe, justified in so feeling because of the numerous other places in which this practical "eristic" attitude is patent.[12]

The fourth chapter of the first book of the *Rhetoric* provides a good illustration of the point we are trying to make. Aristotle starts out bravely by suggesting that a political orator must be concerned with values. "First, then, we must ascertain what are the kinds of things, good or bad, about which the political orator offers counsel."[13] But he immediately drops the "good or bad," leaving it in the realm of conventional response, and proceeds to make several analytical and practical distinctions. He then makes the following very revealing admission: "The truth is, as indeed we have said already, that rhetoric is a combination of the science of logic and of the ethical branch of politics; and it is

---

[11] *Rhetoric* I, 1358 b 20–29. τέλος δὲ ἑκάστοις τούτων ἕτερόν ἐστι, καὶ τρισὶν οὖσι τρία, τῷ μὲν συμβουλεύοντι τὸ συμφέρον καὶ βλαβερόν· ὁ μὲν γὰρ προτρέπων ὡς βέλτιον συμβουλεύει, ὁ δὲ ἀποτρέπων ὡς χείρονος ἀποτρέπει, τὰ δ᾽ ἄλλα πρὸς τοῦτο συμπαραλαμβάνει, ἢ δίκαιον καὶ τὸ ἄδικον, ἢ καλὸν ἢ αἰσχρόν· τοῖς δὲ δικαζομένοις τὸ δίκαιον καὶ τὸ ἄδικον, τὰ δ᾽ ἄλλα καὶ οὗτοι συμπαραλαμβάνουσι πρὸς ταῦτα· τοῖς δ᾽ ἐπαινοῦσιν καὶ ψέγουσιν τὸ καλὸν καὶ τὸ αἰσχρόν, τὰ δ᾽ ἄλλα καὶ οὗτοι πρὸς ταῦτα ἐπαναφέρουσιν. Ross's text.

[12] We have in mind, or course, Plato's conception of eristic as the method in argument which justifies the use of any and all means in order to beat an opponent quite irrespective of the merits or "truth" of the case.

[13] *Rhetoric* I, 1359 a 30–31. Πρῶτον μὲν οὖν ληπτέον περὶ ποῖα ἀγαθὰ ἢ κακὰ ὁ συμβουλεύων συμβουλεύει. Ross's text.

partly like dialectic, partly like sophistical reasoning. But the more we try to make either dialectic or rhetoric not, what they really are, practical faculties, but sciences, the more we shall inadvertently be destroying their true nature; for we shall be refashioning them and shall be passing into the region of sciences dealing with definite subjects rather than simply with words and forms of reasoning."[14] In this curious statement, we are justified in applauding Aristotle's effort to see rhetoric as he thought it truly to be, but at the same time, in so doing he reduces it to be nothing more than a matter of words. It is in this way that Aristotle in effect divorces rhetoric from any firm philosophical undergirding, despite the fact that he made the efforts to establish such an interrelation in the passages we discussed at the outset of the present chapter. Rhetoric thus becomes nakedly the study of that which will practically produce persuasion. "Anything goes," if only persuasion emerges.

We can almost rest our case by presenting a somewhat lengthy passage which brings out crystal clear the value "climate" in which Aristotelian rhetoric operates. In the fifth chapter of the first book of the treatise, he introduces the subject of happiness. "We may define happiness as prosperity combined with virtue; or as independence of life; or as the secure enjoyment of the maximum of pleasure; or as a good condition of property and body, together with the power of guarding one's property and body and making use of them. That happiness is one or more of these things, pretty well everybody agrees.

"From this definition of happiness it follows that its constituent parts are: good birth, plenty of friends, good friends, wealth, good children, plenty of children, a happy old age, also such bodily excellences as health, beauty, strength, large stature, athletic powers, together with fame, honour, good luck, and virtue, [or also the parts of it, practical wisdom, bravery, justice,

---

[14] *Rhetoric* I, 1359 b 8–16. ὅπερ γὰρ καὶ πρότερον εἰρηκότες τυγχάνομεν ἀληθές ἐστιν, ὅτι ἡ ῥητορικὴ σύγκειται μὲν ἔκ τε τῆς ἀναλυτικῆς ἐπιστήμης καὶ τῆς περὶ τὰ ἤθη πολιτικῆς, ὁμοία δ᾽ ἐστὶν τὰ μὲν τῇ διαλεκτικῇ τὰ δὲ τοῖς σοφιστικοῖς λόγοις. ὅσῳ δ᾽ ἄν τις ἢ διαλεκτικὴν ἢ ταύτην μὴ καθάπερ ἂν δυνάμεις ἀλλ᾽ ἐπιστήμας πειρᾶται κατασκευάζειν, λήσεται τὴν φύσιν αὐτῶν ἀφανίσας τῷ μεταβαίνειν ἐπισκευάζων εἰς ἐπιστήμας ὑποκειμένων τινῶν πραγμάτων, ἀλλὰ μὴ μόνον λόγων. Ross's text. Roberts may have over-translated when he renders μὴ μόνον λόγων as "simply with words and forms of reasoning."

and moderation]. A man cannot fail to be completely independent if he possesses these internal and external goods; for besides these there are no others to have. (Goods of the soul and of the body are internal. Good birth, friends, money, and honour are external.) Further, we think that he should possess resources and luck, in order to make his life really secure. As we have already ascertained what happiness in general is, so now let us try to ascertain what each of these parts of it is."[15] Very little is needed by way of comment on this quotation. The definition of happiness is totally lacking in any kind of philosophical or critical discrimination. Aristotle seems rather to have lumped together most of the conventional views of men with respect to the nature of happiness. And the list of the components of happiness which follows contains practically every worldly "good" that anybody could think of. A nod, to be sure, is given to the notion that in some sense happiness must be attended by virtue, but this idea is to all intents and purposes buried in the recital of conventional goods—good birth, friends, wealth, many good children, and so on and on, even to a mention of stature and athletic capability. Where, oh, where is the contemplative philosopher of the *Nicomachean Ethics*? Perhaps he might not be handsome enough, or tall enough, or rich enough to qualify for the value climate of the *Rhetoric*.

Aristotle devotes the remainder of the fifth chapter to more extended descriptions of each of the constituents of happiness, and in the following chapter he continues in much the same vein. The argument is introduced in these words: "Now the political

---

[15] *Rhetoric* I, 1360 b 14–30. ἔστω δὴ εὐδαιμονία εὐπραξία μετ' ἀρετῆς, ἢ αὐτάρκεια ζωῆς, ἢ ὁ βίος ὁ μετὰ ἀσφαλείας ἥδιστος, ἢ εὐθενία κτημάτων καὶ σωμάτων μετὰ δυνάμεως φυλακτικῆς τε καὶ πρακτικῆς τούτων· σχεδὸν γὰρ τούτων ἐν ἢ πλείω τὴν εὐδαιμονίαν ὁμολογοῦσιν εἶναι ἅπαντες.

εἰ δή ἐστιν ἡ εὐδαιμονία τοιοῦτον, ἀνάγκη αὐτῆς εἶναι μέρη εὐγένειαν, πολυφιλίαν, χρηστοφιλίαν, πλοῦτον, εὐτεκνίαν, πολυτεκνίαν, εὐγηρίαν· ἔτι τὰς τοῦ σώματος ἀρετάς (οἷον ὑγίειαν, κάλλος, ἰσχύν, μέγεθος, δύναμιν ἀγωνιστικήν), δόξαν, τιμήν, εὐτυχίαν, ἀρετήν [ἢ καὶ τὰ μέρη αὐτῆς φρόνησιν, ἀνδρείαν, δικαιοσύνην, σωφροσύνην]· οὕτω γὰρ ἂν αὐταρκέστατός <τις> εἴη, εἰ ὑπάρχοι αὐτῷ τά τ' ἐν αὐτῷ καὶ τὰ ἐκτὸς ἀγαθά· οὐ γάρ ἐστιν ἄλλα παρὰ ταῦτα. ἔστι δ' ἐν αὐτῷ μὲν τὰ περὶ ψυχὴν καὶ τὰ ἐν σώματι, ἔξω δὲ εὐγένεια καὶ φίλοι καὶ χρήματα καὶ τιμή, ἔτι δὲ προσήκειν οἰόμεθα δυνάμεις ὑπάρχειν καὶ τύχην· οὕτω γὰρ ἀσφαλέστατος ὁ βίος. λάβωμεν τοίνυν ὁμοίως καὶ τούτων ἕκαστον τί ἐστιν. Ross's text. I have added a rendering for the bracketed section in 23–24, which is omitted in the Oxford version.

or deliberative orator's aim is ultility: deliberation seeks to determine not ends but the means to ends, *i.e.*, what it is most useful to do. Further, utility is a good thing. We ought therefore to assure ourselves of the main facts about Goodness and Utility in general."[16] Then there ensues a popular or conventional discussion of what is good and useful, along with a virtual repetition of the list of all those things which people regard as good, these being in effect the "parts" of happiness already submitted in the preceding chapter. But at the conclusion of the list, Aristotle again makes clear the unrelievedly practical, or non-philsophical, atmosphere in which he proposes to carry forward his analysis of rhetoric, when he observes: "The above are pretty well all the things admittedly good. In dealing with things whose goodness is disputed, we may argue in the following ways: That is good of which the contrary is bad. That is good the contrary of which is to the advantage of our enemies; for example, if it is to the particular advantage of our enemies that we should be cowards, clearly courage is of particular value to our countrymen. And generally, the contrary of that which our enemies desire, or of that at which they rejoice, is evidently valuable."[17] It seems scarcely necessary to point out the essential amoralism of this passage, as well as the striking want of philosophical rigour. For example, a value is determined by its being the opposite of what an enemy values. What a strange defence of the moral value courage is herewith offered. We could not be more clearly in the *milieu* of the worldly.

It has often been argued that such criticisms as we have been making against the *Rhetoric* are not justified on the ground that the treatise is a practical handbook, a "book of directions" for practical public speakers, and therefore its author is not obligated

---

[16] *Rhetoric* I, 1362 a 17-21. ἐπεὶ δὲ πρόκειται τῷ συμβουλεύοντι σκοπὸς τὸ συμφέρον (βουλεύονται γὰρ οὐ περὶ τοῦ τέλους, ἀλλὰ περὶ τῶν πρὸς τὸ τέλος, ταῦτα δ' ἐστὶ τὰ συμφέροντα κατὰ τὰς πράξεις, τὸ δὲ συμφέρον ἀγαθόν), ληπτέον ἂν εἴη τὰ στοιχεῖα περὶ ἀγαθοῦ καὶ συμφέροντος ἁπλῶς. Ross's text.

[17] *Rhetoric* I, 1362 b 29-35. ταῦτα μὲν οὖν σχεδὸν ὁμολογούμενα ἀγαθά ἐστιν· ἐν δὲ τοῖς ἀμφισβητησίμοις ἐκ τῶνδε οἱ συλλογισμοί· ᾧ τὸ ἐναντίον κακόν, τοῦτ' ἀγαθόν. καὶ οὗ τὸ ἐναντίον τοῖς ἐχθροῖς συμφέρει· οἷον εἰ τὸ δειλοὺς εἶναι μάλιστα συμφέρει τοῖς ἐχθροῖς, δῆλον ὅτι ἀνδρεία μάλιστα ὠφέλιμον τοῖς πολίταις. καὶ ὅλως ὃ οἱ ἐχθροὶ βούλονται ἢ ἐφ' ᾧ χαίρουσι, τοὐναντίον τούτου ὠφέλιμον φαίνεται. Ross's text.

to face the problem of the philosophical prior assumptions upon the basis of which the rhetorical theory is being developed. Such a defence can hardly stand examination. In the first place, the *Rhetoric* is found in the corpus of Aristotle in which all the various treatises are in one way or another related to the central view or views of Aristotelian philosophy or metaphysics. Secondly, such an effort to attempt to relate the *Rhetoric* to the basic Aristotelian position is made at the outset of the treatise, but, as we have tried to indicate, this effort tends to fall out of sight as the claims of the mode of the practical handbook move to the fore, and hence the ambivalence we noted has arisen. And finally, like any other subject or discipline, rhetoric demands to be philosophical. Certainly this must be the case if a study of rhetoric is to transcend the limits of a mere collection of the technical tricks of the trade. That rhetoric should be more than a study of techniques, in other words, that rhetoric must be related to philosophy, is the ground of Plato's critique of the Sophists' view of rhetoric in the *Gorgias* and the *Phaedrus*. Therefore, there is legitimate ground to hold that, if Aristotle had equipped himself with a more thoroughgoing theory of value, it would have been impossible for him to have compounded such a worldly and conventional a treatise as his *Rhetoric* proves to be.[18]

No real purpose would be served by a detailed examination of the remainder of the first book of the *Rhetoric*. It will suffice to point to two or three passages where the conventionality of the work may be illustrated.[19] For example, in the seventh chapter, Aristotle sets out to study "relative goodness and relative utility."[20] There follows an analysis of comparative values, a "consideration of degree—the lore of 'less and more,'" as Roberts describes it.[21] Typical of the way in which Aristotle develops his argument is this remark: "Again, that which would

---

[18] It should be remembered, however, that in the second book of the *Rhetoric* where Aristotle is more explicitly concerned with the techniques of argument, the sections involving the enthymeme (especially chapter 22) do exhibit his effort to connect formally rhetorical theory with logic.

[19] Our only exception will be a brief discussion below of the attitude towards pleasure found in the eleventh chapter of *Rhetoric* I.

[20] This is Robert's rendering for περὶ τοῦ μείζονος ἀγαθοῦ καὶ τοῦ μᾶλλον συμφέροντος, *Rhetoric* I, 1363 b 7.

[21] Cf. Roberts, analytical Table of Contents, p. viii, in the Oxford translation.

be judged, or which has been judged, a good thing, or a better thing than something else, by all or most people of understanding, or by a majority of men, or by the ablest, must be so; either without qualification, or in so far as they use their understanding to form their judgement."[22] As is obvious, here we meet again the *phronimos*, the human being who possesses practical wisdom, as a sanction for value, as well as the "majority of men." To mention the latter as a sanction is, of course, nothing more than to raise conventional opinion to a position of over-riding importance.

Let us cite another example. "The most important and effective qualification for success in persuading audiences and speaking well on public affairs is to understand all the forms of government and to discriminate their respective customs, institutions, and interests. For all men are persuaded by considerations of their interest, and their interest lies in the maintenance of the established order."[23] While it is perfectly laudible on Aristotle's side to urge that public counselors should be well versed in the various forms of government, one cannot help but be slightly distressed by the latent amoralism involved in the emphasis upon successful persuasion. In other words, the orator, as Aristotle goes on to point out, must find out what the goal of a given form of government is, deduce from it the interest of a citizen under that government, and in the light of these data persuade the citizen to believe that his interest lies in the preservation of the form of government. So, if an orator is addressing an audience in an oligarchy, he must know that the goal of an oligarchy is money. Therefore the citizen in an oligarchy has as his goal money also. The orator then will be successful in his persuasion if he convinces the citizen that he will achieve his goal, money, only so long as the established oligarchical order is maintained. Note that the orator is not invited to raise any question with respect to the worth of oligarchy

---

[22] *Rhetoric* I, 1364 b 11–14. καὶ ὃ κρίνειαν ἂν ἢ κεκρίκασιν οἱ φρόνιμοι ἢ πάντες ἢ οἱ πολλοὶ ἢ οἱ πλείους ἢ οἱ κράτιστοι ἀγαθὸν μεῖζον, ἀνάγκη οὕτως ἔχειν, ἢ ἁπλῶς ἢ ᾗ κατὰ τὴν φρόνησιν ἔκριναν. Ross's text.

[23] *Rhetoric* I, 1365 b 21–25. Μέγιστον δὲ καὶ κυριώτατον ἁπάντων πρὸς τὸ δύνασθαι πείθειν καὶ καλῶς συμβουλεύειν ‹τὸ› τὰς πολιτείας ἁπάσας λαβεῖν καὶ τὰ ἑκάστης ἤθη καὶ νόμιμα καὶ συμφέροντα διελεῖν. πείθονται γὰρ ἅπαντες τῷ συμφέροντι, συμφέρει δὲ τὸ σῷζον τὴν πολιτείαν. Ross's text.

as a form of government, and, furthermore, he is tacitly invited not to intrude his own convictions on political matters. And in addition to our point about latent amoralism, we must observe again that the discussion is carried forward on the strict level of conventional value thinking.

For another example, there is a passage which we should have before us where the latent amoralism or even immoralism is not so latent. It occurs in Aristotle's treatment of epideictic or display oratory and it runs as follows: "Since we praise a man for what he has actually done, and fine actions are distinguished from others by being intentionally good, we must try to prove that our hero's noble acts are intentional. This is all the easier if we can make out that he has often acted so before, and therefore we must assert coincidences and accidents to have been intended. Produce a number of good actions, all of the same kind, and people will think that they must have been intended, and that they prove the good qualities of the man who did them."[24] The deception invited by this passage is clear. The orator is instructed to say that the actions of the object of his praise, which in fact were *not* done as a result of moral purpose, προαίρεσις, were so done. It is his task to make his "hero's" coincidental and accidental actions *appear* to have been undertaken purposefully. The suggestion is offered that this palpable untruth can be made plausible to the audience by referring to the subject's previous history of purposeful action. It may be urged that this particular illustration is trivial, but, no matter how trivial it may be, it still makes plain Plato's contention that rhetoric, defined as the artificer of persuasion, is a producer of "seeming," and not of truth.

An even more decisive illustration to support the point we have been trying to establish occurs at the very end of the first book of the *Rhetoric*, where Aristotle is treating the question of oaths. "If you have already sworn an oath that contradicts your present one, you must argue that it is not perjury, since perjury is a crime, and a crime must be a voluntary action, whereas

[24] *Rhetoric* I, 1367 b 22–27. ἐπεὶ δ' ἐκ τῶν πράξεων ὁ ἔπαινος, ἴδιον δὲ τοῦ σπουδαίου τὸ κατὰ προαίρεσιν, πειρατέον δεικνύναι πράττοντα κατὰ προαίρεσιν, χρήσιμον δὲ τὸ πολλάκις φαίνεσθαι πεπραχότα· διὸ καὶ τὰ συμπτώματα καὶ τὰ ἀπὸ τύχης ὡς ἐν προαιρέσει ληπτέον· ἂν γὰρ πολλὰ καὶ ὅμοια προφέρηται, σημεῖον ἀρετῆς εἶναι δόξει καὶ προαιρέσεως. Ross's text.

actions due to the force or fraud of others are involuntary. You must further reason from this that perjury depends on the intention and not on the spoken words. But if it is your opponent who has already sworn an oath that contradicts his present one, you must say that if he does not abide by his oaths he is the enemy of society, and that this is the reason why men take an oath before administering the laws."[25] There is no escaping the fact that the orator is here advised to operate on an egregious moral double standard. If he is caught in a situation involving perjury, *i.e.*, having sworn two oaths that contradict each other, he is urged to wriggle out of his trouble by employing rather dubious means such as denying that it was really perjury, by hinting that the first oath was taken under duress, and hence was involuntary, and hence not a crime. And it is even suggested further that in fact "perjury depends on the intention and not on the spoken words." Whereas, if his opponent on the other hand is discovered in an identical situation, our good orator is exhorted to assume a lofty moral line by asserting that anyone who breaks an oath is a subverter of society—"He destroys everything." No further comment is needed.

The opening chapter of the second book of the *Rhetoric* gives further evidence that Aristotle's view of persuasion is based ultimately upon it as an instrument to produce "seeming." Since rhetoric has to do with the making of decisions, Aristotle argues, "The orator must not only try to make the argument of his speech demonstrative and worthy of belief; he must also make his own character look right and put his hearers, who are to decide, into the right frame of mind. Particularly in political oratory, but also in lawsuits, it adds much to an orator's influence that his own character should look right and that he should be thought

---

[25] *Rhetoric* I, 1377 b 3–9. ἐὰν δὲ ᾖ γεγενημένος ὑφ' αὐτοῦ καὶ ἐναντίος, ὅτι οὐκ ἐπιορκία· ἑκούσιον γὰρ τὸ ἀδικεῖν, τὸ δ' ἐπιορκεῖν ἀδικεῖν ἐστι, τὰ δὲ βίᾳ καὶ ἀπάτῃ ἀκούσια. ἐνταῦθα οὖν συνακτέον καὶ τὸ ἐπιορκεῖν, ὅτι ἔστι τὸ τῇ διανοίᾳ ἀλλ' οὐ τῷ στόματι. ἐὰν δὲ τῷ ἀντιδίκῳ ᾖ ὑπεναντίος καὶ ὀμωμοσμένος, ὅτι πάντα ἀναιρεῖ μὴ ἐμμένων οἷς ὤμοσεν· διὰ γὰρ τοῦτο καὶ τοῖς νόμοις χρῶνται ὀμόσαντες. Ross's text. The Oxford translation is rather free, but nonetheless it seems to preserve accurately the meaning of the original. In connection with the phrase ὅτι ἔστι τὸ τῇ διανοίᾳ ἀλλ' οὐ τῷ στόματι, one cannot fail to be reminded of the famous line in Euripides' *Hippolytus*, "It was not my heart but my tongue that swore" *(ἡ γλῶσσ' ὀμώμοχ', ἡ δὲ φρὴν ἀνώμοτος,* 612). Cf. Aristophanes' satiric use of the line, *Frogs*, 101–102, and 1471.

347

to entertain the right feelings towards his hearers; and also that his hearers should be in just the right frame of mind."[26] The elements of "seeming" or "appearance" are obvious. The orator must make his own character "look right." He should carefully calculate how he may put his hearers into a proper attitude of mind. He must then believe that he is rightly disposed towards them, or in other words he must "appear" to be so disposed. Perhaps Aristotle would answer this criticism by insisting that in the context of rhetoric it is not necessary to raise the question whether the orator does in fact possess a good character or is in fact rightly disposed towards his audience. He might even add that it would not be too easy for a man to make his character "look right" unless actually his character was good. Such an answer may mitigate the criticism to a degree, but the fact remains that the text itself emphasizes "seeming" and "appearance," and again it must be recalled that it is exactly this type of rhetoric against which Plato inveighs in the *Gorgias*.

The same tone of amoralism is apparent when Aristotle turns to the topic of the emotions. "The Emotions are all those feelings that so change men as to affect their judgements, and that are also attended by pain or pleasure. Such are anger, pity, fear, and the like, with their opposites. We must arrange what we have to say about each of them under three heads. Take, for instance, the emotion of anger: here we must discover (1) what the state of mind of angry people is, (2) who the people are with whom they usually get angry, and (3) on what grounds they get angry with them. It is not enough to know one or even two of these points; unless we know all three, we shall be unable to arouse anger in any one."[27] This indeed sounds like an excerpt from a

---

[26] *Rhetoric* II, 1377 b 22–28. ἀνάγκη μὴ μόνον πρὸς τὸν λόγον ὁρᾶν, ὅπως ἀποδεικτικὸς ἔσται καὶ πιστός, ἀλλὰ καὶ αὐτὸν ποιόν τινα καὶ τὸν κριτὴν κατασκευάζειν· πολὺ γὰρ διαφέρει πρὸς πίστιν, μάλιστα μὲν ἐν ταῖς συμβολαῖς, εἶτα καὶ ἐν ταῖς δίκαις, τό τε ποιόν τινα φαίνεσθαι τὸν λέγοντα καὶ τὸ πρὸς αὐτοὺς ὑπολαμβάνειν πως διακεῖσθαι αὐτόν, πρὸς δὲ τούτοις ἐὰν καὶ αὐτοὶ διακείμενοί πῶς τυγχάνωσιν. Ross's text.

[27] *Rhetoric* II, 1378 a 19–26. ἔστι δὲ τὰ πάθη δι' ὅσα μεταβάλλοντες διαφέρουσι πρὸς τὰς κρίσεις οἷς ἕπεται λύπη καὶ ἡδονή, οἷον ὀργὴ ἔλεος φόβος καὶ ὅσα ἄλλα τοιαῦτα, καὶ τὰ τούτοις ἐναντία. δεῖ δὲ διαιρεῖν περὶ ἕκαστον εἰς τρία, λέγω δ' οἷον περὶ ὀργῆς πῶς τε διακείμενοι ὀργίλοι εἰσί, καὶ τίσιν εἰώθασιν ὀργίζεσθαι, καὶ ἐπὶ ποίοις· εἰ γὰρ τὸ μὲν ἓν ἢ τὰ δύο ἔχοιμεν τούτων, ἅπαντα δὲ μή, ἀδύνατον ἂν εἴη τὴν ὀργὴν ἐμποιεῖν. Ross's text.

manual for demagogues. One might suppose that Aristotle would defend himself by referring to the rather mundane doctrine of the *Nicomachean Ethics* which honours an angry man in these words: "The man who is angry at the right things and with the right people, and, further, as he ought, when he ought, and as long as he ought, is praised."[28] But, on the other hand, the element of calculation urged upon the orator so that he can successfully play upon the emotions of his hearers, as in the case of anger, seems to be open to question. The spirit of calculation is best seen in the analysis of how to arouse the emotion under the "three heads," without a complete grasp of which a speaker will be powerless "to arouse anger in any one." Aristotle, be it noted, does not ask the question here whether it is right or justifiable for the speaker to arouse anger or whether the indulgence in anger is a meritorious action. Without such questions, the advice suggested could well be used by the most unscrupulous rabble-rouser in order to defend himself. It might be added that the underlying ethical position of this quotation cannot be acceptable either to Platonic or Christian feeling, and we can recall as well that the Christian position may even question the validity of "righteous indignation," particularly if an individual is obviously luxuriating in it.

Two more quotations, taken almost at random, should suffice to bring our discussion of the element of deception, amoralism, immoralism—call it what you will—in Aristotelian rhetorical theory. The first occurs in a discussion of the use of maxims, or gnomic sayings, "To declare a thing to be universally true when it is not is most appropriate when working up feelings of horror and indignation in our hearers; especially by way of preface, or after the facts have been proven. Even hackneyed and commonplace maxims are to be used, if they suit one's purpose: just because they are commonplace, everyone seems to agree with them, and therefore they are taken for truth."[29] All we need note is the

[28] *Nicomachean Ethics* IV, 1125 b 31–32. ὁ μὲν οὖν ἐφ᾽ οἷς δεῖ καὶ οἷς δεῖ ὀργιζόμενος, ἔτι δὲ καὶ ὡς δεῖ καὶ ὅτε καὶ ὅσον χρόνον, ἐπαινεῖται. Bywater's text.

[29] *Rhetoric* II, 1395 a 8–12. καθόλου δὲ μὴ ὄντος καθόλου εἰπεῖν μάλιστα ἁρμόττει ἐν σχετλιασμῷ καὶ δεινώσει, καὶ ἐν τούτοις ἢ ἀρχόμενον ἢ ἀποδείξαντα. χρῆσθαι δὲ δεῖ καὶ ταῖς τεθρυλημέναις καὶ κοιναῖς γνώμαις, ἐὰν ὦσι χρήσιμοι· διὰ γὰρ τὸ εἶναι κοιναί, ὡς ὁμολογούντων πάντων, ὀρθῶς ἔχειν δοκοῦσιν. Ross's text.

approval of Aristotle given to a bare-faced prevarication, if only it achieves the desired effect among the hearers. We cannot refrain from mentioning one of the illustrations offered, which even for a fourth-century Greek is rather grisly. "Or, if he (*i.e.*, the orator) is urging people to destroy the innocent children of their enemies, (*sc.*, he may quote), 'Fool, who slayeth the father and leaveth his sons to avenge him.' "[30] Perhaps we may be wrong to expect moral elevation in a practical handbook on rhetoric, but it does not seem unreasonable to ask that Aristotle exhibit a little more ethical sensitivity than he does in this passage.

Our second quotation is taken from the treatment of the spurious or apparent enthymeme. "Among the lines of argument that form the Spurious Enthymeme the first is that which arises from the particular words employed. One variety of this is when—as in dialectic, without having gone through any reasoning process, we make a final statement as if it were the conclusion of such a process, 'Therefore so-and-so is not true,' 'Therefore also so-and-so must be true'—so too in rhetoric, a compact and anti-thetical utterance passes for an enthymeme, such language being the proper province of enthymeme, so that it is seemingly the form of wording here that causes the illusion mentioned. In order to produce the effect of genuine reasoning by our form of wording it is useful to summarize the results of a number of previous reasonings: as 'some he saved—others he avenged—the Greeks he freed.' Each of these statements has been previously proved from other facts; but the mere collocation of them gives the impression of establishing some fresh conclusion."[31] One

---

[30] *Rhetoric* II, 1395 a 17–18. καὶ ἐπὶ τὸ ἀναιρεῖν τῶν ἐχθρῶν τὰ τέκνα κα μηδὲν ἀδικοῦντα

νήπιος ὃς πατέρα κτείνας παῖδας καταλείπει. Ross's text. Robert's translation. The line of poetry is from the *Cypria*, Fragment 22. Cf. Kinkel, *Epicorum Graecorum Fragmenta* (Leipzig, Teubner, 1877).

[31] *Rhetoric* II, 1401 a 1–13. τόποι δ' εἰσὶ τῶν φαινομένων ἐνθυμημάτων εἷς μὲν ὁ παρὰ τὴν λέξιν, καὶ τούτου ἓν μὲν μέρος, ὥσπερ ἐν τοῖς διαλεκτικοῖς, τὸ μὴ συλλογισάμενον συμπερασματικῶς τὸ τελευταῖον εἰπεῖν, "οὐκ ἄρα τὸ καὶ τό, ἀνάγκη ἄρα τὸ καὶ τό", ἐν τοῖς ἐνθυμήμασι τὸ συνεστραμμένως καὶ ἀντικειμένως εἰπεῖν φαίνεται ἐνθύμημα (ἡ γὰρ τοιαύτη λέξις χώρα ἐστὶν ἐνθυμήματος)· καὶ ἔοικε τὸ τοιοῦτον εἶναι παρὰ τὰ σχῆμα τῆς λέξεως. ἔστι δὲ εἰς τὸ τῇ λέξει συλλογιστικῶς λέγειν χρήσιμον τὸ συλλογισμῶν πολλῶν κεφάλαια λέγειν, ὅτι τοὺς μὲν ἔσωσε, τοῖς δ' ἑτέροις ἐτιμώρησε, τοὺς δ' Ἕλληνας ἠλευθέρωσε· ἕκαστον μὲν γὰρ τούτων ἐξ ἄλλων ἀπεδείχθη, συντεθέντων δὲ φαίνεται καὶ ἐκ τούτων τι γίγνεσθαι. Ross's text. The quotation in 10–11 is from Isocrates, *Evagoras*, 65–9.

need only call attention to the words which emphasize the production of "seeming" and appearance.

There remains but to consider briefly the eleventh chapter of *Rhetoric* I, in which Aristotle discusses the topic of pleasure. It is not necessary to examine it in detail save to note how broadly important pleasure seems to be in his eyes in the context of rhetoric. Take his opening definition: "We may lay it down that Pleasure is a movement, a movement by which the soul as a whole is consciously brought into its normal state of being; and that Pain is the opposite."[32] This definition is bound to be somewhat surprising in the light of the assertion of the *Nicomachean Ethics* that pleasure is an activity, and hence not a "movement."[33] In any event, this eleventh chapter attempts to establish an equivalence between pleasure and "what is natural" and proceeds to list in conventional terms almost everything which can in any way be regarded as pleasurable. The range is imposing as it covers the areas of the intellect, the body, and the emotions. Anger is called pleasant, for example, as is revenge. Victory also is designated as a pleasure, and should even be so regarded in games like "knucklebones, ball, dice, and draughts."[34] The purport of it all is that pleasure must be regarded as an important value or sanction for value by the rhetorician as he practices his craft of producing persuasion.

It is our hope that we have been able to delineate the *Rhetoric* as basically ambivalent, which opens with an attempt to fix philosophical grounds for the theory about to be offered but which as it moves forward becomes detached from its philosophical base and is transformed into a technology of persuasion. We hope also to have shown in this latter aspect that the treatise gives frequent evidence of amoralism or even on occasion immoralism when, as Cicero might have put it, the orator is advised to throw dishonest "dust in the eyes of the jury." And we should like to repeat our contention that Aristotle might not have been guilty of this amoralism, had he been able to be guided by a firm theory of value of his own construction.

---

[32] *Rhetoric* I, 1369 b 33–35. Ὑποκείσθω δὴ ἡμῖν εἶναι τὴν ἡδονὴν κίνησίν τινα τῆς ψυχῆς καὶ κατάστασιν ἀθρόαν καὶ αἰσθητὴν εἰς τὴν ὑπάρχουσαν φύσιν, λύπην δὲ τοὐναντίον. Ross's text.

[33] Cf. above, Chapter VII, pp. 299–301.

[34] *Rhetoric* I, 1371 a 2–3. ἀστραγαλίσεις καὶ σφαιρίσεις καὶ κυβείας καὶ πεττείας. Ross's text.

PART II

THE *POETICS*

In analyzing the evidence of the *Poetics* which has a bearing upon our study of the question of value in Aristotle's thought, we shall omit to mention those passages which have to do with literary form or technique. Rather we shall attempt to concentrate, as we should, on the points where the phenomena of evaluation in some form or another are apparent. Perhaps our position may be clearer if it is viewed in the light of the doctrine that a work of art is an amalgam, or organic compound, of matter, form, and content. According to the theory, these three components are not capable of separate existence. They are analytically distinct, but at the same time are inextricably bound up with one another. We might in fact express the interrelation by saying that the artist imposes form on his raw material, the matter, in such a way that content, or meaning, or significance emerges. In general, one might say that much in Aristotle's *Poetics* has to do exclusively with matter and form, and in these areas, again generally speaking, the questions of value with which we are primarily concerned do not naturally emerge. However, when Aristotle does address himself to the meaning or significance or content of a work of art, whether it be epic or tragedy, or comedy and so on, we shall be able to discern the ways in which Aristotle deals with the problem of evaluation. It will be our attempt to show that six different sanctions for value are invoked in the *Poetics*, *viz.*, the conception of Nature, conventional Greek value thinking, pleasure, reason, intuitive value reaction, and the man of practical wisdom, the *phronimos*. As will be readily recognized, we are meeting again for the most part conceptions we have found operative virtually throughout the Aristotelian corpus. Let us now see how they function in the *Poetics*.

A. NATURE

As Aristotle begins to develop his theory of poetry as imitation, we see him immediately appealing to his familiar conception of Nature: "It is clear that the general origin of poetry was due to two causes, each of them part of [human] nature. Imitation is natural to man from childhood, one of his advantages over the lower animals being this, that he is the most imitative creature in the world, and learns at first by imitation. And it is also natural for all to delight in works of imitation."[35] If we take the term "imitation" to denote basically the relation between the artist and the "material" in all its aspects with which he works, and if we recognize that Aristotle holds imitation theoretically to be fundamental not only with regard to the origin of poetry but also for the artistic production of poetry, imitation or, if you will, "successful" imitation is going to be a source of worth or value for the poetic work thus produced.[36] Clearly, then, by arguing that "imitation" is grounded in Nature, φύσις, Aristotle is strengthening his claim for the validity of the theory which he is advancing. It should also be noted that in this quotation Aristotle appeals again to Nature to explain the delight or pleasure which all men experience when coming in contact with works of imitation.[37]

[35] *Poetics*, 1448 b 4–9. ᾿Εοίκασι δὲ γεννῆσαι μὲν ὅλως τὴν ποιητικὴν αἰτίαι δύο τινὲς καὶ αὗται φυσικαί· τό τε γὰρ μιμεῖσθαι σύμφυτον τοῖς ἀνθρώποις ἐκ παίδων ἐστὶ καὶ τούτῳ διαφέρουσι τῶν ἄλλων ζῴων ὅτι μιμητικώτατόν ἐστι καὶ τὰς μαθήσεις ποιεῖται διὰ μιμήσεως τὰς πρώτας καὶ τὸ χαίρειν τοῖς μιμήμασι πάντας. Bywater's text. The reader is advised to consult the comments on the passages quoted of G. F. Else, *Aristotle's Poetics: The Argument* (Cambridge, Harvard University Press, 1957). Else is by no means convincing in all of his interpretations, but nonetheless no one can fail to be stimulated by them. Note that I have bracketed "human" in Bywater's version since the original does not warrant its insertion.

[36] It should be pointed out that Aristotle in the fourth chapter of the *Poetics* invites us to believe that he is submitting a history of the origin and development of poetry. It is, of course, not strictly the case, for the assertion that poetry begins in imitation, is not history but rather speculation. In this respect the chapter resembles in some degree the opening section of *Metaphysics* A. In any event, Aristotle gives more of the appearance of history by saying that Homer occupies a peculiar position in that tragedy stems from the *Iliad* and *Odyssey*, whereas comedy derives from his *Margites*. (How careful an historian are we to suppose Aristotle to be when he ascribes the *Margites* to Homer?) But the point we wish to make is that he is really approaching poetry from the point of view of a biologist. It has an origin in imitation, it develops, it breaks up into several species, and each species has its own development. So far as tragedy is concerned, in Aristotle's view, it has reached its completion, its entelechy, in the tragic poets of the fifth century. So he can write: "It was in fact only after a long series of changes that the movement of Tragedy stopped on its attaining to its natural form." *Poetics*, 1449 a 14–15. καὶ πολλὰς μεταβολὰς μεταβαλοῦσα ἡ τραγῳδία ἐπαύσατο, ἐπεὶ ἔσχε τὴν αὑτῆς φύσιν. Bywater's text.

[37] For the argument as to whether "pleasure" is the second "cause" referred to in our quotation, cf. the discussion of Else, *op. cit., ad loc.*

There are two other passages out of several which we can well have before us as illustrations of the way in which Nature acts decisively in Aristotle's poetic theory. The first occurs when he is discussing the development of drama and is pointing to the adoption of the iambic metre. "As soon, however, as a spoken part came in, nature herself found the appropriate metre."[38] The other illustration is found in the analysis of the so-called "six parts" of a tragedy, Plot, Character, Diction, Thought, Spectacle, and Melody, if we may use Bywater's English terms. In speaking of actions of agents, Aristotle observes: "There are in the natural order of things, therefore, two causes, Thought and Character, of their actions, and consequently of their success or failure in their lives."[39] For the moment, we are not concerned with the extreme importance which Aristotle placed upon "action," $\pi\varrho\tilde{a}\xi\iota\varsigma$, as, for example, when he says "Tragedy is essentially an imitation not of persons but of action and of life, of happiness and misery. All human happiness or misery takes the form of action; the end for which we live is a certain kind of activity, not a quality."[40] This, as we know, is an elaboration of the famous definition of tragedy, which we shall examine later. Our present purpose is rather to note how Nature acts as a guarantor not only for the significance of action, but also for thought and character as "causes" for action.[41] So much, then, for our consideration of Nature as it functions in the analysis offered by the *Poetics*.

---

[38] *Poetics*, 1449 a 23–24. λέξεως δὲ γενομένης αὐτὴ ἡ φύσις τὸ οἰκεῖον μέτρον εὗρε. Bywater's text.

[39] *Poetics*, 1450 1–3. a πέφυκεν αἴτια δύο τῶν πράξεων εἶναι, διάνοιαν καὶ ἦθος, καὶ κατὰ ταύτας καὶ τυγχάνουσι καὶ ἀποτυγχάνουσι πάντες. Bywater's text.

[40] *Poetics*, 1450 a 16–19. ἡ γὰρ τραγῳδία μίμησίς ἐστιν οὐκ ἀνθρώπων ἀλλὰ πράξεως καὶ βίου καὶ εὐδαιμονίας ** καὶ ἡ κακοδαιμονία ἐν πράξει ἐστίν, οὐ ποιότης. Bywater's text. He appears to be correct in supplying εὐδαιμονία in his translation for the space indicated by the asterisks. If we are correct in assuming that in Aristotle's thought there is a connection between his concern for πρᾶξις in the *Poetics* and his conceptions of πρᾶξις and ἐνέργεια in the *Nicomachean Ethics* and the *Metaphysics*, we can see in this passage which asserts that happiness and misery are "in action," ἐν πράξει, the same problem involved in the notion of a "bad" actuality or activity. Cf. our discussions above, Chapter VI, pp. 191–196 and Chapter VII, pp. 308–310.

[41] Cf. also, as further illustrations *Poetics*, 1451 a 22–24 and 1460 a 2–5.

B. THE VALUES OF CONVENTION

The second chapter of the *Poetics* illustrates, perhaps better than any other passage, the way in which Aristotle relies on conventional thinking in making his value judgements. Let us, therefore, examine the relevant portions of the chapter. "The objects the imitator represents are actions, with agents who are necessarily either good men or bad—the diversities of human character being nearly always derivative from this primary distinction, since the line between virtue and vice is one dividing the whole of mankind. It follows, therefore, that the agents represented must be either above our own level of goodness, or beneath it, or just such as we are."[42] After pointing out that Polygnotus in his painting portrays men "better" than we are, Pauson worse, and Dionysius men such as we are, and after noting that the same situation obtains in other arts, Aristotle continues: "Homer's personages, for instance, are better than we are; Cleophon's are on our own level; and those of Hegemon of Thasos, the first writer of parodies, and Nicochares, the author of the *Diliad*, are beneath it. . . . This difference it is that distinguishes Tragedy and Comedy also; the one would make its personages worse, and the other better than the men of the present day."[43] Clearly Aristotle is appealing to a conventional value response when he asserts that people in action are either good or bad, or that "virtue and vice divide the whole of mankind." It is in the same spirit that he classifies the objects of imitation as either "better" than, "worse" than, or the "same" as we are. Tragedy deals with the "better" and comedy with the "worse." Obviously no criterion is offered other than that everyone, it is assumed, will be in agreement with the value judgements offered.[44]

---

[42] *Poetics*, 1448 a 1–5. Ἐπεὶ δὲ μιμοῦνται οἱ μιμούμενοι πράττοντας, ἀνάγκη δὲ τούτους ἢ σπουδαίους ἢ φαύλους εἶναι (τὰ γὰρ ἤθη σχεδὸν ἀεὶ τούτοις ἀκολουθεῖ μόνοις, κακίᾳ γὰρ καὶ ἀρετῇ τὰ ἤθη διαφέρουσι πάντες), ἤτοι βελτίονας ἢ καθ᾽ ἡμᾶς ἢ χείρονας ἢ καὶ τοιούτους. Bywater's text.

[43] *Poetics*, 1448 a 11–18 (omitting 14–16). οἷον Ὅμηρος μὲν βελτίους, Κλεοφῶν δὲ ὁμοίους, Ἡγήμων δὲ ὁ Θάσιος <ὁ> τὰς παρῳδίας ποιήσας πρῶτος καὶ Νικοχάρης ὁ τὴν Δειλιάδα χείρους. . . . ἐν ταύτῃ δὲ τῇ διαφορᾷ καὶ ἡ τραγῳδία πρὸς τὴν κωμῳδίαν διέστηκεν· ἡ μὲν γὰρ χείρους ἡ δὲ βελτίους μιμεῖσθαι βούλεται τῶν νῦν. Bywater's text.

[44] The following passages may be cited as illustrating a similar reliance upon the values of convention: *Poetics*, 1448 a 25–27 [Sophocles and Homer both imitate good men, σπουδαίους]; 1448 b 24–26 [the more serious poets imitate

Another passage where apparently convention is invoked occurs when Aristotle observes: "Again: to be beautiful, a living creature, and every whole made up of parts, must not only present a certain order in its arrangement of parts, but also be of a certain definite magnitude. Beauty is a matter of size and order."[45] We said that this remark is apparently conventional since it seems to presuppose immediate agreement on the part of any reader of this portion of the *Poetics*. On the other hand, it must be said that Aristotle may have expected one to recall the passage in the *Politics* where he also discussed the subject of size and order.[46] There, however, it is interesting to remember his remark to the effect that the introduction of order was attributed to the work of a "divine power."

Another case in point can be found in Aristotle's definition of the tragic hero as "a man not preeminently virtuous and just, whose misfortune, however, is brought upon him not by vice and depravity but by some error of judgement, of the number of those in the enjoyment of great reputation and prosperity."[47] He then adds that the hero in the tragedy must pass from a state of happiness to misery, "and the cause of it must lie not in any depravity, but in some great error on his part; the man himself being either such as we have described, or better, not worse, than that."[48] Here again we find a congeries of unkeyed value terms, *viz.*, virtuous, just, vice, depravity, reputation, prosperity, happiness, misery, better, and worse. And again we appear to have no other alternative than to conclude that Aristotle depends for his meaning upon the general acceptance of some kind of conventional scheme of values.

---

noble actions, while the meaner imitate the ignoble]; 1449 b 9–10 [epic like tragedy deals with σπουδαῖα]; 1449 b 17–18 ["Hence a judge of good and bad in Tragedy is a judge of that in epic poetry also." διόπερ ὅστις περὶ τραγῳδίας οἶδε σπουδαίας καὶ φαύλης, οἶδε καὶ περὶ ἐπῶν. Bywater's text.

[45] *Poetics*, 1450 b 34–37. ἔτι δ' ἐπεὶ τὸ καλὸν καὶ ζῷον καὶ ἅπαν πρᾶγμα ὃ συνέστηκεν ἐκ τινῶν οὐ μόνον ταῦτα τεταγμένα δεῖ ἔχειν ἀλλὰ καὶ μέγεθος ὑπάρχειν μὴ τὸ τυχόν· τὸ γὰρ καλὸν ἐν μεγέθει καὶ τάξει ἐστίν. Bywater's text.

[46] *Politics*, 1326 a 29–40. Cf. above, Chapter VII, pp. 332–333 and note 177.

[47] *Poetics*, 1453 a 7–10. ἔστι δὲ τοιοῦτος ὁ μήτε ἀρετῇ διαφέρων καὶ δικαιοσύνῃ μήτε διὰ κακίαν καὶ μοχθηρίαν μεταβάλλων εἰς τὴν δυστυχίαν ἀλλὰ δι' ἁμαρτίαν τινὰ τῶν ἐν μεγάλῃ δόξῃ ὄντων καὶ εὐτυχίᾳ. Bywater's text. I have adhered to the traditional view of taking ἁμαρτία to mean "error," despite the argument of Else, *op. cit.*, pp. 378–385.

[48] *Poetics*, 1453 a 15–17. μὴ διὰ μοχθηρίαν ἀλλὰ δι' ἁμαρτίαν μεγάλην ἢ οἵου εἴρηται ἢ βελτίονος μᾶλλον ἢ χείρονος. Bywater's text.

Another almost perfect piece of evidence for our argument can be found in the opening of the fifteenth chapter of the *Poetics* where Aristotle addresses himself to the topic of character. "In the Characters there are four points to aim at. First and foremost, that they shall be good. There will be an element of character in the play, if (as has been observed) what a personage says or does reveals a certain moral purpose; and a good element of character, if the purpose so revealed is good. Such goodness is possible in every type of personage, even in a woman or a slave, though the one is perhaps an inferior, and the other a wholly worthless being. The second point is to make them appropriate. The Character before us may be, say, manly. But it is not appropriate in a female Character to be manly or clever. The third is to make them like the reality, which is not the same as their being good and appropriate, in our sense of the term. The fourth is to make them consistent and the same throughout."[49] At first sight, it seems as though we might be introduced into something more than conventionalism when we are told that the goodness of a character is related to moral purpose. We might even be a little hopeful as Aristotle remarks that goodness is possible even in a woman or a slave, but the standard conventional position is quickly reasserted when he adds that a woman is inferior and a slave is absolutely worthless. And when he comes to deal with the notion of appropriateness, we find that it is not fitting for a woman to be "manly" or "clever." One might wonder whether the word for "manly" might not possibly connote the virtue of courage, but in any case, so far as cleverness is concerned, it might be interesting for us to ask what would have been Aspasia's reaction if it had been possible for her to have read this quotation.[50]

[49] *Poetics*, 1454 a 16–26. Περὶ δὲ τὰ ἤθη τέτταρά ἐστιν ὧν δεῖ στοχάζεσθαι, ἓν μὲν καὶ πρῶτον, ὅπως χρηστὰ ᾖ. ἕξει δὲ ἦθος μὲν ἐὰν ὥσπερ ἐλέχθη ποιῇ φανερὸν ὁ λόγος ἢ ἡ πρᾶξις προαίρεσίν τινα [ἥ], χρηστὸν δὲ ἐὰν χρηστήν. ἔστιν δὲ ἐν ἑκάστῳ γένει· καὶ γὰρ γυνή ἐστιν χρηστὴ καὶ δοῦλος, καίτοι γε ἴσως τούτων τὸ μὲν χεῖρον, τὸ δὲ ὅλως φαῦλόν ἐστιν. δεύτερον δὲ τὸ ἁρμόττοντα· ἔστιν γὰρ ἀνδρεῖον μὲν τὸ ἦθος, ἀλλ᾽ οὐχ ἁρμόττον γυναικείῳ τὸ ἀνδρείαν ἢ δεινὴν εἶναι. τρίτον δὲ τὸ ὅμοιον. τοῦτο γὰρ ἕτερον τοῦ χρηστὸν τὸ ἦθος καὶ ἁρμόττον ποιῆσαι ὥσπερ εἴρηται. τέταρτον δὲ τὸ ὁμαλόν. Bywater's text.

[50] It might be added that Aristotle supports his analysis of character in tragedy by appealing to his so-called law of the necessary and the probable. Cf. *Poetics*, 1454 a 33–36. We shall examine this "law" briefly below.

Among other passages which show Aristotle's dependence upon convention, there are two more which merit our attention. The first occurs likewise in his discussion of character. "As Tragedy is an imitation of personages better than the ordinary man, we in our way should follow the example of good portrait-painters, who reproduce the distinctive features of a man, and at the same time, without losing the likeness, make him handsomer than he is. The poet in like manner, in portraying men quick or slow to anger, or with similar infirmities of character, must know how to represent them as such, and at the same time as good men, as Agathon and Homer have represented Achilles."[51] It is scarcely necessary to point out that the terms such as "better", "handsomer," and "good" have no further support than the meanings ordinarily attached to them by the conventional mind.

Our other passage occurs towards the close of the *Poetics*. "As for the question whether something said or done in a poem is morally right or not, in dealing with that one should consider not only the intrinsic quality of the actual word or deed, but also the person who says or does it, the person to whom he says or does it, the time, the means, and the motive of the agent—whether he does it to attain a greater good, or to avoid a greater evil."[52] One, of course, is immediately reminded of similar passages in the *Nicomachean Ethics*, in which Aristotle demands that in any moral decision, full account must be taken of the individuals involved as well as of the circumstances in all their ramifications. But in our present quotation, as is the case so often

---

[51] *Poetics*, 1454 b 8–15. ἐπεὶ δὲ μίμησίς ἐστιν ἡ τραγῳδία βελτιόνων, ἡμᾶς δεῖ μιμεῖσθαι τοὺς ἀγαθοὺς εἰκονογράφους· καὶ γὰρ ἐκεῖνοι ἀποδιδόντες τὴν ἰδίαν μορφὴν ὁμοίους ποιοῦντες καλλίους γράφουσιν· οὕτω καὶ τὸν ποιητὴν μιμούμενον καὶ ὀργίλους καὶ ῥαθύμους καὶ τἄλλα τὰ τοιαῦτα ἔχοντας ἐπὶ τῶν ἠθῶν τοιούτους ὄντας ἐπιεικεῖς ποιεῖν [παράδειγμα σκληρότητος], οἷον τὸν Ἀχιλλέα Ἀγάθων καὶ Ὅμηρος. Bywater's text. The Greek text is full of difficulties, but since they do not effect the essential point we are trying to make concerning conventionalism, I have chosen to follow the text and rendering of Bywater. For a discussion of the textual problems, cf. Else, *op. cit.*, pp. 475–482. Incidentally, Else translates the bracketed words, omitted in Bywater's version, as "example of stubbornness."

[52] *Poetics*, 1461 a 4–9. περὶ δὲ τοῦ καλῶς ἢ μὴ καλῶς ἢ εἴρηταί τινι ἢ πέπρακται, οὐ μόνον σκεπτέον εἰς αὐτὸ τὸ πεπραγμένον ἢ εἰρημένον βλέποντα εἰ σπουδαῖον ἢ φαῦλον, ἀλλὰ καὶ εἰς τὸν πράττοντα ἢ λέγοντα πρὸς ὅν ἢ ὅτε ἢ ὅτῳ ἢ οὗ ἕνεκεν, οἷον ἢ μείζονος ἀγαθοῦ, ἵνα γένηται, ⟨ἢ⟩ μείζονος κακοῦ, ἵνα ἀπογένηται. Bywater's text.

in the *Nicomachean Ethics*,[53] Aristotle does not indicate that he has any particular value criterion or criteria in mind, and so again we are compelled to suppose here that "morally right" and "a greater good" are nothing other than what they are generally agreed to be. With this passage, then, we can conclude our consideration of the way in which the "values of convention" function in the *Poetics*.[54]

C. PLEASURE

Very early in the treatise, as we have already seen, after having established the notion that imitation is "natural," Aristotle inserts pleasure as a value when he says that "it is also natural for all to delight in works of imitation."[55] The remark which immediately follows clarifies his position with respect to this value. "Though the objects themselves may be painful to see, we delight to view the most realistic representations of them in art, the forms for example of the lowest animals and of dead bodies. The explanation is to be found in a further fact: to be learning something is the greatest of pleasures not only to the philosopher but also to the rest of mankind, however small their capacity for it."[56] The first point worth noting is the way in which this passage exhibits the characteristic method of Aristotle as an empiricist. And secondly, the quotation has implicitly within it the doctrine that the purpose of art is to delight and to teach. But quite apart from these considerations, we do find explicit evidence of the extent to which Aristotle considers pleasure to be absolutely central as a value in his analysis of an individual's experience when he comes in contact with a work of art.[57]

[53] Cf. above, Chapter VII, pp. 288–295.

[54] For further evidence on the question of the influence of conventional value thinking, the reader is invited to examine the twenty-sixth chapter of the *Poetics*, where Aristotle gives his answer to the question: Which is better *(βελτίων)*, Tragedy or Epic?

[55] Cf. above, Chapter VIII, pp. 352–353.

[56] *Poetics*, 1448 b 10–15. ἃ γὰρ αὐτὰ λυπηρῶς ὁρῶμεν, τούτων τὰς εἰκόνας τὰς μάλιστα ἠκριβωμένας χαίρομεν θεωροῦντες, οἷον θηρίων τε μορφάς τῶν ἀτιμο-τάτων καὶ νεκρῶν. αἴτιον δὲ καὶ τοῦτο, ὅτι μανθάνειν οὐ μόνον τοῖς φιλοσόφοις ἥδιστον ἀλλὰ καὶ τοῖς ἄλλοις ὁμοίως, ἀλλ᾽ ἐπὶ βραχὺ κοινωνοῦσιν αὐτοῦ. Bywater's text.

[57] Other passages which can be cited in support of this view are the following: *Poetics*, 1449 a 32–37 [Comedy as involving the ridiculous does not produce

By far the most important doctrine of the *Poetics* with respect
to pleasure is expressed in the following quotation: "Not every
kind of pleasure should be required of a tragedy, but only its
own proper pleasure. The tragic pleasure is that of pity and fear,
and the poet has to produce it by a work of imitation."[58] And
there is the further relevant passage in which Aristotle describes
the ways in which the epic is like tragedy. "The construction
of its stories should clearly be like that in a drama; they should
be based on a single action, one that is a complete whole in itself,
with a beginning, middle, and end, so as to enable the work to
produce its own proper pleasure with all the organic unity of a
living creature."[59] Aristotle is thus asserting that each poetic
form can and, indeed, must produce its own proper pleasure,
and, we may assume, he would be willing to have this principle
generalized so that it would apply as well in other artistic media.
Tragedy must produce a pleasure peculiarly its own, as must epic
and comedy. So far as one may conjecture, this pleasure may be
viewed in two ways. First, in the case of works of art, the pleasure
can be seen as a kind of a completion of the function of the work.
In this respect, the doctrine of the *Poetics* resembles that of the
tenth book of the *Nicomachean Ethics*, where pleasure is presented
as an inevitable concomitant, a "completion" of a virtuous
activity. And secondly, it does seem at times as though Aristotle
is looking at pleasure as in some sense the ultimate value in the
activity of art. In other words, as in the *Nicomachean Ethics*,
there is some kind of final ambiguity, or perhaps lack of clarity,
in his attitude towards pleasure in the *Poetics*.

As a conclusion to our analysis of this subject, we should be

---

pain]; 1450 b 16 [melody is the greatest of the producers of pleasure]; 1451 b 25–
26 [known stories, though known only to a few, are a delight to every one];
1453 a 30–36 [the double plot of the *Odyssey*, with opposite outcomes for the
good and the evil; such plots are designed to please the spectators, but it is the
pleasure of comedy and not of tragedy]; 1460 a 17–18 [the marvelous is a source
of pleasure, explaining why we elaborate our stories in order to produce pleasure].

[58] *Poetics*, 1453 b 10–13. οὐ γὰρ πᾶσαν δεῖ ζητεῖν ἡδονὴν ἀπὸ τραγῳδίας ἀλλὰ
τὴν οἰκείαν. ἐπεὶ δὲ τὴν ἀπὸ ἐλέου καὶ φόβου διὰ μιμήσεως δεῖ ἡδονὴν παρα-
σκευάζειν τὸν ποιητήν. Bywater's text.

[59] *Poetics*, 1459 a 18–21. ὅτι δεῖ τοὺς μύθους καθάπερ ἐν ταῖς τραγῳδίαις
συνιστάναι δραματικοὺς καὶ περὶ μίαν πρᾶξιν ὅλην καὶ τελείαν ἔχουσαν ἀρχὴν
καὶ μέσα καὶ τέλος, ἵν' ὥσπερ ζῷον ἓν ὅλον ποιῇ τὴν οἰκείαν ἡδονήν, δῆλον.
Bywater's text.

aware of the way in which Aristotle exploits pleasure as a value
in his argument to demonstrate the superiority of Tragedy over
the Epic. He offers four points to support his position. First:
"Tragedy has everything that the Epic has (even the epic metre
being admissible), together with a not inconsiderable addition
in the shape of the Music (a very real fact in the pleasure of the
drama) and the Spectacle."[60] The second argument is to the
effect that Tragedy possesses clarity or "reality" even when read
as well as when acted. And third: "The tragic imitation requires
less space for the attainment of its end; which is a great advantage,
since the more concentrated effect is more pleasurable than one
with a large admixture of time to dilute it—consider the *Oedipus*
of Sophocles, for instance, and the effect of expanding it into the
number of lines of the *Iliad*."[61] The final argument urges the
superiority of Tragedy on the ground that the Epic perforce
must be less unified. The important point for us is the decisive
rôle assigned to pleasure in the first and third arguments, and as
we study them, we are tempted, at least in this context, to take
more seriously than ever the extent and the depth of Aristotle's
hedonism. Our contention is surely strengthened by the final
summary statement: "If, then, Tragedy is superior in these
respects, and also, besides these, in its poetic effect (since the two
forms of poetry should give us, not any or every pleasure, but
the very special kind we have mentioned), it is clear that, as
attaining the poetic effect better than the Epic, it will be the
higher form of art."[62] Here Aristotle appears virtually to identify
"poetic effect" (which is Bywater's reasonable rendering for τῷ

---

[60] *Poetics*, 1462 a 14–17. ἔπειτα διότι πάντ' ἔχει ὅσαπερ ἡ ἐποποιία (καὶ γὰρ
τῷ μέτρῳ ἔξεστι χρῆσθαι), καὶ ἔτι οὐ μικρὸν μέρος τὴν μουσικὴν καὶ τὰς ὄψεις,
δι' ἧς αἱ ἡδοναὶ συνίστανται ἐναργέστατα. Bywater's text. His rendering might
be criticized in that the force of the Greek indicates that both music and spectacle
are regarded as sources of "pleasure,"—and here Bywater might well have
reproduced the plural of the original, ἡδοναί.

[61] *Poetics*, 1462 a 18–b 3. ἔτι τὸ ἐν ἐλάττονι μήκει τὸ τέλος τῆς μιμήσεως
εἶναι (τὸ γὰρ ἀθροώτερον ἥδιον ἢ πολλῷ κεκραμένον τῷ χρόνῳ, λέγω δ' οἷον
εἴ τις τὸν Οἰδίπουν θείη τὸν Σοφοκλέους ἐν ἔπεσιν ὅσοις ἢ Ἰλιάς). Bywater's
text.

[62] *Poetics*, 1462 b 12–15. εἰ οὖν τούτοις τε διαφέρει πᾶσιν καὶ ἔτι τῷ τῆς
τέχνης ἔργῳ (δεῖ γὰρ οὐ τὴν τυχοῦσαν ἡδονὴν ποιεῖν αὐτὰς ἀλλὰ τὴν εἰρημένην),
φανερὸν ὅτι κρείττων ἂν εἴη μᾶλλον τοῦ τέλους τυγχάνουσα τῆς ἐποποιίας.
Bywater's text.

τῆς τέχνης ἔργῳ) with the peculiar pleasure produced by the form of the poetry, and it is on the basis of "poetic effect" and its pleasure that the final accolade is given to Tragedy.

D. REASON

To appraise accurately the way in which reason functions as a sanction for value in the *Poetics* poses a difficult problem, since for the most part we must rely upon inference rather than explicit statement. By way of introduction, we may examine briefly the so-called "law of the necessary and the probable." As is well known, Aristotle frequently relies upon this law to establish the value, or worth, or literary merit, of a work or a portion thereof. So far as one can tell, the law is ultimately based upon reason or some kind of ratiocinative process and hence can be properly considered here. For example, when Aristotle is discussing the proper length for a dramatic story or plot, he appeals to the law of the necessary and the probable in these words: "As a rough general formula, 'a length which allows of the hero passing by a series of probable or necessary stages from misfortune to happiness, or from happiness to misfortune,' may suffice as a limit for the magnitude of the story."[63] Or again, when praising the unity of the *Odyssey*, he applauds the poet for not having included certain episodes which "had no necessary or probable connexion with one another."[64] Or, for another example, Aristotle says this with respect to a poet's activity, "From what we have said it will be seen that the poet's function is to describe, not the thing that has happened, but a kind of thing that might happen, *i.e.*, what is possible as being probable or necessary."[65] And finally, we have his condemnation of episodic plots expressed in this way: "Of simple Plots and actions, the

---

[63] *Poetics*, 1451 a 11–15. ὡς δὲ ἁπλῶς διορίσαντας εἰπεῖν, ἐν ὅσῳ μεγέθει κατὰ τὸ εἰκὸς ἢ τὸ ἀναγκαῖον ἐφεξῆς γιγνομένων συμβαίνει εἰς εὐτυχίαν ἐκ δυστυχίας ἢ ἐξ εὐτυχίας εἰς δυστυχίαν μεταβάλλειν, ἱκανὸς ὅρος ἐστὶν τοῦ μεγέθους. Bywater's text.

[64] *Poetics*, 1451 a 27–28. οὐδὲ θατέρου γενομένου ἀναγκαῖον ἢ εἰκὸς θάτερον γενέσθαι. Bywater's text.

[65] *Poetics*, 1451 a 36–38. Φανερὸν δὲ ἐκ τῶν εἰρημένων καὶ ὅτι οὐ τὸ τὰ γενόμενα λέγειν, τοῦτο ποιητοῦ ἔργον ἐστίν, ἀλλ᾽ οἷα ἂν γένοιτο καὶ τὰ δυνατὰ κατὰ τὸ εἰκὸς ἢ τὸ ἀναγκαῖον. Bywater's text.

episodic are the worst. I call a Plot episodic when there is neither probability nor necessity in the sequence of its episodes."[66]

Perhaps there is no other passage where reason seems to be operating more powerfully than in Aristotle's famous definition of tragedy: "A tragedy, then, is the imitation of an action that is serious and also, as having magnitude, complete in itself; in language with pleasurable accessories, each kind brought in separately in the parts of the work; in a dramatic, not in a narrative form; with incidents arousing pity and fear, wherewith to accomplish its catharsis of such emotions."[67] Let us offer the suggestion that in the definition it is really reason that draws together and, here at least, gives ultimate warranty to the various values that have been attributed to tragedy, each of which in turn has been supported by one or another different value criterion. For example, imitation is grounded in nature. Action is definitely to be related to the high value which Aristotle places upon activity or actuality in both his metaphysical and ethical thinking.[68] Seriousness, completeness, and magnitude may probably find their sanction in the values of convention, while pleasure as a value guarantees the validity of the point about "language with pleasurable accessories." And finally, the introduction of the emotions, pity, fear, and the like, certainly would be expected of the author of the *Rhetoric*. Perhaps we may be wrong in attributing this interweaving of these several different value schemes to the power of reason. Nonetheless, it may very well be true that the scope, compression, and profundity of the definition derive from the fact that Aristotle has managed to combine within brief compass

[66] *Poetics*, 1451 b 33–35. τῶν δὲ ἁπλῶν μύθων καὶ πράξεων αἱ ἐπεισοδιώδεις εἰσὶν χείρισται· λέγω δ' ἐπεισοδιώδη μῦθον ἐν τῷ τὰ ἐπεισόδια μετ' ἄλληλα οὔτ' εἰκὸς οὔτ' ἀνάγκη εἶναι. Bywater's text. Cf. also 1452 a 18–21; 1450 a 22–24; 1455 a 16–18.

[67] *Poetics*, 1449 b 24–28. ἔστιν οὖν τραγῳδία μίμησις πράξεως σπουδαίας καὶ τελείας μέγεθος ἐχούσης, ἡδυσμένῳ λόγῳ χωρὶς ἑκάστῳ τῶν εἰδῶν ἐν τοῖς μορίοις, δρώντων καὶ οὐ δι' ἀπαγγελίας, δι' ἐλέου καὶ φόβου περαίνουσα τὴν τῶν τοιούτων παθημάτων κάθαρσιν. Bywater's text. It is not to our purpose to enter into the catharsis dispute. I am not convinced by Else's interpretation, *op. cit.*, pp. 221–232 and 421–452. I would rather take it quite simply to be Aristotle's way of describing that strange feeling of exhilaration and elevation which any one experiences after having seen a great tragedy.

[68] Cf. above, Chapter VIII, p. 354 and our remarks on *Poetics*, 1450 a 16–19 in note 40.

363

the force of several of the differing value schemes which he has been accustomed to employ.

Without doubt, it is reason which is the force underlying the value judgement of the well known comparison of poetry and history. "The distinction between historian and poet is not in the one writing prose and the other verse—you might put the work of Herodotus into verse, and it would still be a species of history; it consists really in this, that the one describes the thing that has been, and the other a kind of thing that might be. Hence poetry is something more philosophic and of graver import than history, since its statements are of the nature rather of universals, whereas those of history are singulars. By a universal statement I mean one as to what such or such a kind of man will probably or necessarily say or do—which is the aim of poetry, though it affixes proper names to the characters; by a singular statement, one as to what, say, Alcibiades did or had done to him."[69]

We do not here need to enter upon the question of Aristotle's view of the nature of history in so far as it may be inferred from the foregoing passage. Aristotle, perhaps despite his reference to Herodotus, appears to be thinking of chronicle history, or to put it somewhat less elegantly, "laundry-list" history, consisting of a series of factual statements uninformed by any critical or interpretive point of view. Such history would indeed be made up of a congeries of "singular statements," and in no sense would be regarded as first-rate historical writing which is always animated by some "philosophical" dimension.[70] Rather we are interested

---

[69] *Poetics*, 1451 a 38–b 11. ὁ γὰρ ἱστορικὸς καὶ ὁ ποιητὴς οὐ τῷ ἢ ἔμμετρα λέγειν ἢ ἄμετρα διαφέρουσιν (εἴη γὰρ ἂν τὰ Ἡροδότου εἰς μέτρα τεθῆναι καὶ οὐδὲν ἧττον ἂν εἴη ἱστορία τις μετὰ μέτρου ἢ ἄνευ μέτρων)· ἀλλὰ τούτῳ διαφέρει, τῷ τὸν μὲν τὰ γενόμενα λέγειν, τὸν δὲ οἷα ἂν γένοιτο. διὸ καὶ φιλοσοφώτερον καὶ σπουδαιότερον ποίησις ἱστορίας ἐστίν· ἡ μὲν γὰρ ποίησις μᾶλλον τὰ καθόλου, ἡ δ' ἱστορία τὰ καθ' ἕκαστον λέγει. ἔστιν δὲ καθόλου μὲν, τῷ ποίῳ τὰ ποῖα ἄττα συμβαίνει λέγειν ἢ πράττειν κατὰ τὸ εἰκὸς ἢ τὸ ἀναγκαῖον, οὗ στοχάζεται ἡ ποίησις ὀνόματα ἐπιτιθεμένη· τὸ δὲ καθ' ἕκαστον, τί Ἀλκιβιάδης ἔπραξεν ἢ τί ἔπαθεν. Bywater's text. Note the repetition of the "law" of the probable or necessary, from the sentence preceding the present passage, which we have already quoted above, Chapter VIII, p. 362.

[70] For a very interesting discussion of this whole problem, cf. A. W. Gomme, *The Greek Attitude to Poetry and History* (*Sather Classical Lectures* 27, Berkeley and Los Angeles, University of California Press, 1954). The book is in fact an extended study of the implications of the Aristotelian passage which we are now discussing.

in Aristotle's conviction that "poetry is more philosophic and of graver import than history." His ground is, of course, dependent upon the difference between "universals" and "particulars," here expressed by "universal statements" and "singular statements." In the first place, we should be clear that Aristotle does not equate poetry and philosophy, but simply insists that poetry is "more philosophic than history," thus making it evident that he believes poetry to be superior to history because of its relation to philosophic universals. Such a conviction is based on a conclusion derived from his rational metaphysics to the effect that universals are in some way "superior" to singulars or particulars. From Aristotle's point of view this is true in the area of epistemology. Universals are more "knowable," and in this sense are more "philosophic" and hence more valuable, and this is why poetry is superior to history. But, as will be recognized, here we have another manifestation of what we have called Aristotle's "epistemological dilemma."[71] On the one hand, there is his metaphysical belief that the individual particular is ultimately real. On the other hand, the particular is ultimately unknowable, while it is the universal, which ontologically holds a secondary status, that is knowable. In our quotation from the *Poetics*, the superior value of poetry has its source in the universal, whereas history, with its affiliation with the particular, that is, the ultimately real, is inferior in value. Such seems to be the rather paradoxical consequence in the realm of literary criticism for Aristotle as a result of his having permitted Being and Value to fall apart.

E. THE PHRONIMOS

As a corollary to our consideration of values based upon reason in the *Poetics*, there is one passage which we can cite in order to show that Aristotle has not forgotten his man of practical wisdom as a court of appeal in the making of value judgements. The topic under discussion is the "impossible" and the "improbable," and the value at stake is truth. Aristotle observes: "The

[71] Cf. above, Chapter III, pp. 73–74 and note 36, as well as Chapter VI, pp. 181–183, p. 213 and note 103.

contradictions found in the poet's language one should first test as one does an opponent's confutation in a dialectical argument, so as to see whether he means the same thing, in the same relation, and in the same sense, before admitting that he has contradicted either something he has said himself or what a man of sound sense assumes as true."[72] Nothing more need be said other than that this quotation reflects precisely the same spirit as is found in the definition of virtue in the second book of the *Nicomachean Ethics*, where reason or the man of practical wisdom are invoked as the instruments whereby one can discover the mean wherein virtue lies.[73]

F. INTUITIVE VALUE RESPONSE

One final quotation must come before us because in it Aristotle in his value judgements seems to be relying on a sanction which appears to be somewhat different from any we have met heretofore. In examining the kinds of tragic plots which he believes should be avoided, he introduces the following argument: "It follows, therefore, that there are three forms of Plot to be avoided. (1) A good man must not be seen passing from happiness to misery, or (2) a bad man from misery to happiness. The first situation is not fear-inspiring or piteous, but simply odious to us. The second is the most untragic that can be; it has no one of the requisites of Tragedy; it does not appeal either to the human feeling in us, or to our pity, or to our fears. Nor, on the other hand, should (3) an extremely bad man be seen falling from happiness into misery. Such a story may arouse the human feeling in us, but it will not move us to either pity or fear; pity is

---

[72] *Poetics*, 1461 b 15–18. τὰ δ' ὑπεναντίως εἰρημένα οὕτω σκοπεῖν ὥσπερ οἱ ἐν τοῖς λόγοις ἐλέγχοι εἰ τὸ αὐτὸ καὶ πρὸς τὸ αὐτὸ καὶ ὡσαύτως, ὥστε καὶ αὐτὸν ἢ πρὸς ἃ αὐτὸς λέγει ἢ ὃ ἂν φρόνιμος ὑποθῆται. Bywater's text.

[73] Cf. above, Chapter VII, pp. 271–275. Incidentally, the principle of the mean or moderation is introduced once in the *Poetics* when Aristotle is talking about poetic vocabulary: "The rule of moderation applies to all the constituents of the poetic vocabulary; even with metaphors, strange words, and the rest, the effect will be the same, if one uses them improperly and with a view to provoking laughter. The proper use of them is a very different thing." *Poetics*, 1458 b 12–15. τὸ δὲ μέτριον κοινὸν ἁπάντων ἐστὶ τῶν μερῶν· καὶ γὰρ μεταφοραῖς καὶ γλώτταις καὶ τοῖς ἄλλοις εἴδεσι χρώμενος ἀπρεπῶς καὶ ἐπίτηδες ἐπὶ τὰ γελοῖα τὸ αὐτὸ ἂν ἀπεργάσαιτο. τὸ δὲ ἁρμοττόντως ὅσον διαφέρει κτλ. Bywater's text.

occasioned by undeserved misfortune, and fear by that of one like ourselves; so that there will be nothing either piteous or fear-inspiring in the situation."[74]

These lines are, of course, those which immediately precede the definition of the tragic hero, which we have already examined.[75] For us, they are primarily interesting, first, because they under-score the importance of the emotions of pity and fear as they are conceived by Aristotle in tragedy. For him, there can be no genuine tragedy, as we all know, unless these emotions and their like are aroused in the spectator or reader. But, secondly and more importantly, the passage does introduce another and a new criterion for genuine tragedy, and that is, it must arouse what we may call an appropriate intuitive or instinctive value response in the member of the audience. In other words, according to the passage, genuine tragedy must arouse all three together, pity, fear, and a proper instinctive value reaction, if it is to succeed. No one of the three can be lacking. An absolutely perfect man in a play cannot be revealed as falling from happiness to misery, because our instinctive feelings will be outraged or as Aristotle says, the situation will be odious, μιαρόν, to us. In the light of the three necessities, the presence of pity, fear, and a proper instinctive reaction, the situation of an evil man passing from misery to happiness, will fail in an absolute sense: there will be no pity, no fear, and no proper instinctive "human feeling." And finally, in the third situation, that of a thoroughly wicked man changing from happiness to misery might arouse a degree of sympathy, an instinctive human feeling, but, as Aristotle shows, the situation will be faulty since it is impossible for pity and fear to be produced. In the light of this evidence which demonstrates how in the given context Aristotle summons a new means of

---

[74] *Poetics*, 1452 b 34–1453 a 7. πρῶτον μὲν δῆλον ὅτι οὔτε τοὺς ἐπιεικεῖς ἄνδρας δεῖ μεταβάλλοντας φαίνεσθαι ἐξ εὐτυχίας εἰς δυστυχίαν, οὐ γὰρ φοβερὸν οὐδὲ ἐλεεινὸν τοῦτο ἀλλὰ μιαρόν ἐστιν· οὔτε τοὺς μοχθηροὺς ἐξ ἀτυχίας εἰς εὐτυχίαν, ἀτραγῳδότατον γὰρ τοῦτ᾽ ἐστὶ πάντων, οὐδὲν γὰρ ἔχει ὧν δεῖ, οὔτε γὰρ φιλάνθρωπον οὔτε ἐλεεινὸν οὔτε φοβερόν ἐστιν· οὐδ᾽ αὖ τὸν σφόδρα πονηρὸν ἐξ εὐτυχίας εἰς δυστυχίαν μεταπίπτειν· τὸ μὲν γὰρ φιλάνθρωπον ἔχοι ἂν ἡ τοιαύτη σύστασις, ἀλλ᾽ οὔτε ἔλεον οὔτε φόβον, ὁ μὲν γὰρ περὶ τὸν ἀνάξιόν ἐστιν δυστυχοῦντα, ὁ δὲ περὶ τὸν ὅμοιον, ἔλεος μὲν περὶ τὸν ἀνάξιον, φόβος δὲ περὶ τὸν ὅμοιον, ὥστε οὔτε ἐλεεινὸν οὔτε φοβερὸν ἔσται τὸ συμβαῖνον. Bywater's text.

[75] Cf. above, Chapter VIII, p. 356.

backing up a value judgement, man's intuitive value response, we are all the more able to sustain our contention that Aristotle in the realm of value operates on an *ad hoc* basis. In other words, he will use a value scheme which appears to suit the situation, without apparently being disturbed by the fact that the several schemes thus invoked do not cohere with one another. How natural it is for him to say that a really good man's fall from happiness to misery outrages our feelings, if seen in a play, that is, it produces a violently unfavourable value reaction on our part. And yet in this same treatise, the *Poetics*, as the occasion demands, we have seen Aristotle also turning to Nature, to the values of convention, to pleasure, to reason, and to the *phronimos*, in order to persuade us of the soundness of the various value decisions which he submits. It is in this way that the evidence of the *Poetics* corroborates our thesis with respect to Aristotle's method of meeting the question of value.

CHAPTER IX

CONCLUSION

IN this book, we have attempted to study the philosophical problem of the relation of Being and Value by a comparative analysis of the metaphysical positions of Plato and Aristotle. In our introductory chapter, we submitted the various grounds upon the basis of which one can argue that in reality Being and Value are deeply interrelated or "conjoined." As a consequence we urged that it is necessary for a thinker to be continually aware of this interrelationship whenever he faces questions either of axiology or ontology. In this connection we took occasion to cite the attitude of Saint Augustine as an individual who always kept Being and Value together in his philosophical speculation. And we further argued for the superiority of an "objective" view with respect to Being and Value over any of the various "subjective" positions which have been propounded in the history of thought. Finally, we insisted, and, I believe, quite reasonably, that in any "system" there must be consistency and coherence in the views put forward concerning Being and Value.

In our second chapter, we presented an analysis of Plato's Theory of Ideas or Forms, which, as is well known, does not dissociate Being from Value, but rather offers simultaneously solutions to questions of ontology and axiology, as well as to those of logic and epistemology. We were then in a position to face the main question of our book: What were the consequences for the thought of Aristotle as a result of his rejection of the Platonic Theory of Ideas? To introduce our study of the Aristotelian corpus, we devoted two chapters to a conspectus of his "metaphysics of the individual particular" in which we emphasized the fact that for Aristotle from first to last Being is primary. Our remaining chapters were then devoted to the task of identifying the various and often mutually incoherent ways in which Aristotle deals with questions of value and evaluation.

Our first step was to study the logical, physical, psychological, and biological treatises of Aristotle, in particular in those systematic passages which do illuminate his attitude towards the question of value. For example, at the conclusion of the section devoted to physics, we were able to list the following differing values or sanctions for value which we could identify: happiness, intelligence, Nature, the goal or *telos*, pleasure, and God or the divine.[1] Note how these are divided between the "subjective" and the "objective." Next we turned to the *Metaphysics*, really the fundamental document in which Aristotle advances the basic principles of his empirical and rational philosophy. Here we attempted to show first how Aristotle often looks at Value as related to the Final Cause. Next we studied Value as a quality and thus something which must occupy a status secondary to that of Being. We also pointed to the way in which Aristotle tends to associate Value with his conceptions of "substance," οὐσία, and activity or actuality, ἐνέργεια and ἐντελέχεια. We then studied the value "force" of the Good, the Beautiful, and the *Telos* in Aristotle's hands, as well as the implications for Value of his doctrine of God, the Prime or Unmoved Mover. In these sections of the *Metaphysics* it must be pointed out that Aristotle in the main is holding to an "objective" point of view, but at the same time he never retreats from his conviction that Being is primary. And finally, we attempted to appraise the influence of a lack of a doctrine of creation upon Aristotle's approach to the question of Value.

The *Nicomachean Ethics* proved to be a rich mine of evidence and showed the differing value schemes which Aristotle is prepared to use according to the exigencies of any given situation where it is necessary to make a value judgement. In this respect, the philosopher does not maintain the "objective" attitude which characterized his approach in the *Metaphysics*, but rather he tends to oscillate between the "subjective" and the "objective." In the *Nicomachean Ethics*, we found value sometimes treated as a quality, as in the *Metaphysics*. Happiness is advanced as the supreme human good or value. Aristotle also relies often upon conventional value thinking to support his own expressed or implied

---

[1] Cf. above, Chapter V, pp. 141–142.

views. The virtues themselves are considered to be values, and, of course, pleasure is likewise so regarded. Happiness, the conventional values, the virtues as values, and pleasure, as we argued, are all "subjective" in nature. But we also noted Aristotle's effort somehow to inject an element of the "objective" into his thinking on the problem through his doctrine of the mean, reason as a value sanction, the *phronimos* or the *spoudaios* as guarantors of values, as well as God or the Divine. It should be clear that Aristotle's metaphysics of Being cannot by its very nature provide the ground for making these "subjective" and "objective" elements come together in any kind of coherent fashion.[2]

And finally, after noting the ambivalence of the *Rhetoric* and the obviously crass conventionality of much of its contents in its function as a practical handbook, we turned to the *Poetics* where we were able to discover once again a varying set of value schemes in operation. Again we met, either as values or sanctions for value: Nature, the values of convention, pleasure, reason, and the *phronimos*, with a new notion added, namely, that of a human being's intuitive or instinctive value response.

Here we must rest our case. We hope we have shown the shifting character of Aristotle's approach to the problem of Value. Our task has been made more difficult by the fact that, despite his metaphysical break with Plato, Aristotle retained consciously or unconsciously much of Platonic influence. In the light of this situation, Aristotle must have always faced a kind of compulsion towards an "objective" value theory after the manner of Plato, but he must, one would think, also have been aware in some degree that such a theory could not be made to derive coherently from his own metaphysics of the individual particular, or more generally put, his metaphysics of Being. We have said that he must have been aware of his predicament. Perhaps we have expressed the point too vigorously. He may not have been aware of the problem of value as such. If this is indeed the case, we could argue that he was content to face the consequences of his rejection of the Platonic Theory of Ideas, as we have said before,[3]

[2] Cf. above, Chapter VII, especially pp. 320–321.
[3] Cf. above, Chapter II, pp. 55–56.

by taking over Platonic logic without change save in that he "relocated" the universal by making it inhere in the particular. He then forged an empiricist and rational ontology and epistemology, and really never constructed an adequate or coherent axiology. That Aristotle's axiology (or axiologies) is such, we hope we have been able to establish, and this result cannot fail to reinforce our view that a metaphysician would be well advised to keep always before him Being and Value as tightly conjoined.

As a final word, one can observe that Saint Thomas in his adaptation of Aristotle went far to repair the weaknesses of Aristotelian axiology, but nonetheless, it is fair to say that the Thomist emphasis upon Being and its rationalistic theology have perpetuated in Christian thought some of the difficulties in Aristotle with which we have been concerned. As Christian thought develops, the genius of Saint Thomas must be illuminated by the insight of Saint Augustine, in particular in his realization that Being and Value must never be permitted to become severed from each other.

SUBJECT INDEX

Academy, 63

accidents, 77, 89, 144, 145; and essence, 78–79; dualism of, 80, 81

action, 354, 355, 363; as goal of practical knowledge, 174

activity, 62, 275–76, 300, 310, 311, 321, 354, 363, 370; conceptions of, 275; life, 207; the state, 268; of thinking, 243; as potentiality, 240–41

actuality, 226, 235, 309; as activity, 89, 90–91, 112, 202; dualism of, 93; as activity and potentiality, 99; analysis, 102; bad, 193, 194, 204; complete, 82; conception of, 101; and essence, 102, 111, 112; good, 193–94; as perfection, 112; and potentiality, 100, 201–4; priority of over potentiality, 149

actualization, bad, 200, 201, 241

Allegory of the Cave, 22; and reality, 28n

alteration, 95

amoralism, in rhetoric, 343–351

Anaxagorean principle, 168

argument from the third man, 53–54

Aristotelian approach, 4

Aristotelian position, 56

Aristotelianism, 9, 51; effectiveness of, 5

art, 164; components of, 352; purpose of, 359

astronomy, 107, 115

bad, conception of the, 114

Becoming, 310; analysis of, 109; realm of, 49, 54; and realm of Being, 28–31, 37; world of, 24

Being, 66, 120, 132, 144, 170, 231, 320, 321, 370, 371; coming into and passing away, 87, 247, 305; conception of, 175; and knowledge, primacy of, 176; meaning of, 190; metaphysics of, 100; and non-being, 21, 22; and potentiality and actuality, 201; primacy of, 275, 369; *qua* being, 176–77, 178, 179; question of,

195; realm of, 41, 49, 54, 55; relation of to value, 146; shift of to value, 140, 141; as source of value, 140, 141; Thomist emphasis on, 372

Being and Value, 6, 11, 12, 13, 14, 15, 25n, 43, 49–50, 108n, 134, 146, 156, 192–93, 253; conjoined, 15, 372; and doctrine of natures, 12; human view of, 16; Plato's theory of, 16, 18; problem of, 128; relation of, 4, 10, 120, 138, 162, 183, 194, 195, 208–11, 246, 256, 260, 369; metaphysical problem, 111; naturalist, 14; source of, 16; Theory of Ideas, 17; and wisdom, philosophic and practical, 264

categories, 62, 247n; doctrine of the, 78–79, 97, 190; of entities, 219; of events, teleological, 218–19; generation of, 247

cause, 132, 204, 353–54; analysis of, 104, 105, 106

efficient, 104, 105, 106, 107, 108, 109, 110, 111, 115, 152, 169, 214, 218, 219; as wisdom, 213

essential, 102, 112

final, 104, 105, 107–8, 109, 111, 113, 114, 115, 124, 133, 141, 158, 159, 161, 166, 171, 212, 213, 217, 219, 220, 222, 229, 230, 231, 236, 251, 252, 255n, 256, 284, 370; analysis, 214; cosmic, 252–53; as end, 218; and the Good, 206, 207; value, related to, 370

first, 157, 159, 177, 178; formal, 104, 105, 107–8, 169, 213n, 214, 218, 307; fundamental, 103; material, 102, 104, 159, 167, 169, 214, 218

chance, 130–31, 132

change, 96

character, 357, 358

Christianity, 10, 249, 252

Christians, 57

class, 43

comedy, 352, 355, 359n, 360

INDEX OF NAMES

INDEX OF CLASSICAL WORKS CITED

One of the most significant moments in the history of Western thought occurred when Aristotle determined to reject the Theory of Ideas, the basic metaphysical doctrine of his master Plato. The Platonic hypothesis, which postulates the ultimate reality of non-spatial and non-temporal Ideas, is remarkable for its philosophical economy. It has four distinguishable functions: it forms the basis of a logic, for an Idea does the work of a logical universal; it supplies Plato with an ontology, for an Idea is that which is in the full sense real; it gives Plato the ground for his epistemology, for one can know completely only that which is fully real, *viz.*, an Idea; and finally it provides Plato with an explanation of the problem of value, for an Idea is not only that which is ultimately real but also that which is ultimately valuable.

The present volume attempts to explore the consequences for Aristotle's thought when he asserted that Ideas do not exist. Professor Oates, in a brilliant and lucid analysis of the problem of being in relation to value, points out how Aristotle is able to retain Plato's logic by maintaining that the logical universal does not exist "apart" but rather inheres in the individual particular, the ultimate reality of which Aristotle holds in his own metaphysics of Being. This ontology is primary for him and he builds a corresponding epistemology which is basically empirical in character. But in the construction of the metaphysics of the individual particular, with its heavy emphasis upon ontology, Aristotle's attitude toward the question of value becomes i